BY FAWN M. BRODIE

Thaddeus Stevens

SCOURGE OF THE SOUTH

If we have not yet been sufficiently scourged for our national sin, to teach us to do justice to all God's creatures, without distinction of race or color, we must expect the still more heavy vengeance of an offended Father.

Thaddeus Stevens
December 18, 1865

The Norton Library
W · W · NORTON & COMPANY · INC ·
NEW YORK

SBN   393   00331   0

PRINTED IN THE UNITED STATES OF AMERICA

6789

Contents

———— ◆ ————

Foreword

THE FIRST biographies of Thaddeus Stevens—Alexander Hood's study in the *Biographical History of Lancaster County* (Lancaster, 1872), and Alexander Harris' *Political Conflict in America . . . Comprising Also a Résumé of the Life of Thaddeus Stevens* (New York, 1876)—were written by men who lived in his own city and knew him well, men who were apparently equally exposed to the adulation heaped upon him by his friends and the defamation circulated by his enemies. But where Hood revered Stevens as one of the great American statesmen, "towering high above the millions around him," Harris denounced him as the American counterpart of Robespierre—a divergence in point of view that set a historical pattern persisting to this day.

The two most recent biographies, by Richard N. Current and Ralph Korngold, reflect the contrast even in their subtitles. Professor Current in *Old Thad Stevens, a Story of Ambition* (Madison, Wisconsin, 1942), though writing with the restraint and scholarship of an able and disciplined historian, nevertheless finds it difficult to hide his "just indignation" over Stevens' career. His public actions, Professor Current writes, were determined not by "mysterious motives" but by "frustrated personal ambitions." And whatever there was in Stevens' life that could be called tricky, unscrupulous, and demagogic is here meticulously assembled and copiously documented. Ralph Korngold in his biography *Thaddeus Stevens* (New York, 1955), uses as a subtitle "A Being Darkly Wise and Rudely Great," a quotation from a favorite poem of Stevens, Alexander Pope's *Essay on Man*. Mr. Korngold's admiration for Thaddeus Stevens permeates every chapter, and his occasional derogatory criticisms are offered with apology and regret.

Both Professor Current's and Mr. Korngold's biographies were of great value to me. They drew upon newspaper and manuscript material not seriously explored in the earlier studies by Edward B. Callender (1882), Samuel W. McCall (1899), James A. Woodburn (1913), and Thomas Frederick Woodley (1937). Both concentrated, however, not on the man but on the political story. Neither grappled with the contradictions in Stevens' nature nor uncovered the details of his diverse personal tragedies.

Other historians and biographers have usually been passionately for Stevens or against him, with the latter certainly in the majority. The late George Fort Milton and James G. Randall did not hesitate to use adjectives like "vindictive" and "malignant," and epithets like "Caliban," "madman," and "apostle of proscription and hate."

This biography does not pretend to absolute detachment. The reader will find value judgments explicitly stated throughout. But it tries to suggest what may have been the basis of Stevens' extraordinary capacity for hatred, which was an energizing force for good and evil right up to his death. It attempts to explain Stevens' radicalism not only in terms of his active role in what Clemenceau called "the second American revolution," but also as an outgrowth of his own desperate inner needs. For much of what would otherwise remain inexplicable in Stevens' life becomes clearer when one scrutinizes his relations with his parents, the stories about his clubfoot, the long-buried details of a Gettysburg murder in which he was mysteriously involved, the hitherto unused material on his unhappy relations with his nephews, and the gossip concerning his relations with his mulatto housekeeper.

Since, however, Stevens' impact on American history was made as a man of politics, most of this book is given over to a description of his turbulent career in Washington during the Civil War and Reconstruction. His relations with Lincoln, which have been much distorted in the past, are here redefined. The special nature of his economic radicalism is also explored. His role as the father of the Fourteenth Amendment and the chief architect of Reconstruction are described with special emphasis on the facts of what was happening to the Negro in 1866 and 1867.

Thaddeus Stevens' battles for Negro suffrage and Negro schooling have a special timeliness now, because he used all three weapons—persuasion, legislation, and force—which are under scrutiny as solutions for the racial problems of our own time. And his equalitarian legislation, which for so many years was a dead letter in the statute books and even in the Constitution, is now reborn and vigorous. This book tries to make evident why Stevens aroused such divergent passions during his lifetime, and why he is today for the American Negro a hero second only to Lincoln, and for the Southern white man the most hated statesman in American history.

FAWN M. BRODIE

Pacific Palisades
June, 1959

Acknowledgments

———————— ◆ ————————

Thaddeus Stevens destroyed many of his letters and papers before he died. But Edward McPherson collected several-score boxes of material which may be seen today as the Stevens Papers and the McPherson Papers in the Library of Congress. To Edward McPherson, then, all biographers of Stevens must admit a formidable debt. Other collections, particularly the papers of Robert Todd Lincoln, Andrew Johnson, and Benjamin F. Butler in the Library of Congress, the Charles Sumner papers in the Harvard University Library, the Salmon P. Chase letters in the Historical Society of Pennsylvania, the Francis Lieber papers in the Huntington Library, and the Stevens papers in the Dartmouth College Library and the Lancaster County Historical Society, were also of value to me. The collected Thaddeus Stevens notes of the late Elsie Singmaster Lewars in the Adams County Historical Society in Gettysburg proved fruitful for information on Stevens' personal life.

Everywhere my research in collections, newspaper files, and government documents was enriched by the friendly aid of librarians and historians. It was Roger W. Shugg who first pointed out to me the exciting possibilities in a study of Stevens. Robert Fortenbaugh of Gettysburg College, extremely generous with his time and information, gave me clues to important new material and read a portion of the manuscript. Arthur Weaner of the Adams County Historical Society did valuable detective work, and N. L. Oyler graciously permitted the reproduction of important material from an old Gettysburg legal file. I am grateful also to the late Mary L. Callahan of the *Gettysburg Times,* and to John H. Knickerbocker of the Gettysburg College Library.

David C. Mearns, Donald C. Holmes, and James O. Sutton, all of the Library of Congress, gave me material aid, as did Leslie E. Bliss of the Huntington Library, Carolyn E. Jakeman of the Harvard University Library, John E. Kephart of the Wheaton College Library, Floyd C. Shoemaker of the State Historical Society of Missouri, Hermann R. Muelder of Knox College, Mary A. Ranck of the Lancaster County Historical Society, and Francis S. Perry of Peacham Academy, Vermont.

I am especially grateful to the librarians of Dartmouth College, Yale University, and the University of California at Los Angeles. The Huntington Library gave me permission to quote from several Charles Sumner letters, and letters from the Francis Lieber Collection. The Frick Art Library and Museum of New York City permitted reproduction of the portrait of Lydia Smith.

Andrew W. Marshall of the Rand Corporation was of great assistance in evaluating Stevens' role in financing the Civil War. Harvey A. DeWeerd gave me much friendly advice and continuing moral support. I am also grateful to William W. Kaufmann, Samuel Flagg Bemis, Herbert S. Bailey, Jr., Joel E. Ricks, David Donald, and the late Bernard DeVoto.

For aid in understanding the special problems of Thaddeus Stevens as a cripple I am indebted to Nathan Leites, Ralph Greenson, Milton Wexler, and Hanna Fenichel, all of whom contributed time, enthusiasm, and expert clinical advice. Dore Schary kindly permitted me to see a private showing of the film *Tennessee Johnson,* and Sylvia Richards provided me with a copy of the script.

But most of all I am grateful for the detailed critical readings by my husband, Bernard Brodie, and for his continuing stimulation and support through all the difficulties of the research and writing.

CHAPTER ONE

The Old Commoner

Scholar, wit, zealot of liberty, part fanatic, part gambler, at his worst a clubfooted wrangler possessed of endless javelins, at his best a majestic and isolated figure wandering in an ancient wilderness thick with thorns, seeking to bring justice between man and man—who could read the heart of limping, poker-faced old Thaddeus Stevens?

Carl Sandburg,
Abraham Lincoln, The War Years

ON MAY 23, 1867, a newspaper editor from Alabama made his way to an unpretentious red brick residence in Lancaster, Pennsylvania, the house and law office of Thaddeus Stevens. He looked sharply at the woman who let him in, afterwards describing her as "a mulatto woman . . . a neat, tidy housekeeper . . . polite and well trained," who "receives or rejects his visitors at will, speaks of Mr. Stevens and herself as 'we,' and in all things comports herself as if she enjoyed the rights of a lawful wife." Stevens was in the library, where the shelves were piled high with books. He was seventy-four, large-boned but thin of flesh, and enfeebled by an erratic liver and bad heart. His bald head was covered with a massive brown wig that made small pretense to being anything but what it was. A specially made boot hid his well-known clubfoot, but it could not disguise the deformity when Stevens walked. Then the limp was painfully evident, and it was only when he stood erect that one realized he was six feet tall.

The Southern editor, George M. Drake, had sought Stevens out for several reasons, including curiosity, but chiefly to ask him his precise terms for readmitting Alabama to the Union. Stevens was not a Senator nor a cabinet member, nor did he even hold so important a post as Speaker of the House. He was simply a Congressman from Pennsylvania. Nevertheless Drake's errand was not quixotic, for Stevens actually held more political power than any man in the nation, more power, in fact, even than Andrew Johnson, whom he very nearly toppled from the Presidency a year later.

Upon Lincoln's death Thaddeus Stevens had become leader and whip of the Republican Party, leader also of its Radical wing, which was determined to block the return of the Confederate states until they had granted the newly freed slaves equality of civil rights with the white man and the right to vote. Stevens had just succeeded in forcing through Congress his Military Bill, which placed all the seceded states save Tennessee under the rule of the Union Army and provided for a revolutionary reorganization of the old state governments, with the black man voting alongside—or in many cases instead of—his former master, and the poor white voting uneasily alongside the ex-slave. It was the beginning of what would later be called with such fury and resentment "Negro-carpetbag rule."

Stevens was frank but not friendly to the Alabama editor, who found the old man "intellectually vigorous, prompt, and lucid," but also "cold and pitiless." Drake shortly sent back to the *Union Springs Times* two editorials which were such brilliant pieces of defamation they were reprinted by other editors who detested Stevens' policies. In one he wrote as follows:

I have no wish to wrong even this wicked man, whose terrible wretchedness gapes frighteningly at him from the hopeless grave upon whose brink he stands—this patricide and murderer—this demon who will soon leave an immortality of hate and infamy for an eternity of unutterable woe—this traitor who gives in the years to come a new and more damnable meaning to treason—this malicious, pitiless, pauseless enemy of an entire nation—this misanthrope, whose curses of mankind shall be written upon his loathed tomb an awful epitaph—this viperous, heartless, adulterous beast, whose horrid life has converted an 'image of God' into plagiarism of devils—this living sepulchre of all hideous things, upon whose body in his mother's womb was fixed hell's seal of deformity, an omen and surety of the deeper and more dreadful crimes he was to teach the world. I would, that man, woman, or innocent child in all this broad land, knew one kind look, happy thought or charitable deed that this lonely, friendless, and unfriendly man ever blessed the world with, that going down into death, he might have the sorrows of one regretful heart, the tears of one sad eye, to even slightly soothe the terrible damnation which shall blast his soul . . .[1]

This was only part of the editor's fulmination, but it expressed better, perhaps, than anything written since the explosive hatred of the Southerner for Thaddeus Stevens. Drake, it will be noted, called him a traitor, adulterer, misanthrope, and murderer. Insinuating that his clubfoot was "hell's seal of deformity . . . fixed in his mother's womb," he echoed the old superstition that cripples are really demons in mortal form.

None of these charges was new. Stevens had been accused of murder when he was thirty-two years old. Rumors that he was a rake and adulterer had followed him almost all his adult life. That he was a misanthrope even his friends would admit. Only a year earlier, the President of the United States had publicly called him a traitor to his country. But the clubfoot had been with him always, and with it the faint but ineradicable smell of brimstone.

For every Southern white man who detested Thaddeus Stevens there was, nevertheless, the counterweight of a Northern white man who looked to him as a great champion of freedom and democracy. Negroes everywhere counted him hero second only to Lincoln. If he was called "Old Clubfoot," he was also called "the old Commoner," leader of leaders, after William Pitt, Earl of Chatham, who for so many years had controlled the House of Commons with his wit and eloquence. Stevens and Pitt both had unrivaled powers of invective; both were great parliamentarians. Like Pitt, Stevens could look back on triumphs and satisfactions denied to men who roused less passion, either of love or hate.

For over thirty years Stevens had been an abolitionist. He had lived not only to experience an exaltation of spirit when the slaves were finally freed, but also a fierce satisfaction in having led the advance guard in the fight. Great foe of ignorance, he had brought free schools to the children of Pennsylvania a full generation before they might otherwise have been established. He could point now to the scattered but significant beginnings of Negro education all over the South.

Along with slavery and ignorance he detested caste, and was devoting the remaining months of his life to legislating against it. For this he was being denounced as a revolutionist and Jacobin, a Constitution-breaker, an American Robespierre. Even the Conservative Republicans believed him to be dangerous, but found themselves slowly but inexorably following his lead and voting as he pointed. Agreeing with him that a constitution is primarily an instrument to distribute political power, they were intent on a redistribution that would lessen the power of the Southern white, who until 1860 had had proportionately more than the Northern white, and give some to the Negro, who had

had none at all.

A powerful minority of Radical Republicans went still further with Thaddeus Stevens, believing that all the equalitarian ideals of the Declaration of Independence were the proper heritage of the Negro as well as the white man, and should be translated into legislation. They agreed with him that the black man had a right to dignity as well as freedom, and that wherever the ex-slave was stunted the cause lay in poverty, ignorance, and a denial of opportunity, and not in an Old Testament curse.

Since Stevens' death the number of Northern whites who might revere his memory has been whittled down to a relative few, for the Republican Party long ago lost its Radicals, and the Democratic Party, however metamorphosed since 1867, has no incentive for adopting Stevens as hero even if his party label could be forgotten. The smell of brimstone, the suspicion of fanaticism, the aura of revolution, surround him still.

His reputation remains many-sided partly because his character and history were full of paradoxes and contradictions. He was a humanitarian lacking in humanity; a man of boundless charities and vindictive hates; a Calvinist convinced that all men are vile who nevertheless cherished a vision of the Promised Land where all men should be equal before the law; a revolutionary who would carve up the estates of the "bloated aristocrats" of the South, but in the same breath offer to defend Jefferson Davis in his trial for treason. He was an equalitarian who would pinion the Southerner for his racial bigotry and caste prejudices, but who for twenty years would live with a colored woman as his mistress, apparently content with a relationship common in the Southern aristocracy, and one that Northern abolitionists generally pointed to with horror.

Stevens' reputation for political evil has been remarkably tenacious, despite the fact that his most significant political achievement, the Fourteenth Amendment, is now recognized to be an integral part of the Bill of Rights in the Constitution. School children are taught that Stevens was a thorn in Lincoln's side, but few learn that the pricking was always in the direction of Negro freedom, and that Lincoln, recognizing the difference between fanaticism for freedom and fanaticism for slavery, managed to make of Stevens not a friend but a powerful if erratic and demanding ally.

White historians almost unanimously agree that when Stevens fastened military rule upon the South in 1867 it was a catastrophic political blunder, but few take pains to point out, as Negro historians are careful to do, that in 1866 probably more Negroes were lynched than in any year before or since. No one can read the story of the impeachment trial of Andrew Johnson and not deplore Stevens' vindictive role as prosecutor, but it is important to remember that Johnson had publicly called Thad Stevens a traitor to his country as deserving of hanging as Jefferson Davis. One may regret that Stevens imposed Negro suffrage on the South when the ex-slave was still largely illiterate, but who is to say how it could ever have become a part of the Constitution after the Southern states returned to white supremacy and home rule?

Stevens' fathomless pessimism makes him singularly a man for our own day. Unlike most of his contemporary New England reformers, he never completely rejected Calvinism in favor of a sentimental belief in human perfectibility. Since he, being crippled, could never be perfect, he would not be deluded by the pleasant fantasy that the world was moving ineluctably toward sweetness and light.

He believed in education and legislation as twin instruments for increasing freedom and justice, but was always vigilant against the counter forces that would oppress the specific minorities he chose to champion. There is no doubt he would have agreed readily with his British contemporary, John Stuart Mill, writing "On Liberty" in 1859, who insisted that truth does not always triumph over persecution, and that "persecution has always succeeded, save where the heretics were too strong a party."

He saw slavery for the horror that it was, and had no illusions that education and persuasion would ever be instrumental in bringing about its disappearance, intertwined as it was with the Southerner's economic and caste traditions. He saw with special clarity, like Lincoln, that the pre-war compromises with slavery were almost certain guarantees of its expansion. But when war finally came, he saw too, unlike William H. Seward, who predicted blithely that it would "all be over in sixty days," that it would be a grim and bloody agony lasting three or four years.

It was this pessimism that made Stevens so impatient with Lincoln's tardiness in freeing the slaves and later so insistent upon the kind of reconstruction that would provide legal guarantees against a slipping backward into slavery or near-slavery. He had no faith in gradualism, and perhaps too much faith in the omnipotence of legislation over human conduct.

On paper his legislation was mighty. The slave had become a citizen, with the right to vote, to hold office, and to share equally in the civil rights so long cherished by the white man. He was not granted his parcel of land, as the Russian serfs had been when they were freed in

1861. But in the Fourteenth Amendment the Negro had what Stevens believed was a strong legal bulwark against the white man's seemingly ineradicable impulse to degrade him. And the Fifteenth Amendment, which passed the House of Representatives shortly after his death, was supposed to provide a permanent guarantee of his right to vote.

Still he was not content. Like most revolutionists he had not only an arbitrary righteousness mingled with cynicism but also a compulsion to punish. It stayed with him to the end, resulting in the sordid impeachment proceedings, which were all the more impolitic because, coming near the close of Johnson's administration, they were unnecessary. And afterward, looking back over his long years, he had no sense of triumph. "I have no history," he said. "My life-long regret is that I have lived so long and so uselessly." [2]

This ravaging pessimism stemmed partly from his clearsighted recognition of man's wish to oppress. Before he died, the Ku Klux Klan had swelled to half a million men. But his gloom would have persisted, one suspects, had every white Southerner bowed abjectly to his will and assumed the mask of the New England conscience. For it is in the nature of the crusader—the radical, the Jacobin, the revolutionary, the true believer: call him what you will—that he is never sated. No triumph brings him to the border of the Promised Land. This is because his crusade is likely to be a substitute for deeper needs, and there is no success but finds him empty and lonely still.

CHAPTER TWO

The Branding

I am a *cripple* in my limbs, but what decays are in my mind, the reader must determine.

John Dryden

THADDEUS STEVENS was born into a blighted family. His father, Joshua Stevens, a farmer and surveyor in an isolated village in northern Vermont, had a local reputation as a wrestler and little else but a special talent for staying poor. The first calamity fell in 1790 when his eldest son was born with clubfeet. In any generation this would have been a tragedy, but it was certain then to be looked upon as punishment for some secret sin. Joshua and Sarah Stevens were Baptists, heirs to the Calvinist tradition of an austere God, whose exactions of the human spirit were inflexible and severe. We know from letters written by Sarah Stevens that she was deeply and articulately religious, and there could have been nothing in her creed to spare her a devastating sense of guilt.

Seventeen months later, April 4, 1792, Thaddeus was born. When his parents saw in the first moments that here was another crippled child—although only one foot was twisted instead of two—they must have felt inexorably cursed. Joshua Stevens in his spare time was a maker of shoes. So in any of his roles in society—farmer, cobbler, surveyor, or wrestler—he could hardly escape being reminded of the lameness of his sons. He failed at farming, like others who have challenged Vermont boulders, and then, unable to live with his own bankruptcy he took to liquor, and finally to running away. He came back long enough to father two more sons, Abner and Alanson—who escaped the lameness of their brothers—but at some time during Thaddeus' early adolescence he finally disappeared altogether. The family learned finally that he had been killed in the War of 1812.

Upon Sarah Morrill Stevens, "a woman of great energy, strong will, and deep piety," [1] fell the burden of raising four boys to be better than their father. Vowing that her two eldest would rise above the merciless handicap of their birth, she moved from Danville to Peacham, where there was a school, enrolled the boys in the academy, and earned their tuition by domestic labor and nursing. With his mother Thaddeus Stevens learned to endure failure, to fight and eventually overpower it. Desertion, however, he never forgave. Whether in later life it was the defection of friends from his political party, or the desertion of the Southern states from the Union, he responded with explosive protest and a sense of acute, personal betrayal.

All his life Thaddeus Stevens was aggressive and implacable in his hatreds. It is easy to speculate that he hated his father first, and that all his subsequent dislikes stemmed from the corroding hostility of his childhood. About all we actually know, however, is that he chose never to talk about him. Now and then, however, in his political speeches he inadvertently bared the childhood scar. Once in the Pennsylvania Constitutional Convention of 1837, when fighting the legal distinctions drawn between poor and rich pupils, he said bluntly: "There is no disgrace in being the son of a poor man or a drunkard." Later, urging an appropriation for the District of Columbia schools, he said: "Now I care not whether the people here are worthless or not; they have children who are to grow up and become men and women, and the more worthless the people here are, the greater the necessity for taking care that their children are properly educated." And in his plans for the District school system he penalized those who might refuse to send their children to school by denying them the right to vote.[2]

Shortly before his death he indicated to one reporter that what had counted most over all the years was his success in partially blotting out his father's financial failure: "The greatest gratification of my life resulted from my ability to give my mother a farm of two hundred and fifty acres, and a dairy of fourteen cows, and an occasional bright gold piece, which she loved to deposit in the contribution box of the Baptist Church which she attended. My mother was a very extraordinary woman, and I have met very few women like her. . . . She worked day and night to educate me." [3]

Alexander McClure wrote that when Stevens spoke of his mother, "all the harsh lines of his countenance disappeared to give place to the tenderness of a child. That one devotion was like an oasis in the desert of his affections, and, regardless of his individual convictions, he reverenced everything taught him by his mother. In his will he provided that the sexton of her little churchyard in the bleak hills of Vermont should ever keep her grave green, 'and plant roses and other cheerful flowers at the four corners of said grave every spring.' " When Stevens willed $1,000 toward the building of a Baptist Church in Lancaster, Pennsylvania, he wrote: "I do this out of respect to the memory of my mother, to whom I owe what little prosperity I have had on earth, which, small as it is, I desire emphatically to acknowledge." [4]

Once, in a cynical mood, Stevens said to some friends that he believed all men mercenary and all women unchaste. When one in the group pointedly asked him about his mother's virtue, "he left the room and never spoke of women in this manner afterward." [5]

Like every other crippled child, Thaddeus Stevens had to learn to live with his deformity and face up to the cruelty of his fellows. "He was still and quiet-like," reported an old neighbor, "different from the rest of the boys, and they'd laugh at him, boy-like, and mimic his limping walk. They didn't mean any harm; but Thaddeus was a sensitive little fellow and it rankled him. I've always thought that's the reason, perhaps, he has never been back to the old homestead." [6]

That Stevens was never really reconciled to his lameness is suggested in a story told by his friend William Hall. He was sitting in the Pennsylvania legislature, Hall said, "with his distorted foot up on the edge of his desk, an attitude in which he seemed to like to place himself, as if to obtrude the deformity upon the vision, perhaps from a feeling that it would not be manly to conceal his defect, when a bright little boy in the innocence and bravery of childhood, advanced near to and looked intently at it. With a scowling expression of countenance Stevens thrust his foot close to the little fellow's face and frightened him with the fierce remark, 'There, look at it! it won't bite! it's not a snake!' " [7]

[The widespread superstition that there was something sinister about cripples seems to have haunted Stevens always.] Late in life he said to two youths who were riding in his carriage: "You have heard that I am one of the devil's children, and that this club foot of mine is proof of my parentage." [8]

As if it was not enough to have the devil for a parent, Stevens suffered too from the rumor that he was actually the bastard son of Count Talleyrand, who was said to have visited New England in the year before Stevens' birth. The fact that the French statesman and Thaddeus Stevens were both lame, that both were gamblers and rumored to have enjoyed favors from mulatto women, and that there was a similarity in their political genius, seemed good enough evidence to those who never bothered to check significant dates. Actually Talleyrand did not visit New England till 1794, when Stevens was already two years old.[9]

Stevens suffered many accusations in silence, whether they were true or false, including this one. But often, choosing his own time and battlefield, he would hurl his javelins with great ferocity, directing them against faults and sins that had in the past been laid at his own door. That the taint of bastardy rankled him is suggested by his not infrequent use of the epithet himself. A celebrated example was described by John W. Forney. When a politician in the Pennsylvania legislature betrayed a promise to support Stevens for senator, Forney related, Stevens protested acidly: "You must be a bastard for I knew your mother's husband and he was a gentleman and an honest man." [10]

After his college years Stevens tried desperately to compensate for his twisted foot. Like Lord Byron, another clubfoot, he became an expert swimmer. William Hall reported that he "could throw the 'long bullet' further and kick a hat off a higher peg than any other man in Gettysburg." The *Philadelphia Press* described him as "a great athlete . . . one of the most daring and best trained riders in the country." His friend T. H. Burrowes wrote that "few could lift a heavier weight or heave a sledge further." And he related that Stevens once said to him: "I never feel myself so much a man as when mounted on a fine horse." [11]

Stevens became the quiet benefactor of many crippled boys, and in later years gave orders to his personal physician in Lancaster to send him the bill for aid to any "deformed or disabled" boys who came his way. But this was only the most obvious evidence of his identification with those handicapped by accident of birth. A lame man is a minority of one wherever he walks. And there was, in fact, no persecuted minority in America for whom Stevens did not at some time speak out. Over and again in his speeches the words "branded" and "marked" crop up like specters that will not be exorcised. "He seemed to feel," said one Congressman, "that every wrong inflicted upon the human race was a blow struck at himself." [12]

Stevens defended the Indians, Seventh Day Adventists, Mormons, Jews, and Chinese,[13] and he battled over thirty years to bring freedom and civil rights to the Negro. Where the crusading zeal of most young men slips into apathy, sours into disillusion, or simply changes to a serenity that accepts the world for what it is, with Thaddeus Stevens the fight was never fiercer than in the year he died at seventy-six. One reason surely was that through all his life no day came without reminding him that he, like Richard III, was "cheated of feature by dissembling nature, deform'd, unfinish'd . . . scarce half made up."

Thaddeus Stevens' older brother, Joshua, became a cobbler and drifted west, where he remained humble and obscure. But Thaddeus, who also learned cobbling from his father,[14] took to books thirstily. He was a bright student, with an encyclopedic memory and a fine talent at debate. His mother, having a proper value for his gifts, managed to raise the tuition for his education first at Peacham Academy, then at Dartmouth College.

Stevens was remembered at the Academy as a "wilful, headstrong" youth with an "overmastering burning desire to secure an education." Once his books and hat were destroyed in a school fire. Coming down the hill afterward, bareheaded and desolate, he met John Mattocks, who later became his law teacher. "Here Thad," said the lawyer, handing him ten dollars, "take this and buy some books and go to college without a hat."

Shortly before graduating, Stevens along with several others broke a school rule by putting on a play "by candlelight" instead of in the daytime. Forced to sign an apology and a promise of future obedience, he yielded, it was said, only because he had to, and "never forgot his chagrin." In later years, after he became famous, the Peacham headmasters repeatedly invited him back to make a speech, but he always refused. He did, however, in his will generously endow the school Juvenile Library Society, which he had founded as a student.[15]

Stevens graduated from Dartmouth College in 1814. Most of his biographers have erroneously stated that he was once expelled, their evidence being an undated and misfiled letter in the Stevens Papers in the Library of Congress. Actually this letter was written by Stevens' nephew, also named Thaddeus, who was in fact expelled from Dartmouth four times.[16]

Stevens' official record at Dartmouth was good. He did get involved in a scandal at Burlington College, where he attended two terms when the Dartmouth buildings were requisitioned by the government for troops during the War of 1812.[17] The Burlington campus was small but unfenced, and the local farmers used it freely to pasture their cows. Student sentiment against the resulting piles of manure ran high, and the cows became the target of much mischief. After one episode, where the cows were hidden in a cellar and the farmers stoned the college building, Stevens and a friend borrowed an ax from one of the most pious students in the college and killed one cow. The owner of the ax was unjustly blamed and threatened with expulsion. Whereupon Stevens privately confessed to the farmer, who was unexpectedly considerate, dropped all charges, and publicly blamed the cow's death on soldiers who had passed through the town. Stevens, who later told the story himself, eventually sent the farmer "a draft for the price of the best cow in the market, accompanied by a fine gold watch and chain by way of interest," which the farmer silently acknowledged later by sending Stevens a hogshead of cider.[18]

This episode cannot be dismissed as an ordinary college prank. Killing a cow with an ax is an act of extreme brutality, and we have to note the fact that the youthful Stevens was capable of it. It is significant that he avoided public confession at the time but in later years paid for the damages in full and then freely told the story. Many crimes were to be laid at Stevens' door, including fornication, bastardy, adultery, and even murder. Rarely did he choose to answer the charges publicly at the time. He might counterattack with a libel suit, or delay many years and then, when there seemed to be no real need to discuss the charge at all, make an oblique denial in print. But from Stevens one almost never gets forthright denial or forthright confession. One must look for more subtle evidence either of atonement for real crimes or of that rage which is likely to possess a man unjustly accused.

There is no evidence that Stevens at Dartmouth was in any kind of rebellion against his conservative, anti-Jefferson professors or their ideas. But there is one remarkable letter written by his roommate, Joseph Tracy, that reveals much about his incapacity to live easily with his fellow students. Tracy was asked to write an obituary for *The Dartmouth* when Stevens died. He refused, saying in part: "I could not honestly write such a sketch as it would be expedient, at present, to publish in the Dartmouth. Perhaps I knew him quite as well as any person who was in College with him. . . . He was then inordinately ambitious, bitterly envious of all who outranked him as scholars, and utterly unprincipled. He showed no uncommon mental power, except in extemporaneous debate. He was tolerably attentive to college exercises. He indulged in no expensive vices, because he could not afford them, and because his ambition so absorbed him, that he had little taste for any thing that did not promise to gratify it. He was not popular enough with the class to get into Phi Beta Kappa, or even to be nominated for membership. This was a source of great vexation to him, though he was very careful not to express his vexation. Yet it burst out once in our room, in an unguarded moment.

"It seems proper that the Dartmouth should take some notice of him, and that notice should be prepared by some one who never knew him so thoroughly as I have done." [19]

It can be seen that Stevens, like several other celebrated cripples—including Alexander Pope, whose poetry he read and admired—chose to be quarrelsome with those he envied or feared. He seems to have decided early that advance attack and deliberate alienation were less degrading than servility or silence. Perhaps he felt that it was better to be despised for being nasty than for not being whole.

His wit became a formidable weapon, and what he lacked in physical dexterity he more than made up for in verbal skill. He used his tongue like the hunchback Danish philosopher, Soren Kierkegaard, who described himself in his *Journal* in words that could equally well be used to describe the youthful Stevens: "Delicate, slender, and weak, deprived of almost every condition for holding my own with other boys: melancholy, sick in soul, in many ways profoundly unfortunate, one thing I had: an eminently shrewd wit, given me presumably in order that I might not be defenseless." [20]

The fact that Stevens was not elected to Phi Beta Kappa left a raw wound. In a letter to a friend, written in anger when he learned of the election of another student to the fraternity, Stevens said: "Charles Leverett has entered into the service of the aristocracy, in the capacity of scullion; and it is expected as a reward for his services, he will be Knighted, i.e., elected Phi Betian. Those fawning parasites, who are grasping at unmerited honors, seem for once to have blundered into the truth. That they must flatter the nobility, or remain in obscurity; that they must degrade themselves by sycophancy, or others will not exalt them." [21]

[This youth would bludgeon but never flatter, and in this regard remained unchanged as a man. He would give freely of his money, his professional aid, and his affection, but only to those below him in power or status. He could not curry favor with men who had something he wanted, and as a politician this was to prove a lifelong handicap.]

The commencement address Stevens delivered at Dartmouth has luckily been preserved.[22] Here one may find germinal ideas that grew to form part of his philosophy of government. Paradoxically this youth, who in his old age was to be denounced as a revolutionary and Jacobin, and who was to be called even by his friends "the great leveler," began his speaking career with a defense of luxury and wealth. "Luxury," he said, "considered as the effect of improvement in the arts of convenience and comforts of life, is more entitled to applause than censure." Man's capacity for invention and improvement, he insisted, would never have been developed unaided by motives of pleasure and profit, and the combination had "banished barbarism, despotism, and superstition from a great portion of the globe."

His speech was not merely the defense of a poverty-stricken but pious youth ambitious to be rich; it was an attempt to express the Calvinist compromise between love of God and love of money, the sanctification of the pursuit of wealth. The New England virtues of thrift, sobriety, and pertinacity had become in the eighteenth century guarantees of both a house on Beacon Street and the Kingdom of Heaven, and the students at Dartmouth College were taught to expect that one would inevitably accompany the other.

The Calvinist compromise need not be dismissed as mere hypocrisy, nor the men who subscribed to it jeered at as crafty and covetous. Stevens, who was considered in the days of his greatest power a kind of caricature of the New England conscience, would never be troubled by a suspicion that wealth was sin. For him poverty was sin, and ignorance, and slavery—and none of these three was likely to be banished by men who were contemptuous of gold or power. Already at twenty-two he had an ineradicable respect for American capitalism. And when he finally embraced the cause of revolution, it was not a revolution against wealth and property but against an agrarian aristocracy battening on the irrevocable inequalities of slavery.

Thaddeus Stevens would remain a bachelor all his life. Nothing is known of his early loves if he had any. Of his attitude toward love itself during his Vermont years there remain only two suggestions. One is in his commencement address, where he said, ". . . if the lofty mansion sometimes becomes the habitation of costly excess, the hovel and the cabin are as frequently polluted by the gratification of baser passions." Another is in a letter to his friend, Samuel Merrill, who had gone to teach in York, Pennsylvania. After describing recent marriages of their Peacham friends as "newly licensed copulations," he went on: "Friend Sam, I assure you, you can hardly conceive the anxiety your friends feel for you in that distant country. Considering you exposed to the invincible charms of those fair Dutch wenches, with their dozen pair of petticoats they are really afraid, that you will lose your heart. . . . and then we shall despair of seeing you again; for I suppose it is as much impossible to transport those 'fair lumps of earth' into another climate as it would be to people America with crocodiles." [23]

In later years, as a rich lawyer in Pennsylvania, he paid court to the daughter of a prominent attorney, John Sergeant, who, according to William Hall, was pleased with the idea of her marrying Stevens. In the prime of life he was said to have been "a remarkably fine-looking man," six feet tall, with a clear, ruddy, smooth skin and beautiful chestnut hair.[24] When he was thirty-eight he had his portrait painted by Jacob Eichholtz, who portrayed a handsome, clear-eyed man with a direct, unsmiling but pleasant expression, straight nose and rather heavy chin. His mouth, which later photographs invariably caught in a dour twist, was here relaxed and almost gentle. But the courtship of Sarah Sergeant ended abruptly in a jewelry store when the girl "playfully suggested to Stevens to buy her a diamond ring, which she admired." Hall surmised that Stevens' ideas of propriety were shocked, or perhaps he thought that the young lady was mercenary or ambitious rather than loving, and he took offense at this and ceased his attentions."[25]

Why did Stevens, faced suddenly with the finality symbolized by the ring, flee from the marriage? His Pennsylvania friends, according to one acquaintance, blamed his bachelorhood on "his sensitiveness on account of his club foot." Soren Kierkegaard broke off his only engagement because of his fear of passing on what he called "the decoration on his back," and Stevens may also have been obsessed with the fear of fathering a crippled child.[26] It is likely too that he feared sharing the sight of his deformity, which would have been inevitable in marriage. The long, specially-made boot hid little enough by day, but at night it must come off altogether. And if Stevens did, in fact, suffer from a corrosive fear of being disliked by men, this fear seems to have been doubly magnified in regard to the "fair lumps of earth."

When he was about thirty-nine, an attack of "brain fever," possibly typhoid fever, left him entirely bald. Eventually he took to wearing a reddish-brown wig, an inevitable target of trite, good-natured ridicule. Once, when he was old and famous, and a foolish woman admirer begged him for a lock of his hair, he replied by bowing gallantly and handing her the whole wig. But at thirty-nine the sudden disappearance of his hair must have been a tormenting humiliation. He could cover up his bald head, as he could feebly disguise his lameness, but there was no camouflage in the bedroom.

Except for one instance, when his name for a time was linked in scandal with the young daughter of a friend, Stevens seems to have largely insulated himself against intimacy with any women his social equal. Eventually he found one woman he could trust to love him, one also crippled by accident of birth. With her, apparently, he could give of himself freely, perhaps since she too, for no cause save a casual edict of Heaven, had known indignity and shame.

Thaddeus Stevens went from Vermont to Pennsylvania in 1815, when he was twenty-three. He taught for a year in the academy at York, and spent his spare time studying law. He was known to be quiet, circumspect, and studious, but he made few friends. Later it was said that someone in York blackballed him when his name was presented as a candidate to join the Freemasons.[27] If true, it meant that for the second time in three years he had been shut out of a secret fraternity for no cause that he could recognize as just.

As if this were not enough, the County Bar Association passed a resolution, apparently aimed at Stevens, forbidding anyone to take the bar examination who was not studying law full time.[28] Had he won the friendship of a single influential lawyer in the city this rebuff need not have happened. But Stevens would lick no one's boots, and until he was admitted to the bar he could not win preferment on his own merit. There was a two-year residence requirement for lawyers in York, but Stevens felt himself ready after a single year's study, since he had read law for a year with John Mattocks. So in August, 1816, he went across the border to Bel Air, Maryland, where passing the examination consisted of answering a few questions on Coke, Blackstone, and Gilbert and presenting a gift of two bottles of Madeira wine to the examining judge.

Once admitted to the bar he could practice anywhere, and in September 1816, he opened an office in Gettysburg. The early months were lean, but he hung on precariously until the summer of 1817, when a murder case brought him local fame. One of his clients, James Hunter, was a feeble-minded farmer who had been jailed for debt. After his release he attacked and killed with a scythe the constable who had jailed him. The countryside was in a furor over the slaying, and for a time it was feared that Hunter would be lynched.

Stevens defended him before an immense, hostile crowd with the plea that he was insane. Though an uncommon defense for the time, it did not serve to convince the jury, and Hunter was hanged.[29] Nevertheless, Stevens won for himself a reputation for audacity and talent, and never thereafter lacked for clients. Later, with the mockery he sometimes affected when talking about justice, he pointed out that he had handled fifty murder cases, in many of them using insanity for the defense. Of all fifty only one had been hanged, and he, Stevens said, was the only one really insane.

Eventually Stevens became the leading lawyer of the state, winning nine out of the first ten cases in which he appeared before the Pennsylvania Supreme Court. The first case seems to have been critical in Stevens' life, for it thrust him headlong into a labyrinth he was never afterward to escape—the Negro problem. By 1821 he had been practicing five years in Gettysburg. He owned a house and lot, several other properties, and had saved enough to buy his mother a farm in Vermont. He was behaving circumspectly, and was extremely intent on winning cases. Norman Bruce, a Maryland slaveholder, asked his help in regaining possession of a slave, Charity Butler, who was claiming freedom under Pennsylvania law.

Bruce had leased the slave to a seamstress who lived near the border and who often crossed into Pennsylvania taking the slave with her. Charity Butler, knowing that a residence in Pennsylvania totaling more than six months meant legal freedom, had carefully tallied the days until the visits totaled over six months, then flatly refused to go back to Maryland. Stevens accepted the case for her owner and fought it through to the State Supreme Court. Insisting that unless a single visit exceeded six months the slave could not claim freedom, he won the case.[30]

The victory seems to have been ashes in his mouth. Vermont had been the first state to abolish slavery, and every schoolboy there had been made conscious of the honor. Stevens could have slipped into the facile rationalizations of the border lawyers, and continued to follow the hair-splitting regulations that casually changed a man into a chattel or a chattel into a man. But this slave, whose hopes of freedom he had smashed, apparently taught the twenty-nine-year-old lawyer something he had not learned in books—that the law can be an instrument of terror as well as justice.

Two years later at a Fourth of July public dinner he made a toast that was reported in the *Gettysburg Sentinel:* [31] "The next president. May he be a freeman, who never riveted fetters on a human slave." Professor Richard N. Current has held that Stevens joined the abolitionists in 1837 to further his political fortunes,[32] and that there is no earlier evidence of his antislavery position. This toast is one of several proofs that he took a public stand much earlier, and at a time when it was professionally hazardous for him to do so.

It was not only unfashionable but dangerous to be antislavery in southern Pennsylvania in 1823.[33] Ever since the Missouri Compromise of 1820, when the specter of disunion had frightened men in North and South alike, abolitionism had been considered officially extinguished, though its occasional sputters of flame could be seen starting up here and there across the North. Those who looked upon slavery as the nation's curse could do little else but subsidize the feeble colonization societies, dedicated to resettling free Negroes in Africa.

Few public leaders had the prescience of Thomas Jefferson, who in 1820 predicted that slavery extension would mean "the knell of the Union," and John Quincy Adams, who in the same year wrote an equally astute prophecy: "If slavery be the destined sword in the hand of the destroying angel which is to sever the ties of this Union, the same sword will cut in sunder the bonds of slavery itself." [34]

Thaddeus Stevens, who more than any other American political figure would take upon his own shoulders the staggering burden of achieving Negro freedom and civil rights, indicated in 1823 that he was on public record as opposing a slaveholder for President. By the end of the following year he was deeply involved in a personal tragedy that helped to entangle him even more in the problems of the Negro people.

CHAPTER THREE

———————————◆———————————

The Gettysburg Tragedy

Tamper not with idle rumor,
Lest the truth appear to lie.

Samuel M. Hageman

THE GETTYSBURG tragedy, as pieced together from fragments in the early town newspaper files and court records, began with the following notice in the *Adams County Centinel* of September 29, 1824:

> On Friday morning last, [September 23, 1824] a small negro woman, servant of Mr. Hersh, of this place, was found dead in a small pond or rather well of water, (about 3 or 4 feet deep,) near the Presbyterian Church —where it is supposed she had lain all night. A coroner's inquest was called, who reported that she came to her death by drowning, but in a manner unknown to the Jury. Every circumstance is in contradiction to the idea of its being accidental; and the generally received opinion is, that violent hands were laid on her. There was but one mark of violence, which was near the right eye, and when opened, a considerable quantity of extravasated blood was found there. This leads to the suspicion, that if she has been murdered, a blow was given on the temple, and her immediately thrown into the water, where she was drowned, before she could recover her senses. She was very far advanced in pregnancy.

A series of anonymous letters that appeared in the *Gettysburg Compiler* from 1824 to 1831, and some scribbled notes, unfortunately undated and unsigned, which were recently found among the correspondence of a lawyer, Moses McClean, who opposed Stevens in a libel suit arising out of the murder mystery, suggest that Gettysburg was seething with rumors. Some believed that Dinah, the servant girl, was pregnant with Thaddeus Stevens' child, and that on the day of her drowning she admitted it with pride to at least one friend. The woman was found dead near the Presbyterian Church—since torn down—which was around the corner from Stevens' law office. Suspicion of murder seems to have fallen upon a colored man, Black Peter, a servant in the John B. McPherson family, and also upon Thaddeus Stevens, who, it was said, had attended the coroner's inquest and strongly urged the opinion that the woman had committed suicide.

Unfortunately the coroner's records were not preserved, and no evidence has come to light that an autopsy was ever actually performed. Because of the extreme aversion in which autopsies were held at the time, it is unlikely that it would have been performed in any case. It was rumored at the time that a Dr. Miller had examined the dead woman and had stated that the child had been fathered by a white man, but without the evidence of an autopsy he could only have been echoing local gossip. What the coroner, Dr. David Horner, Jr., stated as to the cause of the death is not known. We have only the *Adams Centinel* account, reporting that the coroner's jury returned the verdict of death by drowning "in a manner unknown." It is most important to scrutinize the sources of these numerous rumors with an eye to the chronological order of their appearance, and to remember that the stories were never subjected to any examination in a court of law.

Ten weeks after the death notice in the *Adams Centinel* an anonymous letter was published in the *Gettysburg Compiler*. It was signed "Philanthropist," and complained that no action had been taken since the colored woman's death, though suspicion clearly rested on one person. The letter concluded: ". . . the girl was pregnant and within a few days of her delivery of a child, which, the respectable Physician who attended the coroner's inquest, I understood, has said was begotten by a white man." [1]

This was the first in a series of unsigned letters that continued to appear at various intervals for almost seven years. The second letter, signed "Caesar" and published on December 29, 1824, said in part: ". . . I find there is some person in your place strongly suspected of being guilty of the murder of the colored girl spoken of," and urged that his name be revealed. New details were added with each new letter. On February 2, 1825, the letter took the form of a conversation between a "Countryman" and a "Townsman," the Countryman noting that the girl "was pregnant to a white man," and that "suspicion rests against a colored man." The Townsman replied that the colored man was guilty of nothing but making an appointment for the white man to see the murdered girl, "a thing, it is believed, he had often done before." And he went on to hint that the colored man had been given a good deal of money to silence him.

Another anonymous letter on March 9, 1825, scouted the notion that the girl had committed suicide, noting that "the evening of her death, before her departure from her master's, [she] was more than usually cheerful; and about nine o'clock, when she went out, told her fellow servants not to bar the door against her, for that she would be in again shortly . . . she never appeared to be cast down, or in the least concerned, as respected by her character, about her situation of pregnancy; but rather seemed to value herself upon it."

Even the children of Gettysburg talked freely of the scandal, this letter went on. "For, one day, when the person suspected passed where a number of them were at play, one of them, in a low voice, says to his companion—'I don't see any blood on that fellow's hands, as Mother said there was.' 'Oh,' says the other, 'you see he keeps his hand in his pocket: I suppose that is the one that is bloody.' A third child said, that, when he passed him, he thought he saw something like black wool sticking between his fingers."

On March 25, 1825, another letter urged an investigation so that the suspected man be either "washed clean from the foul imputation" or "suffer the penalty which the laws of God and man have affixed to such crimes." The sixth appeared on May 18, 1825, and a seventh, which was particularly explicit, on July 5, 1826. The latter said:

. . . Suppose a man to have destroyed the life of a colored female, while in a state of pregnancy by him:

Suppose him to be unmarried, who, in his criminal intercourse with the opposite sex, makes mistress, maid, and colored females, the indiscriminate objects of his seductive practices:

Suppose, too, that he is a gambler, who has essentially contributed to ruin several men, who were doing good business for the support of themselves and families:

And suppose a person of the above description to be countenanced by a few men, whose situation might afford them an opportunity of assisting in giving a tone to the morals of the society in their neighborhood:

Could, or ought, such a state of things to exist, in the present state of society, without our special wonder and surprise?

On January 3, 1827, the anonymous writer reported in a new letter that a subscription amounting to $300 had been signed by various Gettysburg citizens and offered as a reward for information.

We know from what happened later that although none of the letters up to this point mentioned Stevens by name, they were undeniably aimed at him. From other sources we know that during the years these letters appeared Stevens was becoming a successful lawyer and a popular figure in Gettysburg politics. In May 1822 he had been elected to the Borough Council, and by unanimous choice had been named President.[2] In 1824–1825, critical years so far as the murder rumors were concerned, he was returned to the Borough Council again. He had been steadily accumulating property. In 1823 he owned three houses, two lots, and two other pieces of land assessed at $4,060. By 1827 the assessed value of his Borough property had jumped to $8,325, and by 1829, according to the tax records in Gettysburg, he would be the wealthiest man in the city.[3]

After the anonymous letter of January 3, 1827, no others appeared for over three years. It is possible that they would have ceased altogether and that the Gettysburg general public would have forgotten that the suspicion of murder had ever been directed at the president of their Borough Council and leading lawyer. But another murder by drowning which had taken place several hundred miles northeast of Gettysburg, reactivated the local mystery.

One September night in 1826, in Batavia, New York, five masked men smashed in the door of a printer's shop, clubbed the owner and set fire to the proofs of a new book on his presses, an exposé of the secret rites and oaths of the Freemasons, written by a local author, William Morgan. Several days later Morgan himself was kidnapped, carried to Canandaigua for a secret Masonic trial, and then taken to Fort Niagara on the Canadian border. There he disappeared, and the evidence seemed to indicate that his abductors, a handful of fanatical Masons, had taken him out on Lake Ontario and drowned him.

Five prominent citizens of Canandaigua were tried for the murder; and although the evidence was damning, three were acquitted and the remaining two received sentences of less than a year. The judge, a Mason, was denounced in the press, and deep-seated but hitherto quiet resentment against the order flamed into shrill protest all over the country. Other Masons were brought to court for collusion in the kidnapping, and their trials dragged on during 1828. By the time they, too, were acquitted, the American public was in the throes of one of its great periodic witch-hunts. Masonry was charged with being morally and politically sinister, and lodges everywhere were melting away in mass resignations.

What started out as a legitimate protest against bookburning, kidnapping, and probable murder was soon canalized into political uses. Antimasonry quickly mushroomed into a formidable political party. Since Andrew Jackson was a Mason, and openly scornful of the Morgan hysteria, his opponents were quick to identify Masonry with the Democrats. In late 1827 New York State sent 33,000 Antimasons to the polls; the following year saw the membership swell to 70,000.

[Thaddeus Stevens embraced Antimasonry with passionate enthusiasm.⁴] Within two years he had left far behind him the relative anonymity of his Gettysburg law practice and had become a figure in national politics, with the reputation of being a tough and talented organizer. It was not, however, until with John S. Ingram he started the *Adams County Anti-Masonic Star and Banner* early in 1830 that Stevens' preoccupation with the murder and drowning of William Morgan revived the rumors about the alleged murder and drowning in Gettysburg six years before.

Jacob Lefever, Masonic editor of the *Gettysburg Compiler*, who had published the anonymous letters in the previous years, said pointedly to the editor of the *Anti-Masonic Star* on June 8, 1830, that "if he wishes to preserve consistency and propriety of conduct, he should endeavor to ferret out the perpetrators of that diabolical deed. For, if he shall continue to speak of a crime committed in the State of New York, and neglect one of a similar character at home there would be just cause to suspect the purity of his motives."

Neither Stevens nor Ingram chose to reply. In early July the name of the paper was changed to *Star and Republican Banner*, and Robert W. Middleton became the new editor, though it was generally recognized that Stevens was still the power behind him.⁵ Middleton continued to hammer on the Antimasonic theme. Early in August he editorialized: "Murder cannot be covered up forever—blood once shed by a brother has a voice that will pierce the skies—the mark of the first murderer is upon the forehead of the murderers—and, although slow, but sure, justice will sooner or later overtake the guilty wretches —will yet be dragged to light and expiate their crimes upon the scaffold."

Lefever pounced upon the paragraph and republished it on August 10, 1830 with the following comment:

On the 24th of September, 1824 [two years before the abduction of William Morgan], the dead body of a colored woman was found in one of the back streets of our Borough. This fact is generally known to our citizens, and it is generally believed that her death was produced by violent means —in other words, that she was murdered. Notwithstanding the enormity of the circumstances attending the case, and our frequent reference to it, there has never yet been even a reward offered for the discovery of the perpetrators. The late Editor of the Star refused (or neglected) to assist us in unravelling the mystery which envelopes the subject, though his attention was twice called to it. We hope, however, the present Editor will pursue a different course. . . .

On August 31, 1830, another anonymous letter published in his paper struck the same note. Then on September 7, 1830, a letter signed "A member of the ABOLITION SOCIETY" offered $20 reward for information leading to the solution of the colored girl's death, and pointed out that the old subscription paper promising a $300 reward had unaccountably disappeared. The same issue called for a public meeting of the citizens of Gettysburg "for the purpose of devising means to discover the dastardly villain, that could murder, in cold blood, an unhappy woman far advanced in pregnancy." [6]

The *Star* continued to ignore the matter until an explicit letter signed "Justice," appeared in the *Compiler* October 5, 1830:

Some time has elapsed since I requested the Anti-masonic Editor to inform me, upon what grounds he remains altogether silent concerning the Gettysburg murder. . . . The quiet kind of contempt that Mr. Middleton has bestowed upon a fair and reasonable question will not win the applause of even his own partisans. . . . I am acquainted with men, who are well known to be respectable, upright, worthy persons—that are willing to let the matter sleep. They say, and with good intentions too: "Why disturb the filth? It is some time since the deed was committed—it is better to let the matter rest—it will be forgotten." I give this as the language of many well meaning men: They forget that to conceal murder is to commit it. They do not remember that they do injustice to one of our most eminent citizens —one with whom we are all acquainted—and who has ever been considered the principal in this atrocious crime. The man is possibly innocent—then why not relieve him of the load of agony which the general suspicion has laid upon his heart. . . .

Whereupon the *Star* editor briefly commented that he knew nothing of the murder and "cannot conceive how it can have any connexion with the Morgan affair." [7]

That Thaddeus Stevens was the man suspected of the murder was not publicly revealed by the tenacious letter writer until the following June, 1831. Stevens had made a particularly vitriolic Antimasonic speech in Hagerstown, Maryland, early in the month. He had read aloud many of the bloodthirsty Masonic oaths and had described Masonic rituals in detail. "The presiding officer . . . *personates the ALMIGHTY GOD*," he said, "*while the hood-winked candidate is made to represent MOSES*. And then, amid the lurid glimmerings of their midnight den, this feeble band of lowly reptiles aspire to enact the sublime and terrific scene, before which mortals veiled their faces, and Mt. Sinai trembled to its center!" He accused the Masons of drinking wine out of human skulls, and of keeping each other's secrets, "murder and treason not excepted." Masonry, he said, "was a base-born issue of a foreign sire. . . . a prostituted harlot" who had "entered the Courts of Justice and seduced the venerable Judges with her foul embraces." It encourages crime by promising immunity from punishment. "*It corrupts the fountains of justice. It stays the arm of the law. It stops the regular action of government. It binds the mind in darkness.*" [8]

Stevens' anonymous enemy, who heard this speech, at once wrote another letter to the *Gettysburg Compiler*. Describing Stevens as "a stout man, about forty years of age, with bald head and lame," he attacked the speech as a "compound of vile slander, barefaced falsehood and pandemoniac malignity." Then he thrust deep. "Any men who attempt to change our course, must come to us with pure hearts and clean hands. If they talk to us of cries and murder, we must *know* that they have no blood on their skirts. If a change in politics or religion be their object, we must have assurance that they are honest. Those must not come, in whose wake is heard the wail of the widow and orphan, or rioting in the spoils of the unfortunate." [9]

Immediately Thaddeus Stevens sued the *Compiler* editor for criminal libel and instituted a civil suit for damages. Lefever tried to get James Buchanan, a lawyer in Lancaster who would later become President of the United States, to be his counsel, but Buchanan refused.[10] With another lawyer, Moses McClean, Lefever apparently set to work dredging up evidence pointing to Stevens' guilt.

A file which presumably contained all they had found was preserved in a Gettysburg law office for 125 years. Of all the letters and papers in the file only one document, however, has any real bearing on the possibility of Stevens' guilt. This consists of three pages of almost illegible notes, which are not written in the handwriting of the lawyer. Internal evidence in the document itself indicates that it was not written by Lefever either. It appears to have been written about 1831, seven years after the alleged murder.[11]

[Page 1]

The morning this woman was found— Dinah She boasted to Sarah Wright, wife of John Wright—she was pregnant to Stevens— She was found by David Fletcher of Starboro [?] —in the mud hole—the roads being dry & dusty in peach time. Wm. McPherson was a boy and was sent out by Mrs. McPherson to their fathers farm for peaches—they went out along the turnpike—Black Peter was along—they came to

the fork of the Road they discovered a group of men standing
by [?] church. When Peter observed them—he remarked to Wm. Wonder what those men are doing there
—*I bet they found a dead negro*—Wm. McPherson
will prove this—Bill let us go and see what they
are about— They turned back till they came to North
street—there they met Mrs. Gilliland & [words crossed out] on her
way out—Peter asked her, *have they found Dinah*
says what them men doing over there—where you going.
The intimacy between Peter & Stevens to be proven—and
Peter has said he got many a half dollar to get her
out for Stevens—John Barret will prove this)—It
cannot be proven that Stevens requested to be put on
the Inquest—but he was on it—and wanted the
verdict suicide—after Dr. Miller had examined her
and thought she had been injured—and that she
was pregnant with a white child. Suspicion attached
itself upon Stevens at once before there was any
publication on the subject.

The Council met and offered a resolution for a
reward by resolution—he got to know what they were
doing—and he went in to them—and plead that
they had no authority to offer the reward and prevailed upon them to desist— It was then moved
by a member of the Council—to draw an individual
subscription paper for the purpose— He then made
an ill natured remark or two and left the room

[Page 2]

They went on and raised a sum of money—they all
signed it but himself and circulated it through
Town and raised a considerable sum—(It is supposed
his name is not to it)—John B. Clark has it—
It is said Clark kept it on account the suspicion
getting so strong against Stevens.

~~John L~~ [?] McNeely ⎱ will prove about the muddy shirt
  Ephraim's wife ⎰ of ~~shirt~~ Stevens.

Ephraim will prove about Stevens conduct—and
He will prove that Stevens gave him a lot of ground
within two weeks.

                                    suspected him of
      John Garvin said he thought Stevens   knowing more
than he did & he was afraid of his life. And
he believes Stevens shot at him.

Dobbins [12] pistol was taken about that time—and was
afterwards found in Stevens closet—loaded with two
balls.

Get Lefever to write to John Smith to ascertain
what woman told him about the murder of the
black woman—and where she lives—and her name.

Martha McNeely. The whole family know he was out late
that night—
Dinah was a bound servant of Hersh—

[Page 3]

Ask John Macfarlane—if Stevens said (when they talked
of raising a subscription for a reward)—that it was
all folly for him to pretend he did not know
there was a suspicion—in the matter. And then
went off and left them.

When it came to the trial, Lefever's lawyer did not introduce a
single detail from this document or from the anonymous letters. And
of the six or seven persons mentioned in the paper as apparently
knowing something pertinent to the case, none was called as a witness.
Lefever refused to discuss even the name of the anonymous author
and kept absolutely close-mouthed throughout the trial. This he did
in spite of the fact that Stevens' lawyer, Frederick Watts, waived the
rule excluding the facts from the evidence and offered to hear all that
Lefever might have to justify the libelous insinuations about "blood
on their skirts." [13] The result was that Lefever was found guilty and
sentenced to three months in the Adams County jail.

Continuing to edit the *Compiler* from behind bars, Lefever wrote
a defiant announcement of his own defeat on August 30, 1831, explaining why he had not introduced evidence of Stevens' guilt, and
insinuating strongly that he still believed in it.

In the LIBEL suit brought against us by Thaddeus Stevens, Esq. it was
deemed expedient to submit to a verdict of guilty—because the law would
not permit, nor could the Court with propriety allow, the facts to be proved,
even if the publication were known to be every word true. We were sentenced, on Wednesday, to an imprisonment of *Three* calendar months, a
fine of FIFTY DOLLARS, and the costs. This sentence was rather unexpected, and is deemed somewhat severe, because there is a CIVIL suit yet
pending, for the same publication, in which the whole merits of the matter
can be fully investigated.

Shortly after this, Lefever was pardoned by the Governor, George
Wolf, who was a Mason and who disliked Stevens. The civil suit
dragged on for several years. Lefever's lawyer promised in court that
"although they had not given the truth in evidence on that trial [the
criminal suit] yet they would be prepared to prove the truth of their
allegations on the trial of the civil suit." [14] But at the last moment
it was decided to fight the case on only one issue—the truth or
falsity of Stevens' remarks about Freemasonry. So the murder story
disappeared without ever having been examined in court.

Thaddeus Stevens managed to turn the trial into an Antimasonic theatrical. He brought witnesses from many miles away in New York State to testify about Masonic infamies and to verify the truth of his own Antimasonic charges. The suit finally ended in August 1835, with damages of $1,800 awarded to Stevens.

Since Stevens was more interested in clearing his own reputation than in ruining Lefever financially, he now made the editor the following offer:

Thaddeus Stevens proposes to Defendant, that if he will give up the name of the author of the libel on which suit was brought in this case, and will appear against him as a witness and testify—and if said author be a man of good standing and responsibility, and resident in the county of Adams —said Stevens will exact no more of the verdict against Defendant than will cover actual expenses.[15]

Lefever in his reply admitted that the author was "in possession of desirable real and personal property," and tried to get a definite commitment from Stevens as to the precise amount of the "actual expenses." Stevens replied that the sum would be "the same amount as paid by you to your counsel and the taxed costs. That amount can be ascertained by a statement to be made by yourself. If you are not chargeable with the whole guilt, I wish to punish your colleagues." Lefever protested that the sum would exceed $900 and he simply could not raise the money.[16] Here the correspondence ceased, and Lefever's property went under the sheriff's ax to pay the $1,800 damages. Stevens purchased the property, and then, in a gesture of mixed magnanimity and contempt he turned it back to Lefever and assigned to Mrs. Lefever the judgment remaining unsatisfied by the sale.[17]

The minutes of the trial were shortly published in Gettysburg as an Antimasonic pamphlet titled *Free-Masonry Unmasked.* Stevens may well have financed the publication, ostensibly as an attack on the brotherhood, but actually as a defensive measure to help clear his own name.

So ended the story. It will be seen that even Lefever's lawyer found no evidence worth introducing in court. The charges were all advanced by rumor and insinuation, spread, it is possible, entirely by one man, who succeeded in keeping his name out of print and out of the courtroom. Stevens' counsel, Frederick Watts, later a distinguished judge, apparently knew who this man was but did not identify him. He wrote his recollections of the episode as follows:

"At an early period of my knowledge of Mr. Stevens he had taken up the crusade against Masonry and was surrounded by the most vindictive opponents who charged him publicly and privately with the worst crimes on the criminal calendar, not excepting murder, and when I first met him at the bar my own impression had been poisoned by the thousand stories which I had heard of his cunning, his artifice, his deceit, as well as his crime. I soon, however, unlearned all this, for it was easy to trace to its source the origin of all these calumnies. I can say, without fear of contradiction, that a more candid, truthful, fair opponent at the bar never lived in our state. As a practitioner he was as honorable as he was powerful." Watts noted with bewilderment that all of Stevens' personal companions and all the influential men of his time were Masons, yet "not one of them with whom he dealt so harshly would not seek opportunity to render him personal service." He explained this vaguely in terms of a "mysterious influence" which Stevens had on all who surrounded him.[18]

Watts' implication that Stevens was persecuted because of his Antimasonry is not adequate, however, to explain the venomous accusations of murder. As we have seen, the accusing finger was pointed at Stevens two years before William Morgan's disappearance. And the first notice of Dinah's death, it will be remembered, where the editor had protested against the coroner's verdict, was not published by Stevens' enemy, Jacob Lefever, but by the editor of the *Adams County Centinel*.

Most of Gettysburg's citizens, however, seem to have agreed with Frederick Watts that Stevens was innocent and that the murder rumors had stemmed from the vicious pen of one or two personal enemies—perhaps men who blamed Stevens for their financial ruin —who happened also to be Freemasons. The townspeople showed their confidence by electing Stevens to the State Legislature in 1833 and sending him back six times in the next ten years. The faculty and administration of Gettysburg College honored him by making him a trustee, a post he was to hold for thirty-four years. The McPherson family, who employed Black Peter and were probably in a position to know the true facts of the story, remained on friendly terms with Stevens until his death. Edward McPherson became his law student and protégé. Later as Clerk of the House and unofficial historian for the Republican Party he planned to write Stevens' biography, though he did no more than assemble the mass of Stevens papers found in the Library of Congress today.

The murder rumors died away and were not revived, as they might well have been, in the numerous political campaigns when Stevens was running for Congress. Nevertheless, Stevens knew that there were men in Gettysburg who continued to believe in his guilt. When a young abolitionist preacher, Jonathan Blanchard, sought out Stevens in Harrisburg in 1836, hoping to enlist him formally in the abolitionist movement, he was told "by people near him that he was a blasphemer of God, the father of an illegitimate child or children, a gambler, and that he was open and fearless in his vices as in the advocacy of his principles." When Blanchard was criticized for enlisting aid from a man with Stevens' reputation, he wrote him a frank, ingenuous note: "Dear Sir: As you cannot help supposing that I know what vices and sins your enemies and others impute to you, you must think me a strange Christian if I am indifferent to them. . . . *I sought your acquaintance as that of a wicked man of influence in favor of a good cause . . .*"

To which Stevens replied: "*Probably between us and our God we are all of us somewhat deficient: I know I am deplorably so. But I feel certain that no living creature is the worse off for me,* and therefore my habit is to disregard things said to my prejudice, as either intentional or malicious."

Blanchard, later president of Wheaton College, Illinois, became Stevens' good friend and stout defender, though he never ceased being dismayed at Stevens' lack of religious enthusiasm, and at what he called the "prolonged personal sin" of Stevens' private life. Some weeks before Stevens' death, he visited him in Washington, with the hope of winning him to confession and baptism. He reported that Stevens said to him: "I have tried to deal justly with my fellow-men; I think— well, I will say, I *know* I have wronged or defrauded no person who lives or has lived on earth! Yet I do not trust to that fact, and have no right to, for my salvation, any more than any common sinner on the street." [19]

This was of course an overstatement; in his long life Stevens did his share of wronging and defrauding along with the rest of his fellow-men. But the *fear* of having wronged or defrauded, or of being charged with having done so, seems to have been something Stevens lived with constantly. Even his will betrayed him here. "I bought John Shert's property at sheriff's sale at much below its value," one paragraph in the codicil said. "I want only my own. All except $300, the proceeds and interest I direct shall be returned to the estate." [20]

Bound up with this fear was Stevens' passionate preoccupation with punishment. One devoured by a sense of grievance normally finds some solace in the punishment of others, and the need to punish can with some become a necessity. If Stevens found it legally impossible to punish sufficiently the men who falsely accused him of bludgeoning and drowning a woman said to have been his mistress and the mother of his child, he could nevertheless punish the Freemasons who refused to do penance for the murder and drowning of William Morgan.

Other men of his time were also outraged by the Morgan story. John Quincy Adams, Chief Justice Marshall, John C. Calhoun, Edward Everett, and William H. Seward were all sucked into the Antimasonic frenzy. But Stevens pursued Antimasonry with an intensity almost pathological in its nature, and did not relinquish the crusade until several years after it had been generally abandoned as a dead cause. Later the Southern slaveholder became for Stevens a still more satisfying object for attack. [The desire to punish deepened with his advancing years, until after the Civil War it became an obsession.]

It is possible, of course, that Thaddeus Stevens was the father of Dinah's child but absolutely innocent of her death. It is possible that Black Peter was a jealous suitor and the actual murderer, or that the death was in fact entirely accidental. It is also possible that Stevens was guilty of murder, and that he won the libel suits simply because no man had sufficient evidence to bring against him in the Gettysburg law court. One could even speculate that his bludgeoning of others might be subtle evidence not of a grievance but of a need for denial of his guilt, and on a deeper level a need for self-punishment.

But if Stevens did have a reputation for seducing "mistress, maid and colored females," as one letter to the *Gettysburg Compiler* said, why should he have been induced to murder one of them? There was no special penalty for cohabiting with Negro women this close to the Mason-Dixon line. Carl Schurz reported later that Stevens' Pennsylvania neighbors "did not, indeed, revere him as a model of virtue; but of the occasional lapses of his bachelor-like life from correct moral standards, which seemed to be well known and freely talked about, they spoke with affectionate lenity of judgment." [21]

One can, in fact, imagine a motive for murder. A child, were it really his, might be clubfooted, which would make his paternity apparent to all. Against this possibility is the fact that Stevens apparently took the risk of siring a bastard child quite frequently. Gossip was circulating in the Gettysburg area in 1832 that he might be the father in the case of an unmarried pregnant woman, the daughter of a widow, living near "the Forge." [22] Later, as we shall see, he was named in a paternity suit involving the daughter of a good friend, though here again, there was no real evidence to substantiate the charge. [23] Whatever may have been his actual behavior, his *reputation* for being a rake was well established.

Stevens' passionate crusading against the Freemasons and the slave-holders can much more easily be explained in terms of a continuing rage against his persecutors—or, indeed, simply against the emptiness of his own life—than in terms of penance for murder. He could have hated the Masons for a number of reasons, among them that they had shut him out of their brotherhood, and that they had revived and intensified a campaign of slander which had been hideously unjust from the beginning. As far as his crusade against slavery is concerned, the evils of that institution hardly needed to be underlined to him.

It is a fact that the local insinuations of murder died with the libel suit which ended in 1835.[24] From this time forward Stevens was a power in Pennsylvania politics, and after 1859 a national figure of ever-increasing stature. His own Lancaster district so respected him that it sent him to Congress with no serious opposition from the beginning of the Civil War until his death. And though many in his own state hated him with an intensity accorded few statesmen in American history, they did not revive the charge to include murder among the many crimes laid at his feet.

CHAPTER FOUR

———————— ◆ ————————

The Early Crusades

If it were once shown that the Bible authorized, sanctioned, and enjoined human slavery, no good man would be a Christian.

Thaddeus Stevens, June 10, 1850

IN THADDEUS STEVENS, more than in most men, the entanglement of good and bad lay on the surface for all to see. He could not hide behind a façade of urbanity either his affection or his hatred, his charity or his cruelty. First one and then the other is visible, like the faces of a coin. In his Gettysburg years a kind of Jekyll-and-Hyde character can be seen in his business dealings, his law practice, his relations with his servants, his attitude toward religion, and in his crusades against Freemasonry and in favor of free schools. He seemed always to have had two reputations, one black and one white.

By some he was disliked for his sharp business practices, and by others he was honored for his generosity. As early as 1822 he was accused of legal trickery when he bought at a sheriff's sale for $650 the farm and law library of James Dobbins, an old lawyer said to be senile and "half lunatic." Dobbins brought suit against Stevens, charging that the latter had discouraged prospective buyers who were willing to pay as much as $2,000, by warning them that the farm was loaded with liens. The local Gettysburg jury found Stevens guilty. The decision was reversed, however, by the Pennsylvania Supreme

Court, Justice Gibson pointing out that fraud had not been intended because the advice given by Stevens was actually correct. There *had been* liens on the land, and Stevens had bought the farm with these written into the contract.

The reversal did not clear his reputation with everyone in Gettysburg, for the heckling cry of "Dobbins! Dobbins!" followed him for years in the election rallies. The extraordinary measures that Stevens took to placate the old man suggest that he was deeply troubled, though whether in fear for his reputation or in guilt for having wronged another is not clear. "Quietly and without his knowledge, or the knowledge of anyone," William Hall related, "he sought out and provided a home for the old man in a comfortable room on the outskirts of town, and made him a boarder at his expense with the old lady who occupied the house." When he became unmanageable, Stevens had him placed in the almshouse with the understanding that he would be Attorney for the Directors of the Poor. This had been Stevens' position. He resigned it, and turned the office and library over to Dobbins—though quietly continuing to do all the work—and the old man "lived and died in the pleasant delusion that he was again a lawyer of importance." [1]

We have already seen how the anonymous letters to the *Compiler* accused Stevens of contributing "to ruin several men," and of "rioting in the spoils of the unfortunate." But his first biographer would write emphatically of Stevens' "thorough detestation of everything like trickery and meanness, his perfect fairness in all his business transactions." [2]

There is no doubt that Stevens became wealthy rapidly. First he bought town property and then timberland, hoping, like the other speculators in the area, to capitalize on Pennsylvania's mountains of iron ore. Local iron refining was a primitive process done in charcoal-burning furnaces, but Stevens was quick to catch the contagion of the local ironmasters, who dreamed of building an industry to rival that of the hated British. He invested heavily in 1826 in the Maria Furnace on South Mountain, and became half owner with James D. Paxton. In 1831 the two men built Mifflin Forge near the forks of the Conococheague, and in 1837 a still more ambitious furnace named Caledonia, after Stevens' native county in Vermont.

As Stevens grew rich, his private charities multiplied, until they became, as Hood expressed it, "almost one of the necessities of his being." No one ever approached him for aid, Hood continued, "who did not obtain it, when he was possessed of the means. His money was given freely and without stint, when he had it. And with this unbounded liberality was associated a strong feeling of pride, which but few of his most intimate friends ever suspected to exist. He would never confess to a want of money, no matter how straitened his circumstances . . . he preferred to have the reputation of harshness and cruelty, rather than be suspected of even occasional poverty. Beggars of all grades, high or low, are very quick in finding out the weak points of those on whom they intend to operate; and Mr. Stevens was always, but more particularly when he was a candidate, most unmercifully fleeced." [3]

He loved making the "magic gesture." He gave recklessly, without regard to merit or necessity, perhaps offering the kind of benevolence to others that as a child he had fondly dreamed might be offered to him. One Lancaster lawyer told of riding home with him from a trial and coming upon a sheriff's sale where a widow was about to lose her farm. Stevens joined the bidding and won the farm for $1,600, the actual debt due. He wrote out the check, ordered the sheriff to make the deed to the widow, and continued on his way. This kind of story became commonplace. In a speech in 1839 he said tersely: "Croesus is remembered only to be despised." [4]

"Mr. Stevens was far too observant, far too good a judge of men's motives," Hood said, "not to know that he was almost universally imposed upon. This knowledge led him to believe that nearly all men were corrupt and unfit to be trusted. As he grew older this feeling became stronger, and he came to regard the great bulk of mankind as mercenary creatures, only fit to be the tools of those who were strong enough, rich enough, and skillful enough to use them for their own advantage."

Nevertheless, Stevens' charities continued all his life. When he died there were found among his papers small notes totaling a hundred thousand dollars, which he had never pressed for payment.[5] Such compulsive giving is one measure of the intensity of Stevens' hunger. As Eric Hoffer has aptly put it, "Craving, not giving, is the mother of a reckless giving of oneself." [6]

But disillusionment was inevitable. Perhaps because of a certain ambivalence in his own feelings about giving, the gifts seldom seem to have brought him the satisfaction for which he hungered. Even his gift of a dairy farm to his mother, in which he had taken such obvious pleasure, turned out in the end to be a kind of poison for him. "Poor woman!" he once said. "The very thing I did to gratify her most hastened her death. She was very proud of her dairy and fond of her cows; and one night going to look after them, she fell and injured herself, so that she died soon after." [7] Still, Stevens' mother at her death was about eighty years old, and it is singular that her son should have felt guilt for an accident that was none of his doing.

In Stevens' Gettysburg years there was an even more unhappy ending to a story that began with a conspicuous act of benevolence. It concerned two of his servants, one a slave-girl named Keziah, who had fled from Shippensburg, Maryland, into Pennsylvania. Stevens had saved her from being returned to her master by proving in court that she was free by the old Pennsylvania law of 1780, which provided that all children of slave mothers in Pennsylvania would be free at the age of twenty-eight. Keziah was married to a mulatto youth in Maryland, whose owner, a tavernkeeper, was planning to sell him. She walked twice to Gettysburg to beg Stevens to prevent it. Stevens agreed to stop by the tavern on his return from the races at Hagerstown. He found the landlord engaged with a slave-trader, haggling over the price of the young mulatto, the owner demanding $500, and the trader offering $400. Taking the landlord aside, Stevens quietly proposed to buy the slave for an even smaller sum than the trader had offered, with the promise that after a period of indenture he would free him. The owner agreed.

When he was writing the bill of sale, Stevens slyly asked what he should put down as the slave's last name. The landlord blushed and stammered. "Oh, I'll put your name in," Stevens said. "These fellows always go by the name of their owners."

"I saw," he remarked in telling the story later to Alexander Hood, "he was the landlord's own son, or I never should have bought him for only $350."

The freed slave indentured himself to Stevens for seven years, agreeing to work for $100 a year, plus his food and clothing, and his wife became Stevens' housekeeper. Alexander Hood stated that the youth worked for Stevens for four years, and then was given money to set himself up in a trade. But Stevens' housekeeper of later years, Lydia Smith, who knew Keziah, told a reporter a quite different story.

"He went bad within one year," she said, and Stevens sent him away. Keziah in anguish hanged herself in the attic chimney corner on the last day before she was to leave the house. Her unconscious body was found and revived by Lydia's own mother. Again she tried suicide and was frustrated. She died finally "of consumption and beatings from her husband." [8]

Like all of the stories of Stevens' close personal relationships, this one survives in fragments. Its special significance derives from the pattern of tragedy that appears so often in his life. It will crop up later in his relations with his nephews, whom he took as his own sons when their father died. With them, too, the story began in an aura of warmth and friendliness, and ended with frustration and disillusion.

There was one woman whose relations with Stevens did not end in hatred or tragedy, Lydia Hamilton Smith, daughter of the woman who found Keziah attempting to hang herself in the attic. At the time of this near-suicide, about 1831 or 1832, Lydia was eighteen or nineteen. She was a very light mulatto, of considerable beauty, and was said to have been the daughter of a white man, a Mr. O'Neill, from Russell's Tavern.[9] However, her name would not be linked with Thaddeus Stevens in local gossip for another fifteen years. Not, in fact, until after the death of her husband, Isaac Smith, in 1848, would she become Stevens' housekeeper in Lancaster, and bring a certain serenity to his turbulent personal life.

When they came to write about his legal reputation, Stevens' contemporaries were agreed that he had extraordinary talent. But few of them failed to mention the violent contrast in his methods depending on whether he looked upon his opponents as weak or strong. O. J. Dickey wrote that Stevens "was as remarkable for his consideration, forbearance, and kindness when opposed by the young, weak, or diffident, as he was for the grim jest, haughty sneer, pointed sarcasm, or fierce invective launched at one who entered the lists and challenged battle with such weapons." Significantly, Stevens never acted as prosecutor in a capital case. And he frequently urged the abolition of capital punishment.[10]

Alexander McClure wrote of Stevens that he "was one of the strongest men before a law court that I have ever heard. He was thoroughly master of himself in his profession, and his withering invective and crushing wit, so often employed in conversation and political speeches, were never displayed in a trial of a case unless it was eminently wise to do so; and he was one of the most courteous of men at the bar whether associate or opponent. He was especially generous in his kindness to young members of the bar unless they undertook to unduly flap their fledgling wings, when they were certain to suffer speedy and humiliating discomfiture."[11]

His court audiences were always guaranteed a display of legal dexterity and good theater. "He was a lucky lawyer," said George W. Woodward, "who would go through an argument with Mr. Stevens without being laughed at."[12] Once when replying to a charge that he was "leading" a witness, he replied: "He looked so young and innocent I felt it my duty to lead him." And when one antagonist hurled an inkstand at him, he dodged it and said: "You don't seem competent to put ink to better use."

Frequently he was brutal. When prosecuting an uncommonly ugly man charged with acquiring land by fraud—a charge hurled at Stevens himself more than once—he said: "The Almighty makes few mistakes. Look at that face! What did He ever fashion it for, save to be nailed at the masthead of a pirate ship to ride down unfortunate debtors sailing on the waves of commerce." [13]

Stevens' most conspicuous talent, according to Alexander Hood, was "his faculty of seizing instantly upon the turning point of the case, without regard to the quantity of legal rubbish accumulated around it." When his colleagues came to court with sheaves of papers, Stevens appeared without even a portfolio, and while they scribbled notes, he sat preoccupied and quiet. But when he spoke, it was from a tenacious memory that had mastered the evidence and authorities and integrated the whole into a simple, overpowering argument.

Where Stevens was admired for his legal virtuosity, he was reviled for his attitude toward religion. Despite his pew in the local Presbyterian Church, and his Number 10 pew in the Gettysburg College chapel, he was no churchgoer, and made no secret of his independence of any sect. Once, when a clergyman asked him, after a long argument on predestination, "Stevens, did you ever study with a view to the pulpit?" he turned the question aside brusquely.

"Umph! I have read the books." [14]

He rejected much in Calvinist theology, but never completely abandoned the doctrine that man is by nature inherently evil. "I do not believe, sir, in human perfection," he said in a speech in 1837, "nor in the moral purity of human nature. 'Lead us not into temptation,' was the prayer of Him who knew the hearts of men." [15]

His deep distrust and suspicion was peculiarly concentrated in the clergy. In defending a Seventh Day Adventist who had broken Pennsylvania's rigid Sabbath laws he outraged the local ministers:

"How dangerous is the apparently pious doctrine that the Christian religion is a part of the common law. If it be true, all who disbelieve that religion are habitual breakers of the law. The Jew, the Hindoo, the Pagan, are perpetual malefactors." Pleading for a rigorous separation of church and state, he went on: "It is a melancholy truth, that those who believe in one God, have been more intolerant than Pagans. Polytheism, however erroneous, by allowing the worship of numerous Gods, became indulgent to the introduction of many new ones. But the Mohammedans, the Jews, and above all, I am compelled to say, the Christians, have been guilty of the cruelest persecutions that ever afflicted the human race." [16]

Later, as he became more absorbed by the slavery question and discovered that the noisiest defenders of slavery were often preachers, he came to hold the whole profession in contempt. "I will say," he once said in Congress, "that these reverend parasites do more to make infidels than all the writings of Hume, Voltaire, and Paine. If it were once shown that the Bible authorized, sanctioned, and enjoined human slavery, no good man would be a Christian. It contains no such horrible doctrine. But if it did, it would be conclusive evidence to my mind that it is a spurious imposition, and not the word of God who is the Father of men, and no respecter of persons." [17]

To a Gettysburg seminary student going to a nearby town to preach, he once said urbanely, "I have some advice: Preach the Gospel, but don't attempt to prove it." [18] Few of his contemporaries knew that he supported several theological students through their academic careers.

Pro-slavery clergymen who felt his lash were quick to denounce him as an infidel, and the antislavery ministers feverishly sought the honor of converting him. They could not understand how a man so open and unashamed in his vices could still be in so many respects virtuous—a denouncer of slavery, corruption, and intolerance, fiercely honest and defiant in the face of tyranny. He had even become a teetotaler, having renounced liquor early in his thirties.[19]

For the most part Stevens ignored in contemptuous silence the accusation that he was an atheist. Once, however, when an editor went so far as to accuse him of blasphemously "administering the sacrament to a dog," he brought suit and sent the man to prison for libel. If the editor had not denied it, Stevens said to a friend, "it would have broken my mother's heart." [20] And late in life Stevens was persuaded to repudiate publicly the widespread belief that he was an infidel.

"I am not surprised nor much moved at any scandals which may be publicly or privately uttered about myself. I do not usually contradict them. He is a fool who disbelieves the existence of a God as you say is charged on me. I also believe in the existence of a hell for the especial benefit of this slanderer. I have said that I never deny charges however gross. I make an exception when my religious belief is brought in question. I make no pretension to piety (the more the pity), but I would not be thought an infidel. I was raised a Baptist and adhere to their belief." [21]

Stevens was steeped in Bible lore and used Biblical symbols in his speeches with telling effect. He called the Book of Job, "the grandest drama in any language," and perhaps felt a certain kinship with this Old Testament hero. Evidence of his rigorous Calvinist upbringing permeated his thinking all his life. Nevertheless his reputation stuck to him. "He is an infidel, and, of course, recognizes no moral responsibility," wrote the editor of the Alabama *Union Springs Times* on July 24, 1867, after visiting him in Lancaster.

Shortly before his death Jonathan Blanchard wrote to him in mixed exasperation and sorrow: "At present in every part of the United States, people believe that your personal life has been *one prolonged sin;* that your lips are defiled with blasphemy! your hands with gambling!! and your body with women!!! . . . You owe it to yourself and to your mother's God to leave some means of correcting this belief if false, or to show that you have always condemned and despised yourself on account of these besetting sins! I have, after all, a strange hope that you are not to be lost. . . . But as I have studied you the last quarter century you seem to me to have been able at times to say 'With the mind I serve the law of God, but with the flesh the law of sin! . . .* The good you have done the country (and none has done more if so much) is no offset for vice such as I have named above." [22]

Long after Stevens' death Jeremiah S. Black, an old political opponent, said of him: "When he died he was unequalled in this country as a lawyer. He said the smartest things ever said. But his mind, as far as his sense of obligation to God was concerned, was a howling wilderness." [23]

The sharp split between the destructive and the constructive in Stevens' behavior is nowhere more dramatically demonstrated than in the two crusades he carried on simultaneously in the early 1830's. One was his Antimasonry, the other his championship of Pennsylvania's free public schools. We have already explored possible explanations for the intensity with which Stevens hounded the Freemasons. But it should be pointed out that there were other factors than the Morgan mystery to make Freemasonry suspect to Stevens and many other Americans.

In eighteenth-century France an astonishing number of nobles, bankers, and intellectuals had become Freemasons, many of these men playing an active role in the revolution, and the aura of revolutionary conspiracy had accompanied the Masons to America. Clergymen, suspicious of the semireligious pageantry and of the Masonic oaths with their threats of throat-cutting and disembowelment, believed that Freemasonry encouraged freethinking and blasphemy.

Even to those sophisticated Antimasons who refused to believe Masonry actually dangerous, it still represented mysteries, shadows, enchantment and fakery, as opposed to reason, freedom, and enlightenment. Morgan's disappearance, and the unsatisfactory nature of the trials of his abductors, kindled a national rage, however, that was genuinely hysterical in nature, and therefore certain to be short-lived.

Many politicians joined the movement cynically. William H. Seward, for example, admitted later that he had entered the party because it was the only one opposed to Jackson that had any life.[24] Stevens met Seward at the Antimasonic Convention of 1831. The two men shared a hotel room, and argued through the night for their favorite candidates. Stevens favored John McLean, justice of the U. S. Supreme Court, but finally abandoned him to support the convention favorite, William Wirt. Seward was amiable and winning, a gifted storyteller, politically ambitious, but with no burning convictions at this time. Stevens, on the other hand, was a genuine convert. Hatred of the Masons had brought meaning and purpose to his life.

Their candidate was matched against two giants, Andrew Jackson and Henry Clay, and in the election of 1832 Wirt carried only the seven votes of Vermont. Seward and Thurlow Weed were astute enough to see that the strength of Antimasonry was spent, and joined forces with Henry Clay in forming the Whig Party. As the excitement subsided, and men realized shamefacedly that Masonry was mostly innocuous symbolism and pure theater, they forgave their neighbors or themselves for their Masonic connections, and the lodges slowly began to fill up again.

But Stevens refused to abandon Antimasonry, and almost single-handedly whipped up the frenzy in Pennsylvania for another four years, so that by 1838, out of 116 lodges in the state only 46 were left. He retained the admiration of ex-president John Quincy Adams, who described him in his diary on January 17, 1836 as "the great anti-Masonic leader in Pennsylvania," and on September 13, 1837 as "a remarkable man, likely hereafter to figure in the history of this Union."[25]

Antimasonry was easy to keep aflame in rural Pennsylvania, with its numerous Mennonites, Dunkers, Moravians, Quakers, and Scotch-Irish Presbyterians, all of whom abhorred ritual and oath-taking. In 1833 the party elected Stevens to the Pennsylvania House of Representatives. It is not surprising, in the light of his experience with the Masonic editor Jacob Lefever, that once in the legislature he chose to fight for an investigation of the influence of Masonry in the Pennsylvania courts. But he was outvoted and outmaneuvered, and failed to win even the power to subpoena witnesses.

Meanwhile a "committee to investigate Anti-Masonry" kept up a running barrage of ridicule. Stevens returned sarcasm with venom.

When one Democrat denounced him as the "Arch Priest of Antimasonry," he replied: "Mr. Speaker, it will not be expected of me to notice a thing which has crawled into this House and adheres to one of the seats by its own slime." Thomas M'Elwee, Democratic whip and a prominent Mason, at one point challenged Stevens to a duel, but he contemptuously refused to fight.[26]

When one Antimason voted against a bill Stevens cherished, he asked caustically: "Are you a married man?"

"Yes," came the reply.

"Have you any children?"

"Yes, several."

"I am sorry to hear that," Stevens said. "I was in hopes, sir, that you were the last of your race." [27]

In 1835 an unexpected split in the local Democratic Party permitted the Antimasons to win a majority in the House and Senate, and the post of governor. Stevens now set out to hound the Masons out of existence. He introduced a bill to suppress all secret societies, and in the hearings subpoenaed many prominent Masons, including ex-Governor Wolf, who had pardoned his enemy, Jacob Lefever.

Huge crowds swarmed into Harrisburg, their appetites whetted by the promise of scandal. The Masons rightly reckoned Stevens' attack to be potentially calamitous and united for the defense. On January 11, 1836, every Masonic witness appeared but refused to be sworn, and instead read an earnest statement that Stevens' committee was violating his constitutional rights. This defense, now so commonplace, caught Stevens unprepared. His temper was not improved when one witness needled him about his having been blackballed for lodge membership. When finally in a display of exasperation he told one witness to hold his tongue, he handed the opposition a weapon they were quick to turn against him. Several in his own party were angered, and the House on January 21, 1836, by a vote of 50 to 43 discharged the witnesses and ended the investigation.[28]

The Democratic press, which had denounced the whole episode as a recurrence of Salem witchcraft days, triumphantly proclaimed Stevens' career as "Chief Inquisitor" to be finished. Still he maneuvered through the House a bill making membership in a secret society good cause for the challenge of a juror. It passed by one vote. This was his only triumph in the cause of Antimasonry. His own people failed to re-elect him, and let him cool his heels for a year before returning him to the legislature. "He was a terror to an arbitrary majority," said one member of the House later, "and he laid a heavy hand when he had a chance, on a minority. I am free to say that I look back to the session of 1835–6, when he guided or rather governed us, with great regret." [29]

Long after every other politician had ceased pelting the Masons, Stevens finally stopped, but he remained an Antimason to his death. In the last year of his life, when he was trying to unseat the President of the United States for "high crimes and misdemeanors," he wrote to the Clerk of the House asking for the names of the United States Senators who were members of the Masonic Order.[30] No doubt he feared that the Masons in this last great battle would once more conspire to defeat him.

The Jekyll-and-Hyde character of Stevens' career in the Pennsylvania Legislature was apparent even to the men who hated him. When it came to his fight for free schools, he demonstrated that in this cause he could cooperate with Mason and Democrat, and would if necessary turn against his own party.

Here was a crusade he had every reason to lose. There were no free schools in America in the 1830's except in certain New England states and several large cities. Well-to-do parents paid tuition or a state tax, and free education was provided only for those whose parents publicly admitted their poverty. The children were thus invidiously divided into paupers and non-paupers. While few openly criticized the system, which existed in church and private schools as well, resentment was reflected in the school statistics, for thousands of parents, unable to pay the fees and too proud to admit it, simply kept their children at home.

Stevens began making speeches on behalf of free schools as early as 1826. The *Gettysburg Sentinel* on July 26 reported his toast at a local banquet: "Education. May the film be removed from the eye of Pennsylvania and she learn to dread ignorance more than taxation." In 1832 he helped the Gettysburg Lutherans obtain a state charter for their Pennsylvania College—which became Gettysburg College—deeded them land for the site at a nominal fee, and in 1834 against vigorous opposition won for the school an appropriation of $18,000 in the legislature.

Those who opposed the college bill he described as men who "deem it of much more importance that mudholes in their roads should be filled up, that their horses may go dry-shod to the mill, than that the rubbish of ignorance should be cleared away from the intellects of our children." If a bill had been introduced to improve the breed of hogs, he said, it would have passed handily, but a measure to improve the breed of men was certain to expect nothing but trouble.

The speech was applauded by *The Pennsylvanian*, a Jackson paper, on February 4, 1834, as "one of the most beautiful, classic and pungent pieces we ever heard," and Stevens was rewarded by having the next new building on the college campus named Stevens Hall. The *Lancaster Examiner* praised him as an orator with "few equals and no superior in the state." [31] But his own party was violently opposed to public education. One handbill in the election of 1833 proclaimed: *Thaddeus Stevens and Gettysburg College against the Farmers and Mechanics of Adams County.*[32] The German sects dotting the area, each with its own school and a good deal of instruction in German, saw in his free-school agitation a threat not only to their pocketbooks, but also to the preservation of their integrity as transplanted German communities and to their sanctity as holy societies. Soon the other Antimasonic leaders threatened to ride Stevens out of the party for his radical notion that education was the responsibility of the state. Stevens met this attack with an angry public letter:

"I would sooner lose every friend on earth than violate the glorious dictates of my own conscience—the clearest commands of my official oath. Pardon me, therefore, while I tell you that I cannot obey your orders. I will not sacrifice your posterity to selfish views. . . . I have already resolved that the sight of my name shall never again burthen your ticket. . . . I shall withdraw from your county to some place where the advocates of *Anti-Masonry* may still be the advocates of *knowledge.*" [33]

There then developed the spectacle of Stevens ardently collaborating with the Democratic Governor Wolf while simultaneously denouncing him as a Freemason. Wolf was as ardent as Stevens in this cause, and the two men succeeded in pushing the state's first free-school law through the legislature with only one opposition vote. The legislators went home at the end of the session to find the voters furious. About 32,000 signed petitions for repeal; a mere 2500 asked for its continuance. Legislators were sent back with orders to repeal or be replaced in the next election.

On the day set for the vote to repeal, April 11, 1835, the Chaplain of the House solemnly asked God "to bare His strong right arm and save the State from that poverty and bankruptcy which are sure to follow if the people are to have their property wrested from them for the education of all the children." Speeches against the school law followed. "Free schools," shouted one, "are the hot beds where idle drones, too lazy for honest labor, are reared and maintained . . . and the school tax is a thinly disguised tribute which the honest, hard-working farmer and mechanic must pay out of their hard earnings to pauper, idle and lazy schoolmasters."

The Senate quickly passed the repeal bill, but the House waited for the expected speech by Thaddeus Stevens. Curious to hear him, the Senators filed into the House galleries. He did not disappoint them. First he demonstrated with simple statistics that a free-school system was not only more efficient but less costly. He defended schoolmasters as able and industrious, and struck at the greed of the rich. Then, out of the sufferings of his own youth he spoke with special passion. The repeal law, he said, was simply a re-enactment of the old pauper law which set apart the poor men's children as a distinct class. "Hereditary distinctions of rank are sufficiently odious," he said, "but that distinction which is founded on poverty is infinitely more so. Such an act should be entitled, 'An act for branding and marking the poor, so that they may be known from the rich and the proud.'"

"I know," he went on, "how large a portion of the community can scarcely feel any sympathy with, or understand the necessities of the poor; or appreciate the exquisite feelings which they enjoy, when they see their children receiving the boon of education, and rising in intellectual superiority above the clogs which hereditary poverty had cast upon them. . . . When I reflect how apt hereditary wealth, hereditary influence, and perhaps as a consequence, hereditary pride, are to close the avenues and steel the heart against the wants and rights of the poor, I am induced to thank my Creator for having, from early life, bestowed upon me the blessing of poverty."

He urged the legislators to ignore the misguided petitions and to lead their people as philosophers, with courage and benevolence. "Build not your monuments of brass or marble," he pleaded, "but . . . make them of everliving mind!" [34]

When he finished and limped back to his seat, the House members broke into cheers. Suspending the rules, they amended the repeal bill into an act actually strengthening the school law and passed it that night. The Senators filed back into their chamber and did the same. It was an astonishing victory. New York, Connecticut, Rhode Island, and New Jersey—to say nothing of the whole South—were not to have statewide free-school systems until after the Civil War.[35] Stevens had dealt a blow to illiteracy in Pennsylvania at least a generation before it could otherwise have been expected.

The school fight taught Stevens something he never forgot, that reform inevitably was followed by reaction, that what one legislature passed could blithely be tossed out by the next. "This light of knowledge is so easily extinguished, and so hard and tedious to be rekindled," he said in a later speech, "that it ought to be as carefully guarded, night and day, as was ever the sacred fire by the vestal virgins. . . .

Render learning cheap and honourable, and he who has genius, no matter how poor he may be, will find the means of improving it."

[If Stevens' crusades against Freemasonry and in favor of free schools had anything in common, it was that both were attacks on privilege derived from position rather than merit. Yet there is no doubt about which one brought him the deepest satisfaction. Shortly before he died, he had his speech on free schools reprinted. Handing a copy to Alexander McClure, he said: "That was the proudest effort of my life." [36]]

CHAPTER FIVE

———————◆———————

The Radical Beginnings

I wish I were the owner of every Southern slave, that I might cast off the shackles from their limbs, and witness the rapture which would excite them in the first dance of their freedom.

Thaddeus Stevens, 1837

WHEN A slave crossed the Mason-Dixon line into Pennsylvania, he was not unconditionally free, for his master had the right to follow and track him down. The Maryland border was an exposed salient, hilly and wooded, running high into Northern territory, a favorite crossing for fugitives. Unscrupulous slaveholders, hunting their lost property in the southern Pennsylvania counties, frequently took back any convenient Negro when they could not find their own. The free colored population lived in terror of these kidnappings. Word soon spread among them that a lame lawyer in Gettysburg could be counted on to win them a hearing in court.

In questioning a slaveholder about the identification of his property, Stevens was brilliant and ruthless. Had he not been so able a lawyer, this activity could well have cost him his profession. "He stood almost alone in his community," Hood reported, "whereas to have taken the popular side would have given him immediate professional preferment." "He was an abolitionist," O. J. Dickey said later, "before there was such a party name." [1]

In 1831 the New England abolitionists had found a powerful voice in William Lloyd Garrison, who started the publication of his *Liberator* in Boston in that year with words that made him famous:

I do not wish to think, or speak, or write with moderation. . . . I will be as harsh as truth and as uncompromising as justice. . . . I will not equivocate—I will not excuse—I will not retreat a single inch—and I WILL BE HEARD.[2]

Garrison, like Thaddeus Stevens, was the son of a drunkard who abandoned his wife. He was also a teetotaler and an Antimason, and had already suffered imprisonment in Baltimore for his antislavery sentiments. When reproached by a friend for the heat and severity of his language, he said: "I have need to be all on fire, for I have mountains of ice about me to melt." [3] He did not say slavery was a financial stupidity, a political folly, or a social anachronism; he said "Slavery is sin!" And a Puritan community listened.

Thaddeus Stevens at first was content to attack slavery in his own independent, quietly personal fashion, and avoided the organized antislavery groups. But by 1835 he had become active in forming a colonization society—the most conservative of all antislavery activities.[4] This satisfied him for less than a year.

Stevens never followed Garrison, who was a pacifist and advocated peaceful dissolution of the Union. Nor did he at first go so far as Theodore Weld, leader of the western abolitionists, who advocated "gradual emancipation immediately begun." [5] He was content to attack slavery within the framework of the existing state governments and legal system. In 1836, when the Antimasonic candidate, Joseph Ritner, became Governor of Pennsylvania, every other governor in the North condemned the abolitionists in their annual messages, and some even recommended legislation against the agitation. But Ritner made a stout attack against "bowing the knee to the dark spirit of slavery." It was widely believed that Thaddeus Stevens had written the message, and he was blamed in the press for making the governor an abolitionist.[6]

In 1836 Jonathan Blanchard, who was then a young agent for the National Anti-Slavery Society, was attending the first meeting of the Pennsylvania Anti-Slavery Society in Harrisburg. He called on Stevens, who, with most of the Antimasonic legislators, was living in Nagle's Hotel. Blanchard, a native Vermonter, had been mobbed in several Pennsylvania towns, and hoped to get from Stevens letters of introduction which would permit him to lecture freely in the Gettysburg area. Stevens invited him to dinner at the hotel, Blanchard related, "where sat a hundred members of his own party in the Legislature, most of whom would have, from choice, sooner dined with the devil than with me." Blanchard urged him to make antislavery a political issue. "If you can turn your Anti-Masons into abolitionists, you will have a party whose politics will not bleach out. The Slaveholders will not 'possum like the Freemasons, but will die game."

As they were parting, Stevens handed him ninety dollars, saying with his characteristic sardonic wit: "If they Morganize you we will make a party out of it."

Blanchard at first refused the money, but Stevens pressed it on him, saying: "I am one and twenty in such things and know they cannot be done without money."

Blanchard led the first free public discussion against slavery in Gettysburg. He was savagely assailed by the county judge, who demanded a public vote of condemnation, and as he left the hall he was showered with rotten eggs. This news enraged Stevens. Returning from Harrisburg, he called another town meeting to reconsider the vote of censure. After pillorying the judge for denying the preacher a basic constitutional right, he said: "There comes along a Universalist here, and you put him up and hear him. He passes on and no harm done. But there comes along another man to preach in favor of universal liberty, and him you answer with violence and rotten eggs! Oh shame! SHAME! Shame! What free man does not feel himself covered all over with burning blushes to find himself surrounded by such *free* men!!" Singlehanded, he persuaded the audience to reverse its former resolutions and invite Blanchard to return.[7] He did come back, and was treated with courtesy, but the *Gettysburg Sentinel* reported on March 20, 1837, that nine-tenths of the community were opposed to his views.

Stevens was now hailed in the antislavery press as the foremost abolitionist in Pennsylvania. But he had a different role from itinerant crusaders like Blanchard, evangelists like Wendell Phillips, or editors like Benjamin Lundy and William Lloyd Garrison. [He worked for the cause of antislavery chiefly in two ways: as a lawyer defending fugitive slaves, and as a legislator attacking proslavery legislation.]

Memorials from Southern legislatures urging the passing of bills to suppress abolitionist newspapers were flooding the legislatures of the North. In Pennsylvania these petitions were referred to the House Committee on the Judiciary, of which Stevens was chairman. He saw to it that the committee rejected them, declaring that "every citizen of the non-slave states has a right to think and freely to publish his thoughts on any subject of national and State policy."[8]

Stevens' first big challenge from the proslavery legislators came in the Pennsylvania Constitutional Convention of 1837. This convention had been instigated by the radical wing of the Democratic Party—the Loco Focos—who wanted to broaden the suffrage by giving the vote to every man past twenty-one. At this time only taxpayers with a two-year residence were permitted to vote, and the Democrats, doing their best to carry out the egalitarian reforms advocated in the past by their great idol, Andrew Jackson, hoped to include as voters the working-men who had no property.

The same radical Democrats also wanted to limit the suffrage to white men. At this time prosperous Negroes who owned property could vote, though the right was largely theoretical, since in the larger cities such Negroes were simply kept off the tax rolls so that they would not show up at the polls. Here, then, in a microcosm, was the dilemma of the nation in 1837—that the revolutionary party of Andrew Jackson, which so strengthened the democratic processes in the United States, should simultaneously have pushed the clock back wherever the black man was involved. Jackson was himself a slaveholder, and had denounced the abolitionists in his message to Congress, December 1835, as plotters of a civil war.

When the Democrats in Pennsylvania tried simultaneously to bring the vote to the white laborer and deny it permanently to the Negro, they saw no betrayal of the Declaration of Independence. The Pennsylvania laboring man hated the black man who fled North, fearing not only his economic competition but also the social degradation of sharing his job. The first Negro riot in Philadelphia had come in 1834, and now petitions streamed into the legislature to stop the immigration altogether.[9]

Thaddeus Stevens, leader of the most reactionary wing of the Whig-Antimasonic coalition, compounded the paradoxes of the convention by opposing both the widening of white suffrage and the abolition of black suffrage. He fought off the resolutions prohibiting Negro immigration with every parliamentary trick he knew, and succeeded in keeping them out of the new constitution. With the Negro-suffrage issue he was not so successful, for he lacked the full support of his own party. He ridiculed the Democrats as sycophants of southern slave-holders and berated Whigs and Antimasons for cowardice. "Let those who stand in fear of the South," he said, "truckle to their debasing tyranny." When one Democrat replied that "God pronounced that Ham and his descendants should be the servants of servants to their breth-ren," Stevens responded that he was appalled to hear "the Holy Scrip-tures cited as an apology and license for oppression." [10]

He "went about the hall like a buffalo bull," one convention member said later, "tossing men great and small on his horns, this way and that, upon the slightest provocation, or without any. He was the terror of the whole body, and the members huddled and hurried out of his way." [11]

Hoping to win popular support for the anti-Negro resolution, the Democrats arranged a public demonstration against the state's abolitionists. Seven hundred men, calling themselves "Friends of the Integrity of the Union," gathered in Harrisburg to hear Stevens and his allies denounced. Stevens himself walked boldly into the hall, and after the first speech asked permission to reply. "Every spitbox was kicked and rattled," one observer wrote. "Hundreds hissed and those that did not hiss groaned and howled. It was bedlam uncapped. . . . I looked at Mr. Stevens. He turned with calm haughtiness and looked that storm of howls and hisses in the face! Then with an emphasis utterly indescribable, above the uproar, he said, 'Mr. President, we're not slaves here in Pennsylvania and if, sir, the attempt is made to make us such, there are some of us in this Court House who will make resistance enough to let Pennsylvanians outside know the doom that awaits them.' "

The hisses died away and an immense quiet filled the hall. Then Stevens proceeded with a droll mock solemnity to mimic the proslavery preacher who had preceded him until the audience was shouting with laughter. Thereafter, whenever the Chairman offered proslavery resolutions, Stevens would move to amend them with phrases from the Bill of Rights and the Pennsylvania Constitution. He turned the whole meeting into a farce, and it shortly broke up in a roar of laughter.[12]

But this triumph served only to alienate Stevens still further from the proslavery wing in his own party. "Thaddeus Stevens! a man who has taught the NEGROES to contend for the rights of a white man at the polls! by his zealous support of the accursed doctrines of ABOLITION," trumpeted the Bedford *Gazette*.[13] When it came to a final vote on whether or not the Negro should continue to have the ballot, Stevens could muster only forty-four allies. Seventy-seven voted against him, a dozen or more from his own party. These men clearly believed that Stevens, despite his reputation as a conservative, was in reality a dangerous radical. No man, they said, could be an abolitionist without being subversive and revolutionary at heart.

During this period Southern protests against abolitionism became even more violent. "I warn the abolitionists, ignorant and infatuated barbarians as they are," said Congressman J. H. Hammond of South Carolina in 1836, "that if chance shall throw any of them into our hands, they may expect a felon's death." [14] The *Louisiana Journal* in 1835 made a gesture that was to become commonplace in the South. For the kidnapping of abolitionist Arthur Tappan it offered to pay $5,000. Later the city of Savannah offered $10,000 for Amos A. Phelps; East Feliciana and Mt. Meigs, Louisiana, each offered $50,000 for Arthur Tappan or any other prominent abolitionist; New Orleans offered $100,000 for Tappan or LaRoy Sunderland.[15]

But the proslavery men of the North needed no such encouragement, and were quite capable of independent action. In 1838 a mob in Philadelphia sacked and burned Pennsylvania Hall, built by the abolitionists because they were denied a hearing in every public building in the city.[16] William Lloyd Garrison in 1835 was dragged around the streets of Boston with a rope about his neck and very nearly lynched. John Greenleaf Whittier, poet and editor of the *Pennsylvania Freeman,* had his office sacked and burned in Philadelphia in 1838. And in the Far West, where North and South met along the Mississippi River, Elijah Lovejoy in 1837 met a worse fate. Hounded out of St. Louis because he protested editorially against the public burning of a Negro murderer, he crossed the river to Alton, Illinois, and set up his press again. When he began urging abolition, a mob crossed the river from Missouri, wrecked the press and riddled him with bullets.

Stevens embraced the cause of antislavery in a decade when it was not merely inexpedient but dangerous. He was thereby branded a visionary and fanatic, and also a revolutionist. He had, in reality, become a convert to the religion of antislavery, and had been captured by an insubstantial vision, a Promised Land. Never thereafter would he turn his back upon it. "I wish I were the owner of every Southern slave," he said, "that I might cast off the shackles from their limbs, and witness the rapture which would excite them in the first dance of their freedom." [17] Fate had branded him with a mark of inequality, and it must have eased his torment to strike against another kind of branding, which he also pictured in terms of shackled limbs and a longing for freedom to dance.

Thaddeus Stevens now occupied a peculiar position in Pennsylvania politics. Leader of a stultifying, anti-intellectual party that was now almost dead, still unwilling to join formally the conservative Whigs, and a vigorous foe of the liberal Democrats, he had nevertheless won the reputation for being a radical, which he undoubtedly was. Radicalism is a state of mind, which in the generic sense represents the desire to "root out" or get at the root of a social problem, often by way of revolution rather than evolution. The compulsion to overthrow something is the important ingredient in the radical state of mind.

Although Stevens was eager to overthrow slavery, he was nevertheless deeply committed to the sanctity of other forms of private property, and was suspicious of men who had not acquired any. Like many who have pulled themselves up from poverty against great odds, he felt small sympathy for those white men who could not do likewise. And though in the Pennsylvania Constitutional Convention he did his best to keep suffrage in the hands of propertied Negroes, he also tried to penalize the whites without property by continuing to deny them the right to vote until they had proved themselves virtuous and responsible by acquiring a little. To one proposal that the residence requirement be reduced to six months within the state and ten days within the precinct, he protested that it would "confound the poor man with the vagabond," since it gave him the vote "if he had lodged in a barn in the district for ten days, and washed his cravat in a mudhole." He would have no truck with "the vile, the vagabond, the idle and dissipated." "Government," he argued, "ought to be kept in the hands of men of some little principle."

The Democrats derided him for this stand as "ultra conservative," and he replied by ridiculing the "burning thirst of the reformers," who "make the people their idol, and who say prayers to the people, at the corner of the streets, twenty times a day." Nevertheless his own jeremiads were made in the name of the people. He condemned the reform resolutions because they would "bind the people hand and foot," and denounced the Democrats as "demagogues, the little corrupt demagogues, who occupy the high stations [and] . . . drive their armed chariots with cold, sardonic smiles, over the subdued and prostrate people." [18]

Stevens failed to block the widening of white suffrage, just as he failed to retain suffrage for the Negro. Bereft of voting support as the Antimasons dwindled, he retained only a certain measure of power as "the ruler behind the governor." Ritner was sensitive to the charge of being under Stevens' thumb. "He's a dangerous leader," he once confided to Alexander McClure, "and useful as he was I never permitted him to control my administration." But McClure felt differently. "Ritner was thoroughly honest and intelligent," he wrote, "but of a confiding nature, and certainly permitted Stevens to shape some of the most objectionable features of his administration." [19]

To many observers who looked at Stevens' voting record, he seemed to be a sound Whig, dedicated to the advancement of business and to increasing its share in the political power of the state. As Canal Commissioner he helped develop a complicated system of water transportation, and became involved in the building of the local railroads. He believed in liberal state appropriations to help public utilities.

McClure gave him credit for keeping the administration "clean and free from any corrupt profligacy for individual benefit"—something the Democrats never conceded—but accused him of shaping every public measure to serve the ends of the party. There is no doubt that he forced through the legislature pork-barrel legislation designed to strengthen the Whig-Antimasonic coalition as well as the transportation system. And in regard to the Gettysburg Railroad, which was designed to run past his own iron furnaces, he laid himself open to more serious charges.

Most Whigs believed Stevens sound on economic matters and fanatical only on free schools and antislavery, the virtues of which a few were willing to concede. What almost no one in his party realized, however, was that Stevens' radicalism was becoming so dynamic that it spilled over into economic provinces the conservatives held sacrosanct, with results that were potentially more revolutionary than anyone suspected. There is no more ironic illustration of this than the story of Stevens and the United States Bank.

Banking history is so undramatic it is not easy to believe that a particular bank would once have been regarded by many Americans as a gigantic ogre dedicated to fattening the rich and strangling the poor. The United States Bank was a Philadelphia corporation chartered by Congress through which the government did most of its business. Although it operated as the bank of the nation, and five of its twenty-five directors were appointed by the government, it had been kept remarkably independent of political control.

Andrew Jackson believed the bank to be a dangerous monopoly, and set out to destroy its power. He was quietly encouraged in this by businessmen in his own party, who hoped to free their own banks from any kind of federal credit regulation, and he was openly supported by hard-money theorists, radical intellectuals who believed that business in government meant business control of government. When Congress renewed the bank's charter in 1832, Jackson vetoed the bill in a volcanic denunciation. The bank, he said, "was an evil concentration of power" in the hands of a few men who were not responsible to the people, "making the rich richer and the potent more powerful." The veto was enormously popular, for debtors all over the nation wanted not hard but cheap money. They were delighted to see the bank fall, because it had been strong enough to prevent the inflationary issue of paper money by their local banks.

Actually the United States Bank had given the nation extremely useful service, which was not properly evaluated until its operations were curtailed. With its twenty-five branches scattered throughout the nation, it had made possible the development of an extensive national credit system, had provided a uniform currency, and had helped greatly to stabilize the nation's economy. Nicholas Biddle, the able and incorruptible director of the Bank, whose vision of the need for a regulatory central banking system was far in advance of his time, denounced Jackson's veto as "a manifesto of anarchy, such as Marat or Robespierre might have issued to the mob of the Faubourg St. Antoine." [20]

Thaddeus Stevens, like many Whig businessmen, believed that though there were defects in the operation of the bank's paper-currency system the remedy was certainly not to destroy the bank itself. With Governor Ritner he worked out an agreement with Biddle whereby the United States Bank, instead of going out of business altogether, was to continue as a state bank under a charter granted by the State of Pennsylvania. Stevens believed paper money to be indispensable to the functioning of commerce and refused to believe that the United States Bank was the "monster of corruption" described by Andrew Jackson.

Unlike other Whigs, however, he believed in making the bank pay for its privileges in money and loss of power. The bank bill expressly stated that the legislature would revoke the charter if the bank "was found injurious to the interests of the people." In return for exemption of the bank dividends from taxation, Stevens demanded that the bank pay the State of Pennsylvania a bonus of $2,000,000, that it lend the state up to $6,000,000 at a low interest rate and subscribe $675,000 for public works. He insisted further on a bonus of half a million dollars in 1837 and $100,000 every year for twenty years thereafter, all earmarked for the state's new free schools. This gigantic windfall made it possible to lower personal-property taxes and help the state recover at least temporarily from the financial bankruptcy into which it had plunged by developing its canal and railway system.[21]

Stevens' bank bill was a sensationally hard bargain to which Biddle had to accede or close the bank altogether. It was not only a measure of crude control over this bank, but also in effect a tax on the rich to lessen the taxes of the poor. The whole scheme was remotely kin to the economic radicalism inaugurated one hundred years later in the regime of Franklin Roosevelt. But the true nature of the bill went largely unrecognized. Stevens was hailed by the Whigs as the saviour of the business community and denounced by the Democrats for selling the liberties of the people to the monied aristocracy.[22]

This attempt to control the bank by making it subject to periodic charter renewal in the state legislature greatly heightened the opportunity for corruption of legislators by the banking lobby. Stevens and Ritner were themselves accused of bribery, but were cleared by a Senate investigating committee. By 1838 the United States Bank's lobbyists had become appalled at what the "gang of boodlers" in the legislature demanded in return for the charter renewal. When they went for advice to the bank president, he replied: "What's the use of praying when you're in hell. Pay the d—d scoundrels and let's go home." [23]

If Stevens' unorthodox banking control system was inadequate, Andrew Jackson's was no better. He destroyed the monopoly of the United States Bank, but could not get through Congress supplementary legislation to control the currency-making power of the state banks. There resulted the maddest speculative binge in America's erratic banking history, the wildcat era leading up to the Panic of 1837. Scores of new banks were organized overnight, some of which had barely enough capital to pay the engraver for printing their new bank notes. Illegal bills and counterfeits—the yellow dogs, blue pups, smooth monkeys, and sick Indians—circulated everywhere. The inflationary nature of this banking hysteria, catalyzed by the gigantic speculation in western lands, resulted in a boom as short-lived as it was preposterous.

Jackson pricked the bubble in a deliberate deflationary move when he issued the famous Specie Circular, demanding gold and silver as payment for public land, for the United States Treasury was gradually filling up with a thousand different kinds of almost worthless paper. By the spring of 1837 the Panic was on. The month of May saw 800 banks, containing $120,000,000 in deposits, suspend specie payments. Cities were full of suffering and want, with a resulting tide of fury against bankers and banking which was not to be duplicated again in American history until 1932.

The Panic dramatized the anarchical nature of the banking system, the ineptness of the government at reform, and the primitive character of economic and banking theory. The country desperately needed a uniform and stable currency. Whigs and Democrats alike bellowed for reform. Stevens raised his own voice in a speech before the Pennsylvania Constitutional Convention of 1837 which was not listened to, and is not remembered. Nevertheless, in this speech he pleaded for a government-controlled system such as was finally adopted many years later.

He attacked the "almost insupportable" evils of paper currency and local banks, sitting "like an incubus upon all the States of the Union," with "every petty corporation and every knavish speculator issuing their paper," and insisted, like Alexander Hamilton before him, that the actual power to incorporate banks and issue currency lay not with the states but with the federal government. He begged for a national banking system under which "the currency would be rendered uniform and stable, throughout the country, exchange facilities, and funds of the Government transmitted in a single week from Maine to Louisiana, without disturbing the regular business of the country." [24]

[Stevens' conviction that the government had a legitimate right to legislate banking rules as a protection for her citizens, and his corollary faith in a strongly centralized federal power, made no impression in 1837. But after 1860 this conviction and this faith were to have an unmistakable impact in Washington.]

CHAPTER SIX

———— ◆ ————

The Desperate Years

"Thaddeus Stevens . . . the great unchained of Adams County . . ."

Gettysburg Sentinel, May 28, 1839

THE BUCKSHOT WAR was tough and dirty. It marked a low in the history of Pennsylvania politics to which the state mercifully has never sunk since. Thaddeus Stevens was partly the cause and partly the victim. He got a lesson in political skulduggery and a first-hand acquaintance with the might of the *coup d'état*. All this he learned from the Democratic Party, and he pondered the lesson well because he lost the war.

In 1838 Stevens was hardly a political innocent. His reputation for being crafty, hard, and fearless was justified enough, but he had nevertheless the good lawyer's respect for the law. For three years he had been content to be manipulator behind the scenes and had asked for no political office. But this had sharpened his appetite for prestige as well as power. More than anything else he wanted to be a United States Senator. This is never an easy office to win, but in these years, when Senators were elected by state legislatures instead of the direct vote of the people, one had to be the darling of the party in order to go to Washington. Stevens hoped to see the election of 1838 send enough Whigs and Antimasons to Harrisburg to guarantee the senatorship for himself.

As a first step he persuaded Governor Ritner to appoint him Canal Commissioner, the office with the fattest bag of patronage in the state. The Pennsylvania Canal and Portage Railway, begun in 1824, a gigantic public works program intended to link Philadelphia and Pittsburgh, was designed to carry freight a distance of 320 miles over a terrain crisscrossed by mountain ridges rising to 2,500 feet. The project took imagination and vision; it was also outrageously costly, and was to be outmoded by the steam railroad even before it was finished.

Since it was an elementary political fact that a clever Canal Commissioner controlling the hiring of thousands of workmen could manipulate a sizable bloc of votes, the Democrats took alarm. "The appointment of Mr. Stevens has thrown the Loco Focos into consternation here," William McPherson wrote to his father. "They say it is a *gunpowder* plot to blow them up." [1]

The election of 1838 was probably the filthiest in the history of Pennsylvania. Joseph Ritner was derided as an illiterate, a "damned Dutch hog," guilty of perversions the press hinted at in obscene poems. David R. Porter, the Democratic candidate, was called a fraud and a perjurer. One colored woman signed an affidavit swearing that he was the father of her two children, and Whig editors gleefully published it. [2]

In assaulting Thaddeus Stevens, the Democrats concentrated on his pet project, the Gettysburg Railroad, accusing him of squandering the state's money on a winding serpent intended solely to increase the profits from his iron furnaces, which were on the proposed route. The Gettysburg Railroad project had, in fact, been badly bungled. Most of the original appropriation of $200,000, derived from the bonus from the United States Bank, had been spent before the route was even properly surveyed. When engineers finally did lay out the full road, the plan was so tortuous-looking they were afraid to publish it. However, the Democrats snared a copy, delightedly labeled it "The Tapeworm," and advertised it widely. It was said that the thirty-five miles of track through the mountains could not be finished for less than five million dollars.

The Panic of 1837 had forced Stevens' Maria Furnace to close, and it was unlikely to reopen without the railroad. Since the Democrats vowed to choke off all appropriations for its completion, Stevens was threatened with financial as well as political annihilation if his party lost the election. He proceeded to use his position as Canal Commissioner without scruple, firing Democratic laborers, granting contracts only to men who contributed to the Whig campaign fund—thinly disguised as an educational fund for the children of canal workers—

and compelling workmen to bet a part of their earnings on Ritner, under the assumption that votes would follow the bets.[3] Alexander Hood wrote that Stevens himself spent and bet one hundred thousand dollars on the campaign.

The whole state was swept by a mania for betting. Stakes as high as ten thousand dollars were reported in the press, and citizens without money bet their farms and livestock. With so many personal bankruptcies possible there could have been no worse outcome than a contested election. Everyone conceded that the Democratic Porter had won as governor, and that the Whigs had retained a majority in the Senate. The fight centered in the House, where both sides claimed victory. Fraud was particularly charged in Philadelphia. There the Democratic majority on the Returns Board tossed out the total vote of seven wards and rushed the returns to Harrisburg by special courier. The indignant Whig minority on the Returns Board sent its own set of returns by way of the sheriff, as was required.

When the Secretary of State, Thomas H. Burrowes, who was also leader of the Whigs, received the two sets of returns, he sent for Thaddeus Stevens. The two men mapped out an audacious plan of strategy. Burrowes was to introduce to the House only the Whig returns, withholding the others on the ground that they had not been delivered in the legal manner. With a temporary Whig majority they planned to have Stevens elected United States Senator and Whigs appointed to key posts. Afterward they would proceed to examine the charges of fraud. Then they went on to make a foolish mistake. Burrowes issued a letter to his party calling for an investigation of the election, including the office of governor, though there was no doubt Porter had won. He ordered his party to treat the election "as if they had not been defeated," until the investigation was over. This meant in effect: "Don't pay your election bets. If we win the legislature, we may even keep Porter out."

Shrewder politicians would have concentrated on the Philadelphia districts, where they stood to win, instead of infuriating the whole Democratic Party. It was a characteristic Stevens blunder to overplay his hand. One politician, George W. Woodward, described it later as "the capital mistake of his life." [4] The Whig record was hardly spotless. Alexander McClure later impartially described the "fearful pollution of the ballot" on both sides. The most flagrant Whig fraud was in Lycoming County, he said, where Stevens had poured in workmen to repair a "convenient break on the canal," with a resulting majority of over 500, which was more than the entire legal vote.[5]

In the six weeks before the legislature convened, the Democratic press whipped up the general irritation into hysteria, one editor threatening that unless the Democrats were given their seats "twenty thousand bayonets should bristle in Harrisburg." [6] But to the Whigs, "too respectable to win elections," all this seemed bombast. Stevens had once accused his own party of "a guilelessness which fitted them well for the other world, but which did not so well qualify them for contending against the mammon of unrighteousness in this." [7] But even he, though expecting a bitter legal battle, was unprepared for violence.

When he walked into the House on December 4, 1838, he saw the galleries packed with strangers, big, well-muscled, their pockets bulging with pistols and bowie knives. He described them later as a gang of "brothel-keepers, journeymen butchers, professional boxers, and discharged convicts" imported by the Democrats from Philadelphia. They spilled over into the chamber, and when he elbowed his way through, he found eight of them surrounding his own desk. Several friends, alarmed for his safety, pushed their way past and stood beside him. The room was in an uproar.

The Clerk of the House pounded for silence and began to read the election results. When it became clear that he was reading only the Whig names of the Philadelphia delegates, the galleries howled. The Clerk, a Democrat, now entertained a motion that the Democratic delegates be admitted as well, and it carried. Seeing that he had lost the first round, Stevens quickly got the floor, held his stand amid jeers, and tried to direct the House to the legal procedure he had mapped out.

Pointing out that under the constitution no decision could be made on contested elections until a speaker had been nominated and the uncontested delegates sworn in, he swept through the preliminaries and nominated Thomas S. Cunningham. At this point the galleries began hissing and stamping. Stevens now suggested as a compromise the election of two speakers, hoping, he said, that the House would be courteous enough to find room for both on the speaker's platform "until the law decided between them."

The Democratic whip, Thomas B. M'Elwee, nominated William Hopkins, and the two parties balloted simultaneously on different sides of the hall. Both speakers were escorted to the chair. Then a grim-faced body of armed men converged on the Whig speaker from behind, and he fled the chamber in fright. Confused and dismayed, most of his party soon followed. Left in tumultous triumph, the Democrats passed a resolution forbidding the Whigs to return.

Stevens had been defeated by a mob. Still he refused to recognize disaster, confident that the Whig-dominated Senate, when it met that afternoon, would recognize the Cunningham rather than the Hopkins House. He paid no attention to the alarm of his friends, who brought rumors of his impending assassination, including one report that the Sheriff himself had vowed that day to see Stevens' body at the bottom of the Susquehanna. Taking a stand before the fireplace in the Senate Chamber, he waited for the proceedings to begin, noting angrily that the same hoodlums who had terrorized the House were now in the Senate galleries. Here and there he saw a friendly face, including some of his canal contractors, who had a great stake in the outcome of the crisis.

The Senate first voted on two contested seats from Philadelphia. When it was announced that the Whig delegates had won, the galleries began to stamp. Charles Brown, a Democratic contender, demanded the floor. The speaker, Charles B. Penrose, denied the request on the ground that Brown was not an accredited Senator. At this point the gallery mob began to chant: "Brown! Brown! We will hear Brown!" As the excitement mounted the mob broke through the railing and rushed with a roar into the chamber itself.

"Death to Penrose, Burrowes, and Stevens!" one shouted.

"Build a gallows and hang the speaker!" yelled another. Tar-and-feather threats echoed through the hall.

Trembling with fear and disgust, Penrose flung down his ivory gavel, left the chair, and joined Stevens and Burrowes, who were surrounded by a knot of loyal supporters near the fireplace. Brown now harangued the crowd in what was probably the most incendiary speech ever made in the Pennsylvania Legislature. He shouted that the constitution was defunct, that the people were in the midst of a revolution and must take the government into their own hands.

"Are you ready," he yelled, "in order to defend the rights of which you have been robbed by Burrowes, Stevens, and Company, to drench the Senate Chamber with the best blood of the State?"

"We are!" shouted the crowd.

Then, in the adroit manner of demagogues, Brown put himself in the clear by saying with manifest lack of conviction: "By God, I hope not."

The mob was now shrieking: "Blood! Blood! Ride him! Ride him on a rail!" Stevens, Penrose, and Burrowes slipped out a side door, crossed an empty committee room, climbed through an open window and jumped to the ground. Two men rushed into the room a moment later, one swinging a club and the other brandishing a dirk.

"By Jesus, they have got away," one cried, and the two men ran back into the corridor and down into the street. But Stevens and his friends, hiding in the bushes, were not seen in the twilight. They crept down a back fence, and escaped in safety to Burrowes' home.

Meanwhile, back in the Senate chamber, George W. Barton was urging the mob to return in the morning and compel the Senate to seat the Philadelphia Democrats. "Tomorrow the Capitol of Pennsylvania will smoke," he threatened, "I will not say with the blood of Senators, nor with the torch of the incendiary—but tomorrow it shall smoke."

All night men milled about the streets, spreading rumors of war and assassination. One boasted that he had trailed Stevens as he left the capitol, and almost shot him as he passed under a street lamp. Meanwhile Stevens and Burrowes consulted with Governor Ritner and decided to meet force with force. Ritner stationed twenty-five loyal men in the state arsenal, which the Democrats were threatening to attack. For some time it looked as if there would be a battle, as the Democrats threatened to blow up the building, but the keeper of the arsenal worked out a compromise by promising not to issue arms to either side.

The Cunningham House, or "Stevens' Rump" as it was called, barred from the capitol building, held an unhappy session or two in Wilson's Hotel. Then the frightened proprietor, after being threatened with arson by the Democratic "Committee of Safety," barred his doors to the Whig legislators and drove Stevens from his hotel room.

The desperate governor now called on the President of the United States to send federal troops. But Martin Van Buren chose not to interfere on behalf of a party opposed to his own, and through his Secretary of War politely turned Ritner down. Whereupon the Governor called out the state militia. General Patterson obediently ordered his troops to assemble in winter uniform, "with knapsacks provided with thirteen rounds of buckshot, cartridge, etc." A local wit, reading the order, dubbed the disorder "The Buckshot War," and the name stuck.

Thomas B. M'Elwee, Stevens' most venomous opponent, convinced that the militia would consist of hand-picked Whig supporters, talked openly about blowing up the troop trains. But Governor Ritner, appalled by the crisis, saw to it that the militia acted with scrupulous impartiality, interfering with neither the Hopkins House nor the "Stevens' Rump," which was now permitted to hold session in the Supreme Court room. The talk of murder and riot died away; no shots were fired. Nevertheless, the threat of violence had done its work. The Cunningham House shortly lost three men through intimidation and bribery to the Hopkins House, and the Whig Senate, believing the cause hopeless, reversed its original resolution not to deal with the Democrats. By a seventeen-to-sixteen vote they recognized the Hopkins House, and the war was over.[8]

Smashed were Stevens' high hopes for election to the United States Senate; gone were the appropriations to finish the Gettysburg Railroad; and permanently blasted were certain of his illusions about the nature of representative government. But it would be almost thirty years before the whole nation would be made to see exactly what Thaddeus Stevens had learned from the Buckshot War.

Stevens was now so full of bitterness that he refused to take his seat in the Hopkins House. In one last furious flourish he brought criminal suit against the Democratic leaders, but it resulted in such a fiasco of wrangling over the makeup of the juries that he finally withdrew the charges. After this defeat he bowed to the dissatisfaction of his own constituents, who resented his absence from the legislature. Swallowing his dignity, he announced on May 8 that he was ready to take his seat. Only then did he learn the depths to which his prestige had plummeted.

M'Elwee, who had vowed he would bar Stevens altogether from the legislature, accused him of contempt of the House and ordered a committee to investigate his fitness as a legislator. Stevens refused to appear before the committee on the correct legal ground that under the constitution he could not be tried until he had been sworn in. But M'Elwee had him tried anyway, and Stevens was barred from office on the ground that he had resigned his seat.

Thirty-eight House members protested the illegality of these proceedings, but this was far from a majority. Stevens could not even command the total vote of the Whig-Antimasonic coalition. Too many, already alienated by his brusqueness, his political unorthodoxy, and the brutality of his wit, were now ready to believe in the "sundry personal improprieties" suggested by the investigating committee. The fact was that another personal scandal had broken over his head, and the state was greedily feeding on the details.

In late 1838 the unmarried daughter of his friend Robert Smith had become a mother, and Stevens was fastened upon by the gossips as being responsible for the child's paternity. He was now a bachelor of forty-seven, with a considerable reputation as a rake. In an article cleverly written to evade a libel suit, the *York Gazette* accused Stevens of "the corruption of youthful innocence," of stealing into a neighbor's family under the pretense of friendship "for the base purpose of utterly destroying the fair name and happiness of his child, and, viper-like, desolating the fireside at which he had been welcomed and warmed." [9]

Stevens suspected that the poison was being spread by Thomas B. M'Elwee, but he had no way of proving it in court. Then the father of the girl swore out a warrant for Stevens' arrest on a charge of fornication and bastardy. The lame lawyer wrote a desperate letter to his friend, John B. McPherson:

". . . I pretend to no prudish sanctity, but the pretence in the case referred to is so perfectly false, that I shall shew beyond doubt that the girl was courted—and worse than merely courted, by a man who turned out to be married at the time—and that too just nine months before the birth of the child. So far from being a seducer, I vow to God I have never learned (except by description) the meaning of maidenhead! Nevertheless I wish this cursed matter were ended. But I shall never make advances. I shall carry on the war in the same spirit in which it has been begun, and regret it more for the sake of the weak girl—the instrument of her father's cupidity—than for my own." He insisted that five of his political enemies in Gettysburg had instigated the whole calumny, that they had often visited the girl's father "and urged him by all manner of arguments to bring suit . . . assuring him that he could recover twenty thousand dollars and offering to back him with money." [10]

Sometimes a scandal will blast a man's career with such violence that no frantic assembling of bits and pieces can ever again restore it. The suit for "fornication and bastardy," like the old innuendoes of murder, fell short of being this kind of calamity. Slowly—perhaps as the true identity of the child's father became known—the conviction grew among most of the townspeople that Stevens was wholly innocent. The girl's father dropped the suit and Stevens was never tried.[11]

With this forfeiture came a surge of indignation against Stevens' political enemies. Still more sympathy came his way when M'Elwee, the chief despoiler of his reputation, was expelled from the Senate for slandering another legislator. In the special election of June 14, 1839, Stevens was elected by an overwhelming majority and sent back to the House.

However heartened he may have been by this demonstration of personal loyalty from people among whom he had lived and worked for twenty-two years, Thaddeus Stevens was profoundly shaken by the calamitous events of the year. Seared and poisoned by the paternity suit, which involved against him several men he had hitherto thought good friends, he could not suppress the impulse which comes to every man in trouble, to shake the dust of the city from his heels. It would be three years before other reverses would finally drive him out of Gettysburg, but the impact of this one may well have hastened his decision.

Stevens was now a man without a party. He still refused to join the Whigs, and they in turn, humiliated by the fiasco of the Buckshot War, refused to grant him leadership as an independent. Horace Greeley described him aptly in 1840 as "a *leetle* too savage a politician," and the *Gettysburg Sentinel* called him "the great unchained of Adams County." [12] The fact was that the party was not yet born to which this man could give undeviating allegiance. But he continued to work on the periphery of the Whig group and managed by his energy and talent to remain a force not only in Pennsylvania but also in national politics. The revolution of Andrew Jackson had run its course; Martin Van Buren had been ruined politically by the Panic of 1837, and the Whigs looked forward to the election of 1840 with absolute certainty of victory.

For Henry Clay, the leader of the conservative Whigs, and their apparent favorite for the presidency, Stevens had neither affection nor respect. The fact that he was a slaveholder was enough to damn him. As early as 1836 Stevens had swung his small bloc of Antimasonic votes away from Clay to General William Henry Harrison, the antique hero of the almost forgotten Battle of Tippecanoe in the War of 1812. As the 1840 election approached, and it became clear that Harrison might be a strong candidate, Stevens began campaigning for him with vigor.

Nicholas Biddle had once cynically recommended that any Harrison campaign be conducted as follows: "Let him say not one single word about his principles, or his creed—let him say nothing—promise nothing. Let no Committee, no convention—no town meeting ever extract from him a single word, about what he thinks now, or what he will do hereafter. Let the use of pen and ink be wholly forbidden as if he were a mad poet in Bedlam." [13]

But the aging general made promises right and left. He wrote a private letter to Thaddeus Stevens promising him the office of postmaster general if he would swing the Pennsylvania delegation for him in the nominating convention. [14] This Stevens was able to do. With the aid of Thurlow Weed and other Clay enemies, he managed to push Harrison into first place. In the uproarious campaign that followed, the Whigs abandoned all pretense of respectability and transformed the general, who was something of an aristocrat, into a cider-drinking man of the people. Stevens, who had a remarkable facility for converting the snobbish Whig symbols into democratic shibboleths that would appeal to the common man, was so effective a campaigner that the Van Buren Democrats took time out to spread an anti-Stevens smear. Capitalizing on his reputation as an infidel, they published a story that he had blasphemously administered the Holy Sacrament to a dog and pronounced impious "Tippecanoe prayers" at a secret rally. Stevens at once sued the editor for libel and won, but the Democratic governor pardoned the editor just as his prison term started.[15]

The election campaign continued to its climax, with slogans, music, and bonfires overwhelming sober argument. When the returns came in, it was clear that the Whig cry, "Van, Van, is a used-up man!" had been good prophecy. Van Buren had 60 electoral votes; Harrison 234. For Stevens it was a personal triumph. With Harrison's letter burning in his pocket, he sat back to wait the announcement of the cabinet. He did not reckon with the enmity of the Whig giants, Daniel Webster and Henry Clay, who disliked him as an upstart and radical. Nor did he try to placate his enemies in the local Whig Party. He had quarreled with Charles Penrose, who had been his close ally through the Buckshot War but who was now scheming for a cabinet position himself and publicly denouncing Stevens as "a bold, bad man."[16]

Harrison wrote to Daniel Webster on December 27, 1840: "I tell you, however, in confidence, that I have positively determined against S———; there is no consideration which would induce me to bring him into the cabinet. We should have no peace with his intriguing, restless disposition. We will have nobody of that character . . ."[17] And in March, 1841, when the new President announced his official family, Stevens' name was absent.

It was a sickening blow. Respected even among his enemies as a politician who kept his word, Stevens now felt tricked and cheated. For obvious reasons he never made Harrison's letter public, and bottled up his wrath. President Harrison seems to have felt some measure of guilt about the matter, for after he took office he sent one of his cabinet to Stevens asking him to call for "a long talk." Stevens "sent back word that he had appealed a case of seventeen dollars at Gettysburg which he was going to see to, and he considered that case much more important than any long conversation with the present President of the United States."

Stevens told this story twenty-six years later to Jonathan Blanchard. "I have tried to be charitable," he concluded. "I was looking over my papers a while ago, and I destroyed that letter of Gen. Harrison's lest it might give somebody a little trouble when I am gone."[18]

A longing to reconstruct his life and begin anew in some unfamiliar city now seems to have possessed Stevens. Politics had failed him; his personal life in Gettysburg was cursed with loneliness, betrayal, and scandal. Added to this was a terrifying burden of debt, for his iron furnaces, into which he had poured immense sums, were not paying their way. He was in debt for over $200,000. He had lost heavily in election bets, and the friends and clients to whom he had loaned money in his compulsively careless fashion had not paid him in return. When Jonathan Blanchard wrote urging him to put his talents and money at the service of the antislavery forces, he described something of his financial problem, concluding: "I know of no way out of such things," he said, "but to pay the uttermost farthing." [19]

In 1842 in one swift gesture he severed his roots in Gettysburg, sold his home and office, and moved east to Lancaster. On the day he left he said wryly to a client, "Well, I've got my debts down to two hundred and fourteen thousand dollars, and I reckon now I'll be able to pay them." [20] Later he wrote to Blanchard: "I have moved up to this rich country to earn the means to pay my honest debts." This was his official reason; it may well have been the compelling one. But Stevens was fifty years old, an age when most lawyers with an established practice are amiably reconciled to their status and their community.

Temperamentally he was unfit to be a businessman, for he could never look upon money as an end in itself. He had what Eric Hoffer has described as the radical's fundamental contempt for the present. His vast property holdings seem to have given him small pleasure. He found bill-collecting offensive and alien, and simply could not get back money legitimately owed him. Since the management of his furnaces bored him, he had turned them over to his partner, who proved to be inept. It is not surprising, then, that although his law practice in the bigger and wealthier Lancaster flourished so that he was soon making the handsome income of twelve to fifteen thousand dollars a year, the specter of bankruptcy came closer than ever.

Many years later Stevens told a reporter what happened. "I have failed financially three times," he said. "The first was through going bail and security, and it broke up a very fine practice I had in Adams County. The second was through the carelessness of a partner in some iron mills. Notes were presented to me for payment which I had never executed or known of. I went to my partner and asked him how it was. He explained that he had been losing money for some time, but as he had induced me to embark in the enterprise he had not the courage to tell me of the losses, and had signed the firm name to notes without consulting me. 'Well,' I said, 'what's to be done?' He began to make a piteous mouth, but I cut him short. 'I don't come to upbraid you,' I said; 'I come to get at the facts.' I looked over the books and saw that we were deeply involved. Then I said to him, 'You take the works and pay all the claims, releasing me entirely.' He declined, and I at once said, 'Then I will'; and it was thus the works near Chambersburg came into my possession. The third time I failed was when the rebels burned these works." [21]

Renouncing politics, his costly and faithless mistress, Stevens now set about patiently and realistically reducing debts that would have sent a less proud man scurrying to the bankruptcy court. One by one he sold his wooded tracts and farms. He managed to hold on to the Caledonia Iron Works, for which he paid his partner $20,000, but it was several years before it ceased losing money, and even in the good years of the 1850's, competing as it was with the newer and more efficient anthracite furnaces, it never made its owner wealthy. When his partner went into bankruptcy in 1848, and his friends suggested that he do the same, Stevens replied wryly: "I may be forced to take advantage of the bankruptcy laws in the next world, but that I will never do in this." [22]

CHAPTER SEVEN

———————◆———————

Lydia

LYDIA SMITH, Thaddeus Stevens' housekeeper for twenty years, was described by Jonathan Blanchard as "young, clear-minded and capable . . . in complexion a dark brunette." Others reported that she was "comely in appearance, light in color, and exceedingly intelligent and entertaining." [1] Rumors that she was Stevens' mistress began early and persisted long after his death, ever increasing in richness of detail. When Thomas Dixon in 1905 created a thinly disguised Thaddeus Stevens as the villain of his novel, *The Clansman*—later made into the movie, *The Birth of a Nation*—he gave him as mistress one Lydia Brown, "a mulatto woman of extraordinary animal beauty and the fiery temper of a leopardess." He painted her a woman greedy for wealth and power, who dominated the lame politician's life and exerted a vicious influence on his legislation. [2]

It was widely believed even during Stevens' lifetime that Lydia had been one of the many fugitive slaves he had helped to freedom. Speculation varied about when and where their alliance began. William Hall, who knew Stevens but was not careful to distinguish fact from gossip in his *Reminiscences,* wrote flatly that Stevens "became intimate" with her in Harrisburg. [3] One newspaper editor said that Stevens "separated a handsome mulatto woman from her husband . . . deemed it his duty to provide for her; and their relations were such as to almost entirely exclude him from other female society—a fact which never seemed to give him the slightest concern." [4]

Some of Stevens' defenders have dismissed all the rumors about their intimacy as scurrilous gossip. Judge Charles I. Landis, who was angered by the slime heaped upon Stevens in *The Clansman* and *The Birth of a Nation*, interviewed several old citizens in Lancaster who had known Mrs. Smith. He reported that she visited often at the homes of Stevens' friend, Thomas H. Burrowes, and his physician, Dr. Carpenter, and "was on terms of intimacy with their families." In her will she left small legacies to their children. "If she had been a woman of bad character," he insisted, "is it likely that ladies of this standing would have shown her any regard?" [5]

The serious historians who have written about Stevens have been content usually with insinuations about the relationship between the man and his housekeeper, reluctant to do more in the absence of evidence.[6] The fact is that there is a good deal more evidence than has been realized.

We have already seen that Lydia was not a fugitive slave, but was born in Gettysburg, the child of a white father. Her mother, Mrs. Hamilton, was a good friend to at least one of Stevens' servants, the girl Keziah who attempted suicide. When Lydia Hamilton was about twenty, she married a barber, Jacob Smith, considerably darker than herself, and bore him two sons, one in 1835 and one twelve years later, in 1847.[7] Judge Landis, who knew the younger son, Isaac, as a local barber and the leader of a Negro band, described him as "very black."

Lydia Smith came to work for Stevens in 1848, after the death of her husband. She had been recommended by her cousin, Anna Sulkey, who had been employed briefly by Stevens and was leaving to get married. Judge Landis, who uncovered part of this information, stated that she brought her sons with her, the oldest then thirteen and the youngest a baby of one year. While the boys were young, the three lived in a cottage at the rear of her employer's lot. Later she moved into Stevens' house.

When she came to work for Thaddeus Stevens, Lydia Smith was thirty-five. He was fifty-six. The fact that he was no longer young did not keep the scandalmongers in Lancaster—whose speculations about Stevens' sex life had hitherto covered a considerable geographic area —from concentrating on the new housekeeper. The only photograph of her is a stiff, dignified likeness made in her late fifties. She was not then beautiful, but it is easy to see why those who remembered her described her as "comely." There has recently come into public light, however, a fine portrait of Lydia Smith which indicates that she was at one time a woman of considerable beauty. One who looks carefully will see the resemblance between the portrait and her photograph. In the latter the eyes are sunken, the mouth tight. But the hair is fashioned similarly in both; there is the same broad chin and slightly pointed nose, the same attractive brow and rather heavy neck.

This portrait was painted by Jacob Eichholtz, who had done Stevens' portrait in 1830. The significance of the fact that Stevens commissioned it should not be underestimated. He had the artist paint her as a woman with beauty and status; the fact of her part-Negro ancestry was almost totally disguised. It would be hard to believe that he took the trouble to hire one of the most distinguished portrait painters of his time to paint a picture of a colored woman who was merely his respected housekeeper. The act suggests something of the intensity of his affection, and perhaps, too, a need to leave some kind of quiet evidence of it for the historical record.[8]

Letters to Stevens from his niece and nephews indicate that he insisted she be spoken of as "Mrs. Smith," rather than "Lydia," deferential treatment almost unheard-of in his day. "How is Mrs. Smith," wrote one nephew from Indianapolis in 1862. "As well and lively as ever I hope? Give her my best wishes and tell her that I shall remember her." A letter from young Lizzie Stevens to her uncle in 1864 concluded: "How is Mrs. Smith, bring her with you when you come. Give her a great deal of love for me." Later, after a visit to Washington, Lizzie wrote again: ". . . much love to you and Mrs. S. How is she. I'd like to hear from her—she was so kind to us and made our visit so pleasant. I always think of her with many pleasant thoughts. If any thing should happen to influence you to come out this spring tell her she has a standing invitation also." [9]

The rare letters written by Lydia Smith preserved in the Library of Congress among the Stevens Papers indicate that she had received more education than might have been expected. That she profited under the stimulation of Stevens' tutelage is clear. "She was a member of St. Mary's Church," a preacher who had known her in her old age wrote, "and I recall personally that she was as smart as a steel trap, bright, and a good conversationalist because of her many years of life with Stevens at Washington." [10]

The Democratic press took it completely for granted that she was Stevens' mistress, and either delicately or indelicately so referred to her through the last twenty years of Stevens' life. The press insinuations did not dwindle when he took her to Washington in 1859 to care for his house behind the Capitol, though he had then reached the age of sixty-seven.

In his earlier years Stevens had sued many editors for libel, but except in one instance he ignored all newspaper speculation on his relations with Lydia Smith. It took the merciless article we have already noted, by George Drake in the *Union Springs Times,* to stimulate the only letter in which he ever publicly discussed the rumors. Drake had written as follows:

Radicals have a good deal to say about the close relationship some of the former slaves bear to their masters and their masters' friends. They tell Southern people that numbers among their servile class are too yellow to be white, and too white to be black. They must stop this. It is horribly unkind to their great leader and master. In the city of Lancaster, Pa., in the godly North, nigh unto the pure city of Philadelphia, Thaddeus Stevens has for years lived in open adultery with a mulatto woman, whom he seduced from her husband, a full-blooded negro. This mulatto manages his visitors at will, speaks of Mr. Stevens and herself as "we," and in all things comports herself as if she enjoyed the rights of a lawful wife. I have no word of unkindness or abuse for her. She is a neat, tidy housekeeper, and appears to be as polite and well-trained as negroes generally are. As to Mr. Stevens' connection with her, it is his own business, and entirely a matter of taste. I only mention the fact, that the ultra-godly, super-sanctified saints of the African ascendency may get the beam out of their own eye before they gouge so mercilessly at the mote in ours.[11]

Stevens at this date was old and sick, but he found sufficient strength to write a precise and bitter letter to his friend, W. B. Mellius, who had sent him the press account:

Lancaster, Sept. 14, 1867

I rec'd your letter of the 8 containing a printed libel from Union Springs Times. In the course of my life I have rec'd a very large number of such attacks— Perhaps no man in the State has received more slanders or been charged with more vices or more great crimes than I have. It has been my fortune for forty years to be the bitter object of attack by violent partisans. I have seldom noticed them—never to contradict them unless they affected my moral character aside from politics or was required by the interests of others. You tell me that this charge may influence your next election— Hence I notice it—

I have already denied a part of it on application from a distant State— The rude doctrines ascribed me by the fellow who wrote them I pass over, with a general denial of their accuracy—

As to the domestic history I have only to say that the whole is totally without foundation except so far as follows. From the time I began business (40 odd years ago) I have kept house through the agency of hired servants, having no female relatives. Those servants were of various colors; some white, some black and others of all intermediate colors. My only inquiry was into their honesty and capacity. They have resided with me for various periods from one month to fifteen years. Generally more than one at a time—Indeed I believe always so. I believe I can say that no child was ever raised or, so far as I know, begotten under my roof. Sometimes husband and wife have worked the one for me and the other for another, generally at the same time, cohabiting together on Saturday nights. But I believe none of them became pregnant during the time.

This is a larger disclosure than I believe I have ever made before of my private affairs, and have done it now only out of what you think required by public affairs.

These calumnies and worse have been perennially published against me, by fellows living within sight of my door— I know of no one who has believed one of them, or scarcely pretended to believe them. Having no ambition for office; no aspirations for fame, I have not found it pleasant to turn aside to encounter the offensive odor of diseased dog secretions— [12]

For all its preciseness this letter is more remarkable for what it denies obliquely than what it denies directly. There is first of all the general repudiation—"As to the domestic history I have only to say that the whole is totally without foundation." Afterward comes the specific denial—"I believe I can say that no child was ever raised, or, so far as I know, begotten under my roof," and no servant "became pregnant." The curious fact is that Drake had made no reference whatever to children. He accused Stevens only of seduction and adultery. But Stevens, without any necessity for it, chose to deny the accusation of paternity. He was in effect saying once again that he had not fathered a colored child.

A few months later Stevens privately indicated to an old friend that the rumors about his alliance with Lydia Smith were in fact true. Jonathan Blanchard paid him a visit in the spring of 1868 to discuss his "personal errors and vices," and to urge him to be baptized. Stevens, with what seems to have been sly pleasure in shocking the preacher, took the occasion to discuss his private life, and compared himself to other statesmen of his time with unexpected frankness. He was not as lewd as Henry Clay, he said, nor as profane as Ben Wade, nor as much a gambler as General Sickles. Nor was he a "bloated mass of personal vices," like Lord Lyndhurst. His personal habits, he avowed, were "at least less vicious than those of Daniel Webster." But he went on to say that he might favorably be compared with Richard M. Johnson, save that Johnson had been a slaveholder and a disrespecter of the Sabbath.

Richard M. Johnson of Kentucky had been elected Vice-President under Martin Van Buren in 1836 despite the fact that he had lived openly with his mulatto housekeeper, Julia Chinn. She had borne him two daughters, noted for their beauty, whom Johnson had educated and endeavored to introduce into society. When Julia Chinn died, he became enamored of another high-yellow slave girl, but she fled from his plantation with an Indian lover. Johnson recaptured the fugitives and in a fury sold the girl down the river. Shortly after his nomination he transferred his affections to the fugitive girl's beautiful sixteen-year-old sister, and made little effort to keep the alliance clandestine. The North was shocked by the facts, and the South by Johnson's failure to conceal them. But the scandals astonishingly did not prevent his becoming Vice-President.

By the standards of Calvinist New England, Richard Johnson was guilty of slave-trading, concubinage, and lechery. But the country knew him also as the most sweet-tempered of men, a foe of debtor's prisons, a champion of the rights of frontier settlers and Indian education. He loved his daughters and saw to it that they eventually married white men and inherited his estate.[13] This took courage of so highly specialized a nature that most people found it incomprehensible.

"Johnson's slaveholding," Stevens said to Blanchard ironically, "sanctified his vices, so that a family of mulatto children did not prevent his being the idol of the negro-hating democratic party . . . and Vice-President of the United States." He himself on the other hand, Stevens went on, "with three times the ability and a thousand times his honesty, never held any office but that of a direct representative of the people." He "could not be United States Senator even: and though he made presidents, he could not be a member of their cabinets!" [14]

The implication is clear that Stevens blamed his liaison with Lydia Smith as having been a factor in wrecking his ambitions for high political office. What was forgiven when "sanctified" by the slave relationship was not forgiven in a free society. But if he paid a penalty in political preference he seems never to have thought seriously of abandoning his housekeeper.

Two years before he died Stevens bought a deed to a cemetery lot in Lancaster, only to return it when he discovered that the burial of Negroes was forbidden there. When the unfriendly editor of the *Lancaster Intelligencer* learned of this, he wrote the following editorial on July 6, 1867:

Nobody doubts that Thaddeus Stevens has always been in favor of negro equality, and here, where his domestic arrangements are so well known, his practical recognition of his pet theory is perfectly well understood. . . . There are few men who have not given to the world such open and notorious evidence of a belief in negro equality as Thaddeus Stevens. A personage, not of his race, a female of dusky hue, daily walks the streets of Lancaster when Mr. Stevens is at home. She has presided over his house for years. Even by his own party friends, she is constantly spoken of as Mrs. Stevens, though we fancy that no rite of Mother Church ever gave her a right to it. It is natural for men to desire to sleep their last with those they loved in life. If Thaddeus Stevens insists on being buried side by side with the woman he is supposed to have taken to his bosom, it is entirely a matter of taste. But why did he not purchase a lot in an African burying ground at once? There no white man's bones would have jostled his own, and she who has so long been his most intimate associate might have been gathered to his side without exciting public scandal.

Stevens chose to ignore the editorial. He searched about until he found that Schreiner's Protestant cemetery, while not a Negro cemetery, made no discrimination as to the color of its occupants, and purchased a lot there. Jonathan Blanchard was convinced that Stevens was intent on seeing that Lydia Smith should be buried at least in the same cemetery, if not actually by his side. "I saw him cry till the big tears ran heavily down his sunken cheeks," he wrote later, "while relating his efforts to get his bones into a spot where a devilish spirit of caste and proscription could not cast out as a dead brute the corpse of the woman who had taken care of him for more than twenty-five years with the ability and fidelity of a wife; though not permitted by a law, mightier far than the statute, to become his wife." [15]

It is important to note, however, that Stevens knew that his housekeeper was a Roman Catholic, and was likely therefore to be buried in a Catholic cemetery. When it came to willing his estate, he left the bulk of it not to Mrs. Smith but to his nephew, though he bequeathed her a generous legacy. "I give to Mrs. Lydia Smith, my housekeeper," he wrote, "$500 a year during her natural life, to be paid semi-annually, or at her option she may receive $5,000. . . . Mrs. Smith has some furniture of her own used in common with mine, some bought with her money, as well as other which it would be difficult to distinguish. Now she must be trusted on honor to take such as she claims without further proof." [16]

After his death she chose to take the $5,000 and used part of it to purchase the Lancaster home which she had shared with him for so long. She seems to have invested her money wisely, and at her death left some money, including $500 for the upkeep of Stevens' grave.[17] She did not choose, however, to be buried in the same place, directing in her will that her body be interred in St. Mary's Catholic cemetery.

How much Lydia Smith influenced Stevens' life and thinking must remain a matter for inference and speculation. If this vivacious and intelligent woman brought to Stevens the affectionate warmth so long denied him, this did not mean that there was a mellowing in the man or any tempering of the violence of his hatreds. Marriage was impossible; he could share nothing with her in public. The most he could do would be to exact from his kin and his friends behavior toward her that indicated respect for her dignity as a person. To

everyone else she was a Negro, and subject to every public humiliation the white man chose to impose. The fact that she was nearly
white would only underline for him the relentless cruelty of the caste
system.

Stevens had long had a special perspective on color. As early as
1837, in presenting a memorial from Pennsylvania Negroes to the
Constitutional Convention, he said wryly: "Probably many of those who
signed the memorial are as white as many of us, although they do not
rank according to the technical terms of 'white' and 'black.'" [18] He
was fond of quoting the Bible, *He hath made of one blood all nations
of men,* and of arguing that the great variety in mankind of color, form,
and intellect was actually the effect of climate, habits, food, and
education.[19]

But if Stevens convinced himself intellectually of the irrationality
of the public's attitude toward color and scoffed at caste traditions,
he was nevertheless trapped in exactly the behavior he abominated in
the Southern aristocrat. And this the Southern editors never let him
forget.

CHAPTER EIGHT

———— ◆ ————

The Tyrant Father

When you have passed through the romantic period of your existence, and found your warm sympathies and ardent hopes all chilled or blasted; and the milk of human kindness which flows in your breast is in danger of being curdled by the cold ingratitude of those upon whom you have continually bestowed nothing but benefactions, you will learn to appreciate the truth of the remark 'that he is a happy man who has one true friend; but he is more truly happy who never has need of a friend.'

Thaddeus Stevens

THIS BITTER note, unsigned and undated, was preserved among Thaddeus Stevens' papers in the Library of Congress. He did not destroy it, as he did many letters and documents before his death; it is written in his characteristic impatient and almost indecipherable scrawl—a handwriting so confused and tortuous that one cannot but wonder if it betrayed contempt for his correspondents or a deep-seated fear of discovery. The note is melancholy enough in itself, but coming from the pen of a man who kept no diary, and who wrote letters that were usually remarkably free of self-revelation, it is poignant evidence of his continuing loneliness.

Stevens seems to have kept a barrier always between himself and his friends. Even his law students, his stoutest defenders, stood somewhat in awe of him long after they left his office. He had always attracted students, and when after 1842 he temporarily abandoned politics and concentrated on his law practice in order to reduce his debts, they swarmed to him. He had the best law library in the region and a distinguished collection of books on politics and history, all of which he loaned freely. Before long his office became the acknowledged "law school" of southern Pennsylvania. To a new student, asking the cost of reading with him, Stevens would reply: "Two hundred dollars. Some pay; some don't." The fact was, as one student observed later, "there were . . . two recommendations which never failed to procure an entrance into his office: ambition to learn, and inability to pay for the privilege." [1]

His students, several of whom became Congressmen, repaid him with admiration and devotion that continued until his death. One of them, Alexander H. Hood, later wrote a warm and sympathetic biography. This was an important counterweight to the vitriolic memoir published by Alexander Harris, a Lancaster historian who detested Stevens.[2] Harris, it was said, met Stevens on a narrow path one day and refused to give him the space to pass, saying, "I never stand aside for a skunk." Stevens hesitated, then bowed and stepped to one side, replying with gravity, "I always do."

Stevens became especially fond of one student, Simon Stevens, who, though not a relative, he came to treat almost like a son. The letters from Simon Stevens which have been preserved show an enduring friendship. "Can't you go to Vermont this summer when I go in June," Simon wrote to him on April 25, 1865. "Come what do you say? . . . You are uncle to us all." [3] Thaddeus Stevens helped him financially, made him a law partner, took a paternal interest in his wife and son —who was named Thaddeus in his honor—and remembered him in his will.

During the Civil War, Simon became embroiled in some unsavory ammunition deals, and was accused on the floor of Congress of purchasing defective guns already rejected by the U. S. Army, and of selling them, after retooling, to the Army of the West for an exorbitant profit. Thaddeus Stevens, obviously pained by the scandal, pointed out in Congress that Simon Stevens was not his kin but a former law student. He defended his character with slight mockery as being "as unimpeachable as anyone in his law office," and got the expected laugh from the House in reply. But he did not gloss over the charges. "It was a speculation which may not be very pleasant to look at," he said, "but it was a legitimate business transaction, and involves no officer of the Government." [4]

When accused by one Congressman of taking "good care of his bantling," Stevens replied brusquely: "I take care of nobody; I do not care much for anybody." It was a characteristic denial and retreat. However deeply committed, he could not admit his affections. But Simon Stevens' reputation, at least in the Lancaster area, remained somewhat unsavory,[5] and it is quite possible that he was one of many whose "cold ingratitude" chilled Stevens into ever deeper moroseness and pessimism.

Thaddeus Stevens saw little of his brothers, but he sent them money and befriended their children. His niece, Lizzie Stevens, who lived in Indianapolis, was a lively, warmhearted girl who sent him affectionate letters. But she died in 1867 before reaching the age of twenty. Her brother, Thaddeus, who became a physician, seems to have visited his uncle seldom. The other two nephews, however, came to live with him in Lancaster after the death of their father, Abner Stevens, in Vermont in 1847.

With these youths, Alanson and Thaddeus, Stevens was demanding and uncompromising in a fashion that did not carry over to his students. From his own kin he expected much, and though he acquired these substitute sons late in life, he was feverishly intent on seeing them become successful men. Thaddeus Jr.—as he was called to distinguish him from his uncle—[6] after graduating from an academy in Pennsylvania, was sent in 1854 to the University of Vermont, where it was expected that he would be under the supervision of his aged grandmother, Sally Stevens. His academic record in Pennsylvania had been bad, and Stevens wrote him a stern letter which revealed both his ambitions for the boy and his apprehensions:

. . . Mere meditating should not be your ambition. Be first in your class. You can if you will. It will take intense application, but the prize is worth all the toil. . . .

Knowledge cannot be had per order when you want to use it, as you can order dinner at a restaurant. Not only your classic, but general information should be mastered. History, biography, the whole circle of knowledge should be traversed while in college.

I fear indolence is your besetting sin for sin it is. But now in the midst of stimulants to effort, I trust you will raise your energies, and do honor to yourself. You need not partake of your grandmother's fear that you will be injured either in body or mind by close study. I have never known such a case.

Let strict morality guide all your actions, or your acquirements will be a curse. *Never* taste intoxicating drink—a little is folly—much is crime.

This is a fascinating letter on many counts, not the least of which is the suggestion of a troubled relationship between Thaddeus Stevens and his mother. When he wrote: *You need not partake of your grandmother's fear that you will be injured either in body or mind by close study,* could he have been indicating that she, who had given so many years of toil to provide for his education, was now bitter because this schooling, instead of producing an upright minister, had resulted instead in a lawyer-politician slandered by charges of fornication and atheism? It was said that he visited her almost annually. Still she would write begging him to visit her instead of going "to them Hote Springs." She did not go south to visit him,[7] and it may have been that her resentment, such as it was, stemmed rather from the feeling that her most promising son, like her husband, had abandoned her.

Thaddeus Stevens Jr. failed at the University of Vermont, and was expelled four times from Dartmouth College. One of his penitent letters has been preserved in the Library of Congress. Significantly enough, it was addressed to "Mrs. Smith," and not his uncle. ". . . I have been here nearly 3 months and Mr. Carpenter the man with whom I have been studying has expressed his willingness to give me testimonials of good behaviour at any time. He even offered to write to the faculty of the college and try and get me back at the commencement of the spring term but I told him that I thought it would be of no avail. . . . I will go to Peachem and fix my things there and try and be there when Uncle arrives let him know how all my affairs stand he knows the worst part of them. . . ."[8]

The letters Stevens wrote to his nephew in college show a growing exasperation. "I fear also you love rum and sometimes drink it," he wrote. "If so, the sooner you are abandoned the better, as there is no hope for one who ever tastes strong drink." Later he wrote an angry ultimatum:

I have read your letter with pain. It is grievous to lose your near relatives by death. But it is still more painful to see them disgraced and worthless men.

I foresaw that your indolence and habits would lead you to ruin unless reformed. It seems that instead of reforming, you have continued them, and they have produced the natural result . . .

I must say that until you have redeemed yourself from disgrace, I have no desire ever to see you.[9]

Yet Stevens softened when Thaddeus Jr. within a month left college and came back to Lancaster to throw himself upon his uncle's mercy. He took him into his office as a law student, and the two seem to have worked out an uneasy truce. Thaddeus Jr. became a lawyer and helped his uncle in the management of the Caledonia Ironworks. Stevens had him appointed Assistant Clerk of the House for a time, which brought down upon him the charge of nepotism.[10]

Still their relationship continued to be subtly poisoned. This became clear after Stevens' death with the publication of the provisions of his will. He made it specific that Thaddeus Jr. would inherit his estate only if he "abstained from all intoxicating drinks." He was to be given $800 a year for five years, and if during that time he remained a teetotaler he would inherit one fourth of the estate. At the end of a second five years without liquor he was to be given another fourth. After a third five-year period he would inherit the remainder. If, however, he went back to his rum, the estate was to be used for the endowment of an orphanage.

The Pennsylvania Supreme Court opinion on the will said pointedly: "It is clear that he did not intend that his estate should go to his heirs as such." [11] Whether out of contempt for his uncle, or because as a real alcoholic he was incapable of living up to the stipulated pledge we do not know, but Thaddeus Jr. had no part of his uncle's property. When he died on June 1, 1874, only six years after the elder Stevens, he had received nothing.[12]

Stevens seems to have found it impossible to disentangle the uses of money from the uses of affection. He gave money lavishly to utter strangers and went on his way fortified by their surprise and gratitude. To his nephew he could not give without exacting something in return. But using his purse as a weapon resulted only in alienation and failure. Still he could not cease manipulating the youth's life, and trying to make his decisions for him.

When his second adopted nephew, Alanson, was killed in the Civil War, he took measures at once to bring Thaddeus Jr. home from the battle front and had him made provost-marshall in Lancaster, well out of reach of Confederate guns.[13] Like so many well-meaning parents he would save the life but relentlessly punish the spirit.

In his early years Thaddeus Stevens had been a convivial drinker, and had belonged to a club where the members drank regularly when they met to play cards. Late one night a member of the club, a bank cashier, left the party very drunk and died shortly after reaching home. Stevens, it was said, was so shocked he went down into his cellar, carried up his wine and whisky barrels and demolished them with a hatchet in the middle of the street. The sight of so much liquor running down the cobblestones made a great impression on the townspeople, who seem also to have heard the thunderbolt.[14]

From this moment forward, according to local legend, he refused to touch alcohol altogether. Like so many of his antislavery friends, he formally joined the temperance movement which had mushroomed in the late 1830's, and for a time worked for anti-liquor legislation in Pennsylvania. But unlike many temperance crusaders, he was a practical politician, and soon became disillusioned with the whole notion of legislating against liquor. "I should be glad if legislation would cure intemperance," he said in Congress in 1864, "but I have seen it tried, and tried in vain. . . . When I was a young man, and I would not object to being so again, I was in a State Legislature, and moved that the sale of liquor should be prohibited in my district, and the motion was carried. I did not find that I thereby made one drunkard the less—they would only drink the more when they had a chance." [15]

Stevens eventually owned a brewery and a tavern. In a genial debate on liquor taxes in Congress he defended the beer-drinkers of Pennsylvania as honest and industrious, though admitting that the effects of his own lager beer were "sometimes eccentric and amusing." Mindful of his beer-loving German constituents, Stevens argued to keep the liquor taxes low. "The gentleman from Maine," he said, "says he wants the wages of sin to be as high as possible. I want them to be low. I think the bill makes the price of sin as high as it ought to be. . . . Now, how high does the gentleman suppose the price of sin ought to be?"

Congressman Rice answered him adroitly: "If the gentleman is a better judge upon that subject than I am—"

Whereupon Stevens neatly interrupted: "Well, sir, the gentleman places it higher than I do." And he urged the end of the debate. "I think our thirsty friends had better *dry* up upon this subject. This is not a law to prohibit the sale of liquor or to correct the morals of the country. We should never attempt that in Congress." [16]

Urbane and realistic though he may have sounded here, Thaddeus Stevens clearly had a different set of rules for his nephews and himself. True to the logic if not the theology of his Calvinist upbringing, he demanded from himself and those he loved behavior becoming to the Lord's élite, and counted the rest of the world beyond saving in any case. His renunciation of alcohol was real, and lasted nearly to the end of his life, when under doctor's orders he began to drink small quantities of brandy and wine as a stimulant for his failing heart. His years of self-denial apparently gave him a bitter pleasure, and filled a deeper need than the best Bourbon or Madeira. Unhappily and futilely he chose to exact from his nephew the same kind of self-denial. It is even possible that the smoldering memories of his father's drunkenness were at work here, and in humiliating his nephew he was unwittingly working off an ancient hate.

Stevens' relations with his nephew Alanson were no less uneasy than with Thaddeus Jr., and at the end took on the coloring of tragedy. For a time Alanson read law with his uncle, but soon gave it up and went to work as a clerk in the Caledonia Iron Works. Soon the foreman, John Sweeney, brought Stevens word that his nephew had "taken up housekeeping" with a fourteen-year-old girl, Mary Jane Primm. In describing this occasion years later Sweeney said: "Mr. Stevens said it was very bad behavior on the place; that was all that was said on the subject, and Mr. Stevens remarked as we parted, 'Charge him with whatever he gets.'" [17]

Mary Primm in 1859 bore Alanson a son who died at the age of nine weeks. There was no public funeral for a child born out of wedlock; the neighbors simply stood at their windows to watch the parents weeping together on the way to the graveyard. Mary Primm, suing later to collect money from Alanson's inheritance, insisted that she had been married to him in Harrisburg. The couple did in fact go to Harrisburg on April 19, 1861, a few weeks before their second child, Alanson Jane, was born. When they returned, Alanson said to Jacob Tuckey in Caledonia: "Now we are married, and it's nobody's damn business." But it is clear from the court records and several letters that actually there had been nothing in Harrisburg but a generous exchange of promises.

Mary Primm could never produce a marriage certificate to make good her claim as Alanson's widow, although she maintained stoutly that it had been burned by the rebels during the raid on Caledonia. Many of her old neighbors testified that she had never been known as anything but Mary Primm. One witness, Mary Rea, stated in court that Mary Primm had told her Alanson had promised to marry her when he came back from the war. "She told me if Alanson would marry her the old gentleman would disinherit him—meaning Thaddeus Stevens."

So Stevens emerges again in the role of a harsh and uncharitable father. He wrote a letter to Alanson at the battle front May 22, 1863, which said in part:

> . . . I am glad you remained well. I could wish you were safely back. . . . I think when you come we'll have to take the management of the works. . . . I must say to you . . . you are bestowing the money you send here on a very worthless, dissolute woman—Stage, hack drivers and others speak freely of it—
> This is all I intend to say as I have made no inquiry into the subject.
> Y uncle
> Thaddeus Stevens

The cruelty of this letter is easy to see. Stevens was not only repudiating Alanson's mistress—while clinging to his own—but also by implication repudiating their illegitimate child. And he was bargaining again with his purse, saying in effect: "Give up this dissolute woman and her child and you may be manager of Caledonia."

When Alanson received this, and other apparently more detailed letters from neighbors, he wrote a tortured letter to Mary Primm accusing her of entertaining "persons of very low caracter" and neglecting their daughter, Jennie. She replied angrily:

. . . Lance I think you must of been drunk when you wrote this letter for I dont think you could meane it after living with me one year and knowing me as long as you have. . . .

Yours truely untill death

M J P [18]

Shortly after their bitter exchange, the youth was killed in the Battle of Chickamauga. Mary Primm, now eighteen, was left with the two-year-old Jennie and no claim to honorable widowhood save a slip of paper signed by Alanson Stevens which said: "I hereby acknowledge Mary Primm to be my lawful wife, as I go forth to battle." She took the paper to the foreman, John Sweeney, and begged him to help her obtain a pension as Alanson's widow.

"She showed me a paper and asked me what I thought of it," Sweeney said at the trial. "I just laughed and treated it as a joke. She made no claim to be his wife." Nevertheless Sweeney admitted signing affidavits to help her obtain the pension. However, with her extraordinary incapacity for holding on to the last shreds of respectability, Mary Primm lost even this evidence.

She continued to insist that she was Alanson's legal widow, and used the title in 1866 when trying to enter Jennie in school. When the school superintendent asked Thaddeus Stevens about the relationship, he coldly disavowed her. Lydia Smith, distressed over the child's plight, wrote a delicate letter to Thaddeus Jr.: "Mary Primm has been applying to this district," she said, ". . . to get her child in representing herself the widow of Alanson Stevens and Mr. Burrowes inquired of your uncel about it and he told them that thair was no such widow. Mr. Stevens have you seen the child . . ."

But young Thaddeus, too, hardened his heart against the girl. Alanson had inherited $2,400 from his father, which Mary Primm tried to collect. It was in the form of a promissory note, made payable on demand, and signed by Thaddeus Stevens, who had invested the money for his nephew. When Mary Primm learned that the note had been found among Alanson's possessions, she went to Thaddeus Stevens in Lancaster and begged the money on behalf of her child. Later she testified in court "that Thad Stevens told her his nephew Thaddeus had the note and she would have to look to him for it. But that he would do all he could; that he meant he would do right by me; that he would try and see that young Thaddeus would do right by me; that it was out of his hands entirely."

When, however, she approached Thaddeus Jr., he refused to give it to her. The note remained among his papers, mute reminder of a formidable unkindness. Young Thaddeus could not bring himself to collect on the note for his own pocket, and old Thaddeus retained an uncomfortable memory of the whole matter. According to Simon Stevens, he mentioned the note shortly before his death, expressing surprise that it had never been presented for payment because Alanson had left a widow and child. "Simon," he said, "you know all about this note; that I hold the money in a fiduciary capacity, and if it is ever presented you can explain that it must be paid to the legal holder."

The girl Jennie died at the age of eleven, and Mary Primm drifted from one man to another. In 1894, twenty years after Thaddeus Jr.'s death, the note was found by Simon Stevens, and on behalf of Mary Primm, then Mrs. Clason, he tried to collect the money from the Thaddeus Stevens estate. The suit was lost, not because the court decided against the legality of the claim, but simply because according to the statute of limitations the note had been permitted to expire.

So ends the story. No one of the characters emerges untarnished, least of all Thaddeus Stevens, whose role as the tyrant parent was ugly from the beginning.

CHAPTER NINE

Congress and Compromise

IN LANCASTER Thaddeus Stevens made good his financial losses and reinstated himself as the most formidable lawyer in Pennsylvania. With the fiasco of the Buckshot War largely forgotten, he made hundreds of new friends, many of whom talked freely about sending him to Congress. Although generally avoiding politics, he did campaign for Henry Clay in 1844,[1] and he took pains to establish himself as a member of the Whig Party, on the antislavery or "Conscience Whig" fringe. Since antislavery sentiment was growing fast in the Lancaster area, he was no longer considered dangerous on this issue. That he was still independent and erratic in regard to party discipline he demonstrated by quietly urging New England Whigs to vote for James G. Birney, who was running for president on the antislavery Liberty Party ticket.[2]

In 1848, deeply disturbed by what was happening in Washington as a result of the Mexican War, he decided to run for Congress. He was elected by a memorable majority, 9,500 as against 5,500. On August 29, 1848, the Democratic *Lancaster Intelligencer* commented sourly on his victory:

We have ascribed the nomination of Mr. Stevens to the homage awarded to his commanding intellect, but . . . yet more potent reasons exist at the bottom. *He is the sworn foe of the South*—avowedly selected as a champion able and willing to "worry" the representatives from beyond Mason and Dixon's line. He goes into Congress the predetermined agitator of sectional jealousies and divisions. . . . His mission is to be one of Strife, of Division, and of Hatred, and surely there is no one so well qualified to fulfill it.

As yet, Stevens was not the sworn foe of *the South* but only the sworn foe of *slavery*. But for him to be elected at all with this reputation showed an extraordinary change in Pennsylvania's politics. Actually he had won only with a combination of factions—Silver Greys, Native Americans, and Woolly Heads [3]—any one of which might cancel its support two years hence. He was a member of a minority faction in a minority party. But he represented, nevertheless, a point of view about slavery and slavery extension that would eventually dominate the North. This point of view began with a special perspective on slavery history.

When Stevens and thoughtful men of his persuasion looked backward, they remembered that most of the men who made the nation had been antislavery. They knew that Thomas Jefferson's first draft of the Declaration of Independence had contained an arraignment of slavery, left out of the final version to spare South Carolina and Georgia. They remembered that Jefferson had introduced an ordinance in the Continental Congress in 1784 which would have forbidden slavery in territory that afterward became Alabama, Mississippi, Tennessee, Kentucky, and the old Northwest Territory. They recalled that it lost, tragically for the nation's future, by one vote.

In 1820 the bill that would have prohibited slavery in Missouri lost by three votes, all of them Northern. By such narrow and accidental margins slavery had been permitted to spread until it had become a paralyzing incubus which could not be pulled off without danger of ripping open the nation.

Although all the Northern states had abolished slavery, the number of slaves had jumped from 700,000 in 1790 to three million in 1850.[4] The once-flourishing emancipation and colonization societies in the South had all disappeared, and the old regret and apology for slave labor had been replaced by a militant defense, all the more aggressive for being rooted in a now-buried stratum of guilt. John Quincy Adams had described this in his diary, April 19, 1837: "In the South it is a perpetual agony of conscious guilt and terror, attempting to disguise itself under sophistical argumentation and braggart menaces." [5]

Thaddeus Stevens had opposed the annexation of Texas, like many others in the North, chiefly because it meant that slavery would jump out of the bonds in which he had hoped it would be contained forever. He could not agree with those who held blithely that since Oregon would come in as free territory the nation would still be as nicely balanced as before. This was not his kind of mathematics.

Even those antislavery men who were captivated by the spoils of the Mexican War—a great slice of continent, later to become California, New Mexico, Arizona, Utah, and part of Colorado and Wyoming—and who believed that these gains would insure the nation against Balkanization and guarantee its bright promise as a great power, were deeply troubled. They could see that in fifty-six years slavery had swept across the southern half of the continent to the Rio Grande, covering an area the vastness of which could scarcely have been dreamed of in 1789. Lincoln held the view, though he did not state it publicly until 1854, that in the beginning slavery was "hid away, in the constitution, just as an afflicted man hides away a wen or cancer, which he dares not cut out at once, lest he bleed to death; with the promise, nevertheless, that the cutting may begin at the end of a given time." [6]

In 1846 most antislavery men, including Stevens, were demanding not that the cancer be cut out but only that the growth be stopped. But when David Wilmot, Representative from Pennsylvania, formally demanded that slavery be forbidden in all the territory acquired during the Mexican War, a frightening furor broke out. As the legislatures of New York, Michigan, Massachusetts, and Vermont passed resolutions acclaiming the "Wilmot Proviso," the Southern states furiously denounced it. President Polk called it mischievous and foolish, and clearheaded observers saw the portentous beginning of a split in the nation, no longer between Whigs and Democrats, but between the North and the South. As Bernard De Voto stated it in *The Year of Decision, 1846*, "At some time between August and December, 1846, the Civil War had begun."

As the Wilmot Proviso went down to defeat, both parties began to splinter. There were Barnburners, Hunkers, Freesoilers, Cotton Whigs, Conscience Whigs, Silver Greys, Woolly Heads, Native Americans—a name for every political complexion. The Freesoilers and Conscience Whigs were sizable enough to elect men with antislavery convictions, so that in 1848 Congress had not a scattering but an actual bloc of men dedicated to the "containment" though not the abolition of slavery. This was something new, and long overdue. The leadership of the antislavery movement had finally shifted from independent but politically inept or uninfluential reformers like Garrison, Weld, and Wendell Phillips, to the floor of Congress, where it rightly belonged.

The coalition that elected Thaddeus Stevens in 1848 did so with full knowledge that he would fight against slavery expansion. He had made it explicit in this election, as he did right up to the outbreak of war, that though he detested slavery and was in favor of abolition, he would not trouble the institution in those states where it had been guaranteed by the Constitution. This was a common approach. Two other men destined for future power, who were also elected for the first time in 1848, William H. Seward and Salmon P. Chase, took about the same stand. Lincoln, elected for a single term in 1846, would adopt it cautiously and with reservations later, saying that he agreed with the makers of the Constitution, whose intention had been to put slavery "in the course of ultimate extinction." [7]

There were, in fact, all shades of opinion among the antislavery men about the proper time for the extinction of slavery. Some were for immediate and total abolition, others for "immediate abolition gradually begun." Stevens would "encircle the slave states of this Union with free States as a cordon of fire, [so] that slavery, like a scorpion, would sting itself to death." [8] The conservative Lincoln said in 1858 he did not expect that "in the most peaceful way ultimate extinction would occur in less than a hundred years at the least." [9]

The exact shade which made a man an "abolitionist" instead of merely "antislavery" was never easy to determine at any given time. Many Southerners, perhaps rightly from the long view, looked upon all antislavery men as abolitionists, believing that "ultimate extinction" was just as pernicious as "gradual abolition immediately begun." They had fastened the label "abolitionist" upon Thaddeus Stevens long ago.

Among the new faces in Congress in 1848 Stevens was recognized immediately as a potential leader. In the acrimonious fight for Speaker of the House, which lasted a stormy three weeks, he once received twenty-seven votes. But when a Southern Democrat, Howell Cobb, finally won the speakership and filled the important committees with Southerners and doughfaces, there was little left for Stevens but agitation. Having a realistic understanding of legislative processes he disliked agitation for its own sake. His friends expected him to speak out defiantly, and there were certain things he wanted badly to say. But he did not speak out until the great legislative battle over slavery extension in 1850. On February 20 and June 10 he made his stand clear in two brilliant, acid speeches. If he could not expect to influence legislation in a committee, he could at least explode what he believed to be some contemporary Southern fictions.

During preceding generations two ideas with great vitality had taken hold in the South. Like many enduring fables, they were chiefly but not wholly untrue, and were compounded in part of the daydreams of white men. The one which particularly outraged Stevens was the conception of the happy slave. Senator Solomon W. Downs of Louisiana spoke glowingly on this theme the day before Stevens made his first major speech in the House. "They are the gayest, happiest, the most contented, and the best fed people in the world," Downs said. "We frequently hear the remark made, and we are conscious of it ourselves, that our slaves not only a happy people, but that they are much happier than we are ourselves." [10]

In one profound sense this was true. The oppressed has somewhat of an advantage over his oppressor in peace of spirit. But this was hardly what Senator Downs was seeking to convey. Actually few Southerners were ignorant of the whippings, brandings, and earcroppings, of the continual breaking-up of Negro families—during the fifties Virginia alone sold 6,000 slaves a year to the Cotton Kingdom—and of the widespread plantation concubinage which had resulted in one mulatto child for every eight to ten black ones.[11] "God forgive us, but ours is a monstrous system, a wrong and an iniquity!" Mary Boykin Chesnut would write in her diary on March 5, 1861. "Like the patriarchs of old, our men live all in one house with their wives and concubines; and the mulattoes one sees in every family partly resemble the white children. Any lady is ready to tell you who is the father of all the mulatto children in everybody's household but her own. Those, she seems to think, drop from the clouds." [12]

No one knew better than the Southern legislators how the corrosive fear of slave insurrection pervaded the South. Periodic panics, deliberately unreported in the Southern press, swept through portions of the slave states. After the Nat Turner massacre in Virginia, in August 1831, when seventy slaves killed fifty-seven white men, women, and children, few plantation owners were ever entirely at ease. The English actress, Fanny Kemble, after a winter on her husband's Georgia plantation, wrote: "I know that southern men are apt to deny that they do live under an habitual sense of danger, but a slave population, coerced into obedience, though unarmed and half-fed, *is* a threatening source of constant insecurity, and every southern *woman* to whom I have spoken on the subject, has admitted to me that they live in terror of their slaves." [13]

That many slaves were happy even Thaddeus Stevens could not deny. But when Senator Downs insisted that slaves were happier than white men he seems to have been only fantasying a perfect Platonic society, where all white men were aristocrats, where the slaves worked hard, minded their manners, sang pleasantly, and never tried to burn down their master's cotton gin or run away.

Actually the humane Southern planter was trapped in a dilemma, which no one phrased better than the great fugitive slave Frederick Douglass: "Beat and cuff your slave, keep him hungry and spiritless, and he will follow the chain of his master like a dog; but feed and clothe him well, work him moderately, surround him with physical comfort, and dreams of freedom intrude. Give him a *bad* master, and he aspires to a good master; give him a good master and he wishes to become his own master." [14]

The second cherished Southern notion that outraged Thaddeus Stevens was that the Negro had been rescued from savagery to be tamed and civilized in America by Christianity and the white man's society. Jefferson Davis expressed this concisely in the Senate on February 13, 1850: "The slave trade, so far as the African was concerned, was a blessing; it brought him from abject slavery and a barbarian master, and sold him into a Christian land. It brought him from a benighted region, and placed him in one where civilization would elevate and dignify his nature." [15]

Here, too, truth and fiction were blended. Africa was neither as barbarous as the white man thought,[16] nor was civilization in the South as elevating as Jefferson Davis implied. The teaching of slaves to read was everywhere forbidden by law. Some, like Frederick Douglass, learned surreptitiously; others were educated by their masters in defiance of the statutes; many free Negroes quietly taught each other; [17] but these were exceptional. Judge Lumpkin of the Georgia Supreme Court in 1853 stated the case for perpetual illiteracy: "A white man is liable to a fine of five hundred dollars and imprisonment for teaching a *free* negro to read and write, and if one *free* negro teach another, he is punishable by fine and whipping, or fine or whipping . . . these severe restrictions . . . have my hearty and cordial approval. . . . Everything must be interdicted which is calculated to render the slave discontented." [18]

Instead of following the theory of "barbarism to civilization" to its logical conclusion—emancipation—the South was busy passing or strengthening laws prohibiting manumission of any kind. There was even talk of re-enslaving or deporting free Negroes lest they incite the slaves to rebellion, and free Negro sailors entering Southern ports were imprisoned in their boats and forbidden shore leave.[19] Such contradictions between theory and behavior bothered few. "James H. Hammond got at the crux of the matter," Kenneth M. Stampp has pointed out, "when he asked whether any people in history had ever voluntarily surrendered two billion dollars worth of property." [20]

In assaulting the fictions that all slaves were happy and that slavery was a divinely ordered transition between African barbarism and American civilization, Thaddeus Stevens brought before Congress a relentless and savage talent for satire:

Gentlemen on this floor, and in the Senate have repeatedly, during this discussion, asserted that slavery was a moral, political, and personal blessing, that the slave was free from care, contented, happy, fat, and sleek. . . . Instances are cited where the slave, after having tried freedom, had voluntarily returned to resume his yoke. Well, if this be so, let us give all a chance to enjoy this blessing. Let the slaves, who choose, go free; and the free, who choose, become slaves. . . . We will not complain if they establish societies in the South for that purpose—abolition societies to abolish freedom. Nor will we rob the mails to search for incendiary publications in favor of slavery, even if they contain seductive pictures, and cuts of those implements of happiness, handcuffs, iron yokes, and cat-o'-nine tails. . . .

If it will save the Union, let these gentlemen introduce a "compromise," by which these races may change conditions into that happy state where he can stretch his sleek limbs on the sunny ground without fear of deranging his toilet; when he will have no care for to-morrow; another will be bound to find him meat and drink, food and raiment, and provide for the infirmities and helplessness of old age. Impose, if you please, upon the other race, as compensation for their former blessings, all those cares, and duties, and anxieties.

It may be objected that the white man is not fitted to enjoy that condition like the black man. . . . He may soon become so . . . Homer informs us that the moment a man becomes a slave, he loses half the man; and a few short years of apprenticeship will expunge all the rest except the faint glimmerings of an immortal soul. Take your stand, therefore, courageously in the swamp, spade and mattock in hand, and uncovered, and half naked, toil beneath the broiling sun. Go home to your hut at night, and sleep on the bare ground, and go forth in the morning unwashed to give you a color that will pass muster in the most fastidious and pious slave-market in all Christendom. . . . Deprived of all education, cut off from all ambitions and aspirations, your mind would soon lose all foolish and perplexing desires for freedom; and the whole man would be sunk into a most happy and contented indifference.

Forsaking sarcasm, Stevens then went on to defend the abolitionists. "Throughout the country, the friends of liberty are reproached as 'transcendentalists and fanatics.' Sir, I do not understand the terms in such connection. There can be no fanatics in the cause of genuine liberty." He reminded his listeners of Moses and Aaron, "those fanatical abolitionists, guided by Heaven," leading the Children of Israel to freedom, and concluded with a grim warning: "And you, in the midst of slavery, who are willing to do justice to the people, take care that your works testify to the purity of your intentions, even at some cost. Take care that your door-posts are sprinkled with the blood of

sacrifice, that when the destroying Angel goes forth, as go forth he
will, he may pass you by." [21]

Representative Millson of Virginia said Stevens' speech filled him
with "loathing and indignation"; Marshall of Kentucky said tartly his
words were "suited to a fishmarket." [22] The most venomous attack,
however, came from Stevens' own colleague, the Democrat Ross, from
Bucks County, Pennsylvania.

"Surely," Ross said, "language so offensive, and impudence so un-
blushing, have never before been seen or heard. . . . It is an old
proverb, and as true as it is old, that the bad tongue of a bad man can
defame no one. Pennsylvania knows that member. With deep humiliation she acknowledges the acquaintance. His history has been the
history of her wrongs and misfortunes . . . the Democracy of Pennsylvania may well laugh to scorn his vulgar, indecent and unmanly
abuse." [23]

When Stevens arose to reply to these attacks, he showed the House
something new in the art of vituperation:

To such remarks there can be no reply by one who is not willing to place
himself on a level with blackguards. I cannot enter that arena. I will leave
the filth and slime of Billingsgate to the fish-women, and to their worthy
coadjutors, the gentleman from Virginia, from North Carolina, from Kentucky, Tennessee, and all that tribe. With them I can have no controversy.
When I want to combat with such opponents and such weapons, I can find
them any day by entering the fish market, without defiling this Hall.

I beg those respectable fish-ladies, however, to understand that I do not
include my colleague from Bucks County among those I deem fit to be
their associates. I would not so degrade them.

There is, in the natural world, a little spotted, contemptible animal, which
is armed by nature with a foetid, volatile, penetrating *virus*, which so pol-
lutes whoever attacks it, as to make him offensive to himself and all around
him for a long time. Indeed, he is almost incapable of purification. Nothing,
sir, no insult shall provoke me to crush so filthy a beast! [24]

Howell Cobb, Speaker of the House, after listening to Stevens, said
privately: "Our enemy has a general now. This man is rich, therefore,
we cannot buy him. He does not want higher office, therefore we
cannot allure him. He is not vicious, therefore, we cannot seduce him.
He is in earnest. He means what he says. He is bold. He cannot be
flattered or frightened." [25]

The acrid controversy of 1850 was essentially a sectional fight for
power, never seriously affected by the moral argument that slavery
was sin. The slaveholders, being a minority, believed that Thaddeus
Stevens was right when he predicted boldly that confining slavery would

"bring the States themselves to its gradual abolition." A constitutional amendment passed by two-thirds of the nation's states could legally end it. This was the most elementary political fact in Southern thinking. Faced by the frightening population growth in the North—speeded as it was by the flood of European immigrants, few of whom chose to settle in slave territory—Southerners believed there were only two ways to prevent the extinction of slavery. The first was secession, the second expansion. Threat of the first was constantly used as a weapon to win the second.

"How often," Stevens protested in his maiden speech, "have these walls been profaned and the North insulted by the insolent threat, that if Congress legislate against southern will, it should be disregarded, resisted to extremity, and the Union destroyed. . . . You have too often intimidated Congress. You have more than once frightened the tame North from its propriety, and found 'doughfaces' enough to be your tools." [26]

Militant Southerners demanded now that slavery be permitted in all the territories. "Slavery is national, freedom sectional," thundered Calhoun. He hoped that by carving out a series of four states from Texas, and by splitting California in two, the South could hold its own in the battle for near parity in Washington. When Henry Clay and Daniel Webster insisted that California was designed by her topography to be a free state, Jefferson Davis replied: "I hold that the pursuit of gold-washing and mining is better adapted to slave labor than to any other. . . . I also maintain that it is particularly adapted to an agriculture which depends upon irrigation." [27]

Since the Constitution held that as far as representation in Congress was concerned a slave should be counted as three-fifths of a man, the Southerners had an immense advantage tactically over the Northern legislators. They represented the aristocratic class and voted as a unit on key issues, yet their numbers were determined by *all* Southern classes, including white and black labor. The fact that the South was an oligarchy rather than a democracy infuriated Stevens. "There are twenty-five gentlemen on this floor," he said, "who are virtually the representatives of slaves alone, having not one free constituent. This is an outrage on every representative principle." [28] Still this was the heritage of the Constitution, and not even Stevens dared yet suggest that the sacrosanct document needed amending.

Henry Clay, architect of past compromises, was busy preparing what he hoped would be the compromise to end all slavery agitation. It was an ingenious scheme, which would win him an extraordinary reputation for statesmanship despite the fact that the compromise lasted less than four years. To please the North he would have California admitted as a free state, and the slave trade—though not slavery—abolished in the District of Columbia. To please the South he would have Utah and New Mexico admitted as territories without any kind of slavery law; he would settle the Texas boundary dispute largely on Texas terms—by paying $10,000,000 to cover the Texas debt—and he would provide for a stringent fugitive slave law designed not only to block the Underground Railroad but also to bring back the slaves who had escaped by it.

There is no doubt that Clay had a remarkable talent for arbitration; unhappily his compromise would see slavery extended rather than curtailed. In earlier years Clay had worked for gradual emancipation in Kentucky, but his efforts were all blocked, and he had now come to represent the almost schizophrenic attitude of the border-state people, who disliked slavery but feared abolition more.

"I have during my life emancipated some eight or ten . . ." Clay wrote to Joshua Giddings in 1847. "Of the remainder (some fifty odd), what I ought to do with them, and how, and when, is a matter of grave and serious consideration often with me. I am perfectly sure that to emancipate them forthwith would be an act of great inhumanity and extreme cruelty. . . . They would perish if I sent them forth in the world." [29]

If the freeing of eight or ten required so much deliberation, what of an eventual eight or ten million? For if ever a problem was certain to accelerate with the years it was this one. Lincoln, who was acutely aware of the dilemma but did not speak out publicly on the issue for some years, would write somberly to George Robertson in 1855: "I think, that there is no peaceful extinction of slavery in prospect for us. The signal failure of Henry Clay, and other good and great men, in 1849, to effect any thing in favor of gradual emancipation in Kentucky, together with a thousand other signs, extinguishes that hope utterly." [30]

Daniel Webster, who had often thundered against slavery expansion, was expected to oppose the Clay compromises. One Washington reporter stated that Thaddeus Stevens and Joshua Giddings had been permitted to see a draft of the expected Webster speech and had privately reported it to be "a powerful exposition and vindication of Northern sentiment." [31] But if this draft was ever written, it certainly was not delivered.

As his speech unfolded on March 7, 1850, Stevens was appalled to hear him support the compromise proposals, including the fugitive slave law. Had he been content to defend them as the only way to preserve the Union, Stevens might have forgiven him. But Webster went on to a blistering tirade against the abolitionists. "If the infernal Fanatics and abolitionists ever get the power in their hands," he said, "they will override the Constitution, set the Supreme Court at defiance, change and make laws to suit themselves. They will lay violent hands on those who differ with them politically in opinion, or dare question their infallibility; bankrupt the country and finally deluge it with blood." He called them "a race of agitators," "shallow men, ignorant men, and factious men,—whose only hope of making or of keeping themselves conspicuous is by incessant agitation." The whole antislavery agitation was "theoretical, fanatical, and fantastical," leading away "silly women and sillier men." [32]

There was little applause when he sat down. A voice rang out in the gallery: "Traitor!" and a slight scuffle followed as the man was ejected. Thomas Hart Benton, the stout old antislavery Missouri lion, sat scowling and enraged. William Seward sat unhappily scribbling notes. The triumphant Southern Senators pressed forward to shake Webster's hand. Thaddeus Stevens sat morosely in the gallery. "As I heard it," he said later to a Webster admirer, "I could have cut his damned heart out!" [33]

Stevens continued to attack the compromise plan in the House, denouncing it as an "extraordinary conspiracy against liberty," an act that would "*compromise* away the Constitution." Webster he censured with indirect irony. "Least of all would I reproach the South," he said. "I honor her courage and fidelity. Even in a bad, a wicked cause, she shows a united front. *All* her sons are faithful to the cause of human bondage, because it is *their* cause. But the North—the poor, timid, mercenary, drivelling North—has no such united defenders of her cause, although it is the cause of human liberty." [34]

Other Whigs in Congress were infuriated by Webster's defection, and he carried very few party votes with him. But the death of Zachary Taylor, who had been an unexpected ally to antislavery men, greatly strengthened the power of the compromisers. The new President, Millard Fillmore, appointed Webster his Secretary of State, and the two worked together with Clay. Aided by the skillful strategy of Stephen A. Douglas and the solid support of the Democrats, they pushed through the bills which came to be called collectively the Compromise of 1850. [35]

California came in as a free state and the slave trade was abolished in the District of Columbia. But New Mexico and Utah were admitted as territories with the right to legislate either for or against slavery, a clear victory for the South, since it introduced the rule of Congressional noninterference and made possible the future imbroglio over

Kansas. [Nine years later New Mexico's territorial legislature would legalize slavery.] Texas got her $10,000,000. And the nation was saddled with a fugitive slave law ingeniously designed to inflame an already raw and sensitive North.[36]

Clay admitted that the compromise was "substantially a Southern triumph," but he looked upon it as the crowning achievement of his life and threatened political annihilation to the Whigs who would not support it—"a novel test for office," as Charles Sumner later pointed out, ". . . which would have excluded all the fathers of the republic—even Washington, Jefferson, and Franklin!"[37]

Across the nation the majority of people, frightened by the war talk and tired of all the argument, accepted the compromise with relief. The secession hotheads, leaderless since the death of Calhoun late in March, subsided into apathy. There were few Americans who did not fondly hope that the compromise had brought peace in their time. But Thaddeus Stevens, who had Cassandra's gift for gloomy political divination, truly predicted that it would become "the fruitful mother of future rebellion, disunion and civil war."[38]

CHAPTER TEN

———— ◆ ————

Born out of Violence

It was conceived in violence, passed in violence, is maintained in violence, and is being executed in violence.

Abraham Lincoln, on the Kansas-Nebraska Act, August 24, 1855 [1]

THADDEUS STEVENS lived in the heart of an area scattered with stations on the Underground Railroad. For years the Quakers, Scotch Presbyterians, and Negroes had quietly cooperated in aiding the fugitives from the South, and by a conspiracy of hostile silence had frustrated most of the attempts of the slavehunters who infiltrated the region continuously, searching for lost property. Under the fugitive slave law of 1850, however, all that was needed to establish the identity of a slave was an affidavit made out by the slaveowner's agent, and any unfortunate Negro, unlike even the Roman slave, was presumed to be a slave until he proved himself free. Since he was expressly denied by the new law the right of speaking on his own behalf, and of a jury trial, he had to rely upon the uncertain justice of the marshal and the intervention of white friends. "The Union is not worth a curse as long as distinction exists between negroes and horses," a Representative from Louisiana had declared in Congress in 1850. He had gotten his way.

One of the first slaveowners to claim a fugitive in Pennsylvania under the new law secured the arrest of a colored woman, Euphemia

Williams, who had run away twenty-two years before. He claimed also her six children, all born in Pennsylvania. There was great excitement, and the judge decided, whether out of prudence, humanitarianism, or the legal facts of the case, that she was not the slave the Marylander was seeking. But for every Negro so freed many were carried over the border.[2] All across southern Pennsylvania the Negroes quietly began to arm themselves and organize for action.

On the night of September 11, 1851, Edward Gorsuch, a Maryland slaveholder, led five armed men, including a United States marshal, in a hunt for four escaped slaves said to be hiding near Lancaster. It was just breaking daylight when they converged on a little stone house near Christiana. When the marshal hammered on the door, it was opened by a massive Negro, William Parker.[3]

The marshal pushed his way in and started for the narrow staircase. Parker darted up ahead and grabbed a long, five-pronged harpoon.

"Take another step and I'll break your neck," he said.

"I've heard many a nigger talk as big as you, and then have taken him."

"You haven't taken me yet," said the Negro, flinging the harpoon and then grabbing an ax he had hidden on the landing.

The marshal retreated to Gorsuch's side. At this point Parker's wife, who was upstairs with the four fugitives, blew a horn out the window. Within minutes the house was surrounded by a crowd of Negroes armed with guns, scythes, clubs, and corn cutters.

A tall, thin young miller named Castner Hanway, riding by on his horse, stopped to watch. The marshal, learning that a white man was outside, showed him the warrants and demanded his help. The new law "commanded" all citizens to aid in its execution, including the capture of fugitives. It threatened fine and imprisonment to anyone who aided runaways, and made him liable for the value of each escaped slave, which was fixed at $1,000. The marshals were guaranteed $10 if they restored a suspected slave to his owner and only $5 if they discharged him. "The law," quipped Anson Burlingame, "fixed the price of a Carolina Negro at one thousand dollars, and of a Yankee soul at five."[4] Lincoln was to point out that Northerners were under legal obligation to do "a sort of dirty, disagreeable job, which . . . as a general rule, the slave-holders will not perform for one another."[5]

Hanway heard the marshal out, and replied shortly: "I'll do nothing to help the Fugitive Slave Act or any other act." Two Quakers also refused the marshal's order and advised him coldly to get off the place and avoid bloodshed. The three white men then turned away.

What happened after is not too clear from Parker's narrative nor from the trial records. Shots were exchanged; the marshal and his men ran away leaving Gorsuch with only his son and nephew. The latter two were wounded but escaped. Edward Gorsuch, after emptying his gun, went down under four Negroes. When they finally left him, bleeding and unconscious, the women moved in with scythes and corn cutters and hacked him to pieces.

By nightfall every runaway slave from Baltimore County was on his way to Canada, and the hay mows and straw stacks on the Underground Railway were crawling with fugitives. The Christiana riot immediately became a national emergency. This, the first killing resulting from the Fugitive Slave Law, wrathful Southern editors laid squarely at Thaddeus Stevens' door. Maryland's Governor E. Louis Lowe threatened secession.

The Pennsylvania Governor, acting under orders from Secretary of State Daniel Webster, and Attorney General John J. Crittenden, indicted Castner Hanway, the two Quakers, and thirty-eight Negroes for treason against the United States. Hanway at once appealed to Thaddeus Stevens. He accepted the case and conducted it largely by himself through the preliminary hearings. Realizing then that his own antislavery record might hinder his clients, he secured three other lawyers, among them a prominent Democrat, John M. Read, who presented the final argument for the defense in the federal court in Philadelphia.

When the thirty-eight Negroes filed into the court room on the second floor of Independence Hall, they were dressed and barbered exactly alike, each one wearing a red, white, and blue scarf about his neck. Lucretia Mott, the well-known Quaker feminist and antislavery agitator, sat near them, knitting with red, white, and blue yarn.

The prosecution, led by Maryland's Senator Cooper, described Lancaster County as a hotbed of abolitionism, with armed bands of Negroes patrolling the area to recapture runaways from their lawful owners. Stevens countered with evidence that professional kidnappers were invading the county and carrying off free blacks. Hanway and the Quakers, he insisted, had come upon the riot accidentally; there was no "previous combination" to resist the United States Government. Fortunately, the prisoners had been indicted not for defying the Fugitive Slave Law but for "wickedly and traitorously intending to levy war against the United States," an accusation so palpably absurd that Judge Grier took pains to advise the jury that while the prisoners were clearly guilty of aggravated riot and murder, the riot did not "rise to the dignity of treason or levying war."

Having discharged his duty as a judge, Grier went on to complain against abolitionists, calling them "infuriated fanatics and unprincipled demagogues . . . teaching that theft is meritorious, murder excusable and treason a virtue." Lashing indirectly at Thaddeus Stevens and Lucretia Mott, he said: "With the exception of a few individuals of perverted intellect . . . male and female vagrant lecturers and conventions, no party in politics, no sect or religion, or any respectable numbers or character can be found within our borders who have viewed with approbation or looked with any other than feelings of abhorrence upon this disgraceful tragedy. . . . The guilt of this foul murder rests not alone on the deluded individuals who were its immediate perpetrators, but the blood taints with even deeper dye the skirts of those who promulgated doctrines subversive of all morality and all government." [6]

The jury, out twenty minutes, returned with a verdict of not guilty.

The Christiana riot was the bloodiest of a series of protests against the Fugitive Slave Law. In February, 1851, an escaped slave named Shadrach, detained in a court room in Boston, was rescued by a mob of Negroes. Richard H. Dana, Jr. saw him carried down the steps, "his clothes half torn off, and so stupified by his sudden rescue and the violence of his dragging off that he sat almost dumb," his rescuers moving off "like a black squall, the crowd driving along with them and cheering as they went." [7] The Reverend Theodore Parker wrote in his journal: "This Shadrach is delivered out of his burning, fiery furnace without the smell of fire on his garments. . . . I think it is the most noble deed done in Boston since the destruction of tea in 1773." [8]

The number of rescues was small, but every one was given tumultuous publicity. It is hard to say which converted more people to abolitionism, the stories of rescues or the sadder tales of recapture. Thomas Sims, a Georgia slave, was arrested in Boston on April 3, 1851, and three hundred policemen ushered him to the ship bound for Savannah. He was the first slave to be sent south from Boston by legal process since Revolutionary days. Southerners noted with dismay that his recapture cost his owner fully $5,000. [9]

One index of what the Fugitive Slave Law meant in the North was the 1851 election returns. The Governorship in Massachusetts went to the Radical antislavery Democrat, George S. Boutwell, and the Senatorship to Freesoiler Charles Sumner. Ohio sent Ben Wade to the Senate. These three radicals, along with Thaddeus Stevens, were to be among the chief architects in charge of rebuilding the smashed political structure of the South after the Civil War. It is worth noting at this point, then, that all three went into office on a platform in which the chief plank was indignation.

Boutwell was a self-righteous and pedantic abolitionist, honest and sincere enough to win some respect, but too much of a scold to be effective in a minority. Ben Wade was a compound of New England Puritan, visionary philanthropist, and Western backwoodsman. He created a sensation in Washington shortly after taking his Senate seat. Challenged by a Southern Senator, he broke the anti-duelling tradition of the Northern Congressmen and accepted. When asked to choose the weapons he named squirrel rifles at twenty paces "with a white paper the size of a dollar pinned over the heart of each combatant." The Southerner hastily withdrew.[10]

Neither Boutwell nor Wade was to leave so ineffaceable a mark on the nation as either Charles Sumner or Thaddeus Stevens. Sumner was six-feet-four, a handsome, earnest bachelor, whose mop of wavy hair falling over his forehead gave him a perennially boyish look. His friends, who included some of the most influential literary and political figures in England and France, saw him as a gentle, amiable man with an eager mind and disarming unworldliness, clumsy at repartee and uncomfortable with a jest. All agreed that he had courage, learning, and a superior talent at formal oratory.

Men who disliked him found him pedantic, opinionated, and egocentric. George S. Hillard, who criticized him in his letters to Francis Lieber for his "absolute incapacity to bear contradiction or dissent," and his "cool assumption of moral superiority," wrote on December 8, 1854: ". . . he is essentially a man of emotions and sentiments, and . . . it is very easy for him to believe anything to be true that he wishes to. His nature is facile, impressible, and feminine. . . ."[11]

Sumner was no doubt tactless and arrogant, but in speaking out against slavery he saw no necessity for being genteel. "I have been attacked bitterly," he wrote to his brother in 1848, "but I have consoled myself by what John Quincy Adams said to me during the last year of his life: 'No man is abused whose influence is not felt.'"

More than any other man in American history—more even than Thaddeus Stevens—Sumner personified the Puritan in politics. "We are told," he said in attacking the Fugitive Slave Law in the widely proclaimed speech that assured his election, "that the slavery question is settled. Yes, *settled—settled,*—that is the word. *Nothing, sir, can be settled which is not right.* Nothing can be settled which is against freedom."

After the election, Reverend Theodore Parker wrote to him: "You told me once that you were in morals, not in politics. Now I hope you will show me that you are still in morals although in politics. I hope you will be the senator *with a conscience*." Sumner went into the Senate with the aspiration to be not just *the Senator with a conscience*, but to be the conscience of the whole nation. Unlike Stevens, whose Puritanism had been attenuated by years in the Machiavellian school of Pennsylvania politics, he believed in government by exhortation. "The Senate chamber," he wrote, "is a mighty pulpit from which the truth can be preached." And the remarkable thing is that Sumner's exhortation actually became and continued for years to be an undeniable political force. Massachusetts, turning her back on Daniel Webster, as the symbol of compromise, kept him in the Senate until his death twenty-three years later.

Sumner had begun his war on caste in 1849, when he defended the right of Negro children in Boston to attend white schools. The Massachusetts Supreme Court had decided against him. But in 1855 the legislature reversed the court and prohibited separate schools.[12] The state was moving fast—faster on this issue by over a hundred years than the states in the deep South—but the direction of the national revolution against caste was here resolutely defined, and while often temporarily checked, it was never to be completely reversed.

Although Massachusetts was sprinting ahead, Pennsylvania at this moment was somersaulting backwards. Revolted by the bloody Christiana riot, Lancaster County saw enough votes turn against Thaddeus Stevens so that the same ferment that sent Sumner to the Senate knocked him out of the House. Moreover, it was Pennsylvania rather than Massachusetts that reflected the majority opinion of the United States in 1852. However rapidly the Fugitive Slave Law was making converts to the antislavery cause, it did not yet materially affect the over-all election returns. The proslavery New England Democrat, Franklin Pierce, became President, defeating the Mexican War general, Winfield Scott, who as an antislavery Whig had campaigned with a proslavery platform.

Stevens, bitterly pessimistic, believed the country lost to the compromisers and his own political career at an end. He made a brief, informal statement in the House, saying in parting: "It is more than probable that hereafter I shall never meet any member here or anywhere else officially, and I desire to part with no unfriendly feeling toward any."[13]

He was now sixty-one. Looking back on the past four years, he felt mostly frustration—he had once written to a friend of his "foolish absence in Congress"—and he seems to have returned to his law practice with relief as well as vexation. His practice had not disappeared, since he had frequently left the House to conduct cases before the Pennsylvania Supreme Court—thereby giving the Democratic press a chance to snipe at him—nevertheless it needed rebuilding if his iron-works, perennially losing money, were to be saved. Actually he was as lost to politics as an addict to his drug. But now, as never before since he first tasted the intoxication of this life, he was truly a man without a party.

The Whig organization was shattered beyond repair by the defeat of 1852. Out of its ruins, like an evil spirit released from an ancient corked bottle, emerged a new political apparition. This was the Native American or Know Nothing Party, which mushroomed briefly into power in 1854. The Native Americans were dedicated to checking the political power of new immigrants, chiefly Irish Catholics. The American Party demanded that immigrants be residents for twenty-one years before receiving voting privileges, and that only the native-born hold public office. This was the kind of demagoguery of which Antimasonry had been compounded, and which in the future would fire the crosses of the Ku Klux Klan. What was new about the American Party was the secrecy shrouding its organization. Every member swore oaths promising never to vote for a Catholic or a foreigner, and vowing to keep all party secrets. Horace Greeley, irritated by his failure to elicit any information for his *Tribune* other than "I know nothing," called it the "Know Nothing" party, and the name stuck.

A good many Freesoilers and Conscience Whigs, disgusted with the proslavery trend of national politics, were sucked into its ranks. Sumner was a notable exception. "A party which, beginning in secrecy, interferes with religious belief, and founds a discrimination on the accident of birth, is not the party for us," he said.[14] Seward kept clear, and Lincoln made no secret of his distaste. "I am not a Know-Nothing," he wrote to Joshua F. Speed on August 24, 1855. "That is certain. How could I be? How can any one who abhors the oppression of negroes, be in favor of degrading classes of white people? Our progress in degeneracy appears to me to be pretty rapid. As a nation, we began by declaring that '*all men are created equal.*' We now practically read it 'all men are created equal, *except negroes.*' When the Know-Nothings get control, it will read 'all men are created equal, except negroes *and foreigners and catholics.*' When it comes to this I should prefer emigrating to some country where they make no pretence of loving liberty—to Russia, for instance, where despotism can be taken pure, and without the base alloy of hypocrisy." [15]

Thaddeus Stevens joined the Know Nothings in 1854, taking the

oath of secrecy and participating in the party rituals.[16] Some of his
friends found this inexplicable. They were reluctant to believe him
guilty of the cheapest kind of political cynicism, grabbing at power in
the first party that came along to fill the vacuum created by the Whig
collapse. That Stevens, the great foe of Masonry, should have joined
an organization steeped in secrecy and intolerance showed that what
had become more necessary to him than any set of principles was the
sense of belonging and the exhilaration of fighting, and also, perhaps,
that one constant ingredient in his hatred of the Masons had been
envy. But let it be said that he joined the party late and deserted it the
moment a party more consonant with his lifelong principles appeared.
He made no speeches against Catholics and foreigners, content to work
secretly for the Know Nothing slate of candidates, a hodgepodge
drawn from all party factions.

To everyone's astonishment the party managed to elect nine governors and claimed 104 out of 234 members of the House of Representatives. "Our surprise may be understood," wrote Alexander Mc-
Clure on the Pennsylvania results, "when I state the fact that when
the vote was counted an entire ticket was elected not one of whom
was publicly known as a candidate. . . . I confess that I never saw
political highjinks played to the limit as it was by the Know Nothings
in 1854. . . . It practically absorbed the Whig Party." [17]

The country was ripe for a third party; mercifully, it was not to be
this one. The Native Americans split on the slavery issue into North
Americans and South Americans and shortly disappeared inside the
Republican and Democratic parties, carrying with them their traditions of bigotry and violence.

The party Thaddeus Stevens had been waiting for so long began
when it did largely as a result of a political blunder by Stephen A.
Douglas. Early in 1854 the Little Giant, pugnacious leader of the western Democrats, coolly shattered the Compromise of 1850 by persuading Congress to swallow his witches' brew known as the Kansas-
Nebraska bill. This provided that the question of slavery in the two
new projected states be settled by "squatter" or popular sovereignty,
and threw open almost the whole far west as fair game for slaveholders.

At once leading Missourians announced their intention of carrying
slavery into Kansas. Already many Southern politicians were claiming
New Mexico, and talking about annexing Cuba as an additional slave
state. The illegal slave trade—made possible by the fact that ships
were fitted out by unscrupulous New York businessmen—was actually

increasing and had become a national scandal.[18]

A great many Northerners, uneasily feeling that they had been duped, for the first time began to look at the record. Hitherto optimistic or apathetic, they were troubled to see what an aggressive minority— a minority even in the South—had won over the years by bluff, intimidation, and the deft use of the presidential ambitions of Northern legislators. "If a Southern man aspires to be President," Lincoln would note, "they choke him down instantly, in order that the glittering prize of the presidency may be held up on Southern terms to the greedy eyes of Northern ambition. With this they tempt us and break in upon us." As Thaddeus Stevens put it bitterly: "Somebody has said that in the South they hunt slaves with dogs—in the North with Democrats." [19]

Clergymen, lawyers, journalists, and teachers, joined by some businessmen, now moved decisively into the antislavery ranks, and the cause for the first time became a genuine mass movement, energized not only by indignation and idealism but also by a belated awareness that Northern politics must no longer be played by wholesale default of power. Abolitionism ceased being synonymous with fanaticism, and the Fugitive Slave Law, which had been actively supported by many in the North who did not approve of it, now was openly flaunted.

[The Republican Party, organized in 1854 in Michigan and Wisconsin as a party of protest against the extension of slavery into Kansas, spread with considerable speed. Although the party was slow to take hold in Pennsylvania, Thaddeus Stevens joined it early in 1855.] He was one of seventeen to attend the first meeting in Lancaster, no other leading Whig appearing. His year-old flirtation with the Native Americans over, he carried into the Republican Party none of their proscriptions but a shrewd awareness of the strength of their appeal. In the new party he found at last a political organization that would command his affection and unflagging dedication. And in Thaddeus Stevens the Republican Party won a gifted political tactician who could be counted on to pursue the party ideals with a frightening intensity.

The young party quickly attracted able leaders. Within eighteen months it had acquired, in addition to Stevens, Salmon P. Chase, Henry Wilson, James G. Blaine, Charles Francis Adams, Joshua Giddings, Owen Lovejoy, David Wilmot, Schuyler Colfax, and John Sherman. Significantly, Lincoln and Seward hesitated longer before officially abandoning the Whig name, though by 1857 Lincoln would describe the members of the new party as "the best hope of the nation, and of the world." [20]

The antislavery movement now had an efficient political weapon.

It had, moreover, something equally important, most of the North's young intellectuals. It had a philosopher in Ralph Waldo Emerson; it had poets in John Greenleaf Whittier, William Cullen Bryant, Henry W. Longfellow, Oliver Wendell Holmes, and Walt Whitman. It had the nation's most talented newspaper editor in Horace Greeley, essayists and editors of conspicuous ability in Henry J. Raymond and James Russell Lowell, and a propagandist of formidable proportions in Harriet Beecher Stowe. Antislavery literature poured forth now in an irresistible flood of pamphlets, speeches, poems, and essays. The North's intellectuals, who in normal times would never permit themselves to be organized on behalf of a faith or a cause, had turned, like Milton, from poetry to polemics. They made a small but mighty phalanx.

One thing was needed to turn the antislavery movement into a dynamic political force—a serious outbreak of Southern violence. Accustomed by the traditions of slaveholding to a fairly steady diet of violence, the South was not long in providing it. Here the tradition of vigilante action, which normally died out as the frontier moved west, was still strong. More than three hundred persons were hanged or burned by mobs in the South between 1840 and 1860, only ten per cent of them Negroes, and the area, as W. J. Cash has pointed out, "had become peculiarly the home of lynching." [21] Some Southern editors openly encouraged the fashion. One in Virginia offered a reward of $50,000 for the head of William H. Seward; another $10,000 for the kidnapping and delivery to Richmond of Joshua R. Giddings, or $5,000 for his head. Southern postmasters publicly burned whatever books they considered dangerous, and their actions were pronounced constitutional by Caleb Cushing, Attorney General under President Pierce.[22]

Violence came at the end of May, 1856, with burning and pillaging in Kansas, and with the beating of Charles Sumner upon the floor of the Senate. The story of the Brooks assault bears retelling briefly here in light of the fact that it transformed Sumner for some years into a cripple, so that he shared for a considerable period something of the same kind of suffering endured by Thaddeus Stevens over a lifetime. In a long speech on May 19 and 20, 1856, Sumner blistered the Democratic administration for its Kansas policy, describing it as "the rape of a virgin territory, compelling it to the hateful embrace of slavery." He singled out particularly the two Democrats he believed most responsible for making Kansas a slave state, Senators Andrew P. Butler of South Carolina and Stephen A. Douglas. Comparing them to Don

Quixote and Sancho Panza, he said: "The senator from South Carolina has read many books of chivalry, and believes himself a chivalrous knight, with sentiments of honor and courage. Of course he has chosen a mistress to whom he has made his vows, and who, though ugly to others, is always lovely to him; though polluted in the sight of the world, is chaste in his sight: I mean the harlot Slavery. For her his tongue is always profuse in words."

Douglas made a witty and insulting answer on the floor of the Senate, but Senator Butler was not present to make his own reply. Preston Brooks, a young Congressman from South Carolina, decided to avenge his honor. Arming himself with a heavy gutta-percha cane— the punishing instrument for schoolsboys—he confided to two colleagues, Keitt of Virginia and Edmundson of South Carolina, that he was going to teach Sumner a lesson.

What Brooks and his Southern colleagues seem to have particularly loathed in Sumner's speech were not the Latin phrases and moral indignation, which they had heard before, but the sexual allusions. Slavery was a sexual problem as well as a moral, economic, and political problem, but to insinuate such was to violate an ancient and respected Senate taboo. Sumner was a bachelor of forty-five who lived with his mother and maintained a reputation for singular purity in his private life. When he identified slavery as a mistress and harlot, and spoke feelingly of the "rape" of Kansas, he seems to have kindled a special fury among those who held him in contempt as a man.[23]

Brooks waited until the Senate adjourned on May 22, and then entered with Representatives Keitt and Edmundson. Sumner was sitting at his desk writing. "I have read your speech twice over," Brooks said. "It is a libel on South Carolina, and Mr. Butler, who is a relative of mine." Then without warning he raised the heavy cane and struck Sumner on the head with all his strength.

The first blow was paralyzing. Sumner's long legs were caught beneath his desk, which was bolted to the floor. With a mighty effort he wrenched the desk loose and staggered upward. But Brooks continued to batter him until the cane broke in two. Still he kept on with the butt of the cane until the reeling Senator fell senseless and bleeding to the floor.

Several Senators rushed to Sumner's aid, but Keitt intercepted them, brandishing his pistol and shouting: "Let them alone!"

There were cries, "Hit him, Brooks!" "He deserves it!" Senator Toombs of Georgia stood by, openly applauding. "I approved it," he said bluntly, when a Senate committee later questioned him. Senator Slidell said pointedly to the same committee: "I did not think it necessary to express my sympathy or make any advances toward him." [24]

There were two gashes at the back of Sumner's head, both two inches long and so deep that the bones of his skull were laid bare. Lesser wounds and bruises covered his face, arms, shoulders, and hands. Men finally broke past Keitt and raised him from the floor. After a time he regained consciousness and was helped to an ante-room, where the worst of his wounds were hastily stitched.

News of the beating swept over the North like a prairie fire, kindling a rage that would not be extinguished. Southerners recklessly fed the flames. Jefferson Davis, a cabinet member, and Senator Mason, wrote letters of esteem for Brooks; Representative Savage of Tennessee said Sumner "did not get a lick more than he deserved." The *Richmond Examiner* called Sumner "a foul-mouthed poltroon, [who] when caned for cowardly vituperation falls to the floor an inanimate lump of in-carnate cowardice." Students of the University of Virginia voted Brooks a gold-headed cane "bearing the device of the human head badly cracked and broken." [25]

The House voted 121 to 95 for Brooks' expulsion, less than the neces-sary two-thirds. Whereupon Brooks made a speech threatening to "commence a line of conduct which would result in subverting the foundations of the government, and in drenching this hall in blood." Afterward he announced his resignation and marched out of the House, to be met at the entry by several Southern women who rap-turously embraced him. [26] He was tried for assault in the Circuit Court of the District and fined $300.

Brooks' constituents sent him back to the House in two weeks, with only six dissenting votes. Seven months later he died unexpectedly of what was called acute inflammation of the larynx and sudden strangula-tion. Massachusetts diagnosed it less clinically as the fingers of God about his throat.

Sumner's wounds became infected and refused to heal. He suffered from high fever and loss of weight, and for months afterward staggered as he walked. Southern editors meanwhile taunted him with cowardice. "You are aware that the whole South persists in believing that he is afraid to go back to Washington," Francis Lieber wrote to George S. Hillard, December 13, 1856. "If he resigns they will glory in it as a new proof of cowardice." [27]

He returned to the Senate two or three times to cast his vote on key issues. After a day there in February, 1857, he wrote to Theodore Parker: "After a short time the torment to my system became great and a cloud began to gather over my brain. I tottered out, and took to my bed. I long to speak but cannot." [28]

Searching for relief from his shattering headaches, he went abroad, where he fell into the hands of one of the most sadistic quacks in Europe, Dr. Brown-Séquard, whose celebrated "fire cure" consisted of applications of burning agaric cottonwood to the back and neck for five or ten minutes at a time. The treatment brought on Sumner's first heart attack, and resulted in ghastly burns that refused to heal.

"He applies fire to my neck and spine. Fire is fire . . . as I have ample occasion to know," Sumner wrote to a friend from Paris June 22, 1858. A few months later he wrote: "I am a poor cripple, halting about in torment. It came upon me suddenly. Perhaps it is the result of a cure." [29] Eventually he went on to another physician who tormented him with "dry cupping along the spine."

Between Preston Brooks and European doctors, Sumner was kept an invalid for three and a half years. Massachusetts re-elected him in his absence, and his empty seat in the Senate remained a mute reminder to the nation's lawmakers. When he was abroad Sumner led a fairly active social life despite his illness, as the Southern press continually pointed out. The charge of cowardice continued to be flung at him, and may well have scarred him as severely as the Brooks' beating.

Charles Sumner and Thaddeus Stevens were to become the joint chief architects of Southern Reconstruction after the Civil War. It will be seen that each in his own fashion had special reasons for wanting to scourge the South. Stevens took no pains to hide his hatred. Sumner on the other hand openly forgave Brooks and insisted that he bore him no malice. He likened him "to a brick that should fall upon my head from a chimney," and called him "the unconscious agent of a malign power." [30] But Sumner's hatred was possibly no less an energizing force than Stevens', though it seems to have been buried so deep that he could deny that it was there at all.

CHAPTER ELEVEN

---•---

The Road to War

We insist that our government is neither an accident or a trifle. It is the best yet devised by the wit of man, and is worth a dozen wars to keep.

Indianapolis Daily Journal, January 17, 1861

THADDEUS STEVENS did not rise rapidly in the Republican Party. Men of lesser talents and slighter reputation became Senators or leaped into cabinet posts. In 1854, when the party was born, Stevens was sixty-two. It took him eleven years to become the most powerful Republican in the nation, and the remarkable fact then was that an ill old man of seventy-three, who was simply a Representative from Pennsylvania, could so dominate legislation in the political crisis following Lincoln's murder.

There were many reasons, some personal, some political. Stevens was erratic, impulsive, and contemptuous even with his friends. He was too radical even for this, the most revolutionary party since the days of Thomas Jefferson. Pennsylvania never elected him Senator, though he was a perennial aspirant for the office. Moreover, although Stevens had uncanny foresight about election outcomes, he never managed to ally himself with a winning candidate. In a politician this is unforgivable.

Stevens opposed the nomination of John C. Frémont in 1856, and of Abraham Lincoln in 1860. In both elections he preferred instead an aged Conservative Republican, John McLean, who had been appointed Justice of the Supreme Court by Jackson in 1830.] Stevens and McLean had roomed in the same bachelor's quarters for a time when Stevens first came to Washington. In his youth McLean had had the reputation of being a fighter and dissenter, and according to Alexander McClure, Stevens admired him "chiefly because McLean had dared to disobey the commands of Jackson when in his Cabinet." Normally Stevens' attitude toward a man in power was likely to be aloof if not hostile. He could never bring himself to court favor, a political weakness certain to be reflected in his career.[1] With younger men, his students and lesser politicians, he could be gentle and encouraging. But of men in authority he had a perpetually alienating suspicion. The one exception was McLean, whom Stevens seems to have admired without reservation.

Lincoln, too, supported McLean in 1856. But as yet there was no real communication between him and Thaddeus Stevens.[2] The majority of Republicans were enthusiastic about the romantic explorer and soldier hero, John C. Frémont, and the seventy-one-year-old McLean was privately regarded by the militant younger party men as a marrowless old fogy. Although Stevens fought vigorously for his friend, who won as many as 196 votes on one ballot, his defeat was certain. "I never heard a more feeling and eloquent appeal than Mr. Stevens made to them at this meeting to give their support to Judge McLean," wrote E. B. Washburne. "His knowledge of Pennsylvania politics, and his great experience in political affairs entitled his opinions to the greatest possible weight. I never heard a man speak with more feeling or in more persuasive accents. He closed his speech with the assertion that the nomination of Frémont would not only lose the State of Pennsylvania to the Republicans, but that the party would be defeated in the presidential election." [3]

Stevens believed Frémont would lose the Know-Nothing vote in Pennsylvania because he was suspected, mistakenly, of being a Catholic. But McLean was clearly not the appropriate candidate for the aggressive young party. And in 1860, when Stevens championed the seventy-five-year-old McLean against both Seward and Lincoln, the choice of such a candidate was absurd.

In 1856, after Frémont won the nomination, some who had endorsed him had uneasy second thoughts. Horace Greeley wrote privately to Schuyler Colfax: "I am afraid several volumes might be filled with what he don't know about the first elements of politics. I am afraid we shall be sorry if we get him elected. And I'm afraid we can't elect him." The *Richmond Enquirer* suggested as a slogan for the Republican campaign: "Free niggers, free women, free land, and Frémont." [4]

Stevens was deeply pessimistic over the election outcome. "The north is a dastard & Slavery I fear will always triumph," he wrote to E. D. Gazzam in August. "The cry of Fremont's Catholicism has . . . lost us the Nation." [5] Nevertheless he campaigned tirelessly, doing his best to unite the Republicans, the old Whigs, and the Know Nothings into what was called in Pennsylvania the People's Party. But the Know Nothings organized independently to nominate Millard Fillmore, thus splitting the anti-Democratic vote.

Worse still, from Stevens' point of view, the Democrats nominated James Buchanan, a native of Stevens' own Lancaster, for President. Long ago he had refused to defend Stevens' enemy, Jacob Lefever, in the libel suit growing out of the Gettysburg murder mystery, and afterward had become Stevens' friend. But when as ambassador to England and as Senator he had openly favored the extension of slavery, Stevens turned against him. "Until he attempted to make Kansas a slave State, he and I were on intimate terms," Stevens said. "Since then we have never spoken to each other." [6] Enmity between the two became personal as well as political. It was said that when they met at the wedding of Dr. Henry Carpenter, who was friend to both, Buchanan refused to shake Stevens' outstretched hand.[7]

Stevens had now come to believe Buchanan to be a shallow, vacillating opportunist, unprincipled and inept. When he chose to make no speeches throughout the campaign, Stevens attacked his silence venomously: "There is no such person running as James Buchanan. *He is dead of lockjaw.* Nothing remains but a platform and a bloated mass of political putridity." [8]

The Democrats channeled enormous sums of money into Pennsylvania—$150,000 from the slave states and as much again from Wall Street, where the business interests were terrified that a Frémont victory would mean disunion and the loss of Southern markets. Stevens did his best with the small funds of the Republican Party, expending them chiefly in what he euphemistically called "securing" opposition newspapers.

Buchanan carried Pennsylvania, as Stevens had foreseen, and won the election. It must have been humiliating for Stevens to see this politician he so disliked rise to the nation's highest office out of a political district he counted peculiarly his own. He was tempted to get back into public office, and particularly to turn the President's home district against him in 1858. With good luck, he believed, he might regain his old seat in the House. It was a modest ambition. Later he would jest about the President being "one of my constituents."

[Three things made it possible for Stevens to win in 1858. First was the Panic of 1857, which had paralyzed the Pennsylvania iron industries, and which he blamed on the Democratic low tariff act of March, 1857. Second was the continuing struggle in Kansas, where a minority of 2,000, supported by prominent Democrats in Washington, including President Buchanan, succeeded in legalizing the proslavery Lecompton Constitution over the protests of almost 10,000 antislavery Kansas citizens.[9] The third was the Dred Scott decision.]

Dred Scott, as is well known, was a Missouri slave whose master had taken him for long periods into free territory in the northwest, and who had been encouraged to sue for freedom on the ground that his residence in free territory had made him a free citizen. After a complicated court history, the case went to the Supreme Court. On March 6, 1857 the judges handed down a split decision that convulsed the nation.

Chief Justice Taney, who until now had had an excellent judicial record—and who had, in fact, emancipated his own slaves—wrote the decision most often quoted, and was supported in the majority of his arguments by six justices. He declared that Dred Scott had been correctly denied the right of freedom, and then went on to declare not only that Dred Scott was not a citizen, but also that no *free* Negro had ever been one. The word "people" as used in the Constitution, he said, was synonymous with "citizen," and he implied that Negroes were neither. They had, in fact, long been regarded as "beings of an inferior order, and altogether unfit to associate with the white race, either socially or politically; and so far inferior that they had no rights which the white man was bound to respect." Not content with this, Taney passed judgment on the right of Congress to legislate for or against slavery in the Territories, declaring that Congress had no power to regulate slavery there, and implying that the Missouri Compromise had never been constitutional.[10]

The decision, actually a classic pronouncement of the principles of John C. Calhoun, left the Republicans aghast. Lincoln said bluntly it was "erroneous" and based on "assumed historical facts which were not really true." The next Dred Scott decision, he pointed out ominously, would mean the nationalization of slavery. ". . . there is vigor enough in Slavery to plant itself in a new country even against unfriendly legislation," he insisted. "It takes not only law but the *enforcement* of law to keep it out. That is the history of this country upon the subject." [11]

Thaddeus Stevens in 1860 pilloried the Chief Justice in a speech at Cooper Union Institute, in New York. "It had been better for the

reputation of this old man, had he been silent upon this political question. In order to sustain his partisan views, and crush a persecuted
race, he was obliged to write a false chapter in the most important part
of the history of his country. Instead of brightening the characters of
the illustrious men of the revolution . . . he has perverted the meaning of their immortal words. He contends that 'all men' means less
than one-third of the human race. That 'people' means 'white folks.'
That the authors of the Declaration of Independence and of the constitution, while inaugurating a new and startling epoch in the science
of government—an epoch of Liberty and equality—were preparing
a system which denied that a whole race of God's immortal creatures
had 'any rights that white men were bound to respect.'" Taney and six
justices, he went on, had promulgated a doctrine more infamous than
'the divine right of kings'—the divine right of color.'" [12]

Lincoln too had noted with alarm the decline in the reputation of
the Declaration of Independence. "In those days, our Declaration of
Independence was held sacred by all, and thought to include all;
but now, to aid in making the bondage of the negro universal and
eternal, it is assailed, and sneered at and construed, and hawked
at, and torn, till, if its framers could rise from their graves, they could
not at all recognize it."

Wendell Phillips trumpeted harshly: "To-day the triumph of the
Slave Power is written on the forehead of the Government! and that
is why the necessity of the hour is revolution." But the majority of
Republicans had too great a reverence for the Supreme Court to make
a general outcry for repudiation of the decision. "We know the court
that made it, has often over-ruled its own decisions," Lincoln said,
"and we shall do what we can to have it over-rule this. We offer no
resistance to it." [13]

Wrongheaded, injudicious, and inhumane, the decision destroyed
the faith of many Americans that slavery could ever be wiped out by
legal process, and thereby increased forebodings of civil war. But it
remained theoretically in force for a full decade, until, in fact, Thaddeus Stevens forced the Fourteenth Amendment through Congress and
set in motion the legal machinery for undoing its mischief.

Stevens was elected to Congress in 1858 with an impressive majority
—Lancaster County gave him 75 per cent of its votes—and his party
swept the state. President Buchanan wrote ruefully to his niece: "We
have met the enemy in Pennsylvania, and we are theirs." [14] The election
had been one of triumph for the Republicans through the whole
North. One critical defeat had been that of Abraham Lincoln, cam-

paigning for Senator in Illinois against Stephen A. Douglas. But Lincoln in his public debates with Douglas had analyzed the issues that were splitting the nation apart with a clarity unparalleled since the days of Thomas Jefferson.

William Seward had also rocketed to leadership in the party in a bold speech at Rochester, New York, October 25, 1858. "I know, and you all know," he said, "that a revolution has begun. I know, and all the world knows, that revolutions never go backward."

Although far more radical than Seward, Thaddeus Stevens had not yet been so rash as to use the dangerous word "revolution," with its connotation of conspiracy and anarchy. He wanted revolutionary change, but as yet in the tradition of Jefferson and Jackson—in peace and within the law. This was never more certainly demonstrated than in his reaction to the news of John Brown's attack at Harper's Ferry.

When the news trickled into Lancaster that a handful of white men and Negroes had led a raid on the federal arsenal at Harper's Ferry, less than sixty miles away in Virginia, with the apparent intention of starting a general insurrection among the slaves, all work stopped, and the troubled citizens gathered together in little knots. Stevens was in his law office with Judge Penrose and several others when the telegraph brought word that John Brown had failed. He had been captured alive by Virginia troops; two of his sons had died in the battle; there had been no slave revolt.

"Why, Mr. Stevens," said one, "they'll hang that man."

To which he replied: "Damn him, he ought to be hung!" Later in Congress he said to a Virginia Congressman who insisted that his state had executed John Brown and his men according to law: "You hung them exactly right, sir." [15]

John Brown was a true conspirator. Impatient, visionary, and obsessed, he looked to revolution by violence. What he had failed to recognize was the most elementary fact of revolution, that serious revolt almost never starts among slaves or untouchables, who lack organization and intellectual leadership, and whose first hunger is likely to be more for bread and ease of pain than for freedom. A rare exception had been the bloody Haiti revolution, which had generated in both the North and South unwarranted fears about the nature and probability of serious slave revolt in the United States.

The Democratic Party, handed an explosion that served to unite the South and embarrass the North, was quick to lay the blame for Harper's Ferry upon the Republicans. Stephen A. Douglas said it was the "natural, logical, inevitable result of the doctrines and teachings of the Republican party." William Seward and Thaddeus Stevens were particularly singled out for complicity in the raid. Republican leaders somersaulted backward lest they be tainted with responsibility. "John Brown was no Republican;" said Lincoln, "and you have failed to implicate a single Republican in his Harper's Ferry enterprise." [16]

That the party suffered little was largely due, in the end, to John Brown. Once he had the brief leisure in his cell to reflect on the magnitude of his failure, the death of his sons, and the certainty of the gallows, he cast off the disagreeable evidences of his short-sightedness and self-delusion. He wrote and spoke in his own defense with a dignity and eloquence that won him even the grudging admiration of his jailors, and turned him in four weeks into a folk hero in the North.

Recognizing with a true martyr's insight that he was worth "inconceivably more to *hang* than for any other purpose," he refused all suggestions for rescue. As he walked forth to the gallows he handed a bystander a slip of paper, at once an apology and a prophecy: "I John Brown am now quite *certain* that the crimes of this *guilty land: will* never be purged *away;* but with Blood. I had *as I now think:* vainly flattered myself that without *very much* bloodshed; it might be done." [17]

"It would be vain to kill him," said Henry Thoreau. "He died lately in the time of Cromwell, but he reappeared here . . . when you plant, or bury, a hero in his field, a crop of heroes is sure to spring up."

"Virginia did not tremble at an old gray-headed man at Harper's Ferry," said Wendell Phillips; "they trembled at a John Brown in every man's own conscience. He had been there many years. . . . and every man keeps his right hand pressed on the secret and incurable sore, with an understood agreement, in church and state, that it shall never be mentioned."

Thaddeus Stevens came to modify his original harsh judgment. "The motive of John Brown," he said in 1865, "honest, upright, but mistaken in his means—no man who loves freedom can help applauding, although none of us would justify the means. But upon the principle which I have mentioned, when the gentleman from New York and myself will be moldering in the dust and forgotten, or only unpleasantly remembered, the memory of John Brown, I will venture to predict, will grow brighter and brighter through coming ages." [18]

John Brown went to the gallows on Friday, December 2, 1859. On the following Monday the Thirty-sixth Congress assembled. When Thaddeus Stevens took his seat in the House, he could hardly have been unaware of the atmosphere of anarchy. The spectre of John Brown stalked the halls. Senator James W. Grimes wrote to his wife: "The members on both sides are mostly armed with deadly weapons, and it is said that the friends of each are armed in the galleries." [19]

On the second day of the session Representative Lawrence Keitt, who, it will be remembered, had helped Preston Brooks in his attack on Sumner, made a blustering speech in which he laid the John Brown raid squarely at the feet of the Republican Party. He finished with a threat: "The South here asks nothing but its rights. As one of its representatives, I would have no more; but, as God is my judge, I would shatter this republic from turret to foundation-stone before I would take one tittle less."

Thaddeus Stevens rose to make a brief, sardonic reply. He did not blame the gentlemen of the South, he said, for using "the language of intimidation, and using this threat of rending God's creation from the turret to the foundation. All this is right in them, for they have tried it fifty times, and fifty times they have found weak and recreant tremblers in the North who have been affected by it, and who have acted from those intimidations."

There followed a lively exchange of insults between Stevens and Crawford of Georgia. William Barksdale of Mississippi was so infuriated he sprang toward Stevens brandishing a bowie knife. At once Roscoe Conkling, Elihu Washburne, and several other Republicans rushed to Stevens' defense. For a moment riot threatened, but the clerk thundered for order, and the Southerners retreated to their own side of the House. Stevens laughed off the episode as "a mere momentary breeze," [20] but he was shaken by it, and in later years referred to it grimly, without laughter. This was the second time knives had been drawn against him in a legislative hall.

The Republicans had a plurality but not a majority in the House, and the balance of power lay in the hands of a few Native Americans. It took eight weeks to elect the Speaker. During this struggle Stevens rose repeatedly to point out that legally there could be no debate until the Speaker was chosen. But the speeches went on nevertheless. Stevens hoped to see Galusha Grow made Speaker, and worked quietly to discipline the new party members into a voting unit. "He was continually rallying the timid and wavering," Grow wrote later, "and many a one remained firm during that contest as much from fear of Mr. Stevens as from any other cause."

Stevens vowed publicly that he would vote for Grow for Speaker "till the crack of Doom." When finally both sides compromised to elect Pennington of New Jersey, and Stevens cast his vote for him, one

Republican twitted him about his promise. "I thought you would vote for Grow till the crack of Doom."

Stevens replied with a quick smile, "I thought I heard it cracking." [21]

Congress in 1860 ceased being a legislative body and became the battleground for what might be called the "cold war" before the Civil War. The Republicans, new to the responsibilities of government, were fumbling and inept, and the Southern fire-eaters, eager for secession, were impatient of normal committee work and contemptuous of compromise. In one acrimonious session Galusha Grow walked over to the Democratic side of the House to confer with Hickman of Pennsylvania. The obstreperous Keitt called out: "Go back to your side of the House, you black Republican puppy!"

"This hall belongs to the American people," Grow answered. "I shall stay in it where I please and no slave-driver shall crack his whip over my head." Keitt lunged at his throat, but Grow caught him with a blow under his ear that sent him sprawling. Within seconds about thirty members were swinging wildly at each other. Grow described it with immense satisfaction in a letter on February 9, 1860: "It was the first free fight that ever came off in Congress and the alacrity with which the Republicans rushed to the encounter took Southern men entirely by surprise. They have labored under the delusion that Northern men would not fight." [22]

Tempers remained ugly, and more Congressmen took to wearing arms, though Stevens, who had never worn a gun in his life, refused now to change his habits. Speeches became more violent. Owen Lovejoy, brother of the abolitionist Elijah Lovejoy who had been lynched by Missouri slaveholders in 1837, made a blistering attack on slavery April 5, 1860. With his coat off and collar open, he advanced toward the Democrats shaking his fist and crying: "There is no place in the universe outside the five points of hell and the Democratic party where the practice and prevalence of such doctrines would not be a disgrace."

Roger Pryor of Virginia, putting his hand menacingly in his pocket, called to the Speaker: "*He shall not*, sir, come upon this side of the House shaking his fist in our faces."

Mississippi's Barksdale shouted: "Order that black-hearted scoundrel and nigger-stealing thief to take his seat, or this side of the House will do it!"

"Nobody can intimidate me!" Lovejoy shouted back.

Thirty or forty men were soon milling about, brandishing weapons. When order was restored, and Lovejoy resumed his speech, he reminded his listeners grimly: "You shed the blood of my brother on the banks of the Mississippi twenty years ago, and what then? I am here to-day, thank God, to vindicate the principles baptized in his blood."

Barksdale interrupted again, crying, "Perjured villain! Perjured negro-thief!" But Lovejoy ignored him.

"I cannot go into a slave State and open my lips in regard to the question of slavery," he went on.

"No," shouted Pryor. "We would hang you higher than Haman!" [23]

The incident passed. It had been said before. Senator Foote of Mississippi had long been called "Hangman Foote" because of his declaration in the Senate that if the abolitionist Senator John P. Hale would come to Mississippi he would be hanged to one of the tallest trees in the forest, and that he himself would assist in the operation.[24]

One result of the fracas was that Pryor challenged Potter of Wisconsin to a duel. He accepted, choosing bowie-knives for the weapons. Pryor's second canceled the duel on the ground that the bowie-knife was "vulgar and barbarous," and not the weapon for gentlemen. Whereupon Thaddeus Stevens acidly suggested that the appropriate weapon should be dungforks.

That night Stevens went to dinner at Joe Hall's. Looking down the long table he said to a Senator at the other end: "Have you seen the bill I offered to-day in the House?"

"No; what was it?"

"It is a bill to change the name of Pryor to Posterior." [25]

The incivility and comedy were a release for the ever-increasing tension. No Republican, including Stevens, properly evaluated the secession threats. Who could foresee that Roger Pryor one year later would be one of four men faced with the decision of whether or not to order the bombardment of Fort Sumter? By then the brawling in the House would be over, and Pryor himself in his famous Charleston speech would signal the beginning of the war:

Gentlemen, I thank you, especially that you have at last annihilated this accursed Union, reeking with corruption, and insolent with excess of tyranny. Thank God, it is at last blasted and riven by the lightning wrath of an outraged and indignant people. . . . As sure as to-morrow's sun will rise upon us, just so sure will Virginia be a member of this Southern Confederation. *And I will tell you, gentlemen, what will put her in the Southern Confederation in less than an hour by Shrewsbury clock—STRIKE A BLOW! The very moment that blood is shed, Old Virginia will make common cause with her sisters of the South.*[26]

When the Democratic Party split in two in the spring of 1860, it was clear to everyone that the Republican Party might well elect the next president. Had Thaddeus Stevens chosen to abandon his allegiance to John McLean, he could easily have been president-maker. Instead it was the slippery Simon Cameron who unified the votes of the critical Pennsylvania delegation under Lincoln's banner. Stevens stayed stubbornly with McLean, presenting, as Alexander McClure described it, "the anomaly of the most radical Republican leader of the country, Giddings excepted, supporting the most conservative candidate for the Presidency."

An inflexible dissenter even in his own party, Stevens refused to swing his own vote in the preliminary caucus where the delegation decided to vote for Lincoln instead of Seward. A letter to the *Philadelphia Press* May 21, 1860, reported his stand: "The attachment and devotion of your old, able, and distinguished Representative in Congress, Hon. Thaddeus Stevens, of Lancaster, to the nomination of Judge McLean, of Ohio, who was his favorite in 1856, as in this Convention, was exhibited by him to the last, he voting for him even on the last ballot when Lincoln was nominated." On the Wigwam floor Stevens shared neither in the unexpected humiliation of Seward's followers, nor in the contagious delirium of the Lincoln men, but stood alone in his own defeat. It was a familiar spot.[27]

Afterward he campaigned vigorously for Lincoln and Hannibal Hamlin, doing his best, as party strategy prescribed, to minimize the sectional fight over slavery, to emphasize the tariff issue and to ridicule the secession challenge. In his public campaigning he said that "only a few old women in pantaloons" believed in the secession threat. Others in his party called it "humbug," "bullying game," "scare stuff," "empty sham," and "chronic disease." [28]

Three weeks and two days after Lincoln's victory, every state of the deep South save Louisiana had initiated secession proceedings. Buchanan seemed incapable of grasping what was happening. "All our troubles have not cost me an hour's sleep," he wrote on December 20, 1860, "though I trust I have a just sense of my high responsibility. I weigh well and prayerfully what course I ought to adopt, and adhere to it steadily, leaving the result to Providence." [29]

His course consisted of letting the great majority of forts, arsenals, customs houses and navy yards in the South fall like ripe fruit into the hands of the secessionists. Republican Senator James W. Grimes wrote to his wife on December 16, 1860: "Mr. Buchanan, it is said, about equally divides his time between praying and crying. Such a perfect imbecile never held office before." [30] Thaddeus Stevens, ill in Lancaster during these weeks, wrote despairingly to Edward McPherson: "I do not care to be present while the process of humiliation is going on—Buchanan is a very traitor." [31]

Within his own party Buchanan had little support for drastic measures to save the Union. The Democratic press clamored for compromise, and almost universally indicated that it preferred peace and disunion to coercion. "Far better that the Union should be dismembered forever," said the *New York Herald* on February 5, 1861, "than that fraternal hands should be turned against one another to deluge the land in blood." Many Democratic leaders accepted disunion as inevitable. Horatio Seymour, soon to be Governor of New York, wrote to ex-President Franklin Pierce on December 5, 1860: "The Union is about gone already . . . we have deferred cutting throats long enough. . . . I should like to begin with the Abolitionists at once." Rodman M. Price, ex-governor of New Jersey, publicly advocated that New Jersey secede and join the South. Fernando Wood, Democratic mayor of New York City, spokesman for a widespread movement among the merchants, talked earnestly of making New York a free city, independent of both the United States and the Southern Confederacy.[32]

Other leading Democrats busied themselves with compromise schemes. Senator John J. Crittenden of Kentucky wanted to extend the old Missouri Compromise line all the way to California. Andrew Johnson of Tennessee urged a constitutional amendment providing for an even division of the Supreme Court into justices from free and slave states, and guaranteeing that the office of either president or vice-president always be held by a slave-state man. Even for this he was burned in effigy by the secessionists of Tennessee.[33]

Secession shocked but did not shatter the Republican Party. The Republican press in December, 1860, as Kenneth Stampp has pointed out, "was like the blare of bugles calling men to the colors." [34] But there were many influential dissenters. The extreme abolitionists in New England, in a display of incredible political naivete, applauded disunion. "We rejoice in their departure," said Wendell Phillips, "because we know their declaration of independence is the jubilee of the slave. . . . Slavery will drop to pieces by the competition of the century." Garrison said, "All Union-saving efforts are simply idiotic." Even the doughty Horace Greeley momentarily lost his head. "We hope never to live in a republic, whereof one section is pinned to the residue by bayonets," he said, and advised the South to "depart in peace." [35]

Charles Sumner for a time privately advocated disunion. Thurlow Weed bowed to pressure from the terrified New York merchants, and came out openly for the Crittenden proposal to extend the old Missouri Compromise line to California.[36] Lincoln, who deliberately remained silent on policy until after his inauguration, was alarmed and wrote privately to Representative E. B. Washburne on December 13, 1860: "Prevent, as far as possible, any of our friends from demoralizing themselves, and our cause, by entertaining propositions for compromise of any sort on 'slavery extention.' There is no possible compromise upon it but which puts us under again, and leaves all our work to do over again. . . . On that point hold firm, as with a chain of steel." [37]

Stiffened by this, and by vigorous opposition from the extreme antislavery wing of the party, the Republicans united in rejecting the Crittenden compromise. But as the crisis deepened, and as it became clear that the seceding states could be won back, if at all, only by drastic concessions, the split between the conservative and radical Republicans widened. Soon it became clear that Thaddeus Stevens and William Seward were at opposite party poles. Seward, who fancied himself the new premier and real power in the government, cheerfully occupied himself with one compromise scheme after another. "I do not know a man on earth," he said on December 24, 1860, "who—even though his wife was as troublesome as the wife of Socrates—cannot keep his wife if he wants to; all that he needs is, to keep his own virtue and his own temper."

On January 12, 1861, he made a conciliatory speech in the Senate. When it was over, Senator Hemphill of Texas said, "That would have been a fine address for the Fourth of July, but we are going to secede." Thaddeus Stevens was equally unimpressed. "I have listened to every word," he said, "and by the living God I have heard nothing!"

Men who are at war with the present are often peculiarly well-equipped to take the measure of a revolution. The true magnitude of the approaching crisis seems to have been best understood by the political extremists on both sides. After the secession of South Carolina, Stevens saw that "concession, humiliation, and compromise," could "have no effect whatever." The decisive evidence for him was the action of six states in the deep South refusing to attend the Peace Conference called by Virginia. "Thus ends negotiation;" he said, "thus ends concession; thus ends compromise, by solemn declaration of the seceding party that they will not listen to concession or compromise." [38] And he comprehended perfectly that the real choice was not between compromise and disunion, but between compromise and war.

"I see these States in open and declared rebellion against the Union," he said on January 29, 1861, "seizing upon her public forts and arsenals, and robbing her of millions of the public property . . . I see the batteries of seceding States blockading the highway of the nation, and their armies in battle array against the flag of the Union. . . . I see, sir, our flag insulted, and that insult submitted to. . . .

"Sir, has it come to this? Cannot the people of the United States choose whom they please President, without stirring up rebellion, and requiring humiliation, concessions, and compromises to appease the insurgents? Sir, I would take no steps to propitiate such a feeling. Rather than show repentance for the election of Mr. Lincoln, with all its consequences, I would see this Government crumble into a thousand atoms. If I cannot be a freeman, let me cease to exist." Though counseling patience, he took small pains to hide his conviction that war was likely. "Let there be no blood shed until the last moment; but let no cowardly counsels unnerve the people; and then, at last, if needs be, let every one be ready to gird on his armor, and do his duty."

Later he did his best to block the reception of the Memorial of the Peace Congress, saying: "I think we had better go on with the regular order. We have saved this Union so often that I am afraid we shall save it to death." [39]

Two weeks before the inaugural of Lincoln he said pointedly that he agreed with what the President-elect was "authentically reported to have said," that it was "his intention to retake all the public property of which we have been robbed—to retake it by such means as are necessary, using gentle means at first, and if those fail, then such as become necessary." When Representative Martin J. Crawford of Georgia, with whom he had often battled, resigned from Congress and cheerfully bade him goodbye, saying, "The next time I return it will be minister from the Southern confederacy," Stevens shook hands and replied with a grim smile:

"The next time you come to Washington, it will be as a convicted rebel!" [40]

Other Republicans, less hesitant than Stevens to talk openly of coercion, nevertheless faced up squarely to the fundamental problem. "This is either a Government to be sustained or a thing to be destroyed," wrote Senator Zachary Chandler. "If it is a Government let us stand by and sustain it—if it is a thing without the power of self protection *let it perish* and the sooner the better." "The issue now before us," Senator Grimes wrote to the Governor of Iowa, "is whether we have a country, whether or not this is a nation." [41] Lincoln himself defined the problem in his first inaugural: "Is there in all republics this inherent and fatal weakness? Must a government, of necessity, be too strong for the liberties of its own people, or too weak to maintain its own existence?"

Seward, however, was confident that a compromise settlement that would restore the Union was still possible. "Seward is infatuated," Sumner wrote to John Jay on March 7, 1861, "he says in sixty days all will be well." [42] In December Seward had suggested the passage of a new constitutional amendment guaranteeing that the Constitution would never be altered so as to allow Congress to abolish or interfere with slavery in the states. After much bitter debate this had passed Congress a few days before Lincoln's inaugural. Stevens in the House voted against it, along with sixty-four others, but a combination of Democrats and Conservative Republicans carried it through.[43]

Lincoln himself urged ratification in his first inaugural. It was a notable step backward from his stand that slavery should be put "in the course of ultimate extinction." A determined effort was made by the compromisers to bring New Mexico into the Union, ostensibly as a slave state, but it failed.[44] The Dakota, Colorado, and Nevada territories were all organized without any provision to exclude slavery. As Stephen A. Douglas put it on April 25, 1861: "For the first time in the history of this Republic, there is no prohibitory act of Congress upon the institution of slavery, anywhere within the limits of the United States." [45]

But such concessions, as Thaddeus Stevens perfectly understood, were straws in the wind. Six states were out permanently and had no interest whatever in compromise. Their leaders not only had no intention of returning, but could not. "After the extent to which they have gone," Stevens pointed out, "condemnation which is now felt for their conduct would degenerate into contempt." [46]

In February 1861 Jefferson Davis had been elected President of the Confederacy and Alexander H. Stephens Vice-President. A constitution had been written; an army was being organized. Alexander Stephens had stated bluntly the philosophic principle underlying the new government: "Our new Government is founded upon . . . the great truth that the negro is not equal to the white man. That slavery —subordination to the superior race, is his natural and moral condition." [47]

The fact was that the differences between the North and South were far too profound to be bridged by compromise. It was not only that slavery was profitable, that the price of slaves was higher than it had ever been, and that agitation for reopening the slave trade was growing ever more insistent. It was even more that owning slaves had become a badge of nobility. Individual emancipation usually meant a drop out of the aristocracy. And though eighty per cent of the Southerners owned no slaves, the majority identified in fantasy with the plantation owner and followed him willingly out of the Union.

The old traditions of dignity and status were certainly at stake. Many Southerners believed, too, that their actual survival was in doubt. "The honor of our children, the honor of our females, the lives of all our men, all rest upon you," Senator Yancey of Alabama had said at the Charleston Convention of April, 1860. "You would make a great seething cauldron of passion and crime if you were able to consummate your measures."

The pervading Southern terror that the Negroes would someday be free—free for revenge and free for equality—could probably not have really been dissipated by any Northern concession except the nationalization of slavery. "You can never convert the free sons of the soil into vassals," cried Judah P. Benjamin in his farewell speech in the Senate, December 31, 1860, "and you never, never can degrade them to the level of an inferior and servile race. Never! Never!"

CHAPTER TWELVE

Stevens and Lincoln—the Secession Crisis

> Give him all kindness: I had rather have
> Such men my friends than enemies.
>
> Julius Caesar, Act V, Scene 4

[STEVENS and Lincoln were neither friends nor enemies. There was a guarded mutual respect but no affection and very little personal communication.] "Stevens never saw Lincoln during the war except when necessity required it," said Alexander McClure, who was friend to both. "It was not his custom to fawn upon power or flatter authority, and his free and incisive criticism of public men generally prevented him from being in sympathetic touch with most of the officials connected with the administration." [1]

Temperamentally the two men were alien. John W. Forney, editor of the *Philadelphia Press,* pointed out that "no two men, perhaps, so entirely different in character, ever threw off more spontaneous jokes." [2] But where Stevens used his stories as a weapon, Lincoln loved storytelling for its own sake, finding in it relief from tension as well as the chance to make a political parable. "Were it not for these stories, I should die," he once confided, "they are vents through which my sadness, my gloom and melancholy escape." [3]

144

Where Lincoln's wit was usually droll and kindly, Stevens' was sardonic, sharp, and earthy. He could convulse the House by saying, "I yield to the gentleman for a few feeble remarks." And while most of his cloacal witticisms were edited out of the *Congressional Globe,* it is on record that he once said in the House: "There was a gentleman from the far West sitting next to me, but he went away and the seat seems just as clean as it was before."

Justin Morrill, Stevens' colleague on the Ways and Means Committee, described another special quality of Stevens' humor. "His wit was all his own, and he had no skill in working ores mined by others, failing even in the common art of story-telling . . . nor did I ever know him to reproduce or to give a new edition of the good things of which he was the constant and prolific author. Born in a jovial moment, often glowing with passion, they were foundlings never after to be nursed by parental solicitude." Carl Schurz wrote that Stevens "shot out such sallies with a perfectly serious mien, or at best he accompanied them with a grim smile not at all like Abraham Lincoln's hearty laughs at his own jests."⁴

Lincoln, unlike Stevens, never used frankness as a weapon to deride and humiliate others. Where he was tactful and forbearing with many shades of political opinion, Stevens cut himself off from men whose principles did not largely coincide with his own. Where Lincoln's compassion was boundless as the sea, Stevens'—like that of most men— was channeled into estuaries of his own making. Both men were honest and incisive to a degree almost unknown among politicians. But Lincoln was incomparably abler as a statesman, and also shrewder as a tactician.

Stevens had one touchstone by which he tested his superiors and supported or abandoned his friends—the vigor with which they moved in the antislavery cause. This was his test for Lincoln. When he praised the President, it was because he had moved decisively in the direction of Negro freedom; when he attacked him, it was because he believed Lincoln dilatory in pushing emancipation, or in prosecuting the war.

"I am quite sure," wrote McClure, "that Stevens respected Lincoln much more than he would have respected any other man in the same position with Lincoln's convictions of duty. He could not but appreciate Lincoln's generous forbearance even with all of Stevens' irritating conflicts, and Lincoln profoundly appreciated Stevens as one of his most valued and useful co-workers, and never cherished resentment even when Stevens indulged in his bitterest sallies of wit or sarcasm at Lincoln's tardiness. Strange as it may seem, these two great characters, ever in conflict, and yet ever battling for the same great cause, rendered invaluable service to each other, and unitedly rendered incalculable service in saving the Republic. . . . Stevens was ever clearing the underbrush and preparing the soil, while Lincoln followed to sow the seeds that were to ripen in a regenerated Union." [5]

Lincoln was, in fact, the driver of an eight-horse team. In front were the Radical Republicans, galloping furiously forward, heedless of obstacles in the road. The second team were the Conservative Republicans, headed in the same direction, but less impulsive and often fearful. Behind them came the War Democrats, leaping forward in a great cooperative lunge in the beginning, and afterward doing their best to swerve the lead team from its fixed goal of "the Union with emancipation," to "the Union as it was and the Constitution as it is." Eventually they did their best to unhorse the driver. Finally, there were the copperheads, who did nothing but sit on their haunches and stall. As could be expected, it was on the Negro question that they pulled off in all directions.

Lincoln's skill and adroitness as a driver were certainly not obvious to his contemporaries in harness, each of whom felt that his own direction and pace should be enforced upon all the rest. In recent years several historians have derided Thaddeus Stevens, Charles Sumner, and their followers particularly for the crime of opposing Lincoln.[6] It is true that Lincoln was often grieved by the hostility of these men, but he was not one to lose sight of the difference between being damned for not prosecuting the war vigorously enough, and being damned for prosecuting it at all. Sumner wrote to Massachusetts' Governor Andrew early in December 1861: *"The Presdt. tells me* that the question between him & me is one of 4 weeks or at most 6 weeks, when we shall all be together." [7] Actually the time span was longer.

Stevens' attitude toward the President was always distorted by being way out in front of him. "He and Lincoln worked substantially on the same lines," McClure said, "earnestly striving to attain the same ends, but Stevens was always in advance of public sentiment, while Lincoln never halted until assured that the considered judgment of the nation would sustain him. Stevens was the pioneer who was ever in advance of the government in every movement for the suppression of the rebellion, whether by military or civil measures. . . . Lincoln possessed the sagacity to await the fulness of time for all things, and thus failed in nothing." [8]

The relations between Stevens and the president-elect started out badly when Lincoln—who had been committed against his wishes— appointed Simon Cameron of Pennsylvania to his cabinet. Stevens, with many others, believed Cameron to be unscrupulous and dishonest. And he was infuriated by Cameron's recent statement that he was willing to see slavery extended to the Pacific. Alexander McClure rushed to Springfield to fight the appointment, urging that Thaddeus Stevens or David Wilmot be selected instead. He wrote back to Stevens on January 10, 1861:

> I urged Lincoln to appoint either yourself or Wilmot. He finally answered that General C. would not consent to any other appointment than himself in Penna. . . . I found the Cameron retainers about Springfield . . . are against you, and do not fear Wilmot. . . . I found rumors rife there that you had an odious history in Penna. politics. I think you have been struck there as far as that element could do it! But I do not know that it has to any extent succeeded with Lincoln. . . . Lincoln asked very specially as to your position here with regard to our divisions, and I need not say that my answer was all you could desire. . . . I hope the arch scoundrel of the State is thrown, and if I am entitled to any credit for it, I am willing to retire. I shall have done my State essential service.[9]

Stevens meanwhile had been led to believe that Cameron had not only declined the post but had actually swung to his own support. "Some ten days ago it was rumored that Gen'l Cameron had declined a seat in Mr. Lincoln's cabinet," he wrote to E. B. Washburne. "One of my colleagues suggested my name for the place. I objected until it was ascertained from Gen. Cameron himself if it were true as I would have no contest on my account. A short time afterwards General Cameron called on me as he said to inform me that he had absolutely declined going into the Cabinet, and wished me to allow my name to be used as most likely to unite all factions. I asked him, as a question of honor, whether he might not yet be induced to reconsider his determination and accept. He answered that there was no earthly contingency which would induce him to go into Mr. Lincoln's Cabinet; and again urged me to allow my name to be presented. I consented. His friends in the House who had signed his recommendation joined on mine under his advice." [10]

Stevens went on bitterly to say that he feared Cameron had "forgotten his honor," and consented to become a candidate again. What had actually happened was that Lincoln had revoked his offer to Cameron, but that the Pennsylvania politician had tenaciously refused to give it up. On February 3 Stevens wrote angrily to Salmon P. Chase: ". . . with Cameron to make whatever department he may occupy a den of thieves, I have but little hope that we shall be able to survive the next election." [11]

When Lincoln arrived in Washington, Stevens with other Republicans went to him privately to protest the Cameron appointment. "We did not think that he was the proper person to go there," Stevens said later in the House, "nor did we think that he had the capacity. We gave other strong reasons why he should not be appointed. It is true that those reasons did not appear very strong, for the executive power treated them as I expect they deserved to be treated, with silent contempt." [12]

During one interview with Lincoln, the president-elect questioned Stevens pointedly: "You don't mean to say you think Cameron would steal?"

"No," said Stevens drily, "I don't think he would steal a red-hot stove."

Lincoln partly as a joke and partly perhaps by way of delicate warning, repeated the statement to Cameron. He was not amused.

Stevens later returned to demand of Lincoln: "Why did you tell Cameron what I said to you?"

"I thought it was a good joke and didn't think it would make him mad."

"Well, he is very mad and made me promise to retract. I will now do so. I believe I told you he would not steal a red-hot stove. I will now take that back." [13]

It is not altogether surprising that Cameron said of Stevens after his death: ". . . from the time of his entry into public life no man assailed him without danger or conquered him without scars." [14]

For a time the press spoke of Stevens as a possible Attorney-General, though it was the Treasury post he wanted. But after all the intrigue was over, Stevens was left out. Cameron became Secretary of War; the conservative Edward Bates became Attorney General, and the Treasury went to Salmon P. Chase, who had as great prestige among the Radical Republicans as Stevens but who lacked his reputation for irascibility. McClure disclosed that Stevens felt "personally aggrieved, although few even of his most intimate acquaintances had any knowledge of it." [15]

It was characteristic of Stevens that he stifled his hostility to Simon Cameron the moment Cameron first spoke out publicly for Negro freedom. It was said at the time that Stevens forgave Cameron as a result of a deal on some horse contracts. This he angrily denied in Congress, pointing out that he and Cameron were not on speaking terms until Cameron's first official recommendation that slaves be confiscated, freed, and used in Union armies. Stevens had applauded the gesture, whereupon Cameron had sought a personal reconciliation.

"I replied," said Stevens, "that I had not the slightest objection. I told him that I would support him so long as he followed out the course which he had started. I told him further, that I would look upon his past record as a blank sheet, and that I would judge him by his official conduct as a Cabinet officer. That is how General Cameron and I came to speak." [16]

Time and again Stevens forgave his enemies, but he required conversion first. Later, when Cameron's ineptness and careless bookkeeping became intolerable, and the House publicly censured him, Stevens tried to soften the severity of the corruption charges. But his realistic suspicions of Cameron died hard. When Lincoln tactfully ousted his War Secretary by naming him Minister to Russia, Stevens was heard to comment: "Send word to the Czar to bring in his things of nights." A. B. Ely wrote ruefully to Charles Sumner: "Thaddeus Stevens said Cameron would add a million to his fortune. I guess he has done it." [17]

In the first momentous decision facing Lincoln—whether to abandon Fort Sumter or re-enforce it at the risk of war—the President stood almost alone in the cabinet. At first every member except Montgomery Blair was opposed to re-enforcement save Chase, who said he was neither for it nor against it. Seward, who had so lost his usual sagacity that he had seriously proposed provoking a war with France or Spain in order to unify the country, was vehemently opposed, and had, in fact, secretly promised Southern commissioners that the fort would be evacuated. General Scott, head of the Army, was for letting Sumter go. Steven A. Douglas was strongly urging evacuation, and even the radical Sumner was for the moment wavering and silent.[18]

"It cannot be denied," said the *New York Times* on March 21, 1861, "that there is a growing sentiment throughout the North in favor of *letting the Gulf States go.*" Lincoln in his decision on Sumter had the support of the Republican governors who met with him on April 4, and also a handful of aggressive Senators and Congressmen who met secretly and demanded that reinforcements be sent to General Anderson. Ben Wade, Zachariah Chandler and Lyman Trumbull were delegated to bring direct pressure on the President. Thaddeus Stevens, who had taken the position even before the inaugural that Lincoln must retake all the "stolen forts," using "gentle means at first, and if those fail, then such as become necessary," was now an active belligerent. Many years later he wrote: "Had it not been for a few determined men in 1861 the Union would have been dissolved." [19]

After the firing on Sumter, Stevens was one of the few Congressmen who refused to vote for the resolution introduced by John J. Crittenden stating that the war was not to be waged to destroy slavery. He agreed with Albert G. Riddle, who when attacked by his colleagues for voting against the Crittenden resolution said bluntly: "You all believe that it [slavery] is to go out, when it does, through convulsion, fire, and blood. That convulsion is upon us. The man is a delirious ass who does not see it and realize this. For me, I mean to make a conquest of it; to beat it to extinction under the iron hoofs of our war horses." [20]

When some weeks later it was proposed that the Crittenden resolution be reaffirmed, Stevens returned to the argument. He was curt, as usual, and harshly eloquent: "I, for one, shall never shrink from saying, when these slaves are once conquered by us, 'Go and be free.' God forbid that I should ever agree that they should be returned again to their masters. I do not say that this war is made for that purpose. Ask those who made the war what is its object." [21]

Stevens now became, as Alexander McClure described him, "the master-spirit of every aggressive movement in Congress to overthrow the rebellion and slavery." He was never cowed, never dismayed or discouraged into retreat, and never guilty of considering what was "safe." Godkin of the *Nation*, who was generally critical of Stevens, later wrote: "A manlier man never sat in the House. He had what Congressmen so often wanted—a conscience of his own, opinions of his own, and a will of his own, and he never flinched from the duty of asserting them. . . . No political puppet or intriguer could look at him without envy." [22]

More than most abolitionists Stevens looked upon the war with a tough and pragmatic understanding of the nature of political power. "If this nation were broken into fragments, and two or three republics were to arise upon its ruins," he said, "we should be a feeble people, incapable of self-defense. The Old World would shape our institutions, regulate our commerce, and control all our interests." [23] From the beginning he demonstrated that he was no mere stinging gadfly but a genuine man of action.

Upon Stevens more than any other single person would fall the burden of raising four billion dollars in loans and taxes to feed, clothe, and arm 2,300,000 soldiers. As Chairman of the Ways and Means Committee, which at that time handled both appropriations and taxes, he held the most important post in the House. By virtue of this position he had a notable privilege, the right of precedence to take the floor of the House at any time. When Lincoln took office the United States Treasury was practically empty. Within twenty-four hours after his appointment to the Ways and Means Committee, Stevens reported a bill authorizing a national loan. In exactly one hour he introduced a bill appropriating six million dollars to pay the soldiers Lincoln had called into service and sent it through the House. With similar speed he pushed through the bill Lincoln had requested authorizing the Secretary of the Treasury to borrow up to $250,000,000 for the prosecution of the war. When Lincoln asked for 400,000 troops, he saw to it that the House Army Bill provided for 500,000.[24]

Within a week he had discovered a silencer for copperhead filibustering: he simply moved a suspension of the rules so that the House could go into the "Committee of the Whole on the State of the Union," to consider the bill, then moved that debate be limited to one hour —or in some cases five minutes—and in one case half a minute. It worked as long as his party was with him.

Once his good friend, Owen Lovejoy, protested at the speed with which a bill was being pushed. "If the Committee of Ways and Means expect to drive this thing through with a tandem team, I reckon they will find obstacles in the way." To which Stevens good-humoredly replied:

"We do not expect to drive the bill through with a tandem team. There are too many mules here." [25]

To speed up the tedious process of legislation he had a constant supply of witticisms. "I cannot yield the floor for the purpose of being praised." "Debate is exhausted on the amendment and everybody is exhausted with the debate." "There are no grave questions in this bill except the question of sending it to the grave."

Against the copperheads he was merciless. Of Alexander Long of Ohio, who was censured by the House for treasonable statements, he said: "I would as soon be hanged in chains alongside of a gibbeted traitor, as to be thus connected with a moral carcass before the House." Fernando Wood, he said, "would not even rise to the dignity of a respectable demagogue." To John W. Chanler, another copperhead from New York, he retorted: "There are some reptiles so flat that the common foot of man cannot crush them." [26]

Stevens came to be called "the old Commoner," leader of leaders, and it was said that "whoever cracked Thaddeus Stevens' skull would let out the brains of the Republican Party." "He was a skirmisher rather than a regular debater," said the *New York World*, "direct, pungent, concise, adroit, a great master of sarcasm and unsparing in his use of it." [27] Always he was out in front, badgering and demanding, months in advance of others, exactions that the cruel progress of the war made inevitable. Lincoln's first call for troops limited the service to three months, and Cameron so misunderstood the nature of the crisis that he actually turned back regiments eagerly offered by the state governors with the excuse that he had no place for them. Stevens, one of the few men in the North who did not underestimate the strength and tenacity of the South, urged enlistment for the duration of the war, or at least a term of three years.

When Lincoln, at Seward's urging, declared a blockade of the Southern ports, thereby inadvertently giving the Confederacy the status of a belligerent with full war privileges, Stevens went at once to the President and pointed out to him that he had thereby recognized a state of war and could no longer describe the conflict as a local revolt. Before Lincoln took office Stevens had urged a blockade, but in a different fashion, proposing that the government abolish the laws establishing ports of entry in the seceding states, thus making it impossible for any ship to leave a Southern port with proper clearances. "The vessel," he had said, "would be without papers, without nationality, and a prize to the first captors." [28] It was now too late for this.

As Stevens described the conversation later, Lincoln frankly admitted his error: "Well, that is a fact. I see the point now, but I don't know anything about the law of nations and I thought it was all right."

"As a lawyer, Mr. Lincoln, I should have supposed you would have seen the difficulty at once."

"Oh, well, I'm a good enough lawyer in a western law court, but we don't practice the law of nations up there, and I supposed Seward knew all about it, and I left it to him. But it's done now and can't be helped, so we must get along as well as we can." [29]

The incident served to strengthen Stevens' fears that Seward and not Lincoln was the real executive in office, and to confirm a growing conviction that the Secretary of State was capable of nothing but blunders and compromise, a conviction he was never thereafter able to shake off, despite Seward's able statesmanship in the later war years.

Stevens was one of the first men in the government to see that handing belligerent rights to the Confederacy, however advantageous to the South as far as foreign relations were concerned, gave one great advantage to the Union. It solved the theoretical problem of a nation fighting to preserve itself and its Constitution and using unconstitutional means of doing it. Actually there was an immense body of opinion in the North holding that the war must somehow be fought without interfering with either the state governments or the domestic laws of the seceding states. Stevens recognized the folly of this position from the military point of view, and took advantage of the declaration of blockade to insist that as far as the Confederacy was concerned the Constitution was now entirely superseded by the laws of war. In a thorny debate on whether or not the Union had the right to confiscate rebel property, including slaves, he withered the protesting Democrats:

> Mr. Speaker, I thought the time had come when the laws of war were to govern our action; when constitutions, if they stood in the way of the laws of war in dealing with the enemy, had no right to intervene. Who pleads the Constitution against our proposed action? Who says the Constitution must come in, in bar of our action? It is the advocates of rebels, of rebels who have sought to overthrow the Constitution and trample it in the dust. . . . Sir, it is an absurdity. . . .
> When a country is at open war with an enemy, every publicist agrees that you have the right to use every means which will weaken him.[30]

Emboldened by this speech, other Radical Republicans accepted the position, and later the Conservative Republicans one by one came to recognize that the war could be fought on no other theoretical basis. Lincoln's most energetic measures were taken in the name of his "war powers." When he roused public furor by suspending the privilege of the writ of habeas corpus, Stevens introduced a bill expressly granting him the authority, and in what Nicolay and Hay described as an "energetic, not to say arbitrary, manner," succeeded in getting it passed the same day it was introduced.[31]

The timing of the President and Thaddeus Stevens was not often, however, so neatly synchronized. When it came to the problem of Negro freedom, as we shall see, Lincoln seldom succeeded in matching Stevens' pace, though both were moving toward the same bright horizon.

CHAPTER THIRTEEN

Stevens, Lincoln, and the Negro

Emancipation of the negroes was not what the North fought for, but only what it fought with. The right to secede was not what the South fought for, but only what it fought with. The great majority of the Southern people loved the Union, and consented to its destruction only when there seemed to be no other way to save slavery; the great bulk of the North consented to destroy slavery only when there seemed no other way to save the Union.

George Washington Cable: *The Negro Question* [1]

BOTH ABRAHAM LINCOLN and Thaddeus Stevens passionately desired to see an end to slavery. But Lincoln, a strict constitutionalist, who had always declared himself to be antislavery but not an abolitionist, could not for some time be persuaded that the outbreak of war had given him any special power to destroy it. Moreover, he was desperately intent upon holding the slave-holding areas still loyal to the Union—Maryland, Delaware, Kentucky, and portions of Missouri, Virginia, and Tennessee. For some time Washington itself was in grave danger of being swallowed up in the Confederacy. Lincoln waited seventeen months after war broke out before issuing the Emancipation Proclamation. During this period, punctuated as it was by heartbreaking military defeats, Thaddeus Stevens in the House and Charles Sumner in the Senate led the struggle against widespread apathy and fear, pushing through Congress the limited emancipation measures that prepared the nation for general emancipation and the Thirteenth

Amendment.

One of the reasons for their exasperation with the President was that he never caught up with them. And since he chose not to confide in them, they could never be certain that he would even follow in their direction. Anyone who looks at the chronological record now, however, can see that actually Lincoln was never very far behind. As Wendell Phillips expressed it, if Lincoln was able to grow "it is because we have watered him." [2]

In July 1861 Stevens secured the passage of an act seizing the property of certain rebels and freeing those slaves that were being used for war purposes, such as digging entrenchments and driving teams. He predicted then that if the war lasted two years general emancipation would be "the doctrine of the whole free people of the North." [3]

In September Lincoln was still urging caution. "I think Sumner and the rest of you would upset our applecart altogether if you had your way," he said to a group of Radical Republicans. "We'll fetch 'em; just give us a little time. We didn't go into the war to put down slavery, but to put the flag back; and to act differently at this moment would, I have no doubt, not only weaken our cause, but smack of bad faith. . . . This thunderbolt will keep." [4]

In the same month Lincoln tactfully rebuked John C. Frémont, now a general in Missouri, for independently issuing a proclamation freeing all the slaves of the Missouri rebels. He asked him to modify his proclamation to conform to Congress' Confiscation Act, lest it "alarm our Southern Union friends, and turn them against us—perhaps ruin our rather fair prospect for Kentucky." [5] This caused great indignation among the friends of emancipation. "How many times," wrote James Russell Lowell, "are we to save Kentucky and lose our self-respect?" Stevens said pointedly in the House on January 22, 1862: "We have put a sword into one hand of our generals and shackles into another. Freemen are not inspirited by such mingled music."

[In November 1861 Stevens introduced a bill providing for total emancipation. It did not pass. On December 2 he introduced a resolution asking Lincoln to free every slave who aided in the rebellion, with compensation for loyal masters.] Lincoln in the same week, much behind Stevens, delicately suggested in his Message to Congress that the border states agree to abolish slavery by 1900, selling their slaves to the government, which would then provide for their emancipation and colonization.[6]

Three months later, March 6, 1862, Lincoln had only moved forward far enough to make a cautious recommendation that Congress pass a joint resolution promising compensation to any border state choosing voluntarily to emancipate its slaves. Even this was enough to make Congressman William H. Wadsworth of Kentucky apoplectic. "I reject it now," he said. "I utterly spit at it and despise it . . . emancipation in the cotton States is simply an absurdity. . . . There is not enough power in the world to compel it to be done." Stevens at the opposite extreme derided the resolution as "the most diluted milk-and-water-gruel proposition that was ever given to the American nation." [7]

The resolution passed and was signed by Lincoln April 10, 1862. But it did nothing but demonstrate that loyal slaveholders as well as rebel would still cling to slavery. The border states repudiated the resolution, and despite Lincoln's patient urging obstinately refused to accept emancipation with compensation until it was too late, and they were forced by growing Radical strength in their own legislatures or by the passing of the Thirteenth Amendment to emancipate without payment.

Congress itself, though overwhelmingly Republican, at first seemed terrified to move in the direction of emancipation. As late as May 1862, the House, to the despair of the Radicals, voted down a bill freeing the slaves of the armed rebels. Nevertheless, as the war progressed and it became increasingly apparent that the South could not be subdued in a single battle, or a single year, the Conservative Republicans gradually were won over to the realization that there was nothing to be gained by carrying on the elaborate pretense that the war could somehow be fought without doing anything about slavery.

First they swung to the support of the Radicals in abolishing slavery in the District of Columbia. In the debate on this bill a Democrat from Pennsylvania moved to amend it so that it would not operate unless a majority of the District citizens voted in its favor. Stevens rose with a waggish objection: "I am opposed to the amendment and I would recommend to my colleague with great respect, an amendment in another document. It is somewhere provided that the wicked shall be damned. I would suggest to my colleague that he propose a proviso to that, 'provided that they consent thereto.' It would be just as decent an amendment as the one he has proposed." The amendment was lost. [8]

Lincoln signed the District of Columbia emancipation bill April 16, 1862. It provided compensation amounting to an average of $300 per slave. For Stevens this was just the beginning, and he quickly introduced a bill abolishing slavery in all United States territories. When a Rhode Island Representative opposed it because it might give offense to the South, Stevens shut him up with an anecdote: "A captain, who was a little timid, unlike my friend, raised a company to go out and fight the British—it may be that they were from Rhode Island—and when his company were brought in front of the enemy, he cried out, when they were about to shoot, 'For God's sake, don't fire, for don't you see it will only make them a great deal madder!' " [9]

After this bill passed, the Radical Republicans tried to persuade Congress to declare free the slaves of rebels fighting the Union, and to enlist them as soldiers in the Union Army. This met with tremendous resistance. "Pass these acts," one Congressman warned, "confiscate under the bills the property of these men, emancipate their negroes, place arms in the hands of these human gorillas to murder their masters and violate their wives and daughters, and you will have a war such as was never witnessed in the worst days of the French Revolution, and horrors never exceeded in San Domingo." [10]

Nevertheless, the Negro problem would not be put down. Tens of thousands of fugitives gathered in the wake of the Union armies in a pathetic quest for food and liberty. The slaves were treated in fashions as varied as the commanding officers. Many were driven away as potential spies; loyal slaveholders were freely permitted to enter the Negro compounds and carry off whatever slaves they cared to identify as their own,[11] and soldiers were detached to escort them—a practice that caused a ferment in the armies. General Benjamin F. Butler called the slaves "contraband of war," and put them to work on the abandoned estates, a practice that eventually became official.

General David Hunter, angered by the continuing obeisance of Lincoln to the Fugitive Slave Law, stepped out of rank, as Frémont had done, and peremptorily ordered the slaves freed in three states under his jurisdiction. Lincoln repudiated the order. "No commanding general," he wrote to the protesting Salmon P. Chase, "shall do such a thing, upon *my* responsibility, without consulting me." When, however, Thaddeus Stevens managed to get through Congress a bill forbidding any member of the armed forces to return fugitive slaves, Lincoln approved it without question. This was March 13, 1862. On July 17 he approved that portion of the new tough Confiscation Act which provided that all slaves coming into the Union lines from rebel owners be freed and used in the prosecution of the war. Theoretically this act freed about as many slaves as would the Emancipation Proclamation. Both were dependent upon the success of the Union armies.

Thaddeus Stevens was convinced the President had the necessary war power to free all the slaves, and now went repeatedly to the White House. "Stevens, Sumner and Wilson, simply haunt me with their importunities for a Proclamation of Emancipation," Lincoln complained one day to Senator John B. Henderson of Missouri. "Wherever I go and whatever way I turn, they are on my trail, and still in my heart,

I have the deep conviction that the hour has not yet come." They reminded him of a story from his childhood, he said, when the children in school stood in line to read passages from the Bible.

Our lesson one day was the story of the Israelites who were thrown into the fiery furnace and delivered by the hand of the Lord without so much as the smell of fire upon their garments.

It fell to one little fellow to read the verses in which occurred for the first time in the chapter the names of Shadrach, Meshach, and Abednego. Little Bud stumbled on Shadrach, floundered on Meshach, and went all to pieces on Abednego. Instantly the hand of the master dealt him a cuff on the side of the head and left him wailing and blubbering, as the next boy in line took up the reading.

But before the girl at the end of the line had done reading, he had subsided into sniffles and finally become quiet. His blunders and disgrace were forgotten by the others of the class until his turn was approaching to read again. Then like a thunderclap out of a clear sky, he set up a wail which alarmed even the master, who with rather unusual gentleness, asked what was the matter now. Pointing with a shaking finger at the verse which a few moments later, would fall to him to read, Bud managed to quaver out, "Look there, marster, there comes them same damn three fellers again!" [12]

For a time during 1862 it seemed to the Radical Republicans that Lincoln would never use his war power to destroy slavery, and that the war might end with it relatively intact. "Patch up a compromise now," Stevens warned on January 22, 1862, "leaving this germ of evil and it will soon again overrun the whole South, even if you free three fourths of the slaves. Your peace would be a curse. You would have expended countless treasures and untold lives in vain." During the summer it seemed to him that the President was completely dominated by "border-state counsellors," and was oblivious to the danger that a war that did not end slavery would one day have to be refought.

Actually Lincoln read his Emancipation Proclamation to his cabinet as early as July 22, 1862, but at Seward's urging agreed to withhold it until after a military victory; and the secret that it had been written at all was well kept. As late as August 22 Lincoln would say evasively in a public reply to Horace Greeley's "Prayer of Twenty Millions" pressing for emancipation: "My paramount object in this struggle *is* to save the Union, and is *not* either to save or to destroy slavery. If I could save the Union without freeing *any* slave, I would do it, and if I could save it by freeing *all* the slaves, I would do it; and if I could save it by freeing some and leaving others alone, I would also do that." [13]

On September 5, 1862, just nineteen days before the Emancipation Proclamation was issued, Stevens wrote despairingly to Simon Stevens: "The removal of Hunter and Butler, and the continued refusal to receive Negro soldiers convince me that the Administration are preparing the people to receive an ignominious surrender to the South. It is plain that nothing approaching the present policy will subdue the rebels. Whether we shall find *anybody* with a sufficient grasp of mind, and sufficient moral courage, to treat this as a radical revolution, and remodel our institutions, I doubt. It would involve the desolation of the South as well as emancipation; and a re-peopling of half the Continent. This ought to be done but it startles most men." [14]

Stevens' impatience and pessimism blinded him to the President's true intentions. He believed Lincoln to be "honest" and "amiable," but misled by Seward, Weed, and the border-state men, particularly Montgomery Blair. He described him with irony as "our very discreet Executive," having no suspicion that Lincoln was being driven by what the President himself described later to a young cavalryman as "a great impulse moving me to do justice to five or six millions of people." [15] This was something, in fact, that very few men were ever permitted to see.

To Isaac Arnold and Owen Lovejoy on July 13, 1862, Lincoln expressed his hopes: "Oh, how I wish the border states would accept my proposition," he said. "Then you, Lovejoy, and you, Arnold, and all of us, would not have lived in vain! The labor of your life, Lovejoy, would be crowned with success. You would live to see the end of slavery." [16] And when he told his cabinet of his final decision to issue the Emancipation Proclamation, he made such a poignant admission of religious faith that both Chase and Welles noted it in their diaries. "When the rebel army was at Frederick," Lincoln said, "I determined, as soon as it should be driven out of Maryland, to issue a Proclamation of Emancipation such as I thought most likely to be useful. I said nothing to anyone; but I made the promise to myself and (hesitating a little)—to my Maker. The rebel army is now driven out, and I am going to fulfil that promise." [17]

The Proclamation went to the world on September 23, 1862, with the understanding that it would take effect January 1, 1863. It did not free the slaves in the loyal slave states, nor even in those areas in Louisiana and Arkansas that had been overrun by Union armies. This could legally be done, Lincoln believed, only by a Constitutional amendment. But Stevens seemed to be satisfied. In an open letter to his constituents he praised Lincoln's patriotism and promised him full support. "Lincoln's proclamation," he said, "contained precisely the principles which I had advocated." [18]

When Representative Wadsworth of Kentucky protested in the House, "As to that proclamation, we despise and laugh at it. . . . The soldiers of other States will not execute it. May my curse fall upon their heads if they do!" Stevens put to him a single question: "Will it take Kentucky out of the Union?"

"No: by St. Paul," he replied. "She cannot be taken out of the Union by secession and abolition combined!" [19]

On the hotly debated issue of whether or not Negroes should be used as soldiers, Lincoln again moved slowly from the Conservative to the Radical side. As early as January 12, 1862 Stevens introduced a bill calling for the enlistment of 150,000 Negro troops. It passed the House but was killed in the Senate. Still he persisted. "I would raise a hundred thousand of them to-morrow and have them drilled," he said in an earnest speech on July 5, 1862. When Kentucky's Mallory protested first that the slaves would turn against their masters with "indiscriminate slaughter of men, women, and children," and second that "one shot of cannon would disperse thirty thousand," Stevens questioned drily:

"Why then object to them as a savage and barbarous race, if one gun will disperse an army. . . . History tells us that they make the best and most docile soldiers in the world. They are not barbarians in nature. They are a people as well calculated to be humanized as any other." [20]

Despite the urging of Vice-President Hamlin, Edwin M. Stanton his new Secretary of War, and the whole growing Radical faction in Congress; despite the mounting pressure crisply expressed by Governor Samuel J. Kirkwood of Iowa, who said he wanted to see, before the war was over, "some dead niggers as well as dead white men"— Lincoln would not at first consent to arming the blacks. [21] Stevens blamed Seward for Lincoln's reluctance. "I have accused the prime minister to his face for having gone back from the faith he taught us," he said, "and instead of arming every man, black or white, who would fight for this Union, withholding a well-meaning President from doing so." [22]

When it was protested in Congress that to employ Negro soldiers would mean Negroes commanding white troops, Stevens pointed out that the bill authorizing the use of the blacks specified "soldiers or non-commissioned officers only." He went on bitterly: "I do not expect to live to see the day when, in this Christian land, merit shall counterbalance the crime of color. True, we propose to give them an equal chance to meet death on the battle-field. But even then their great achievements, if equal to those of Dessalines, would give them no hope of honor. The only place where they can find equality is in the grave. There all God's children are equal." [23]

Lincoln eventually moved decisively over to the Radical position. Stevens was successful not only in getting him to authorize the use of colored troops but also to secure the passage of an act providing that slaves in the border states be drafted into the army and freed, their masters being compensated at the rate of $300 for each slave. This speeded the movement toward emancipation, especially in Maryland. Stevens also led the fight to equalize the pay between white and colored soldiers, which had originally been fixed at $13 per month for white and $10 for colored troops.

"I despise the principle that would make a difference between them in the hour of battle and of death," he said passionately. ". . . The black man knows when he goes there that his dangers are greater than the white man's. He runs not only the risk of being killed in battle, but the certainty, if taken prisoner, of being slaughtered instead of being treated as a prisoner of war." The ugly Fort Pillow massacre, where Negro troops and some white officers had surrendered to General Nathan B. Forrest only to be indiscriminately slaughtered, was less than four weeks old. It gave strength to his argument.[24]

Lincoln and Stevens were not as far apart on the issue of colonization of Negroes abroad as has been commonly supposed. Both were opposed to compulsory deportation, though at least two members of Lincoln's cabinet, Blair and Bates, were in favor of it.[25] When Lincoln saw to it that the bill freeing slaves in the District of Columbia had a rider providing steamship tickets to Liberia or Haiti for any freed slave who cared to go, Stevens made a motion to raise the $100,000 appropriation by $500,000 more. But later, when Lincoln encouraged the development of two new sites for Negro colonies—Chiriqui on the Isthmus of Panama and the Ile la Vache off the coast of Haiti—Stevens deplored the choices as "so unhealthy as to be wholly uninhabitable."

"I moved the appropriation of half a million for general colonization purposes," he wrote to Chase, "but never thought new and independent colonies were to be planted."[26] Chase read the letter to Lincoln, who ordered an investigation. When it was discovered that unscrupulous speculators were behind both schemes, the sites were abandoned and the Negroes repatriated.

Where Stevens had long realized that it would be an economic impossibility to deport the whole labor force of the South, and encouraged colonization chiefly because it served to lessen the fears of apprehensive Congressmen, Lincoln was more genuinely converted to the idea of general repatriation of the Negroes in Africa. "I am so far behind the Sumner lighthouse," he said in discussing this, "that I shall stick to my colonization hobby."[27]

This was not a reflection of hostility for the Negro people but rather of pessimism concerning the ineradicable nature of the white man's prejudice. To a group of Negroes who visited him at the White House he said:

"Your race are suffering, in my judgment, the greatest wrong inflicted on any people. But even when you cease to be slaves, you are yet far removed from being placed on an equality with the white race. . . . The aspiration of men is to enjoy equality with the best when free, but on this broad continent, not a single man of your race is made the equal of a single man of ours. Go where you are treated best, and the ban is still upon you. I do not propose to discuss this, but to present it as a fact with which we have to deal. I cannot alter it if I would. . . . But for your race among us there could not be war, although many men engaged on either side do not care for you one way or the other. Nevertheless, I repeat, without the institution of Slavery, and the colored race as a basis, the war could not have an existence. It is better for us both, therefore, to be separated." [28]

Lincoln treated everyone according to his measure as a man, and not according to his color, status, or pretensions. He greeted the ex-slave, Frederick Douglass, by saying, "Sit down; I am glad to see you." And later, when he learned that Douglass was being turned away from a White House reception by the guards, he ordered that he be permitted to enter, and greeted him warmly by name in a frank gesture of friendliness.[29]

When the Radical Republicans succeeded in passing a bill recognizing the republics of Haiti and Liberia, snobbish Washington society was distracted by the possibility of a black ambassador or minister invading their drawing rooms as an equal. When the Haitian President tactfully let it be known to Lincoln that he would not send a colored minister against Lincoln's wish, the President drawled to the messenger: "You can tell the President of Hayti that I shan't tear my shirt if he sends a nigger here!" [30]

Thaddeus Stevens, after listening to Representative Cox of Ohio express horror at the idea of a black diplomat in Washington, said ironically in the House: "I hope that we shall not be less liberal than a very rich colored merchant in Jamaica that I heard a gentleman from Boston, who had dined with him, speak of. He said to this gentleman . . . that he had no prejudices about color; that he would never prefer a man of color, and that he would just as soon dine with a man as white as his tablecloth." [31]

Stevens and Lincoln both treated individual Negroes as equals and as friends, without self-consciousness or self-righteousness. But Stevens never agreed with Lincoln about the necessity or justice of colonizing all the Negroes abroad, and Lincoln eventually came to recognize the idea as largely impracticable, though he never completely abandoned it.[32] [In one sense Stevens was more realistic than Lincoln, since he understood that the Southerners themselves would be the first to prevent the deportation of their labor force. In another sense he was less realistic, since he believed that the Negro could be made the white man's equal—at least in political and civil rights—through the single instrument of legislation.]

One of the thorniest matters dividing Lincoln and the Radical Republicans was the proper choice of Union generals. Lincoln never measured his generals by their attitude toward slavery, but for Thaddeus Stevens this was the first yardstick. Civil War history was to demonstrate in the most perverse fashion that military genius had little or nothing to do with a man's convictions about slavery. Robert E. Lee could write to his wife in 1856: ". . . slavery as an institution, is a moral and political evil in any Country . . . a greater evil to the white than to the black race," but this attitude did not noticeably damage his genius in directing a war to preserve it. William T. Sherman, on the other hand, could write in December, 1859: "I would not if I could abolish or modify slavery."[33] Grant's wife held slaves up to 1862. Frémont and Ben Butler, the most articulate antislavery generals, were also the most inept.

The Civil War was to demonstrate, however, that a *preoccupation* with the politics of slavery usually indicated an incompetent general. If Frémont was the pet general of the Radical Republicans, McClellan was their *bête noir*. The story of this vain young man has been told countless times, and the complicated and disheartening tale of his military failures cannot be related here.[34] But since McClellan was one of Thaddeus Stevens' hates, and Lincoln's patient support of him served to infuriate all the Radical Republicans, something must be said about what made this general anathema to them, in addition to his inertia and his defeats.

Stevens would have forgiven much had McClellan moved with boldness and vigor. (He did not protest Sherman's conservative views on slavery when he captured Atlanta.) But as the months went by, it seemed to Stevens that despite the fact that McClellan's army was superior in numbers and in equipment, he was little better than a competent drill sergeant when compared with Lee. Gradually the suspicion took hold in his mind that McClellan refused to destroy Lee because he did not want to. Along with others in the party, including many Conservatives, he began slowly to total up what seemed to be the evidence.

Shortly after McClellan's appointment, he announced to the people of western Virginia that his army did not come to interfere with their slaves in any way. "We will, on the contrary," he said, "with an iron hand, crush any attempt at insurrection on their part." He took no pains to hide his contempt for the abolitionists, surrounded himself with a clique of young proslavery officers, and spurned personal relations with the older antislavery officer group. He told Secretary of the Navy Welles that he "detested both South Carolina and Massachusetts, and should rejoice to see both States extinguished." [35]

He took pains to help loyal slaveholders recapture Negroes who had fled to the army, and permitted soldiers to be used as escorts for their return. He ordered out of the Army of the Potomac the Hutchinson family singers, who had entertained the troops by singing Whittier's antislavery songs. And he refused to let Robert E. Lee's spacious Arlington home and grounds be turned into a hospital, though his wounded men were dying in the swamps below it, because he had promised Mrs. Lee the estate would not be damaged.

Stevens made a stormy attack on these practices on July 5, 1862. "There are many things in the conduct of this war of which I cannot approve. I cannot approve of setting our generals who sympathize with slavery at the head of our armies, or setting our generals, under express orders, to pursue and return fugitives from traitors. I cannot consent to that portion of the conduct of the war which sets our armies to watch the property of rebel soldiers in arms against us, rather than allow it to be occupied by our own troops, while, in the meantime, our soldiers, sick and wounded, are placed in swamps filled with deadly miasma, which destroys health and unfits our men to meet the enemy." He laid the immediate blame not on Lincoln—for against no other man in power was his hostility so mitigated by respect—but upon his advisers. "I believe the President—and I do not mean to flatter—is as honest a man as there is in the world; but I believe him to be too easy and amiable, and to be misled by the malign influence of Kentucky counsellors, and following that advice, that he has permitted the adoption of the policy which I have just stated without rebuke." [36]

Lincoln entertained the Hutchinson family singers in the White House and gave permission for them to sing for the soldiers wherever invited. And he ordered the Lee mansion to be turned into a hospital. [37] An Act of Congress of March 13, 1862, prohibited the practice of returning fugitive slaves.

The President did not know that McClellan was capable of writing a confidential letter on July 11, 1862, to the Confederate, Hill Carter, owner of a great Virginia estate, expressing regret for the losses his armies had wrought and affirming that he had not come to destroy slavery. But he did know that McClellan had taken time to write him a long lecture against Radicalism. It said in part: "Neither confiscation of property, political executions of persons, territorial organization of States, or forcible abolition of slavery, should be contemplated for a moment. . . . A declaration of radical views, especially upon slavery, will rapidly disintegrate our present armies." [38]

The fact that Fernando Wood and other prominent Democrats had suggested to McClellan at this time that he be the next Democratic candidate for President did not escape Lincoln's notice. Horace Greeley said bluntly in the *New York Tribune* February 20, 1862 that McClellan had ambitions to win the presidency with Southern support and therefore deliberately prevented decisive military action. Senator Henry Wilson said scornfully in Congress that some commanders "seem more anxious to catch negroes than to catch rebels." [39] And Senators Wade and Chandler brought McClellan before the Committee on the Conduct of the War, where they openly accused him of cowardice.

The full extent of the arrogance with which McClellan treated Lincoln, and his hopes for saving the Union without giving it over to what he called "the abolitionists and other scoundrels," were not fully known by anyone till the publication later of his letters to his wife and the revelations of John Hay. Lincoln's patience with McClellan remains one of the most remarkable records of forbearance in military history. But finally, after the Battle of Antietam and McClellan's failure to follow up the victory, Lincoln with great reluctance came to accept the view so long held by the Radicals. "I began to fear he was playing false," he confided later to John Hay, "—that he did not want to hurt the enemy. I saw how he could intercept the enemy on the way to Richmond. I determined to make that test. If he let them get away I would remove him. He did so & I relieved him." [40]

[On several critical issues Lincoln never came to agree with Thaddeus Stevens. One was the idea of paying compensation for the slaves of the rebels. Stevens was always violently opposed, but Lincoln, even though he had no support in his cabinet, toyed with the idea almost up to the day of his death. The most irreconcilable disagreement, however, concerned the confiscation of the Southerners' estates. Stevens was certain that the evils inherent in the political oligarchy of the South could not be eradicated unless the vast holdings of the aristocrats were broken up.] To Lincoln, the confiscation of title to land "beyond the lives of the guilty parties" was a revolutionary excess to which he would not be a party.

Actually the tradition of confiscation—the usual accompaniment of revolution—was not alien even to the United States. During the Revolutionary War thousands of Tories had been driven into Canada and their property expropriated by the young Republic. Despite British indignation, the property was never restored. The Radical Republicans felt, therefore, that they had respectable precedent on their side. And in 1862 many Conservative Republicans and War Democrats agreed with them.

Andrew Johnson, former Democratic Senator, and now military governor of Tennessee, said emphatically: "Treason must be made odious, and traitors must be punished and impoverished. Their great plantations must be seized, and divided into small farms, and sold to honest and industrious men. The day for protecting the lands and Negroes of those authors of the rebellion is past."

Thurlow Weed, visiting in England, said to the British: "We shall treat the South as William the Conqueror did England. We shall divide it into territories, make a military man the governor of each territory, give the estates to well-deserving officers and men, and let the slaves, who cultivate them for the rebels, now cultivate them for loyal men." [41]

Weed and Johnson would eventually somersault backward from this position. But Thaddeus Stevens until the end of his life deviated very little from the extreme stand he took on July 5, 1862: "I would seize every foot of land, and every dollar of their property as our armies go along, and put it to the uses of the war and to the pay of our debts. I would plant the South with a military colony if I could not make them submit otherwise. I would sell their lands to the soldiers of independence; I would send those soldiers there with arms in their hands to occupy the heritage of traitors, and build up there a land of free men and of freedom, which, fifty years hence, would swarm with its hundreds of millions without a slave upon its soil." [42]

The extreme Jacobin position was perhaps best expressed by Wendell Phillips: "Now, while those large estates remain in the hands of the defeated slave oligarchy, its power is not destroyed. But let me confiscate the land of the South, and put it into the hands of the negroes and white men who have fought for it, and you may go to sleep with your parchments. I have planted a Union sure to grow as an acorn to become an oak. You do not build governments like a clap-board house; you plant them like an oak. Plant a hundred thousand negro farmers and by their side a hundred thousand of white soldiers, and

I will risk the South, Davis and all." [43]

When Lincoln was confronted with the tough Second Confiscation Act passed by Congress in July 1862, he made it clear that he would veto the whole bill—which included confiscation and freeing of rebel slaves—unless the act was amended to state that confiscation did not include the rebel landowner's fee or title. The change was made. It seemed to many Radicals that Lincoln had knocked out the most important part of their bill. George W. Julian found it "inexpressibly provoking," and the obstreperous Ben Wade threatened that "the scenes witnessed in the French Revolution were nothing in comparison to what we should see here." [44]

Lincoln at a later date permitted some of the captured estates to be sold for failure to pay taxes, and a few of these, notably on the sea islands around Port Royal, and the rice plantations along the coast, were broken up and sold in small parcels to the ex-slaves. [But his insistence against confiscation of land titles in July 1862 successfully checked a movement which would have had incalculable political and economic consequences. In effect, he knocked the teeth out of a movement which would have directed the Republican revolution into channels traditionally followed by revolutions of the past, with the thorough-going economic destruction of a privileged class. By quietly smashing the legislation calculated to start this movement he effectively aborted the revolution. The slaves would be freed and granted suffrage, but the Southern aristocracy, except for certain changes wrought by the economic ravages of the war itself, would remain a powerful political force.]

No other single act of Lincoln's served so efficiently to checkmate Radical Republican intentions. Stevens recognized this, and frequently growled about what he called "the error of the President." By January 1864, the old Congressman had retreated so far on this point as to demand only confiscation of the estates of "the leading traitors." But later he amended this to include "the property of the guilty morally as well as the politically guilty." [45]

Lincoln, unlike Cromwell and the leaders of the French Revolution, or later Lenin, was able to say, in effect: "Thus far shall the revolution go, and no farther." Considering the hatred and passion generated by the terrible bloodletting, it is one of the most extraordinary facts of history that he was able to block this kind of revolutionary excess, and that even after his death, when the Radical Republicans took over control of the government, the barrier remained intact. That Lincoln should have wanted to block it at all shows not only his conservative attitude toward the sanctity of property, but also his capacity for magnanimity toward an enemy *during* war. Stevens' compassion was always concentrated upon the handicapped Negro, and if there had to be a choice between justice for the black and justice for the white he unhesitatingly chose the former.

CHAPTER FOURTEEN

---◆---

Economic Heretic

THADDEUS STEVENS has often been cast in the role of a capitalist tyrant whose chief ambition was to destroy the agrarian economy of the South and make the whole area an economic colony of eastern capital. The Republican Party, dominated, it has been said, by the nation's big-business interests, deliberately promoted the Civil War with this end in view.[1] It is dangerous to generalize about the motives of any economic group in America, where the degree of mobility and interfusion among classes has been extraordinarily high, and it is particularly hazardous to imply that a lust for economic power was the dominating motive in the life of Thaddeus Stevens.

There is no doubt that big business eventually became interfused with the Republican Party, but not until after the war began. Alexander McClure long ago pointed out that only two of the leading business houses in Philadelphia contributed to aid Lincoln's election. George Fort Milton has shown that wealthy New Yorkers refused to support even Stephen A. Douglas, lest they offend Southern customers.[2] Once the shooting started, however, the majority of Northern businessmen moved decisively into the Republican ranks. Gradually they took over power from the idealists and reformers, but they did not fully control the party until after Thaddeus Stevens' death and the election of Grant. Through the war and through the regime of Andrew Johnson the party was roughly split into the Conservative—Old Cotton

Whigs—and Radical factions, with the businessmen clearly on the Conservative side; but the Radicals usually dominated the ideology if not always the tactics of the party.

Stevens was a Radical first and a businessman last, and the story of his economic and financial activity is one of contradiction and paradox. When it came to the tariff, he seemed to be completely old-line Whig. In railroad legislation his record is mixed—he favored railroad expansion but dismayed his railroad friends by insisting on federal controls—and on matters of confiscation and war finance he was an absolute heretic. But in no one of these four areas did his party act as a unit, nor did it ever reveal a united conspiratorial intention to destroy the Southern agrarian economy.

There is no doubt that Stevens was determined to wreck the *political* oligarchy of the South after the war, and he never lost his conviction that the only decisive way was to break up the big plantations. This would obviously have altered the economic structure, but it would hardly have destroyed it. Confiscation—with all its attendant political and psychological evils—would actually have meant decentralization of economic power, and a consequent strengthening of the political and economic autonomy of the small landholder such as prevailed in the West. After World War II, when General Douglas MacArthur ordered the Japanese Diet to insist on the breaking-up and sale of the vast holdings of the Japanese landlords to their tenant farmers, the move was hailed throughout America as an essential prerequisite to the spreading of democracy in Japan. But the Republican Party of the 1860's steadfastly refused to pass Stevens' confiscation measures, or to substitute less drastic land reform, and economic power in the South remained in the hands of about as small a number of men after the war as before, though some of these men were Northerners.[3]

It is forgotten that Stevens fought the one scheme that would have devastated the Southern economy, deportation of the Negro labor force. On this issue he differed from Lincoln, and it is the rare historian who will note the fact that in this special instance Stevens, in effect if not in intention, was the truer friend of the South.[4]

[When it came to the tariff issue, however, Stevens was wholly against Southern interests. As chief legislator for the Pennsylvania iron industry, he wanted as high a tariff as possible.] The American iron industry was still small; British competition appeared often to be threatening to ruin it, though actually it needed very little protection in order to survive and expand. Stevens always looked upon American iron manufacturing as weak (an important factor in his championship), and dreamed of eliminating British iron competition altogether.

He did not count it immoral that his own private foundries benefited from the higher prices; nor did it trouble him that it was the American public that paid.

During the war tariff duties soared, with particularly heavy additions to the duty on British iron.[5] Still the tariff did not go as high as he wanted it to, and he failed to push through the tariff bill in 1863. Many Republicans had been Democrats until 1856 and 1858, and they carried their free-trade sentiments into the new party. Not until after the war did many of them slip back to their old party allegiance; then the Republicans were completely unified on the tariff issue, and the South was severely pinched by their uncompromising protectionist policies.

Stevens' tariff policy was not good economics when measured in terms of the national interest over a long period. But his Pennsylvania constituents believed the tariff necessary to accelerate the development of their cherished industry. They considered him a tough partisan and faithful representative of his state.[6] They did not believe it to be politically immoral for a Congressman to legislate on the tariff even though his own personal fortune was involved—nor would they feel so today. Only once did Stevens oppose a raise in the duty on any article, and this a tariff on the importation of rice. He spotted it at once as a discriminatory measure aimed at the California Chinese, and exposed it as such in an acid speech.[7]

Although Republican businessmen considered Stevens sound on the tariff, they came to distrust him on other issues as an unpredictable economic heretic. This was especially true in his role as chief legislative spokesman on the proper way to finance the war. His fight with the banking interests needs retelling, if only briefly, for the facts belie the widespread notion that Stevens acted chiefly to serve the financial interests of the businessmen of his party.

Perhaps because he had been on the brink of financial ruin twice and knew what it meant to have to beg for credit, Stevens disliked bankers. When his ironworks were destroyed in a Confederate raid in 1863, his fortune was wiped out again, and he had to go deeply in debt to rebuild them. So he carried over into the complicated problems of war finance the debtor's point of view. This, plus his consistent bent toward radicalism, so molded his ideas on war inflation that at times he seemed to stand outside his party altogether.

Lincoln, on coming to power, had inherited an empty treasury and a $100,000,000 debt, contracted during the regime of his bungling predecessor. The government's financing system was primitive; less than twenty-five per cent of federal revenue came from taxation; most of the remainder came from the sale of public lands and hand-to-mouth borrowing. There was no national banking system and no national currency. The public did its business with gold and silver coin, a variety of treasury notes, and an appalling conglomeration of notes issued by 1,600 individual banks. The country's credit system was unstable and capricious, subject to the slightest fluctuation in the nation's business.

The coming of the war brought a financial crisis. The Secretary of the Treasury, like all of Lincoln's cabinet appointments, had been selected because of his political status. The crisis called for imagination and audacity, qualities for which the pedantic and self-righteous Chase was not noted, and he had no experience whatever in finance. Not surprisingly, his first recommendations were timid. Instead of asking for a stiff tax program, he recommended that the regular taxes be used to pay the ordinary expenses of the government and that war expenditures be met by new loans.

Most Northerners cheerfully counted on victory in six months; the blackest pessimist could not have predicted that war would last four years, costing the unheard-of sums of two to three million dollars a day, and totaling in the end four billion altogether. In the first weeks of newly kindled patriotism the bankers rushed to take up the first war loan—$250,000,000—and Chase's program seemed successful. But the *Trent* crisis laid bare its fragile structure. When an impetuous American captain boarded the British steamer and carried off Confederates James Mason and John Slidell, the British Government sent a sharp note which seemed a thinly veiled threat of war. The news caused a panic on the New York stock market. Banks were besieged with runs on their gold supply, and within a fortnight suspended specie payments.

The country was left to do business with its fantastically mixed paper money, which neither the issuing banks nor the federal treasury would redeem in coin. The government had to take the final installment—$50,000,000—of the first war loan in currency, at a loss to itself of $5,000,000, and soon found itself unable to negotiate a loan at any satisfactory price.

At this time Thaddeus Stevens, chairman of the committee that bore the triple burden of appropriations, tariff, and taxes, came forth with an audacious program for ending the crisis and financing the war. He had been hard at work with his committee drafting a program based on taxation plus a national currency secured by government bonds. Justin Morrill of Vermont was made responsible for the war tax program; E. G. Spaulding of New York for the currency bill, and Stevens for the task of pushing the committee bills through the House.[8]

Stevens' currency bill, later to be blamed for ninety per cent of the economic ills accompanying the war, deserves a brief examination. Its author was Spaulding, a Buffalo banker and former state treasurer of New York. Stevens, after some initial misgivings, worked closely with him, and succeeded in forcing the bill through the Committee of Ways and Means, despite the fact that half the members were violently opposed. The bill provided for an issue of $100,000,000 in legal tender United States notes—the nation's first greenbacks. Unlike previous issues of treasury notes, these were to bear no interest, and could not be redeemed in coin; but they were to be interchangeable for six per cent twenty-year bonds, of which the Secretary of the Treasury was authorized to issue $500,000,000. What this bill meant was that the government was for the first time creating a genuine national currency, and moreover, one not immediately redeemable in gold.

Stevens felt strongly that "if a currency not immediately redeemable in coin must be used by the Government it had better issue its own notes; it would be more secure than the State banks, and would save the Government a large amount of interest." It is clear that he expected a return to "hard money" within twenty years and fully expected that the principal of the twenty-year bonds would be redeemed in gold, but this was not stipulated in the bill. But he hoped to demonetize gold completely for the war period, and he provided that the interest on these bonds be paid in paper money.[9]

Stevens' faith in the triumph of the Union was as solid as his Pennsylvania mountains, and had it been shared by the whole North the greenback problem would never have become so perplexing. He believed that it was possible to eliminate gold at least temporarily as a medium of exchange in the nation's domestic economy, and that the true basis of the government's credit lay in the productive capacity of its people plus the tax power. He made no pretense to being an economist, but unlike his colleagues he did make some effort to study the measures Great Britain had used in financing the Napoleonic Wars—when specie payments had been suspended and the nation used Bank of England notes for currency—and drew many of his arguments from the speeches of the British anti-bullionists in that period.

During the war and for years afterward Stevens was bitterly blamed for the wartime inflation that followed the greenback issues. But in recent years, with the experience of two world wars behind us, some economists have come to believe that a moderate amount of inflation during war is not a pernicious evil in itself but an acceptable and probably necessary way of helping to pay for it, constituting as it does an alternative and supplement to taxation. We have had some inflation in every war, and that in the Civil War was no more serious, relatively, than in that of either the First or Second World War.[10]

Stevens and his colleagues did have an alternative proposal, one strongly urged by the New York bankers. This would have been a program of selling long-time government bonds at their market value rather than par, plus heavy taxation. The taxation came, but slowly. In the beginning the Republican Party, unsure of its power and conscious of its minority status, was afraid to impose a heavy tax burden. Stevens wanted no more than Chase to test by this means the uncertain patriotism of the North. [The first income tax in the nation's history saw a levy of 3 per cent on incomes from $600 to $10,000, and 5 per cent on incomes in excess of $10,000—by modern standards no tax at all, though unprecedented for its day. But the excise taxes were made more and more severe so that in the last years of the war 25 per cent of the total cost of the war came from taxes. This was a good record, particularly in view of the limited experience of the time in financing a really big war.[11]]

[margin note: income & excise taxes]

The struggle between Stevens and the bankers over the war loans crystallized in the matter of interest payments. The bankers wanted to buy the bonds at their market value, with interest paid in gold. Stevens, who believed the cost to the government would be ruinous, wanted to sell the government bonds at par, and make the interest payable in currency.[12] The Senate finance committee was convinced, however, that the bankers simply would not buy the loans at par with this condition and sent Stevens' bill back to the House with amendments providing that the interest on the government loan of $500,000,-000 be paid in gold.

Stevens, blaming the amendments upon the insistent lobbying of the "bankers and brokers," was filled with anguish. Gold was now reintroduced into the monetary system with the result, as he saw it, that there were now "two classes of money—one for the banks and brokers, and another for the people." He had, he said, a "melancholy foreboding" that they were "about to consummate a cunningly devised scheme which will carry great injury and great loss to all classes of people throughout the Union, except one."[13] Already in January, 1862, a hundred dollars in paper money was worth ninety-seven on the gold exchange. So the soldier was being paid in depreciated currency, and the banker who loaned to the government was being paid in coin. But the Senate remained inflexible.

Since the government now had to secure gold to pay the interest on its loans, Stevens insisted that all import duties be payable in specie. This had the ultimate effect of raising the tariff by about 30 per cent, an outcome he looked upon with satisfaction. Once he had wrung this concession he acquiesced in the hated Senate amendments. He never ceased belaboring the Senate for mangling his bill, and came to look upon the amendments as the chief cause for all the financial problems that followed.

The fact is that had Stevens had his way, and had the interest on the government loans been paid in currency rather than gold, the bankers almost certainly would have refused to buy the bonds at par. There really was no way the government could prevent the bankers from acting like bankers. It was a professional obligation, as well as in their interest, to provide themselves with a hedge against the certain inflation that would follow the issuing of the greenbacks and the economic dislocations normal to a war period. The bankers had the power to safeguard themselves against inflation; the salaried people, including all the soldiers, did not. This Stevens furiously resented; he believed in equality of sacrifice for the war effort.

Characteristically, he fought the soldiers' draft provision that exempted anyone who could pay $300 to the Treasury for a substitute, calling it "a rich man's bill, made for him only who can raise his $300, and against him who cannot raise that sum." [14] He failed to eliminate the $300 exemption provision (which proved to be one of the most unpopular of all the war measures), and he failed, too, in all his efforts to prevent the bankers from benefiting from the war at the expense of the rest of the population. Yet he remained blind to the fact that his tariff on iron resulted in the same kind of preferential discrimination he tried to block in the fiscal field.

After Stevens was defeated in his efforts to have gold completely demonetized, there was a fever of speculation in gold on the New York Stock Exchange. Soon there were three other stock markets, including one lively place called "The Gold Room," where the "copperhead bulls" chanted *Dixie* when war news was being reported, and the "bears" competed with *John Brown's Body*. The volume of transactions in gold became enormous, as many physicians, lawyers, clergymen, and small merchants—as well as bankers and big businessmen—now became speculators. It was theoretically possible for a group of speculators to corner the gold market temporarily, and this was attempted frequently when importers needed gold to pay tariff duties and the government was about to pay the semi-annual interest on its loans. The rise in the price of gold was temporary, but infuriating and demoralizing to government officials and manufacturers alike. Stevens pointed out angrily that gold-holders could clear thirty per cent on their capital by a single operation.

Public indignation soon reverberated through the halls of Congress. Even Lincoln was incensed. Frank Carpenter, the portrait painter, heard him say to Andrew Curtin: "What do you think of those fellows in Wall Street, who are gambling in gold at such a time as this?"

"They are a set of sharks," Curtin replied.

"For my part," Lincoln went on, hitting the table with his fist, "I wish every one of them had his *devilish* head shot off!" [15]

Stevens was so angry at the speculation in gold that as early as December, 1862, he introduced a bill providing for a return to his original plan of making the interest on government loans payable in greenbacks. "The bullion mongers would lose; the merchants and the Government would gain," he insisted. "I object to the payment of specie for interest as it sets the Government and the merchant in competition and puts them both in the power of bankers and brokers. Besides it is a shame to use one currency for the Government and another for the people." [16] The bill raised a furor in financial circles; Stevens was accused of advocating repudiation, and it was voted down. Throughout the war he made repeated but futile efforts to revive the issue.

Actually, the speculation in gold had little effect on the total problem of war financing, but it was a serious political liability for the government nonetheless. As the war went on, bringing monetary inflation along with full employment and increasing scarcities in commodities important to the standard of living, prices began to rise. The Treasury was empty sooner than had been expected. Two new legal-tender bills were passed, raising the total authorized issue of greenbacks to $450,000,000. There was no further issue after March 3, 1863. By then an improved revenue system had been worked out, based on heavier taxation and a more efficient negotiation of loans. In the meantime, however, the price of everything, including gold, had rocketed.

Stevens was disturbed by the inflation and sensitive to the general criticism that it had resulted from issuing the greenbacks. For a while he blamed the inflation on the expansion of currency in the state banks, and proposed—unsuccessfully—a tax of fifty per cent of all their circulation beyond one-half of their capital. Actually the expansion in the state banks was moderate and seems to have contributed little to the problem. [17]

As the war wore on, speculation on the gold market became an increasing political scandal. Although actually the rise in the price of gold was not out of line with the rise in other key commodities and for the most part simply reflected the general inflation, it seemed to many men in the government that the speculators were out to swindle the Treasury. Few men were dispassionate enough to see that the speculators acted more as a reflection of the instability of government credit rather than as its manipulators.

By March, 1864, gold was selling at $1.80—that is, one dollar in gold could be exchanged for $1.80 in greenbacks—and Stevens correctly predicted that it would eventually go over $2.00. In discussing this he said ironically: "Iron is rising in price, brass is rising in price, lead is rising in price, just as much as gold is rising in price. My friends about me say copper, too. Well, that is owing more to the amount used in making copperheads than anything else." [18]

Secretary Chase finally proposed the sale of government gold in an effort to force down the market price. Stevens was quick to support him. When the bill passed the price of gold fell sharply, but only to rise again higher than before. Chase was now extremely angry. "The price of gold must and shall come down," he wrote to Horace Greeley on June 16, 1864, "or I'll quit and let somebody else try." [19] And he worked out with Stevens what became the famous Gold Bill, whereby the government, having failed to control the gold market, tried to abolish it altogether.

This bill prohibited under heavy penalties all contracts for the sale of gold for future delivery and forbade brokers to sell gold outside their offices. During the several days of debate the price of gold rose from 190 to 197½. Once the bill passed there were no organized gold markets and no regular quotations. By June 27 there was a difference of nineteen points between the lowest and the highest selling rates. Businessmen brought violent pressure to bear in Washington for repeal. Chase wrote to Stevens urging higher taxes: ". . . There is no good reason, in general, except over-supply for any considerable difference in purchasing power between a United States five dollar coin and a United States five dollar note. . . . The injurious influences of over-supply have now, however, been aided by fear of ill-success in military operations, and by other alarms excited by the unscrupulous acts of enemies and traitors. . . . Every dollar now collected by tax will, in my judgment, save three dollars of debt." [20]

At this point Chase resigned as Secretary of the Treasury. His leaving office had nothing to do with the Gold Bill; nevertheless, one effect was to depreciate the currency still more. When it became obvious to everyone in Congress that the bill had not abolished gold speculation but had actually advanced the price, it was repealed on July 1, 1864, having been on the statute books only twelve days. Ten days later Confederate General Jubal Early carried a raid into Maryland to within ten miles of Washington. The next day gold touched 285, the highest value of the war. One hundred dollars in greenbacks could now be purchased with only $35.09 in gold.

Bankers who had invested early in government bonds were now reaping fat profits. Stevens protested in the House: "There is no reason why a man who holds $20,000 in bonds issued in 1858 should be paid in gold, or its equivalent, at the rate of two hundred per cent. . . . It is a perversion of the law. It is injustice to the people. It is a favor to a few moneyed men. I do not begrudge the money to the men who hold these bonds, but it is not their right." [21]

The late summer and fall of 1864 saw substantial victories for the Union armies, which greatly strengthened the government's credit, and sent the price of gold down again. But Stevens never lost his conviction that the gold speculators were somehow responsible for the continuing general inflation. "I have no knowledge which would justify me in theorizing in financial matters," he admitted frankly, "and I have not much faith in theories against facts." But it became almost an obsession with him that "the gold gamblers have deluded us . . . we have not sense enough to confound them." [22]

In December, 1864, Stevens introduced a bill trying to equalize the value of greenbacks and gold by making it a criminal offense for anyone to exchange paper dollars for anything but an equal number of dollars in gold. But he found no support in his own party. His friend, James G. Blaine, attacked the bill as "absurd and monstrous." "You cannot," he insisted, "make a gold dollar worth less than it is, or a paper dollar worth more than it is, by Congressional declaration." And he added that it was like trying to make the mercury in a thermometer regulate the weather.[23] Charles Francis Adams Jr. wrote contemptuously to his father: ". . . your old friend, Thad. Stevens, as soon as he has fixed our currency, is going to regulate by law the rising of the sun, so that the days shall be of equal length all the year round." [24]

Rumor had it that the mere announcement of the bill sent the price of gold up 12 per cent, and it was decisively beaten. Stevens was still leader of the House, but not on matters of finance. When he introduced a resolution asking for power to investigate conspiracies among the speculators, he was forced to withdraw it at once. In conceding defeat he said ruefully: "I would not willingly again throw my excellent friend from Maine [Blaine] into convulsions, or the House into epileptic fits." [25]

It was unfortunate that Stevens' fixation on the "traffickers in gold" cost him the respect of so many Republicans. For some of his criticisms of the government's financial policy were sounder than those of his colleagues. The speculation in gold was a scandalous political liability for the government which was entirely avoided in World War II. Stevens' continued insistence on the need for a national currency brought a desperately needed reform in 1863. But he failed to get the greenbacks accepted for this purpose. So great was Congressional suspicion of federal money that the National Banking Act provided only that a national currency be issued through the state banks belonging to a national banking system. The degree of federal control was mild, and Stevens was greatly disappointed in the act's provisions.[26] No serious attempt was made to eliminate any other of the multitudinous banking evils, though Stevens had repeatedly urged federal regulatory controls. "When, a few years hence, the people shall have been brought to general bankruptcy by their [the bankers'] unregulated enterprise," he said, "I shall have the satisfaction to know that I attempted to prevent it." [27]

After the war, when the greenback issue became a political football, the gulf between Stevens and his party on this matter became a chasm. If we step ahead in our narrative long enough to finish the account of Stevens' relations to the greenback controversy, we will see that though he was old and ill, and spent most of his energy on Reconstruction, he never wholly abandoned the problem.

With the end of the fighting, the whole monetary activity of the government was expected to go into reverse. Specie payments were to be resumed, and the $450,000,000 worth of greenbacks taken out of circulation. Hugh McCulloch, the Secretary of the Treasury, was an uncompromising "hard money" man. He urged that all the obligations of the government on $2,800,000,000 worth of government bonds be paid immediately in gold, and that the greenbacks be withdrawn from circulation as soon as possible.

A good portion of the bonds had been purchased for 40 cents on the dollar. Greenbacks had by no means appreciated to par, and the men who held the bonds and greenbacks formed a small but highly influential group controlling the bulk of the nation's newspapers—which they did not hesitate to use. Immediate contraction of the currency and resumption of payments in gold would mean for these creditors profits that would make many of them millionaires overnight.

Stevens saw no justice now in making haste, when haste meant milking the public treasury. The North was prosperous; business and agriculture were flourishing, and he saw no reason why, with the end of government borrowing, the currency would not appreciate to par and inflation taper off. There had been, in fact, a precipitous decline in prices after January 1865. By March gold had fallen to 150. Stevens, along with Radicals Benjamin F. Butler and Oliver P. Morton, preferred to defer any large-scale currency contraction, which would certainly have had a further and probably disastrous deflationary impact. [Eventually he urged the issuance of even more greenbacks, to be used—dollar for dollar instead of gold—to pay the nation's bondholders.[28] No other financial gesture of his ever raised such a storm in his own party. The *New York Tribune* called the proposal "swindling so barefaced that no blackleg in New York or Washington could resort to it without being cut by his fellow blacklegs as a low, contemptible villain." For a while it seemed that Stevens' only friends on this issue were Democrats. At one point he even threatened to vote Democratic if the bondholders were paid in coin.[29] Nevertheless his general theory of delay and more delay, before contracting the currency and resuming specie payments, was accepted by his party as being good politics, though few could see that it was good economics as well. Specie payments were not resumed for thirteen years after the war's end.[30]

[Thaddeus Stevens was always an enthusiastic promoter of railroads.] His fervor has been explained by unfriendly historians as stemming from greed for profit from his ironworks—which did indeed manufacture iron rails—just as his eagerness for property confiscation has been explained as revenge for the fact that Confederate raiders burned his ironworks in 1863. Both explanations are too simple.

The Caledonia ironworks were destroyed by Jubal Early, who led a cavalry unit in advance of Lee's army in the campaign that ended in the battle of Gettysburg. The Confederates carried off Stevens' horses, mules, grain, and bar iron, and the contents of the local company store, and then burned the furnace, sawmill, two forges, rolling mill, office, and storeroom. Early said to the foreman he was sorry Stevens was not on hand to be captured too. When the foreman asked if he would take Stevens to Libby Prison, Early spat out the reply: "No, sir, I would hang him on the spot and divide his bones and send them to the several States as curiosities."[31]

Stevens wrote to his law partner, Simon Stevens, on July 6, 1863:

I suppose my loss to be about $75,000. But as they were now (for the first time) in profitable operation, I suppose the loss might well be called $15,000 more.

The Government does not indemnify for such losses.

But all this gives me no concern, although it was just about the savings of my life, not the earnings. The rest has been lavished in the payment of other people's debts. As to my personal wants nature will soon take care of them.

We must all expect to suffer by this wicked war. I have not felt a moment's trouble for my share of it. If, finally, the government shall be re-established over our whole territory, and not a vestige of Slavery left, I shall deem it a cheap purchase.

On July 11 he wrote in another letter to Simon Stevens: "They could not have done the job much cleaner. It is rather worse than I expected." [32]

Simon Stevens launched a fund-raising drive to remunerate the old Congressman for his losses. Later, in discussing this with a reporter, Thaddeus Stevens said: "The third time I failed was when the rebels burned these works. My friends in Lancaster and elsewhere raised about $100,000, which they tendered to me, but I declined it, and it went to the poor fund, but I did not give it. I managed to get through my trouble, and have never taken advantage of a bankruptcy law yet." [33]

The *New York World* accused Stevens of pressing for confiscation of Southern estates so that he would be reimbursed by the government for his own losses. The truth of the matter is that Stevens was urging confiscation two years before his ironworks were burned. Moreover, he never put in a claim for reimbursement and specifically instructed the federal agent who was investigating the damage to property in Pennsylvania to ignore all of his properties in and about Caledonia "as no remuneration is claimed for it." He rebuilt the ironworks on borrowed money. [34]

The same fierce pride that had in the past kept Stevens from asking or accepting even legitimate favors continued to bind him. He wanted to be beholden to no man. Nevertheless, the destruction of his property infuriated him, deepened his hatred of the South, and no doubt served to accelerate his zeal for railroad building, since selling rails was his best hope of getting out of debt.

Railroads were "great civilizers," Stevens said,[35] and their cost was inconsequential when weighed against the agricultural, mineral, and timber resources open to the people wherever the rails went down. He favored federal aid to all railroads that could not be built without it, and his particular interest lay with the first railroad to bridge the continent, the Union Pacific.

The first Pacific Railroad bill passed in 1862. Stevens had urged it as a solution to the blockade of the Mississippi, as an aid to the thousands of unemployed refugee laborers from the South, and as a binding chain to keep the West from breaking off into a separate empire.

It should be finished before the war's end, he said, when the "arrogant, insolent dictation" of the returned Southern states might block construction by insistence on a Southern route.[36]

The bill provided for a grant of eleven million acres to the Union Pacific and Central Pacific, and $50,000,000 in a federal loan. Its control measures were tight enough to satisfy even the suspicious Washburne brothers, Elihu and Cadwallader, watchdogs of the Treasury, who were anti-monopoly and had sensitive noses for fraud.[37] But most businessmen looked upon the Pacific Railroad as a certain invitation to bankruptcy, and little was done until 1864. Then a second bill was introduced in Congress almost doubling the land grants to the Union Pacific and granting another federal loan of $27,000,000. Cadwallader Washburne raged against the bill as surrendering "nearly all the rights reserved to the people," and he later accused the government of giving away land almost twice the size of the British Isles and nearly equal to the acreage of France. Worse still, he said, the government had relinquished its first-mortgage rights by permitting the company to borrow an amount equal to the government loan by selling first-mortgage bonds, a provision, he insisted, that reduced the value of the government bonds to zero.[38]

Thaddeus Stevens, who became chairman of the Committee on the Pacific Railroad December 16, 1863, defended the bill. He showed an intimate knowledge of the geography of the proposed route, and evidence of having read Lewis and Clarke and many subsequent accounts. He upheld the land grants by pointing out that without the railroad the land would remain worthless; with it, the products raised upon the land would ultimately be worth many times the value of the land itself. "I think, sir," he said, "that this is one of the greatest enterprises of the age." The House laughed when an enemy of the bill asked him later if he had taken care that the Union Pacific be built only of American iron, but he was unperturbed. "It says so in the bill. I go for nothing but American iron, of course." [39]

Lincoln also favored the bill. "Ames, take hold of this;" he said to the millionaire Congressman from Massachusetts who was helping to finance the Union Pacific, "and if the subsidies provided are not enough to build the road, ask double and you shall have it. That road must be built, and you are the only man to do it. . . . you will become the remembered man of your generation." [40]

The Senate returned the bill with extraordinary favors to the company. As Cadwallader Washburne later described it, "nothing that the ingenuity of man could invent for their benefit was withheld." But the bill was "gagged through; the opponents of the measure were not permitted to have it printed and postponed, so that they could see what it was. I struggled in vain for the printing of the report and for its delay until the members of the House could have an opportunity of reading it; but the gentleman from Pennsylvania [Mr. Stevens] demanded the previous question. . . . even the yeas and nays were refused."

Washburne accused the vice-president of the Union Pacific Company of spending almost half a million dollars in Washington to secure passage of the act of 1864, and caused a sensation by intimating that many members of Congress had secretly bought stock in the company on unusually favorable terms.[41] There was no Congressional investigation, however, until five years after Stevens' death, when the Credit Mobilier scandal broke in 1873. In the subsequent hearings Congressman John B. Alley testified that Thomas C. Durant, vice-president of the Union Pacific Company, told him he had paid Thaddeus Stevens "$80,000 in a roundabout way for getting bills through Congress." Alley went on to insist that he had always believed the charge to be false. "Mr. Stevens' character and position forbid its belief," he said, and he implied that Durant was a scoundrel who had personally embezzled most of the $400,000 lobbying fund turned over to him by the Union Pacific executive board.[42]

Oliver Ames, who had been president of the Union Pacific at the time, testified that the expense account showed no record of any payment to Thaddeus Stevens, and Thomas C. Durant repudiated the whole story under oath.[43] Stevens' name seemed to be completely cleared when Oliver J. Dickey, the executor of his estate, testified that the Caledonia Iron Furnace had not been sold to anyone, and that Stevens' estate at his death included no Union Pacific bonds.[44] But Dickey's account, though earnest and detailed, did not quite clear the record.

Six weeks before his death Stevens did own Union Pacific Railroad stock, and a lot of it. Among his private papers preserved in the Library of Congress is the following letter:

Washington D.C.
June 24, 1868

Sir: In reply to your favor of the 19th Inst.—I will state that in the event Congress shall provide for the Extension of the road of the Union Pacific R Way Co. to the Pacific—and shall grant the necessary *aid* in land and bonds, therefore, I will give you Government *or first mortgage bonds* of the said Company for the twenty nine (29000) thousand dollars of full paid stocks held by you in said Rway Co. which is an acceptance of your proposition.

Very respectfully
John D. Perry

How damaging is this letter in the light of what is known about Stevens' personal financial history? He had lost $90,000 in the burning of his ironworks in 1863, and tried for a time to sell them.[45] He had rebuilt them on borrowed money, and had been hard-pressed for credit in 1866. Yet by 1868 he owned $29,000 worth of full-paid Union Pacific Railroad stock which never seems to have been accounted for in the settling of his estate.

There are at least three possible explanations for disappearance of this stock. The first, and most likely, is that he sold it before his death so that the several personal bequests listed in his will might be easily fulfilled. It is also possible that the stock was taken by his partner, Simon Stevens, who bought and sold stock of all kinds. As early as February 5, 1864, he had written to Thaddeus Stevens on the stationery of the Union Pacific Company requesting "to have the *full paid certificates* held by you to have them transferred to me on the books of the Company. Will you let me have them for that purpose . . ." [46]

A third and least likely explanation might be that Stevens had become involved with Credit Mobilier. This was a holding company organized by Oakes Ames, a multimillionaire Representative from Massachusetts, who meshed its dealings with the Union Pacific Company in such fashion as to concentrate the profits of the railroad in the hands of a few leading stockholders. Using the credit obtained by the federal loan and land grants, these men mortgaged the road for $27,000,000 and the land grants for $10,000,000. Then by contracting with themselves at three times the normal cost of the work, they swallowed up the proceeds of these mortgages, leaving the Union Pacific Company broke.

To ward off a Congressional investigation expected in December 1866, Oakes Ames was given 343 shares of Credit Mobilier to distribute in Washington, "where," he wrote in a private letter to H. S. McComb, "they will do most good to us." [47] This stock he sold at par, though it was already worth two or three times par value. To those who could not pay he promised to hold the stock with the understanding that they could pay for it out of the first dividends. Three dividends were issued in 1868 before Stevens' death. They were so fat several red-faced Congressmen hastily returned the stock.[48] Others were not so circumspect.

It is hard to believe that Stevens did not know about Congressman Oakes Ames' Credit Mobilier dealings, for he had a reputation for smelling out bribery, though he was never one to press charges against his colleagues. Once, when a member of his railway committee was thought to have accepted a $10,000 bribe for going against Stevens on a railroad bill, Stevens exploded: "Mr. Speaker—While this House has slept, the enemy has sown tares among our wheat. The gigantic corporations of this country, who have neither bodies to be kicked nor souls to be damned, have, alone stolen away from the majority of my committee the member from Connecticut. The enemy are now in a majority of one. I move to increase the number of that committee to twelve." James M. Scovel, who retold the story, said that the motion was granted, and the "member from Connecticut," fearful of Stevens' wrath, dared not show his face in the House for a week thereafter.[49]

The lengthy Credit Mobilier investigations showed that at least fifteen Congressmen had been involved,[50] but Thaddeus Stevens' name never appeared on anyone's list. The fact that he possessed Union Pacific stock in 1868 does not by itself prove anything; Senator Grimes, whose reputation remained spotless, held Union Pacific stock from the beginning. There is, however, a good yardstick for measuring Stevens' integrity regarding railroad legislation—his voting record. An examination of his votes from 1862 to 1869 shows that he acted as a kind of buffer, on the one hand fighting the rapacity of the railroad men and on the other loosening the reins that several suspicious Congressmen were using to curb the railroad men more than he thought advisable.

In 1866 he insisted on amendments to the Union Pacific bill specifically providing that the railroad did not get mineral lands.[51] He did not want to preserve the Union Pacific as a monopoly, but feverishly promoted the Northern Pacific and Southern [or Kansas] Pacific as well.

The critical vote as far as Credit Mobilier was concerned came on the issue of whether or not the government should fix the Union Pacific rates. Cadwallader Washburne, who was afraid that the gigantic corporation would bleed the people along the route, introduced a resolution calling for government control. To kill this resolution Oakes Ames handed out railroad stock with a lavish hand. It is a matter of record that every Congressman known to hold Credit Mobilier stock voted against it. Thaddeus Stevens voted in its favor. In the final tally in the House, the resolution failed by seven votes.[52] The Ames gamble had paid off.

Stevens died just before Credit Mobilier issued its fourth fabulous dividend. There is no way of knowing what he would have done about the gigantic swindle had he lived. But he was clearly on record as voting against Credit Mobilier, and in favor of government control of railroad rates, just as he favored government regulation of the nation's banks. This would be heresy in the Republican Party for many years.

Credit Mobilier did not damage Stevens' reputation. But it did destroy the popular faith in the honesty and integrity of many other Republican leaders. These men were ruined by what Godkin of the *Nation* had once warned against—"that most dangerous of all kinds of corruption, the corruption of men who profess to be serving great moral ideas." [53]

CHAPTER FIFTEEN

The Jacobins

I have no sympathy with that spirit of Jacobin ferocity displayed by some of the leaders of the Administration, who, in their thirst for blood and confiscation, are already rivaling the worst days of the French Revolution.

> Representative Joseph K. Edgerton, in the House of Representatives, January 28, 1864

THE EPITHET *Jacobin* was repeatedly hurled at the Radical Republicans by their political enemies, and Thaddeus Stevens was the favorite target. It was a smear word, smelling of the guillotine. Even Lincoln was called Robespierre by irresponsible copperhead journalists and Confederate editors, but most newspapers correctly styled the President a Conservative Republican, and never placed him in the Radical camp. The word *conservative*, however, confused an already complicated semantic problem. Lincoln was a conservative leader when matched against Thaddeus Stevens, but when compared with War Democrat Horatio Seymour, copperhead Clement Vallandigham, or Confederate Jefferson Davis, he could more properly be described as a radical or revolutionary leader in the tradition of Washington and Jefferson.

The word *radical* did not yet have the odor of conspiracy and tyranny it would acquire during the Bolshevik Revolution. The Radi-

cal Republicans were, in fact, proud of their label, and counted themselves kin, at least on civil-rights issues, to the Liberals in England,
led by Richard Cobden, John Bright, and John Stuart Mill. But the
word *Jacobin* was something evil—as *radical* has become in our own
time—and the Radical Republicans were constantly defending themselves against it.

The distinction between the conservative and radical wings of
the party was real and vital. It had something to do with timing and
something to do with compassion. It had a great deal to do with the
difference between devotion to principle and surrender to principle.
The Radical Republicans had certain things in common with the
Jacobins, but the guillotine was not one of them. Up to a certain point
Thaddeus Stevens could properly be compared with Robespierre, for
both were doctrinaire idealists intent on making a paradise of human
brotherhood. There was some similarity too in their theories of confiscation.

"The Republican Party," Edwin L. Godkin would write, "is often
called, jokingly or contemptuously, 'the party of great moral ideas,'
and it *is* essentially a party of ideas, while the Democratic party is
essentially now, whatever it may once have been, a party of habits,
prejudices, and traditions." [1] Where the Democrats were callous,
complacent, self-interested, or merely inept, the Radical Republicans
had a burning thirst. Many, like Thaddeus Stevens, were agitators,
delighting in the prickly and unpleasant truth, careless of personal
popularity, reckless with their own reputations and capacity for vote-
getting, and compulsively intent on a political and social ideal. As
Richard Hofstadter has pointed out, they thoroughly understood "the
revolutionary dynamics of the war." [2] But Stevens and his colleagues,
unlike the Jacobins, never came to have more faith in killing than in
conversion.

Most Radical Republicans championed not only antislavery but a
whole galaxy of causes. With Horace Greeley it was prohibition,
women's rights, the abolition of sweatshops, free homesteads, and
Brook Farm socialism. Wendell Phillips advocated "the overthrow of
the whole profit-making system, the extinction of monopolies, the
abolition of privileged classes, universal education . . . obliteration
of poverty . . . a ten-hour day for factory work and eight hours
hereafter," and equal pay for equal work done by women. [3] Many
Radicals advocated the ten-hour day, and almost all were prohibition-
ists. Vice-President Hamlin abolished the sale of liquor in the Senate
restaurant, and Charles Sumner forbade the use of liquor in his committee room. (The Conservative Lincoln also left liquor alone. "It is

unpleasant to me and always makes me feel flabby and undone," he confessed to a friend.) [4]

Yet even among the Radicals there was nonconformity and dissent. Senator Zachariah Chandler was notorious for his profanity and liquor consumption, the *New York World* saying his "thirst of blood intermits with his thirst of Bourbon." [5] Stevens, although a teetotaler, was against temperance legislation. Where Charles Sumner looked pained at obscene language, Ben Wade told the most ribald jokes in the Senate, and Stevens time and again made witticisms that had to be expunged from the *Congressional Globe*. Once, when reproached for his "foul" language, Stevens convulsed the House by replying: "That gentleman has complained that my language was foul, and talked about its being learned in Billingsgate, and Cripplegate and Newgate. Sir, with all the gates that the gentleman has gone through and that he refers to, there is one gate which the gentleman will enter which I shall try to avoid." [6]

In personal character the Radicals were as unlike as any other group of men. Chase and Sumner were pompous; Stevens, Wade, and Chandler were forthright and unpretentious. Stanton, on the other hand, was conspiratorial and intriguing. Chase was so pious he frequently refused the communion cup in church because he felt unworthy, but Stevens was contemptuous of all organized religion. The *New York World* said Stevens had "all the intolerance of the Radicals without their hypocritical cant." [7]

Unlike other Radicals, Stevens was an inveterate gambler. Almost every night he visited one of the many casinos lining Pennsylvania Avenue east of the Capitol. Since gambling had not yet become a certain badge of corruption and sin in Washington, he never felt it necessary to defend his presence there. Pendleton's, the biggest faro house in the city, had been patronized in the 1850's by Congressmen, editors, and cabinet members, and when the owner died, President Buchanan himself had attended the funeral, and several Democratic Congressmen had acted as pallbearers. [8]

Stevens was known as a small-scale bettor, seldom winning or losing more than fifty dollars, though one acquaintance reported seeing him win $1,400 on a twenty-dollar gold piece. He clearly preferred male to female company, and found in the gambling houses the conviviality he needed without the threat of intimacy he seems to have feared, and which he might have encountered had he let himself be drawn into fashionable partygoing. The impersonal excitement of the faro table was exactly to his taste. He was hardly a compulsive gambler, yet it is clear that the casinos had for him a steady fascination. [9]

The "American Jacobins" were constantly derided for their Puritanism. Democrat Samuel Cox of Ohio attacked them as "selfish, pharisaical, egotistic, and intolerant," and declared that their Puritan ambition "to make government a moral reform association," was the special curse of the nation. Like many other War Democrats, he blamed the Radical Republicans for causing the war. "What is known as Abolition is, in the moral sense, the cause of the strife," he said.[10] Down in the Confederacy Howell Cobb acidly observed in 1863: "Only two things stand in the way of an amicable settlement of the whole difficulty: the Landing of the Pilgrims and Original Sin."

There was, in fact, a notable similarity between the language of the War Democrats in blistering the Radicals, and that of the Confederates in attacking the Yankees. The *Richmond Examiner* called the Union war effort "plunder perpetrated under the guise of canting humanity," and insisted that "Universal liberty and equality, universal elections, absolute majorities, eternal demagogism and free competition, have leveled, degraded, demoralized and debased Northern society." [11]

In all Radical Republican thinking there was a strong religious component. Secretary Stanton wrote to an old friend, Reverend Heman Dyer, on May 18, 1862: "I was never taken for a fool, but there could be no greater madness than for a man to encounter what I do for anything else than motives that overleap time and look forward to eternity. I believe that God Almighty founded this government, and for my acts in the effort to maintain it, I expect to stand before Him in judgment." [12] Even the hardheaded Conservative Republican editor Godkin occasionally echoed the current millennialism: "It is no slight task to convince a whole nation of great moral principles, but it is a labor that promises, in the long run, a certain reward. . . . We have faith in the indefinite progress of the human race." Stevens, according to one colleague, "denied the power of time to sanctify injustice . . . he believed that the true end of government was to right all the wrongs men suffer." [13] And interwoven with this revolutionary philosophy was his Calvinist conviction that all who did not accept it must be cast out of the city of the saints.

What detracted from the strength of the moral position of many Radical Republicans was their certainty of having a monopoly on righteousness. Garrison defined the true radical as "the sworn enemy of every known evil or wrong . . . the uncompromising enemy of the sin." In the last issue of his *Liberator* he wrote: "Better to be in a minority of one with God—branded as madman, incendiary, fanatic . . . mobbed by the populace, in defence of the *Right*, than like

Herod, hearing the shouts of the multitude, crying, 'It is the voice of a god and not of man!' " [14]

Thoreau had said it neatly in his *Civil Disobedience* in 1849: "Moreover, any man more right than his neighbors constitutes a majority of one already." But the story that best illustrates the narrow bridge between conviction and arrogance in the Radical Republicans is one George W. Curtis told about Charles Sumner. "I was one day talking with him upon some public question, and as our conversation warmed, I said to him, 'Yes, but you forget the other side!' He brought his clenched fist down upon the table till it rang again, and his voice shook the room as he thundered in reply, 'There is no other side!' " [15] Sumner would have been only mystified had Lincoln said to him, as he did to another Radical, "Mr. Moorhead, haven't you lived long enough to know that two men may honestly differ about a question and both be right?" [16] Stevens, more flexible and less doctrinaire than Sumner, nevertheless shared his certainty that there was only a single road to justice.

Nothing kindled so much fury against the Radical Republicans as the notion that they favored amalgamation of the white and black races. There was a great outcry after Wendell Phillips' sensational speech on July 4, 1863, when he argued that miscegenation was "God's own method of crushing out the hatred of race, and of civilizing and elevating the world." [17] Lincoln's most conservative cabinet member, Montgomery Blair, who paled at the prospect of the Negro rising even to political equality, publicly accused the whole "Abolition party" of favoring "*amalgamation,* equality, and fraternity." And though this was a year after the Emancipation Proclamation, he told his Maryland listeners not to fear that the government would deprive them of their slaves.[18]

Blair was already disliked by the Radicals, and this speech made him political poison. Thaddeus Stevens, who was himself so vulnerable that he may well have looked upon Blair's references to amalgamation as a peculiarly personal assault, wrote angrily to Salmon P. Chase that if Blair was retained it was "time to look for a successor to Lincoln." To Sumner he wrote: "The speech of the P. M. Gen'l. is so vulgar, so infamous that I think it becomes necessary for the true men of the party to bring it to the attention of the President with a request for his removal—He has done us more harm in our election than all the copperhead speeches of the campaign—If the President persists in retaining such men as Blair and Seward we must take care that his reign shall not be prolonged. We must think of a successor. What shall be done?" [19]

Wm. Lloyd Garrison later published in *The Liberator* a letter from Blair that added fuel to the rising Radical fire: "You think freedom and equality possible for the masses of blacks and whites in the same community; we think all history proves the contrary." [20]

Stevens eventually went to the White House with Simon Cameron to deliver what was virtually an ultimatum to the President. "In order that we may be able in our State to go to work with a good will I want you to make us one promise," he said, "that you will reorganize your cabinet and leave Montgomery Blair out of it." According to John Nicolay, to whom the conversation was reported, the discussion lasted two hours, and Lincoln became impatient and indignant.

"Am I to be the mere puppet of power?" he asked. "To have my constitutional advisers selected beforehand, to be told I must do this, or leave that undone? It would be degrading to my manhood to consent to any such bargain—I was about to say it is equally degrading to your manhood to ask it."

It is probably no accident that this, the most acrimonious of all the conversations reported between Lincoln and Stevens, should have been partly stimulated by the miscegenation firebrand. Wherever it was thrown it kindled trouble.[21]

Many Radicals said openly they believed the Negro should have the right of intermarriage. Horace Greeley in the *Tribune* of March 16, 1864, stated that, while he believed intermarriage unwise, it should not be forbidden, and was certainly preferable to the "promiscuous concubinage which has so long shamelessly prevailed upon the Southern plantations."

Racial attitudes among the Democrats, on the other hand, were full of curious contradictions. Some insisted that to permit intermarriage would automatically mean amalgamation, and others that the Negro must amalgamate or be exterminated. William T. Sherman had written in 1860 that the Negro "must amalgamate or be destroyed. Two such races cannot live in harmony save as master and slave." By the second year of the war he had not changed his mind. "When the negroes are liberated either they or their masters must perish," he wrote privately. "They cannot exist together except in their present relation." [22]

To add to the confusion, some Democrats voiced the odd notion that the product of amalgamation, the mulatto, was inferior to both races and sterile. Representative Cox of Ohio said in Congress on February 17, 1864: "The mulatto does not live; he does not recreate his kind; he is a monster." [23]

As late as 1862 in the District of Columbia there were laws on the statutes providing that if a free Negro married a white person, or if a black woman permitted herself even to be seduced by a white man, the penalty was to be sold into slavery. It was the Radical Republicans, led by Senator Henry Wilson, who abolished these legal evidences of the white man's conviction that in matters of miscegenation only the Negro could sin.[24]

[Men wrangled over whether or not there were physical differences between Negroes and whites in addition to color. The arguments reflected not only sexual fears but also the practical question of whether or not the Negro was in fact capable of suffrage and citizenship. Thaddeus Stevens himself admitted on several occasions that he did not believe the Negro to be the white man's equal in intelligence, but usually with an oblique qualification that left his listeners puzzled as to his real meaning. "I do not know," he once said in Congress, "that I shall ever come across men of dark color of the same intelligence as white men. I have seen some that I thought not much inferior to most of us." He insisted that he had never held to the doctrine of Negro equality—"not equality in all things—simply before the laws, nothing else." [25]]

Lincoln's attitude toward the Negro's capacity for citizenship evolved rapidly during the war. Back in 1858 he had said: "I am not, nor ever have been in favor of bringing about in any way the social and political equality of the white and black races . . . I am not, nor ever have been in favor of making voters or jurors of negroes, nor of qualifying them to hold office nor to intermarry with white people; and I will say in addition to this, that there is a physical difference between the white and the black races which I believe will for ever forbid the two races living together on terms of social and political equality. And inasmuch as they cannot so live, while they remain together there must be the position of superior and inferior, and I as much as any other man am in favor of having the superior position assigned to the white race." [26]

The President was greatly impressed, however, by his first-hand acquaintance with articulate Negro groups, and even more by the fighting record of the Negro soldier. He signed without hesitation a bill forbidding segregation on the District of Columbia streetcars— which had passed the Senate by only one vote—another bill belatedly equalizing pay for white and colored soldiers, a bill prohibiting in all United States courts the exclusion of Negroes as witnesses, and a bill allowing the school tax exacted from colored people in the District of Columbia to be used for colored schools. Until this time all the school tax money had gone for white schools.[27]

When that portion of Louisiana conquered by the Union Army was organized with a loyal Union government, Lincoln wrote to the newly elected Governor, Michael Hahn:

"I congratulate you on having fixed your name in history as the first-free-state Governor of Louisiana. Now you are about to have a Convention which, among other things, will probably define the elective franchise. I barely suggest for your private consideration, whether some of the colored people may not be let in—as, for instance, the very intelligent, and especially those who have fought gallantly in our ranks. They would probably help, in some trying time to come, to keep the jewel of liberty within the family of freedom. But this is only a suggestion, not to the public, but to you alone." [28]

Shortly before his death Lincoln openly advocated Negro suffrage "for the very intelligent" and "those who served our cause as soldiers." And in a private letter to General James S. Wadsworth early in 1864 he made it clear that he was seriously considering *universal* suffrage.[29] Lincoln had no quarrel with the Radicals of his party over Negro civil rights. On this, as on so many other issues, he moved more slowly, but in basic moral conviction he was wholly their kin. But because he was always a little behind them—for proper political reasons—the idealists of his party suffered in a state of chronic exasperation at his slowness.

The fact is that Lincoln understood his Jacobins far better than they did him. Needing their energy and moral strength, he was willing to forgive them their intolerance and self-righteousness. "Mr. Lincoln," wrote one observer, "was the only man living who ever managed Charles Sumner, or could use him for his purpose." [30] He patiently endured many public criticisms from the Massachusetts Senator, and managed to preserve an amicable personal relationship.

Lincoln was especially fond of the veteran abolitionist and Radical, Owen Lovejoy, whom he visited several times in 1864 during the latter's last illness. After Lovejoy's death, he wrote a letter of tribute which he read aloud to Frank B. Carpenter, who was painting his portrait. It said, in part: ". . . it would scarcely wrong any other to say, he was my most generous friend." [31]

Henry Winter Davis, a Radical Republican from Maryland, whose hostility to Lincoln was a "source of chagrin and disappointment," [32] never became friendly, despite Lincoln's repeated tactful attempts to win him over. But the Radical Republicans who irritated Lincoln most were Senators Ben Wade and Zachariah Chandler, who ran the Committee on the Conduct of the War. They carped at Lincoln continually, and did their best to wreck the careers of any general they suspected of being a slavery sympathizer. They went so far as to call a meeting to discuss the loyalty of Mrs. Lincoln, who had half-brothers in the Confederate Army. Lincoln himself appeared unexpectedly at the meeting and shamed the committee into silence. It was this kind of hostility that led Lincoln privately to characterize some Radicals as having "a petulant and vicious fretfulness." [33]

Lincoln had two ardent Radicals in his cabinet, Salmon P. Chase and Edwin M. Stanton. With Chase his relations were frequently difficult, but it is well known that the problems arose not from the Secretary of the Treasury's Radical views but from his corrupting passion to be President in Lincoln's place. Stanton, unlike his predecessor, Simon Cameron, was a gifted administrator, aggressively incorruptible, and a man of ferocious drive. Although he had a reputation for being irascible with subordinates, sycophantic with his superiors, and an intriguer, Lincoln defended him against every attack. "Gentlemen," he once said to Radicals Julian and Lovejoy, "I do not see how he survives, why he is not crushed and torn to pieces. Without him I should be destroyed. He performs his task superhumanly." [34]

Lincoln was just as quick to defend his conservative Secretary of State as his radical Secretary of War. He and Seward had become fast friends, delighting in each other's stories. They were temperamentally kin, confirmed middle-of-the-road men. Seward no longer patronized his chief, and had come to have a deep, abiding respect for him. "The President is the best of us," he wrote to his wife.

Seward was under constant attack from the Radical Republicans, who felt now that he had misled them when in 1858 he had talked of revolution. Appalled by his compromise attempts before Sumter, the Radicals rejected him completely when they learned of his lukewarm attitude toward emancipation in 1862. Seward wrote an unfortunate letter to Charles Francis Adams, ambassador in England, on July 5, 1862, saying that the rebels and antislavery leaders were "acting in concert together to precipitate a servile war [that is, an insurrection among the slaves]. . . . the latter by demanding an edict of universal emancipation." Sumner had seen the dispatch, and the whole radical faction soon learned of it. Later Sumner wrote to a friend that Seward "lost his head after he lost the nomination at Chicago and has done nothing but blunder since. *He never understood our war.*" [35]

Thaddeus Stevens never forgave Seward what he considered a betrayal of Radical principles. "It were a great blessing if Seward could be removed," he growled privately in a letter to Simon Stevens on November 17, 1862. "It would revive hope, now nearly extinct. But I fear it cannot be done. But Fessenden is not the man for his successor. He has too much of the vile ingredient, called conservatism, which is worse than secession. He is not as great as at one time I hoped he would prove. Bancroft would be better. But no one will succeed." [36]

After the war, when Seward abandoned almost the whole Republican Party to stand by Andrew Johnson, Thaddeus Stevens reflected on the fact that the Secretary of State had been almost killed by Lewis Payne at the time of Lincoln's assassination. Never one to suppress his death wishes, Stevens shocked his friend Albert G. Riddle by saying, "What a bungler Payne was!" [37]

The Radical Republicans abominated Montgomery Blair even more than William Seward, and considered the conservative Attorney General Edward Bates a fossil. "How are these men to be of service to you in any way?" Zachary Chandler wrote to Lincoln after the elections of 1863. "They are a millstone about your neck. You drop them and they are politically ended forever. . . . Conservatives and traitors are buried together. For God's sake don't exhume their remains in Your Message. They will smell worse than Lazarus did after he had been buried three days."

To which Lincoln replied with what was for him rare irony: "I am very glad the elections this autumn have gone favorably, and that I have not, by native depravity, or under evil influence, done anything bad enough to prevent the good result. I hope to 'stand firm' enough to not go backward, and yet not go forward fast enough to wreck the country's cause." [38]

[It cannot be too greatly emphasized that the major cause of the Radicals' dissatisfaction with Lincoln in 1863–1864 was the fact that the war was going badly.] The victories of Vicksburg and Gettysburg receded with the passing months. Decisive results remained elusive. Many Republicans believed that Lincoln, if nominated, was certain to lose the election, and for a time in the late summer of 1864 Lincoln himself was by no means certain that he could win it.[39] There was a good deal of subterranean Radical intrigue over a possible successor. Late in 1863 it was no secret that Thaddeus Stevens favored Chase for President and considered Lincoln a "dead card" in the political deck. In November, when Lincoln and Seward left Washington to dedicate the Gettysburg cemetery, someone asked Stevens where the President and Secretary of State were bound.

"To Gettysburg," he replied.

"But where are Stanton and Chase?"

"At home, at work," he said curtly. "Let the dead bury the dead."

The story was carried to Lincoln, who wryly repeated it in a cabinet meeting.[40]

Stevens was not reluctant to contribute to the growing impression that Lincoln was without political support. In introducing a Pennsylvania editor to Isaac N. Arnold, Congressman from Illinois, he said: "Here is a man who wants to find a Lincoln member of Congress. You are the only one I know, and I have come over to introduce my friend to you."

Arnold replied seriously: "Thank you. I know a good many such, and I will present your friend to them, and I wish you, Mr. Stevens, were with us." [41]

Nevertheless Stevens and other Radical leaders remained remarkably reluctant to endorse Chase publicly for President. J. M. Winchell, Henry Winter Davis, and Senators Ben Wade and Samuel Pomeroy collaborated secretly, devising a circular criticizing Lincoln for his tendency to compromise, and suggesting Chase for President, but Pomeroy was the only one who actually signed it when it was released in February, 1864. The circular, a kind of trial balloon, collapsed before it was scarcely afloat, and Chase found himself in a humiliating position in regard to his chief.[42]

There was no other significant Radical rival to Lincoln in the 1864 election save John C. Frémont, who was actually nominated by a group of Radical Germans in the West. Horace Greeley and Wendell Phillips endorsed him, though not William Lloyd Garrison, who stood staunchly by Lincoln. But the Congressional party leaders, including Stevens, left Frémont severely alone.

Still the intriguing persisted, as the Union armies failed to win a decisive victory in the East. In August Henry Winter Davis, Chase, and even Sumner talked privately about forcing Lincoln to withdraw, and perhaps substituting Benjamin F. Butler as a candidate. Nicolay and Hay, who were alive to the rumors, do not mention Thaddeus Stevens as being among the Butler supporters. But in mid-August, Stevens let it be known in Lancaster that he was no longer supporting Lincoln.[43]

The moment, however, that George B. McClellan was nominated to oppose Lincoln on the Democratic ticket, the Radical Republicans, recognizing a real enemy, began to work feverishly for Lincoln's victory. As Charles Sumner put it privately, "Lincoln's election would be a disaster, but McClellan's damnation." [44] Thaddeus Stevens quietly urged Carl Schurz to repair the split in the Republican Party by swinging the Frémont Radicals to Lincoln's side. And Zachary Chandler finally succeeded in getting Frémont to withdraw from the race.[45]

The Radicals exacted a price for this, however—the conservative, anti-Negro Montgomery Blair went out of the cabinet.

Stevens now campaigned vigorously for Lincoln in Philadelphia and Lancaster, telling the voters that the President had risen above "the influence of Border State seductions and Republican cowardice." "Let us forget," he said, "that he ever erred, and support him with redoubled energy." [46]

Lincoln had an exact knowledge of the Radical opposition to his nomination and seemed not to be unduly depressed by it. Shortly before the Republican convention Shelby Cullom visited him in the White House and told him that he had "been in Washington some ten days or more, and that everybody seemed to be against him."

"Well, it is not quite so bad as that," Lincoln said. He took down his directory, Cullom related, "and I soon discovered that he had a far more intimate knowledge of the situation than I had. He had everyone marked, and how he stood, and the list made a better showing than I had expected." Later after the convention Lincoln reminded Cullom of the conversation, and went on to tell a little story:

"A couple of Irishmen came to America and started out on foot into the country. They travelled along until they came to a piece of woods. They thought they heard a noise, but did not know what it was. They deployed on either side of the road to find out, but were unable to do so, and finally one called to the other, 'Pat, Pat, let's go on; this is nothing but a domned noise.' So the opposition to him, he said, was apparently nothing but a noise." [47]

Though he could jest in this fashion, it is clear that Lincoln was actually extremely sensitive to the Radical Republican charge that he was not prosecuting the war with vigor, and knew what it could cost him politically. After the election he said to Hugh McCulloch, his new Secretary of Treasury: "I am here by the blunders of the Democrats. If, instead of resolving that the war was a failure, they had resolved that I was a failure and denounced me for not more vigorously prosecuting it, I should not have been re-elected, and I reckon that you would not have been Secretary of the Treasury." [48]

What Lincoln really thought of the extreme Jacobins in his party is best suggested by two entries in John Hay's diary in 1863. On September 30 a group of "ultra" Radicals from Missouri, who were extremely bitter against the President, interviewed Lincoln in the White House. "The President never appeared to better advantage in the world," Hay wrote. "Though he knows how immense is the danger to himself from the unreasoning anger of that committee, he never cringed to them for an instant. He stood where he thought he was right and crushed them with his candid logic." Nevertheless, four weeks later Lincoln said thoughtfully to his secretary in discussing these same men: "I believe, after all, those Radicals will carry the State & I do not object to it. They are nearer to me than the other side, in thought and sentiment, though bitterly hostile personally. They are utterly lawless—the unhandiest devils in the world to deal with—but after all their faces are set Zionwards." [49]

---◆---

CHAPTER SIXTEEN

The End of Slavery

JAMES TRUSLOW ADAMS in his *Epic of America* called Thaddeus
Stevens "perhaps the most despicable, malevolent and morally deformed character who has ever risen to high power in America." Other
judgments have been equally harsh. Claude G. Bowers, in *The Tragic
Era,* said of Stevens: "This man in his den was as much a revolutionist
as Marat in his tub. Had he lived in France in the days of the Terror,
he would have pushed one of the triumvirate desperately for his place,
have risen rapidly to the top through his genius and audacity and will,
and probably have died by the guillotine with a sardonic smile upon
his face." [1] These judgments are not noticeably different from those
of the copperheads and Confederates during the Civil War.

The Radical Republicans have been labeled "the Vindictives" by
historians James G. Randall and George Fort Milton. James G. Randall
called "the avenging force of Puritanism in politics" a major cause
of the war. And T. Harry Williams has described Lincoln's difficulties
with the Radicals over Reconstruction as "a struggle to the death"
against "cunning and implacable foes." [2]

Lincoln would probably have been astonished by such descriptions.[3]
It is true that in 1864 Stevens and other Radicals were opposing his
reconstruction policies as being too hurried and too lenient, but these
same men were also fighting passionately to carry through Congress
the legislation he most wanted—a Thirteenth Amendment abolishing

slavery. The story of their aid and dedication, though told many times, is often neglected or forgotten in the final historical judgment.

In 1863 the Radicals were by no means certain that Lincoln, if faced with a sudden collapse of the Confederacy, would not fall back into some kind of compromise on slavery. Charles Sumner had written to the English Liberal, John Bright, shortly after the Battle of Gettysburg: "We are too victorious; I fear more from our victories than our defeats. If the rebellion should suddenly collapse, Democrats, copperheads, and Seward would insist upon amnesty and the Union, and 'no question asked about slavery.' God save us from any such calamity! If Lee's army had been smashed, that question would have been upon us. Before this comes, I wish two hundred thousand negroes with muskets in their hands, and then I shall not fear compromise." [4]

Senator Chandler, often a bitter critic of Lincoln, gave him unexpected support now. "I have little fear that the President will recede," he wrote to Lyman Trumbull. "He is stubborn as a mule when he gets his back up & it *is up now* on the proclamation. Seward and Weed are shaky but this peculiar trait of stubbornness (which annoyed us so much 18 months ago) is *now* our Salvation." [5]

When Lincoln in his Message to Congress, December 8, 1863, said firmly, ". . . I shall not attempt to retract or modify the emancipation proclamation; nor shall I return to slavery any person who is free by the terms of that proclamation, or by any of the acts of Congress," he quieted Radical fears on this point. John Hay, who had been in Congress when the message was read, wrote in his diary: "Men acted as if the millennium had come. Chandler was delighted, Sumner was beaming, while at the other political pole Dixon & Reverdy Johnson said it was highly satisfactory." Henry Wilson said to Hay: "The President has struck another great blow. Tell him for me, 'God bless him.'" [6]

But everyone recognized that the Emancipation Proclamation left great sections of slave territory untouched, and no one could be sure that the legality of military emancipation would be honored by future governments. Lincoln had urged a constitutional amendment abolishing slavery in December, 1862, and Stevens had been quick to introduce in the House a resolution implementing this request. The appalling fact for the Radical Republicans was that as late as June 15, 1864, the House of Representatives still could not muster the necessary two-thirds vote. There were always enough Democrats to kill the measure. George Boutwell later wrote: "I do not recall the name of one man who favored emancipation as a policy and adhered to the Democratic Party." All Democrats, in the words of Representative Anson Herrick of New York, were for "closing this war the moment it can be done with honor, irrespective of the fate of the negro." [7] The Democratic platform in 1864, though disavowed by General McClellan, explicitly declared the war was a mistake and should be brought to an immediate end.

The Radicals were greatly encouraged when in October, 1864, Maryland by popular vote amended her constitution and abolished slavery. Lincoln, elated, said to a friend: "It is worth many victories in the field. It clears up a piece of ground." [8]

In November he was returned to the White House, and the Republican majority in the House was greatly strengthened. But experienced politicians knew that two or three votes could still defeat the Thirteenth Amendment. Lincoln once again urged its passage in his Message to Congress, and firmly repudiated the idea of a negotiated peace. Thaddeus Stevens greeted this speech with what was for him extraordinary praise:

"I wish to say a few words upon the President's message. It is brief (a great virtue in public documents), it treats of subjects of deep importance, not only to this nation but to the whole family of man. I do not think I am extravagant when I say that it is the most important and best message that has been communicated to Congress for the last sixty years." He went on then to plead for the Thirteenth Amendment in language that astonished those who were quick to call him an infidel:

Those who believe that a righteous Providence punishes nations for national sins believe that this terrible plague is brought upon us as a punishment for our oppression of a harmless race of men inflicted without cause and without excuse for ages. I accept this belief; for I remember that an ancient despot, not so cruel as this Republic, held a people in bondage— a bondage much lighter than American slavery; that the Lord ordered him to liberate them. He refused. His whole people were punished. Plague after plague was sent upon the land until the seventh slew the firstborn of every household; nor did they cease until the tyrant "let the people go." We have suffered more than all the plagues of Egypt; more than the first-born of every household has been taken. We still harden our hearts and refuse to let the people go. The scourge still continues, nor do I expect it to cease until we obey the high behest of the Father of men.

We are about to have another opportunity to obey this command. We are about to ascertain the national will by another vote to amend the Constitution. If gentlemen opposite it will yield to the voice of God and humanity and vote for it, I verily believe the sword of the destroying angel will be stayed and this people be reunited. [9]

Abraham Lincoln, like Thaddeus Stevens, did not often take the responsibility for justifying the ways of God to man. But he, too, had pondered deeply on the problem of expiation for the collective national guilt. In a widely publicized letter to Kentucky editor Albert G. Hodges, he wrote earnestly, somberly: "I am naturally anti-slavery. If slavery is not wrong, nothing is wrong. I can not remember when I did not so think, and feel." After giving his reasons for military emancipation, which had resulted, he said, in "a gain of quite a hundred and thirty thousand soldiers, seamen, and laborers," he concluded: "If God now wills the removal of a great wrong, and wills also that we of the North as well as you of the South, shall pay fairly for our complicity in that wrong, impartial history will find therein new cause to attest and revere the justice and goodness of God."

Later, in his Second Inaugural, he returned again to the theme of retribution and punishment: "Fondly do we hope—fervently do we pray—that this mighty scourge of war may speedily pass away. Yet, if God wills that it continue, until all the wealth piled by the bondman's two hundred and fifty years of unrequited toil shall be sunk, and until every drop of blood drawn with the lash, shall be paid by another drawn with the sword, as was said three thousand years ago, so still it must be said 'the judgments of the Lord, are true and righteous altogether.'" [10]

Thaddeus Stevens closed the debate on the Thirteenth Amendment in the House on January 13, 1865. Isaac Arnold, a Republican from Chicago, described the scene later: "As he came limping with his club foot along down the aisle from his committee room, the members gathered thickly around him. He was tall and commanding in person, and although venerable with years, his form was unbent and his intellect undimmed. The galleries had already been filled with the most distinguished people in Washington. As the word ran through the Capitol that Stevens was speaking on the Constitutional Amendment, senators came over from the Senate, lawyers and judges from the court rooms, and distinguished soldiers and citizens filled every available seat, to hear the eloquent old man speak on a measure that was to consummate the warfare of forty years against slavery." [11]

It was short, like all of Stevens' speeches, and more reflective than argumentative, as if he was already confident of the vote.

From my earliest youth I was taught to read the Declaration of Independence and to revere its sublime principles. As I advanced in life and became somewhat enabled to consult the writings of great men of antiquity, I found in all their works which have survived the ravages of time and come down to the present generation, one unanimous denunciation of tyranny and of slavery, and eulogy of liberty. Homer, Aeschylus the Greek tragedian, Cicero, Hesiod, Virgil, Tacitus, and Sallust, in immortal language, all denounced slavery as a thing which took away half the man and degraded human beings, and sang peans in the noblest strains to the goddess of liberty. And my hatred of this infernal institution and my love of liberty were further inflamed as I saw the inspired teachings of Socrates and the divine inspirations of Jesus . . . . when I first went into public assemblies, forty years ago, I uttered this language. I have done it amid the pelting and hooting of mobs, but I never quailed before the infernal spirit. . . .

When, fifteen years ago, I was honored with a seat in this body, it was dangerous to talk against this institution. . . . I did not hesitate, in the midst of bowie-knives and revolvers and howling demons upon the other side of the House, to stand here and denounce this infamous institution. . . .

I recognized and bowed to a provision in that Constitution which I always regarded as its only blot. . . . Such, sir, was my position . . . not disturbing slavery where the Constitution protected it, but abolishing it wherever we had the constitutional power, and prohibiting its further expansion. I claimed the right then, as I claim it now, to denounce it everywhere.[12]

Lincoln was so disturbed lest the Thirteenth Amendment be lost in the House by one or two votes that he quietly let it be known to several key Congressmen that they must be procured regardless of cost. Later there was talk about patronage, about a bargain over an odious New Jersey railroad monopoly, and about the release of Confederates who were kin to several Democratic Congressmen. Thaddeus Stevens commented cryptically: "The greatest measure of the nineteenth century was passed by corruption, aided and abetted by the purest man in America." [13]

When, however, the roll was called on January 31, 1865, no one could be certain that all the fervent oratory and all the backstage bargaining had changed the proper number of votes from Nay to Aye. The House, crowded with anxious spectators, was hushed when the clerk began the decisive call. The Republicans voted Aye, as was expected. But when the first Democrat, Alexander H. Coffroth of Pennsylvania, who had been expected to vote Nay, also voted Aye, cheers shook the galleries. Slowly the voting went on, every Democratic Aye meeting the same wild applause. At the end of the alphabet, copperheads Ben and Fernando Wood, of New York City, voted for slavery. George H. Yeaman of Kentucky voted for freedom. Then Speaker Schuyler Colfax, violating precedent, asked that his name be added with an Aye behind it. The total was announced, 119 Ayes and 56 Nays.

The shout that went up fairly shook the Capitol. "The cheering in the hall and densely packed galleries exceeded anything I ever saw before and beggared description," George W. Julian wrote in his diary. "Members joined in the shouting and kept it up for some minutes. Some embraced one another, others wept like children. . . . I have felt, ever since the vote, as if I were in a new country." [14]

Messengers raced outside, some to the White House, some to the soldiers manning artillery for the defense of the city. The young gunners at the Capitol shot off a hundred-gun salute, and the city knew at last that slavery in the United States was irrevocably dead.

On the following night Lincoln spoke to a crowd from the window of the White House. He called the Amendment "a great moral victory." It was, he said, "a king's cure for all the evils. It winds the whole thing up." To his portrait painter, Frank B. Carpenter, he said soberly: "It is the central act of my administration, and the great event of the nineteenth century." [15]

"Hail, ye ransomed millions," wrote the jubilant William Lloyd Garrison in the next issue of his *Liberator*, "no more to be chained, scourged, mutilated, bought and sold in the market, robbed of all rights, hunted as partridges upon the mountain. . . . 'Great and marvellous are thy works Lord God Almighty; just and true are thy ways, thou King of saints!' "

The names of the men who fought the Thirteenth Amendment to the last vote were destined to be forgotten. Among them was George H. Pendleton, vice-presidential candidate on the ticket with McClellan in 1864. Thaddeus Stevens, who had never undervalued the tenacity of the proslavery men in Congress, paid his respects to Pendleton on the floor of the House: "He may have his epitaph written, if it be truly written, 'Here rests the ablest and most pertinacious defender of slavery and opponent of liberty.' " Then Stevens went on in a poignant definition of his own hopes for a proper perspective of his role in antislavery history: "And I will be satisfied if my epitaph shall be written thus: 'Here lies one who never rose to any eminence, and who only courted the low ambition to have it said that he had striven to ameliorate the condition of the poor, the lowly, the downtrodden of every race and language and color." [16]

CHAPTER SEVENTEEN

---◆---

Blueprints for Utopia

The radical has a passionate faith in the infinite perfectibility of human nature. He believes that by changing man's environment and by perfecting a technique of soul forming, a society can be wrought that is wholly new and unprecedented.

Eric Hoffer: *The True Believer*

THADDEUS STEVENS through the war had been the lead scout in the antislavery wagon train—beckoning, urging, cursing—faithfully keeping it headed toward the Promised Land. In 1864, surmounting the last ridge and looking down into what seemed to be a valley of peace and freedom, he began to organize for Utopia. This is a heady, dangerous pastime for a politician in power. But to Stevens something had happened that rarely comes to a pessimist and misanthrope; he had seen a dream fulfilled. The approaching end of slavery, instead of satisfying, generated in him a ferment. He was like the fisherman's wife who demanded from the magic flounder a cottage, then a castle, then the palace of an emperor, only to remain dissatisfied and unfulfilled.

At seventy-two he still pinned his hope on the scrap of paper and on the legal phrase, having more faith in the majesty of the law and the ultimate authority of ideas than in the hearts of men. He was never a moral optimist, like Emerson. Most of all he distrusted the Southern aristocrat, who, he was certain, would make every effort to re-enslave the Negro.

Stevens wanted the freedmen to have not only personal liberty but also suffrage, free schools, and forty acres. He was convinced that the only way to get them would be to insist that specific provisions guaranteeing these rights be written into the constitutions of the seceded states *before* they were readmitted into the Union. So he set about making blueprints for Reconstruction, sabotaging every plan that did not meet his specifications.

He smashed headlong into Lincoln, who was threading his way delicately through the end-of-the-war political labyrinth. Lincoln wanted the seceded states back in the Union as soon as possible after they had been conquered by the Union armies, asking, however, that the new governments be set up by loyal Union men, and that they repudiate slavery. He had appointed military governors in Tennessee, Louisiana, and Arkansas, and had quietly succeeded as early as February 9, 1863, in getting accepted into the House of Representatives—over Thaddeus Stevens' protest—two loyal Congressmen from Louisiana, Michael Hahn and Benjamin F. Flanders. On December 8, 1863, he issued a special proclamation on political reconstruction,[1] providing that if ten per cent of the citizens who had voted in 1860 would take a loyalty oath promising to support the Constitution and respect the edict of emancipation, they would be permitted to set up a government and elect representatives to Washington. The "Ten Per Cent Plan" specifically excepted all Confederate officials and military men above the rank of colonel.

Stevens took a hard look at the Ten Per Cent Plan, and went before the House with mingled censure and praise. "The idea that the loyal citizens, though few, *are the State,* and in the State municipalities may overrule and govern the disloyal millions, I have not been able to comprehend," he said. "If ten men fit to save Sodom can elect a Governor and other State officers for and against the eleven hundred thousand Sodomites in Virginia, then the democratic doctrine that the majority shall rule is discarded and dangerously ignored. When the doctrine that the *quality* and not the *number* of voters is to decide the right to govern, then we have no longer a republic, but the worst form of despotism."

But he went on to say that basically he and Lincoln agreed in their theory of reconstruction. Lincoln's plan, he said, "proposes to treat the rebel territory as a conqueror alone would treat it. His plan is wholly outside of and unknown to the Constitution. But it is within the legitimate province of the laws of war. . . . The President may not strike as direct a blow with a battering-ram against this Babel as some impetuous gentlemen would desire; but with his usual shrewd-ness and caution he is picking out the mortar from the joints until eventually the whole tower will fall." [2]

Congress, as always, was jealous of the executive power, and counted Reconstruction peculiarly its own province. Conservative and Radical Republicans alike made this clear when they passed a bill on July 4, 1864, introduced by Radicals Henry Winter Davis and Senator Ben Wade, which provided for a much more stringent oath than Lincoln's. No one could take part in the reconstruction governments, the bill said, except those who could swear an oath that they had not volun-tarily borne arms against the United States nor given aid to those who had. The bill prohibited slavery, disavowed Confederate debts, and barred Confederate officeholders from holding any post in the new governments.

Lincoln was disturbed by the stringency of the loyalty oath. "On principle," he had written to Stanton, "I dislike an oath which requires a man to swear he *has* not done wrong. It rejects the Christian princi-ple of forgiveness on terms of repentance. I think it is enough if the man does no wrong hereafter." [3] For this and other reasons he decided to kill the Wade-Davis Bill by a pocket veto. Believing, however, that he owed Congress an explanation, he issued a proclamation on July 8, 1864, which said in part: "I am . . . unprepared, by a formal ap-proval of this Bill, to be inflexibly committed to any single plan of restoration. . . ." Believing that what might be good for Tennessee might be quite wrong for Louisiana or Arkansas, he asked, in effect, for a free hand. [4]

Thaddeus Stevens, who wanted a fixed blueprint for Reconstruction, had nothing but contempt for Lincoln's seeming lack of policy. Though he had himself opposed the Wade-Davis Bill because it was not harsh enough—he had hoped for a severe confiscation measure—he was furious at Lincoln's veto. "What an infamous proclamation," he wrote to Edward McPherson. "The idea of pocketing a bill and then issuing a proclamation as to how far he will conform to it. . . . How little of the rights of war and the law of nations our Prest. knows! But what are we to do? Condemn privately and applaud publicly!" [5]

What particularly angered Stevens was that he could never get Lincoln to admit in principle what he was actually doing in practice —that is, treating Louisiana, Arkansas, and Tennessee very much like conquered provinces. They were in fact ruled by military governors, and Lincoln was in effect dictating the terms upon which the new state governments must be organized. But with consummate evasive skill he managed to avoid the impression that he was handing down

Thaddeus Stevens at the age of seventy-four
(A Matthew B. Brady photograph, 1866)

Courtesy of the Frick Art Museum and Library

Lydia Hamilton Smith as painted by Jacob Eichholtz

Courtesy of the Lancaster County Historical Society

Thaddeus Stevens at thirty-eight
Engraved by John Sartain from

Courtesy of the National Archives

Thaddeus Stevens (A late Matthew B. Brady photograph)

Courtesy of the Lancaster County Historical Society
Lydia Hamilton Smith
(A photograph made after Stevens' death in 1868)

Abraham Lincoln

Salmon P. Chase

Edwin M. Stanton

William H. Seward

Charles Sumner

Wendell Phillips

Leading Radical Republicans

Benjamin F. Wade

Zachariah Chandler

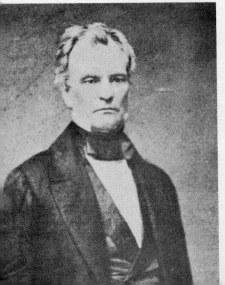

Thomas Nast cartoon depicting Andrew Johnson
as king and Thaddeus Stevens on the block
— *Harper's Weekly, November 3, 1866*

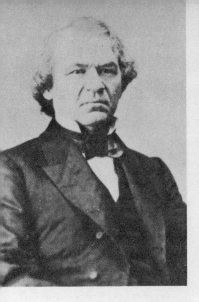

Andrew Johnson

James Buchanan

Eminent Thaddeus Stevens Foes

Montgomery Blair

General George B. McClellan

THE IMPEACHMENT MANAGERS   *Courtesy of the National Archives*

Standing: James F. Wilson, George S. Boutwell, and John A. Logan
Sitting: Benjamin F. Butler, Thaddeus Stevens, Thomas Williams, and John A. Bingham
(A Matthew B. Brady photograph)

conqueror's terms. By many acts the President had acknowledged the belligerent status of the Confederates. Still he insisted that no state had actually seceded, but had only tried to. To admit that they were out of the Union, he said, would be to admit their right to secede. In his last public address he dismissed the question of "whether the seceded States, so called, are in the Union or out of it," as "a merely pernicious abstraction." [6]

Stevens found this kind of reasoning absurd and unrealistic. "The theory that the rebel states, for four years a separate power and without representation in Congress, were all the time here in the Union," he said later, "was a good deal less ingenious and respectable than the metaphysics of Berkeley, which proved that neither the world nor any human being was in existence." [7] Stevens insisted that the South *had* seceded, that the Union Government had officially admitted it, and by the laws of war could exact any terms it wanted from the enemy. This "conquered province" theory was the base upon which he erected his pyramid of exactions. He saw very clearly what many of his Radical Republican contemporaries did not, that once it was officially admitted that a Southern state was under the protecting banner of the Constitution, the federal government forfeited almost all legal right to dictate anything concerning civil or economic rights or suffrage.

Stevens was accused on every hand of holding the Constitution in contempt. Attorney-General Bates wrote in his diary on April 29, 1864: " 'Uncle Thad.' Stevens always full of whims and oddities. He is, at once ignorant and careless of the constitution. He thinks of it only as a bar of Juniata Iron—that may be forged into any shape, and cut into any pieces, to suit the fancy of any Pa. blacksmith." [8]

Actually Stevens in his special fashion was still scrupulous of the Constitution. All through the war he held that the government was acting outside the Constitution, and that any pretense at finding a sanction for either the war or reconstruction measures in the sacred document was hypocrisy. When the loyal section of Virginia broke away from the parent state and was welcomed into the Union as West Virginia, and there was a strenuous effort to make it appear that her creation was strictly constitutional, Stevens laughed at his colleagues. The new state could come in, he said, only "in virtue of the laws of War; and by the laws of nations those laws are just what we choose to make them so that they are not inconsistent with humanity." [9]

Like all practical politicians Stevens was adept at counting, and he was one of the first in his party to see that the Thirteenth Amendment markedly altered the arithmetic of Southern politics. The Negro—

formerly counted as three-fifths of a man when it came to determining a state's representation in Congress—was now rated a whole man. This meant that the fifteen slaves states of 1860—which had among their representatives twenty-four whose seats derived from counting black faces alone—would now be entitled to thirteen more. As Stevens figured it, there would be thirty-seven Southerners in Congress simply because of the presence, though not the ballots, of the black population. Altogether there would be thirty Senators and eighty-eight Congressmen who could be counted upon to vote "Southern." [10] Other Republicans who did this elementary figuring were, like Stevens, appalled to discover that freeing the slave had actually strengthened the voting power of his former master.

Soon Republican caucuses were buzzing with questions. Could not the Southern Congressmen, in unholy alliance with the Northern Democrats, even try to restore slavery? Could they not be counted on in any case to make the Union pay the Confederate war debt, as the Union had paid the Texas debt back in 1847? And with such a postwar Congress could the freedman hope ever to win either civil rights or suffrage? With the bitter pessimism born of his reading of pre-war history, Stevens was certain they could not.

He was not alone in this fear. The Conservative Republican Senator, John Sherman, wrote to his brother on May 16, 1865: "As to negro suffrage, I admit the negroes are not intelligent enough to vote, but some one must vote their political representation in the States where they live, and their representation is increased by their being free. Who shall exercise this political power? Shall the rebels do so? If yes, will they not now in effect restore slavery? . . . After all, how much more ignorant are these slaves than the uneducated white people down South?" [11]

Lincoln himself was acutely conscious of the postwar problem of political power, which he described to John Hay as the problem of "how to keep the rebellious populations from overwhelming and outvoting the loyal minority." He was just as aware as Thaddeus Stevens of the Republican Party's minority status and by no means as ready to welcome the ex-rebels back into power as some historians have made him out to be. "There must be a test by which to separate the opposing elements," he said, "so as to build only from the sound; and that test is a sufficiently liberal one, which accepts as sound whoever will make a sworn recantation of his former unsoundness." [12]

Lincoln's reconstruction policy in 1864 was embryonic, and in a state of rapid evolution. The best clues as to what he hoped to see in the South can be found in his correspondence concerning Louisiana.

At this time two-thirds of Louisiana's citizens were under Union Army rule. No more than 50,000 voters had ever cast a ballot in this state, and now, under the direction of the military governor, General Nathaniel P. Banks, 11,400 citizens took the loyalty oath and sent delegates to make a new state constitution. It was decided that the slaveholding planter could be partly deprived of his former influence if only the whites were counted in determining the basis of representation.

The convention set in motion what was for the Louisiana aristocrats an appalling revolution. Led by a new social class which had never held power—consisting of tradespeople, artisans and small farmers, and a good many naturalized immigrants, the Free State Party under the leadership of former Bavarian Michael Hahn proceeded to abolish slavery, inaugurate a system of progressive income taxation, open the public schools to every child, white or black, between six and sixteen, and establish a nine-hour day. The new Louisiana constitution, according to Lincoln, was "better for the poor black man than we have in Illinois." [13] This was not high praise, for the black code in Illinois was as savage as that in Kentucky, and included an ordinance passed in 1853 that provided imprisonment for any Negro coming into the state.[14]

It is generally forgotten that Lincoln approved of the Louisiana convention, though it disfranchised rebel soldiers of high rank, Confederate officials, and wealthy planters. He regretted only that it did not grant the Negro the vote, and said so publicly.[15] It did, however, empower the legislature to confer suffrage upon the colored man in the future.

When the Constitution was voted upon, about 6,000 ballots were cast in its favor and 2,000 against. The 6,000 represented nearly the whole loyal citizenry of the state. To Thaddeus Stevens the vote showed not the strength but the weakness of the Louisiana revolution. He was afraid that once the rebel soldier returned to vote he would toss out this constitution like garbage. For Stevens and many other Radical Republicans there seemed only one answer to the reconstructed rebel vote, suffrage for the ex-slaves.

Stevens came to this conclusion with some reluctance. "In my county there are fifteen hundred escaped slaves," he said to W. W. Holden. "If they are specimens of the negroes of the South, they are not qualified to vote." Could he have had his order of preference he would have seen the freedman granted first a piece of land, then a free school, and after four or five years the right to vote. "Seek ye first for the negro a little land," he said, "and all other things will be added unto him." [16] Still he could see that there was much to be said for the argument of the ex-slave Frederick Douglass, who believed that the school-house door would never open for the Negro unless he had the ballot.

"It is said that the colored man is ignorant," Douglass said early in 1864, "and therefore he shall not vote. In saying this, you lay down a rule for the black man that you apply to no other class of your citizens. I will hear nothing of degradation nor of ignorance against the black man. If he knows enough to be hanged, he knows enough to vote. If he knows an honest man from a thief, he knows much more than some of our white voters. If he knows as much when sober as an Irishman knows when drunk, he knows enough to vote. . . . All I ask, however, in regard to the blacks, is that whatever rule you adopt, whether of intelligence or wealth, as the condition of voting, you should apply it equally to the black man." [17]

For the Radical Republicans it was a disagreeable political fact that in the North only six states permitted the Negro to vote, and one of these, New York, required a property qualification for the Negro that was not required of the white. Nevertheless, when Louisiana elected new Congressmen to Washington, Thaddeus Stevens and Charles Sumner set about blocking their admission chiefly on the ground that the Louisiana constitution did not permit Negro suffrage.

Sumner had written to a friend just after Lee's surrender that Lincoln "saw with his own eyes at Richmond and Petersburg, that the only people *who showed themselves were negroes,* all others had fled or were retired in their houses. Never was I more convinced of the utter impossibility of any organization which is not founded on the votes of the negroes." [18]

The joint Congressional resolution recognizing the Louisiana delegates had Lincoln's warm support. Senator Lyman Trumbull deserted the Radicals on this issue to marshal support for the President. It did not help his cause when one of the newly elected Congressmen, A. P. Field, a former Louisiana circuit-court judge, started a brawl in a Washington restaurant with Congressman Wm. D. Kelley, and ended it by gashing him seriously with a knife. For Stevens it was proof that the Southerners had not yet lost a perennial capacity for senseless acts of violence. Senator Ben Wade trumpeted against the admission of the whole Louisiana group. "God knows I never will sanction such fatal heresies as these," he said. ". . . Are unwashed rebels to be brought in here, men who have not taken the oath, and who, without perjuring themselves to the lowest hell, cannot take it?"

Despite Radical Republican opposition, it was fully expected that the resolution would pass. But Charles Sumner started a filibuster in the Senate, attacking it as a "mere seven months abortion, begotten by the bayonet, in criminal conjunction with the spirit of caste, and born before its time, rickety, unformed, unfinished, whose continued existence will be a burden, a reproach, and a wrong." Because the end of the session was only a few days off, Sumner had his way; the resolution lost by a single vote.

Lincoln, whose political philosophy did not include the word "heresies," and who did not, like Ben Wade, divide citizens into the washed and unwashed, was deeply disappointed. In his last public address he pleaded again for the admission of Louisiana, though frankly admitting that the new government had many faults, and expressed the hope that educated Negroes and the colored soldiers would be permitted to vote. "Concede," he concluded, "that the new government of Louisiana is only to what it should be as the egg is to the fowl, we shall sooner have the fowl by hatching the egg than by smashing it." [19]

Thaddeus Stevens never lost his suspicion that Lincoln by his amiability and gentleness would let slip away the revolutionary gains won by the carnage of battle. Peace proposals suggesting compromise and negotiation sent him into a fury of anxiety even when they came from his own Radicals. On November 20, 1864 he wrote to Lincoln from Lancaster: "This twaddle about new peace propositions promulgated by Butler and others is as unwise, and nearly as injurious as Sherman made three or four months ago, which nearly ruined us— All such feeble stuff enervates the public—I am happy in believing that you will give no countenance to such superficial suggestions." [20]

When the President went to Hampton Roads to meet with Confederate commissioners on February 1, 1865, and the War Democrats insinuated that he had gone to negotiate a peace and repudiate emancipation, Stevens growled privately to Noah Brooks that "if the country were to vote over again for President of the United States, Benjamin F. Butler, and not Abraham Lincoln, would be their choice." [21]

Nevertheless, when Lincoln returned, and at Stevens' specific request reported to Congress the results of the Hampton Road talks, the old Commoner arose with praise upon his lips: "The President has made the peace effort," he said, "in such a masterly style, upon such a firm basis and principle, that I believe even those who thought his mission was unwise will accord to him sagacity and patriotism, and applaud his action." [22]

Everyone knew Lincoln was no man for hangings. "The President is full of tenderness to all & several times repeated 'Judge not, that ye be not judged,'" Sumner wrote to a friend. "This he said—even when

Jeff Davis was named as one who should not be pardoned." [23] In his last cabinet meeting Lincoln said, "I hope there will be no persecution, no bloody work after the war is over. No one need expect me to take any part in hanging or killing these men, even the worst of them. Frighten them out of the country, open the gates, let down the bars, scare them off"—throwing up his hands as if scaring sheep, Welles said. "Enough lives have been sacrificed." [24]

There were men hungry for hangings in both parties. It is generally forgotten that the new Vice-President, Democrat Andrew Johnson, repeated in speech after speech that traitors must be hanged for treason and their families impoverished. Even Secretary Welles, also a Democrat, though sagely anticipating that the Confederate leaders would in the end go unpunished, nevertheless went on record in his *Diary* on June 1, 1864, as favoring the hanging of a few "for present and future good," and the impoverishment of leading aristocrats by property confiscation. But the notion of a Carthaginian peace was generally and rightly identified with the Radical Republicans, with men like Senator Zachary Chandler, who defined the rights of the Southern rebel as "the constitutional right to be hanged and the divine right to be damned."

Nevertheless, as the war's end neared, some of the Radicals were coming to have mixed feelings about executions. Sumner found the idea repugnant, and wrote to John Bright May 16, 1865, that he was sorry Jefferson Davis had not escaped.[25] Thaddeus Stevens, who had many times called for the hanging of Davis and other leaders in the rebellion, amazed John W. Forney early in 1865 by signing an appeal to Lincoln to pardon a fire-eating secessionist. When Forney twitted him about it, he said drily: "I saw you were going heavily into the pardon business, and I thought I would take a hand in it myself." And he offered to sign any pardon Forney would write.[26]

Soon he astonished all his colleagues by saying that Jefferson Davis and his chief aides should never be hanged as traitors. Legally they could not, he said, since Lincoln by granting the Confederacy belligerent rights had acknowledged their status as leaders of an independent government. Later he offered his services as a lawyer to defend both Jefferson Davis and Clement C. Clay against the treason charge.[27]

This about-face was not taken as evidence of an unexpected welling-up of humanity in Thaddeus Stevens. The switch was demanded, most of his contemporaries believed, by the logic of his conquered-province theory, and it was considered further evidence of the legalistic, doctrinaire quality of his radical thinking. He would free the Confederate leaders in order better to destroy the political power of the whole white aristocracy. Jefferson Davis understood Stevens' motives. "When I was in prison waiting trial," he said, "Thaddeus Stevens twice sent a message to me volunteering to defend me. I declined, not from any lack of confidence in his ability, because he was a man of great natural endowment, but I was aware of his line of argument. It would have been that the seceding States were conquered provinces, and were to all intents and purpose a foreign power which had been overthrown. Therefore, their property was subject to confiscation and the people to such penalties and conditions as the conquerors might impose. That would have been an excellent argument for me, but not for my people." [28]

Stevens in 1867 talked about putting Davis on trial for "the murders at Andersonville, the murders at Salisbury, the shooting down of our prisoners of war in cold blood," [29] but it was empty talk, for he took no active steps to push the matter. Had he actually been the vindictive Robespierre he has been made out to be, Stevens would have had his Utopia *and* his hangings, and he would have modified his theory to include both. But like so many other Americans of every political complexion, he tossed about the word "extermination" in the heat of passion, but when confronted with the task of making an actual list for the gallows, he could no more face it than could Lincoln.

As a small boy he had seen his father desert his mother and return, to be forgiven and, presumably, once more become beloved. But it was impossible for Stevens to forgive except on the basis of elaborate and somehow humiliating conditions for good behavior. Just as he had affronted his nephew by the conditions he exacted in his will, so he would deal with the Southern aristocrat. He would spare the life, but only at the price of mortifying the spirit. And the humbling would consist—as it doubtless had in the fantasies of his childhood—in equalizing the status of the cripple and the whole man, in raising the black to the exalted level of the white.

The last time Thaddeus Stevens talked to Abraham Lincoln seems to have been late in March, 1865, well after the adjournment of Congress. The President was only fifty-six, seventeen years younger than Stevens, but his face was as haggard and deeply lined. Both men had suffered in the war, but Stevens had been stiffened through the years by his capacity to hate. Lincoln was bowed by the weight of a double burden, for he had, as he once himself admitted, suffered *with* the South.

William Crook of the White House staff later described what he remembered of their conversation. "Mr. Stevens was one of the ablest, as well as one of the most radical men then in Congress," he said, "but he was a very impatient man. The President listened patiently to Mr. Stevens's argument, urging 'a more vigorous prosecution of the war,' which was the watchword of those men of his own party who criticized the President, and when he had concluded he looked at his visitor a moment in silence. Then he said, looking at Mr. Stevens very shrewdly:

" 'Stevens, this is a pretty big hog we are trying to catch, and, to hold when we do catch him. We must take care that he doesn't slip away from us.' Mr. Stevens had to be satisfied with the answer." [30]

So Stevens left the President, as so many men before him, with the memory of a homely metaphor but no real certainty of having left so much as a thumbprint on Lincoln's policy. Several of Lincoln's private acts, had Stevens known of them, would have filled him with rage. One was the President's suggestion to his cabinet on February 5th that the Union offer to pay $400,000,000 in compensation to the Southerners for the loss of their slaves. Grant was bludgeoning his way toward Richmond, with the most appalling casualties of the war, and Lincoln was willing to do almost anything to hasten Southern capitulation. Since the war was costing three million a day, he pointed out, it would be a cheap way to end it, if successful. But the cabinet unanimously rejected the proposal, and it was kept a secret from members of Congress. [31]

Another project of Lincoln's was his decision to proclaim universal amnesty as soon as possible after the Confederate armies surrendered. Booth's bullet interfered with this. Stevens, on the other hand, always violently opposed universal amnesty. Three years after the end of the war, though he was ill and close to death, he would still say bluntly in his last major speech before the House: "I despise the doctrine." [32]

CHAPTER EIGHTEEN

The Tailor in the White House

Men of weak abilities set in great place are like little statues set on great bases, made to appear the less by their advancement.

Plutarch [1]

EARLY IN 1864 Abraham Lincoln had a conference with Thaddeus Stevens, Simon Cameron, and others, to discuss the forthcoming election. With what was probably calculated carelessness, he suggested the idea of sacrificing his Vice-President, Hannibal Hamlin, in favor of a War Democrat, and forming a coalition government under the banner of a Union Party. "Why," he ventured, "would not Johnson be a good man to nominate?"

Stevens looked stonily at the President and replied: "Mr. President, Andrew Johnson is a rank demagogue, and I suspect at heart a damned scoundrel." [2]

This was a savage judgment even for Stevens. In 1864 Johnson was something of a war hero. As Senator from Tennessee he had seen three-fourths of his state slide into the Confederacy, but he had stayed with the Union, smearing the secessionists with the ripe language of the Tennessee mountain stump orator, demanding hanging for the rebel leaders and impoverishment for their families. [3] He had been burned in effigy in his home state and had narrowly missed assassination. Lincoln had appointed him war governor at Nashville, where he held on tenaciously, though the city for a time was besieged by Confederate armies. His courage had become a kind of symbol of the unexpected good, for who in the North could have predicted that this former slave-holder would have stood steadfast before so much calumny and personal danger from his own people?

He had a strong, masculine, impassive face that effectively masked his real thoughts, and a gentle, slightly formal manner, which he discarded only when he stood before an audience. There he invariably opened his heart in fierce assaults against men and issues he disliked. Like Thaddeus Stevens, he abominated the Southern aristocrat. But where Stevens hated with the passion of the dedicated abolitionist, Johnson hated with the special intensity of an ambitious man ill-at-ease with his own origins.

Johnson's father, a poor-white in North Carolina, had died when Andrew was four years old. The boy grew up in poverty and without education, for the state had no free schools. He was apprenticed to a tailor at fourteen, but eventually fled from this semi-slavery to Tennessee, where he went into the business of tailoring for himself. As an apprentice he learned to read; the girl he married taught him to write. His rise to fame followed the familiar frontier-hero pattern—alderman, mayor, state legislator, United States Congressman, Senator, and Governor—but Andrew Johnson had the special distinction of being a plebeian elected to high office in the South. This was possible only because he represented the small farmers and artisans of East Tennessee; in the big plantation country to the west he was looked upon contemptuously as an upstart poor-white.

Especially was he derided for his trade as a tailor, which was considered effeminate and degrading. Southern Senators in Washington treated him like something slightly soiled. Like many men on the defensive he became pugnacious, striking out at the aristocracy and glorying publicly in his humble background. Jefferson Davis said that he had "the pride of having no pride." [4]

Andrew Johnson, again like Thaddeus Stevens, was a torch-bearer for free schools. As Governor of Tennessee he had succeeded in forcing through the legislature the first bill taxing property for public education, despite violent opposition from the plantation slaveholders. [5] He shared with Stevens a contempt for organized religion, though he declared himself to be no atheist, and was in some respects more puritanical than Stevens, since he scowled upon gambling and took pride in the fact that he had never been to the theater. Unfortunately for his career he was not a teetotaler. Both men were labeled bastards in whispering campaigns, although Stevens, as the purported son of Talleyrand, was given a much more exalted paternity. Where Johnson furiously attacked the imputation in public, Stevens refused even to mention it.

Johnson shared Stevens' horror at the disintegration of the Union, and made its restoration the paramount object of his career. Like Stevens, he did not consider the government bound by the narrow confines of the Constitution when it came to fighting a war. "Whenever you hear a man prating about the Constitution," he said when military governor of Tennessee, "spot him as a traitor." [6]

Stevens and Johnson were both fighters and foes of compromise. But despite all these likenesses, the chasm between them was virtually bottomless. Johnson had been a slaveholder, and though he had owned only five or six Negroes and had voted against the extension of slavery, Stevens was convinced that having embraced the moral corruption associated with owning one, he was no better than the owner of a thousand.

Johnson was a Southern Radical Democrat, who was genuinely grieved at the plight of the white working man but indifferent to slavery. He had opposed its extension not so much because it was unjust to the black laborer but because it degraded the white. Back in 1855 he had argued that voting registration in Tennessee should be based on the white population only, so that the plantation owners, who had extra votes based on the number of their slaves, would no longer be able to legislate against the poor whites. "How do you like to see your wives and daughters offset by the greasy negro wenches of Shelby, Davidson, Fayette, Sumner and Rutherford counties?" he asked, and demanded an end to the system that placed Negro women "on an equality with the fair daughters and virtuous wives of laboring men." [7] He opposed the abolitionists, saying in the Senate February 6, 1861: "Thank God, I am not in alliance with Giddings, with Phillips, with Garrison, and the long list of those who are engaged in the work of destruction, and in violating the Constitution of the United States." [8] Later he did approve the Emancipation Proclamation, but chiefly because it would "break down an odious and dangerous aristocracy," and "free more whites than blacks in Tennessee." [9]

His chief project as Senator had been the passage of a Homestead Law to provide free western land to impoverished small farmers, who were normally either treated as trespassers or ensnared by speculators. The Homestead Act had been favored also by many Radical Republicans, notably Galusha Grow, George Julian, and Ben Wade—who said he preferred "giving lands to the landless instead of niggers to the niggerless"—and they all collaborated with Johnson in pushing the bill through Congress in 1862. Thaddeus Stevens, however, had opposed the Homestead Act. "It would be a very unhappy condition in society if that country was to be settled altogether by paupers—by men who had no means," he said, and voiced his fears of "wrongdoers and trespassers" in language characteristic of large landowners the world over.[10]

Despite his homestead policy, Johnson as military governor had shown himself to be very tender of the property rights of the Tennessee slaveholders, refusing to farm out the many abandoned plantations even on a temporary war basis, though the state was swarming with destitute whites.[11] Stevens, on the other hand, was eager to be reckless with these particular property rights. So the relationship between the two men was full of contradictions.

Stevens was full of compassion for the downtrodden black man, Johnson for the downtrodden white. Johnson's hatred of the Southern aristocrat was compounded partly of envy, an envy that could be dissipated the moment he began to be courted by members of this class. Stevens' hatred had the ineradicable, passionate quality of the boy who sees his father abusing his mother. Both men in temperament were alien to Lincoln, who was an unconscious aristocrat, suffering neither from class envy nor from a gnawing awareness of deformity.

In turning to Johnson as a potential vice-president, Lincoln was turning simply to a distinguished War Democrat. But he indicated his preference to only a few key men, and Stevens was not aware that he sent secret instructions to the nominating convention. When Alexander McClure told him that he had presidential orders to carry the Pennsylvania delegation for Johnson, he "turned his cold gray eye" upon McClure and said "with an expression of profound contempt," "Can't you get a candidate for vice-president without going down into a damned rebel province for one!"[12]

Some Radical Republicans, however, mistakenly believing Johnson's special brand of radicalism to be the same as their own, were delighted at the choice. Charles Sumner is said to have told two delegates he wished the ticket was turned around.[13]

When news of his nomination reached Nashville on June 19, 1864, Andrew Johnson said to a friend: "What will the aristocrats do, with a railsplitter for President, and a tailor for Vice President?"[14] This was a characteristic and revealing question. With Lincoln, the fact that he had been a railsplitter was the most incidental aspect of his life; with Johnson the consciousness of having been a tailor would cling to him like a wet garment even in the White House.

It may well have been this ravaging self-contempt that was responsible for the blunder of his drunkenness at the inauguration. The story is now well-known that he had been ill with typhoid fever, and had come from Nashville to the ceremony in Washington only because Lincoln had urged him to. Exhausted and still somewhat ill, he asked for some whiskey shortly before the ceremony. Some said later that he filled his glass three times.[15]

By the time Johnson had entered the Senate Chamber to take the oath, his taciturnity—a habitual defense against self-revelation—was completely dissolved in alcohol. He began characteristically by expressing pride in coming from the ranks of the people rather than from high descent. Then in a rambling, incoherent address he proceeded to commit what is for any politician the unforgivable sin: to lay bare an unconscious conviction of inferiority. The audience first began to squirm when he turned to the special gallery for foreign diplomats and said: "And you, gentlemen of the Diplomatic Corps, with all your fine feathers and gewgaws . . ." Again and again he returned to the theme of his humble origin—"Humble as I am, plebeian as I may be deemed. . . . I'm a-going for to tell you—here to-day—yes, I am a-going for to tell you all that I am a plebeian. I glory in it. I am a plebeian. The people—yes, the people of the United States, the great people—have made me what I am. . . ."[16]

Many reporters in the gallery heard little because of the chatter of dismayed voices declaring: "What a shame!" "Has he no friends?" "Is there no person who will have mercy upon him?" Gideon Welles whispered to Stanton: "Johnson is either drunk or crazy."[17] Hamlin tugged at his coat, vainly whispering to him to stop, while Lincoln heard him, according to John W. Forney, "with unutterable sorrow."

Lincoln delivered his own inaugural address on the steps of the Capitol, where the crowd had no intimation of the humiliating episode inside. But they learned it all in the scolding press the next day. Charles Sumner offered a resolution in the Senate asking Johnson to resign, but Lincoln, with characteristic magnanimity, simply said: "It has been a severe lesson for Andy, but I do not think he will do it again."[18]

Many Republican newspapers discreetly ignored the incident, but the Democratic editors, who considered Johnson a traitor to the party, sharpened their knives on him. Thaddeus Stevens could have read in the *Lancaster Intelligencer* of March 7 that the country now had "a buffoon for President and a drunken boor for Vice President." The *New York World* called Johnson "an insolent drunken brute, in comparison with whom Caligula's horse was respectable." What Stevens himself thought of Johnson's inaugural one cannot say, since he did not choose to be quoted. But he kept a clipping of the *New York World* libel, and a year later found an occasion to dust it off and give it some publicity.

Forty-one days after the inaugural, Lincoln was dead, and the nation was in a state of shock from which it took weeks to recover. The defeated South was in an agony of apprehension. "We are shattered and stunned," wrote Mrs. Chesnut in her diary, "the remnant of heart left alive within us filled with brotherly hate. We sit and wait until the drunken tailor who rules the United States of America issues a proclamation, and defines our anomalous position." [19]

A cry for vengeance echoed over the North, as many who had formerly talked of a soft peace clamored for hangings. Men who said they were glad Lincoln was dead were beaten on the streets and sentenced to jail, and preachers who did not eulogize him on Easter Sunday were dismissed by their congregations. But there were unseeing men in his own party, men too close to Lincoln to measure his stature, who were shocked but not dismayed by the assassination. George Julian, a Radical who had been extremely critical of the President, described in his journal of April 15 exactly how he reacted to the news of Lincoln's death.

"I was still half asleep and in my fright grew suddenly cold, heartsick, and almost helpless," he wrote. Then he went on to describe a caucus held that afternoon with Wade, Chandler, Covode, Judge Cartter, and Wilkinson, correspondent of the *New York Tribune*. "Their hostility towards Lincoln's policy of conciliation and contempt for his weakness were undisguised; and the universal feeling among radical men here is that his death is a godsend. It really seems so, for among the last acts of his official life was an invitation to some of the chief rebel conspirators to meet in Richmond and confer with us on the subject of peace." [20]

Thaddeus Stevens was in Lancaster when Lincoln was murdered, and we do not know how the death of Lincoln moved him. Two years later he said of Lincoln in the House: ". . . there is no danger that the highest praise that the most devoted friends could bestow on him would ever be reversed by posterity. So solid was the material of which his whole character was formed that the more it is rubbed the brighter it will shine." At this time Stevens was fiercely embroiled with Andrew Johnson in the fight over Reconstruction, and whatever troubles he had had with Lincoln must have seemed insignificant and trifling. In a thoughtful vein he went on to talk about Lincoln's death. It told much about Stevens' attitude that when he compared Lincoln with the heroes of the past he went far back to the Old Testament—to the imagery of Moses, and Elijah, and the Promised Land.

Death is terrible. Death in high places is still more lamentable; but every day is showing that there are things more terrible than death. It was better that his posthumous fame should be unspotted than that he should endure a few more years of trouble on earth. All must regret the manner of his death; yet, looking to futurity and to his own personal position, it may be considered happy. From the height of his glory he beheld the promised land, and was withdrawn from our sight. In the midst of the most exquisite enjoyment of his favorite relaxation he was instantaneously taken away without suffering one pang of death. Like the prophet of the Lord who knew not death, he was wrapt from earth to heaven along a track no less luminous than his who ascended in a chariot of fire with horses of fire. Would to God that some small portion of the mantle of our Elijah had fallen on his Elisha.[21]

When Andrew Johnson took office, the South feared him as an Avenger; the Democratic Party looked upon him as a renegade, and most Radical Republicans claimed him for their own. When several members of the Committee on the Conduct of the War met with Johnson, Senator Ben Wade greeted him: "Johnson, we have faith in you. By the gods, there will be no trouble now in running the government!" Johnson thanked him, replying formally: "I hold that robbery is a crime; rape is a crime; murder is a crime; *treason* is a crime, and *crime* must be punished. Treason must be made infamous, and traitors must be impoverished."

Ten days before, in a speech on the fall of Richmond he had said the same thing in public: "My notion is that treason must be made odious, that traitors must be punished and impoverished, their social power broken . . . wealthy traitors should be made to remunerate those men who have suffered as a consequence of their crimes." [22]

In the first fortnight of his term Johnson seemed to be the Avenger in fact as well as in sentiment. He repudiated General Sherman's peace terms, which would have permitted the South to return to its immediate pre-war status, with the old state governments recognized and no demands made for the repudiation of slavery.[23] And he permitted Stanton to order the Union armies to dismiss the legislatures of South Carolina, Mississippi, and Georgia, which had met to re-establish relations with the Union.

On May 2, 1865, he offered a reward of $100,000 for the arrest of Jefferson Davis and $25,000 for Clement C. Clay, as supposed accomplices in Lincoln's assassination plot. Thaddeus Stevens scorned the idea that these men were guilty, telling George Shea that the evidence was "insufficient and incredible." "Those men are no friends of mine," he said. "They are public enemies; but I know these men, sir. They are gentlemen, and incapable of being assassins." [24]

Stevens called on Andrew Johnson with a delegation from Pennsylvania on May 3. The new president again promised punishment for Confederate leaders. But he also said—and to the sharply watching Stevens this must have seemed more significant than a whole quiver of threats—that it was nonsense to speak of the seceded states as having gone out of the Union or having (in Sumner's favorite phrase) committed suicide.[25]

A fortnight later, with as much circumspection and courtesy as he could muster, Stevens wrote to Andrew Johnson from Caledonia his first letter:

May 16, 1865

I hope I may be excused for putting briefly on paper what I intended to say to you only—Reconstruction is a very delicate question. The last Congress (and I expect the present) looked upon it as a question for the Legislative power exclusively. While I think we shall agree with you almost unanimously as to the main objects you have in view, I fear we may differ as to the manner of effecting them. How the executive can remodel the *states in the Union* is past my comprehension. I see how he can govern them through military governors until they are reorganized. . . . My one object now is to suggest the propriety of suspending further reconstruction until the meeting of Congress. Better call an extra session than to allow many to think that the Executive was approaching usurpation. . . .[26]

Johnson, who was as thankful as Lincoln had been that Congress was not in session when the war ended, made the mistake of ignoring Stevens. He did not call a special session but went ahead trying swiftly to speed restoration before the return of the Congress in December complicated further an already labyrinthine political puzzle. In the crucial seven months from May to December, 1865, there came about one of the most extraordinary realignments of political sympathy in American history.

By the opening of Congress Andrew Johnson and the Radical Republicans were scarcely on speaking terms. Thaddeus Stevens was ready with a detailed plan to nullify everything Johnson had done over the summer. Charles Sumner, who had been delighted with his April interviews with the President, describing his attitude as "excellent" and even "sympathetic" toward Negro suffrage, now reported him to be "changed in temper and purpose . . . no longer sympathetic or even kindly," but "harsh, petulant and unreasonable." After a final stormy session on December 2, 1865, the two men never spoke to each other again.[27]

Northern Democrats, meanwhile, were welcoming the President back into their party like a prodigal son, and the ex-Confederates were generally agreeing with the provisional governor of South Carolina, Benjamin F. Perry, who said publicly on July 3, 1865, that Johnson was "in all respects, a better, wiser and greater man than Lincoln." "I said," Perry wrote later in his *Reminiscences,* "we ought to look upon his death as the act of God! We had more to expect from Johnson, as a Southern man, a slaveholder and a Democrat." W. W. Boyce of South Carolina write for *DeBow's Review:* ". . . an overruling Providence, not blind chance, selected President Johnson for the great mission of being the restorer of his country." [28]

What had happened in these seven months? The first shock to the Radical Republicans was Johnson's recognition by executive order of the Pierpont Government in Virginia, the little Union fragment stationed in Alexandria that had pretended to be a state government throughout the war. When he heard of it, Stevens wrote angrily to Sumner from Philadelphia: "Virginia is recognized! I fear before Congress meets he will have so be-deviled matters as to render them incurable. But I almost despair of resisting Executive influence." [29]

Late in May Johnson carried out Lincoln's plan of issuing a proclamation of general amnesty, with restoration of all property rights, save slaves, to those who would take a loyalty oath supporting the Constitution and the emancipation laws. It specifically exempted, however, Confederate government officials, high-ranking military and naval officers, and all who owned property worth more than twenty thousand dollars. The last provision, Johnson's own idea, was aimed specifically at the Southern aristocrat. Anyone, however, could regain his citizenship status by obtaining a Presidential pardon.

And Johnson proceeded to issue pardons with a lavish hand— nearly fourteen thousand in less than nine months.[30] The result was predictable. When a plantation owner humbled himself in the difficult act of penance, and the President forgave him his past errors, the consequence for Johnson was warmth and friendliness. He had not been in office two months before he told friends from Tennesee: "Give yourselves no uneasiness. I am not going to hang anybody." [31]

He did, however, hang Mrs. Surratt, believing her to be equally guilty with Booth, Herold, Payne, and Atzerodt in plotting the assassination of Lincoln, Seward, and himself. But even this mistake seems to have been the result of the fact that the military court's recommendation for mercy for Mrs. Surratt was deliberately withheld from him by the chief prosecutor, Judge Advocate General Joseph Holt.

Thaddeus Steven later called the Surratt hanging a "cruel, unnecessary murder." [32]

The growing Radical Republican resentment against Johnson was reflected by the *New York Tribune* journalist Whitelaw Reid: "All summer long the capital was filled with the late leaders in Rebel councils, or on Rebel battle-fields. . . . They asked him if he was going to let Massachusetts Abolitionists lead him now and control his Administration, while his own native South lay repentant and bleeding at his feet. He was ambitious, proud of his elevation, but stung by the sneer that after all he was only an accidental President. They cunningly showed him how he could secure the united support of the entire South and of the great Democratic party of the North, with which all his own early history was identified, for the next Presidency." [33]

Late in May and early June, 1865, Johnson appointed provisional governors in all the Confederate states that did not already have one, with instructions for the calling of constitutional conventions to set up new state governments along the line of Lincoln's Ten Per Cent Plan. But the Radicals noted that he differed significantly from Lincoln in one respect. As George Boutwell described it, "Mr. Lincoln, during his administration, was very careful, in the provisional governments which he established or authorized, to act exclusively in his capacity as commander-in-chief of the army, and not at all as President clothed with civil authority. And, further, he either appointed an officer of the army to be the provisional or military Governor of a State, or, if civilians were appointed, they received commissions in the military service. But Mr. Johnson . . . exercised authority merely in his civil capacity . . . he pardoned rebels . . . then appointed them Governors of these various States." [34]

What disturbed Thaddeus Stevens most was that Johnson, by announcing minimum rather than maximum requirements for restoration had forfeited all his political bargaining power. The two things the South most feared in defeat were property confiscation and interference with the political status of the Negro. On both Johnson had capitulated in advance without exacting anything in return. From Philadelphia on July 6, 1865, Stevens wrote the President a blunt letter:

Sir: I am sure you will pardon me for speaking to you with a candor to which men in high places are seldom accustomed. Among all the leading Union men of the North with whom I have had intercourse, I do not find one who approves of your policy. They believe that "Restoration" as announced by you will destroy our party (which is of but little consequence) and will greatly injure the country. Can you not hold your hand and wait the action of Congress and in the meantime govern them by military rulers? Profuse pardoning also will greatly embarrass Congress if they should wish to make the enemy pay the expense of the war or a part of it.

With great respect
your obedient servant
Thaddeus Stevens

Johnson paid no attention to Stevens' letter, a political indiscretion of which Lincoln would never have been guilty.[35]

It is a common historical misconception that Johnson's restoration ideas were identical with those of Lincoln, and that had Booth's bullet missed its target Lincoln would have had exactly the same battle as Johnson with the Radical Republicans. Forgotten is the fact that Lincoln had had four years of experience keeping the Radicals in line, utilizing their energies and moral indignation, and keeping a firm thumb on their wilder revolutionary impulses. What is also forgotten is that Lincoln was a Republican and Johnson a Democrat. If Thaddeus Stevens was interested in "the perpetual ascendancy of the Republican Party," so too was Lincoln. Johnson could hardly have been less interested.

Lincoln was not afraid of a policy of exclusion. To Johnson himself he had written on September 11, 1863, concerning reconstruction in Tennessee: "The whole struggle for Tennessee will have been profitless to both State and Nation, if it so ends that Gov. Johnson is put down, and Gov. Harris is put up. It must not be so. You must have it otherwise. Let the reconstruction be the work of such men only as can be trusted for the Union. Exclude all others, and trust that your government, so organized, will be recognized here. . . ."[36]

On the single most critical issue for Reconstruction—Negro suffrage —Lincoln had made himself unmistakably clear a year before his death in a letter to General Wadsworth:

I cannot see, if universal amnesty is granted, how, under the circumstances, I can avoid exacting in return universal suffrage, or . . . suffrage on the basis of intelligence and military service. How to better the condition of the colored race has long been a study which has attracted my serious and careful attention; hence I think I am clear and decided as to what course I shall pursue in the premises, regarding it a religious duty, as the nation's guardian of these people, who have so heroically vindicated their manhood on the battle-field, where, in assisting to save the life of the Republic, they have demonstrated in blood their right to the ballot. . . . *The restoration of the Rebel States to the Union must rest upon the principle of civil and political equality of both races; and it must be sealed by general amnesty.*[37]

Andrew Johnson, on the other hand, stated frankly to many men that he was afraid of Negro suffrage. To a delegation from South Carolina he said that he was opposed to it because he was afraid "the late slaveholder would control the Negro vote against the white man." To a friend from Tennessee he said that the Negro "would vote with his late master, whom he does not hate, rather than with the nonslave-holding white, whom he does hate." To George Boutwell he said: "If you extend suffrage to the negroes, there will at once be quarrels between the whites and blacks, and bloodshed." [38]

He privately advocated limited Negro suffrage in a letter to the provisional governor of Mississippi, but only as a sop to disarm Radical Republican hostility. "If you could extend the elective franchise to all persons of color who own real estate valued at not less than $250, and pay taxes thereon, you would completely disarm the adversary and set an example the other States would follow. This you can do with perfect safety, and you thus place the southern States, in reference to free persons of color, upon the same basis with the free States. I hope and trust your convention will do this, and, as a consequence, the radicals, who are wild upon negro franchise, will be completely foiled in their attempts to keep the southern States from renewing their relations to the Union by not accepting their Senators and Representatives." [39] Here was the President, after three months in office, calling the Radical Republicans "the adversary," a word that to this Bible-reading population was synonymous not only with "enemy," but also with "the devil."

What misled many Radical Republicans into believing in the beginning that Johnson favored Negro suffrage was his taciturnity. When confronted with arguments he listened politely and did not disagree, but his silence often conveyed the impression of agreement. Sumner and Chase had no notion at first how futile had been their conferences with him. Stevens distrusted him from the beginning. So, too, did the Negro leader Frederick Douglass, whose feeling was crystallized by an incident at the inauguration.

"I was standing in the crowd by the side of Mrs. Thomas J. Dorsey," Douglass later wrote, "when Mr. Lincoln touched Mr. Johnson, and pointed me out to him. The first expression which came to his face, and which I think was the true index of his heart, was one of bitter contempt and aversion. Seeing that I observed him, he tried to assume a more friendly appearance; but it was too late; it was useless to close the door when all within had been seen." [40]

Thaddeus Stevens peppered Charles Sumner with anguished letters through the summer of 1865. On August 26 he laid bare his future strategy:

I am glad you are laboring to arrest the President's fatal policy—I wish the prospect of success were better—I have twice written him urging him to delay his hand until Congress meets—Of course he pays no attention to it—Our editors are generally cowards and sycophants—I would make a speech as you suggest if a fair occasion offered—Our views "reconstruction & confiscation" were embodied in our resolutions at Harrisburg, amidst much chaff—Negro Suffrage was passed over as heavy & premature—get the rebel states into a territorial condition, & it can be easily dealt with.
That I think should be our great aim—Then Congress can manage it—We need a good committee on elections—I fear Dawes—can he be brought to right—to exclude all rebel state members until final reorganization of *all*. I wish you would sound him, & let me know, as it may be proper to "reconstruct" that committee.[41]

In the late summer and early fall of 1865 there was a marked change in the temper of the politicians of the South. In June, as *The Nation* put it, "most Southern men looked forward to exemption from hanging and forfeiture of goods as the utmost they could hope for. . . . They laid down their arms, denounced all attempts at guerilla warfare, acknowledged that their slaves were free, and, in fact, gave the Government to understand that it had only to name the terms on which it would restore civil government in order to have them normally acceded to." But as a result of what Godkin called Johnson's "excessive tenderness," the Southerners had been roused "to their old audacity." [42]

They proceeded with a series of political acts that not only infuriated even Conservative Republicans, but also pained and humiliated the President. The legislature of South Carolina repudiated slavery but refused to ratify the Thirteenth Amendment, because, according to Governor Perry, they believed the second section "might be construed to give Congress the power of legislating for the freedmen in the Southern States." [43] Andrew Johnson found himself in the position of having to beg Perry by telegraph not to "lose all that she had done and so well done," and at Perry's urging, the necessary measure was passed. It took special telegrams from Johnson to force the Georgia and North Carolina legislatures to repudiate the Confederate war debts. The Georgia Assembly, in abolishing slavery, declared that it had not thereby relinquished the right of compensation.[44]

Mississippi refused to ratify the Thirteenth Amendment, and elected as her governor an ex-Confederate brigadier-general, Benjamin G. Humphrey, who didn't even wait for a presidential pardon before assuming office. Georgia, against Andrew Johnson's explicit advice, proceeded to elect to the Senate the late vice-president of the Confederacy, Alexander H. Stephens, while he was still in prison awaiting trial for treason. Altogether the Southern states elected to Congress four Confederate generals, five Confederate colonels, six Confederate cabinet officers, and fifty-eight Confederate Congressmen. No one of these men could take the oath of allegiance; they could not therefore accept office without Johnson's special pardon.[45]

From a Southern point of view these choices made sense. Some were old statesmen; many were war heroes; almost all of them knew something of the difficult art of government. But to Radical and Conservative Republicans alike these selections were abhorrent.

Even by midsummer of 1865 the Thirteenth Amendment had not yet been ratified. Kentucky, Maryland, and New Jersey, whose legislatures were all dominated by Democrats, had all refused to ratify, on the ground that ratification was a denial of States' Rights. Slavery was still legal in Kentucky, though the Negroes there were deserting the plantations by thousands and fleeing to the cities on the Ohio. General Palmer, who knew a dead law when he saw one, gave them all passes, writing to Andrew Johnson that he always "presumed" the applicant was free.[46] Stevens' journalist friend, Whitelaw Reid, was reporting from the South that in the rural areas slavery was far from dead. "The masters tell them that slavery is to be restored as soon as the army is removed; that the Government is already mustering the army out of service; that next year, when the State is re-organized, the State authorities will control slavery." [47]

To the impatient and apprehensive Stevens it seemed that if the Amendment failed of ratification the clock might well be turned back to 1860. The President's policies seemed popular throughout the country; the South was solidly behind him. Young Georges Clemenceau, describing the American scene for the Paris *Temps*, wrote on September 28, 1865: "Republicans and Democrats vie with each other in expressing their friendship for Mr. Johnson, the Democrats seeking to win him over, and the Republicans to keep their claim on him. Both parties have held their conventions, in Albany, New York, and the copperheads praised Johnson to the skies, the same Johnson whom three short months ago they were calling "Dionysus the Tyrant." [48]

Stevens feared that nearly everyone in the North was content to leave the freed slave to the mercy of his former master. Anti-Negro sentiment, which had flared up in the ugly draft riots during the war, now seemed to be spreading through the North. Connecticut, Minnesota, and Wisconsin all rejected Negro suffrage in 1865, and the fact that in all these states greater numbers voted in its favor than ever before did not alter the fact of the rejection.

New England, which through the war had been a unified force for liberation, was now torn by ideological party ruptures. William Lloyd Garrison, believing the work of the abolitionists to be finished, stopped publication of the *Liberator*, and came out against the forcing of Negro suffrage upon the South. For this he was blistered by Wendell Phillips, who believed that the liberation of the Negro had just begun.[49] Of all the New England states, only Massachusetts in its Republican convention took a stand against Johnson. In no other state save Pennsylvania did this occur, and for Pennsylvania's stand Stevens was responsible.

In the cabinet itself, as far as Stevens knew, Stanton, Harlan, and Speed were against Johnson; McCulloch, Welles, and Seward were with him. Montgomery Blair and his father, who had taken Johnson to their Silver Springs home after the humiliation of the inauguration, were said to be completely in his confidence.

Stevens was deeply pessimistic. "Is there any hope that Congress will overrule the Pres't?" he wrote to Sumner on October 7, 1865. "I fear we are ruined, for I have little faith in Congress." But instead of resigning himself to the inevitability of the postwar reaction and the seemingly imminent death of the Republican revolution, he began making battle plans. Among other things, he made a study of the recent emancipation measures in Russia. "Where can I find *in English* a correct history of the condition of the Russian serfs, and the terms of their liberation," he wrote to Sumner. "I know not where to look for it."[50] Especially was he eager to learn the terms upon which the serfs had been granted parcels of land.

In a sensational speech in Lancaster, September 6, 1865, Thaddeus Stevens flung his first real challenge to Andrew Johnson. The unfriendly *Lancaster Intelligencer* on September 7 called the speech "a tissue of sophistical fallacies." Lincoln's cabinet member, Edward Bates, who despised Stevens, read a half-column report of the address and condemned it in his diary with a pointed quotation from Richard III: "Wrens make prey, where eagles dare not perch."[51] Even Stevens' friends who read the speech were inclined to dismiss him as an absurd old Don Quixote galloping after impossibilities. Only the *New York Tribune* published it in full, September 11, 1865, but after the opening days of Congress, when the press belatedly realized the extent of Stevens' power, many editors revived it in their editorials, and the *New York Herald* republished it in its entirety on December 13, 1865.

"The sovereign power of the nation is lodged in Congress," Stevens said, but not even Congress, much less the Executive, "has the power to meddle with the domestic institutions of the several states. *In reconstruction therefore, no reform can be effected in the Southern States if they have never left the Union.*" To impose Negro suffrage upon a

state already in the Union would be, he said, "a mischievous imper-
tinence."

"But reformation must be effected; the foundation of their institutions—political, municipal and social—must be broken up and relaid
or all our blood and treasure have been spent in vain. This can only
be done by treating and holding them as a conquered people. Then all
things which we can desire to do follow with logical and legitimate
authority."

Stevens then went on to define exactly what he would do with the
South. "We especially insist that the property of the chief rebels should
be seized and appropriated to the payment of the national debt, caused
by the unjust and wicked war which they instigated. . . . There are
about 6,000,000 of freedmen in the South. The number of acres of
land is 465,000,000. Of this those who own above 200 acres each
number about 70,000 persons, holding in the aggregate—together with
the States—about 394,000,000 acres. By this forfeiting the estates of
the leading rebels the government would have 394,000,000 of acres,
besides their town property, and yet nine-tenths of the people would
remain untouched. Divide the land into convenient farms. Give, if
you please, forty acres to each adult male freedman. Suppose there are
1,000,000 of them. That would require 40,000,000 of acres, which de-
ducted from 394,000,000 leaves 354,000,000 acres for sale. Divide it
into suitable farms, and sell it to the highest bidders. I think it, including town property, would average at least $10 per acre. That
would produce $3,540,000,000."

This money, he said, could be used to pay for damage done to loyal
men, for soldiers' pensions, and to apply toward the national debt. "It
is fashionable to belittle our public debt," he said, "lest the people
should become alarmed, and political parties should suffer. I have never
found it wise to deceive the people.

"If the South is ever to be made a safe republic," he went on, "let
her lands be cultivated by the toil of the owners, or the free labor of intelligent citizens. This must be done even though it drive her nobility
into exile. If they go, all the better. . . . It is far easier and more
beneficial to exile 70,000 proud, bloated and defiant rebels than to
expatriate 4,000,000 of laborers, natives to the soil and loyal to the
government. This latter scheme was a favorite plan of the Blairs,
with which they had for a while inoculated our sainted President. But
a single experiment made him discard it and his advisers . . ."

Under Johnson's plan, he warned, "every rebel State will send rebels
to Congress, and they, with their allies in the North, will control Congress, and will occupy the White House. Then restoration of laws

and ancient constitutions will be sure to follow, our public debt will be repudiated, or the rebel national debt will be added to ours, and the people be crushed beneath heavy burdens."

Near the close of the speech he digressed long enough to declare the Blairs a family "of considerable power, some merit, of admirable audacity and execrable selfishness," and warned Andrew Johnson that however pure and patriotic he might be, if he followed their advice he would become "the most unpopular Executive—save one— that ever occupied the Presidential chair." [52]

This prophecy, like so many others of Thaddeus Stevens, seemed fatuous when it was pronounced, but it would nevertheless come true. Stevens was only partly responsible. He had unexpected assistance from the Southern whites.

CHAPTER NINETEEN

———◆◆———

Stevens Views the South

They began to pass in the road yonder while the house was still burning. We couldn't count them; men and women carrying children who couldn't walk and old men and women who should have been home waiting to die. They were singing, walking along the road singing, not even looking to either side. The dust didn't settle for two days, because all that night they still passed; we sat up listening to them, and the next morning every few yards along the road would be the old ones who couldn't keep up any more, sitting or lying down and even crawling along, calling to the others to help them; and the others—the young strong ones—not stopping, not even looking at them. I don't think they even heard or saw them. "Going to Jordan," they told me. "Going to cross Jordan."

William Faulkner: *The Unvanquished* [1]

WHEN A SLAVE was told that he was free, whether by a Union soldier, by his master, or by the clandestine whisperings of his own people, he usually tested the truth of the matter in a direct and simple fashion—he began to walk. The mass movement of Negroes in 1865, in the words of one Union officer, was like "the oncoming of cities." [2] Trailing in the wake of a single Union army in the East, there were at one time eight thousand ex-slaves. "They were detailed from us and sent off," said General O. O. Howard. "It took three or four hours for them to pass my quarters, and they made a great impression on me. There were a great many old people and women and children. They were bound for freedom."

"For nothing were the Negroes more eager than for transportation," wrote another Union officer. "They had a passion, not so much for wandering, as for getting together; and every mother's son among them seemed to be in search of his mother; every mother in search of her children." [3]

The roads from Texas, where 125,000 slaves had been shipped for safe-keeping in the early years of the war, were lined with Negroes going back home. Brigadier-General W. E. Strong, reporting to a Congressional committee on February 3, 1866, described the condition of the freedmen in Texas as worse than in any other Southern state. "They are frequently beaten unmercifully, and shot down like wild beasts, without any provocation, followed with hounds, and maltreated in every possible way," he said. Despite the fact that they had harvested an immense crop of cotton, corn, and sugar, he continued, "two thirds of the freedmen in the section of the country which I travelled over have never received one cent of wages since they were declared free. . . . I saw freedmen east of the Trinity river who did not know that they were free until I told them. . . . In the vicinity of the Mount Jordan and Jasper . . . the freedmen are still held in a state of slavery." [4]

General Strong was but one of scores of observers in the South who brought back word to Washington that while the Negro was free—except in rare and isolated areas—he was also in trouble. No longer looked upon as liquid capital, worth $500 to $1,500 in the open market, he had lost the protection of the one man who—though he might use the lash himself—would also see to it that no one else did. The result, as W. J. Cash has described it, was that "the road stood all but wide open to the ignoble hate and cruel itch to take him in hand which for so long had been festering impotently in the poor whites." [5]

If he was ill, there was no free medical service; if he was old, he must either beg or steal to stay alive. Many planters, who were willing to pay wages and continue the old plantation tradition of charity to the aged, were themselves homeless and bankrupt. In the wide swathes ravaged by Sherman's and Grant's armies there were no railroads, no granaries, or factories. Bridges were burned, locomotives wrecked, and rails torn up and twisted for hundreds of miles. In these areas destitution rested upon white and black alike.

In the suffering of the Confederate white man Thaddeus Stevens had no interest whatever; with the Union white and the ex-slave he was passionately concerned. From scores of different sources he could learn what was happening to every kind of Southerner. During the summer of 1865 the South was overrun with Northern journalists. Correspondents of the *New York Tribune*, *The Nation*, and the *Chicago*

Tribune, several Boston papers, and the old abolitionist presses, all reported widespread atrocities being inflicted upon the ex-slaves and indignities being heaped upon Southern Union men.

Detailed periodic reports streamed into Washington from agents of the Freedmen's Bureau, an agency set up early in 1865 under the direction of Major-General O. O. Howard to care for the hordes of dislocated and destitute ex-slaves. The Bureau agents mediated between whites and blacks in the matter of work contracts, helped set up colored schools—which were supported by Northern philanthropy, not Bureau funds—reported injustices and atrocities to the military, and gave free rations to white and black alike in the hardship areas.

"I was placed at the close of the war at the head of a bureau of impossibilities," General Howard said in a speech early in 1866. "I could not forget all the prejudices and hate, the battles and prisons. But I remembered the refugee, the sacked towns, and cities, and the terrible state of the people. Labor must first be settled, and that, too, immediately, without compulsion." In the first year General Howard saw to it that 7,000 Negro fugitives were returned to the plantations.[6]

The Freedmen's Bureau was the nation's first large-scale experiment in social welfare. It functioned on a small budget, $12,000,000 for the first year, and suffered from three grave disabilities in addition to lack of funds: the universal hostility of the ex-Confederates, bad publicity in the Democratic press, and the suspicion and lack of cooperation on the part of Andrew Johnson.

The President was not actively anti-Negro, but he believed that the old Southern paternalist tradition was perfectly adequate to secure the colored man justice. So it was possible for him on the one hand to give an Episcopal minister from South Carolina a thousand dollars for his Negro school in Charleston, but still actively oppose spending any federal money for Negro education through the Freedmen's Bureau.[7]

General Howard, who was an imaginative and able administrator, compassionate toward white and black man alike, was extremely sensitive to the criticisms hurled at the Bureau. 'Some of our papers charge that the object of the bureau is to support the negroes in idleness," he said. "I emphatically deny it. The object is diametrically opposite. If we can hold a steady hand now, in five years there will be no need of a Government control over these people."[8] Major-General Clinton B. Fisk described the typical Southern attitude toward the Freedmen's Bureau January 23, 1866: "The bureau is a good thing when burdens are to be borne. It is odious when it enforces justice."[9]

In addition to the Freedmen's Bureau reports and the dispatches of Northern journalists, Thaddeus Stevens could read the elaborate report on the South compiled by Carl Schurz, who had spent three months touring the South in 1865 at the bidding of the President. Schurz, the most distinguished German-American of his time, leader of the western Radical Republicans, was a conscientious and lucid journalist. He reported that almost everyone in the South conceded that slavery was extinguished and secession was a dead cause. He noted widespread relief that the Negroes had not risen in insurrection during the war. But carnage and defeat had not rooted out the old slavery attitudes. " 'You cannot make the negro work without physical compulsion.' I heard this," Schurz wrote, "hundreds of times, heard it wherever I went, heard it in nearly the same words from so many different persons, that at last I came to the conclusion that this is the prevailing sentiment among the southern people." [10]

A few planters, he reported, bewildered and infuriated when their Negroes tried to leave the plantations, dealt with them as they had formerly treated runaway slaves, by whipping and shooting. Some turned their shotguns upon the colored men who came to claim their wives and children. "There are certainly many planters," Schurz pointed out, "who, before the rebellion, treated their slaves with kindness, and who now continue to treat them as free laborers in the same manner." These planters had no labor problem. But the men with a reputation for cruelty saw their harvests rotting in the fields. The rice plantations in particular, where the mortality among slaves had been shockingly high, were practically deserted. [11]

The Schurz report, which had sixty pages of appended documents— letters, city ordinances, speeches of Southern politicians, and Army, Freedmen's Bureau and hospital reports—contained scores of items certain to infuriate Thaddeus Stevens. There were copies of recently passed ordinances in several Southern communities which indicated that all the possible devices of local legislation were being utilized to restore the Negro to conditions of near-slavery.

Schurz had personally authenticated in hospitals a great many stories of individual brutality, and had reports from Freedmen's Bureau agents detailing murders of freedmen all over the South. He noted widespread resistance to Negro education, in which Thaddeus Stevens had taken a special personal interest. "Hundreds of times I heard the old assertion repeated," he wrote, "that 'learning will spoil the nigger for work' and that 'negro education will be the ruin of the south.' " (It had not helped the cause of Negro education when Northern-bred teachers in the newly founded Negro schools taught their pupils to sing "John Brown's Body" and "Hang Jeff Davis to a Sour Apple

Tree.") [12]

From many sources it was evident to all who cared to read that in early December, 1865, labor relations in the South were in a state of chaos. The rumor had spread everywhere among the colored people that the big plantations would be divided up among them at Christmas. Stevens' speeches on confiscation were in part responsible, but more important, the knowledge of the sea island and Port Royal experiments in plantation subdivision had been spread through the South everywhere by colored soldiers. General Sherman's Field Order No. 15, of January 16, 1865, had provided that all the sea island plantations and a wide strip of rice plantations along the coast not already disposed of by the government be set aside for the Negroes following his army. The Freedmen's Bureau under General Rufus Saxton had divided 485,000 acres among 40,000 Negroes, who mistakenly believed that they held title to the land. [13]

Unscrupulous tricksters in surrounding areas did a thriving business selling red, white, and blue stakes at $2.00 each to the unsuspecting freedmen, telling them that all they had to do to obtain their forty acres was to mark out the land of their choice. In other areas, returning colored soldiers, having better information, were prepared to spend their army pay purchasing land. One regiment in Louisiana had saved $50,000, and was endeavoring to negotiate the purchase of five big plantations on the Mississippi River. But it was a rare Negro who would consent to sign a work contract until after Christmas, although the Freedmen's Bureau agents worked strenuously to destroy the rumor. [14]

For some Negroes freedom from slavery meant freedom from work. For others the mere hope of owning land had been enough reason for declaring a holiday through the whole autumn. "What with trapping rabbits by day and treeing 'possums by night, dances which lasted till morning, and prayer-meetings which were little better than frolics, they contrived to be happier than they had 'any call to be,' considering their chances of starving to death," wrote Freedmen's Bureau agent John DeForest. Many lived by petty pilfering, though DeForest believed that it was less common than in slavery days, "when they held, not without reason, that it was no harm 'to put massa's chicken into massa's nigger.'" [15] A further complication in the labor picture was the fact that many Negro men, following the example of their late masters, proudly refused to let their wives go into the fields to work.

The Southern legislators, most of whom met in the fall of 1865, had set about briskly repairing what seemed to them the abominable results of abolition. The resulting "black codes," most of which came into Thaddeus Stevens' possession before the opening of Congress and during the month of December, 1865, provided him with more am- munition for his program than the reams of copy from Northern journalists.

In Maryland the black code provided that if a Negro was convicted of any penitentiary offense he would be "sold," either in or out of the State "for such term as a white man for the same offence would be sentenced to the penitentiary." In Louisiana, where the Radical Re- publican government had been largely replaced by ex-Confederates— as Stevens had feared—the new black code provided that if a Negro refused to work according to contract he could be fined double the amount of wages for the time lost, or forced to work on public roads or levees until he agreed to return to his employer. Any Negro could be arrested as a vagrant upon the complaint of any white man, and if unable to give bond and security, would be sentenced to be hired out for a year, preferably to the white man bringing the complaint. The law declared that "every adult freedman or woman shall furnish themselves with a comfortable home and visible means of support within twenty days after the passage of this act." Failure meant being hired out at public auction for the remainder of the year.

The black code of Mississippi, approved November 25, 1865, pro- vided that any laborer who quit his job would forfeit his wages for the year. Negroes were forbidden to rent or own land outside of towns or cities, or to have any kind of independent business, and those already renting were compelled to give up their leases. The result, according to one former Union Army officer, was that the Negroes "stampeded." [16]

The Alabama black code, approved December 15, 1865, declared that "stubborn and refractory servants, and servants who loiter away their time," were to be treated as vagrants, fined fifty dollars, and in default of payment "hired out at public auction for a period of six months." The South Carolina code of December 19, 1865, made it a penal offense for any Negro to pursue any trade but that of farmer or house servant. Masters had the right to "whip moderately" any servant under eighteen. Colored children over the age of two whose parents were not "teaching them habits of industry and honesty," could be apprenticed to white persons until maturity. A Negro, unlike a white man, could be hanged for stealing a horse, a mule, or a bale of cotton, as well as for rape and murder. In Florida a Negro could be pilloried for an hour and whipped thirty-nine lashes for "intruding himself into any religious or other public assembly of white persons, or into any rail- road car or other public vehicle set apart for the exclusive accom- modation of white people."

The black codes were widely publicized in the Radical Republican press.[17] The editor of the *Chicago Tribune*, who printed the Mississippi code on December 1, 1865, commented: "We tell the white men of Mississippi that the men of the North will convert the state of Mississippi into a frog pond before they will allow any such laws to disgrace one foot of soil in which the bones of our soldiers sleep and over which the flag of freedom waves."

As George W. Cable described it later: "Emancipation had destroyed private, but it had not disturbed public subjugation. The ex-slave was not a free man; he was only a free negro." [18]

Thaddeus Stevens went to the opening of Congress in December, 1865, knowing that there was only one weapon in the whole Congressional arsenal that could be used to change at least the legal machinery of race relations in the South: the right of Congress to deny admission to its own members. He was now seventy-three, and had been ill through much of the summer. A semi-invalid, unable to walk any distance, he was carried everywhere in a special chair. Carl Schurz, who had not seen him for eighteen months, was shocked at his appearance. "He looked very much aged since our last meeting and infirm in health. In repose his face was like a death-mask." But his spirits seem to have been high, keyed up by the expectation of battle. There was good authority for the story, said Schurz, that he once said to the two young men who carried him to his seat in the House: "Thank you, my good fellows. What shall I do when you are dead and gone?" [19]

On December first, at a meeting of party leaders, Stevens outlined his plan, and on the following night a party caucus gave him unanimous support for a resolution he said he would introduce on the first day of Congress. It provided that instead of the Senate and House voting separately on their own members, a joint committee of fifteen, composed of nine members of the House and six of the Senate, be appointed to study the condition of the "so-called Confederate States of America," and that no member from these states be admitted to Congress until the Committee had made its report.

It was unprecedented for the Senate—normally extremely jealous of its power in relation to the House—to hand over so large a measure of authority on an issue of such magnitude. Secretary Welles, who privately opposed Negro suffrage and equality of civil rights, went to Andrew Johnson in great alarm, calling the whole proceeding "revolutionary, a blow at our governmental system." Johnson, less acute than Welles, refused to be disturbed, saying the Radicals "would be knocked in the head at the start." Tennessee, he pointed out, had elected Horace Maynard, a Union leader in East Tennessee, who had been active in the nominating convention that selected Lincoln and himself in 1864. To Johnson it was inconceivable that Maynard would be denied admission.[20]

Welles was not so sanguine. Nor was the editor of the Democratic *New York World*, Manton Marble, who in reporting the caucus wrote on December 4, 1865, that Thaddeus Stevens had "strangled the infant 'Restoration,' stamped upon it with his brutal heel, and proclaimed his plan for keeping the Union disunited."

As the House convened on December 4, 1865, Edward McPherson began to call the roll. This young lawyer and editor from Pennsylvania was Stevens' devoted disciple, who would one day collect his papers with the intention of writing his biography. Stevens had coached him well. As he read down the list he omitted all the representatives newly elected from the seceded states. When he skipped the name of Tennessee, Horace Maynard jumped to his feet, demanding the floor. McPherson said shortly:

"I decline to have any interruption of the call of the roll." When Maynard still protested, Stevens rose:

"I call the gentleman to order."

James Brooks of New York, Democratic floor leader, then objected, whereupon Stevens pointed out, as he had done thirty years earlier in the Buckshot War, that until the House was organized no question was in order except the election of a speaker. He was polite but firm, and all Brooks' flailings could not budge him.

When Brooks flung out a final taunt, "Talleyrand, the great diplomatist, said that language was given to man to conceal ideas; and we all know the gentleman's ingenuity in the use of language," there were few in the House who missed the veiled reference to Stevens' clubfoot and the rumor of his bastardy. But Stevens remained unmoved. Unlike the days of the Buckshot War, the galleries were now friendly, and by virtue of his careful preparation in the caucus he had not only a majority but two-thirds of the House committed to follow him on this procedure. There was, moreover, a still more profound difference. The Southern record through the summer and fall had shaken and angered Conservative Republicans as well as Radicals, and Stevens' adroit parliamentary maneuvering succeeded because he had behind him an immense reservoir of indignation. The House stayed with him, and Tennessee, the President's own state, was blocked.[21]

Howell Cobb wrote anxiously to his wife in Macon, Georgia: "We have just seen the first day's proceedings of Congress and it presents a gloomy future for the South. If the movements of Sumner in the Senate and Thad Stevens in the House foreshadow the future policy of the Govt. then indeed are our darkest days yet to come." Old Edward Bates, describing the proceedings in his diary, called Stevens "ignorant and vicious." But young Rutherford B. Hayes, who would one day be President, wrote cheerfully to his wife that Stevens was "witty, cool, full and fond of 'sarcasms,' and thoroughly informed and adequate." "He is radical throughout, except, I am told, he don't believe in hanging. He is leader." [22]

Stevens' resolution establishing the Joint Committee of Fifteen passed both houses handily, though the Senate abandoned the critical section denying any state readmission into the Union until the Committee had made its report. William Pitt Fessenden of Maine, the ablest Conservative Republican in the Senate, was made chairman of the whole committee as well as chairman of the Senate six; Stevens was made chairman of the House nine. Of the fifteen, three were Democrats.

No other committee of Congress ever wielded the power of the Joint Committee on Reconstruction or left so permanent an imprint on the country's history. It has long been traditional to say that Stevens dominated it with his malicious tongue, whipped it into submission, and made it the organ of his spite. This would be no mean accomplishment with fifteen members of Congress picked at random any time. This particular fifteen had some able and courageous men, proud of their independence, and not easily coerced by anyone. The Chairman, Senator Fessenden, said to be the ablest constitutional lawyer in the Senate since Webster, was an effective practical legislator, free from vanity, and an extremely able debater. He wrote to his family on January 14, 1866. "It is very unlucky for me that I have been forced to take hold of this reconstruction business. . . . The work of keeping the peace between the President and those who wish to quarrel with him, aided as they are by those who wish to quarrel with us, is a most difficult undertaking. The fools are not all dead, you know." [23]

Elihu B. Washburne of Illinois and Justin S. Morrill of Vermont, though friends of Stevens, had clashed with him on many issues and were suspicious of his fanaticism. Senator James W. Grimes of Iowa was described by one journalist as a man "who speaks little and accomplishes much . . . one of the pillars against whom weaker men lean and are propped into strength." [24] Neither he nor Senator Ira Harris of New York was an intense partisan. John A. Bingham of Ohio was leader of the Conservative Republicans in the House. Roscoe Conkling of New York, George S. Boutwell of Massachusetts, Henry T. Blow of Missouri, and Senators Jacob M. Howard of Michigan and

George H. Williams of Oregon, could, however, be counted upon to follow Stevens' lead and generally obey his orders.

The three Democrats on the Committee of Fifteen were violently anti-Stevens, especially Henry Grider of Kentucky and Andrew J. Rogers of New Jersey. The third, Senator Reverdy Johnson of Maryland, the most brilliant Democrat in the Senate, had worked with Thaddeus Stevens on a law case back in 1854,[25] but his political record thereafter—which included representing the defense in the Dred Scott Case, supporting McClellan in 1864, opposing the Emancipation Proclamation, and fighting the Freedmen's Bureau—had put him foremost on Stevens' blacklist.

Reverdy Johnson had, however, voted for the Thirteenth Amendment, which was not true of Representative Rogers, who boasted in Congress: "I thank God I never did. I could not lie down on my bed at night with a clear conscience if I had been guilty of being engaged as a participant in robbing a portion of the people of this country of millions of dollars invested under the Constitution in property in negroes." [26] Stevens recognized in Reverdy Johnson an able opponent; Rogers he looked upon as an unwitting asset to the Republican Party, and he let him talk all he pleased. Once, after listening to him make a two-hour diatribe against Negro suffrage in the District of Columbia, Stevens said: "I move that he be allowed to go on for the rest of the season!" [27]

From mid-January to the end of March, 1866, the Joint Committee on Reconstruction held hearings in Washington, interviewing 144 witnesses—Union Army officers, Freedmen's Bureau agents, Northern journalists, Southern Union men, and a handful of Negroes. Almost forty Confederate politicians and editors were also included, among them the former vice-president of the Confederacy, Alexander H. Stephens, but the selection of witnesses was heavily weighted on the side of men who would talk freely about the race problem. As is usual with committee hearings, the men with grievances got the publicity. But these grievances, piling up week after week, by sheer weight of numbers and by the horror of their details, shook Congress to the core.

Southerners who had steadfastly opposed secession testified that they were still treated like pariahs, despised, insulted as "damned Tories," and frequently threatened with death. One United States district judge, a native of Virginia, described how a returned rebel surgeon had shot to death on an Alexandria street the only man in his county who had voted for Lincoln. The surgeon had not been punished.

"A Union man in Virginia," said one witness from Lynchburg, is treated "like a weed upon a current" with "nothing honorable attached to him." [28] Such stories were re-enforced by Stevens' own private correspondence. One ex-Confederate wrote to him from Virginia: "I think you could afford to let *our* so-called representative into the show; he is a *preacher* and a plain man, who could not do you any harm if he were to try. We had to hunt a long time for a man who could swallow the nauseous test oath, and we found him in a 'corner obscure and alone.' " [29]

Most witnesses testified that where the Southern Union man was treated chiefly with contempt, the Negro was the real victim of the Confederate soldier's humiliation and rage in defeat. Major General George A. Custer, in command of the cavalry in Texas, said: "The people of the north have no conception of the number of murders that have been committed in that State during and since the war. . . . It is of weekly, if not of daily occurrence that freedmen are murdered." Into the record went a letter from a Freedmen's Bureau agent in Mississippi, who had written to his chief, November 27, 1865: ". . . almost daily murders are reported to this office, many of which are perpetrated by the militia or black cavalry, as they are called, who seem to have special fears of an 'insurrection.' These organizations are particularly adapted to hunting, flogging, and killing colored people." [30]

Reports of armed bands of "regulators," or "moderators" were sporadic; there was as yet no hint of widespread organization, but the stories came from every Southern state including Kentucky. Many witnesses testified that Southerners made no effort to bring the members of these bands to justice, and that the Freedmen's Bureau agents were powerless unless supported by sizable numbers of Union soldiers.

The famous Civil War nurse, Clara Barton, who had been south searching for names of missing Union Army men at Andersonville, testified briefly of a single incident. A young pregnant colored woman, flogged for failing "to fulfill a requirement for spinning properly," had come to her for help. "I found across her back twelve lashes or gashes," she said, "partly healed and partly not, some of them cut into the bone. She must have been whipped with a lash half as large as my little finger—it may have been larger; any of these gashes was from eight to ten inches in length; the flesh had been cut completely out most of the way." [31]

Freedmen's Bureau agent John William DeForest wrote: "My impression is that most of the murders of the Negroes in the South are committed by the poor-whites, who do not mean any harm to the 'black'uns' because they are black, but simply kill them in the exercise of their ordinary pugnacity. They could not shoot slaves in the good old times without coming in conflict with the slaveowner and getting the worst of it. Now, the Negro is no better than they are, and they pay him the compliment of fighting him as an equal." [32]

Several Freedmen's Bureau agents reported the burning of colored churches and schools, and there were scattered instances of assaults and indignities upon teachers of colored children. But these were isolated cases; on the whole the attitude of the Southern whites toward Negro schools seemed to be one of contempt but toleration so long as there were no taxes imposed for the purpose. Many Southern churches were actively cooperating in the Negro education movement.

The Freedmen's Bureau officer in charge of Negro education read his official report, issued January 1, 1866, into the hearings. It radiated optimism. There were nearly 100,000 Negro children in 740 schools, he said, largely financed by benevolent associations in the North. Five hundred schools had been set up and financed by literate Negroes. Everywhere there seemed to be an extraordinary zeal for learning. The total number of students, including soldiers, he estimated at 125,-000, and concluded cheerfully: "This is a wonderful state of things." [33]

But the committee members carefully noted reports that in certain areas colored schools were burned after the Union troops were withdrawn. Four schools in Franklin, Louisiana, and two in Terrebonne had been so destroyed. Four colored churches being prepared for use as schools had been burned in Mobile, Alabama.[34] Later these stories were to multiply.

Former Confederates who were questioned about the interracial violence either denied its existence or blamed it upon the Freedmen's Bureau and the colored troops stationed in the South. William L. Sharkey, provisional governor of Mississippi from June 13 to October 16, 1865, declared bluntly that "the Freedmen's Bureau and the colored troops there have done more mischief than anything else." The Negro, he said, was "destined to extinction, beyond all doubt," and declared the percentage of deaths among them "alarming, appalling." [35]

Southern writers were echoing this theme. Dr. J. C. Nott, of Alabama, said emphatically in *DeBow's Review*, March 1866: "History proves, indisputably, that a superior and inferior race cannot live together practically on any other terms than that of master and slave, and that the inferior race, like the Indians, must be expelled or exterminated. . . . I was born among the negroes at the South . . . and feel confident in the prediction that they are *doomed to extermination*." The editor of the *New Orleans Daily South* said on November 19, 1865: ". . . the whites must and shall rule to the end of time, even if the fate of Ethiopia be annihilation." [36]

There were certain things upon which all the witnesses testifying before the Joint Committee on Reconstruction agreed: first, that the Negro was bitterly hated by the poor-white, who could only see in the elevation of Negroes evidence of his own degradation; second, that Negro suffrage would be opposed everywhere with extreme violence; and third, that nearly all ex-Confederates approved of the policies of Andrew Johnson. The hearings convinced many Conservative Republicans that the Radicals were right when they held that there had been no real change in the South, that the same society that had tolerated organized violence and brutality before the war, now bitter and impoverished in defeat, shrugged at disorganized violence. It seemed, too, that even the most thoughtful and educated Southerners blanketed their real antipathy to the Negro with talk of inevitability and fate.

Alexander Stephens did not help the cause of the South by testifying in April 1866 that he still believed in the right of secession *and* return without submitting to any conditions precedent. Members of the committee like Washburne, Grimes, and Fessenden now found it impossible to continue to support the President and Secretary Seward in their efforts for a speedy restoration of the seceded states. They did not share Johnson's certainty that the racial violence was an inevitable and temporary result of the dislocations of the war and emancipation, and that the speediest way to resolve the tensions was to restore the reins of power to the Southern whites and get the federal government out of the South altogether. They were troubled that he could lightly dismiss reports of the new laws apprenticing colored children by saying that he himself had been apprenticed at the age of ten and "he did not suppose they were any better." [37]

The 800-page report of the hearings was eventually printed, and a hundred and fifty thousand copies issued. It became—as Thaddeus Stevens intended—a vital campaign document in the election of 1866. But while the hearings were still going on, the breach between Andrew Johnson and the Republicans widened into a chasm, and the Union Party, always a patchwork, began to disintegrate. By February 23, 1866, a month before the hearings were over, the whole nation knew that the President and Thaddeus Stevens were at each other's throats.

CHAPTER TWENTY

---◆---

The Open Rupture

THROUGH DECEMBER, 1865, and January, 1866, Thaddeus Stevens beat off every attempt to win recognition for the Congressmen elected from the former Confederate states. When Representative Ingersoll from Illinois pleaded for the admission of Colonel James M. Johnson, of Arkansas, saying, "I know him to be a devoted loyalist, one who has fought for three years and more in our Army against the rebellion," Stevens made a reply that brought a guffaw across the House:

"I do not see what that amounts to, except that he shall not be hanged."

When James Brooks of New York protested the injustice of taxing Southerners while denying them representation, Stevens cut him off: "Well, they have taxed us considerably; I call for the previous question." [1]

There were three projects to which he had dedicated himself: first, the continuation of the Freedmen's Bureau for another year, second, the adoption of Negro suffrage in the District of Columbia, and third, the adoption of a fourteenth amendment to the Constitution that would—in his own words—guarantee "perpetual ascendency to the party of the Union; so as to render our republican government firm and stable forever." [2]

Stevens did not anticipate much opposition to the Freedmen's Bureau Bill, which passed the House February 6, 1866, and seems to have had no expectation whatever of a presidential veto. He was especially intent that Union Army officers continue to have authority to set up military courts with power to fine and imprison in those cases where the Negro was denied equal rights with the white man. Since most Southern states still denied the Negro the right to testify in cases where a white man was involved, Stevens believed this provision a basic requirement where martial law was no longer in force.[3]

A second provision in the Freedmen's Bureau Bill was especially dear to his heart. It authorized giving forty-acre tracts to the freedmen from the unoccupied lands owned by the state governments. Although this land was uncleared and relatively valueless compared to the plantation country, it was at least available.[4] Stevens had not abandoned his agitation for confiscation of the big plantations, but knowing that politics is the art of the possible, he was willing to take small favors.

Andrew Johnson had steadily insisted that the Freedmen's Bureau restore to former owners all confiscated land that had not been sold for nonpayment of taxes, even though some estates where the title was not yet clear had long been divided up among the freedmen. The Bureau never held more than two-tenths of one per cent of the land in the seceded states, but most of this was quickly being restored to the former owners. Many Negroes, who had been given to understand that the land was rightfully theirs, were now filled with consternation and bitterness.[5]

When an amendment to the Freedmen's Bureau Bill was introduced, providing that the freedmen buy or rent the land already allotted to them, or else be turned off at the end of three years, Stevens protested that the price was too high and the plan unjust. "The freedmen on the Sea Islands who have gone there upon the faith of these forty-acre grants, and have built for themselves comfortable houses and established communities there, have the right to retain those lands forever; and . . . it is a burning cruelty in us, by a provision of this kind, to allow them to be turned off in three years." He cited the example of the Emperor of Russia, who "set free twenty-two million serfs," and "compelled their masters to give them homesteads upon the very soil which they had tilled; homesteads not at a full price, but at a nominal price; 'for,' said he, in noble words, 'they have earned this, they have worked upon the land for ages, and they are entitled to it.' But, by this bill, we proposed to sell our land at not less than the Government price, or to rent it at prices which these poor people can never pay." [6]

But Stevens was defeated in this and all other of his attempts to secure private land for the freedmen. His party was content to deny the Southerner the right of ownership in man; on denial of other property rights it would not follow Stevens an inch.

What Lincoln would have done about the problem of land for the ex-slave one cannot be sure. He was firmly against confiscation. But one letter that he wrote on the subject of how the ex-slaves should be treated shows a markedly different spirit from that of Andrew Johnson. This letter, written to Alpheus Lewis of Arkansas, January 23, 1864, has been largely forgotten by historians eager to demonstrate that Johnson was carrying out Lincoln's reconstruction plan.

"You have enquired how the government would regard and treat cases wherein the owners of plantations, in Arkansas, for instance, might fully recognize the freedom of those formerly slaves, and by fair contracts of hire with them, re-commence the cultivation of their plantations. *I answer I should regard such cases with great favor, and should, as the principle, treat them precisely as I would treat the same number of free white people in the same relation and condition. Whether white or black, reasonable effort should be made to give government protection. . . . Such plan must not be used to break up existing leases or arrangements of abandoned plantations which the government may have made to give employment and sustenance to the idle and destitute people.* With the foregoing qualifications, and ex-planations, and in view of its tendency to advance freedom, and re-store peace and prosperity, such hiring and employment of the freed people, would be regarded by me with rather especial favor." [7]

This letter indicates not only that Lincoln would have been slow to restore the divided plantations to their former owners, but also that he was firmly committed to "government protection" for white and black, and to the principle of equality of treatment for both races.

Thaddeus Stevens looked upon the District of Columbia as a con-venient laboratory for experimenting with his Utopia. Here Congress had real power, with no constitutional prohibitions. He saw no reason why the Negroes there should not have immediate suffrage. They paid taxes on over a million dollars' worth of property; they owned twenty-one churches and a like number of schools, built and maintained by their own money, and had furnished far more volunteers for the Union Army in proportion to their population than the white men of the District.[8] But in a recent local plebiscite in Washington and George-town, the white citizens had cast 7,369 votes against Negro suffrage and but thirty-six in its favor.

Stevens had no faith that Washington's property owners would ever voluntarily accept Negro suffrage, and he had no compunction about forcing it upon them. A bill with this intent was introduced into the House shortly after Congress opened. This was the first wedge; he was ready for a long hammering.

To secure Negro suffrage in the states, however, in the face of a universal and almost hysterical opposition in the South, and a determined pressure from the Democratic Party in the North, seemed at this point a Gargantuan task. It is usually forgotten that in the beginning Thaddeus Stevens indicated he would be content with less than Utopia in regard to universal Negro suffrage. His first bill for a proposed Fourteenth Amendment, introduced less than a fortnight after the opening of Congress, provided for a change in the basis of representation among the states from total population to actual voters. If the Southerners denied suffrage to Negroes, they would see sliced off the ballot a certain number of men they might otherwise send to Congress. "If," he said, "they should grant the right of suffrage to persons of color, I think there would always be Union white men enough in the South, aided by the blacks, to divide the representation, and thus continue the Republican ascendance. If they should refuse to thus alter their election laws it would reduce the representatives of the late slave States to about forty-five and render them powerless forever."

Until the former Confederate states accepted this amendment, he said, they should be denied statehood and kept in a territorial status, where Congress would have the right to fix their election laws. He insisted that none of these states should be counted in determining the ratification of any amendment. Later, under pressure from other members of the Joint Committee of Fifteen, he abandoned this bill because it would have meant the loss of fifteen to twenty representatives from Northern states based on the 3,800,000 immigrants who were not yet citizens. "It was dear to my heart," he said, "for I had been gestating it for three months." [9]

Stevens' plans for Negro suffrage ran headlong into a political principle already hallowed in the Democratic Party and believed sacred by many in his own, the principle that only white men were fit to govern. The Democratic Convention of Pennsylvania passed a resolution March 5, 1866, saying: "The white race alone is entitled to the control of the Government of the Republic, and we are unwilling to grant the negroes the right to vote." [10] Stevens now proceeded to ridicule this theme with the best that was in him:

Governor Perry and other provisional governors and orators proclaim
that "this is the white man's Government." The whole copperhead party,
pandering to the lowest prejudices of the ignorant, repeat the cuckoo cry,
"This is the white man's Government." Demagogues of all parties, even
some high in authority, gravely shout, "This is the white man's Government."
What is implied by this? That one race of men are to have the exclusive
right forever to rule this nation, and to exercise all acts of sovereignty,
while all other races and nations and colors are to be their subjects, and
have no voice in making the laws and choosing the rulers by whom they
are to be governed. Wherein does this differ from slavery except in degree?
. . . If we have not yet been sufficiently scourged for our national sin
to teach us to do justice to all God's creatures, without distinction of race
or color, we must expect the still more heavy vengeance of an offended
Father. . . .
If equal privileges were granted to all, I should not expect any but white
men to be elected to office for long ages to come. The prejudice engendered
by slavery would not soon permit merit to be preferred to color. But it
would still be beneficial to the weaker races. In a country where political
divisions will always exist, their power, joined with just white men, would
greatly modify, if it did not entirely prevent, the injustice of majorities. . . .
Sir, this doctrine of a white man's Government is as atrocious as the infamous sentiment that damned the late Chief Justice to everlasting fame;
and, I fear, to everlasting fire.[11]

Thaddeus Stevens never stood higher in the estimation of the Republican press than in January, 1866. The Conservative Republican
Harper's Weekly, normally critical of Stevens and as yet a supporter
of Johnson, said on January 6, 1866: "Mr. Stevens certainly keeps his
eye upon the light and scorns the wind. He sees plainly that the end
we must seek is sure rather than swift reconstruction."

Before the month was out, his bill permitting Negro suffrage in the
District of Columbia had passed the House (though not the Senate),
and the *Nation*, on January 25, 1866, called it a "great act of legislative justice." It was the passage of this bill, however, that touched off
the fireworks that displayed to the whole country the nature and magnitude of the chasm separating Stevens from the President.

Andrew Johnson had an interview with Senator James Dixon, in
which—according to the newspaper accounts Stevens had read on the
floor of the House on January 31, 1866—he had called the District
suffrage bill "ill-timed, uncalled for, and calculated to do great harm,"
leading to a war between the races and "certain extermination of the
negro population." This had been the President's first definite pronouncement against Negro suffrage, and to many in the country it came
as a shock. As late as December 23, 1865, Georges Clemenceau had
written to his Paris newspaper: "No one has any doubt that the blacks

will have the right to vote, now that slavery is abolished. It should be so and it will be so, Mr. Johnson wishes it to be so, as much as any radical." [12]

Johnson in the interview had indicated a grudging willingness to go along with the Radical Republicans in supporting a new constitutional amendment "making in each State the number of qualified voters the basis of representation." But his reason had annoyed Stevens. Such an amendment, the President had suggested, would "remove from Congress all issues in reference to the political equality of the races." In any case, he had "doubted the propriety at this time of making further amendments to the Constitution," and urged that the first order of business in Congress be the restoration of the Southern states.

Stevens now caused a sensation in the House by calling the interview a violation of the privileges of the House, "made in such a way that centuries ago, had it been made to Parliament by a British king, it would have cost him his head." The shocked editor of *Harper's Weekly* shortly remarked that Stevens' sarcasm was "but another proof of his singular incapacity as a leader," and condemned the House for lacking the dignity to rebuke him.[13]

In a revealing diary entry on February 13, 1866, Gideon Welles, still Secretary of the Navy, made it clear that Andrew Johnson had come to believe that Thaddeus Stevens was capable of anything. "The unmistakable design of Thad Stevens and his associates was to take the government into their own hands, the President said, and to get rid of him by declaring Tennessee out of the Union. A sort of French Directory was to be established by these spirits in Congress, the Constitution was to be remodeled by them, etc."

This extraordinary statement revealed the dangerous failure of communication between the White House and Congressional leaders. Actually the Joint Committee on Reconstruction—despite Stevens' delaying tactics—was now practically ready for the formal readmission of Tennessee.[14] In Nashville, the Radical Republicans were in control, and the new governor was the flamboyant Unionist "Parson" Brownlow, a long-time enemy of Johnson, who had undergone a quick-change conversion from extreme anti-abolitionism to ultra-Radicalism. The new Tennessee constitution had abolished slavery, repudiated the Confederate debt, and disfranchised leading rebels, but had not yet provided for Negro suffrage.

In what was probably the most foolish mistake of his career Andrew Johnson hurled a grenade into the Radical Republican camp on February 19, 1866, by vetoing the Freedmen's Bureau bill. He did this against the advice of three members of his cabinet, James Speed, Edwin M. Stanton, and James Harlan. The President objected chiefly to the clause continuing to give Union officers in the South the right to try civilian cases where Negro civil rights were at stake, which did in fact preserve a dual court system in the South. But he did not suggest where else the Negro could turn for justice. He objected to what he believed was unnecessary almsgiving, and insisted that economic necessity would force the white man to treat the Negro fairly. But what particularly enraged Congress was Johnson's implication that Congress had no right to enact a measure directing the internal affairs of states denied representation.

Later in a public speech he said of the Freedmen's Bureau: "The cost of this to the people was $12,000,000 at the beginning. The further expense would be greater, and you are to be taxed for it. That's why I vetoed it." [15]

Andrew Johnson could hardly have chosen a worse issue upon which to break with the Republican Party. Horace Greeley gathered editorials on the veto from twenty-two Republican newspapers, most of them Conservative. All deplored it.[16] The Southern press, on the other hand, was triumphant. "The old Tennesseean has shown his blood," said the Montgomery, Alabama, *Ledger*, "and bearded the lion in his lair, 'The Douglass in his hall'—'glory enough for one day'—glorious old man, and let the earth ring his praise to the heavens. The South and the Government are in the same boat one more time, thank the gods!" [17]

The day following the veto message Thaddeus Stevens went to the House with a bomb of his own design. It was a resolution from the Joint Committee of Fifteen designed to prevent the restoration of any state "until Congress shall have declared such State entitled to such representation." Specifically it meant that all plans to admit Tennessee had come to a halt.[18]

When Johnson's supporters realized that Stevens intended to push the resolution through without debate, they angrily accused him of gag rule. Amid the confusion and shouting he sat imperturbable. "It is simply the return of the rebels of 1861," he said. "I sat thirty-eight hours under this kind of fight once, and I have no objection to a little of it now. I am ready to sit for forty hours." When the opposition finally subsided in defeat, Stevens made a characteristic barbed compliment: "I confess, sir, for so small a number they have made a most venomous fight." [19]

So Congress—which until now had been willing to grant Andrew Johnson extraordinary executive power through the Freedmen's Bureau —served official notice on the President that he would no longer be permitted to wield any of the special power exercised by Abraham Lincoln during the war emergency. Under no circumstances would he be permitted to restore the South by executive action. Few Congressmen took the extreme position held by Thaddeus Stevens, that the nation's sovereignty was vested in Congress—as in England it was vested in the Parliament—and not shared equally by the President and the Supreme Court.[20] But the feeling was general that the old pre-war balance had become upset and ought to be restored.

Had Johnson at this point chosen to conciliate the Conservative Republicans, particularly those on the Joint Committee of Fifteen, his future might have been wholly different. His personal relations with Thaddeus Stevens were not yet seriously damaged. In fact, Stevens on February 15, 1866, had strongly urged an appropriation for refurnishing the White House, which had been shamefully plundered by the public after Lincoln's death. The furnishings were being replaced, Stevens said, "as the present humble and economical President deems necessary. I can say to the committee that nothing more is asked by the President and his family than is absolutely necessary to make the house decent." [21]

But Johnson, in a sensational speech on Washington's Birthday, showed himself to be utterly wanting in Lincoln's tact and sagacity, and capable of meeting the impolitic vituperation of Thaddeus Stevens only with bludgeoning of his own. Against the advice of Secretary McCulloch and Senator Doolittle, who warned him against extemporaneous speaking, he addressed a crowd of several thousand supporters who had marched to the White House from a rally at a local theater. He lashed out against the Joint Committee of Fifteen as an "irresponsible central directory" determined to keep the Southern states out of the Union, after a four years' war fought to prove that they had no right to leave. "I am opposed to the Davises, the Toombses, the Slidells, and the long list of such," he said. "But when, on the other hand, men—I care not by what name you call them—are still opposed to the Union, I am free to say to you that I am still with the people."

"Name them," shouted someone in the crowd.

Johnson waited a few seconds before replying. "Suppose I should name to you those whom I look upon as being opposed to the fundamental principles of this government, and as now laboring to destroy them," and he called out with deliberation: "Thaddeus Stevens, Charles Sumner, and Wendell Phillips." When a voice cried out, "Forney!" (John W. Forney, editor of the *Washington Chronicle*, who had turned against Johnson in recent months) he replied with contempt: "I do not waste my fire on dead ducks!"

Johnson went on to say that he would not be governed by friends nor bullied by enemies but would stand by his own honest convictions. Then he made an extraordinary statement of self-revelation, an inadvertent betrayal of his continuing preoccupation with the idea of martyrdom: "They may talk about beheading [an obvious reference to Stevens' recent taunt comparing him with Charles I], but when I am beheaded, I want the American people to be the witnesses. . . . Are those who want to destroy our institutions and change the character of the Government not satisfied with the blood that has been shed? Is their thirst still unslaked? Do they want more blood? Have they not honor and courage enough to effect the removal of the 'Presidential obstacle' otherwise than through the hands of the assassin? . . . Does not the blood of Lincoln appease the vengeance and wrath of the opponents of this government? I do not fear assassins, but if my blood must be shed because I vindicate this Union, let it be so. Let an altar of the Union be erected, and then, if necessary, lay me upon it, and the blood that now warms and animates my frame shall be poured out in a last libation as a tribute to the Union." [22]

According to Carl Schurz, for many in Washington there was only one explanation—that Johnson was drunk again. Senator Doolittle later wrote privately to O. H. Browning that the speech had "lost to our cause" two hundred thousand votes.[23] Godkin in the *Nation* wrote soberly on March 1, 1866: "But, verily, the appearance of the President at the windows of the White House to accuse prominent members of another branch of the Government of the foulest crime of which a man can be guilty, is something new and alarming in American history."

The Northern Democratic press cheered Johnson. The *Chicago Times* suggested that he arrest Sumner, Stevens, and Phillips, and jail them, and if Congress persisted in its policy, that he turn the Senate and House out of the capitol at the point of the bayonet. Stevens' hometown opposition newspaper, the *Lancaster Intelligencer,* labeled him, together with Charles Sumner, "traitors of the present hour." [24] The *Illinois State Register* demanded that Stevens, Sumner, and Wade "be seized in the Halls they desecrate and be imprisoned. Let the southern members of Congress return to Washington and be duly installed in their seats. Then, on promise of amendment, let these revolutionists out, and the Union will be restored indeed." [25]

Thaddeus Stevens waited eighteen days before replying to Johnson's charge that he was destroying the fundamental principles of the government. He began with unaccustomed soberness: "Instead of feeling personal enmity to the President, I feel great respect for him. I honor his integrity, patriotism, courage, and good intentions. He stood too firmly for the Union, in the midst of dangers and sacrifices, to allow me to doubt the purity of his wishes. But all this does not make me fear to doubt his judgment and criticize his policy. When I deem his views erroneous, I shall say so; when I deem them dangerous, I shall denounce them."

Representative Hiram Price of Iowa, who had expected a blast against the President, now interrupted to ask with mock astonishment if this could really be the same Thaddeus Stevens referred to by Johnson "in a certain speech." Whereupon Stevens went on with what seemed at first to be a piece of whimsy.

"Does the learned gentleman from Iowa suppose for a single moment that that speech, to which he refers as having been made in front of the White House, was a fact? I desire at this time to put the gentleman right. . . . that speech . . . was one of the grandest hoaxes ever perpetrated. . . . I am glad to have at this time the opportunity . . . to exonerate the President from ever having made that speech. It is a part of the cunning contrivance of the copperhead party, who have been persecuting our President since the 4th of March last.

"Why, sir, taking advantage of an unfortunate incident which happened on that occasion, they have been constantly denouncing him as addicted to low and degrading vices. To prove the truth of what I say about this hoax, I send to the Clerk's desk to be read, a specimen of this system of slander. It is an extract from the *New York World* of March 7, 1865. Let the Clerk read that vile slander from the leading paper of the Democratic party."

The Clerk read as follows:

The drunken and beastly Caligula, the most profligate of the Roman emperors, raised his horse to the dignity of consul—an office that in former times had been filled by the greatest warriors and statesmen of the public, the Scipios and Catos, and by the mighty Julius himself. The consulship was scarcely more disgraced by that scandalous transaction than is our Vice Presidency by the late election of Andrew Johnson. That office has been adorned in better days by the talents and accomplishments of Adams and Jefferson, Clinton and Gerry, Calhoun and Van Buren. And now to see it filled by *this insolent, drunken brute, in comparison with whom even Caligula's horse was respectable,* for the poor animal did not abuse his own nature! And to think that only one frail life stands between this *insolent, clownish drunkard* and the Presidency! My God bless and spare Abraham Lincoln!

"That was a serious slander," Stevens went on, "which appeared as an editorial in the *New York World.* That party, taking advantage of an incident which it is thought by many they themselves brought about, have been persecuting the President with such slanders as that ever since. . . . We never credited it, but looked with indignation upon the slander."

Then returning again to the President's speech, Steven continued his mockery. "If these slanders can make the people believe that the President ever uttered that speech, then they have made out their case. But we all know he never did utter it. It is not possible, sir, and I am glad of this opportunity to relieve him from that odium." [26]

Stevens' thrust created a roar of laughter in the House. But however deftly inflicted, it was meant to scar. Godkin in the *Nation* called it "a painful incident." "No matter what Mr. Johnson may do or say," he continued, "he is our President, and his shame is our shame. . . . Our quarrels with him are, in some sense, family quarrels, and the less they are exposed to the public gaze the better." And the editor of the *North American Review* wrote: "Mr. Stevens ought to have remembered that it was not so much the nakedness of an antagonist that he was uncovering as that of his country." [27]

CHAPTER TWENTY-ONE

The Rump Parliament

All New Englanders are not Puritans, and all Puritans are not vulgar, ignorant, and half-demented like Thad. and his Rump.

> George Fitzhugh: "Thad. Stevens's Conscience—the Rump Parliament," *DeBow's Review,* November 1866.

SIX WEEKS after he accused Thaddeus Stevens and Charles Sumner of destroying the fundamental principles of the government, Andrew Johnson had lost control of the party that elected him and had begun sliding slowly downhill toward the impeachment morass. The Republican press was increasingly hostile; the Conservative Republicans were divided and drifting, most of them into the Radical camp, some back toward the Democratic Party.

By April 9, 1866, the Radical Republicans had recruited enough members to override Johnson's veto on a decisive issue, the Civil Rights bill. This marked the beginning of real Radical rule, a three-year interregnum, the only period in American history when the Chief Executive was truly politically impotent. That it should be Thaddeus Stevens, and not Charles Sumner, Henry Wilson, Ben Wade, or any other dedicated Radical Republican whom history should hold as the man responsible was no accident. Stevens was more than a symbol, more than the hub of a wheel; he had become a political dynamo, relentless, calculating, indefatigable.

Many in his own party feared and hated him. Senator Grimes described him to Gideon Welles as "a pretty unscrupulous old fellow, unfit to lead any party . . . a debauchee in morals and politics." Representative Martin Kalbfleisch said ruefully of Stevens after one encounter in the House: "I do not mean to say that the gentleman's judgment is not honest, but he slanders most mightily." [1] J. W. Binckley, in a portrait in the *Galaxy*, July 16, 1866, marveled that "the master spirit of the American Congress," who "wielded daily far more power than Henry Clay ever had," was also "the most unpopular man on the floor." His "astonishing mastery over the unwilling minds of other powerful men" was due, said Binckley, to three things: first, "a will of inherent and uncommon might," second, "a perfect indifference to praise or blame," and third, an "invincible and incorruptible moral sense."

"Who believes he could flatter Thaddeus Stevens? Or who supposes that he could be made to blush with mortification?" Binckley asked. "He differs capitally from other partizan managers, in that he acts from no selfish motive, taking this in the ordinary sense. Contemning all applause, defying all censure, incapable of meekness, or of that sense of being belittled which comes of being stripped of external adjuncts, this man has no ambition. On the other hand, his love of power is the master passion of his soul."

Actually Stevens was never to relinquish one ambition, that of becoming Senator. But he never let this hope spoil his independence nor weaken his hand as whip of the Republican Party. He had no political façade, and lacked the ordinary vanity that is easily punctured by malice or defeat. His was the special and invulnerable pride of the man without pretense. He could be churlish in the name of honesty and reckless in the pursuit of principle.

Justin Morrill, of Vermont, who worked closely with Stevens in committees, said of him after his death: "He was wholly untinctured by vanity, and seemed nearly as oblivious to the praise of friends as to the censure of enemies. Without self conceit and iron-clad against criticism, especially newspaper criticism, he never courted flattery nor counted it as any part of his wages. Envious of nobody, careless of his own reputation, he was wholly satisfied when satisfied with the result, and neither revised his own speeches nor paid much attention to the revised speeches of anybody else. Though deaf himself to personal compliments, he cordially praised and remembered all those who voted rightly, and was an inexorable hater of those who did not or dodged. Rarely wounded in any contest his wounds never bled, but healed without scars, as he had no memory for the blows he provoked and received, still less apology or regret for such as he had given." [2]

A great many journalists of the day tried to describe the remarkable versatility of Stevens' parliamentary techniques. "In times of emergency," wrote John B. Ellis, "he would call on every Republican in the House to sustain the party measures, and boldly defy any conservative to oppose them on pain of being 'read out' of the Republican organization. At such times his manner would be expressive of the bitterest sarcasm, and his voice cold and trenchant as steel, would strike terror to the hearts of his weaker followers." [3]

J. W. Binckley said he usually began a speech with a kind of "grandfatherly grumbling . . . monotonous, and sometimes incoherent, always with a tone of muffled good-will, and a total absence of all trace of scorn." He would seem to be "hunting mislaid notes or a dropped handkerchief, with the dull solicitude of dotage," and the House pages would surreptitiously mimic him. "Then, rising erect, the Leader lifts his long right arm with a wide sweep, the elbow in advance of the hand; contracts his beetling brows, throws up and back his towering head, and with a sudden, straight thrust of his long, yellow finger, followed by the whole out-stretch of his arm, he sends forth, in a thundering tone, the iron bolt of his argument." [4]

Alexander McClure sat by him once in the House and heard a leading Pennsylvania Republican protest about committing his party to Negro suffrage in the District of Columbia. Stevens, he said, "with grim face and cold gray eyes," "waved his hand to the trembling suppliant and bade him go to his seat and vote for the measure or confess himself a coward to the world. The Commoner was obeyed." [5]

The Conservative Republican press, though beginning to deride Andrew Johnson, was often inclined to damn Stevens in the same breath. *Harper's Weekly* on April 7, 1866, admitted that Stevens' words had "a gladiatorial strength which would have done honor to the boldest of Rome's orators," but added caustically: "Mr. Stevens has no single quality of a statesman, except strong conviction and fidelity to principle. He is strictly a revolutionary leader: reckless, unsparing, vehement, vindictive, loud for the rights of conquerors, intolerant of opposition, and as absolutely incapable of fine discrimination and generous judgment as a locomotive of singing. Of a pleasant humor and personal kindliness, he is no more fitted for the task of reconstruction which devolves upon Congress than a jovial blacksmith to repair a watch, or 'a butcher to take up hidden arteries and sundered veins in the very region of the heart.' "

The Boston *Republican* put the Conservative Republican dilemma aptly on July 21, 1866: "But to reject Thaddeus Stevens and Charles Sumner and support Mr. Johnson is one thing, and to go to bed with Copperheads and rebels is another; and many eager for the first will hesitate long before doing the last."

The fact that Stevens, despite the hostility from his party press and many leaders in the party itself, was so able to dominate the legislation of reconstruction from April 1866 until his death in August 1868 is an astonishing political phenomenon, which cannot be explained merely as a consequence of adroit and ruthless parliamentary maneuvering. There was a whole complex of contributing circumstances, of which the most important were the political ineptness of Andrew Johnson, the continuing moral bankruptcy of the Democratic Party in the North, and the unfortunate capacity of the Southerners for alienating possible allies by their outbursts of violence.

The most elemental difference between the philosophy of Republicans and Northern Democrats continued to be the same as during the war—whether or not to be inclusive or exclusive about the rights of man. The Democrats who had fought emancipation now fought the Republicans who wanted to guarantee the Negro civil and political rights, with exactly the same arguments. "It is one of the unhandsomest aspects of the Democratic party," said the *Nation,* "that it devotes itself to the derision of the colored population. . . . Mr. John Van Buren [son of Martin Van Buren] in his last speech at Albany in the autumn of 1865, said that colored men were chiefly fit to black boots and cut hair." [6] Gideon Welles wrote bluntly in his diary, September 28, 1865: "Whenever the time arrives that he should vote, the Negro will probably be permitted. I am no advocate for social equality, nor do I labor for political or civil equality with the negro. I do not want him at my table, nor do I care to have him in the jury-box, or in the legislative hall, or on the bench."

The whole influential Blair family, which had taken Andrew Johnson under its wing, was emphatically opposed to equal rights for the Negro, and denounced the Freedmen's Bureau. When Charles Sumner began to champion the Civil Rights bill, Mrs. Violet Blair let it be known through Washington that she would no longer speak to him.[7]

The Republicans, on the other hand, still continued to draw upon as a major source of their strength what James Russell Lowell called "an effort of the ideal America which was to them half a dream and half a reality, to cast off an alien element. . . . They are fully resolved to have the great stake they played for and won, and that stake was the Americanization of all America, nothing more and nothing less." [8]

The Republicans in Congress, coming gradually to believe with Frederick Douglass that "the man who is whipped easiest is whipped oftenest," [9] set about early in January 1866 to pass legislation guaranteeing to the Negro the same civil rights enjoyed by the white man. It is significant that Lyman Trumbull of Illinois, an old and trusted friend of Lincoln, a Conservative Republican who hoped to avoid a break with Andrew Johnson, led the way in introducing the Civil Rights bill in the Senate.

It conferred national and state citizenship upon the Negro—which had been so emphatically denied him by the Dred Scott decision—and made it a criminal offense for anyone to deny a Negro, on account of his color, any civil right accorded a white man. The machinery for enforcement was copied largely from the old Fugitive Slave Law, many Radicals taking a special satisfaction in emphasizing that the old shoe was now on the other foot, but it was unfortunate that more imagination was not employed in working out punishment provisions with a less odious history.

Of all Johnson's cabinet only Welles opposed the bill energetically. Stanton admitted it had defects, yet warmly defended it, along with Harlan, Dennison, and Speed. Seward thought parts of it unconstitutional, but felt that some sort of citizenship law was essential.[10] Nevertheless Johnson vetoed the bill on March 27, 1866, denouncing every aspect.

Senator Trumbull was indignant. In frequent interviews with the President, he said, "he never indicated to me, nor so far as I know to any of his friends, the least objection to any of the provisions of the bill till after its passage." [11] Senator John Sherman, also a Conservative Republican, wrote to his brother, the General: "What Johnson is, is from and by the Union party. He now deserts it and betrays it. . . . Besides, he is insincere; he has deceived and misled his best friends. I know he led many to believe he would agree to the Civil Rights Bill, and nearly all who conversed with him until within a few days believed he would acquiesce in the amendments, and even aid in securing their adoption. I almost fear he contemplates civil war." [12] For the first time there began to be serious consideration of impeachment.

The veto was entirely consistent with Johnson's philosophy of the proper function of the federal government, his deep distrust of further centralization of power. He acted like a true "states rights" man. None of the hundreds of stories of Southern violence to the freedmen had shaken his conviction that the states must be permitted to work out their racial problem without federal interference. Although only a few months earlier he had told a Negro audience in Nashville that he would be their Moses, he now said emphatically in the veto that the Negro was not ready for citizenship. He had had no objection earlier when an identical enforcement machinery had been applied to capturing fugitive slaves, but now this machinery seemed something "fraught with evil" when applied to the white man who maltreated the Negro. The Civil Rights bill would foment instead of reducing racial strife, he insisted. Moreover, it probably repealed the state laws forbidding intermarriage of Negroes and whites.[13]

Radical Republican leaders, believing Johnson to be hopelessly shortsighted and legalistic in the face of a national emergency, now gave up all hope of converting him. Sumner wrote to John Bright on May 21, 1866: "But there is no hint that the President will give way; he is indocile, obstinate, perverse, impenetrable, and hates the education and civilization of New England."[14]

The Liberal leaders in England were watching the contest with keen attention. John Stuart Mill wrote to John Lothrop Motley, May 6, 1866: "It seems to me that things are going on as well and fast as could be hoped for under the un-toward accident of getting an obstinate Southern man, a pro-slavery man almost to the last, in the position of President. . . . If you only keep the Southern States out of Congress till they one by one either grant negro suffrage or consent to come in on the basis of their electoral population alone, they may probably then be let in in safety."[15]

By fair means and foul the Radical Republicans now proceeded to acquire enough votes to override any presidential veto. In the House, with Stevens as whip, this was no problem. The Committee on Elections proceeded to scrutinize every new Representative. When the Chairman told Stevens that in one contested case both men were damned rascals, he simply asked: "Well, which is our damned rascal?"[16]

In the Senate, Democratic Senator Stockton of New Jersey was thrown out of office on a legal technicality involving his election, although no Senator had been disturbed about the matter until it became clear that one or two votes would be decisive in the fight against the President. Senator Foot of Vermont conveniently died, and was replaced by a Radical Republican, G. F. Edmunds.

When the Civil Rights bill came up again for a vote, there was a feverish counting of noses. Senators Dixon of Connecticut and Wright of New Jersey, both Johnson supporters, were gravely ill. When several Senators urged a postponement in view of Dixon's condition, Ben Wade spoke his mind: "I will tell the President and everybody else, that if God Almighty has stricken one member so that he cannot be here to uphold the dictation of a despot, I thank Him for His interposition, and I will take advantage of it if I can." [17]

On April 6, 1866, despite the fact that Senator Dixon had himself brought into the capitol on a stretcher, the Senate overrode the veto, thirty-three to fifteen, with one vote absent. Three votes defeated the President. According to one reporter, when the result was announced, "nearly the whole Senate and auditory were carried off their feet and joined in a tumultuous outburst of cheering such as was never heard within those walls before." [18]

The margin of victory was so slight that the Radicals canvassed desperately every possible means of widening it. They passed a bill admitting Colorado as a state even though the population was but 25,000 and the existing ratio for a member of Congress was one to 127,000. Johnson, stating bluntly that the country could not stand two more Radical Senators, vetoed the bill, and the Senate failed to pass it over his veto. This vote showed that Johnson had not yet been reduced to a mere figurehead. Had he kept the allegiance of a mere handful of Conservative Republicans in the Senate, had he shown some small comprehension of the sustained vigor of the social revolution rushing past him, and diverted or controlled it with some political guile instead of ramming against it, the whole story of the next two years might have been very different.

But he was shy and reticent, misleading friend and foe alike by seeming to agree when he was actually only listening. "Johnson is suspicious of everyone, and I fear will drift into his old party relations," John Sherman wrote to William T. Sherman in March, 1866.[19] Southerners found him no less difficult. "I found that he always postponed action, and was of an obstinate, suspicious temper," wrote the ex-Confederate General Richard Taylor, who interviewed him in 1866. "Like a badger, one had to dig him out of his hole; and he was ever in one except when on the hustings addressing the crowd." [20]

He alienated Republicans by giving jobs to Democrats, and angered Democrats by keeping the Republicans in his cabinet. Worst of all for his own sake, he had no talent for building up a political organization upon which he could depend in any kind of voting crisis. He had always been a lone wolf, fiercely proud of his independence, an attitude he had carried over into the Presidency. It now cost him dear.

"He sought rather than avoided a fight," wrote Shelby M. Cullom of Illinois. "I disliked to follow the extreme radical element, and when the row was at its height, Judge Orth, a colleague in the House from Indiana, and I concluded to go and see the President and advise with him, in an attempt to smooth over the differences. I will never forget that interview. . . . without mincing any words he gave us to understand that we were on a fool's errand and that he would not yield. We went away, and naturally joined the extreme radicals in the House, always voting with them afterwards." [21]

Torn now by his allegiance to the Union Party that elected him, and his quarter-century affiliation with the Democratic Party, Johnson was racked by indecision. Welles, who shared Johnson's political philosophy, in his diary bitterly condemned Johnson's procrastination and costly reserve. Despite his defects as a politician and narrowness of vision, the President could probably have weathered through his term and could perhaps have prevented the excesses of the Radical Republicans had it not been for two calamitous race riots, the first in Memphis, and the second in New Orleans.

Memphis was still in sympathy a Confederate city. Thaddeus Stevens had a friend there, who sent him a clipping from the *Memphis Avalanche* of April 22, 1866, nine days before the explosion.[22] It said in part:

> The Radicals commenced a remorseless war upon the rebels—not the war of one body of armed men against another equally armed, but a war of the triumphant party against the defenseless. They have been actuated by a devilish hate and a fiendish malice. . . . Since they cannot, in this part of the State, assassinate, kill, and murder rebels, and take possession of their property, they propose to give a greasy, filthy, stinking negro the right to crowd them from the polls. . . .
>
> In the late elections in this country. . . . only one hundred and one men were found base enough to vote for the Radical ticket. We have held up the names of a portion of these men, and written small pox over their doors in order that our people might shun them.

A regiment of colored troops, the 3rd Heavy Artillery, had been stationed at Fort Pickering, just outside Memphis, and had only recently been disbanded. They had been disarmed, but were remaining in the fort waiting for back pay. On May 1, 1866, several hundred of these ex-soldiers gathered about the taverns on South Street singing and carousing. Trouble started with that ancient gesture of defiance, the tripping of a policeman.

Relations between the colored troops and the police—ninety per cent of whom were Irish—were already bad.[23] When the police proceeded to arrest two ex-soldiers, there were hoots of scorn and protest. Someone called out: "Abe Lincoln!" and a policeman shouted back: "Your old father, Abe Lincoln, is dead and damned!"

Several ex-soldiers who had managed to keep their pistols now fired at the police. An exchange of shots followed, with the result that two policemen and four colored soldiers were killed. The police went for reinforcements; when they returned there was intermittent firing but no further killings. The soldiers fled back to the fort, and by dark the streets were empty.

The chief of police did not go to the fort and demand custody of the rioters from the commanding officer. Instead he tried to organize an attack on the fort itself. It collapsed almost as soon as it began, and the police then went on a rampage of burning, looting, and shooting in South Memphis. Led by the Judge of the Recorder's Court, John C. Creighton, who was reported to have said: "Boys, I want you to go ahead and kill the last damned one of the nigger race, and burn up the cradle," they killed forty-six colored people, including three women and two boys, and wounded seventy to eighty more, including inmates of the Freedmen's Bureau Hospital. In addition they burned ninety cabins and twelve schoolhouses. As General Stoneman later described it, "the negroes had nothing to do with it after the first day, except to be killed and abused." [24]

Thaddeus Stevens on May 14, 1866, demanded an investigation, and the House shortly sent three of its members to Memphis for hearings. The Democrats protested that the riot was not as bad as the draft riots in New York during the war, when at least eighty-six Negroes had been killed. Republicans were quick to point out the difference that in Memphis it was the police who *carried out* the butchery.

The riot stiffened the Radicals, appalled the Conservatives, and mortified the able Democrats. It came at a time when Congressional debates over the Fourteenth Amendment were at a critical stage, supplying the Radicals with an unexpected arsenal of ammunition. Nowhere can the immediate effect of the riot be more concretely measured than in the speeches of Thaddeus Stevens. Before the riot he had steadily and patiently, and with what was for him a minimum of vituperation, worked to get through the House a constitutional amendment that would guarantee the Negro a minimum of civil rights and that would still pass unscathed through the fire of the state legislatures. The Civil Rights bill was not enough, he argued, since it was a law repealable by a majority. "And I need hardly say," he added, "that the first time that the South with their copperhead allies obtain the command of Congress it will be repealed." [25]

The Fourteenth Amendment had already gone through a complicated history of revisions and rejections. At the time of the Memphis riot Stevens and the Joint Committee of Fifteen had worked out a new version, not one that met his ambitions but one that he hoped would pass. It gave the Negro citizenship and guaranteed him the same civil rights as the white man. It did not grant him outright suffrage, but penalized those states refusing him suffrage by reducing their representation in Congress.

The third section, especially dear to Stevens, denied all Southerners "who had voluntarily adhered to the late insurrection" the right to vote in elections for federal office until July 4, 1870. In effect this meant that practically the whole white South would remain disfranchised until after the 1868 presidential election. Stevens called it "the mildest of all punishments ever inflicted on traitors. . . . It falls far short of my wishes, but it fulfills my hopes. . . . we did not believe that nineteen of the loyal States could be induced to ratify any proposition more stringent than this." [26]

There was, nevertheless, widespread opposition to the disfranchising section. Stevens severely limited debate under the rule of the previous question, and just before the vote on May 10, 1866, made a blistering speech:

"Give us the third section or give us nothing," he said. ". . . that section is there to save or destroy the Union party. . . . Some say it is too lenient. It is too lenient for my hard heart. Not only to 1870, but to 18070, every rebel who shed the blood of loyal men should be prevented from exercising any power in this Government. That, even, would be too mild a punishment for them. . . . They have not yet confessed their sins; and He who administers mercy and justice never forgives until the sinner confesses his sins and humbles himself at His footstool. . . . I shall not agree that they shall come back except as supplicants in sackcloth and ashes. . . . I hear several gentlemen say, that these men should be admitted as equal brethren. Let not these friends of secession sing to me their siren song of peace and good will until they can stop my ears to the screams and groans of the dying victims at Memphis. . . ."

When Representative Russell from Pennsylvania interrupted to say, "I wish to ask my colleague in this connection whether he thinks he can build a penitentiary big enough to hold eight million people," Stevens replied bitterly:

"Yes, sir, a penitentiary which is built at the point of the bayonet down below, and if they undertake to come here we will shoot them. That is the way to take care of these people. They deserve it, at least for a time." [27]

In the vote immediately following Stevens' speech the House passed the Fourteenth Amendment 128 to 37. There were six more "yeas" and four fewer "nays" than in the vote on the Civil Rights bill. This is one yardstick for measuring exactly what the Memphis riot had done to reduce the friends of the South in Washington.

It can be seen that the Fourteenth Amendment, destined to result in more judicial controversy than all the others, was not developed in a political vacuum, but in the savage turbulence of 1866. The influence of Thaddeus Stevens in writing this amendment can clearly be traced in the journal kept by the Joint Committee of Fifteen, and in the *Congressional Globe*. His own measures were more voted against than voted for. But with remarkable flexibility he took what he could get, sometimes with grace and sometimes with contempt, always accepting the possible when he could not have his own special Utopia.

If we look back briefly, we can see how much he subordinated his dreams for a political paradise—and also his hatred of the Southern white—to the necessities of practical politics. The first plan he submitted to the Joint Committee of Fifteen was not his own but the creation of the volatile Robert Dale Owen, son of the English reformer and philanthropist, who brought Stevens a carefully written outline. It called for civil rights for the Negro, a penalty for the whites who denied suffrage to the Negro after five years' preparation; forfeiture of the Confederate debt, and the admission of the Southern states upon their agreeing to the Amendment.

Stevens told Owen he objected to the five-year postponement of Negro suffrage, but that he was pleased with the general outlines of the plan. "We've had nothing before us that comes anywhere near being as good as this, or as complete. It would be likely to pass, too; that's the best of it. We haven't a majority, either in our committee or in Congress, for immediate suffrage; and I don't believe the states have advanced so far that they would be willing to ratify it. I'll lay that amendment of yours before our committee tomorrow, if you say so; and I'll do my best to put it through."

Senator Fessenden became ill with the varioloid, a mild form of smallpox; and by the time he recovered, word of the proposed Owen amendment had spread through Congress. There were violent repercussions from the New York, Illinois, and Indiana Congressmen, who were afraid that if it became known that the Reconstruction Committee planned to give the Negro the vote, it would cost them the fall elections. When Stevens saw Owen again, he admitted that Negro suffrage had been abandoned by the Joint Committee of Fifteen. *"Damn the varioloid!"* he exploded. *"It changed the whole policy of the country."* [28]

The first official version of the Fourteenth Amendment as worked out in the Joint Committee of Fifteen—as with the final version— merely penalized those states denying votes to the Negro by lowering their representation in Congress. With this Stevens was content, and worked strenuously to push the measure through the House with the necessary two-thirds vote. He had not reckoned with the doctrinaire Charles Sumner, who filibustered against the amendment because it did not give the Negro the vote, and succeeded in killing it in the Senate. It was as bad, Sumner said, as the leg of mutton served for dinner to Samuel Johnson, "ill-fed, ill-killed, ill-kept, and ill-dressed." It was "a constitutional recognition of an oligarchy, aristocracy, caste, and monopoly, founded on color." [29]

Stevens and Fessenden, both furious at Sumner, lashed at him in Congress. Stevens said the amendment had been "slaughtered by a puerile and pedantic criticism, by a perversion of philological definition which, if when I taught school a lad who had studied Lindley Murray had assumed, I would have expelled him from the institution as unfit to waste education on." [30] Sumner, easily stung, doubtless remembered this when he said of Stevens after his death: "Nobody said more in fewer words or gave to language a sharper bite. Speech was with him at times a cat-o-nine-tails and woe to the victim on whom the terrible lash descended." [31]

The final version of the Fourteenth Amendment was a far less tough and exacting document than Thaddeus Stevens had hoped for. The first section he approved. It was intended to guarantee the Negro citizenship and equality with the white man in civil rights.

All persons born or naturalized in the United States, and subject to the jurisdiction thereof, are citizens of the United States and of the State wherein they reside. No State shall make or enforce any law which shall abridge the privileges or immunities of citizens of the United States; nor shall any State deprive any person of life, liberty, and property without due process of law; nor deny to any person within its jurisdiction the equal protection of the laws.

Already in the Fifth Amendment the national government was forbidden to deprive anyone "of life, liberty or property, without due process of law." The new amendment extended this rule to individual states, which were now recognized to be potential tyrants as much as the national power. It gave the freedman—and indeed all citizens —the right to look to Congress and the federal courts for the protection of civil liberty, making possible a potential revolution in the equilibrium of state and national power—a revolution that did not really materialize, however, for more than three generations. [32]

The second section of the Fourteenth Amendment provided that the basis of representation should be the whole number of persons in each state, exclusive of Indians, eliminating the old rule that counted each slave three-fifths a man. But it penalized any state that should deny any of its male citizens suffrage by reducing the number of their representatives.

The third section, as amended by the Senate, Stevens looked upon as virtually emasculated. Instead of denying the vote to almost every white man in the South until 1870, as Stevens had hoped, it simply made all leading Southern politicians and generals temporarily ineligible for public office. A fourth section denied the right of Southerners to claim compensation for their slaves and formally declared illegal all Confederate war debt claims.

This, then, in June 1866, seemed to be the declared limit to the exactions of the United States Senate for vengeance. Gone was most of the talk of execution of traitors, confiscation of property and reparations. If the Southerner himself chose to let the Negro vote, he would be rewarded by increased representation; if he denied it, he would sacrifice the old representation based on the number of slaves. And for the time being he must look to the little men—the teachers, farmers, artisans, and obscure Union sympathizers, who had hitherto left politics alone—or to the bellicose opportunists of the "Parson" Brownlow stamp—to take over temporarily the reins of local and state government.

Stevens surveyed the Senate version of the Fourteenth Amendment with regret but resignation. In what was for him a remarkably mellow speech on June 13, 1866, he urged the House to accept it:

In my youth, in my manhood, in my old age, I had fondly dreamed that when any fortunate chance could have broken up for awhile the foundation of our institutions, and released us from obligations the most tyrannical that ever man imposed in the name of freedom, that the intelligent, pure and just men of this Republic, true to their professions and their conscience, would have so remodeled all our institutions as to have freed them from every vestige of human oppression, of inequality of rights, of the recognized degradation of the poor, and the superior caste of the rich. In short, that no distinction would be tolerated in their purified Republic but that arose from merit and conduct. This bright dream has vanished 'like the baseless fabric of a vision.' I find that we shall be obliged to be content with patching up the worst portions of the ancient edifice, and leaving it, in many of its parts, to be swept through by the tempests, the frosts, and the storms of despotism.

Do you inquire why, holding these views and possessing some will of my own, I accept so imperfect a proposition? I answer, because I live among men and not among angels; among men as intelligent, as determined, and as independent as myself, who, not agreeing with me, do not choose to yield their opinions to mine. Mutual concession, therefore, is our only resort, or mutual hostilities. . . . I am anxious for its speedy adoption, for I dread delay.[33]

Shortly after this speech the House adopted the Senate version by a strict party vote: 120 Republicans against 32 Democrats, and the

Fourteenth Amendment went to the states for ratification.

There were a good many Republicans who looked upon this amendment as the final basis for reconstruction, and who were quite willing to admit any Southern state that ratified it. Despite the Memphis riot, Tennessee was admitted back into the Union within a few days after her legislature passed the necessary bill late in July, 1866. Thaddeus Stevens did not hail the return of the President's state with enthusiasm; neither did he oppose it. Of the House bill admitting Tennessee he said wryly that it "deserves special favor as the birth-place or residence of one of the most extraordinary men in his time that has ever appeared on earth. I do not pretend that she is loyal. I believe this day that two thirds of her people are rank and cruel rebels. But her statesmen have been wise and vigilant enough to form a constitution which bridles licentious traitors and secures the State government to the true men. And she has an Executive fit to ride upon the whirlwind. I know that two thirds of the congressional districts will send us secessionists, which will greatly impair our two-third votes. But she has two or three men in her delegation who would saved Sodom." [34]

The Executive "fit to ride upon the whirlwind" was "Parson" Brownlow, Johnson's journalist enemy, who had publicly accused him in the past of being an atheist and a bastard. A determined Unionist throughout the war, Brownlow had come to embrace the Negro's cause with the same fervor he had once defended slavery. His language was always pungent, frequently ribald. Typical of his irreverent political manners was the telegram he sent to the Senate with the news that the Tennessee Legislature had ratified the Amendment:

"We have fought the battle and won it. We have ratified the constitutional amendment in the House, forty-three voting for it, eleven against it, two of Andrew Johnson's tools not voting. Give my respects to the dead dog of the White House!" [35]

Thaddeus Stevens would support any Radical Republican, including Brownlow and Benjamin Butler, in preference to the most statesmanlike conservative. With him political principles came first, and the most exemplary personal behavior or moral rectitude meant nothing if a man's voting record was anti-Negro.

Tennessee was permitted to come back into the Union without Negro suffrage. And there were many sanguine citizens who believed that reunion with the remainder of the seceded states was close at hand. Stevens was not one of them. If he could have his way, no state would get past the icy barrier of his disapproval until it had adopted a Radical Republican government. He knew this would be impossible anywhere in the South except Tennessee without Negro suffrage and some measure of white disfranchisement. Even in Tennessee the Legislature in April 1866 had disfranchised all Confederate civil and military officers for fifteen years and all rebel soldiers and sympathizers for five.

Just before the Memphis riot Stevens had laid before Congress his own reconstruction plan. Its details, by the standards of almost all of his colleagues, were impossibly harsh.[36] Everyone who had sworn allegiance to the Confederate government had forfeited his citizenship, he said, and must be naturalized like any foreigner. He called for new constitutional conventions, to be manned only by loyal whites and Negroes. Although a measure only slightly less severe than this was actually adopted a year later, no one in May 1866, except perhaps Stevens himself in a hopeful mood, entertained any notion that such a measure would ever become law.

By July 28 Stevens had modified his own plan. He would deny suffrage only to the leading men of the South, he said, and that for only three years.[37] This bill, too, came to nothing. It is clear, then, if one looks carefully at Stevens' own special legislation in 1866 that the old Commoner was only the whip in the House; he was not yet its tyrant. *Harper's Weekly* pointed out on October 6, 1866, that "not a single important measure, except the appointment of the Committee, proposed by Mr. Stevens was adopted by the House. It honored his profound conviction, his Roman firmness, his noble fidelity to equal rights, but it did not follow him."

Stevens could not, in fact, become the tyrant until after the fall elections of 1866. But even before they took place, the South unexpectedly and gratuitously handed him what was to become the deadliest weapon in his whole arsenal. It was the massacre at New Orleans.

CHAPTER TWENTY-TWO

New Orleans

Miserable Scoundrel. Hell's dominions are too good for such men. You call me disloyal. Yes *I am disloyal* to any *damned* Government ruled by such men as you are, and *glory that I still live to hate you.* Make us a visit. Some of your *damned blue jacket thieves* are still here— But not enough to keep you from wearing *a coat of Tar and Feathers.* . . .

> *Your Southern Friend*
> and
> *So called Rebel*
> Anonymous letter to Thaddeus Stevens, May 1, 1866

NEW ORLEANS in 1866 was in large part an impoverished city, with immense slums, a generous supply of gambling dens, and a long tradition of violence. Before the war, political murders at election time had become so common that two governors had filed alarmed protests with the state legislature. The Know-Nothing Party had a small unit officially known as "Thugs," who went into the foreign quarter, disguised and painted, and terrorized the immigrant population into staying away from the polls. "Our electoral system is a farce," said the *New Orleans Delta* on May 6, 1860, determined by "fraud, the knife, the sling-shot, the brass knuckles," and it blamed New England, that "fecund source of political infamy," as the source of the Know-Nothing movement.[1]

In 1864 the small Radical Republican minority governed the city, supported by the Union Army, but after the election of 1865 the local offices, as well as the state, were filled almost entirely by ex-

Confederates. The Governor, J. Madison Wells, a Unionist planter, retained office only because he had campaigned on a program of white supremacy.[2] The legislature enacted an extremely repressive black code, and Unionist sympathizers everywhere were dismissed from office. In New Orleans 110 teachers who were suspected of spreading Union sentiments lost their jobs. The new mayor of New Orleans, John T. Monroe, said to have been the leader of the Know-Nothing "Thugs" before the war, replaced all Union men on the police force with ex-Confederate soldiers.[3]

Governor Wells has been dismissed by many historians as an opportunist and a weakling, but there is a good deal of evidence in his correspondence, as published in the documents concerning the New Orleans massacre, that he was honestly trying to do the impossible— steer a middle course. Disturbed by the recrudescence of the old "Thug" organization, he wrote a worried letter to Andrew Johnson on February 10, 1866, including a copy of the by-laws of the new secret Southern Cross Association, and predicting a return of the "atrocious and diabolical outrages" committed before the war.[4]

Meanwhile the Louisiana Republicans refused to be reconciled to their political impotence. They had only one possible route back to power—Negro suffrage. Having little faith in Congress and no faith in the President, a few of the more aggressive leaders, with the sanction of Governor Wells, worked out a scheme by which they hoped to return to office, abolish the black codes, and carry out some of the economic and educational reforms they had mapped out in 1864.

Their plan was legally dubious and inherently dangerous. They decided to reconvene the Constitutional Convention of 1864 for the purpose of amending the state constitution so as to give some or all Negro citizens the right to vote. It will be remembered that Lincoln had urged this Convention, through the provisional governor, Michael Hahn, to give suffrage to the more intelligent Negro civilians and to the Negro soldiers, but the plea had been ignored. The Convention of 1864 had adjourned with a resolution stating it could be reconvened at any time at the call of its president, E. H. Durell, a United States district judge. Durell wired Senator Fessenden for advice, but upon receiving no reply he was sufficiently discouraged to refuse to take action.[5] We must examine with care the complicated story of what followed.

The Louisiana Republicans, ignoring Durell's apathy, managed to assemble forty out of the original ninety-six members of the old Constitutional Convention on June 26, 1866, and appointed a new president, Rufus K. Howell of the Louisiana Supreme Court. Despite the fact that there was no quorum present, Governor Wells cooperated by ordering writs of election to fill the vacancies from counties that had not formerly been represented. At once there was promise of trouble. Edmund Abell, judge of the first district court in New Orleans, summoned a grand jury of 150 men on July 3, 1866, and publicly charged them to indict all convening members of the Constitutional Convention on the criminal charges of misdemeanor in office and perjury. This was three weeks before the Convention was even due to meet.[6]

Nevertheless, on July 8, 1866, Judge Howell reconvoked the Convention, ordering the members to meet on July 30 for the purpose of getting authentic evidence of the vacancies to be filled.[7] He then went to Washington to enlist Congressional support, and, as was to be expected, consulted Thaddeus Stevens. After the massacre Howell testified under oath that Stevens "rather discouraged it [the Convention] because he thought his plan for an enabling act, a bill for which he had already presented, was preferable." The *New York Times* of July 18, 1866 reported that Stevens told Howell the original convention of 1864 "never was legally born; it was a bastard." "I never would have anything to do with it while it was alive," he said, "and now that it is dead, it may stay in H— where it belongs."

But Stevens must have reconsidered this judgment afterward, for he admitted under oath that he told Judge Howell he thought the plan was legal, saying that "if they framed a constitution and presented it to Congress, I had no doubt Congress would consider it, and would consider the question of the admission of delegates under it, for I held that their present government was a bogus government. I remember giving this opinion to him, not in writing, but in conversation."[8]

Judge Howell consulted numerous other Radical Republicans (including George Boutwell, Roscoe Conkling, and General Nathaniel P. Banks), and returned to New Orleans with some optimism, for a reporter there wired to the Washington correspondent of the *New York Times*: "Howell has returned with the assurance that Congress will support the convention."[9] B. F. Flanders, a Louisiana Radical Republican who had been elected to Congress in 1864, claimed to have a letter signed by two members of the Joint Committee of Fifteen urging the Convention and saying, "Do the best you can, and trust to the consequences." Curiously, he withheld the identity of the signatories.[10]

As the time for the meeting of the Constitutional Convention approached, Judge Howell and the other officers agreed that they would go unarmed, and if arrested submit peacefully and then secure release with writs of habeas corpus.[11] The only power in New Orleans that could prevent their arrest if it was ordered by the Mayor was the Union Army, a small force of which was still stationed in New Orleans under General Sheridan. The ex-Confederates at once set about ensuring its neutrality. Joseph A. Rozier was dispatched to Washington to see the President. Later he testified that he and Andrew Johnson came to complete agreement that the military must not interfere.[12]

Since General Sheridan was away in Texas, Mayor Monroe of New Orleans wrote on July 25, 1866, a frank letter to the officer in charge, Major General Absalom Baird, telling him he intended to arrest the Convention members since their "avowed object is to subvert the present municipal and State government," and asking Baird if the military would interfere. General Baird, greatly disturbed, replied: "If the assemblage in question has the legal right to remodel the State government, it should be protected in so doing; if it has not, then its labors must be looked upon as a piece of harmless pleasantry, to which no one ought to object," and he said pointedly that it was the business of the legal branch of the United States Government and not the Mayor to decide.[13]

On July 27, 1866, three days before the Constitutional Convention met, several Radical Republican leaders addressed a large body of colored people before the City Hall, urging their support. The mere massing of these people in an area where Negro insurrection had for generations been a nightmare to white men was already provocative. All the speakers but one, sensing this, spoke moderately. Then Dr. A. P. Dostie, a dentist from the North, an agitator and a fool, began hurling firebrands that cost him his life three days later.

There were many conflicting reports about what he said, but even one of his friends admitted that he had concluded with a threat: "Now friends, go home, peaceably, quietly, make no noise; disturb no person; but, I learn that there are prowling bands of armed men out to waylay you. As you separate, go home. If you are insulted by any of these bands of men, pay no attention to them; go home, right by them, without saying a word to them; but if they strike you, kill them." [14]

It was also reported that he said: "I want the negroes to have the right of suffrage and we will give them their right to vote. We have three hundred thousand black men with white hearts. Also one hundred thousand good and true Union white men who will fight for and beside the black race against the three hundred thousand hell-bound rebels. . . . We can not only whip but exterminate the other party. . . . If interfered with, the streets of New Orleans will run with blood." [15] Yet R. L. Shelley, a correspondent of the *New York Tribune*, said that he had stood within four feet of Dostie and heard nothing of these threats.[16]

The Louisiana Lieutenant-Governor, Albert Voorhies, and the Attorney-General, Andrew J. Herron, telegraphed the President, describing the mass meeting as having ended in a riot—which it had not—and telling him that he had been bitterly denounced. They revealed their plans to arrest the Convention members and asked: "Is the military to interfere to prevent process of court?" Andrew Johnson at once wired back: "The military will be expected to sustain, and not to obstruct or interfere with, the proceedings of the courts. A dispatch on the subject of the convention was sent to Governor Wells this morning." [17] He had wired Governor Wells asking by what authority he convened the Convention and expressing displeasure.

General Baird telegraphed for instructions to his chief, the Secretary of War: "A convention has been called, with the sanction of Governor Wells, to meet here on Monday. The lieutenant governor and city authorities think it unlawful, and propose to break it up by arresting the delegates. I have given no orders on the subject, but have warned the parties that I could not countenance or permit such action without instructions to that effect from the President. Please instruct me at once by telegraph."

It is at this point that the proper measuring of responsibility for what happened becomes fantastically complicated. For Secretary Stanton did not show the telegram to Andrew Johnson; in fact, he did not answer it.[18] General Baird was left to act entirely on his own. The President, on the other hand, told his Secretary of War nothing of his own exchange of telegrams with the Louisiana Lieutenant-Governor and Attorney General. Already Johnson and Stanton, intolerably estranged, were deliberately bypassing each other on matters that cried out for the closest possible consultation.[19] The consequences were ugly.

General Baird was now in a dilemma. The Mayor of New Orleans issued a proclamation saying the Convention would "receive no countenance from the President," and at least one local newspaper published Johnson's wire to Voorhies, the Lieutenant Governor, indicating that the Union Army would "sustain" the courts.[20] But General Baird still had received no direct word from the President through the Secretary of War. Later Baird testified that Voorhies promised him that no arrests would be made, and he agreed to station his troops at the Mechanics Institute one hour in advance of the meeting to prevent trouble. He was told that the Convention would convene at 6 p. m.[21] What happened next may have been the result of an accidental misunderstanding, but it was more likely the consequence of deliberate deception on the part of Mayor Monroe.

The Convention leaders, genuinely fearful of a riot, changed the time of the meeting from 6 p. m. to noon. General Baird insisted under oath that no one told him of this change, though he had seen both Lieutenant-Governor Voorhies and Mayor Monroe shortly before noon. Mayor Monroe, however, insisted under oath that Baird had known about the time change two days in advance.

At two o'clock, Baird said, Mayor Monroe rushed into his office demanding to know when the troops would arrive, whether or not they would be white troops, and whether or not they would act with the police. By this time the massacre was actually well under way.[22]

The best eye-witness account of what happened came from the pen of a correspondent of the New York Times.[23] About twenty-five members of the Convention assembled at noon. Disappointed in the small attendance, they adjourned for an hour, hoping to secure a greater number. Violence started at one o'clock when a parade of colored men, estimated later as consisting of 60 to 130 marchers, approached the Institute. Some said one in ten carried a pistol and the remainder carried clubs; others testified all were unarmed. The riot started when some white bystanders snatched at the American flag. Soon the colored marchers were surrounded by a squad of police led by the Sheriff—ex-Confederate General Hayes—and an immense mob of white men, many brandishing revolvers. When the shooting started, about half the men in the parade fled inside the building.

A white flag appeared at the window. The firing outside momentarily stopped, and the police rushed inside the Institute. There, as General Sheridan later described it in a telegram to the President, "the policemen opened an indiscriminate fire upon the audience until they had emptied their revolvers." The men inside defended themselves with chairs as best they could; finally in terror they broke through the doors and began jumping from windows. They were shot as they jumped and stabbed when they fell. Dr. Wm. H. Hire, a member of the Convention, who was himself wounded, later testified:

At one time I saw a colored man kneel down and pray to go out; the only reply the policeman made was, the click of a pistol discharging a shot into his bowels. I saw men shot in this way by policemen several times, and without provocation. I would state also that when Mr. Horton called out "We surrender—we make no resistance," there was a rush by policemen, and the reply was made by a man in a gray coat, "God damn you, not one of you will escape from here alive." . . . Although I have been here twenty-one years as a practicing physician, I never imagined that such things could happen.[24]

General Sheridan later wired General Grant—a wire that was omitted by Andrew Johnson from the official correspondence—"From my accounts of my own scouts, who saw the affair from first to last, from my own officers, from disinterested and faithful persons, I believe that at least nine-tenths of the casualties were perpetrated by the police and citizens by stabbing and smashing in the heads of many who had already been wounded or killed by policemen." [25]

One spectator, B. Rush Plumly, later testified that one young man triumphantly showed him a weapon covered with black hair and blood, saying: "I have just killed a nigger with that." When Plumly warned him of trouble, the rioter cut him short: "Oh hell! haven't you seen the papers? Johnson is with us." [26]

A few policemen fought valiantly to stop the slaughter. Michael Hahn, former Governor, who was lame and walked with a crutch, was escorted out of the hall by the Chief of Police. Once outside he was beaten with clubs and shot in the back, but the policeman managed to get him into a carriage and took him to jail, thus saving him, according to the *New York Times* correspondent, from certain lynching. Dr. Dostie was beaten and stabbed, and later died of his wounds.

General Baird's Army Surgeon counted forty-eight killed, sixty-eight severely wounded and ninety-eight slightly wounded, all members of either the Convention or the parade. One man was killed and ten policemen were injured, none seriously, on the other side.[27] General Sheridan, returning from Texas two days after the massacre, was horrified at what had happened in his absence. His first telegram to General Grant called the leaders of the Convention "political agitators and revolutionary men," but denounced the police action as outright murder. A second telegram to Grant, on August 2, 1866, said: "The more information I obtain of the affair of the 30th in this city the more revolting it becomes. It was no riot: it was an absolute massacre by the police, which was not excelled in murderous cruelty by that of Fort Pillow. It was a murder which the mayor and police of this city perpetrated without the shadow of necessity; furthermore, I believe it was premeditated, and every indication points to this." [28]

By August 4 Andrew Johnson had two conflicting stories of the New Orleans massacre, the telegrams from General Sheridan on the one hand, and on the other a wholly different—and as it proved later quite fictitious—accounting of casualties from the Mayor of New Orleans and the Lieutenant-Governor. Monroe and Voorhies stated that "forty-two policemen and several citizens were either killed or wounded" by the colored mob. They listed on the other side twenty-seven "rioters" as killed and "a considerable number" as wounded. Moreover, they accused the leaders of the Convention of rousing the "passions and prejudices of the colored population, so as to make them the victims of a riot by urging them headlong into a conflict with the State and municipal authorities." [29] This was the beginning of the myth of the great Radical Republican conspiracy.

Gideon Welles, who heard the Monroe and Voorhies telegrams read in a cabinet meeting on August 3, 1866, promptly accepted the insinuation of the Mayor of New Orleans that the riot had been deliberately planned by the local Radical Republicans, and was quick to include the Washington leaders in the plot. "There is little doubt," he wrote in his diary, "that the New Orleans riots had their origin with the Radical Members of Congress in Washington. It is part of a deliberate conspiracy and was to be the commencement of a series of bloody affrays through the States lately in rebellion. Boutwell and others have stated sufficient to show their participation in this matter." [30]

That Andrew Johnson had embraced the conspiracy theory was not known publicly for several weeks. But he made no secret in his telegram to New Orleans and in his public utterances that he thought the Convention in New Orleans had been "illegal" and "extinct" and that its "usurpation and revolutionary proceedings" caused the riot. [31] *Harper's Weekly* was only one of many journals to point out that something else was involved.

"It is of no importance whether the members of the Louisiana Convention of 1864 were wise or unwise, fanatical or moderate," said the editor on August 18, 1866. "Any body of men, anywhere in the country, have the unquestionable right of assembling under any call whatever to consider public affairs."

Not since Lincoln's assassination had the nation been so shaken as by the massacre at New Orleans. But what cost Andrew Johnson dear was not the fact of the slaughter but his attitude toward it. The *Nation's* editor wrote on August 9, 1866: "The coolness with which he refrained from expressing one word of honest indignation at the slaughter, in an American city, of unarmed men by a mob of their political opponents for political reasons . . . is, perhaps, the most alarming incident in this sad affair."

There can be no doubt that Andrew Johnson felt vulnerable, as did Stanton, Stevens, Boutwell, and all others who had meddled in advance of the massacre. When it became public information that Stanton had withheld a vital telegram from Johnson, he defended himself privately by accusing the President. This we know from a letter Charles

Sumner wrote to John Bright in England: "He [Johnson] is perverse, distempered, ignorant, and thoroughly wrong. You may judge him by the terrible massacre at New Orleans. Stanton confessed to me that he [the President] was its author." [32]

Andrew Johnson hurled his own accusations publicly in a sensational speech in St. Louis on September 8, 1866:

If you will take up the riot at New Orleans, and trace it back to its source or its immediate cause, you will find out who was responsible for the blood that was shed there. If you will take up the riot at New Orleans and trace it back to the radical Congress you will find that the riot at New Orleans was substantially planned. If you will take up the proceedings in their caucuses you will understand that they knew there that a Convention was to be called, which was extinct. . . .

You will find also that that Convention did assemble in violation of law, and the intention of that Convention was to supersede the reorganized authorities in the State government of Louisiana. . . . hence you find that another rebellion was commenced, having its origin in the radical Congress. . . . And there was the cause and the origin of the blood that was shed; and every drop of blood that was shed is upon their skirts, and they are responsible for it.

. . . I have been traduced, I have been slandered, I have been maligned, I have been called Judas Iscariot and all that. . . . If I have played the Judas, who has been my Christ that I have played the Judas with? Was it Thad. Stevens? Was it Wendell Phillips? Was it Charles Sumner? These are the men that stop and compare themselves with the Saviour; and everybody that differs with them in opinion, and try to stay and arrest their diabolical and nefarious policy, is to be denounced as a Judas.

In the days when there was a Christ, while there was a Judas, were there unbelievers? Yes, oh yes; unbelievers in Christ, men who persecuted and slandered, and brought Him before Pontius Pilate, and preferred charges, and condemned and put Him to death on the cross to satisfy unbelievers; and this same persecuting, diabolical, and nefarious clan to-day would persecute and shed the blood of innocent men to carry out their purposes.[33]

No other speech by Andrew Johnson so betrayed the masochistic tendency in his thinking and behavior. His eagerness to believe the preposterous theory that Thaddeus Stevens and others had deliberately planned the New Orleans massacre, his comparisons of himself with Judas and Jesus Christ, his denunciations of the Radicals as "persecuting, diabolical, and nefarious"—none of these can be lightly dismissed as mere Tennessee stump oratory.

In the audience that heard this speech there were cries of "Bully for you!" and cheers. But when a transcript reached the Northern press, there were editorial roars of indignation in every Republican paper. Even those who believed him to be drunk again—which seems not to have been the case [34]—were bewildered by his extreme agitation and the violence of his language. Religious readers were deeply offended by his likening of himself to Jesus Christ. And even the most conservative of Republicans were antagonized by his accusations against Stevens, Sumner, and others in regard to the massacre. It was generally conceded in all camps that the President had become, in fact if not in intention, the partisan champion of the white South.

Many Southerners found the Radical-conspiracy theory thoroughly palatable. Even before the massacre of New Orleans George Fitzhugh of Virginia had written in *DeBow's Review:* ". . . the dominant party of the North, inspired by an insatiate and diabolical spirit of revenge, is ready to see the negroes of the South exterminated or expelled (which would be but a prelude to extermination) in order to further harass, and torture the impoverished and oppressed whites." In August he wrote grimly: "Indians were made to be exterminated. But for abolition negroes might be put to better use." [35]

No one was arrested for riot and murder in New Orleans except the few surviving members of the ill-fated Constitutional Convention.

Thaddeus Stevens made no public reply to the President's charge that he and others had "substantially planned" the New Orleans riot, and that the blood that had been shed was "upon their skirts"—the same phrase, in fact that had been used against him in Gettysburg thirty-five years before. When the House investigating committee held hearings in Washington and questioned him on his interviews and correspondence with Judge Rufus K. Howell, President of the Convention, Stevens frankly admitted that he had encouraged him to go ahead. This was the extent of his responsibility and he was not terrified by it. He did not make evasive motions, like Secretary Stanton, not furiously blame his enemies, like the President.

But the accusation of Andrew Johnson that he had deliberately plotted to bring on the massacre did not really go unchallenged. When in the past Stevens had been seriously libeled, he usually succeeded in bringing his accuser before a court of law. It was really no accident, then, that Andrew Johnson eventually ended up on trial before a court, and that Thaddeus Stevens was responsible for putting him there.

CHAPTER TWENTY-THREE

The Climate of Reconstruction

There is so much right on both sides—so much wrong on both sides—so much reason to hope and expect that the difference may be made up.

Springfield Republican, February 26, 1866

THE ELECTION OF 1866 was a nasty political brawl that spoiled whatever hope there may have been for a statesmanlike settlement of Reconstruction. The National Union Party broke up into its old sections, and men who had been political allies through the war now cursed each other as vile traitors. Both Andrew Johnson and Thaddeus Stevens proved to be obstinate, graceless, and belligerent in this campaign, and the complex problems of reunion were blotted out by their spectacular public feud.

The disintegration of the Union Party speeded up in July, 1866, when Dennison, Speed, and Harlan all resigned from the cabinet in protest against Johnson's reconstruction policies. Many were surprised, not knowing the devious workings of his mind, that Stanton did not follow. But the full measure of the party breakup was not apparent until August, when the President's supporters met in the National Union Convention in Philadelphia. There were a few Conservative Republican leaders present, notably William Seward, Thurlow Weed, and Henry J. Raymond, who according to James Russell Lowell had joined with "the Democratic faction, carefully keeping their handkerchiefs to their noses all the while,"[1] but the Convention as a whole was overwhelmingly Democratic.

All the Southern states were represented, and when Major-General Couch, a Union soldier heading the Massachusetts delegation, walked down the aisle arm-in-arm with Governor Orr of South Carolina the Convention wildly applauded. Radical Republicans derided it as the "Arm-in-Arm Convention," likening it to Noah's Ark, where the animals entered "two and two, of clean beasts, and of beasts that are not clean."[2]

When the official report of the Convention was handed to Andrew Johnson in a public ceremony, he formally expressed pleasure at the evidences of national reconciliation. But he could not resist the impulse to use the opportunity once more to insult Congress. "We have seen hanging upon the verge of the government, as it were, a body called, or what assumes to be, the Congress of the United States," he said, "while in fact it is a Congress of only a part of the States. We have seen this Congress pretend to be for the Union, when its every step and act tend to perpetuate the disunion and make disruption of the States inevitable." The Southerners, he continued, "have the shackles upon their limbs and are bound as rigidly by the behests of party leaders in the National Congress as though they were in fact in slavery."[3]

Stevens, home in Lancaster, was too ill to join in the indignation voiced in the Radical Republican convention which met in Philadelphia September 3, 1866. But he lashed out at Andrew Johnson in a speech to his constituents late in August. The *London Times* singled out and reprinted this paragraph:

You all remember that in Egypt He sent frogs, locusts, murrain, lice, and finally demanded the first-born of every one of the oppressors. Almost all of these have been taken from us. We have been oppressed with taxes and debts, and He has sent us worse than lice, and has afflicted us with an Andrew Johnson.[4]

Hoping to fill the Congress with Democrats, the President on August 28 started on a stumping tour of twenty-one cities. There was no longer much pretense that he was head of a coalition party. The only eminent Republican left in the party was William Seward, who had remained loyal to his chief. Seward once wryly described himself as a man "who has faith in everybody, and enjoys the confidence of nobody."[5] The *Nation* said of him on September 20, 1866: "Seward has no other vocation in life than to be a party leader, and now no party will have him. Distrusted by his old friends, he will never be taken to the bosom of his old enemies. . . . he wanders about, like a restless ghost—a leader without a party."

The defection of Seward was a source of sorrow to many Republicans. Thaddeus Stevens blamed him for Johnson's "betrayal" of the Party. The President was "beguiled," Stevens said. "While he was 'clothed in his right mind' he uttered the thoughts and sentiments of a statesman; but Seward entered into him, and ever since they have both been running down steep places into the sea." [6]

Forgotten were Seward's patience and good-tempered tolerance, his lack of pettiness or false piety. Henry Adams admired him because "he never seemed to pose for statesmanship; he did not require an attitude of prayer." [7] But his unpretentiousness and indifference to the hot-gospeller idealism of the Radical Republicans were now treated as vices by the Party.

The fact is that Seward since emancipation had become genuinely indifferent to the Negro problem. "The North has nothing to do with the negroes," he said privately to editors E. L. Godkin and C. E. Norton on April 12, 1866. "I have no more concern for them than I have for the Hottentots. They are God's poor; they always have been and always will be so everywhere. They are not of our race. They will find their place. They must take their level. . . . The North must get over this notion of interference with the affairs of the South." The most he would say that was that he approved of Negro suffrage in theory, and that he expected to see it prevail "eventually." [8]

Seward stayed with the President on the whole "Swing Round the Circle" from Baltimore through New York and Chicago, to St. Louis and back again to Washington. The reporters watched his sallow, imperturbable face for signs of impatience with the President. Thin, wrinkled and worn, chewing constantly on a cigar, he showed nothing but devotion and approval.

General Grant, too, was with the party, but he left it at St. Louis, saying privately to General Rawlins that he did not care "to accompany a man who was deliberately digging his own grave." [9] For Johnson on this tour probably lost more votes for his party by his speeches than any president in the nation's election history. His defenders have tried to blame the unfavorable press upon the mendacity of the stenographic reporters, and have accused the Radical Republican politicians of deliberately planting hecklers in the crowds to humiliate the President.[10] But it cannot be denied that Johnson in many speeches did get involved with arguments with hecklers, whereas other Presidents have considered such behavior a sign of political ineptness and a degradation of their high office.

In his speech in Cleveland, while freely bandying epithets with the crowd, Johnson once more publicly insulted Thaddeus Stevens:

Who can come and place his finger on one pledge I ever violated, or one principle I ever proved false to? (A voice, "How about New Orleans?" Another voice, "Hang Jeff Davis.") Hang Jeff Davis, he says. (Cries of "No," and "Down with him!") Hang Jeff Davis, he says. (A voice, "Hang Thad. Stevens and Wendell Phillips."). . . .

Why not hang Thad. Stevens and Wendell Phillips? I tell you, my countrymen, I have been fighting the South, and they have been whipped and crushed, and they acknowledge their defeat and accept the terms of the Constitution; and now, as I go around the circle, having fought traitors at the South, I am prepared to fight traitors at the North.[11]

If Johnson had said "Hang Thad Stevens" only once, it might well be blamed on the stimulation of the occasion, or—as many newspapers insinuated—on the possibility that he was drunk again. But there is no good evidence that he was intoxicated, and there is ample evidence that he liked the phrase. On September 8, 1866, in St. Louis, when a heckler called out, "Hang Jeff Davis!" Johnson replied: ". . . I might ask you a question, Why don't you hang Thad Stevens and Wendell Phillips?" And after great cheering he went on: "A traitor at one end of the line is as bad as a traitor at the other." [12] It was later in this speech that he blamed Stevens and others for the New Orleans riot.

Stevens had been warned by his physician not to take part in the election campaign, but he did make two speeches. In the second, shortly before election day, he referred to the President's attacks with a beguiling casualness that misled many into thinking he scarcely cared:

I have amused myself with a little light, frivolous reading. For instance, there was a serial account from day to day of a very remarkable circus that traveled through the country, from Washington to Chicago and St. Louis, and from Louisville back to Washington. I read that with some interest. . . . I expected great wit from the celebrated character of its clowns. . . . they told you, or one of them did, that he had been everything but one. He had been a tailor—I think he did not say drunken tailor. He had been a constable. He had been city alderman. He had been in the legislature. God help that legislature! He had been in Congress; and now he was President. He had been everything but one,—he had never been a hangman, and he asked leave to hang Thad Stevens.[13]

As the tour progressed Andrew Johnson was more and more openly insulted. The Governors of Indiana, Ohio, Pennsylvania, Illinois, Michigan, and Missouri all found excuses to avoid greeting him. In Battle Creek, Michigan, General Grant and Admiral Farragut both received bouquets and the President none, and the crowd sent up three cheers for Thaddeus Stevens and Congress. An observer of this episode wrote to Stevens: "He left us with more curses than any man ever did." [14] In Indianapolis the crowd was so abusive the President could not speak at all.

Periodicals and newspapers that had hitherto supported the President now turned against him. The editor of *Harper's Weekly* described his speeches as "incredible balderdash." Marguerite H. Albjerg has pointed out that by 1867 Johnson had alienated every important New York daily except the *World,* and "might have read his political doom in the change of front of this powerful metropolitan press." [15]

There were certain themes that Andrew Johnson returned to with compulsive repetition. One was his apprenticeship as a tailor. "Like a boy whistling down ghosts," said the *Nation,* "the vehemence with which he boasts of his plebeian origin shows that is a sore spot with him, and the pains which he takes to remind us that he was a tailor only prove that he is constantly haunted by that unwelcome fact." The editor mentioned his address to the tailors of Philadelphia, commenting that Johnson's painful effort to show that he was proud of associations ". . . showed that he was at heart bitterly ashamed." [16]

Another theme Johnson often touched upon by innuendo was the danger of Negro equality. He did not want the Southerners to come back into the Union "a degraded and debased people," he said. "I want them to come back with all their manhood." [17]

Thaddeus Stevens did not believe that elevating the Negro meant degrading or "emasculating" the white man. He sensed, however, that talk of "social equality" was dangerous politics. When he heard that the ex-slave Frederick Douglass—who had been elected a delegate to the National Loyalist [Radical Republican] Convention from Rochester, New York—had paraded arm-in-arm with editor Theodore Tilton, he wrote to Wm. D. Kelley: "A good many people here are disturbed by the practical exhibition of social equality in the arm-in-arm performance of Douglass and Tilton. It does not become radicals like us to particularly object. But it was certainly unfortunate at this time. The old prejudice, now revived, will lose us some votes. Why it was done I cannot see except as a foolish bravado. The Massachusetts and S. Carolina [arm-in-arm spectacle] was disgusting enough. This I fear will neutralize it." [18]

In an aggressive public attack on September 4, 1866, Stevens struck at the white man's fear of "social equality" with great frankness:

The most effective argument (if argument it can be called) which will be issued by our opponents is the effort made by the Republicans to give equal rights to every human being, even to the African. We shall hear repeated, ten thousand times, the cry of "Negro Equality!" "The radicals would thrust the negro into your parlors, your bedrooms, and the bosoms of your wives and daughters. They would even make your reluctant daughters marry black men." And then they will send up the grand chorus from every foul throat, "nigger," "nigger," "nigger!" "Down with the nigger party, we're for the white man's party." These unanswerable arguments will ring in every low bar room, and be printed in every blackguard sheet throughout the land whose fundamental maxim is "all men are created equal."

. . . A deep seated prejudice against races has disfigured the human mind for ages. . . . This doctrine [Negro rights] may be unpopular with besotted ignorance. But popular or unpopular, I shall stand by it until I am relieved of the unprofitable labors of earth.[19]

Back in Lancaster the editor of the *Intelligencer* growled: "If such a policy as Mr. Stevens foreshadows is carried out, or seriously entered upon, nothing on earth is more certain than the utter overthrow and ruin of this Republic." [20] As the campaign progressed, personal attacks on Stevens became ever more violent. A Democratic parade in Carlisle, Pennsylvania, had one banner bearing the inscription, "Thad Stevens' Idea of Reconstruction," and behind it a man painted black to resemble a Negro strolling arm in arm with a white woman.[21]

Montgomery Blair, echoing the President, accused Stevens of instigating the New Orleans riot. The nation was on the eve of a civil war, he said, and if the Radicals won it would lead to the establishment of two Presidents and two Congresses.[22] From Virginia the editor of the *Richmond Enquirer* joyfully joined the attack: "The Satanic puddler of the national foundry grins as he sees the sparks fly off from the mass of metal, that he is manipulating with devilish glee in his fiery furnace. He knows that they will fall cold and lifeless, mere flakes of inert iron. But, Mr. Stevens, God helping us, we do not intend to pass through your rolling: and *the day may not be distant when the fires of your forge will be put out by a thunderbolt from the red right hand of Caesar.*" [23]

Thaddeus Stevens must have been jubilant at the election returns of 1866. Only three states had Democratic majorities: Delaware, Maryland, and Kentucky. Everywhere else in the North the Republicans won decisively. In the Fortieth Congress the Senate would have 42 Republicans and 11 Democrats; in the House 143 Republicans and 49 Democrats, and Stevens at last would have more than a two-thirds majority.

For a brief interval he had hopes that the Pennsylvania Legislature would elect him Senator in January, 1867. The *New York Tribune* urged it:

It is not much to be a Republican today. We take with us now the drift-wood and scum. But it was something to be a lover of freedom and pro-tection forty years ago. . . . He has stood by our party when it was a corporal's guard; he leads it now when its columns cover the nation.

It is said that Mr. Stevens is too old. We wish one-half of his colleagues were as young.[24]

During the Christmas holidays Stevens made a trip to Chambers-burg to win the support of Alexander McClure. When McClure saw his old friend lying on the hotel bed, pale and emaciated, his feet swol-len with dropsy, he did his best to dissuade him, pointing out kindly but sensibly that as a freshman Senator he would have no committee status, whereas in the House he was the acknowledged Commoner—leader of leaders. But Stevens still hoped to sit in the Senate before he died. He had, however, neither the strength nor the temperament to go about seriously soliciting votes for himself, and the wily Simon Cameron ended up with the prize. Stevens got only 7 votes, Curtin 23, and Cameron 46.[25]

Gideon Welles wrote in his diary on January 11, 1867: "The result surprises all, more in the fact that Stevens was so feebly supported than that Cameron succeeded. . . . No worse man than Stevens could be elected. Curtin is limber, deceptive, and unreliable. Cameron is not great but adroit; his instincts are usually right, but he will sacrifice the right for selfish purposes."

Stevens prepared to return to the House in December 1866 with more than a personal score to settle with Andrew Johnson as a result of the election campaign. For during the summer the President had added greatly to the list of what he considered grave political crimes. First, he had actively intervened to encourage the legislatures of the Southern states to reject the Fourteenth Amendment.[26] This they were proceeding to do with alacrity and unanimity. Texas had rejected it in October; Georgia followed in November, and North Carolina, Arkan-sas, Florida, South Carolina, and Alabama in December. Virginia, Mississippi, and Louisiana rejected it during January and February, 1867.

For many Conservative Republicans in Congress the repudiation of the Fourteenth Amendment, which had seemed to them a peace plan of extraordinary mildness, was profoundly disturbing. James A. Garfield expressed bitter regret: ". . . so magnanimous, so merciful a proposi-tion has never been submitted by a sovereignty to rebels since the day when God offered forgiveness to the fallen sons of men. . . . They have deliberated; they have acted. The last one of the sinful ten has at last with contempt and scorn, flung back into our teeth the magnanimous offer of a generous nation. It is now our turn to act. They would not cooperate with us in rebuilding what they destroyed. We must remove the rubbish and rebuild from the bottom." [27]

The President's second crime, in Stevens' eyes, was the fact that he had been turning Republicans out of office. During the campaign he had replaced 1,283 postmasters with Democrats, and had made similar changes in other government departments. In his speech in St. Louis he had said bluntly: "I believe that one set of men have enjoyed the emoluments of office long enough. . . . God being willing, I will kick them out. I will kick them out just as fast as I can." [28] He could not, however, bring himself to remove either Seward or Stanton from his cabinet and make a thoroughgoing break with the Conservative Republicans, and this made him continuously suspect in Democratic eyes.

Third, the President was replacing anti-Southern or pro-Negro officers in the South with men more sympathetic with his own views. He transferred General George H. Thomas from Tennessee to Kentucky [though the Virginia-born General was not noticeably pro-Negro], confiding in Orville Browning in September 1866 that it was because Thomas had supported "Parson" Brownlow.[29]

What disturbed Thaddeus Stevens even more was that the President had found a powerful and unexpected ally in the Supreme Court. Although five out of the nine justices were Lincoln appointees, including the Radical Republican Chase as Chief Justice, the Court on December 17, 1866, announced a ruling in the Milligan Case which struck at the whole concept of military rule as it had been exercised throughout the war and afterward. Lambdin P. Milligan was an Indiana Confederate sympathizer who had been tried in 1864 by a military commission on a charge of conspiracy to seize federal arsenals and free Confederate prisoners. He had been sentenced to be hanged for treason on May 19, 1865. The Supreme Court now decided unanimously that the military commission in this instance was unlawful. It further decided (though here the Court divided five to four) that "neither Congress nor the President possessed the power to institute such a military commission, except in the actual theater of war, where the civil Courts were not open." [30]

Stevens and his fellow Radical Republicans might not have been filled with such consternation by this decision—which has since been hailed as one of the great bulwarks of American freedom—had not the President made it immediately clear that he would use it as a weapon to make the Union Army in the South impotent. He had already declared civil government in the South to be restored and their courts operative, but military courts working with the Freedmen's Bureau were still actively functioning. What the South had in 1866 was one set of courts that could be counted on to take the side of the white man against the black, and another that was likely to hand down decisions for the black man against the white. This was hardly good government by any standard, but for Thaddeus Stevens, who had steadfastly refused to admit that the civil governments in the South had any legal validity, it seemed now that the President and the Supreme Court had joined hands in destroying the one remaining safeguard for the freed Negro against the ferocity of the organized terrorists.

As soon as the Milligan Case decision was announced, Johnson issued orders dismissing all trials of civilians by the military then pending in the South. The result was that a good number of men then on trial for murdering freedmen and Union soldiers were turned out of jail, and those who had already been sentenced began busily applying for release on writs of habeas corpus. To many observers it seemed that even the conviction of the men who planned Lincoln's assassination was now declared "a juridico-military murder." [31] Shortly afterward, the Court handed down two more decisions—four justices dissenting—declaring unconstitutional a Missouri law requiring clergymen to take a loyalty oath, and a Congressional law requiring a loyalty oath of all lawyers appearing in federal courts.

The Milligan Case decision roused almost as much fury in Thaddeus Stevens as had the Dred Scott Case. He was certain it made the Freedmen's Bureau and Civil Rights bills inoperative in the South. In Maryland, Virginia, and Kentucky the State courts had already pronounced the Civil Rights bill unconstitutional, and he feared now that the Supreme Court would do the same.[32] Suddenly all the hard-won victories of the previous Congress seemed threatened. The Milligan Case ruling, he said, while "perhaps not as infamous as the Dred Scott decision . . . is far more dangerous in its operation upon the lives and liberties of the loyal men of this country. That decision has taken away every protection in every one of these rebel States from every loyal man, black or white, who resides there." He called upon Congress "to do something to protect these people from the barbarians who are now daily murdering them; who are murdering the loyal whites daily and daily putting into secret graves not only hundreds but thousands of the colored people of that country." [33]

There was scattered talk among the Radical Republicans of impeaching the justices, but Stevens, it was said, preferred to impeach the President, "from whom all evils flow." [34] Some wanted to abolish the Court altogether; others talked of packing it with additional justices, as had been done in 1807, 1837, and 1863. Even the Conservative Republican *Nation* called the Court "nine elderly men." [35] Rumors spread that the Court might declare invalid both the Thirteenth and Fourteenth Amendments.

Stevens met this, one of the last great political crises of his life, not only with a new series of bills to nullify the power of the President and bypass the rulings of the Supreme Court, but with a whole new theory of government. At no other time in his life did he show more dramatically the destructive flexibility of a truly revolutionary leader. Caught in the meshes of the check-and-balance system of the American constitutional government, he now showed not the slightest hesitation in tossing the whole thing overboard. He would redefine the power relationships in the government in his own terms; and these terms were: first, that Congress was to be sole sovereign power, and second, that none of this power was to be shared with the President or the Court.

In this country, the whole sovereignty rests with the people, and is exercised through their Representatives in Congress assembled. The legislative power is the sole guardian of that sovereignty. No other branch of the Government, no other officer of the Government, possesses one single particle of the sovereignty of the Nation. No Government official, from the President and Chief Justice down, can do any one act which is not prescribed and directed by the legislative power. . . . [the President] is the mere servant of the people, who issue their commands to him through Congress.[36]

From now on Stevens, who had earlier been careful to define what was being done inside or outside the Constitution, seems to have come to look upon the document itself as "a worthless bit of old parchment." He used this contemptuous phrase in a conversation with the ex-Confederate General Richard Taylor, who was careful to record the fact.[37]

There were Radicals even more extreme than Thaddeus Stevens. The *Boston Commonwealth* advocated abolition of the Presidential office, and the *Anti-Slavery Standard* proposed throwing out the Presidency, the Supreme Court, and the Senate, as "the three remaining oligarchies." [38] Charles Sumner, on the other hand, persisted in trying to fit Radical Republican theories inside the Constitution. "Anything for human rights is constitutional," he said. ". . . There can be no State rights against human rights." [39]

Even William Seward had once said privately of the Constitution: "A written Constitution is a superstition that presupposes certain impossibilities. The first is that it can express all the wisdom of the past, and anticipate all the wants of the future. It supposes that its creators were both saints and sages. We have had those two classes, but never the two qualities united in one class. The saints were not sages, and the sages were not saints." [40] There have been few of our great presidents, in fact, who were not at some time troubled by the uncomfortable limitations of the sacred paper. They maneuvered within these limits, or adroitly bypassed them. But Stevens in 1867 would willingly have abandoned the whole constitutional organization in favor of something like the British system, where supreme authority did in fact rest with the elected parliament.

Sustained and invigorated by his ever-mounting fury against the President, the Supreme Court, and the defiant Southern people, he set about planning a series of reconstruction measures that represented, in their potentialities, the most radical change in the American constitutional system in all its history, excepting, of course, the calamitous cleavage imposed by secession.

Stevens justified himself on the ground that he was protecting the ex-slave and Union man in the South. He had the Memphis and New Orleans riots to bulwark his argument, and also the detailed lists of murders and assaults regularly reported by the Freedmen's Bureau. General O. O. Howard later wrote that it seemed to him for a time that "the whole white population [was] engaged in a war of extermination against the blacks," but he also noted that "careful investigation has proved that the worst outrages were generally committed by small bands of lawless men, organized under various names, whose principal objects were robbery and plunder," and "to prevent what was denominated 'negro domination.'" [41] These bands were almost as active in the winter of 1866–1867 as in the previous year. There were "Jayhawkers" and "Black-horse Cavalry" in Georgia, the "Ku Klux Klan" in Tennessee, the "Regulators" in South Carolina and Kentucky.

Major General Scott reported that in South Carolina the Regulators offered—for a fixed sum per head—to kill any freedman who refused to sign a labor contract. All the army officers reported public apathy toward the continued lack of decent policing, and almost universal failure to bring any outlaw to justice. Major General Thomas J. Wood reported from Mississippi that in all his months there only one white man had been convicted for murdering a Negro, and he had only been sentenced to one year for manslaughter. Senator Williams read a letter on the Senate floor from General Custer saying that there had been five hundred indictments for murder in Texas and not a single conviction. [42]

Stevens pointed out in the House that hundreds of Negroes who had been convicted of petty crimes were being legally sold at public auction. In Florida, he said, it was the law that any Negro guilty of assault and battery should be sold into slavery for twenty years.[43] The Memphis Chief of Police was arrested at the order of General Howard for imprisoning Negroes without cause and—for a fee—hiring them out from jail without trial to planters. Freedmen's Bureau agents were constantly interfering to free hundreds of children "apprenticed" out under the black codes in a state of virtual slavery. This continued until October, 1867, when the Supreme Court declared the apprentice system illegal under the Civil Rights Act.[44]

Stevens did not ignore the fact that the Tennessee Democrats nominated for governor early in 1867 Emerson Etheridge, a fanatical foe of emancipation. "The negroes are no more free than they were forty years ago," he said publicly, "and if any one goes about the country telling them that they are free, shoot him; and these negro troops, commanded by low and degraded white men, going through the country ought to be shot down." [45]

What Stevens did not choose to see were the new evidences of peace and reconciliation between the races. Arkansas was the only state to report an actual increase in the persecution of the freedmen in late 1866. General Wager Swayne noted in Alabama "a growing kindliness between the races, and increasing fairness in the application of the laws." Major General J. B. Kiddoo, assistant commissioner in Texas, stated that outrages were decreasing, though there was little respect for law in the Northeastern counties. General Sheridan held that most areas in Louisiana were peaceful, though Franklin and St. Landry parishes were racked with violence. From Florida, Major General J. G. Foster wrote in October 1866 that working conditions between the blacks and whites were good, that 32,000 acres of homestead land thrown open to the freedmen had been occupied, and that there had been a gratifying decrease in opposition to Negro schools. Some planters, he said, had opened schools at their own expense.

From Georgia, General Davis Tillson reported that many planters had driven the freedmen off their plantations without paying them, but this was largely due to the widespread crop failures. The civil authorities, he said, "are on the whole faithful and efficient." From South Carolina, where the black codes were most oppressive, word came from Major General R. K. Scott that thousands of freedmen were migrating to Florida. The Negro had learned quickly that he had one effective weapon, his own mobility.[46]

The black codes were being modified everywhere in the face of the Congressional threat to impose Negro suffrage. In South Carolina the modification was slight; the vagrancy and domestic-relations laws were left unchanged.[47] But the codes were greatly modified in Georgia and entirely repealed in Tennessee.

Still, when Thaddeus Stevens looked at the South in 1866 and early 1867, he saw only misery and injustice, lynching and massacre. Moreover, in the bankruptcy and suffering of the Southern white man he took a sardonic pleasure. White men died of hunger in the mountain districts of Alabama early in 1866, and in March, 1867, famine fell upon the Southern coast. Governor James L. Orr of South Carolina reported in April 1867 that more than 100,000 in the state had not tasted meat for a month, and thousands had no bread. General Sheridan reported acute poverty in Louisiana. General Swayne wrote from Alabama, October 31, 1866: "For freedmen work is plenty, and of such as they are used to, with ample compensation. With refugees, as the whites are called whom war has left in destitution, the case is sadly otherwise. 'Remote, unfriended, melancholy, slow,' the widow and the fatherless, the aged and infirm are scattered through the 'piney woods,' . . . in utter, hopeless desolation."

General Howard, despite some protests at the notion of helping rebels, insisted on throwing open all the facilities of the Freedmen's Bureau, saying: "The rebellion is over; people are starving." General Daniel Sickles in South Carolina ordered a moratorium on all private debts incurred during the war, forbade imprisonment for debt, and stopped all sheriff's sales for twelve months, and the enforcement of old contracts concerning the sale of Negroes.[48]

When the disastrous spring flood of 1866 wiped out many Mississippi levees, there had been talk among Northern Congressmen about appropriating money to rebuild them. But Thaddeus Stevens had expressed his opposition in a barbed joke: "Let them build their own levees. Let them raise their own cotton. I would not be in favor of hanging them, but I do not think I should interfere if the Lord should choose to drown them out." [49]

CHAPTER TWENTY-FOUR

———————◆———————

Puritan Tyrant

By the Puritan idea we mean a feeling of impatience at sin in others, and a disposition to repress it by the strong arm. . . . At the present moment the Republican party is in great danger of suffering itself to be controlled by the Puritan idea.

Nation, September 19, 1867

THADDEUS STEVENS CAME to the Fortieth Congress with two ravaging ambitions, the first to humble Andrew Johnson, and the second to remodel the South in his image of "a perfect Republic." He did not, however, act alone, nor even inaugurate most of the legislation by himself. And though it is largely true that the extraordinary measures passed early in 1867 might never have become law save for his audacity and driving will, it should not be forgotten, as David Donald has pointed out, that "every major piece of Radical legislation was adopted by the nearly unanimous vote of the entire Republican membership of Congress." [1]

Stevens had been ill for more than a year, and rumors of his death had periodically filtered through Washington. But it was soon apparent that the fires smoldering in the old man were far from extinguished. He had always been able to joke about his waning strength. In April he had apologized: "Mr. Speaker, I am not well, and I am afraid that I have been somewhat diffuse. A man is always diffuse when he is feeble, and always feeble when he is diffuse." Now when Horace

Maynard expressed regret that Stevens had not vacationed in Tennessee, he replied: "Well, sir, I made no preparation for a burial down there, so I thought I would stay home until I got ready, or at least until winter was over and the ground was broken." [2]

It was clear that as far as Andrew Johnson was concerned, Stevens' wit was sharper than ever. After listening to the President's Message to Congress, which re-echoed many of the arguments in his veto messages, he said briefly:

I read a newspaper account recently of an aged college president who was reading to his students a chapter in the Bible daily with the intention of reading the Bible through in course. Some roguish student daily placed back his mark until he had read the same chapter daily for a long time. Perhaps some one has been playing a similar prank with our President. We certainly hear the same message all the time, and I wish for variety's sake that some one would change the mark.[3]

Stevens struck at the President on several levels. On December 3, 1866, he introduced a bill designed to curtail the patronage power. This Tenure of Office bill would rob Johnson of his authority to remove office-holders except with the consent of the Senate, and thereby destroy a presidential prerogative that had gone unchallenged for eighty years. By this device Stevens hoped to stop Johnson's wholesale discharging of Republicans from the administration.

The Senate version of the bill specifically exempted cabinet members, but Stevens, seeing that this provision would enable Johnson to fire Secretary of War Stanton, strove desperately to eliminate it. The debates on this section of the bill were confused, and the final wording was thought to be a victory by both sides. Since this section was to be the impeachment trap a year later, the exact phrasing is worth noting. Members of the cabinet, the bill said, "shall hold their offices respectively for and during the term of the President by whom they may have been appointed, and for one month thereafter, subject to removal by and with the advice and consent of the Senate." Since Stanton had been appointed by Lincoln and simply continued in office by Johnson, many thought the President could still dismiss him at will. On the other hand, if the continuation constituted an appointment, Johnson could not remove him.

Stanton, whether from love of power or from the genuinely religious fervor of his radicalism, had convinced himself that he must stay in office to prevent Johnson from vitiating the revolutionary gains made by the war. The fact that he could do this only by intriguing against his chief did not trouble him. Unlike Stevens, whose candor was perennially startling even to his friends, Stanton was devious and evasive, presenting a wholly different face to different men.

Andrew Johnson continued to keep Stanton long after their relations became intolerably strained. Stanton had made it clear before the whole cabinet that he differed on such vital issues as the Fourteenth Amendment and suffrage for Negroes in the District of Columbia.[4] He had shown himself to be capable of dangerous intrigue by withholding the vital telegram before the New Orleans massacre. Still Johnson did not dismiss him.

Stanton, too, had real grievances. He knew that the President secretly bypassed both him and General Grant in issuing orders to the commanding generals in the South. But instead of resigning in protest, he went to Representative George Boutwell and dictated an amendment to the pending Army Appropriation Bill which made it a misdemeanor for the President to transmit orders to any officer except through the General of the Army, whose office should not be removed from Washington. It was also made a misdemeanor for any officer to obey orders except those issued through the General of the Army. Boutwell took the amendment to Thaddeus Stevens, who fastened it as a rider on the important appropriations bill, and saw to it that it was whisked through Congress.[5] Though it was a heavy-handed insult to the Commander-in-Chief, Johnson swallowed his pride and signed the bill on March 2, 1867, saying that he did so only because the bill was essential for the support of the Army.

By March 1867, Stevens had robbed the President of his patronage power, insulted him as Commander-in-Chief, and through Congressman James M. Ashley started an investigation that threatened to end in impeachment. During these months, however, most of his energy went into plans for restoring the South to military rule and guaranteeing Negro suffrage. On December 19, 1866, he tested the sentiment of his colleagues by introducing a bill calling for Negro suffrage and the disfranchisement of most of the white men, defending it on January 3, 1867, in an impassioned speech:

I am for negro suffrage in every rebel State. If it be just, it should not be denied; if it be necessary, it should be adopted; if it be a punishment to traitors, they deserve it.

But, it will be said, as it has been said, "This is negro equality!" about which so much is said by knaves, and some of which is believed by men who are not fools. It means, as understood by honest Republicans, just this much, and no more; every man, no matter what his race or color; every earthly being who has an immortal soul, has an equal right to justice, honesty, and fair play with every other man; and the law should secure him those rights. The same law which condemns or acquits an African should condemn or acquit a white man. . . . Such is the law of God and such ought to be the law of man. This doctrine does not mean that a negro shall sit on the same seat or eat at the same table with a white man. That is a matter of taste which every man must decide for himself.[6]

The bill failed, not because the Republicans disagreed with Stevens about the basic morality and political necessity of Negro suffrage— since the South had repudiated the Fourteenth Amendment, sentiment had swung sharply in favor of Negro suffrage—but because they could not agree with Stevens about disfranchising the Southern white. Lincoln had wanted universal suffrage and universal amnesty, and many Conservative Republicans endorsed the idea. But Stevens successfully buried every bill that recommended the combination.

Most Republicans were now convinced that the freedman could never get police protection without suffrage, and all agreed the party needed the Negro vote. Many went along with Maryland's Radical Congressman, Henry Winter Davis, who had written in a letter to the *Nation*, late in 1865:

> It is insane to dream that the South will, of itself, ever give suffrage or equality before the law, and now is our only time to compel it.
> If, men say, God works slowly, yet will not let a good cause fail, they had better enlighten their piety by a glance at his ways in history, and reflect that he visits wasted opportunities, not less than wickedness, with ruin. I trust we may not be monuments of that wrath.[7]

No Republican leader was happy about Negro illiteracy, but many believed that only the ballot would stop the burning of Negro schoolhouses. Moreover, illiterate whites had been voting in the South for generations [30% of the white males in South Carolina in 1860 could not read or write], and Stevens saw no reason for not offsetting this anti-Republican illiterate vote by a pro-Republican bloc.

Not all Negroes were as ignorant as commonly believed. There was an educated mulatto group in Louisiana which supported a Negro newspaper, the *New Orleans Tribune*, from 1864 to 1869.[8] Many free Negroes had learned to read; the Negro soldiers had studied spelling along with shooting. And as with illiterate people everywhere, such as in much of modern India, there was a reservoir of purely verbal learning. There were skilled mechanics, artisans, and agricultural foremen among them; they were a Bible-quoting if not a Bible-reading people.

Most Southerners, however, would have agreed with the editor of the *Memphis Appeal*, who said on February 26, 1867, in discussing Negro suffrage: "If one had the power and could not otherwise prevent that curse and inconceivable calamity, in many of the southern states, it would be a solemn duty for him to annihilate the race. The right to vote might just as safely be given to so many South American monkeys as to the plantation negroes of Mississippi and Louisiana."

What the Southern white man most feared was not the Negro's ignorance when he went to the polls but his capacity to learn. In Tennessee, the first Confederate state to grant Negro suffrage, word went around the colored districts, "Vote the way you shot—point blank against your oppressors!" The Loyal Leagues carried banners: "The Radicals build schoolhouses and the Conservatives burn them." [9] Republican ballots frequently carried a picture of Lincoln in the upper corner. No other education was necessary.

A few Southerners, believing Negro suffrage inevitable, spoke out in its favor. Some planters hoped to use it as a political lever against the old hill-country opposition.[10] Governor Orr of South Carolina, who had urged defeat of the Fourteenth Amendment, now talked of the ballot for literate Negroes holding property worth $250—as prevailed in New York State. General James Longstreet stated publicly he was willing to test Negro suffrage fully. Alexander Stephens had written in his prison diary June 26, 1865: "Let all the blacks in a state be put into a class, a sort of guild, corporation, or tribe, and let this guild or tribe have representation in legislation." General P. G. T. Beauregard said publicly that "if the suffrage of the Negro is properly handled and directed, we shall defeat our adversaries with their own weapons. The Negro is Southern born. With a little education, and a property qualification, he can be made to . . . fight with the whites." [11]

If the liberal Southern planter was naive in believing that he could persuade the Negro to vote with him, so was the Northern Republican naive when he believed that the Negro ballot by itself would stop the casual killings and whippings, or that the Southern white man could be made to accept equality with the Negro in the voting booth. Even Conservative Republicans fell into the trap of these optimistic assumptions.

Senator William M. Stewart from Nevada said on May 24, 1866: "Give him the ballot, and he will have plenty of white friends, for the people of the United States love votes and office more than they hate negroes." [12] E. L. Godkin wrote in the *Nation* on November 29, 1866, cheerfully, and he thought astutely:

Now, we maintain that the ballot will do for the negro what it does for the poor ignorant Irishman, or German, or Englishman, but no more. It will secure him against flagrant class legislation, or cruel or unusual punishments, and against all oppression which is on the face oppressive. It will do more than this; it will cause politicians and public men—sheriffs, policemen, and the whole race of functionaries, actual and expectant—to treat him with civility, even with deference. . . .

But more than this the ballot will not do for the negro . . . it will not enable him to tell the difference between statesmen and demagogues.

These men had no real comprehension of the Southern white man's pride or his terror. Even before Stevens' Reconstruction Acts passed Congress, measures were being devised in the South to "head off" Negro suffrage. In most Southern states a conviction for a petty crime punishable by a public whipping disfranchised a man. North Carolina now started the fashion of arresting and whipping Negroes by hundreds. "We are licking them in our part of the State," one local legislator said, "and if we keep on we can lick them all by next year and none of them can vote." [13]

Thaddeus Stevens took particular note of this development, reporting in the House that "in North Carolina and other States, where the punishment at the whipping-post deprives the person of the right to vote, they are now every day whipping negroes for a thousand and one trivial offenses." [14] General Daniel Sickles was so incensed he forbade all public whipping in the state. At once the Governor, Jonathan Worth, went to Washington to protest to Andrew Johnson. The President revoked General Sickles' order and the whipping continued.[15]

It was this kind of circumstance that hardened Stevens' conviction that only military rule and white disfranchisement would secure to the Negro either his ballot or his safety. What he failed to anticipate was the extreme vulnerability of the southern Union man, and the phoenixlike vitality of the old master class. Henry J. Raymond, founder and editor of the *New York Times,* who was a Conservative Republican leader in Congress, warned Stevens in vain against "pressing such reforms before the summer has prepared the soil." They must come, he said, "from the culture of the public conscience, from education, from experience of life," and by too much impatience one "may turn the dial backward and ruin all." [16]

But Thaddeus Stevens was feverishly intent on creating before he died what he called "a political paradise," and he was racked with fear that he would not live long enough. "We are now attempting," he said in the House, "to build a perfect Republic. We are now attempting to finish a structure whose foundations were laid nearly a century ago. That structure is the temple of liberty, where all nations may worship." [17]

What Stevens now worked out, in partnership chiefly with Representative Williams of Oregon, was a drastic military bill which declared the "pretended State governments" in the South to be illegal, and returned all the former Confederate states save Tennessee to the rule of the Union Army. Five military districts were to be organized, each controlled by a general. These generals were at liberty to use local political organizations and courts if they so chose, but all were to have power to overrule any decision they thought unjust.

It cannot be too greatly emphasized that this bill was Stevens' response not only to the New Orleans Massacre, the continuing murders of freedmen elsewhere, and the pro-Southern decisions of the President, but also to the action of the Supreme Court. In the Milligan Case decision the Court had denied the validity of all military courts except in war theaters. Stevens by his military bill intended to transform the South—legally at least—back into a war theater, thereby making it certain that Union men and Negroes could get justice in the courts. He described it as "simply a police bill to protect the loyal men from anarchy and murder." [18]

Conservative Republicans were disturbed that there were no definite limits to the duration of military rule and insisted on amendments providing for reconstruction of the Southern states on the basis of universal suffrage. These amendments, introduced in the House by John A. Bingham and James G. Blaine, strongly supported by Samuel Shellabarger of Ohio, were fought by Thaddeus Stevens with jeers, taunts, and parliamentary maneuvers. For a time it seemed that Bingham would win the issue and take over Stevens' leadership in the House. But Bingham was no real match for Stevens, and the Military Bill passed without amendment by a vote of 109 to 55. When the vote was announced Stevens was triumphant. "I wish to inquire, Mr. Speaker," he said, "if it is in order for me now to say that we indorse the language of good old Laertes that Heaven rules as yet and there are gods above?" [19]

The Senate, however, returned the bill with amendments of much the same character introduced by John Sherman, and Stevens found himself facing the same fight all over again. The second fight he won by persuading the Democrats to vote against the amendments. "We began to filibuster with the Democrats," Stevens later related, "promising them something better than Sherman's bill after the 4th of March: they took the bait like so many gudgeons, and with the Sumner contingent in the House we defeated John Sherman's bill, horse, foot, and dragoons." [20] The Democrats foolishly believed they could secure a still milder measure in the Fortieth Congress; Stevens was rightly certain that he could exact a harsher one.

The Reconstruction Act that finally emerged from the committees and passed over Johnson's veto on March 2, 1867, was not as punitive as Stevens would have liked. But even the *New York Tribune* said the terms were "harsher than we wish they were." This bill, together with the Supplementary Reconstruction Bill passed on March 23 by the 40th Congress, acquired the name "Thorough" after the tyrannical policy, also called "Thorough," of William Laud, Archbishop of Canterbury, during the reign of Charles I. In the South, "Thorough" has ever since been a synonym for Reconstruction and tyranny.

Stevens had many allies working with him in both the House and the Senate. Even Chief Justice Chase—never content to restrict himself to the bench—secretly helped draw up the Second Supplementary Reconstruction Act.[21] The Acts provided the following: The South was to be divided into five military districts, each governed by an Army General who should be appointed by the President. All local governments were to be called "provisional only" and were to be subject to the authority of the United States. Martial law was to prevail until each state should call a constitutional convention to which the delegates would be elected by all male citizens, white and black, except those white men rendered ineligible for office under the terms of the Fourteenth Amendment. These Conventions must grant suffrage to the Negro, but could disfranchise ex-Confederates. The constitutions they devised must be submitted to the same electorate that chose the delegates, and then forwarded to Congress for approval. All the new state governments must ratify the Fourteenth Amendment.[22]

What "Thorough" meant was that all Negro men would vote and be eligible for office, and many white men, including the whole former ruling class of the South, would not. This is what Thaddeus Stevens had hoped for from the beginning but had never really expected to get. As George Boutwell put it: "South Carolina is a blank piece of paper on which may be written a new form of government." [23]

Senator Doolittle called it a "declaration of war" against the South; the Democratic *New York World* on March 6 listed "The Infamous Two-Thirds" in a box outlined in black, calling the measure of March 2 "a bill to annul the Constitution of the United States," and "to organize hell." The editor of the *Richmond Examiner* wrote desperately: "Such infamous madness cannot last always. Some great financial or political calamity will scourge our enemies into justice, or the idol of irresponsible power, which they are now worshipping, will fall on them and crush them." [24]

Once he had won the Negro suffrage fight, Stevens concentrated once more on securing for the black man his forty acres. "Homesteads to them are far more valuable than the immediate right of suffrage," he said, "though both are their due." [25] But with the special blindness growing out of his eagerness to punish the Southern white, he could not consider any solution to the economic problems of the ex-slave except that of carving him a farm out of the confiscated plantation of his old master.

He was particularly impenetrable to the idea that economic desolation of the whites added to the black man's problems. His tax committee laid a 3 per cent tax on cotton, including cotton for export. The value of cotton had already declined, since India and Egypt had increased their acreage, and the tax greatly hampered the sale of cotton abroad. Clemenceau wrote to his Paris paper January 5, 1867: "This product, essentially American, cannot compete any longer in the English markets with the cottons of Egypt and India, and the result has been to discourage the growers, cause stagnation in shipping, poverty and privation among the masses, and unheard-of wealth for a few men in high places." [26]

Meanwhile Thaddeus Stevens encouraged ever higher tariffs, though they were calamitous for South and West alike. "The incredible tariff," Clemenceau wrote, ". . . would be unendurable except for the immense resources of this country and the abundance of paper money." Godkin of the *Nation*, who also had a broad economic perspective, wrote angrily: "There have been nineteen new tariffs within the last forty years, and of these we have had eleven within the last five years. Nothing but the extraordinary energy of the people and richness of the soil has prevented these changes from proving ruinous. No other country could possibly have stood them. The tariffs of the last five years have steadily risen, until, if the present one passes, we shall have an average of about seventy per cent on all foreign imports." [27]

Stevens was not content with cotton tax and tariff. In the face of repeated defeats he returned to his confiscation plans, introducing a bill in March 1867 baldly advertised as a measure for inflicting "proper punishment" for "an unjust war." It provided for the seizure of all estates worth more than $5,000, and their division into forty-acre farms, one for every Negro family. The remainder could be sold, he said, and the proceeds used to give $100 to every freedman to build a home, to reimburse loyal Southern whites for damages, and to pay the pensions of crippled Northern soldiers and the families of the war dead.

He could muster little support. "All confiscation is robbery," said Representative John W. Chanler from New York. "It is the tool of the tyrant and the oppressor." [28] Godkin, who was becoming bitterly critical of the Radical Republicans, wrote in the *Nation:* "A bill in which provision is made for the violation of a greater number of the principles of good government and for the opening of a deeper sink of corruption has never been submitted to a legislative body. . . . If it be deemed desirable that he should have land without waiting to earn it, it ought to be given him out of Government lands, and it would be better for the nation to spend five hundred million in settling him on them rather than allow or encourage him to use his ballot for the purpose of helping himself to his neighbor's goods." [29]

Stevens' bill failed. He had succeeded in the Act of June 21, 1866, in getting public lands thrown open to the Negro for homesteads in Arkansas, Mississippi, Louisiana, Alabama, and Florida, but Congress never appropriated money to assist in any kind of resettlement. Much of the public land was worthless, and the Negro preferred to become a sharecropper on good land rather than starve in the pine woods. Many good acres fell into the hands of speculators, and only about 4,000 families were settled on the public lands.[30]

Frances Butler Leigh reported that many of her former slaves accumulated a little money and left the plantation to buy land, paying forty or fifty dollars an acre. "The land was either within the town limits, for which they got no titles, and from which they were soon turned off, or out in the pine woods, where the land was so poor they could not raise a peck of corn to the acre." "Gentlemen," she said, could seldom be persuaded to sell to Negroes at all.[31]

Had Stevens succeeded in getting for the Negroes their forty acres by confiscation, there can be small doubt but that all the cunning, legal manipulation, and intimidation that the white man used to take away the Negro ballot would also have been employed to recapture the land. The Southerner would always have looked upon confiscation as robbery. Already on the sea islands the Negroes were being defrauded of land they had legally purchased from the government. Some were accused of nonpayment of the land tax of 1866; others were swindled by speculators with free whiskey.[32]

Stevens knew that in Russia the feudal lords had been paid compensation, and that the serfs had to redeem the loans by payments extending over a long period of years. But he steadfastly insisted on outright confiscation, and thus lost more for the Negro than he could possibly have imagined. Had he spent the same energy getting Congress to appropriate money for land purchase and resettlement, many Negroes would have been far less vulnerable in the post-reconstruction period.[33]

Stevens' failure in statesmanship on this issue seems to have resulted from his intense preoccupation with punishment. His speeches on the confiscation bill are an unwitting revelation of the obsessional nature of this preoccupation. And they illuminate in the most unexpected fashion something of his own self-hatred.

> The punishment of traitors has been wholly ignored by a treacherous Executive and by a sluggish Congress. . . . To this issue I desire to devote the small remnant of my life. . . .
>
> This bill, it seems to me, can be condemned only by the criminals and their immediate friends, and by that unmanly kind of men whose intellectual and moral vigor has melted into a fluid weakness which they mistake for mercy, and which is untempered with a single grain of justice, and to those religionists who mistake meanness for Christianity, and who forget that the essence of religion is to "do unto others what others have a right to expect from you." It is offensive to certain pretentious doctors of divinity who are mawkishly prating about the "fatted calf, the prodigal son, and the forgiving father."
>
> . . . When the great ancestor of this bloody race had slain his brother, and tremblingly met his Judge and sought for pardon, what was the answer? "The voice of thy brother's blood crieth unto me from the ground. And now art thou cursed from the earth, which hath opened her mouth to receive thy brother's blood from thy hand. When thou tillest the ground it shall not henceforth yield unto thee her strength; a fugitive and a vagabond shalt thou be in the earth." When Cain cried out that his "punishment was more than he could bear," the Judge who administered justice in mercy drove him forth into stern, inexorable exile. He taught no forgiveness for such sins. He prated of no "fatted calves." [34]

That he should have turned to the story of Cain to justify his own harshness was extraordinary, for Cain to many Bible readers was thought to be the ancestor of the Negro race, and with this tragic Biblical figure, set apart from the rest of humanity by the "mark upon his forehead," Stevens was certain to have had a real sense of identity. Superficially it would seem that Stevens was justifying his own severity in terms of the unrelenting Old Testament Jehovah, and simply being true to the Calvinist training of his youth, where justice always outweighed mercy. But if one may hazard a deeper significance, it may be possible that Stevens, by taking on the mantle of the unforgiving father—or the punishing god—was intent on righting an ancient wrong, daring no less, in fact, than to reverse the judgment of Jehovah. He would punish "the father"—the Southern white man—for branding the Negro, in a kind of symbolic punishment of his own father—or of God Himself—for branding and crippling him.

It was characteristic of Thaddeus Stevens that when word came from Mexico in June 1867 that Maximilian of Habsburg had been shot at the orders of the revolutionary President Juarez, he was the only man in Congress to defend the execution. His reason—that Maximilian had sought to usurp power from the weak.[35] He liked seeing men in power topple. It may have been deeply reassuring for him to see men favored by the gods destroyed by the accident of war or the inexorable finger of the law.

To treat an enemy with compassion meant a blunting of his hatred. And for Thaddeus Stevens hatred was an energizing force with the passionate quality of love. "The forgiveness of the gospel," he said, "refers to private offences, where men can forgive their enemies and smother their feeling of revenge without injury to anybody. But that has nothing to do with municipal punishment, with political sanction of crimes. When nations pass sentence and decree confiscation for crimes unrepented there is no question of malignity. When the judge sentences the convict he has no animosity. When the hangman executes the culprit he rather pities than hates him. Cruelty does not belong to their vocabulary. Gentlemen mistake, therefore, when they make these appeals to us in the name of humanity. They, sir, who while preaching this doctrine are hugging and caressing those whose hands are red with the blood of our and their murdered kinsmen, are covering themselves with indelible stains which all the waters of the Nile cannot wash out." [36]

It will be seen that Stevens' paradise, like so many political Utopias, was not without its purgatory. He could not purify without purging. And in this regard his enemies were right when they likened him to Robespierre. He would not go as far as the guillotine, but this was no real proof of compassion. For the American aristocrat he had other cutting weapons.

I have never desired bloody punishments to any extent, even for the sake of example. But there are punishments quite as appalling, and longer remembered, than death. They are more advisable, because they would reach a greater number. Strip a proud nobility of their bloated estates; reduce them to a level with plain republicans; send them forth to labor, and teach their children to enter the workshops or handle the plow, and you will thus humble the proud traitors. Teach his posterity to respect labor and eschew treason. Conspiracies are bred among the rich and the vain, the ambitious aristocrats.[37]

This was in truth Robespierre's "despotism of liberty against tyranny."

CHAPTER TWENTY-FIVE

---◆---

Negro Suffrage—the First Fruits

That's the question, what's for their good, not what pleases them.

Oliver Cromwell

"WHEN THAD STEVENS shall die, his virtues will be better appreciated and his name will be more highly honored than now; for he is one of those men who are very inconvenient when alive, and very valuable when dead. It will be remembered that in the dark hour of his country's history, when other men were afraid to speak, he was *not* afraid to speak, and when other men were afraid to be unpopular, he was *not* afraid to be unpopular." This was the fashionable Brooklyn preacher, Henry Ward Beecher, in a sermon April 14, 1867.[1] Although not good prophecy, it was apt description. Thaddeus Stevens was not only contemptuous of his unpopularity, but like many men who have no real expectation of being loved, he took a certain grim pleasure in it.

"You used to have a good deal of moral courage in old times," he said to a Pennsylvania Democrat in 1867, "have you enough now, to come and pay *me* a visit?" [2] In Congress he referred frankly to his own unpopularity:

I know it is easy to protect the interests of the rich and powerful; but it is a great labor to guard the rights of the poor and downtrodden; it is the eternal labor of Sisyphus forever to be renewed. I know how unprofitable is all such toil. But he who is in earnest does not heed these things. I know, too, what effect it has on personal popularity. But if I may be indulged in a little egotism, I will say that if there be anything for which I have entire indifference, perhaps I may say contempt, it is that public opinion which is founded on popular clamor.[3]

With increasing age he grew more irascible, waspish, and defiant. His skin was gray, his voice hollow and empty. The dark brown wig, sitting carelessly on his head, might well have turned him into a kind of clown but for the dour twist to his mouth, which gave him, in the words of one observer, "the visage of an undertaker." His eyes, topped by enormous brows, though now deeply sunken and faded to an indefinable color, were still capable of lighting up with a fierce gleam.

He resented bitterly the combination of ailments that were robbing him of his old vigor. ". . . how little enjoyment there is when age or disease has withered our mental and physical faculties," he wrote to Simon Stevens August 3, 1867. "Since I returned I have been getting rather worse. What the result of this disease may be, I am doubtful. Nor does it give me much concern. I remember that we are admonished that there is a time when we must no longer attempt to hurl the discus or bend the bow of Ulysses. That day has come with me. I should regret to depart without seeing this government placed on a basis of perfect freedom." [4]

To one visitor, who looked at his pallid face and wasted frame and concluded he could not live a week longer, Stevens insisted that he felt "lively as a trout." But he freely admitted one weakness. "It is not the physical disability; it's the head, the memory. There is no use disguising the fact: I am fast losing my memory, a faculty which was strongest in my youth, and which I have ever relied upon. When a young man, like yourself, I had no more abilities than other young men, but my splendid memory, which I loved to cultivate, enabled me to retain that which I would glance over *verbatim*, and which others would study hard to commit. It is not so now. I find that I have to send out scouts to gather up ideas for me." [5]

According to Justin Morrill, Stevens had always had "a tough and wiry constitution" that was able to bear "any amount of fatigue and some excesses with little pain or injury." A glance at the index to the *Congressional Globe* in any year after 1861 bears out Morrill's statement that Stevens watched "with sleepless vigilance all the bills on the calendar." (Clemenceau would write on January 3, 1868, that Stevens "though dying, proposes more bills in one day than any of his colleagues in a month." [6])

But after the summer of 1867 he spent much of his time lying on a couch in an anteroom to the House chamber. Whereas earlier he had stood erect to give his speeches, reluctant even to lean upon a cane, "firmly poised," said Morrill, "as if conscious that his foundation reached to the very center of the earth," now he could stand no more than a moment, and his voice would give way after a few paragraphs, whereupon he would apologetically turn his speech over to the clerk of the House.

When he was too ill to be carried to the capitol, cabinet officers, foreign ministers, senators, representatives, newspaper correspondents, and the public, visited him in his little two-story brick house at 279 South B. Street. Here in this house, said a *New York Tribune* correspondent, with its seven front windows looking out on a row of fine linden trees, "were born and matured most, if not all, of those important measures of legislation which have become woven into the history of the Republic." [7]

Everyone expected him to die shortly, and many made it no secret that they looked forward to the event with relish. "There is no piece of news comes from Washington of such good augury for the country as the announcement that Stevens is down again," said the *New York Herald* on May 13, 1868, "while if it declares that there is not the slightest hope of his recovery, it is a reason for universal delight."

"There is a hideous significance about this old man," wrote Southerner Edward A. Pollard, "preparing in the last moments of his own life new instruments of torture for the South, and grinning over the work of his bony and unsightly hands, at the very side of his own grave. It is an exhibition of what hate and passions legislate for the South—a picture of diabolism at which the heart shudders." [8]

There was much speculation about who would succeed him as leader of the Republican Party. Charles Sumner had none of Stevens' genius as a parliamentary whip and only a fraction of his capacity for creating legislation. As a Radical he was less flexible and more dogmatic, and frequently blocked radical legislation simply because it was not radical enough. His inordinate vanity made him unpopular in the Senate, and he had fallen into a nasty personal feud with the able Conservative Republican leader, Senator Fessenden, which did not enhance his prestige within the party.

In the fall of 1866, to everyone's surprise, Sumner married. He was fifty-five, and the marriage occurred six months after the death of his mother. The bride, Mrs. Alice Hooper, the daughter-in-law of a Congressman, was twenty-eight years old, a widow with a young daughter. Within nine months, however, the pair had separated, and before a year was out Sumner had instituted divorce proceedings. Unfriendly reporters blamed his arrogance, dictatorial exactions, and his habit of inviting distinguished Negroes to dine. Others hinted that the young widow, finding her new husband "cold and unfeeling," had given her favors to a young diplomat. The *New York World* callously described him as "*Prince Paul* Sumner, the plaintive, the impotent, the thin of leg." [9]

Two months after the divorce he went to Boston to attend his sister's funeral and remained to sell the old family home. "I have buried from this house," he wrote to Longfellow, "my father, my mother, a brother and sister; and now I am leaving it, the deadest of them all." [10]

Stevens' increasing frailty and Sumner's heavy melancholy were symptomatic of what was happening to the Republican revolution. The genuine religious fervor accompanying the abolition of slavery and the passing of the civil-rights measures was dissipated by the Military Bill, and a sense of shock at its severity turned an increasing number of Republicans into critics of the party. Thurlow Weed, as new editor of the *New York Commercial Advertiser*, wrote in his first editorial: "We of the North have become as exacting and aggressive after, as southern men were before the Rebellion." He echoed the sentiments of most Northern businessmen, especially bankers, railroad men, and cotton manufacturers, who favored political moderation as the swiftest way to economic recovery in the South. [11]

The *Nation*, which had consistently applauded Republican efforts to gain suffrage and civil rights for the Negro, now warned that Congress "either through fatuity or through desperation," had entered "on a course in which it will not be sustained by the country. . . . We do not mean to say that we have gained nothing by the war, the moral vision of the nation has not been cleared by it and its moral aims raised. Far from it. We mean simply that the powers of evil are far from being vanquished. . . . the South has not yet revealed its real temper."

"The kind of 'courage' we want in public men," Godkin insisted, "is not the kind which Wendell Phillips so loudly calls for, and which Messrs. Stevens and Butler so lavishly display—the courage to be unscrupulous, dexterous, reckless—but the courage to be right under all circumstances . . . to be faithful not simply to pledges made to blacks, but to pledges made to white men. . . . before very long the whites will reassume their old ascendancy. The worst enemies of the blacks are those who deceive themselves on this point." [12]

When Thaddeus Stevens was likened by the Democrats to Cromwell and Robespierre, the Republican press scorned the imputation as absurd, but certain resemblances caused thoughtful men in the party deep anxiety. Cromwell had divided his domain into twelve military districts, each under a major-general "to forestall conspiracy and watch over public morals," and it seemed to many that Stevens now had gone back to 1655. The *New York World* needled constantly on this issue: "The Jesuits, the Dominican Inquisitors, the Fifth Monarch men, and the French Jacobins, were all parties based upon 'great moral ideas,' " it said. "The Rump Congress are usurpers and revolutionists." [13]

Stevens made matters no better by his frank and frequent admission that he was acting wholly outside the Constitution. "Some of the members of the Senate," he wrote, "seemed to doubt their power under the Constitution which they had just repudiated, and wholly outside of which all agreed we were acting; else our whole work of Reconstruction was usurpation." [14] But the most disquieting thing of all was that Stevens—like the Sibyl who continued to double the price of her books foretelling the destiny of Rome as she destroyed the volumes—became more and more exacting with every Southern refusal. No one could be certain of his final price.

A Southern editor put the question to him exactly in an interview on May 23, 1867: "Suppose, sir, Alabama should organize a government enfranchising the negro, providing for his education and giving ample guarantee for his protection before the courts and in society, and under that government should send good men, who could take the 'Test Oath' to Congress, would you admit her to representation?" Without a moment's pause, the editor noted, "he answered with strong emphasis, 'No, sir,' and thus closed the interview." [15]

During the summer of 1867 the work of registration of whites and Negroes in the former Confederate states had gone busily forward. Registration of Negroes was done largely by Freedmen's Bureau agents, partly because the Negroes trusted them, partly because many agents saw a chance for political office. Political clubs called Loyal Leagues were organized through the South. Many had elaborate initiation rites and flag ceremonies, much singing and memorizing of phrases from the Constitution and the Declaration of Independence. The Negro, so long denied any freedom to organize, found the club activity as exciting as his religious revivals. Some leagues kept their activities secret, partly to escape the wrath of the white Regulators, and partly in imitation of their methods. As white men swore oaths to keep the Negro from voting, so the Negro swore oaths to vote only the Republican ticket and see to it that all Negroes did likewise.

The Loyal Leagues alone would have been enough to rouse among white men their ancient fear of Negro insurrection. But the fear was greatly heightened by the organization of companies of Negro militia. George Fitzhugh reflected the mounting hysteria in *DeBow's Review:*

> We assure you, and your readers, and the entire North, that the freedmen (with very few exceptions) are anxious, impatient, burning with desire to begin the fight—the war of races—at once. They are all around; they are continually drilling in defiance of law. They have everywhere secret military organizations; they daily defy and insult the Federal troops and the Freedmen's Bureau. They are ready and anxious to fight all the whites both North and South.[16]

Even General O. O. Howard, head of the Freedmen's Bureau, admitted that the Negroes generally were "not wisely led." Many of the white organizers told them that their first political job would be confiscation of the plantations.[17] The Negro publishers of the *New Orleans Tribune* urged that Louisiana be made an African state, after the example of Haiti, San Domingo and Liberia.[18] One mulatto leader in Uniontown, Alabama, made a speech which brought the whole Negro colony trouble:

> Gentlemen, I am no nigger, I am neither white nor black. . . . my father, God damn his soul to hell, had 300 niggers, and his son sold me for $1,000. Was this right? No! I feel the damned spirit of damnation in me and will fight for our rights until every rascal who chased niggers with hounds is in hell.[19]

Lewis Lindsay, prominent Negro Radical in Virginia, made a speech in Charlottesville in July 1867 demanding that the state offices be equally divided between the races. One Radical white leader was arrested in November for making a speech to Negroes in which he said: "You colored people have no property. The white race has houses and lands. Some of you are old and feeble and cannot carry the musket, but you can apply the torch to the dwellings of your enemies. There are none too young—the boy of ten and the girl of twelve can apply the torch." [20]

When the registration was finished, it was estimated in the Senate that 672,000 ex-slaves had been added to the voting population, against a possible total white electorate of 925,000. The exact number of white men disfranchised has always been an elusive figure. Andrew Johnson was determined to keep the number as small as possible, and Thaddeus Stevens was equally bent on making it big. Seeing Johnson's intention, especially as expressed through the interpretive decisions of Attorney-General Stanbery, Stevens made sure that the Supplementary Reconstruction Acts of March 23 and July 19, 1867—passed over the President's veto—contained provisions making it increasingly difficult for the former Confederates to pass the required loyalty oath. He saw to it that a Presidential pardon was not enough to guarantee a man suffrage or the right to office.

In some states the hostility of the whites led them to boycott the whole Reconstruction proceedings. "I think most of the gentlemen felt as I did," wrote Frances Butler Leigh, "that the negroes voting at all was such a wicked farce that it only deserved our contempt," and she reflected a widespread misconception in reporting that *all* white men were disfranchised.[21] In the poor-white areas, apathy kept many away from the polls, as in the past, whereas among the Negroes there was feverish activity. In Mississippi and Louisiana there was a mass boycott of the election on the part of white men.[22]

Many Southern leaders, like General Robert E. Lee, sincerely urged their countrymen to take the oath and not remain "unreconstructed." Others were more cynical. "We are in Rome and mean to do as Rome does," wrote George Fitzhugh. "We know our abolition catechism by heart; on a pinch, we could repeat it backwards." [23]

Godkin in the *Nation* persistently opposed oath-taking, saying that it had never succeeded in anything but "a monstrous deal of perjury." [24] But the oath was insisted upon, and made more stringent with the Reconstruction Acts. No man in the South could vote unless he could swear to the following:

. . . I have never been a member of any State Legislature nor held any executive or judicial office in any state and afterwards engaged in insurrection or rebellion against the United States, or given aid or comfort to the enemies thereof . . .

In some states the percentage of white disfranchisement was much higher than in others because of the political sentiments of the general in charge. General Sheridan, in command over Louisiana, interpreted the oath so stringently that the *New Orleans Times* estimated that half the white males were barred from the polls, including all veterans and Democratic office holders.[25] General Schofield in Virginia, on the other hand, was lenient, holding, for example, that "giving aid and comfort to the enemy" did not mean supplying charity but furnishing horses and guns.[26] In Tennessee the new Radical constitution disfranchised more than half the white male citizens.[27]

Paul Lewinson has estimated that at least 100,000 white men were disfranchised or chose to stay away from the polls in the summer of 1867.[28] Negro voters outnumbered the whites in five states—Florida, Alabama, South Carolina, Mississippi, and Louisiana—though only in the latter three did they number 50 per cent or more of the population. In South Carolina the Negroes formed 60 per cent of the population and 63 per cent of the voters; in Mississippi 55 per cent of the population and a majority of the voters; in Louisiana 50 per cent of the population and 65 per cent of the voters; in Alabama 45 per cent of the population and 63 per cent of the voters; in Georgia 44 per cent of the population and 49 per cent of the voters. In Virginia 47 per cent of those registered were colored men.[29]

The heavy proportion of Negro votes was not, however, reflected in the membership of the new constitutional conventions. While in all of them there was a generous sprinkling of "black and tan" faces, only in South Carolina and Louisiana did the Negroes participate in proportion to their population in the electorate. South Carolina elected 48 white delegates and 76 Negroes. Two-thirds of the latter had been slaves. In Louisiana the delegates were evenly divided, 49 Negroes and 49 whites, which stimulated the *New York Herald* to call it "the Zebra Convention." In all other states the proportion of Negro delegates was much smaller. In Mississippi there were only 17 Negro delegates and 83 whites; in Florida, 18 Negroes and 27 whites; in Virginia, 25 Negroes and 80 whites; in Georgia, 33 Negroes and 137 whites; in Alabama, 18 Negroes and 90 whites; in North Carolina, 15 Negroes and 118 whites; in Texas, 9 Negroes and 81 whites.[30]

In only two states, then, if the Negro delegates had chosen to vote as Negro units, could they have controlled the activities of the conventions. But this they did not and could not try to do. Many were illiterate; almost all were bred in the tradition of deference to the white man, and would now simply vote as the white Republican leaders indicated. Still in every convention there was a small core of Negro leaders, educated either in the North or in the free Negro schools in Washington, Richmond, Charleston, and New Orleans, who were articulate and active in the convention proceedings.[31]

The spectacle of Negroes merely sitting at the seat of government in the Southern states was profoundly shocking to the majority of Americans. Even before the conventions met in December 1867 and January 1868, the North had registered in the voting booths its sense of dismay at the thoroughness of Thaddeus Stevens' Reconstruction. Although dedicated in theory to the ideals of the Declaration of Independence, and genuinely devoted to the American creed of equality before the law, many were now appalled at the reality of impartial suffrage.

Connecticut, which had for years voted Democratic, and had rejected Negro suffrage in 1865, rejected it again in April 1867. Although the margin of defeat was by several hundred instead of several thousand as in 1865, the failure to carry Negro suffrage in a New England state that had almost no Negroes was a nasty blow to the prestige of the Radical Congress. But this was only a portent of what happened in the general elections in the fall of 1867.

The Democrats had concentrated largely on one idea. "Any Democrat," reported Clemenceau, "who did not manage to hint in his speech that the negro is a degenerate gorilla, would be considered lacking in enthusiasm. The idea of giving political power to a lot of wild men, incapable of civilization, whose intelligence is no higher than that of the animals! That is the theme of all the Democratic speeches."

William Mungen, Democratic Representative from Ohio, insisted in Congress that the Negro had a nervous system weighing one-third less than the Anglo Saxon. The *New York World* coined the phrase "hybridizing Radicals," and accused the Republican Party of forcing "negro equality and miscegenation upon the people of ten American States." [32]

When James Brooks, Democratic Party whip in the House, spent an hour arguing that the Negro was physically inferior to the white man, Thaddeus Stevens rose briefly to point out that the Negro had an immortal soul which God could damn as well as his if he deserved it. While he conceded, Stevens said, that the "gentleman from New York" had an intellect that "towers above the rest of us," he was willing to match him for the oratorical championship of America against the Negro orator Frederick Douglass. "Let the topic be anything the gentleman pleases except the negro's skin, and if at the end of the discussion he does not 'throw up the sponge,' I will admit that the negro is an inferior animal—not only inferior to the gentleman from New York, but inferior to the rest of us." [33]

In the 1867 elections the Democrats carried New York, New Jersey, Maryland, and Ohio, and showed surprising strength in the states won by Republicans—Massachusetts, Michigan, Wisconsin, Kansas, Missouri, and Illinois. What was worse for the Radical Republicans, Minnesota, Kansas, and Ohio all rejected Negro suffrage. Ohio gave a majority of over 50,000 against it, and Andrew Johnson sent an exultant telegram to the president of the Executive Committee of the Democratic Party: "Ohio has done its duty and done it in time. God bless Ohio."

The *New York World,* crowing over the election results on October 16, 1867, said the people had put the "stamp of their reprobation" upon "the old anarch" Thaddeus Stevens. "Unhappy, unhappy ancient, who devotes the last rags of his life to party hate, not heeding the voice of his countrymen when, in detestation of his principles and pity for his years, they cry, 'Fall to thy prayers, old man; we know thee not.' "

When a reporter interviewed Stevens shortly after the election, they were interrupted by the noise of men outside going to serenade the President. Stevens growled: "Democracy! God! The people are not all crazy. All will be well if they do not act like fools and cowards." [34]

"The nigger whipped us," admitted Senator Ben Wade, in discussing the loss of his own state, Ohio. "We went in on principle, and got whipped. We should have carried the State by a good majority if it hadn't been for the suffrage issue. . . . I had no idea that there were so many Republicans in Ohio who were willing to see negro suffrage in the South, but wouldn't let the few niggers of Ohio vote. That's what got me. . . . Hell is full of such Radicals as we'll have now." [35]

In the border states, as Thaddeus Stevens had feared, the election was disastrous for the Radical Republicans. In Kentucky, where the Democrats had won a slight victory even in 1865, and had consolidated their victory in 1866, they now tossed out all the remaining Radicals with ease and proceeded with plans to nullify the expected Negro suffrage. Because she had stayed in the Union throughout the war, Kentucky avoided carpetbag government and military rule. But as E. Merton Coulter has pointed out, she "carried her proscription of Union men in her own borders so far as almost to bring down reconstruction on her own head. It was often remarked that she waited until after the war was over to secede." Assuming in advance that Negro suffrage was wholly an evil, Kentucky's white men saw to it that it was never seriously tried.[36]

In Tennessee, "Parson" Brownlow, called by the *New York World* "a small fire-engine spouting gutter water," and "an empty, ribald old bruiser," [37] was still in power. The Negroes had been permitted to vote and managed to carry the state for the Radical Republicans. But the victory was accompanied by an ominous rise in violence. General W. P. Carlin reported to General O. O. Howard that from June to October, 1867, there had been recorded at his headquarters in Tennessee 25 murders, 35 assaults with intent to kill, 83 cases of assault and battery, 4 of rape, and 4 of arson, all against the freedmen. Not one murderer had been punished, and almost all the other offenders had escaped the law.[38]

The Ku Klux Klan, which began in Pulaski, Tennessee, in December 1865, had been reorganized at a secret conference in Nashville early in the summer of 1867. General Nathan B. Forrest, former slave-trader, "hero" of the Fort Pillow massacre—"an illiterate, but able and gallant Confederate cavalry officer" [39]—was made Grand Wizard. An elaborate organization was being developed, destined to spread speedily in a gigantic web over the whole South, absorbing most of the scattered bands—the Knights of the White Camelia, White Brotherhood, White League, Pale Faces, Constitutional Union Guards, Black Cavalry, White Rose, and the '76 Association—into a guerrilla underground of terrifying proportions, numbering, it has been said, a half a million men in 1868.[40]

By April 1868 reports were coming in of Klan attacks everywhere in the South. Thaddeus Stevens was not neglected. On May 4, 1868, the New Orleans Klan dispatched him the following letter:

Thaddeus Stevens,
Thou hast eaten the bread of wickedness, and drunk the wine of violence. Thou hast sown to the wind, Then shall reap the whirlwind in the *moon's last quarter*.

> By order of the R H P of the
> Ku Klux Klan
> N.O.L.D.[41]

By this time the Klan had won the support of practically the whole Southern press, and was absorbing into its ranks men from every social stratum, including the old aristocracy. The editor of the *Richmond Examiner*, Edward Pollard, wrote in early April, 1868:

. . . under its cap and bells it hides a purpose as resolute, noble and heroic, as that which Brutus concealed beneath the mask of well-dissembled idiocy. It is rapidly organizing wherever the insolent negro, the malignant white traitor to his race, and the infamous squatter are plotting to make the South utterly unfit for the residence of the decent white man.[42]

Pollard had become the popular historian of the Confederacy. In his new book, *The Lost Cause Regained*, published in 1868, he warned grimly of the consequences of Negro suffrage: "Let the Negro beware of the poisoned gift. . . . It is the declaration of war between the Negro and the white man." [43]

The rise in violence, coming as it did on the heels of the 1867 election defeats, caused a shift in the policy of the Radical Republicans. Whereas Thaddeus Stevens before had employed the most artful tactics of delay, now he reversed himself and urged the utmost speed in reinstatement of the Southern states into the Union. Seeing the gathering power of the counter-revolution, he hoped to forestall it at least until after the presidential election of 1868. He followed the proceedings of the constitutional conventions in the South with meticulous care and drew up an omnibus bill providing for the admission of most of the states back into the Union as soon as their new constitutions had been voted upon.[44]

As the Reconstruction Acts directed, the new constitutions provided for Negro suffrage and equality of civil rights. Six states disfranchised and barred from office the leaders of the Confederacy, as required by the Fourteenth Amendment, and added even harsher provisions to keep ex-Confederates from the polls—notably Arkansas, Alabama, Mississippi, Louisiana, and Tennessee. But the Georgia, North Carolina, South Carolina, and Florida constitutions barred no white men whatever—though the provisions of the Fourteenth Amendment automatically applied in these states. This action was most surprising in South Carolina, where 76 out of 124 delegates were colored, and 57 had been slaves.[45]

Between November 5, 1867 and May 18, 1868, all the Southern states adopted new constitutions except Texas. There were many things wrong with the new experiment in universal democracy, but the quality of these new constitutions was remarkably high. Out of what some historians have chosen to call a mass of ignorance and semi-barbarism came the provisions for the South's first statewide public schools. The South Carolina constitution, in addition to providing universal suffrage, enlarged the rights of women, providing that their property could not be sold to pay their husband's debts, gave the state its first divorce law, outlawed dueling, and provided special education for the deaf and dumb. Even after the Conservatives regained control, they kept this constitution for eighteen years.[46]

The Mississippi convention abolished all property and racial qualifications for suffrage or office, thus opening the ballot box to thousands of white men who had been barred in the past. It forbade distinctions in the possession and inheritance of property and provided for equality in civil rights. Mississippi was content to live under its provisions for twenty-two years.[47]

Many of the constitutions abolished the whipping post, the branding iron, the stocks, and other medieval punishments, and reduced capital felonies from twenty-odd to two or three.[48] But except in the Radical Republican press the men who devised these constitutions met with contumely and contempt in North and South alike. The *New York Times* said of the South Carolina convention: "There is scarcely a Southern white man in the body whose character would keep him out of the penitentiary." [49] Representative James B. Beck from Kentucky said of the Alabama constitution that it "is perhaps republican in form, as a gorilla is human in form, but it has as few of the attributes of a true republican Constitution, especially in its oaths, as the ape has of the cultivated gentleman." [50]

Unquestionably the most notable achievement of the new constitutions was the creation of public-school systems. An attempt was made in Louisiana and Mississippi to provide by statute for the mixing of races in the schools, but no attempt was made to enforce it. As Henry C. Warmoth described it in Louisiana, "The white people were opposed to mixed schools and the colored people loved their children and knew too well what would happen to them if any of them should attempt to force themselves into white schools." [51]

In Tennessee, when the new school law provided for separate schools, John Ogden, professor at the newly chartered Fisk University, raised a lonely voice in protest:

We only ask for equal justice and impartial representation. The law should make no distinction or it provides for oppression. It should not even allow the exercise of a partiality, even though the school may desire it. But let these schools be peaceably provided for by law, and nothing be said about color or caste; and mark my word, in less than fifty years this needless prejudice will be dead. But legislate for it and you make it respectable, and will provide for its continuation. It must die sometime and the sooner the legislature strikes the blow the better. If it hurts somebody, let somebody get out of the way. [52]

Thaddeus Stevens did not publicly object to the separation of the races in the schools, though he was against segregation in theory, and in his will left money for an orphan asylum with the strict provision that it should be open to all colors and races, and that the children should eat at the same table. But he never pressed for legal enforcement of this kind of equality, as Charles Sumner did, believing it achievement enough that the South would have free schools at all.

It was to be four or five years, however, before the new schools could be properly organized and financed, and this period saw an actual and serious increase in the illiteracy of the South. Only the Freedmen's Bureau schools, financed privately and with some small government assistance, kept the ratio from being even higher, and these were gradually abandoned as the public school systems got under way. The Bureau schools were open to both races, but in South Carolina, at any rate, in 1867, only fifteen white children were enrolled. [53] In 1868 about one in eleven of the colored children in the South were being taught in the Freedmen's Bureau schools. As the Ku Klux Klan spread, many schoolhouses were burned, especially in the hill country, and the white teachers were frightened into leaving altogether. [54] Nevertheless, the idea of the necessity of free schools for white and black alike took hold in the South, and was to become ever stronger with passing years.

Thaddeus Stevens dreamed of establishing in the District of Columbia a free-school system that would be a model for the nation. This was "the object of his extremest solicitude," said the *Philadelphia Press,* "and the one that cost him the most labor." He studied the Swiss, German, and Scandinavian systems, and emerged from his planning with a remarkable bill, which was introduced December 3, 1867. It called for compulsory school attendance eight months out of the year, a library in each school, a maximum of sixty pupils to each teacher. It provided a liberal pension fund for the teachers, night schools, and a normal school for teacher training. In discussing this bill Stevens said: "If there be anything for which, above all others, I would feel grateful to a benevolent Providence, it would be for furnishing me an opportunity to unlock the bondmen's chains and carry free education into every poor man's hut throughout the fertile valleys and barren mountains of the whole land." [55]

In the same weeks in which he was drawing the blueprint for his school system, a new threat to Stevens' Reconstruction measures was appearing over the horizon. The obstreperous Southern editor of the *Vicksburg Times,* W. H. McCardle, had been jailed by the military governor, General E. O. C. Ord, for publishing libels on his officers, for intimidating voters and inciting the ex-Confederates to violence. McCardle shrewdly applied for a writ of habeas corpus under the Reconstruction Act of February 5, 1867, which had been designed to help the Southern Negro and Unionist. The old Act of 1789 had given the federal courts the right to issue writs of habeas corpus with only a limited right of appeal to the Supreme Court. The Radical Republicans had amended this in 1867 by permitting appeal in "all cases where any person may be restrained of his or her liberty, in violation of the Constitution or of any treaty or law of the United States." McCardle, with able Democratic counsel, including Jeremiah Black, now used his imprisonment as a challenge to test the validity of the Reconstruction Acts.

The Radical Republicans, fearing that the Supreme Court would divide five to four against them, once more tried to hamstring it by legislation. The House Judiciary Committee drew up a bill requiring a two-thirds vote of the Court to declare laws unconstitutional, and it passed the House. The nation's press raised a furor. The *New York World* in an article entitled "The Rump Revolution," said angrily on January 17, 1868: "Congress is today the Judiciary. . . . These men are traitors."

Only extreme Radical papers argued on the other side, the *New*

York Tribune insisting on January 23, 1868 that inasmuch as two hundred men, many of them better jurists than any on the bench, had concurred in passing the bill, it was monstrous to let the vote of a single judge set it aside.

The bill ran into so much trouble in the Senate that Thaddeus Stevens introduced another one, described by the New York World on January 24, 1868 as "short, sharp, and aimed straight at the mark." It expressly forbade the Supreme Court to take jurisdiction in any case in law or equity arising out of the Reconstruction Acts. The New York World on January 24, while grudgingly admitting that Stevens "has more brains and logic in his little finger than all the rest of the party seem to have in their skulls," and admitting that the bill had "at least the merit of consistency" with Stevens' principles, nevertheless called it "the most flagitious abuse of power ever attempted by a legislative body." It was, in fact, too brazen a challenge of the Supreme Court to pass the House.

Meanwhile hearings on the McCardle Case had begun, and the Radical Republicans turned to guile. Representative Robert C. Schenck slipped past the unsuspecting Democrats, by explaining that it was a routine matter, a bill repealing the Supreme Court's appellate jurisdiction under the Habeas Corpus Act of 1867, and prohibiting the Court from exercising any jurisdiction on any appeals which had already been taken, or might be taken. What this meant in effect was that Congress was now repealing the special rights it had granted to the Supreme Court a year earlier.

When the Senate passed this bill, Andrew Johnson vetoed it, even though his own inconsistency was thereby exposed, for he had also vetoed the original bill. But the new veto was more defensible. If the bill became a precedent, he said, there would no longer be any check on unconstitutional legislation. Here he struck particularly at Thaddeus Stevens, who had made no secret of his intention of making the Court impotent when it came to review the legislation of Reconstruction.

The bill nevertheless passed both houses of Congress on March 26–27, over Johnson's veto, and the Supreme Court abandoned its review of the McCardle Case. The parliamentary maneuver had spared the Radical Republicans an immediate Supreme Court test of the validity of the Reconstruction Acts, and still, according to the Nation, had left the "independence and dignity of the court unimpaired." Pro-Southern Jeremiah Black took a different view. "The court stood still to be ravished and did not even hallo while the thing was being done," he wrote privately to Howell Cobb.[56]

Partly because of accident, and partly because the members of the Supreme Court chose to act gingerly in this matter in succeeding years, the legal validity of the Reconstruction Acts was never seriously tested. Eight months after Stevens died, the Court in *Texas v White* settled the question of whether a state could legally secede by declaring that Texas had always remained a state in the union within the purview of the Constitution. But the impact of this decision, which indirectly rocked the legal structure of such reconstruction legislation, was lessened by the strong dissenting opinions of Justices Grier, Swayne, and Miller, one of whom said bluntly: "If I regard the truth of history for the last eight years I cannot discover the State of Texas as one of these United States." In 1875 in *Raymond v Thomas* the Supreme Court intimated that the Reconstruction Acts might be valid, but the case was decided on a subordinate point.[57]

But the Radical Republicans could not know this in advance, and for several months they continued to bombard Congress with legislation to tie the Court's hands. Senator Wilson in December 1868 tried to increase the number of judges to fifteen, and later introduced a bill giving the judges full pay if they chose to retire at seventy.

The actual legislation that did pass was hardly the monumental threat to the right of judicial review it has been made out to be. Nevertheless, had Thaddeus Stevens had his way, the Supreme Court would have been made truly impotent as far as the legislation on Reconstruction was concerned. And had this become a precedent, Andrew Johnson's fear that the nation would lose its last check on unconstitutional legislation would actually have been realized.

CHAPTER TWENTY-SIX

---◆---

Impeachment Beginnings

At each session they add a shackle to his bonds, tighten the bit in a different place, file a claw or draw a tooth, and then when he is well bound up, fastened, and caught in an inextricable net of laws and decrees, more or less contradicting each other, they tie him to the stake of the Constitution and take a good look at him, feeling quite sure he cannot move this time.

But then Seward, the Dalila of the piece, rises up and shouts: "Johnson, here come the radicals with old Stevens at their head; they are proud of having subjected you and are coming to enjoy the sight of you in chains." And Samson summons all his strength, and bursts his cords and bonds with a mighty effort, and the Philistines (I mean the radicals) flee in disorder to the Capitol to set to work making new laws stronger than the old, which will break in their turn at the first test. This has been going on now for two years, and though in the course of things it is inevitable that Samson will be beaten, one must admit that he has put up a game fight.

Georges Clemenceau, September 10, 1867 [1]

THE IMPEACHMENT OF Andrew Johnson was not an inevitable ending to the personal vendetta between the President and Thaddeus Stevens. Agitation for impeachment swelled and receded, swelled again, and then seemed to disappear altogether. Had the President been a little less inept—and it might even be said, less masochistic— the trial need never have occurred at all. For Stevens, powerful though he was, had no success with impeachment resolutions until Johnson blundered in the manner of his firing the Secretary of War. There was, nevertheless, a kind of inevitability in the thing. Johnson could have prevented it easily, but somehow did not. Stevens, who had truly enchained the President and had nothing further to gain politically by impeachment, still relentlessly pursued it to its climax, and thereby seriously damaged his party and his own reputation.

Agitation for impeachment started in earnest after the President's "Swing Round the Circle" in the campaign of 1866, and had much support in the Republican press. *Harper's Weekly* said on January 26, 1867: "The New Orleans massacre, the stumping and staggering orgy to the grave of Douglas, the exhortations to the late rebel States to reject the Amendment, the Copperhead society in which he loves to dwell, and the coarse vituperation of Senators and Representatives by name . . . have left Andrew Johnson morally impeached, and morally condemned." It did not help Johnson's cause to have the Democratic conventions and papers like the *Washington Constitutional Union* openly threaten armed resistance if Johnson was brought to trial.[2]

The Congressman who in the beginning had assumed chief responsibility for punishing the President was a small-minded Radical Republican, James M. Ashley from Ohio. On January 7, 1867 "Impeachment Ashley" introduced a resolution authorizing the House Judiciary Committee to investigate Johnson's conduct and see if he was guilty of "high crimes and misdemeanors." From January to March the committee industriously questioned the stenographic reporters who had taken down the President's election speeches, thumbed through his private accounts, and dredged up all the gossip and scandal that had ever been circulated about his private life.[3]

Stories of pardon-brokers, harlots, and alcoholism filtered out of the committee hearings to the press. Unfortunately for the President, his son Robert had been so indiscreet that some of the scandal attributed to the President was in fact true in regard to his son. Andrew Johnson was not an alcoholic, though he drank occasionally and sometimes in quantity, but there was no doubt that Robert Johnson was an alcoholic and something of a rake. Mrs. Johnson was an invalid dying slowly of tuberculosis, and the White House was managed by Johnson's sensible and unpretentious daughter Martha, wife of Tennessee's Senator David Patterson. No one could control the dissolute son. The President in despair finally persuaded Secretary Welles and Secretary Seward to give him a commission and send him to Liberia, ostensibly to study the slave trade. Johnson scrupulously insisted on paying his son's expenses.[4]

Thaddeus Stevens was not a member of the House impeachment committee in the beginning, but it cannot be said that he was not therefore responsible for the degrading calumny that issued from the hearings, since he could probably have stopped them had he cared to. For Representative Ashley was not content with aspersions upon Johnson's private life, including hints of adultery, but actually tried to prove that he had been guilty, along with Jefferson Davis and Clement C. Clay, of complicity in Lincoln's assassination.[5]

In the following month Benjamin Butler compounded the slander by insinuating publicly that Andrew Johnson had torn out the missing leaves from John Wilkes Booth's diary to prevent its use in the trial of Lincoln's assassins.[6] Stevens later condemned his own associates on the House Judiciary Committee for their "malignity." "Of all the prosecutions which I have ever witnessed, either in civil or military affairs," he said, "that result was to me the most unsatisfactory. . . . But these innumerable eggs were thrown into the nest of this investigation until it was more than full, and there was great danger of their becoming addled. They thought to break the elephant's back, broad as it was, by piling upon it straws and chaff bags . . . if that would not prove sufficient, to mount upon it two or three buxom damsels seated on pillions; Mrs. Cobb proved too light." [7]

But while the investigation was underway, Stevens let his underlings do their worst without rebuke. He may even have taken a savage satisfaction in seeing Andrew Johnson suffer the same kind of defamation that had been heaped upon himself throughout the years. In any case, he was exacting doublefold revenge upon the President who, sixteen months before, had said publicly, "Why not hang Thad Stevens!"

Stevens never attacked Johnson with Butler's and Ashley's insinuations and perjured testimony, content rather with his own brand of irony. "I'll take that man's record," he said, "his speeches, and his acts before any impartial jury you can get together, and I'll make them pronounce him either a knave or a fool, without the least trouble. My own impression is that we had better put it on the grounds of insanity or whisky or something of that kind. I don't want to hurt the man's feelings by telling him he is a rascal. I'd rather put it mildly, and say he hasn't got off that inauguration drunk yet, and just let him retire to get sobered." [8] When one Congressman tried to excuse Johnson because he was a "self-made man," Stevens quipped: "Glad to hear it, for it relieves God Almighty of a heavy responsibility." [9]

On June 1, 1867, the House impeachment committee decided by a five to four vote that there was no ground for action against the President. Stevens, greatly disappointed, nevertheless admitted fairly: "If nothing can be found which sufficiently implicates him to put him on his trial before the country, it is due to him, it is due to this House and to the country that that committee should be discharged and this matter should be abandoned." [10]

But punishing the President had become an obsession Stevens could not abandon. The case was reopened, and the House committee continued to take testimony. "Well, *have you got anything, anyhow?*" he said to one member after several weeks. "It was more an ejaculation of anger and disgust at failure," according to Senator Edmund G. Ross, "than a query of one seeking hoped for information." [11]

Clemenceau, watching the American scene with fascination, described Stevens to his Paris audience: "What he says, he does, always, and in spite of everything, heeding no obstacles, and accepting no compromise. His horizon is limited, but what he does see, he sees clearly. And he always knows where he wants to go, and goes there. When a man of this kind is irascible, vindictive, and vigorous, and when, moreover, he pursues with quite unusual intellectual powers and an ease in expressing himself which amounts almost to oratory, one sole end, with all his strength, and all his force, and all his passions and prejudices, it is dangerous to stand in his way." [12]

Johnson meanwhile, though fearful of impeachment, and actually scrupulous about carrying out the letter if not the spirit of the Reconstruction Acts he so detested,[13] nevertheless continued unnecessarily to antagonize Congress despite advice from his cabinet. When Secretary of the Treasury McCulloch urged his immediate appointment of the military governors under the "force bill," saying that "it would have a good effect, and would tend to prevent impeachment," the President "got very angry, and swore vehemently, and said they might impeach and be d-m-d he was tired of being threatened." [14]

General Grant went ahead and appointed General John Pope to rule over Georgia, Florida, and Alabama; General E. O. C. Ord in Mississippi and Arkansas; General John M. Schofield in Virginia; General Philip H. Sheridan in Louisiana and Texas, and General Daniel Sickles in North and South Carolina. All had had administrative experience in the South, but they varied a good deal in their attitudes toward the use of force in obtaining civil rights for the Negro.

James G. Blaine noted that Johnson's personal hostility to some of the officers thus assigned was well known, and he expressed surprise that the President did not countermand or qualify General Grant's order in the beginning.[15] Actually Johnson was waiting until Congress adjourned.

In a final contemptuous gesture toward the President, Congress in the last days of the session passed over his veto an amendment to the Military Bill giving the military commanders in the South the power to depose any civil authority, subject only to the disapproval of the General of the Army—Ulysses S. Grant—and virtually denied the right of the President, though commander-in-chief, to overrule his own officers.

One power he still retained in Reconstruction: he could fire the military governors and replace them with men of his own choosing. This he shortly proceeded to do. Against the advice of all his cabinet, and over General Grant's bitter protest, he first replaced General Philip Sheridan, who was making strenuous efforts to combat the violence in Louisiana and Texas. Sheridan had said publicly that if he owned both hell and Texas he would rent Texas and live in hell. The man who replaced him was an affable Democrat, General Winfield S. Hancock, who made it clear in his "Order No. 40" that he intended to interfere as little as possible in the racial difficulties of his area.[16] The immediate result was that murders in Texas, which had averaged about nine a month (in a population of 700,000) jumped to an average of fifty-four a month. In Louisiana Hancock proved so inept that the election crisis of 1868 saw more than two thousand Negroes killed or injured in the state.[17]

Andrew Johnson believed that General Sickles was also too Radical, and replaced him on August 26, 1867 with General E. R. S. Canby. Sickles, who had been in South Carolina since 1865, had rigorously enforced equality of civil rights, had insisted on Negroes serving on juries, and had abolished discrimination on public transportation. Canby was a Southerner, a native of Kentucky, "not so guilty of so many acts that caused resentment."[18]

General Pope was later replaced by General George G. Meade. General Schofield, who worked so closely with the whites in Virginia that the Reconstruction Acts were largely circumvented and Negroes and Unionists were prevented for the most part from being elected to office, was permitted to remain in power. The new generals revoked many of the rulings of their predecessors regarding civil rights for the freedmen, and Hancock in particular made little effort to curb the Ku Klux Klan.

Angered by these changes, the Republicans returned to Congress in December 1867 determined to shear away the last remnant of Johnson's power in the South. In January 1868 they passed over his veto a bill transferring all his authority in Reconstruction to General Grant. The *New York Herald* on January 20, 1868 called this "a bill to dissolve civil society and to abolish the executive," pointing out that "a penalty is imposed upon the President, as upon some burglar or other vile criminal, for any attempt to execute his constitutional functions as the Executive and Commander-in-Chief. Usurpation and revolution cannot go further short of arresting and deposing the President and declaring the office absolutely abolished."

"Arresting and deposing the President" still continued to be Thaddeus Stevens' consuming ambition. He was not content to see Johnson technically impotent during his few remaining months in office; he was determined that the President suffer the humiliation of a trial and be hurled from the White House. One thing made it possible for at least part of this ambition to be realized, the extraordinary relationship between Andrew Johnson and his Secretary of War. Hugh McCulloch, Secretary of the Treasury and one of Johnson's chief defenders, described this relationship honestly and exactly in his memoirs. Stanton, he said, "attended the Cabinet meetings, not as an adviser of the President, but as an opponent of the policy to which he had himself been committed, and the President lacked the nerve to dismiss him. The failure of the President to exercise his undoubted right to rid himself of a minister who differed with him upon very important questions, who had become personally obnoxious to him, and whom he regarded as an enemy and spy, was a blunder for which there was no excuse. In this crisis of his political life, Mr. Johnson exhibited a want of spirit and decision which astonished those who were familiar with his antecedents." [19]

While Johnson was not lacking in courage, it was the peculiarity of his nature that he was never so stout-hearted as when fighting alone. He had been the *only* Southern Senator not to defect to the Confederacy, and he gloried in fighting with his back to the wall against great odds. As President he had alienated most of the strong men, whether Democrat or Conservative Republican, who might have saved him. As early as June 27, 1867, Montgomery Blair made it clear to Secretary Welles that he had become "quite indifferent" to Johnson's fate.[20] Horatio Seymour, Democratic governor of New York, openly mocked him at a political dinner. Conservative Republican John Sherman, who had great influence in the Senate, had never forgiven him for his failure to support the Fourteenth Amendment. "This he could easily have carried," he wrote to his brother William. "It referred the whole suffrage question to each state, and if adopted long ago the whole controversy would have culminated." [21]

All the great metropolitan daily papers in New York except the *World* had deserted him. The *Sun* was calling him "insane and an opium addict." [22] The fact was that Andrew Johnson had no party. He was a traditional hill-country independent. As C. Vann Woodward has pointed out, "there really was no permanent political place of abode" for him.[23] Failing to marshal support in either party, toying futilely with the idea of starting a third, and powerless to halt the humiliating encroachments upon his executive power, he became increasingly friendless. Although he had excellent advice from his cabinet which could easily have prevented his impeachment, he ignored it. It is, then, not surprising to read what Gideon Welles wrote despairingly in his diary on February 24, 1868: "I have sometimes been almost tempted to listen to the accusation of his enemies that he desired and courted impeachment." [24]

Johnson fancied himself a modern Cato, whose character he greatly admired, and whom he described to Colonel W. G. Moore in February 1868 as a man who "would not compromise with wrong, but, being right, died before he would yield." [25] In Stanton, on the other hand, there was a streak of brutality. It had been especially evident in his relations with subordinates, but even at times apparent in his dealings with Lincoln, with whom, despite his enormous respect, he had often been irascible, contemptuous—and as Alexander McClure put it— "offensively despotic." [26]

Stanton was a complicated, turbulent man, who had lost all his buoyancy and good humor with the death of his beloved first wife, and who suffered now from asthma, headaches, and other symptoms of extreme tension. Though he knew himself to be hated by the President, and though he was in complete disagreement with most of Johnson's reconstruction policies, he would not do his chief the courtesy of resigning. Not surprisingly, he believed his own motives to be noble and honorable. "I will not resign," he said to Senator Henry Wilson early in 1867. "I will die in this room rather than leave my post of duty. I know I have done some good and prevented much evil, and our friends may see it when I am gone." [27]

Stanton had, in fact, become as much a convert to the principles of the Radical Republican revolution as Thaddeus Stevens. Though his behavior by Johnson's standards was intriguing, hypocritical and devious, he saw himself as a stalwart defender of justice and righteousness. In justifying before Congress his failure to resign he said: "I had as secretary of war put over a million of men into the field, and I was unwilling to abandon the victory they had won, or to see the 'lost cause' restored over the graves of nearly four hundred thousand soldiers, or to witness four millions of freedmen subjected, for want of legal protection, to outrages against their lives, persons, and property, and their race in danger of being returned to some newly-invented bondage." [28]

Had the President dismissed his War Secretary before the passage of the Tenure of Office Bill, there would have been no impeachment. But he delayed month after month, and it was not in fact until he discovered the shameful fact that Stanton—or General Holt with Stanton's approval—had deliberately and secretly withheld from him the military court's recommendation for mercy in the case of Mrs. Surratt that he was galvanized into action. On August 5, 1867, he sent Stanton a curt note requesting his resignation. Stanton replied just as curtly that he would not resign before the next meeting of Congress.

The President now did a foolish thing. Instead of firing Stanton outright, and justifying his action on the ground that he had the Constitutional right and Congress could not deprive him of it, he merely suspended Stanton under the provisions of the Tenure of Office Act, thereby giving public notice that he recognized its validity. He appointed General Grant to be Secretary of War *ad interim* until Congress should meet in December. The *New York World* on August 13 congratulated the President "that this infamous man is no longer in a position to do mischief," and there was no special outcry in the Republican press, so great was Grant's popularity.

Had the relations between the President and Grant remained amicable, there still need have been no disaster for Johnson. But the President in his characteristic tactless fashion promptly proceeded to antagonize the most popular man in the North. It did not help his cause that many Republicans were looking to Grant to be the next President. And Johnson seemed blind to the fact that he needed Grant far more than Grant needed him.

One week after Grant's appointment, Johnson removed General Sheridan as military governor of Louisiana and Texas. Grant's vigorous letter urging that he be retained found its way into the press and caused a sensation in Washington. The scholarly Francis Lieber, who had only recently become hostile to Johnson, wrote to law professor Theodore W. Dwight at Columbia:

. . . An angry gloom prevails in this city. The letter of Gen. Grant to the President must have stirred the whole country. This is a revolutionary letter, but we are in the midst of a revolution, though, God grant, it be bloodless. The person who is president fears impeachment and yet is defiant and has become heedless. He has again taken to intoxication. The day before yesterday, so I am positively informed, wholly intoxicated. You know he has never given up deep and constant drinking. . . .

Neither you nor I have agreed with everything Congress has done; but when it comes to choosing between Congress and *that* man—a faithless, ruinous and rebellious executive—who can hesitate? Congress is the country.[29]

As soon as Congress met in December 1867, the House Judiciary Committee formally recommended impeachment. The *Nation* commented tartly on December 5:

> . . . the more they thought of their scheme, the more important it appeared; and the more important it appeared, the more stupendous a villain Andrew Johnson became. He started before them as simply a very indecent brawler. . . . grew into a fornicator and adulterer, then a seller of pardons, then a conspirator against the nation, and then the preparer of a *coup d'etat,* and finally General Butler ran him to earth as a common assassin. But all this was done by hint of hallooing and insinuating. No proofs were forthcoming. . . . Mr. Williams . . . has nothing to show that we did not know already.

The majority in the House seem to have agreed with this point of view, for the resolution to impeach was voted down 108 to 57.

Meanwhile Grant was seeking to get out of the cabinet, where he felt uneasy and out of sympathy with the President's views, and increasingly annoyed as the President replaced his generals in the South one by one with less Radical men. Grant had long believed that the South should be treated as conquered territory. He had been consulted and had given his approval of the Reconstruction Acts.[30] By now he was being openly wooed by the Republicans as presidential timber, and he wanted to disassociate himself from Johnson altogether.

The Senate, having examined Andrew Johnson's reasons for dismissing Stanton and Stanton's reasons for refusing to be fired, now proceeded to embarrass the President as much as possible by refusing to concur in the dismissal. This was on January 13, 1868. On the next day Grant assured the President at a cabinet meeting that he would hold on to the office until it could be filled by someone approved by the Senate. Nevertheless he abruptly relinquished the office without warning the President, and Stanton returned to his old post. There resulted a nasty public quarrel in the press between Johnson and General Grant, with the President, not without reason, accusing Grant of bad faith and duplicity, and Grant replying angrily that the only reason he had taken the job in the first place was not to assist the President in ridding himself of Stanton, but to preclude Johnson's appointing someone who would not enforce the Reconstruction Acts.

When the bitter exchange of letters between Grant and Johnson was read on the floor of the House, Thaddeus Stevens listened intently. When the Clerk finished Grant's statement, "I can but regard this whole matter, from the beginning to the end, as an attempt to involve me in resistance of law, for which you hesitated to assume the responsibility in orders, and thus to destroy my character before the country," the old Commoner was heard to say exultingly: "He is a bolder man than I thought him. Now we will let him into the Church." [31]

Almost everyone around the President expected Stanton to resign. Welles said it was reported that Grant and Sherman had told him he must, and Seward was certain that he would.[32] Welles alone in the cabinet had a realistic understanding of Stanton's temper, and was certain he would not. The fact that he did not resign cannot wholly be laid to a discourteous or sadistic desire to humiliate the President. It should not be forgotten that Stanton's self-appointed role as the great defender of Reconstruction was taken very seriously by his fellow Radical Republicans. The day after his reinstatement in the War Department Schuyler Colfax, the speaker of the House, accompanied by fifty Congressmen, made a personal visit to present him with a letter signed by sixty other Representatives who could not be present, urging him to continue in office. Colfax told Stanton he was the "Thermopylæ, the pass of greatest value to reconstruction by Congress." Even the dean of the Conservative Republicans, Senator Fessenden, urged him to "bind into continuity" a government imperiled by the "renegade at the White House." [33]

Stevens believed there was evidence enough in the correspondence between Grant and Johnson to impeach the President, and succeeded in getting his own Committee on Reconstruction to take the impeachment out of the hands of the Judiciary Committee, which he felt had handled the whole matter stupidly. "Old Thaddeus Stevens," Clemenceau wrote on February 14, 1868, "is still keeping himself alive only by the hope of sometime scalping Andrew Johnson on the altar of patriotism, and watches with a feverish and bilious eye from behind the rampart of his Reconstruction laws the least movement of the enemy." [34] But having personal charge of impeachment won him no immediate advantage, for his committee turned down a resolution to impeach by a vote of six to three.

"Damn it," he said to a correspondent of the *New York World,* "don't both the President and General Grant subscribe to this vital fact, that Grant had first considered and that Johnson had insisted upon the proposition that Grant should help Johnson keep Stanton out of office . . . ? What the devil do I care about the question of veracity, as they call it, between Johnson and Grant? That's nothing to do with the law. Both of them may call each other liars if they want to; perhaps they both do lie a little, though the President has the weight of evidence on his side. . . . If they want to settle the question, they may both go out in my back yard and settle it alone. . . .

Grant may be as guilty as the President . . . but Grant isn't on trial; it's Johnson." And when the reporter asked him if the President would be impeached, the old man replied emphatically: "I shall never bring up this question of impeachment again." [35]

Yet one week later a resolution to impeach Andrew Johnson passed the House by a vote of 126 to 47. Sixty-seven Republicans who had voted against impeachment only ten weeks earlier had abruptly changed their minds.

After weeks of disastrous indecision the President, without consulting anyone, had taken the bit in his teeth and had written an order removing Stanton. In his stead he had appointed the somewhat fuzzy-minded Adjutant-General, Lorenzo Thomas, whom Stanton had years earlier promised to pick up with a pair of tongs and drop from the nearest window.[36] Thomas had done able work during the war organizing colored regiments, but the fact that he and Stanton detested each other was well known. Gideon Welles called the appointment an action "incautiously and loosely performed without preparation," and said the President took his friends by surprise.[37] The Senate met in an Executive Session lasting seven hours, and by a vote of twenty-eight to six adopted a resolution saying the President could not remove Stanton from his office.

There followed a sequence of events that more properly belonged to comic opera than to a serious government crisis. Lorenzo Thomas took his order of appointment to Stanton, who proceeded to barricade himself in his office, surround the War Department with soldiers, and dispatch a series of frantic notes for assistance to members of Congress. That night General Thomas boasted openly at a masquerade ball that if Stanton did not relinquish his office he would take it by force. At once Stanton issued an order for Thomas' arrest.

The marshal appeared at Thomas' home with the warrant early in the morning before breakfast. The astonished general begged to be allowed to inform the President, and was permitted to go to the White House. When Andrew Johnson learned what had happened he said simply: "That is the place I want it, in the courts." After Thomas appeared before the judge and was released on bail, he proceeded to the War Department and ordered Stanton to give up his post. Stanton refused. Each man continued stiffly to order the other out, until finally the general, with an increasing sense of the ridiculousness of the situation, said weakly: "The next time you have me arrested please don't do it before I get something to eat."

Stanton at once came over, put his arm around the general's neck, and ran his fingers through his hair in a friendly fashion. A messenger was dispatched for some whisky, and the two men proceeded to relax over several drinks. Thomas then went off to report to the White House.[38]

When rumor swept the city that Johnson contemplated civil war and intended to expel Stanton forcibly with a detachment of Marines, Senator Chandler and Representative Logan personally led a company of one hundred men to guard the War Department, and Grant detailed a special guard for Stanton with powers to call upon all the troops in Washington. A few days later the New York Chief of Police telegraphed the Speaker of the House that a great quantity of nitroglycerine had disappeared and might well be on its way to Washington. The House thereupon adjourned in a panic, and additional police were called to guard the Congress.[39]

There was not the slightest reason for such hysteria. Andrew Johnson was fully aware of the illegality of the farcical activity in the War Department, which constituted real insurrection against him as commander-in-chief. But he chose to treat it with silent contempt and court action rather than violence.

A few Democrats came to the President's defense. James Brooks, a notorious Copperhead, denounced Stanton's failure to resign as "arrogant, impertinent, and insolent," and applauded Johnson for dismissing him. "If the President is impeached," Brooks said, "we will never, never, so help me God! never, never submit!" Four-fifths of the Army were Democrats, he said, and they could be counted on to save the President.[40]

But most Democrats, according to the *New York Tribune*, "recoiled from the President as a ruined man and a political corpse. Not only did they abandon him, but as they went, they turned and cursed him for his folly." Even the *New York World* now explicitly repudiated him.[41]

The House met in special session at noon on Washington's birthday, and the debate carried over to the following Monday. Stevens—"haggard and trembling" according to the *New York World*—closed the debate on February 24, 1868. It had been snowing heavily all day; the hall began to look quite dark, and the gas was lighted. According to the *New York Tribune* his voice was "low, and husky," and often "lost in weakness." Finally, unequal to the effort, he gave his speech to his old friend, Edward McPherson, Clerk of the House, who finished the reading.

"Let us," he said at first, "discuss these questions in no partisan spirit, but with legal accuracy and impartial justice." He charged Johnson with attempting to obstruct and resist the execution of laws, and with violating the Tenure of Office Act, and then went on to get at what he believed to be the heart of the matter: "I agree with the distinguished gentleman from Pennsylvania on the other side of the House, who holds this to be a purely political proceeding. It is intended as a remedy for malfeasance in office and to prevent the continuance thereof. Beyond that, it is not intended as a personal punishment for past offenses or for future example. . . . This is not to be the temporary triumph of a political party, but is to endure in its consequence until this whole continent shall be filled with a free and untrammeled people or shall be a nest of shrinking, cowardly slaves."

But Stevens was the least capable of all men in the House of living up to his own admonition about avoiding a "partisan spirit." And he showed that for all his talk about impartial justice he hoped to see the President in the end imprisoned like a common criminal. "If Andrew Johnson escapes with bare removal from office," he said, "if he be not fined and incarcerated in the penitentiary afterward under criminal proceedings, he may thank the weakness or the clemency of Congress and not his own innocence." [42]

The House now voted 126 to 47, a strict party vote, to bring the President to trial. Shortly afterward Stevens was carried to the Senate in his armchair, and then, leaning on the arm of John A. Bingham and supporting himself with a cane, he entered the chamber, followed by a large delegation from the House. "Pale, emaciated, deathlike in appearance, but in a stern, vigorous voice and in a bold, lofty manner," he made this formal announcement to the Senate:

In obedience to the order of the House of Representatives we appear before you in the name of the House of Representatives and of all the people of the United States. We do impeach Andrew Johnson, President of the United States, of high crimes and misdemeanors in office; and we further inform the Senate that the House of Representatives will in due time exhibit articles against him, and make good the same, and in their name we demand that the Senate take order for the appearance of said Andrew Johnson to answer said impeachment.

As Clemenceau put it: "The black cloud has finally broken. The President called upon the lightning, and the lightning came." [43]

CHAPTER TWENTY-SEVEN

The Trial

BENEATH the clamor, slander, and vituperation of the impeachment process there was a grave political problem. This was the question of whether a president should be removed because he chose to thwart the will of the majority party. Johnson had vetoed over twenty bills in three years; Andrew Jackson, who until now had held the record for vetoes, had vetoed but eleven in eight years. Moreover, Johnson's were not petty vetoes but attempts to block the Congressional solutions for the gravest crises of the time. And when the veto device failed, he often turned, by administrative techniques that could not be called illegal, to thwart the acts that had been approved.

The English obviated this kind of problem following the reign of George III by making the Prime Minister responsible to the Commons. There was never any question but that the man who led the British Government also represented the majority party. Thoughtful Englishmen now watched the American struggle with intense interest. Walter Bagehot wrote in the London *Economist* of December 7, 1867, that he was anxious to see the experiment of impeachment tried in America—"to see the executive obedient to the will of the dominant party, and not gifted with powers which enable him to bring the machinery of government to a dead-lock." A reporter for *Blackwood's Edinburgh Magazine* said bluntly: "And if future Presidents are to be as powerless [as Andrew Johnson] . . . the sooner the cumbrous and costly office is abolished the better for the public peace." [1]

There were some Americans who were convinced that the charge of "high crimes and misdemeanors" should become a convenient fiction and the impeachment process a piece of conventional political machinery to change the executive when he no longer represented the will of his party. Impeachment, insisted the *New York Tribune*, "is not a mode of punishment, but a means of security and of avoiding political maladministration." Editor Horace Greeley was convinced that the conviction of the President would bring about the end of anarchy and violence in the South. "The hammer rusts on the anvil," he wrote, "—loyal men steal through highway and forest like thieves in the night—Rebels triumphantly defy the law. . . . The rebel looks to the President for help, and wars upon the loyalist. . . . Impeachment will end this. The Rebel will see that nothing is left but obedience." [2]

Others, like Senator Lyman Trumbull, though a sharp critic of the President, believed that conviction would set a dangerous precedent. ". . . no future President will be safe who happens to differ with a majority of the House and two-thirds of the Senate on any measure deemed by them important," he said frankly during the trial. "What then becomes of the checks and balances of the Constitution, so carefully devised and so vital to its perpetuity . . . I tremble for the future of my country. I cannot be an instrument to produce such a result." [3] Others were troubled by the paradoxes that while Johnson's defiance of the Tenure of Office Act was a legitimate reason for impeachment, still the President could not test its constitutionality without exposing himself to impeachment, and that he would be tried before the very body that passed the law in the first place.

Thaddeus Stevens emphasized the superiority of the British parliamentary system, and the necessity of removing Andrew Johnson for political betrayal of his party rather than for any personal crimes. But he knew that in order to be got rid of the President must be convicted criminally. Stevens determined therefore to make the articles of impeachment as rigorous as possible.

A special committee selected to frame these articles reported ten of them on February 29, 1868. The first three charged the President with removing Stanton contrary to law; the next five charged conspiracy to prevent Stanton from holding office. The ninth accused the President of illegal intent to control the war department funds; and the tenth, framed by Benjamin F. Butler, charged that Johnson's speeches in the election campaign of 1866 constituted a high crime and misdemeanor.

Stevens looked hard at the articles and decided they were not enough to convict the President. So he fashioned an eleventh and presented it in a speech before the House on March 2, 1868. The *New York World,* always bitter against Stevens, on March 6 described the presentation with a malevolence to match that in the speech itself:

A wig of black, gave by contrast an added and horrid ghastliness to the yellow face—but there was no face, it was an anatomy merely—these were not so much eyes as snakes, that glittered in the deep pit-holes; the voice was as hollow and sepulchral as if it already issued from the tomb. Full of malignant passions, and even now the prey of the grave, he must carry in himself the worst fate he dare imprecate upon his enemies. . . .

Quivering with passion and exultation, this vindictive despot of the despotic majority tottered forward from his place, and shaking a finger above his head, *defied the Senate* to find any verdict but a verdict of guilty.

Stevens began his speech by saying: "Never was a great malefactor so gently treated as Andrew Johnson." He dismissed the ten articles of impeachment as inadequate—"the most trifling crimes and misdemeanors"—and then offered his own, a hodgepodge of charges deliberately drawn to be intricate in form and obscure in meaning, a kind of omnibus of all the other ten, combined in such a fashion that it was extremely difficult to attack. "If there be shrewd lawyers," Stevens said, "and I know there will be, and caviling judges, and, without this article, they do not acquit him, they are greener than I was in any case I ever undertook before a court of quarter sessions." But with the eleventh article he was confident of conviction.

"Let us see now," he exclaimed, "what chance he has to escape. The Senate has four times voted on the constitutionality of the Tenure-of-Office bill. . . . Let him hope who dares to hope that so high a body as that Senate will betray its trust, will forget its own acts, will tread back its own action, will disgrace itself in the face of the nation. Point me out one who dares to do it, and you show me one who dares to be regarded as infamous by posterity. . . . If my article be inserted, what chance has Andrew Johnson to escape, even if all the rest of the articles should fail. Unfortunate man! thus surrounded, hampered, tangled in the meshes of his own wickedness—unfortunate, unhappy man, behold your doom!" [4]

The *Nation* called the speech "painful reading," and the *New York Herald* warned that Stevens was a fit leader for organizing a reign of terror in the United States. "He has the boldness of Danton, the bitterness and hatred of Marat, and the unscrupulousness of Robespierre." [5]

During the trial the *New York Herald* splashed over its front page a hysterical—and spurious—telegram:

STARTLING REVELATIONS REGARDING THE PLOTS OF THE RADICALS
OUR REPUBLICAN FORM OF GOVERNMENT TO BE SUPERSEDED BY A DICTATORSHIP

VIRTUAL ABOLITION OF THE SUPREME COURT
GRANT, THE SENATE AND THE NATIONAL BANKS TO RULE THE NATION
THE GREAT RADICAL CONSPIRACY

The telegram went on to say that the ultimate object of the leading Radical Republicans was to set up "a dictatorship more absolute and arbitrary than of Robespierre and the Commune de Paris." [6] On May 20, 1868 a *Herald* editorial predicted that Wade, Stevens, and Grant would act as "the three Consuls," with Grant "patiently awaiting the occasion which will compel him to re-enact the *rôle* of Cromwell and Napoleon."

It is easy to see now that all the warnings about military despotism and comparisons with the excesses of the French Revolution were exaggerated to the point of absurdity. Impeachment was a legitimate attempt to overthrow the President by constitutional means, and there was never the slightest preparation for a *coup d'état*. Had Johnson been convicted, Ben Wade would have taken his place; there would have been a new cabinet, and the administration of the government would probably have been much like that of Ulysses S. Grant.

But it must be admitted that the language of the Radical Republicans, particularly Thaddeus Stevens and Benjamin F. Butler, echoed Jacobin ferocity. All the hatred they had felt toward Jefferson Davis during the war seemed to be concentrated upon Andrew Johnson. "Davis is charged with sinning against the country," the *New York Herald* said on March 15, 1868, "but the President of the United States is charged with sinning against the party; and this, in the eyes of the radicals, is the worse crime!" It is wholly characteristic of the Jacobin mind—or the revolutionary mind in any age—to consider the deviationist or apostate more traitorous than the man who opposes the revolution altogether.

Seven men were elected by the House to be the impeachment managers. John A. Bingham, chairman, had in the past been opposed to impeachment, and had only recently swung over to the extreme Radical position. "The best-natured and crossest-looking man in the House," he had the reputation of being an eminent and learned lawyer. A stain on his record, only recently exposed by Benjamin Butler, had been his handling of the evidence in the prosecution of Mrs. Surratt.

George S. Boutwell was a fanatical Radical and Puritan stalwart, mediocre in talent and rigid in his thinking. For his lengthy speeches he had been christened privately as "the Steady Wind Blowing Aft." Three other managers—James F. Wilson, Thomas Williams, and John A. Logan—were good Radicals but of no outstanding competence.

Thaddeus Stevens would have been the acknowledged leader of the impeachment managers had it not been for the inclusion among them of Benjamin F. Butler. The latter was chosen presumably for his reputation as a brilliant criminal lawyer, but as the President's most savage and unscrupulous critic he could no more be ignored than Stevens.

Butler was malicious, cynical, and impudent, with a fine "talent for turbulence." The stormier the scene the greater his satisfaction.[7] Had Stevens not been so near death he would never have permitted Butler to wrench from him the leadership of the impeachment trial. But Butler had the vigor Stevens had lost, and seemed to be equally ruthless and intent on punishment. Unlike Stevens, he delighted in secret intrigue, and he could be unscrupulous in his handling of evidence.

Still, Butler's record was not entirely bad. He had fought the bigotry of the Know-Nothing movement, and after his conversion to the cause of anti-slavery with the coming of the war, he had held a consistently enlightened and imaginative attitude toward the Negro people, insisting that they had the potential capacity for becoming good citizens. For all his ruthlessness as Governor of New Orleans, he had brought order and commerce back to the city, and had checked a plague of yellow fever by having the city's countless fetid canals cleaned out. But no one could be sure with Benjamin Butler that his championship of the Negro was not sheer opportunism, or whether his legal and administrative successes were the result of talent, or cunning—or simply the result of his enormous energy. Despite the urging of some of his colleagues that Andrew Johnson should be treated with the dignity due him as President, Butler indicated from the beginning that he would handle the trial like any "horse case." [8]

The Senate was organized as a court on March 5, 1868, and met formally on March 13, with Chief Justice Chase presiding. When Henry Stanbery, who had resigned as Attorney General to be counsel for the President, asked for forty days to prepare an answer to the impeachment articles, Butler objected, saying archly that it took the Almighty only forty days to destroy the world by flood. The Senate granted ten. Later, when the President's counsel asked an additional thirty days, they were awarded six. The Radicals paid for this ungracious behavior, however, for the managers had to prepare their own cases in haste. Butler wrote later that he had only nine hours' sleep in three days, and said it was the hardest labor of his life.[9]

As preparations for the trial proceeded, the frantic activity of the managers, counsel, and newspaper reporters was in sharp contrast with the apathy of the rest of the nation. "Public opinion is remarkably calm in all these matters," Clemenceau wrote on March 6, 1868.[10] But an increasing number of thoughtful Republicans were deeply disturbed at the impeachment proceedings. "Either I am very stupid or my friends are acting like fools and hurrying us to destruction," wrote Senator Fessenden to a friend. "I am very tired of public life, and would gladly retire if I could do so with honor. Passion has banished sense. . . . I still think that whatever may have been his misdemeanors, it would have been better to tolerate him to the end of his term, rather than to expose our party and our country to so great a hazard." [11]

Chief Justice Chase opposed impeachment from the beginning, writing to Gerrit Smith on April 19, 1868: ". . . if I had any option I would not take part in it." [12] He was annoyed by the flood of letters from friends who had the impropriety to write to him, as judge, advising him how to behave at the trial—"and from persons of sense too"— he wrote.[13]

The *New York Herald* pointed out on March 8, 1868, that had there been no impeachment—with "half the country disposed to believe him incompetent, and the other half positively regarding him evil minded and treacherous"—Johnson would have gone down in history as a conspicuous failure along with Fillmore, Pierce, and Buchanan, but that the proceedings had changed all this. "If he shall be found guilty nothing can change the impression in regard to his martyrdom. . . . while if he be acquitted his Presidential term will close with the *éclat* of a triumphal testimonial to his career in office."

The President meanwhile, though by no means certain of the outcome, met the impeachment with a show of outward calm that impressed all his friends. But he had an almost superstitious awe of Stevens' explosive vitality. When a rumor swept through the capital that the old man was dead, Johnson refused to believe it. Stevens, he said was a human Vesuvius. When you thought him extinct it was but a temporary paralysis, soon to be succeeded by "a flow of living passion." [14]

Andrew Johnson selected as his counsel several very able lawyers. The best known was Benjamin Curtis of Massachusetts, the recognized leader of the American bar. Curtis had resigned from the Supreme Court in a disagreement with Chief Justice Taney developing out of the Dred Scott Case, but he had afterward followed an extremely conservative line. He had even issued a pamphlet insisting that Lincoln had no constitutional right to issue the Emancipation Proclamation, and he had openly opposed the reconstruction measures. His dignity and passionlessness were in sharp contrast with the courtroom manners of Benjamin F. Butler.

Curtis was deeply committed to the rightness of Johnson's cause. "There is not a decent pretence that the President has committed an impeachable offence," he wrote to his uncle on March 26, 1868. *"The party* are in a condition to demand his removal from power, and do demand it." The President, he said, "firmly believes he has been right and is right, he knows he is honest and true in his devotion to the Constitution." A fortnight later he was somewhat more critical. Johnson "is honest, right-minded, and narrow-minded;" he wrote; "he has no tact, and even lacks discretion and forecast. But he is a firm as a rock." [15]

In William Evarts the President had as a counsel not only an able and witty lawyer, but one gifted in the art of compromise. He had many friends among the Radicals, and gave the President some very shrewd political as well as legal advice. He persuaded him, for example, to nominate during the trial General John M. Schofield for Secretary of War, an excellent choice, since Schofield was acceptable to the Radicals and yet the least obnoxious of the military governors as far as the Southerners were concerned.

But Evarts was by no means as certain as Curtis and Henry Stanbery that the President was completely in the right. During the trial he accepted an invitation to Sunday dinner with none other than Charles Sumner. And when at the party someone chided him for working on the Sabbath day—for he had been busy with preparations for the trial—Evarts responded wryly: "Is it not written that if thine ass falleth into a pit, it is lawful to pull him out on the Sabbath day?" [16]

The whole strategy of the Radical Republicans, whether reflected in the actual prosecution or in the press, was aimed at making the impeachment trial a political rather than a legal proceeding. The *New York Tribune* declared it to be entirely a political matter, and said that any Republican Senator who refused to convict the President would be expelled from the Party. All talk about the sanctity of the Senatorial oath, Greeley said, was simple cant. [17]

No one treated the Senate as a jury, isolated and inviolable from pressure during the trial. On the contrary, every conceivable influence was brought to bear by Democrats and Republicans alike on those Republican Senators known to be undecided. General Grant importuned Senator Henderson of Missouri twice, urging him to convict. "I would impeach him," said the General, ". . . because he is such an infernal liar." [18] Telegrams and petitions poured in to the seven or eight doubtful men.

When it became clear that Senator Fessenden would vote in Johnson's favor, the Republicans were filled with consternation. "If he was impeached for general cussedness, there would be no difficulty in the case," Fessenden said. "That however is not the question to be tried. . . . I prefer tar and feathers to lifelong regret." [19]

Learning of this attitude, Justin S. Morrill of Vermont wrote him a desperate letter: "You cannot afford to be buried with Andrew Johnson, nor can a poor devil like myself afford to have a cloud of suspicion thrown on the correctness of his vote by a wholly different vote given by yourself." [20]

Pressure for acquittal from the Democratic press was unsubtle and shrill. The *New York World,* which had clamored for Johnson's impeachment after his drunken inaugural address, now published a letter urging the subscription of ten million dollars to "buy a favorable verdict." Even Chief Justice Chase, though presiding at the trial, could not sit quiet and aloof on his bench. "Three senators, at least," wrote James A. Garfield, "were taken in hand by him privately and all the weight of his office and his influence were brought to bear to save Johnson." [21]

Chase's role throughout the trial was fascinating to watch. Since his appointment to the Supreme Court he had continued to meddle in national politics, and everyone knew he still hungered to be President. He had long been considered the likeliest Republican candidate for 1868, with the exception of Grant, who since his quarrel with Johnson had been rapidly growing in Radical Republican favor. Nevertheless, Chase opposed impeachment and brought to the trial dignity and intelligence if not impartiality.

This behavior certainly cost him the Republican nomination, for, after a few rulings that seemed to favor the President, the Radical Republicans turned against him, denouncing him as an apostate and traitor. The rumor swiftly spread that Chase could not endure the thought of Ben Wade, who was President of the Senate, being elevated to the Presidency because he would then win the nomination in the August convention. The *Philadelphia Evening Star* hinted that Chase's lovely and tempestuous daughter Kate had threatened to divorce her husband, Senator Sprague of Rhode Island, if he voted for conviction, and reported that she had said: "The idea of that horrid Ben Wade being put over my father." [22] James A. Garfield wrote that he thought Chase was "trying to break the Republican party and make himself president." [23] The Democrats further complicated the matter by praising Chase for the first time since 1860, and hinting that they might well consider him their candidate.

The embarrassing fact for the Radical Republicans was that no one was happy about the possibility of Ben Wade becoming President. He had recently been defeated in his own state for a new Senatorial term. He was crotchety, irascible and profane. "There was even a sort of fascination about his profanity," George W. Julian wrote. "It had in it a spontaneity and heartiness which made it almost seem the echo of a virtue. It was unlike the profane words of Thaddeus Stevens, which were frequently carried on the shafts of his wit and lost in the laughter which it provoked." [24]

Stevens had long recognized the difficulty of raising Wade to be President. A year earlier he had repeated on the floor of the House what Representative Blaine had said privately: "There will be no impeachment by this Congress; we would rather have the President than the shallywags of Ben Wade." Blaine had taken offense, saying Stevens had no right to repeat a private conversation, and garble it as well. But his original sentiments were widely shared.[25]

Wade was more tactless and obstinate than the man he hoped to replace. But he was also a fierce idealist, with convictions that were considered visionary or dangerous at the time but which would in fact be accepted by most of the nation in succeeding generations. He was a staunch advocate not only of Negro suffrage and civil rights, but also of legal equality and suffrage for women, the abolition of poverty, and the eight-hour working day. "Men should not be compelled to labor until life is worn out and being is a curse," he said. "If you dull heads cannot understand this, the women will." [26]

Benjamin Butler dominated the trial from the beginning. "Active as a cat, and indefatigable, fresh, vigorous and aggressive all the time," according to the *New York World,* he never abandoned his role of chief prosecutor. He had a strong, arrogant face, with a big, hawk-like nose and great protruding eyes. He was quite bald, save for a shaggy fringe of hair hanging about his neck. One eye, permanently cocked, was partly masked by a drooping lid, and this gave his face a Mephistophelean character that was fully exploited by the cartoonists of the time. Once during the trial when he helped Stevens to his chair, a well-known copperhead was heard to say he looked like the devil helping the old man into hell.[27]

Except for two brief observations, Stevens sat silently at the managers' table through the whole impeachment proceedings until time for the final speeches. "Thaddeus Stevens' ghost haunts the courtroom," wrote one reporter. "Occasionally the ghost orders crackers and tea, and astonishes everybody by partaking of lunch." [28] Once, when taking his seat at the managers' table, he missed his foothold and fell heavily to the floor. The sound could be heard all over the hall. Several men rushed to his aid and lifted him to his chair. There he silently went on writing.[29] Descriptions of him varied day by day. On April 10 the *New York World* described him as "a half-decayed corpse risen from the grave," and on April 20 as "a sturdy old man, whose face is the most impressive object in the court room."

Butler had opened the prosecution on March 30 with a three-hour address, in which he accused Johnson of attempting to overthrow Congress and establish a despotism. He likened the President to Napoleon, Caesar, and Cromwell, adding contemptuously that while Johnson had their malignity and will, he conspicuously lacked their ability. The President, he said, was not the choice of the American people, but a man "thrown to the surface by the whirlpool of civil war, carelessly, we grant, elected to the second place in the Government, without thought that he might ever fill the first. By murder most foul he succeeded to the Presidency, and is the elect of an assassin to that high office, and not of the people." [30]

The charge that Johnson was a danger to the liberties of his country and a potential tyrant of the stature of Caesar or Napoleon was patently ridiculous. In 1866, when it was still possible for him to work out an alliance between the Southern and Northern Democrats, he had been a real threat to the Republican Party and its revolutionary aims for the liberty and advancement of the Negro people. But now, as the *Nation* pointed out, he was "completely disarmed, tied neck and heels, and has lost the confidence of the South, and is openly repudiated and sneered at by the Northern Democrats." [31] There were a good many in the Senate who were honestly uncomfortable at the spectacle of the President being kicked in the stomach when he was down.

Senator John Sherman defined his own attitude toward the President in words that were an echo of many Conservative Republicans: "I mean to give Johnson a fair and impartial trial. . . . I regard him as a foolish and stubborn man, doing even right things in a wrong way, and in a position where the evil that he does is immensely increased by his manner of doing it." [32]

Nevertheless, Washington buzzed with the rumor that Johnson was planning a *coup d'état.* "Although," as Carl Schurz admitted later, "it was very difficult to imagine what kind of a *coup d'état* President Johnson could possibly think of, yet he was openly charged with entertaining various hellish designs, and there is no doubt that even the most absurd gossip found much lodgment with the people. . . . I do not exaggerate in saying that an overwhelming majority of the loyal Union men North and South saw in President Johnson a traitor bent upon turning the National Government to the rebels again." [33]

In the trial the President's counsel, William Evarts, adroitly reduced the charge of despotism to absurdity:

The people understand that treason and bribery are great offences, and that a ruler guilty of them should be brought into question and deposed. They are ready to believe that . . . there may be other great crimes and misdemeanors touching the conduct of government and the welfare of the state. . . . But they wish to know what the crimes are. They wish to know whether the President has betrayed our liberties or our possessions to a foreign state. They wish to know whether he has delivered up a fortress or surrendered a fleet. They wish to know whether he has made merchandise of the public trust and turned authority to private gain. And when informed that none of these things are charged, imputed or even declaimed about they yet seek further information and are told that he has removed a member of his cabinet. . . . Was the Secretary of War removed? they inquire. No; he was not removed, he is still Secretary.[34]

Butler called in many witnesses to describe and confirm the accuracy of the reporting of the President's unfortunate speeches in his Swing Round the Circle in the campaign of 1866. But the spectacle of the insolent and malicious-tongued Butler condemning the President for scandalous speech was too much for thoughtful men in both parties. It is worth noting that Butler was not chosen by the managers for this argument; he developed it himself and insisted on emphasizing it— driven compulsively perhaps to attack in the President that which he was most guilty of himself.

The *New York World* said ironically: "Butler, fresh from the plate-closets and bank-vaults of New Orleans, representing the outraged virtue and integrity of the party of 'moral ideas' recalls more vividly even than his language the spectacle of that 'bolting-hutch of beastliness,' old Falstaff, preaching virtue in Mistress Quickly's tavern." [35] When William Evarts defended the President's right to speak as he pleased, Butler replied: ". . . the counsel for the President claim the freedom of speech and we claim decency of speech." [36] But as the trial proceeded, it was the decency of Butler's speech, and not the President's, that became a matter for public judgment.

When Henry Stanbery fell ill, and the defense asked for a delay until he recovered, Butler opposed it: ". . . while we are waiting for the Attorney-General to get well, and you are asked to delay this trial for that reason, numbers of our fellow citizens are being murdered day by day. There is not a man here who does not know that the moment justice is done on this great criminal, these murders will cease."

Butler's professional conduct, said the *Nation* on April 23, 1868, "has been such that he has steadily, little by little, and day by day, been disgusting the Senate, and, what is if possible worse, disgusting the public." So when manager Thomas Williams in his concluding attack reminded the Senate that Andrew Johnson had brought Congress into disrepute by calling one of its members a traitor and another an assassin, and that he had called the whole Congress "a body hanging on the verge of government," it was hard to rouse any special indignation.[37]

In contrast with Butler's bad manners and interminable legalistic quibbling, Benjamin Curtis led the defense with impressive dignity and restraint. He emphasized that the Tenure of Office law did not apply to Stanton because he was simply a hold-over from Lincoln's cabinet and had never been officially appointed by Johnson. Even if the law applied to Stanton, he insisted, it had not been violated because Johnson had not removed Stanton but had only tried unsuccessfully to remove him. Clemenceau, listening to the argument, noted a basic contradiction. Curtis held on the one hand that Johnson had a perfect legal right to remove Stanton because the Tenure of Office Bill did not apply to him, and on the other that Johnson deliberately removed Stanton with the plan of forcing the Supreme Court to decide on the bill's constitutionality. "I confess," wrote Clemenceau, "I cannot see how Mr. Curtis can reconcile his two lines of defense."[38]

Thaddeus Stevens in his final speech seized upon the contradiction and exposed it pitilessly. To prove that Johnson fully believed that Stanton fell within the provisions of the Tenure of Office Bill, he quoted Johnson's letter of August 14, 1867, appointing Grant Secretary of War *ad interim*, which began: "In compliance with the requirements of the act entitled 'An act to regulate the tenure of certain civil offices.'" Then he went on wryly: "How necessary that a man should have a good conscience or a good memory! Both would not be out of place."[39]

Of all the speeches made for or against Andrew Johnson in the impeachment trial, Thaddeus Stevens' was the shortest. He began with a thrust at all the long-winded orators who had preceded him: "Experience has taught that nothing is so prolix as ignorance," adding with the characteristic self-deprecation that no one ever took seriously, "I fear I may prove thus ignorant." Short as it was, the speech was too long for Stevens' feeble body, though he fortified himself by sipping on a concoction of raw eggs and brandy. After twenty minutes of reading, in a voice so low it could scarcely be heard at the speaker's platform, he turned the manuscript over to Benjamin Butler.

It was generally agreed that Stevens made the ablest argument of all the managers. He hammered on the theme that Johnson had deliberately violated the Tenure of Office Act after having given every evidence that he considered his Secretary of War to be included under its terms. He defied the law, said Stevens, because he did not want Stanton carrying out the Reconstruction Acts, and this "mistake in intention" was quite sufficient to warrant his removal from office. Then he went further to insist that the managers did not even need to prove a "corrupt or wicked motive." It was enough that Johnson had violated the law.[40]

In the beginning of this speech Stevens, sensitive to the increasing feeling in the Senate that Butler was damaging the prosecution by his petty nagging and insolence, said firmly: "I desire to discuss the charges against the respondent in no mean spirit of malignity or vituperation, but to argue them in a manner worthy of the high tribunal before which I appear, and of the exalted position of the accused." And for the most part he held himself in control and adhered to the legal argument. But near the end of his speech—written out in advance, it must be remembered—the concentrated fury he felt for the President burst forth again, as it had in the past on so many occasions, though now with extraordinary violence and the symbolism of execution:

"And now this offspring of assassination turns upon the Senate, who have thus rebuked him in a constitutional manner, and bids them defiance. How can he escape the just vengeance of the law? Wretched man, standing at bay, surrounded by a cordon of living men, each with the axe of the executioner uplifted for his just punishment." The Senators who voted against him, he threatened, "would be tortured on the gibbet of everlasting obloquy," and the "track of infamy" would mark their names.[41]

Stevens' exhortations to his colleagues in private had been even more violent. Shortly before the impeachment vote in the House he had gone among the Representatives, leaning on the arm of Mr. Bingham, moving from group to group and constantly repeating: "Didn't I tell you so? What good did your moderation do you? If you don't kill the beast, it will kill you." [42]

When during the trial he learned that Chase had made a ruling that foreshadowed acquittal, Stevens limped into Wade's office, dropped into an easy chair, "opened his invective upon Chase," and ended his criticism of the trial saying: "It is the meanest case, before the meanest tribunal, and on the meanest subject of human history." [43]

A correspondent for *Blackwood's Edinburgh Magazine* reported to his journal an even more revealing story. "Not impeach and remove Johnson?" Stevens had said to him. "I tell you sir, we *must* do it.

If we don't do it, we are damned to all eternity. There is a moral necessity for it, for which I care something; and there is a party necessity for it, for which I care more. In fact, the party necessity is the moral necessity; for I consider that when the Republican party dies, this country will be given over to the so-called Democracy, which is worse than the devil. There need be no fear about *law*. That damned rascal (Mr. Johnson) has violated all the laws that Congress has passed; and especially the Civil Tenure law; and I can prove it, by God! Ay—prove it forty times over—Yes, by God!" [44]

The savagery of Stevens' symbolism—"the axe of the executioner uplifted," "killing the beast," "damned to all eternity," "tortured on the gibbet of everlasting obloquy"—these cannot altogether be dismissed as the luxuriant rhetoric of the time, but are evidences of the pathology of Stevens' hatred. Andrew Johnson had publicly called Stevens a traitor of equal stature with Jefferson Davis. And by accusing him of virtually planning the New Orleans massacre, he had in effect called him a murderer of Negroes. Johnson was a Freemason, as had been the man who had anonymously accused Stevens of the murder of a Negro girl forty-four years before. There was no doubt a whole galaxy of reasons why Stevens should have striven with such ferocity to hurl Johnson from high office, and should have contemplated with such satisfaction the prospect of seeing the President incarcerated in the penitentiary like a common criminal. But in addition to all these, the President may well have unknowingly reopened the old, deep wound.

Stevens had only to look at his own record—the fugitive slaves he had freed in the Pennsylvania courts—the abolitionists he had championed—the tenacious fight for emancipation—the struggle for the use of colored soldiers—the battles for the Thirteenth Amendment, the Freedmen's Bureau, the Civil Rights Bill, the Fourteenth Amendment, and finally the Military Bill and Negro suffrage—and compare this record with that of the President, who though professing to be a friend to the Negro had consistently vetoed every Act of Congress designed to protect the colored man from being reduced to near slavery. Johnson, Stevens said, was worse even than Judas Iscariot. "Would to God," he added, "that such an Executive had the repentance of that remorseful malefactor, who had been guilty of no indictable offense, but had simply indicated by a kiss the identity of the Master who trusted him." [45]

It is curious to note that the morning before his major speech in the impeachment trial he said to his Democratic critics in the House: "For ten years no man on that side of the House has risen and spoken on any important question but what if a person were to enter the gallery he would think that I was on trial—that 'the gentleman from Pennsylvania' was on trial for some offense." [46] Why should Stevens have felt himself on trial? Why should he tell a British reporter that he would be "damned to all eternity" if the President should go unpunished? What was really in Stevens' heart when after the trial he urged an investigation of the Senators who had voted against conviction, saying: "That there has been great, manifold, deep damnation, and that there is somewhere to be found the greatest of all mysteries, the mystery of this great prevalence of evil, no one can doubt." [47] Where was this "great, manifold, deep damnation"?

In this same speech, which is in some respects the most significant of his whole life, Stevens concluded with an extraordinary statement: "I can recollect but two men whom I deem absolutely impenetrable to temptation, he of Athens and He of Bethlehem. . . . we must remember not to place our trust in princes, for we have seen that in the richest heart, the most highly cultivated mind, adorned with every literary grace, keen in argument as the Stagirite,[48] and fortified with an outward shield of bronzed austerity which seemed to forbid the approach of levity or corruption; the richest composition of human mold may be the abode of malignity, avarice, corroding lust, and uncontrollable ambition, as the owl, the prairie-dog, and the rattlesnake nest together in loving harmony in the richest soil of the prairie." [49]

Who was guilty of "malignity, avarice, corroding lust, and uncontrollable ambition"? Who was also "keen in argument as the Stagirite" and "fortified with an outward shield of bronzed austerity which seemed to forbid the approach of levity or corruption"? Could it have been that Stevens here, four weeks before his death, was inadvertently portraying his own pitiless picture of himself?

CHAPTER TWENTY-EIGHT

Defeat

People who sincerely believe that they know how to make heaven on earth are most likely to adopt the conspiracy theory, and to get involved in a counter conspiracy against nonexisting conspirators. For the only explanation of their failure to produce their heaven are the evil intentions of the devil who has a vested interest in hell.

Karl Popper: *The Open Society and Its Enemies* [1]

MOST RADICAL Republicans were confident of the President's conviction up to the eleventh of May, when the Senate met in secret session and many of its members frankly discussed how they were going to vote and why. Charles Sumner, calling Johnson a "Pharaoh," said passionately he would vote for conviction on every article. John Sherman said he would vote against the first, but for the second. But Senators Fessenden, Grimes, and Trumbull boldly rejected all the articles, in speeches of such vigor and authority that they threw the whole Senate into confusion.[2] When word of their opinions filtered through the capitol, the impeachment managers were filled with consternation. A feverish counting of possible votes indicated that if Andrew Johnson was to be convicted at all it would probably be on Thaddeus Stevens' eleventh article. The second and third stood a slight chance—the others none at all. "We are sold out!" cried Butler.[3]

Stevens, who had never really been certain of the outcome, did not wait for the forthcoming vote to confirm his fears. He had already tried to get a bill through the House admitting Arkansas to the Union, but his colleagues, fearful that they be charged with packing the impeachment court, had refused to pass it. Now he brought out of the Reconstruction Committee a bill to admit North and South Carolina, Louisiana, Georgia, and Alabama. During the past month all these states had adopted new constitutions permitting Negro suffrage, and had elected new members to Congress—all but two of them Republicans. But this bill was more a gesture of intimidation than a real political maneuver, for the impeachment vote was due on the following day and Stevens had no expectation that the measure could pass the Senate even if there was a delay. A delay of five days did in fact follow, due to the illness of the Radical Republican Senator Howard, and the Senate briefly debated the bill, but after a blunt warning from Senator Fessenden the matter was dropped.

During the five days the doubtful Senators were bombarded with letters and telegrams; all were told that a vote for Johnson meant political suicide. Senator James W. Grimes—who had said frankly in the Senate, "If the question was, Is Andrew Johnson a fit person for President? I should answer *no*," but who had nevertheless said that he would vote for acquittal because the President had committed no crime—brought down upon himself an avalanche of excoriation. The *New York Tribune* called him a traitor and a Judas. Two days before the vote he suffered a mild paralytic stroke.

Young Edmund Ross, Senator from Kansas, who had refused to commit himself at all, except to intimate that if he voted for conviction it would be on Article Eleven, was subjected to every kind of pressure, including a petty attack upon his sculptress friend, Vinnie Ream, the daughter of his landlady. Vinnie Ream was a moderately talented young artist from Missouri, who had been allowed to use the capitol crypt as a studio for fashioning a statue of Abraham Lincoln. When she refused to use her influence with Ross to induce him to vote against the President, and permitted the crypt to be used as a conference room for the President's friends, there was talk among the Radicals of expelling her from the capitol.[4]

But the pressure was not all one-sided. Jeremiah Black wrote to Howell Cobb: "I think there has been buying and selling enough to save Johnson—that is to acquit him of the impeachment."[5] Stevens himself was pelted with threats. One letter, addressing him as "Fiend Incarnate of Hell," uttered a prayer to God that he with the other impeachment managers be "scorned, spit-upon, detested, loathed . . . and put to death, either by lawful means, by foul means . . . in the Stile of Wilkes Booth." The letter concluded: "Whoever does rid our fair country of all of you, will be a Christian, a patriot, a lover of his country." [6]

May 16, 1868, was voting day. The House adjourned and marched in a long procession, two by two, toward the Senate, preceded by the impeachment managers, Bingham and Boutwell foremost, and Stevens last, carried high above the others in his chair. Every Senator was present, including Senator Howard, who had been brought to the capitol on a stretcher. Even Senator Grimes, though still very ill, made his way slowly to his seat, leaning on the arms of two friends. The managers, realizing that Article Eleven was the most likely to carry, placed it first on the list for voting. Everyone expected the Democratic Senators to vote against conviction, and the calling of their names caused little stir in the crowded galleries. Senator Fessenden was the first of the Republicans to vote "Not guilty." Fowler of Tennessee was the second. When the roll call reached Senator Grimes, the Chief Justice said gently: "Mr. Grimes need not rise." But Grimes struggled to his feet and voted a firm "Not guilty."

Senator Howard also rose to speak, despite his weakness, and voted to convict. Henderson of Missouri surprised no one by voting for the President, since he had spoken his mind freely and indignantly during the previous few days. Finally it became clear that the critical vote might well be cast by Senator Ross. He was a quiet, unassuming man, new to the Senate, who had been elected by an extreme radical constituency in Kansas. Now, suddenly and inexplicably, this mild, blond man found himself a key figure in the trial. He had been sitting quietly, tearing sheets of paper in his fingers, making a little snow storm of litter. When his name was called, he rose and spoke in an even, conversational tone: "Not guilty."

The contest was over. Senators Trumbull and Van Winkle voted not guilty, as had been expected. Thirty-five Senators had voted against Andrew Johnson, nineteen in his favor. The President had been acquitted by a single vote. "The whole aspect of the House," said a *New York World* reporter, "was that of an assemblage just smitten with the news of a great calamity." The galleries now "hurled themselves angrily out of the Senate Chamber." [7] William Crook, sprinting down the marble staircase to carry the news to the White House, came into the Senate corridor and was momentarily stopped by a crowd. In it was Thaddeus Stevens, lifted high on the shoulders of two attendants.

"What was the verdict?" yelled several of the men milling about him. "Thad Stevens' face," said Crook, "was black with rage and disappointment. He brandished his arms in the air, and shouted in answer: 'The country is going to the devil!' " [8]

Instead of proceeding to vote on the remaining articles, the Senate now adjourned for ten days, an act which, according to the *Nation* of May 28, "not only deprived the process of all value, but converted it into a national scandal and disgrace." Many Senators rushed off to attend the National Republican Convention in Chicago, relieved that they were no longer committed to nominate Ben Wade for any office, and eager to push the candidacy of Ulysses S. Grant.

Few serious observers believed that the President, having been acquitted on the strongest article, could now be convicted on any of the others. When Butler in a meeting of the impeachment managers strongly urged a House investigation of the vote, Stevens opposed it, saying there was no use going further, for "impeachment is stone dead and the Republican party gone to the devil." [9] But Butler, who was said to have freely offered bribes himself to convict the President, was certain that at least four Senators had been paid to vote for acquittal. He managed to persuade Stevens to offer a resolution in the House for a complete investigation. It passed by a vote of 88 to 14. Coming as it did before the impeachment was truly over, Senator Ross wrote later, "it was an act of intimidation." [10]

Butler proceeded to have the telegraph files searched, bank balances scrutinized, and the wastebaskets of the President's counsel ransacked. When a well-known gambler, Charles Woolley, refused to answer questions in the hearings, Butler ordered him confined in the Capitol crypt, and Vinnie Ream was ordered out. Fearing that her statue of Lincoln would be ruined if it was moved, the girl went in tears to Thaddeus Stevens, whose bust she had finished modeling some weeks earlier.

Stevens regarded the girl with amiable affection. He had been delighted with his own statue, which had been done in the style of a Roman Senator, and seemed not to mind that she had made little attempt to soften the severity of his eyes or the harshness of his mouth. "I desire to express my gratification at the genius and skill which you have shown in the execution of my statuette as far as you have progressed," he had written her on March 28, 1868. "The taste and genius shewn by a lady who has been taught as you have, great intellectual power and delicacy of tone are not often found." The bust had been presented to the State of Missouri in May and placed in the Executive Mansion. [11]

Stevens was now thoroughly angry at Butler and interceded on her behalf. After some delay she was restored to her studio. She wrote to him gratefully: "I am at a loss how sufficiently to thank you for your great and constant kindness and interest in my behalf, which has just been crowned with success by the restoration of my room. But for you the result so important to me could not have been." [12]

Butler's investigation backfired upon the Radical Republicans when one witness testified that Senator Pomeroy had offered his own vote and that of three or four more Radical Republicans to the President's friends for $40,000. No real evidence of bribery on either side came out of the hearings, but the rumors were widely believed. The abuse heaped upon the seven Republican Senators who had voted for acquittal did the investigators no credit, and served only to strengthen their decision to vote for acquittal on the remaining articles of impeachment. The impeachment managers even sent a formal request to the Resolutions Committee of the Republican Convention that the seven Senators be read out of the party, but this was ignored.

Three prominent Republican journals, however, came to the defense of the seven dissenters, the *Chicago Tribune*, the *New York Evening Post*, and the *Nation*. "The thanks of the country are due to Mssrs. Trumbull, Fessenden, Grimes, Henderson, Fowler, Van Winkle, and Ross," said the *Nation* of May 21, 1868, "not for voting for Johnson's acquittal, but for vindicating, we presume nobody but themselves knows at what cost, the dignity and purity of the court of which they formed a part, and the sacred rights of individual conscience."

The Senate met again as a court on May 26, 1868. The vote on Articles Two and Three was exactly the same as on Article Eleven. Again the Radicals tried to prevent a conclusive vote by adjourning, but Chase stopped the disgrace further by formally declaring the President acquitted. James Gordon Bennett of the *New York Herald* commented on May 29 in his characteristic flamboyant fashion: "Impeachment is broken down completely. . . . So, with Lincoln murdered, with Chase pushed from his moral leadership of the party he made, with all the original heads of the great national movement out of the way, Butler, Sumner and Stevens had their vile hour and gloried in their political reign of terror. But the ninth Thermidor came soon, and their heads are in the sawdust."

After the trial Stevens discovered that he had bitten so hard and deep that he could not let go despite himself. Though he had said publicly, "Impeachment is dead," he was quite incapable of accepting this reality, and long after everyone else had abandoned the cause he worked obsessively, drawing up a new set of impeachment articles. He accused Johnson of abusing the patronage of the government, of usurping Congressional powers, of attempting to induce the Senators-elect of Colorado to perjure themselves, of pardoning 193 deserters on condition that they would vote for the Democratic party, and of restoring forfeited tracts of property in the South without the right. In his defense of these articles he insisted again that the President could be impeached for "malfeasance in office—where there was no actual crime committed . . . but with great injury to the country." The President, he said, "can be impeached, convicted, and punished without having committed a single offense which involved malignity of heart." [13]

His resolution to use the new articles fell flat in the House, however, and he was forced to concede defeat. No one paid him heed when he talked of carving Texas into three states so that six new Republican Senators could be counted upon for conviction. "It is lamentable," said the *New York Herald* on July 8, "to see this old man, with one foot in the grave, pursuing the President with such vindictiveness."

The futility of his obsession even Stevens seems to have recognized. "I have come to the fixed conclusion that neither in Europe or America will the Chief Executive of a nation be again removed by peaceful means," he said darkly on July 7, 1868. "If he retains the money and the patronage of the Government, it will be found, as it has been found, stronger than the law and impenetrable to the spear of justice. If tyranny becomes intolerable, the only resource will be found in the dagger of Brutus. God grant that it may never be used." [14]

For the President the impeachment acquittal was a triumph, but the humiliation of the proceedings left him deeply scarred. One of the little-publicized consequences was that Johnson, who had swung completely away from the idea of hanging the secession leaders, now swung back again. To his secretary, Benjamin C. Truman, he wrote on August 3, 1868: "I shall go to my grave with the firm belief that Davis, Cobb, Toombs, and a few others of the arch-conspirators and traitors should have been tried, convicted, and hanged for treason. . . . If it was the last act of my life I'd hang Jeff Davis as an example." [15]

CHAPTER TWENTY-NINE

The Last Weeks

I see some bright prospects in the future that could almost tempt me to live a little longer, but no matter.

Thaddeus Stevens to his physician, August 1868

STEVENS was to live only ten weeks after the impeachment trial. But it would not be accurate to say that failure had destroyed his will to live. For in these weeks he gave his time and waning strength to an astonishing variety of problems—his free-school system for the District of Columbia, the greenback controversy,[1] railroad bills, the problems of Reconstruction, and the coming election. He even continued to be involved in the Alaska problem, which should be examined briefly here because, as in his railroad legislation, his record for statesmanship was damaged by rumors of corruption.

When Secretary Seward in 1867 negotiated a treaty for the purchase of Alaska for $7,200,000, he had met with opposition that cut across party lines. "Russia," said the *New York World* on April 1, 1867, "has sold us a sucked orange." Despite the fact that he detested Seward, Thaddeus Stevens approved of the Alaska treaty from the beginning. As Chairman of the House Committee on Appropriations he pledged the honor of his country to the full payment. He made several speeches defending the purchase, believing, as he said, that "the vastness of the nation is very often the strength of the nation." When

Sumner insisted that Congress had a right to be consulted in the formation of the treaty, Stevens denied it vigorously: "This, it seems to me, is directly repugnant to the Constitution. . . . If Congress had to be consulted before a treaty was complete then the provisions of the Constitution would be partly thwarted." [2]

Although the treaty for the purchase of Alaska successfully passed the Senate on June 20, 1867, opposition mounted to the point where it was doubtful if the House would appropriate the money. As months passed Baron Edward de Stoeckl, the Russian minister, became increasingly disturbed. Later a Congressional investigation unearthed the fact that he had been authorized by the Czar to use $165,000 of the $7,200,000 purchase price, with the understanding that it be spread where it would facilitate legislation fastest. Seward passed on to Andrew Johnson the gossip that $30,000 had gone to newspaperman John Forney for his support, $8,000 to N. P. Banks, chairman of the House Committee on Foreign Relations, $20,000 to R. J. Walker and F. P. Stanton, and $10,000 to Thaddeus Stevens.

To John Bigelow, however, Seward told a somewhat different story at an after-dinner whist game. After listing several men said to have been bribed by Baron de Stoeckl, Seward said: "One thousand more were to have been given to poor Thad. Stevens, but no one would undertake to give that to him, so I undertook it myself. The poor fellow died, and I have it now." [3] But when questioned under oath at the Congressional hearings on the subject, Seward said emphatically: "I know nothing whatever of the use the Russian minister made of the fund, I know of no payment to anybody, by him, or of any application of the funds which he received." [4]

Whatever really happened to the money, it is clear that Stevens received no part of it, for he died before the bribes were distributed. More important, the record makes clear that it was unnecessary to bribe Stevens at all, since he had championed the purchase from the beginning. Perhaps Seward, who had many times felt Stevens' lash, took pleasure in spreading these stories without caring about their accuracy.

Stevens knew that he was dying, but the nearness of the grave brought no mellowing of his hatred for the President. In late July he was visited by Alexander McClure. "He spoke of the perfidy of Johnson with great bitterness," McClure wrote, "and seemed clouded with gloom as to the achievements of his own life." [5] There can be no doubt that Stevens was nourished and sustained by his hatred, that it kept him from disintegrating under what would otherwise have been an appalling sense of failure. For Stevens, unlike most Utopians, had a disturbing sense of reality. Better than any of his colleagues, he knew what was really happening in the South.

To a superficial observer it would seem that he had obtained everything he had asked for. In June and July, 1868, seven of the former Confederate states were readmitted to the Union. Only Texas, Mississippi, and Virginia remained under military rule. Johnson—obstinate to the end—had vetoed the bills for the readmission of the seven states on the ground that Congress had no right to impose conditions for their re-entry, but the two-thirds majority carried them through.[6] Thanks to the combination of Negro suffrage and partial white disfranchisement, all the new states had elected an overwhelming majority of Republicans to Congress and also to their own legislatures.

There was a strong movement underway in Congress to make suffrage universal by a Fifteenth Amendment. "We propose to go to universal and impartial suffrage as the only foundation upon which the Government can stand," Stevens said on March 18, 1868. "There is no other way . . . you and I and every man can protect himself against injustice and inhumanity." [7] He was enraged that the Republican Convention dared not endorse universal suffrage. "I regret I cannot speak favorably of the Chicago platform," he wrote. "It is like most of the Republican platforms for the last six years tame and cowardly. . . . What did the bold men at Chicago mean by selling the right of suffrage? There is one consolation. The Democrats cannot find as good candidates—But from instinct and long practice will make a much more villainous platform." And in a public letter to John Forney, March 11, 1868, he insisted that universal suffrage "was one of the inalienable rights intended to be embraced" in the Declaration of Independence.[8]

Stevens' own state of Pennsylvania rejected Negro suffrage in March 1868; in April Republican Michigan did the same. There was still much conversion to be done in the North. The Fifteenth Amendment would not, in fact, even pass the House until seven months after Stevens' death, and would not be ratified until March 30, 1870. But Stevens had every expectation of its ultimate success, for the majority of his party was already committed to it in theory. "I have never adopted a political principle which the party do not now hold," he wrote with satisfaction to a Lancaster editor on July 28, 1868. "Excuse this vanity into which I have been goaded." [9]

Although he was not enthusiastic about either Grant or Schuyler Colfax as nominees of the Republican Party, Stevens nevertheless felt confident that they would win and would uphold his Reconstruction policies. All these things he could point to with satisfaction in July 1868. Nevertheless, he saw ominous signs that the Republican Revolution had run its course and that henceforth, while there might be a superficial appearance of victory, a return to the "white man's government" throughout most of the South was likely if not inevitable.

The Negroes were in a numerical majority in only three states, South Carolina, Louisiana, and Mississippi; they were penniless, detested, illiterate, and absolutely lacking in political experience. They owned almost no land, and except for a handful of relatively wealthy Negroes in Louisiana had no knowledge of commerce or finance. They had no political power save the ballot and the knowledge that a Republican government in Washington would, as a last resort, send a limited number of federal troops for their protection. They could at best hold their own at the polls for two or three years, unless they won substantial numbers of white men to their side, and there were no signs of such a thing happening.

On the contrary, the white South was quietly uniting in a massive and deadly opposition. Had Stevens lived four weeks longer he would have read the celebrated statement of Nathan Bedford Forrest, Grand Master of all the Klans, that the number of Southerners who had joined the Ku Klux Klan already amounted to 550,000. There were 40,000 in Tennessee, Forrest said, adding: "There is not a radical leader in this town [Memphis] but is a marked man; and if a trouble should break out, not one of them would be left alive." [10]

The Klan itself, as the *Nation* pointed out, was nothing new. "The South before the war was one vast Ku-klux Klan; every man was a member of the organization, and the State governments made no attempt to interfere with it, and its victims were rare because dissenters from the popular creed did not enter the South." [11] Now that the dissenters were in control, the old complex paraphernalia of enchainment was being rebuilt in secret.

Stevens could see the pattern of the future all too clearly in Mississippi. In the state election of June 22, 1868, the Democrats had won the governorship and four out of five Congressmen. The new constitution calling for Negro suffrage had been defeated. And because of the organized terror of the Klan and similar groups, 22 per cent of the Negroes who had voted for the Constitutional Convention some months earlier now failed to appear at the polls. The best that Stevens could do was to deny Mississippi re-entry into the Union until she accepted Negro suffrage; but this political weapon could be used only once. He knew full well that after she was readmitted there was nothing Congress could do to guarantee continued Negro suffrage except to police the state with the Union Army.

Even the Southern Democrats who deplored violence were urging economic pressure against the Negroes and white Republicans. Wade Hampton, who issued a circular in 1868 advising the Democratic Party in South Carolina to "make no more assassinations," urged his people not to employ "in the future anyone, white or black, who gives his aid to the Republican Party." [12] Benjamin Hill was urging public ostracism for all white Republicans. "Drive them from your society, forsake them in their business, and brand them like Cain, to be fugitives and vagabonds upon the face of the earth." [13] The *Richmond Enquirer* spread hysteria by calling the Republicans a "cannibal and miscegenation party," which would reduce the whites to the level of Negroes, "whose native worship is the adoration of reptiles and the practice of obscene rites and cannibalism." [14]

Stevens was especially disturbed that the Republican whites numbered so small a minority in the South. Twenty-six out of the forty-four men elected to Congress by the governments in the seven newly admitted states were Northern men who had gone South—contemptuously called carpetbaggers by Southern Democrats. Some were able men, others mere adventurers. The Freedmen's Bureau had become the chief political tool of the Republican Party, and suffered under the stigma of being a creation of Northerners. The Union Leagues, local organizations of the Republican Party, were rapidly becoming as secretive and oath-ridden as the Klan. Wherever they armed the Negroes and drilled them as militiamen, the Klan or similar organizations went into action with deadly effect.

Stevens did not live to read about the election lynchings and riots of October and November, 1868. General Oliver O. Howard wrote later that the Negroes in Louisiana never recovered from the election murders of that year. Both Georgia and Louisiana, it was widely agreed, were carried for the Democrats by organized assassination.[15]

In the last weeks of his life, Stevens' pessimism was intensified by what was happening to the Democratic Party in the North. The old War Democrats, shrilly opposed to Reconstruction, were now uniting wholeheartedly with copperheads and ex-Confederates. What others looked upon as heartening evidence of a return to national unity and a healing of the hideous wounds of the war seemed to Stevens nothing but a realignment of the old pre-war groups. He saw only that the Democratic Party was savagely opposed to Negro suffrage and that it mocked the idea of the Negro as a citizen.

The Democratic Party had nominated for president the copperhead governor of New York, Horatio Seymour, who had called abolitionism "malignant philanthropy" and "leprous hypocrisy," and who had labeled the Emancipation Proclamation "a proposal for the butchery of women and children." [16] Salmon P. Chase, who had been supported for the Democratic nomination by the *New York Herald* as the one man in the country who could combine moral leadership with the traditional economic views of the Democratic Party, had received only four convention votes.

For Vice-President the Democrats had nominated Frank Blair, who, though he had fought valiantly for the Union, had never approved of the elevation of the Negro. Shortly before his nomination he had made public a letter to Colonel Brodhead urging that a Democratic President declare the Reconstruction Acts "null and void, compel the army to undo its usurpations in the South, disperse the carpetbag State governments and elect Senators and Representatives." [17] The Democratic platform bluntly declared the Reconstruction Acts to be "usurpations, unconstitutional, revolutionary and void."

Thaddeus Stevens was even fearful that a Democratic victory would see the restoration of slavery. "Blair declares," he said in the House on July 1, 1868, "that the only course for the Democratic party is to elect a President who shall send the armies of the Union to uproot all we have done in reconstructing the South, forcibly deprive the right of suffrage of about half of the legal voters, re-establish the institution of slavery, reorganize the 'white man's government.' . . . Is not that rebellion? . . . The Democratic party! Why, sir, it is the slave party. It is nothing but a slave party, and it will be a slave party until we grind them to powder under our heels." [18]

Stevens' gloom deepened as death approached. To Alexander McClure he said: "My life has been a failure. With all this great struggle of years in Washington, and the fearful sacrifice of life and treasure, I see little hope for the Republic." When a reporter from the *New York Tribune* asked for an interview to get his "history," Stevens said drily: "You newspaper men are always wanting to get at a man's history. As I said to a young girl who came to me some time ago to collect materials for a biography of me, I have no history. My life-long regret is that I have lived so long and so uselessly." To Jonathan Blanchard he echoed the same lament: "I have made but little history." [19]

This despair did not derive wholly from Stevens' realistic fears that his victories for the Negro people were temporary. If his triumphs had been guaranteed a long and vigorous life, there would probably still have been no steady glow of satisfaction in Stevens' breast. Like all Utopians, he could not be content with any triumph, however complete, because his political visions were largely an escape from his own desperate hungers. It is quite possible that he did not really want a happy world. But it cannot be denied that his crusade for a Promised Land where no one who had been crippled by poverty, the accident of fortune, or the color of his skin, should be made to suffer, was the dominating and sustaining passion of his life. The vision never in fact completely deserted him, but served to buoy him up, even at the end.

In his last formal speech in the House the old fire burned up brightly for a moment, long enough for him to make a final declaration of political faith: "Mr. Speaker, Providence has placed us here in a political Eden. All we have to do is avoid the forbidden fruit, for we have not yet reached the perfection of justice. While nature has given us every advantage of soil, climate, and geographical position, man still is vile. But such large steps have lately been taken in the true direction, that the patriot has a right to take courage."

Turning toward the Speaker, he continued: "My sands are nearly run, and I can only see with the eye of faith. I am fast descending the downhill of life, at the foot of which stands an open grave. But you, sir, are promised length of days and a brilliant career. If you and your compeers can fling away ambition and realize that every human being, however lowly-born or degraded, by fortune is your equal, and that every inalienable right which belongs to you belongs also to him, truth and righteousness will spread over the land, and you will look down from the top of the Rocky mountains upon an empire of one hundred millions of happy people." [20]

During his illness Stevens was besieged with clergymen. Knowing his reputation as an infidel, admiring him nevertheless for his crusades, and possibly fascinated by the aura of sin enveloping his private life, they hovered about him, each one hoping to snatch the prize of his confession and baptism. Jonathan Blanchard visited him just before the impeachment trial, and afterward wrote to him in bafflement and anxiety: "I have, after all, a strange hope that you are not to be lost. Though I will not insult your intelligence by arguing that 'whore-mongers and adulterers' are necessarily left outside of heaven with 'dogs, sorcerers and murderers'; or that if you die in these sins where Christ is you cannot come. . . . But if even now you will go to Christ He has all the power in Heaven and earth and can make your Scarlet Sins white!! I have loved and followed you with a strange fascination!! I have prayed and do still pray for you with a terrible earnestness— And now I bid you *farewell!*" [21]

Stevens met most of these overtures with evasion or good humor, though to at least one clergyman who offered to pray for him he said thoughtfully: "Pray that I may have more faith and rely less upon myself." [22] But when Robert Dale Owen, who had become an ardent spiritualist, called upon him with a recital of the views of the spirits of Henry Clay, Daniel Webster, and Stephen A. Douglas on Reconstruction, Stevens cut them short: "Well, present my compliments to the defuncts and tell them for me that if they have nothing better to offer on the subject, I think that since they died they have not been in a progressive state. Especially present my compliments to Douglas, and tell him I think he was the greatest political humbug on the face of the earth." [23]

Other stories indicated that his fortitude and wit did not desert him. When John Hickman remarked that he was looking well, Stevens answered quickly: "Ah, John! it is not my appearance, but my disappearance, that troubles me." [24] To John Law he wrote on July 21, 1868: "I am whittled down to a very narrow *pinte* at one end. If that should not be entirely shaved off before the next session of Congress I hope you will come here and give us a couple of weeks. . . . Don't forget to live yourself if I should die. A little of the old stock will be needed, whoever has the helm." Then he added a postscript: "If you should come up after me, just knock and enquire and I will have it opened." [25] A few days before he died, he said to his physician: "You have changed my medicine have you not?" And when the doctor nodded, he said, "Well, this is a square fight." [26]

Few of his visitors knew that there was torment in his prolonged dying. Only Lydia Smith, who massaged his swollen feet and saw to it that he followed the orders of his Lancaster physician—iron tonic, blue pills, nourishing food, "with as much of the punch, wine, brandy, whisky, or beer, as may be necessary and agreeable," [27]—knew the extent of his pain.

Stevens had drawn up his will some years before. We have already noted that he bequeathed to Lydia Smith $500 a year until her death, and willed the bulk of his estate to his nephew with the understanding that he give up alcohol. Should this condition not be met—and it seems likely that Stevens knew it would not be—the estate was to be sold to endow an orphanage. This was to be open to children of all colors and creeds. "No preference shall be shown on account of race or color in the admission or treatment," Stevens wrote. "Neither poor Germans, Irish or Mohammedans, nor any others on account of their race, or the religion of their parents, must be excluded. All the inmates shall be educated in the same classes and manner without regard to color. They shall be fed at the same table." [28]

Like many men about to die, he had given some thought to the kind of stone that would mark his grave. "I suppose, like the rest of the fools," he said, "we shall have to get something stuck up in the air; let it be plain." [29] But if he cared little about the monument, he took some pains with the inscription, and left orders that the stone should be cut as follows:

> I repose in this quiet and secluded spot,
> Not from any natural preference for solitude
> But, finding other Cemeteries limited as to Race
>   by Charter Rules,
> I have chosen this that I might illustrate
>   in my death
> The Principles which I advocated
>   Through a long life:
> EQUALITY OF MAN BEFORE HIS CREATOR.

In the last days of his illness Stevens was cared for by two nurses, Sisters Loretta and Genevieve, nuns from the Protestant Hospital, a charity for colored people Stevens had aided by helping to secure a Congressional appropriation of $30,000. On the night of August 11, 1868, his Washington physician, Dr. N. Young, told him he was dying. He only nodded. Shortly before midnight the two nuns asked his nephew, Thaddeus, if they might baptize him, and he agreed. He died quietly about ten minutes after the ceremony.

His body was embalmed and lay in state in the Capitol rotunda before being taken to Lancaster for burial. The guard of honor was chosen from a Massachusetts regiment of Negro Zouaves. Visitors filed in and out of the capitol in a winding line until long after dark. One was Representative James G. Blaine, who whispered to his companion: "The death of Stevens is an emancipation for the Republican party." [30]

The editor of the *Washington Daily Chronicle,* noting that five to six thousand visitors filed through the Capitol rotunda, said with some surprise on August 14: "It is a remarkable fact that no man in this District, save Abraham Lincoln, ever had the homage paid to him as he whose mortal remains were conveyed to their final resting yesterday." After the burial in Lancaster, the Republican Party in the area, in an extraordinary gesture of respect, formally nominated Stevens for Congress on the forthcoming election ticket. This, the announcement explained, was meant as a "fitting tribute to the memory of our most able and distinguished champion of freedom and justice." Arrangements to fill the vacancy were made later. Although the Democratic *Lancaster Intelligencer* openly mocked at the idea of voting for a "Corpse for Congress," [31] Stevens' name stayed on the ticket and won an overwhelming victory.

CHAPTER THIRTY

The Stern Pen of History

The new era of American nationality felt his powerful clutch and impetus, and the effect of his work will remain on our Constitution and polity, longer than that of Webster, of Clay, or of Calhoun.

Thaddeus Stevens obituary, *Springfield Republican*
August 12, 1868

"WHAT WE say at the graves of admired friends or statesmen is not biography," Thaddeus Stevens once said. "The stern pen of history will strip such eulogies of their meretricious ornaments." [1] When he died, his Republican friends did him the honor of largely avoiding the unctuous flattery he detested, and the Democrats were overwhelmingly merciless. A few of his enemies grudgingly admitted as virtues his independence and lack of cant; his friends did not ignore the sour and bitter quality of his genius, and the destructive component of his political philosophy. The memorial addresses delivered in his honor when Congress met in December make better reading, therefore, than the usual saccharine obituary speeches.

Perhaps the most impressive tribute came from Ignatius Donnelly, Representative from Minnesota. "He never flattered the people," Donnelly said. ". . . On the contrary, on all occasions he attacked their sins, he assailed their prejudices, he outraged all their bigotries; and when they turned upon him he marched straight forward, like Gulliver

367

wading through the fleets of the Lilliputians, dragging his enemies after him." [2]

The memorial speeches were collected and published in 1869. When one of Stevens' old Gettysburg friends obtained a copy, he inscribed it thus:

> To the Memory of
> Thaddeus Stevens
> Ah, Alas, Alas,
> the
> Great unchained
> is
> Chained at last.[3]

The *New York Times* in a sober appraisal applauded Stevens' war years. "He was one of the few who are not afraid to grasp first principles and lay hold of great truths, or push them to their remotest logical result. . . . though ahead of the Republican party he was a steady co-worker with it through all the stages of the war, sustaining its every measure, and rendering valuable assistance to the Government in the execution of its plans." But on Reconstruction the *Times* called him "the Evil Genius of the Republican Party. . . . defiant, despotic, and in all things irritating."

James Gordon Bennett, who had been damning him as the American Robespierre for over two years, wrote more soberly in the *New York Herald:* "Thad Stevens was, almost independently of his own volition, an instrument for expressing and for working out the predestined purposes of the revolution through which the American people are passing. Malevolent, even malignant, as he appeared to be and was in his capacity as a public man, his friends represent him as courteous and genial in his private intercourse with them. Publicly he was an evil, but a necessary evil."

Even the waspish American correspondent of the *London Times* gave him some praise. "He was a fanatical, bitter and self-willed man, but not mean or deceitful. He is the last of the leading Americans who had the courage to rise above political partizanship." Horace Greeley, as was to be expected, wrote a long and glowing tribute in the *New York Tribune,* predicting that his reconstruction measures would remain "a monument more enduring than bronze," but he could not omit a note of regret for Stevens' confiscation, taxation, and financial theories. The *New York World* admitted his indomitable audacity of spirit, his parliamentary tact and inflexible will, but went on to call him "the author of more evil and mischief than any other inhabitant of the globe since the end of the civil war." [4]

Southern journals frankly crowed with pleasure. "The prayers of the righteous have at last removed the Congressional curse!" said the *Planter's Banner* of Franklin, Louisiana. "May his new iron works wean him from the earth, and may the fires of his new furnace never go out!" "The evil which this man did while living will not die with him," said the *New Orleans Picayune*. "It was too monstrous, too malignant, for oblivion to shroud it from future criticism. . . . It is written that unseen hands strewed flowers upon the tomb of Nero. It may chance flowers may also be scattered upon that of Thaddeus Stevens." [5]

But it remained for Samuel Bowles in the *Springfield Republican* of August 12, 1868, to write a judgment on Stevens that made a proper accounting of his impact on the nation's history:

When the hour came, the man was ready,—not with broad views, wise doctrines, good taste, faultless manners, or exemplary morals,—but resolute, shrewd, unsparing; willing to use friend or foe, careless of both, possessed with his cause and that alone, and equal to every occasion. When his hour passed, as it did long before his death, he was judged to be harsh, coarse, ignorant, unreasonable, and troublesome,—he was a revolutionist in a period of reaction and organization. But to estimate him merely thus is as unjust as to call him the saviour of his country or the first of statesmen. He had passed a long life in training for his work, which began in 1859 and ended in 1867, —by that he is to be measured, and not by what preceded or followed. The new era of American nationality felt his powerful clutch and impetus, and the effect of his work will remain on our Constitution and polity, longer than that of Webster, or Clay, or of Calhoun.

How, then, is Thaddeus Stevens to be judged in our own day? Modern Negro historians, like W. E. B. DuBois, look upon him as an enlightened statesman. Social analysts like Gunnar Myrdal, looking at the origins of the racial problems of our time, have much admiration for Stevens' recognition of the potentialities of the Negro people sixty-five years in advance. Constitutional lawyers, on the other hand, are troubled by his destructive invasion of the executive power. And white historians reared with or sympathetic to the traditions of the South still use epithets like "Caliban," "Marat," "atrabilious sansculotte," and "Lord Hategood of the Fair."

George Fort Milton has written that he had a mouth "of unexampled cruelty," and that he had hatred "stamped upon his brow." Lloyd Stryker styled him a "malignant cancer," a "horrible old man . . . craftily preparing to strangle the bleeding, broken body of the South, and to strike down, if he could, the advocates of justice." Stevens, he said, thought it would be "a beautiful thing" to watch "the white men, especially the white women of the South, writhing under negro domination." W. E. Woodward has described his policy as "simply a set of hates strung together in a definite pattern." Other historians, like Paul H. Buck, give him credit for being "idealistically or at least unselfishly motivated," but damn the Radicals as a whole for being "the sickest of the nerve-shot age." [6]

No one can deny that Thaddeus Stevens was fanatical in the pursuit of principle, but he was fanatical for free schools and universal suffrage at a time when opposition fanatics stood for caste and ignorance. If he was callous toward the Southern white, he was also a great humanitarian for the Negro people. If he made solid contributions to the rapacious railroad and tariff interests, he also contributed enormously to the spread of democracy by extending the suffrage to millions of blacks and poor whites.

But it is on the thorny problem of Reconstruction that Stevens as a statesman must chiefly be judged. Seventy-nine years after his death so able a Southern historian as Professor E. Merton Coulter would still describe the chief problem of Reconstruction as "a question of the survival of the dignity and integrity of the Caucasian race," and insist passionately that the enforcement of Negro suffrage was "sinning against light." [7] Carl Sandburg has perceptively suggested that the whole Civil War was fought over the question of human dignity. Thaddeus Stevens believed that the dignity of the Southern white man should not be dependent upon the degradation of the Negro, who had a right to his own dignity. He believed with Abraham Lincoln, "You must not force negroes any more than white men." [8]

And though little by little both the North and the South have come grudgingly to accept the majority of Stevens' aims for the Negro as just and right, they still damn him for his methods. Negro suffrage was premature, it is said. Negro-carpetbag government was outrageously corrupt. Reconstruction was, in the words of Paul H. Buck, "disorder worse than war and oppression unequalled in American annals," [9]—oppression worse, apparently, than the brandings, whippings, enforced ignorance, and multiple family tragedies of slavery.

There is no doubt that for the Southern white man Reconstruction was a process of humbling and a degradation of the spirit. Any extension of democracy is painful to the aristocrat, and in striving to destroy the aristocratic traditions of the South, Stevens helped purge the nation of what was essentially a remnant of feudalism.

Moreover, he pushed vigorously toward the centralization and consolidation of the federal power, and helped transform what was a sprawling, invertebrate country into a unified nation, responsive to strong central leadership. His assault on Andrew Johnson was actually not so much an attack on the executive power as such—for he defended Lincoln in many of his so-called "usurpations" of power—as an attack on the man because of what Stevens believed to be a betrayal of principle. And if the Republican Party under his leadership continued the work of Lincoln in consolidating the national government as against state government, it also provided in the Fourteenth and Fifteenth Amendments two great potential legal bulwarks against the tyranny of state government.

Thaddeus Stevens was able to foresee the might of the United States, and urged much of his railroad and tariff legislation with the aim of making her a great industrial and commercial nation. Unfortunately he failed to exact guarantees that might have helped to prevent some of the festering corruption and gigantic peculations of the succeeding epoch.

As the "Father of Reconstruction" Stevens must bear much of the blame for the anarchy, violence, and misgovernment that accompanied it. His insistence on the disfranchisement of what had been practically the total political leadership of the South meant that most of the men who stepped into this leadership, even when they were well-meaning and honest, had had no practice in the art of government. This was especially disastrous in the judiciary.

For all his pessimism, Stevens underestimated the strength of the counterrevolution already underway before he died. Despite his intent, he stimulated it by his "all or nothing" demands for the Negro. He correctly foresaw that without economic power the Negro could not preserve his ballot. If, instead of continually crying for confiscation he had fought for a system of land purchase or government loans at a fractional interest rate, he might have succeeded in getting at least a portion of the Negroes their forty acres and a mule. As it was, the Negro had as an economic weapon only his own labor, and the white man very quickly discovered, as George Fitzhugh triumphantly pointed out, that hunger was a better weapon than hickories.[10]

Stevens should not be blamed for the fictions of Reconstruction, which cling tenaciously in the Southern folk memory. One of these holds that Reconstruction consisted of "Negro rule" and the "Africanization" of the South. In only two states, Mississippi and South Carolina, did the Negroes control the state legislature, and in both these states the Negroes greatly outnumbered the whites in the total population. Everywhere else "Negro rule" meant simply that a minority of Negroes were elected to the state legislatures, where they were largely dominated by Radical white men.

Many Negroes in the reconstruction governments could not sign their names, but literacy is not necessarily a guarantee of wisdom and virtue. If these men did nothing but keep silent and vote for their party, they did not thereby legislate any great evil. If in Louisiana they passed laws forbidding Jim Crow in schools, theaters, restaurants, and public transportation, this was indeed premature—and the Negroes themselves made little attempt to take advantage of the laws [11]—but it was not, like the slave codes or the black codes of 1866, legislation to impose injustice or inhumanity. As the great Southern heretic, George Washington Cable, pointed out in 1890: ". . . the struggle had never been by the blacks for and by the whites against a black supremacy, but only for and against an arbitrary pure-white supremacy." [12]

"Is it not time," Howard K. Beale has asked, "that we studied the history of Reconstruction without first assuming, at least subconsciously, that carpetbaggers and Southern white Republicans were wicked, that Negroes were illiterate incompetents, and that the whole white South owes a debt of gratitude to the restorers of 'white supremacy'?" [13] If the reconstruction governments raised land taxes to the point of confiscation, as they did in Mississippi, where 640,000 acres were seized and sold for nonpayment, it was in part because of the almost universal refusal of the white man to sell his land to the black under any circumstances. Basic land changes did not take place in the South. By 1900 only 600,000 acres were owned by nonwhites. [14]

If the Southern states went deeply into debt, it was in part because the transportation system had to be rebuilt, and partly because for the first time in its history the South was developing a system of free public schools. Virginia, which escaped Negro-carpetbag rule, had by 1872 piled up a state debt amounting to $43,690,000, which was a good deal higher than the $18,515,000 debt of South Carolina—even though the latter had for a time a notorious free saloon in the state capitol. [15]

If corruption was rampant in the South, the area held no monopoly. Boss Tweed probably stole from the citizens of New York City more than the total graft in the South up to 1875. "The great thieves," wrote W. E. B. DuBois wryly, "were always white men." And as George Washington Cable pointed out long ago, all the robberies of the carpetbag governments were not as dark and foul as the enormities of Lynch-law. [16]

Another fiction of Reconstruction rule is that it was long-lived, that the carpetbaggers, scalawags, and Negroes held the South in their clutches till after the Hayes-Tilden election of 1876. Even though Thaddeus Stevens expected wholesale return to the white man's government, he would have been dismayed at the speed with which this was accomplished. As C. Vann Woodward has pointed out, "If reconstruction ever set the bottom rail on top, it was not for long and never securely." [17] Texas, like Virginia, never had Negro-carpetbag rule. Tennessee secured "home rule" by 1869; West Virginia, North Carolina, and Georgia in 1870; Alabama and Arkansas in 1874, and Mississippi in November 1875. Only in South Carolina, Louisiana, and Florida did the Reconstruction governments last through the election of 1876.[18] Professor Woodward has demonstrated brilliantly that it was not Reconstruction but the "Redeemers" who truly laid the modern foundations for race relations in the South.

Reconstruction remained a great bogeyman, however, an efficient propaganda device for frightening the white South into remaining "solid." By 1900 the Negro had virtually lost the right to vote and the right to hold office. The Supreme Court had given notice that it was not to be "a perpetual censor" on all the state legislation affecting civil rights,[19] and sat idle while the South defied the Fourteenth and Fifteenth Amendments and enacted a vast network of Jim Crow legislation. The Negro was effectively enchained in a mudsill caste from which there was no easy escape except emigration. He was now completely abandoned by the Republican Party, which had lost its burning, chiliastic faith, and was intent not on remodeling the world but only on possessing it.

For a time it seemed that Reconstruction had cost the Negro far more than it was worth, and that Thaddeus Stevens' legislation against massive antiminority group sentiment had been utterly futile. But in recent years the legacy of Stevens and of his Radical Republican contemporaries has been revitalized. The Supreme Court has taken a hard look at the Fourteenth and Fifteenth Amendments, and seems willing to shoulder the disagreeable burdens it cast off in 1873. The Negro now is a real political power in the North. And because everywhere in the nation he has demonstrated his capacity for education, creative achievement, and a phenomenal gift for self-discipline in the face of the white man's humiliations in both North and South, there seems to be good reason for believing that the Fourteenth and Fifteenth Amendments will eventually become the instruments that Thaddeus Stevens and his colleagues intended them to be.

For Stevens the revolutionist there may therefore come a time when he is judged less harshly than in the past. As Arthur M. Schlesinger Sr. has written, ". . . the shock troops of reform are almost necessarily captained by the headlong and the ungenteel—men of explosive temperament and rude manners." [20] The malice and hatred in Stevens

served to enhance the penetrating power of his ideas. His ruthlessness
and fire won him a far wider audience than mild men usually get. Indignation served him instead of love, and a sense of injustice was his
substitute for hope. It is sobering and disquieting to realize that if he
had truly possessed both love and hope, the Negro might well have
had no such champion.

Notes °

CHAPTER 1 *The Old Commoner*

1. This was the second of two editorials, published July 12 and July 24, 1867, in the *Union Springs Times*. The first was signed "On-the-Wing," but the second acknowledged authorship of the first and was signed George M. Drake.

2. *New York Tribune*, August 14, 1868.

CHAPTER 2 *The Branding*

1. Oliver J. Dickey, Representative from Pennsylvania, and a former law student of Thaddeus Stevens, in *Congressional Globe*, 40 Congress, 3 session, Dec. 17, 1868. Dickey is the source of information on Joshua Stevens' death. For facts about the elder brother, see the Elsie Singmaster Lewars Papers, Adams County Historical Society, Gettysburg, Pa. The elder Stevens was with his family as late as 1804, when Thaddeus was twelve, for he took the boy to visit relatives in Boston that year. See Alexander Harris, *A Review of the Political Conflict in America . . . Comprising Also a Résumé of the Career of Thaddeus Stevens*, p. 17.

2. Pennsylvania Constitutional Convention, *Proceedings and Debates*, V:348–349; *Congressional Globe*, 37 Congress, 2 session, March 3, 1862, p. 1044; *Pennsylvania School Journal*, April 1867, p. 248.

3. *Washington Weekly Chronicle*, August 22, 1868. The earliest detailed record of Stevens' childhood was written by his law student and friend, Alexander Hood, and published as "Thaddeus Stevens," a chapter in *A Biographical History of Lancaster County*, edited by Alexander Harris. A sketchy account had appeared in 1871 in William H. Barnes, *The Fortieth Congress*, II:1–12.

4. Alexander McClure, *Abraham Lincoln and Men of War-Times*, p. 265. See also Stevens' will, a copy of which is in the Stevens Papers, Library of Congress.

5. This story is told in one of fourteen pages of notes from an unidentified writer, in the Stevens Papers.

6. *New York Times*, August 14, 1868, quoting the *Philadelphia Press*.

7. William Hall, *Reminiscences and Sketches, Historical and Biographical*, p. 7.

° Titles of works cited in footnotes are sometimes shortened for quicker reference. For full, exact titles and complete reference data, see the Bibliography.

8. As reported in the reminiscences of one who signed himself "Byng," in the *Gettysburg Star and Sentinel,* July 7, 1874.

9. See the Records of Births, Deaths, and Marriages, Book I, p. 261, in the Town Clerk's Office, Danville, Vermont, as cited in Richard N. Current, *Old Thad Stevens, a Story of Ambition,* p. 4n. See also Anna B. Dodd, *Talleyrand: the Training of a Statesman.* Talleyrand sailed for America February 3, 1794. He created a sensation by escorting a handsome mulatto woman around Philadelphia.

10. John W. Forney, *Anecdotes of Public Men,* II:181.

11. William Hall, *Reminiscences,* p. 6; *Philadelphia Press,* Aug. 13, 1868; T. H. Burrowes, "Reminiscences of Thaddeus Stevens," *Philadelphia Press,* Sept. 2, 1868.

12. Ignatius Donnelly, Representative from Minnesota, *Cong. Globe,* 40 Cong., 3 session, Dec. 17, 1868, p. 139.

13. See especially *Cong. Globe,* 38 Cong., 1 session, May 18, 1864, p. 2342; 38 Cong., 2 session, Feb. 23, 1865, p. 1041; 39 Cong., 1 session, March 1, 1866, p. 1128.

14. Alexander Harris, *Review of the Political Conflict,* p. 12, reported that ". . . in his younger years, when first a candidate for the legislature, he used to boast that he was a shoemaker."

15. Speech of C. A. Bunker, *100th Anniversary of the Caledonia County Grammar School, 1897,* pp. 52–55.

16. This letter was first published by T. R. Witmer in "Some Hitherto Unpublished Correspondence of Thaddeus Stevens," *Lancaster County Historical Society Papers,* XXXV:50, 1931. The "Mrs. Smith" to whom it was addressed was not Stevens' "aunt," as has been said, but Mrs. Lydia Smith, Stevens' housekeeper. The error was discovered by Mrs. Elsie Singmaster Lewars. See her papers in the Adams County Historical Society, Gettysburg.

17. *Washington National Republican,* August 13, 1868, and *Philadelphia Press,* August 12, 1868. Burlington College later became the University of Vermont.

18. Hood, *op. cit.,* pp. 572–573.

19. A copy of this letter, addressed to the Reverend Dr. Smith, dated Aug. 19, 1868, and other information regarding Stevens' Dartmouth years, were kindly furnished me by librarians at Dartmouth. Election to Phi Beta Kappa was not then determined entirely by scholastic standing, as it is today.

20. Walter Lowrie, *A Short Life of Kierkegaard,* p. 42. Theodor Haecker, in his *Kierkegaard the Cripple,* p. 33, noted that Kierkegaard has many references to Richard III and Talleyrand in his writings.

21. Stevens' letter to Samuel Merrill, Jan. 5, 1814, *Lancaster County Historical Society Papers,* 1906, X:396–401.

22. It is handwritten and endorsed "Conference by Sen" Stevens for next commencement, July 9, 1814." The librarian of Dartmouth College kindly furnished me with a copy.

23. Jan. 5, 1814. *Lancaster Co. Papers,* X:396–401.

24. Hood, *op. cit.,* p. 596.

25. Hall, *Reminiscences,* p. 16.

26. Wm. M. Stewart, *Reminiscences,* p. 205; Haecker, *Kierkegaard the Cripple,* pp. 24, 32.

27. *New York Herald,* April 8, 1868; Hall, *Reminiscences,* pp. 24–25; Oscar J. Harvey, *History of Lodge No. 61, and History of Perseverance Lodge No. 21.* There is no record, however, that Stevens ever made a formal application for admission. Erik M. Erikson in "Thaddeus Stevens, 'Arch Priest of Antimasonry,' *Grand Lodge of Iowa Bulletin,* XXVII:40, Feb. 1926, has stated that his "disability in the form of a club foot would have prevented him from becoming a Mason."

28. According to the obituary in the *Philadelphia Press,* Aug. 12, 1868.

29. Commonwealth v. Hunter, October term, 1817, *Minute Book of the Criminal Court,* Adams County Courthouse. An article signed "A Friend to Humanity" ap-

peared in the *Adams County Centinel*, Dec. 3, 1817, describing the whole story in detail and defending Hunter vigorously; it may have been written by Stevens. Twenty-nine years later, when Wm. H. Seward defended Henry G. Wyatt on grounds of insanity, it was still considered most uncommon. See Earl Conrad, *Mr. Seward for the Defense.*

30. Butler *et al.* v. Delaplaine, October 1821, in T. Sergeant and Wm. Rawle, Jr., reporters, *Cases Adjudged in the Supreme Court of Pennsylvania, 1814–1828,* VII:378–379; W. U. Hensel, "Thaddeus Stevens as a Country Lawyer," *Lanc. Co. Historical Society Papers,* 1906, X:252.

31. Gettysburg Sentinel, July 9, 1823. This was pointed out to me by Dr. Robert Fortenbaugh of Gettysburg College.

32. Current, *Old Thad Stevens,* pp. 34–35.

33. See Russel B. Nye's excellent monograph, *Fettered Freedom, Civil Liberties and the Slavery Controversy, 1830–1860,* esp. pp. 139–176, "The Reign of Mob Law." Nye points out that the use of mob action for suppressing abolition agitation in the North reached its climax during the period 1833–1840.

34. See Jefferson's letter to John Holmes, April 22, 1820, quoted in Adrienne Koch and Wm. Peden, eds., *Life and Selected Writings of Thomas Jefferson,* p. 698. The Adams prophecy is in his *Memoirs,* ed. by C. F. Adams, V:210.

CHAPTER 3   *The Gettysburg Tragedy*

1. *Gettysburg Compiler,* December 8, 1824. Presumably this physician was the Dr. Miller mentioned in the transcript of notes from the Lefever file, pp. 41–43 of this book. Mr. Arthur Weaner of the Adams County Historical Society has informed me that the coroner in 1824 was Dr. David Horner, Jr. I am also greatly indebted to Robert Fortenbaugh of Gettysburg College, who first put me on the trail of this mystery, and generously shared his own information concerning the anonymous letters.

2. In 1822, however, he had been convicted by a Gettysburg jury of defrauding James Dobbins of his property and law library, but the Pennsylvania Supreme Court had reversed the sentence. For details, see Chapter IV, pp. 49–50.

3. According to Robert Fortenbaugh; also, see Thomas F. Woodley, *Great Leveler,* p. 31.

4. Harvey, *History of Lodge No. 61,* 81n.; Wm. L. Stone, *Letters on Masonry and Anti-Masonry; Proceedings of the U. S. Anti-Masonic Convention;* Charles McCarthy, *The Antimasonic Party,* pp. 435, 461–489.

5. Stevens was co-editor from April 17, 1830 to July 4, 1830. On August 25, 1835, the *Gettysburg Compiler* published a letter to the editor saying: "It is laughable, when we know that Stevens controls the Editor, to see column after column filled with *Thaddeus Stevens,* Thaddeus Stevens, Thaddeus Stevens."

6. Signed "Justice," *Gettysburg Compiler,* September 7, 1830.

7. As reported in the *Gettysburg Compiler,* October 26, 1830.

8. As reprinted in *Free-Masonry Unmasked, or Minutes of a Suit in the Court of Common Pleas of Adams County, wherein Thaddeus Stevens, Esq. was Plaintiff, and Jacob Lefever, Defendant,* pp. iv–xiii.

9. *Gettysburg Compiler,* June 21, 1831.

10. Buchanan's letter of refusal is now in the possession of Mr. N. L. Oyler of Gettysburg.

11. For permission to reproduce this document I am greatly indebted to Mr. N. L. Oyler, who recently purchased all the law-office records, which date back to 1816. The file also contains several letters mentioning Stevens, none of which is of value as far as this crisis is concerned. This paper, three pages in length, was found among letters dated 1832. Internal evidence indicates that it was written about the time of the criminal libel suit of 1831, but not much earlier. See especially the phrase: "Wm. McPherson was a boy . . ." Arthur Weaner has been

of invaluable assistance to me in the detective work.

12. Dobbins was a "half-lunatic" lawyer who had accused Stevens in 1822 of acquiring his property by fraud. See Chapter IV, pp. 49–50.

13. Hall, *Reminiscences,* p. 25. The brief record of this trial may be seen in the Adams County Court House in Gettysburg. There is no mention whatever of the insinuations of murder.

14. *Free-Masonry Unmasked* . . . , p. iii. This was published by R. W. Middleton, editor of the *Gettysburg Star,* which was largely controlled by Stevens.

15. The offer was filed in the Adams County Court, September 14, 1835, and reprinted in the *Gettysburg Compiler,* September 15, 1835. The letter was dated August 27, 1835. Lefever stated in the same issue that this was the first time Stevens had requested the name of the anonymous letter-writer.

16. The exchange of letters from August 29 through September 11, 1835, was published in the *Gettysburg Compiler,* September 15, 1835. In his commentary on the letters, Lefever pointed out that the *Star* had stated that in the trial it was proved that he had already been indemnified for the costs incurred. This he vigorously denied.

17. Hall, *Reminiscences,* p. 26.

18. Letter dated January 16, 1868, published in Hall, *Reminiscences,* pp. 29–30.

19. *Christian Cynosure,* September 22 and November 3, 1868. Dr. Jonathan Blanchard, founder and editor of *Christian Cynosure,* wrote a revealing series of reminiscences shortly after Stevens' death, which were published in *Christian Cynosure,* September 8 to December 29, 1868. These have been overlooked by Stevens' biographers, though Blanchard's later reminiscences of 1883, which are not as valuable, have been used. Unfortunately all of his correspondence was destroyed in a fire in Wheaton, Illinois, including the Stevens letter quoted here. Blanchard's numerous letters to Stevens may be seen in the Stevens Papers, Library of Congress. Blanchard was a Presbyterian clergyman, Vermont-born, who became president of Knox College in 1845 and of Wheaton College in 1860. He had many friends in Washington. Senator James W. Grimes wrote to his wife from Philadelphia, November 24, 1859: "Dr. Blanchard is an able, honest, ultra-enthusiastic, and somewhat bigoted man—a great friend of ours, and I entertain great respect for him." Wm. Salter, *Life of James W. Grimes,* p. 120.

20. The will and codicil were published in the *New York Tribune,* August 19, 1868. "Shert" was a misspelling for either Schulz or Schurtz. See also the copy in the Stevens papers.

21. Carl Schurz, *Reminiscences,* III:215.

22. This gossip, obviously third-hand, is communicated in a letter from Z. Herbert to Jacob Lefever, dated March 1, 1832. It is in the legal file owned by N. L. Oyler.

23. See pp. 80–81.

24. What may have been a faint echo of the Gettysburg mystery crept into the imagery of one of Stevens' statements two years before his death. The *New York Times* of July 18, 1866, reported that in a private conversation he attacked the Louisiana Constitutional Convention of 1864, saying: "What! revive that d——d bogus concern of Banks'! Sir, it never was legally born; it was a bastard. I never would have anything to do with it while it was alive, and now that it is dead, it may stay in H—— where it belongs."

CHAPTER 4 *The Early Crusades*

1. Dobbins v Stevens, in Sergeant and Rawle, *Reports of Cases* . . . , XVIII: 13–15; W. U. Hensel, "Thaddeus Stevens as a Country Lawyer," *Lancaster Co. Hist. Soc. Papers,* X:266; Hall, *Reminiscences,* pp. 26–27.

2. Hood, *op. cit.,* p. 595.

3. Hood, *ibid.,* pp. 588–589. In this regard Stevens was very like another Radical Republican reformer, Wendell Phillips, whose generosity was "almost pathological,"

according to Richard Hofstadter in "Wendell Phillips: the Patrician as Agitator," *American Political Tradition*, pp. 142–143.

4. *Speech . . . to establish a School of Arts . . .* Stevens Papers.

5. *Washington Daily Morning Chronicle*, August 14, 1868; *Estate of Thaddeus Stevens . . . , Auditor's Report*, April 29, 1893. The gross value of his estate exclusive of these notes was estimated at $116,000.

6. Eric Hoffer, *The True Believer, Thoughts on the Nature of Mass Movements*, p. 75.

7. *Washington Weekly Chronicle*, August 22, 1868.

8. Lydia Smith's account comes from an interview of uncertain date in the *New York Times* that was copied into Notebook No. III of Elsie Singmaster Lewars, Adams County Historical Society. It is clear from internal evidence that the interview occurred after Stevens' death. Lydia Smith stated that Keziah married a mulatto, Ephraim Woolricks (also spelled Ulrich), "whose father tried to sell him." Alexander Hood stated that the purchase took place about 1830 and that the ex-slave stayed with Stevens four years (see Hood, *op. cit.*, p. 576). Godlove S. Orth, Representative from Indiana, stated in his obituary speech on Stevens that the slave's name was John, and that Stevens paid $300 for him, sacrificing money he was going to spend in Baltimore on his law library. See *Cong. Globe*, 40 Cong., 3 session, December 17, 1868, p. 138. In the *History of Cumberland and Adams County*, published in 1886, it is said (pp. 74–75) that Stevens spent "his last dollar when on his way to Baltimore with his carefully garnered gains to buy his first law library and he saw a slave parent and child being sold to be separated; he spent all he had and purchased the slaves and returned to Gettysburg with these instead of his promised books." It is possible that Stevens purchased more than one slave to free him, and that there were both an "Ephraim" and a "John" who worked for him after being freed.

9. See Elsie Singmaster, *I Speak for Thaddeus Stevens*, p. 160; also her Notebook No. III. Lydia Smith's tombstone indicates that she was born on Valentine's Day, 1813.

10. O. J. Dickey, *Cong. Globe*, 40 Cong., 3 session, December 17, 1868, p. 130; Alexander Harris, *A Review of the Political Conflict*, p. 64.

11. McClure, *Abraham Lincoln and Men of War-Times*, p. 270.

12. *Cong. Globe*, 40 Cong., 3 session, December 17, 1868, p. 141.

13. W. U. Hensel, "Thaddeus Stevens as a Country Lawyer," *op. cit.*, X:265.

14. Hood, *op. cit.*, p. 573.

15. Pennsylvania Constitutional Convention, *op. cit.*, I:546.

16. *Argument of Thaddeus Stevens . . . Jacob Specht . . .* Stevens Papers.

17. *Cong. Globe*, 31 Cong., 1 session, June 10, 1850, App. I:767.

18. As reported by Robert Fortenbaugh, Gettysburg College.

19. T. H. Burrowes, "Reminiscences," *Philadelphia Press*, Sept. 2, 1868.

20. As reported in fourteen sheets by an unidentified writer in the Stevens Papers. He states further that Stevens said: "I pursued and brought them to the door of the prison and then the Governor pardoned them out." For the press reports of this libel suit, see *American Sentinel*, August 31, 1840, and *Keystone*, January 30, 1841.

21. Letter to John T. Keagy, January 23, 1867, quoted in Hall, *Reminiscences*, p. 18.

22. February 15, 1868. Stevens Papers.

23. W. U. Hensel, "Thaddeus Stevens as a Country Lawyer," *op. cit.*, X:279.

24. Frederic W. Seward, ed., *William H. Seward: An Autobiography from 1801 to 1834*, pp. 89–91. See also Crane Brinton, *The Anatomy of Revolution*, pp. 53–54; Samuel F. Bemis, *John Quincy Adams and the Union*, p. 275ff.

25. Adams had been elected to Congress on the Antimasonic ticket in 1830. Stevens visited him on September 13, 1837. See Charles Francis Adams, ed., *Memoirs of John Quincy Adams*, IX:273, 372–373. See also Charles H. McCarthy,

The Antimasonic Party, p. 546.

26. Barnes, *The Fortieth Congress,* II:5.

27. Hall, *Reminiscences,* p. 14. Curiously, this is a hope Stevens could well have felt about himself.

28. *Pennsylvania House Journal,* January 11, January 21, 1836; also the *New York Herald,* April 8, 1868, where the incident was recalled.

29. Letter from Wm. D. Reid to Edward McPherson, January 13, 1869, Stevens Papers.

30. Stevens Papers, Vol. IX, no. 54503.

31. Quoted in the *Gettysburg Star,* February 28, 1835.

32. Quoted in Samuel G. Hefelbower, *The History of Gettysburg College, 1832–1932,* pp. 71–73.

33. *Pennsylvania Telegraph,* Harrisburg, January 25, 1834.

34. See *Pennsylvania House Journal,* 1834–1835; *Speech of Thaddeus Stevens on the School Law* . . . , a reprint of which, published in Lancaster in 1865, is in the Stevens Papers; see also John L. Rockey, "Pennsylvania's Free School Laws of 1834 and Their Great Defender, Thaddeus Stevens," *Lebanon County Historical Society Papers,* 1917, VII:363–369.

35. These Northeastern states required parents to pay a school tax in proportion to the number of children taught. See Allan Nevins, *Ordeal of the Union,* I:53.

36. *Speech of Thaddeus Stevens . . . bill to establish a School of Arts . . . ,* Stevens Papers; McClure, *Abraham Lincoln and Men of War-Times,* p. 263.

CHAPTER 5   *The Radical Beginnings*

1. Hood, *op. cit.,* pp. 21–22; also Hensel, *op. cit.,* X:269. Dickey's statement was made in the *Cong. Globe,* 40 Cong., 3 session, December 17, 1868, p. 131.

2. Salutatory of the *Liberator,* January 1, 1831. Until this year most abolitionist writing came from the pens of Charles Osborn or Benjamin Lundy, or Negro abolitionists like David Walker. See John Hope Franklin, *From Slavery to Freedom,* pp. 240, 246ff.

3. Wendell P. and Francis J. Garrison, *Wm. Lloyd Garrison, the Story of his Life as Told by His Children,* I:225; and Oliver Johnson, *Wm. Lloyd Garrison and His Times,* p. 408. David Donald, in his *Lincoln Reconsidered,* has a perceptive essay on the personal and social origins of antislavery leaders.

4. The *Gettysburg Compiler,* July 28, 1835.

5. Garrison's followers numbered only about one-eighth of the antislavery forces, according to Henry Wilson, *History of the Rise and Fall of the Slave Power in America,* II:718; see also Russel B. Nye, *Fettered Freedom, Civil Liberties, and the Slavery Controversy, 1830–1860,* p. 5.

6. Jonathan Blanchard, *Christian Cynosure,* September 22, 1868, I:9; Bedford, Pa., *Gazette,* June 22, 1838; Alexander McClure, *Old Time Notes of Pennsylvania,* I:32.

7. Blanchard told this story in detail in the *Christian Cynosure,* September 22, 1868, and December 29, 1868, Vol. I, nos. 3 and 10. Copies may be seen in the Wheaton College Library, Wheaton, Ill. He repeated the account in the same journal on April 5, 1883, a copy of which is in the Grand Lodge of Iowa's Masonic Library, Cedar Rapids, Iowa.

8. Nye, *Fettered Freedom,* p. 113. See the chapter, "Abolitionism and Freedom of the Press," for attempts of proslavery men to throttle the nation's newspapers, pp. 94–139.

9. Edward R. Turner, *The Negro in Pennsylvania, 1639–1861,* pp. 153, 160. But the laboring classes in the North were not at all anti-Negro; the textile-mill populations of New England were largely abolitionist. See Nye, *Fettered Freedom,* p. 246.

10. For Stevens' part in this fight, see Pennsylvania Constitutional Convention,

Proceedings and Debates, I:220; II:199–200, 243; III:160, 307, 546, 643, 693–694.

11. As described by Judge Black to Albert G. Riddle, in the latter's *Recollections of War Times, 1860–1865,* p. 32.

12. Blanchard's account was first published in the *Harrisburg Telegraph* and reprinted in the *Gettysburg Star,* May 15, 1837. Years later he repeated it in the *Christian Cynosure,* April 5, 1883. For another eye-witness description, see Woodward's account, *Cong. Globe,* 40 Cong., 3 session, Dec. 17, 1868, pp. 140–141.

13. *Bedford Gazette,* November 17, 1837.

14. W. J. Cash, *The Mind of the South,* pp. 88–89.

15. *Cong. Globe,* 36 Cong., 3 session, June 4, 1860, p. 2598; Samuel J. May, *Some Recollections of our Antislavery Conflict,* p. 135; Nye, *Fettered Freedom,* p. 144. Nye points out that public opinion in the North did not shift toward abolition till after 1840.

16. Horace Greeley, *The American Conflict, a History of the Great Rebellion in the United States of America, 1860–64,* I:115.

17. Pennsylvania Constitutional Convention, *op. cit.,* III:694.

18. *Ibid.,* I:547; II:243, 307; III:160, 546.

19. McClure, *Old Time Notes of Pennsylvania,* I:31, 171.

20. See Bray Hammond's brilliant analysis, *Banks and Politics in America,* pp. 286ff., 323–324, 406, 442–443. See also Arthur M. Schlesinger, Jr., *The Age of Jackson,* pp. 74ff.; Chas. G. Sellers, *James K. Polk, Jacksonian, 1795–1843,* pp. 168–232; Ralph C. H. Catterall, *The Second Bank of the United States.*

21. *Pennsylvania House Journal,* 1836–1837, II:745–757; *American Sentinel,* January 30, 1836. Bray Hammond (*Banks and Politics in America,* p. 535) called the conditions imposed by the State of Pennsylvania "outrageous."

22. See *Pa. Hse. Journal,* 1835–1837, II:769ff.; I:407; and Henry R. Mueller, *The Whig Party in Pennsylvania,* pp. 22ff.

23. McClure, *Old Time Notes of Pennsylvania,* I:226. Although when the bank ceased to be the national bank it had a surplus in excess of all losses of over six million dollars, mistakes made in the bank's lending policy from 1836 to 1841 brought about its ultimate collapse. Catterall, *The Second Bank of the United States,* pp. 363, 371; Hammond, *Banks and Politics in America,* pp. 500ff.

24. Pa. Const. Conv., *op. cit.,* I:546.

CHAPTER 6 *The Desperate Years*

1. McPherson Papers. See also Archer B. Hulbert, *The Great American Canals,* p. 176.

2. *Pennsylvania Telegraph,* October 1, 1838. Porter sued for libel after the election and was cleared of this slander.

3. For the House investigation of Stevens' tactics see *Pa. Hse. Jour.,* 1838–1839, Vol. II, Part 2, pp. 4–11, 78–79.

4. *Cong. Globe,* 40 Cong., 3 session, December 17, 1868, p. 141. See also *Pa. Senate Jour.,* 1838–1839, Vol. II, Part I, pp. 928, 975–976; and Mueller, *The Whig Party in Pennsylvania,* pp. 48–49.

5. McClure, *Old Time Notes of Pennsylvania,* I:49–50.

6. See press reports in *Pa. Senate Jour.,* 1838–1839, Vol. II, Part I, p. 806.

7. Pa. Const. Conv., *op. cit.,* III:654.

8. For the complete investigation, see *Pennsylvania Senate Journal,* 1838–1839, Vol. II, Part I, pp. 799ff., Part II, pp. 319–981; and *Pennsylvania House Journal,* 1839–1840, Part II, pp. 96ff. See also *Gettysburg Compiler,* January 11, 1839; Harris, *Review of the Political Conflict,* pp. 44ff.; McClure, *Old Time Notes,* I:47ff. Charles McCarthy, reviewing this episode in *The Antimasonic Party,* wrote that "there seems to be no doubt, however, of the culpability of the Democrats in causing the riot at Harrisburg and using illegal and extreme methods." See p. 501.

9. Quoted in the *Pennsylvania Reporter,* January 18, 1839, and Current, *Old Thad Stevens,* p. 69.

10. May 24, 1839. Stevens Papers.

11. Docket E., Clerk of Courts Office, County of Adams, Pa., April term, 1839. Commonwealth vs. Thaddeus Stevens. Fornication and Bastardy. True Bill. Recognizance of Thaddeus Stevens and Robert Smith forfeited. April 22, 1839.

12. Wm. Harlan Hale, *Horace Greeley, Voice of the People,* p. 317; *Gettysburg Sentinel,* May 28, 1839; Mueller, *The Whig Party in Pennsylvania,* p. 55.

13. Nicholas Biddle to Herman Cope, August 11, 1835, quoted in Schlesinger, Jr., *Age of Jackson,* p. 211.

14. McClure, *Old Time Notes of Pennsylvania,* I:74, and *Abraham Lincoln and Men of War-Times,* p. 283.

15. *American Sentinel,* August 31, 1840, and *Keystone,* January 30, 1841.

16. See R. N. Current, *Old Thad Stevens,* p. 75; see also T. F. Woodley, *Great Leveler,* p. 139.

17. Daniel Webster, *Writings and Speeches,* XVIII:97.

18. *Christian Cynosure,* November 3, 1868, I:21.

19. Stevens Papers.

20. George F. Miller in *Cong. Globe,* 40 Cong., 3 sess., December 17, 1868, p. 136; and James M. Scovel, "Thaddeus Stevens," *Lippincott's Magazine,* April 1898, LXI:548.

21. Interview with a *New York Tribune* correspondent, published in the *Washington Weekly Chronicle,* August 22, 1868.

22. Myra L. Dock, "Thaddeus Stevens as an Iron-Master," *Philadelphia Times,* July 14, 1895, a copy of which is in the Stevens Papers. See also Woodley, *Great Leveler,* p. 141; and Current, *Old Thad Stevens,* p. 81.

CHAPTER 7 *Lydia*

1. For Blanchard's reminiscences see *Christian Cynosure,* November 17, 1868, p. 26. See also Chas. I. Landis, "A Refutation of the Slanderous Stories against the Name of Thaddeus Stevens," *Lanc. Co. Hist. Soc. Papers,* March 1924, XXVIII: 49-52.

2. Thomas Dixon, Jr., *The Clansman, an Historical Romance of the Ku Klux Klan,* p. 57.

3. Hall, *Reminiscences,* p. 16.

4. *Albany Evening Journal,* quoted in the *Georgetown Courier,* August 22, 1868.

5. Landis, *op. cit.,* pp. 49-52.

6. See esp. Korngold, *Thaddeus Stevens,* p. 72ff.; also Woodley, *Great Leveler,* pp. 417-418. Current is somewhat more outspoken in *Old Thad Stevens,* p. 117.

7. According to the inscriptions on their tombstones in St. Mary's Catholic Cemetery, Lancaster.

8. The existence of the portrait was unknown to the public until 1913, when it fell into the possession of Redmond Conyngham. See W. U. Hensel, "Jacob Eichholtz, Painter," *Pennsylvania Magazine of History and Biography,* 1913, XXXVII:62. The late Mrs. Wm. H. Hager, who owned it for several years, only recently permitted it to be photographed by the Frick Art Reference Library, New York City, N. Y., by whose courtesy it is reproduced in this book.

9. November 25, 1862; June 26, 1864; April 1865. Stevens Papers.

10. Letter from Rev. George W. Brown, November 22, 1937, Elsie Singmaster Lewars Notebook No. 3.

11. Letter dated May 10, 1867, signed "On-the-Wing," Alabama *Union Springs Times,* June 12, 1867. July 24, the same correspondent, this time signing his name George M. Drake, gave further details of the interview, describing Mrs. Smith as Stevens' "yellow mistress." See also Chapter I, pp. 17-18.

12. Stevens Papers. This was printed in several New York and Pennsylvania

papers.

13. Schlesinger, *The Age of Jackson,* pp. 212–213.

14. *Christian Cynosure,* November 3, 1868, p. 21.

15. *Ibid.,* November 17, 1868, p. 26. Blanchard seems to have been in error in saying twenty-five years; twenty was more accurate.

16. *Estate of Thaddeus Stevens, Deceased,* Lancaster, 1893, pp. 21–25.

17. Hall, *Reminiscences,* p. 16, and Scovel, *op. cit.,* p. 550. Lydia Smith's eldest son, William, died on May 10, 1860, when he was twenty-five. The younger son, Isaac, who had grown up from babyhood in Stevens' back yard, at twenty seems to have incurred the old man's wrath. On November 9, 1867, he received a curt ultimatum from Stevens which said: "Sir, take notice that before Tuesday night next you have all your things away from my house and that you do not yourself enter my House during my absence to sleep or for any other purpose, under the penalty of being considered a Housebreaker." A copy of this found its way into the Stevens Papers. Isaac Smith died April 7, 1884.

18. Pa. Const. Conv., *op. cit.,* III:686.

19. See esp. *Cong. Globe,* 31 Cong., 1 sess., June 10, 1850, Appendix, I:767.

CHAPTER 8 *The Tyrant Father*

1. O. J. Dickey, *Cong. Globe,* 40 Cong., 3 sess., December 17, 1868, p. 130.

2. Harris, *A Review of the Political Conflict,* was published in New York in 1876. Hood's shorter "Thaddeus Stevens," appeared in 1872 as part of *A Biographical History of Lancaster County,* edited by Harris. Harris was extremely pro-Southern, deplored the freeing of the slaves, and dismissed Lincoln as "a tricky, jocular, village politician of mediocre capacity."

3. McPherson Papers, Box 60 B.

4. *Cong. Globe,* 37 Cong., 2 sess., April 28, 1862, p. 1851. The House Committee investigating war contracts accused Simon Stevens of purchasing 5,000 Hall carbines at $12.50 and selling them to General Frémont for $22 each. They had originally been sold by the Bureau of Ordinance to Arthur Eastmar at $3.50 each. He altered them at a cost of $.75 to $1.25 each, and then sold them to Simon Stevens for $12.50. 37 Cong., 2 sess., House Report No. 2, "Government Contracts," pp. 40–46, 242–248.

5. Stevens' foreman at the Caledonia Ironworks considered Simon Stevens a scoundrel. See his testimony in the court fight over Stevens's will, *Estate of Thaddeus Stevens,* Stevens Papers.

6. But not to be confused with his physician cousin of the same name in Indianapolis.

7. See Luke P. Poland, Repr. fr. Vermont, *Cong. Globe,* 40 Cong., 3 sess., December 17, 1868, p. 131; and letters from Sally Stevens in the Stevens Papers.

8. This letter, dated only March 26, and written in Littletown, N. H., is misfiled in the Stevens Papers, and for many years was mistakenly believed to have been written by the Elder Thaddeus Stevens. It was used as evidence that he was expelled from Dartmouth. See p. 27.

9. December 4, 1854. Stevens' letters to his nephew were first published in Woodley, *Great Leveler.* See pp. 182–184.

10. *Lancaster Intelligencer,* February 22, 1866.

11. October 25, 1894, McPherson Papers, Box 57.

12. *Appeal from the Orphan's Court . . . Estate of Thaddeus Stevens.*

13. Samuel P. Bates, *History of Pennsylvania Volunteers,* 1870, IV:56 and V:1291, gives the details of Thaddeus Junior's service. He was discharged as a Lt.-Colonel of the Emergency and State Militia Troops in 1863.

14. Burrowes, "Reminiscences," *op. cit.;* Hall, *Reminiscences,* p. 21.

15. *Cong. Globe,* 38 Cong., 1 sess., January 19, 1864, p. 270.

16. *Cong. Globe,* 37 Cong., 2 sess., March 20 and March 21, 1862, pp. 1313,

1327–1328.

17. Except where otherwise noted, the story of Mary Prim is derived from two documents: *Estate of Thaddeus Stevens, Deceased. Audit of Notes of Testimony*, and *Appeal from the Orphan's Court of Lancaster County, Estate of Thaddeus Stevens, Deceased*. Both are in the Stevens Papers, Box 57.

18. All the letters quoted in regard to this episode are in the Stevens Papers.

CHAPTER 9 *Congress and Compromise*

1. See the report of his Philadelphia campaigning in the *North American and Daily Advertiser*, Philadelphia, October 2, 1844.

2. Harris, *Review of the Political Conflict*, p. 503n.

3. The Silver Greys were regular Whigs; Woolly Heads were the antislavery or Conscience Whigs; and the Native Americans comprised a group with anti-foreign, chiefly anti-Catholic sentiments.

4. The census of 1850 listed 3,200,000 slaves. Samuel F. Bemis has pointed out that "Since the discovery of the New World, Christian slave-traders from Europe had taken a total of 24,000,000 persons out of Africa to the New World. Half of these died on the way—12,000,000 souls. . . . one of the greatest atrocities in modern history even when measured against the monstrous genocide of our own times." *John Quincy Adams and the Foundations of American Foreign Policy*, p. 412.

5. *Memoirs of John Quincy Adams*, IX:349. Both Adams and Jefferson had suggested constitutional amendments abolishing slavery. For a superb description of Adams' battle with the pro-slavery faction in Congress over the right of petition see Samuel F. Bemis, *John Quincy Adams and the Union*, Chapters 17, 18, 20. See also Gilbert H. Barnes, *The Antislavery Impulse, 1830–1844*, pp. 182ff; also George W. Julian, *The Life of Joshua R. Giddings*, pp. 243–244.

6. Speech at Peoria, Ill., October 16, 1854, in *Collected Works of Abraham Lincoln*, II:274, Roy P. Basler, ed.

7. Speech at Chicago, July 10, 1858; Basler, ed., *ibid.*, II:492.

8. As requoted in *Cong. Globe*, 36 Cong., 1 sess., January 25, 1860, p. 586.

9. Speech at Charleston, Ill., September 18, 1858; Basler, ed., *Collected Works*, III:181.

10. *Cong. Globe*, 31 Cong., 1 sess., App., 1:175, Feb. 19, 1850.

11. According to the U. S. Census, 10 per cent of the Negroes in the slave states were mulattoes, that is, persons with 50 per cent or more white blood, and in 1860, 12 per cent. See Kenneth M. Stampp, *The Peculiar Institution*, pp. 350–361, for a perceptive account of miscegenation under slavery. On the slave traffic, Stampp points out (p. 238) that between 1830 and 1860 Virginia exported nearly 300,000 slaves, almost the whole of her natural increase.

12. Mary B. Chesnut, *A Diary from Dixie*, the unexpurgated version edited by Ben Ames Williams, p. 21.

13. Fanny Kemble, *Journal of a Residence on a Georgia Plantation in 1838–39*, quoted in Herbert Aptheker's expertly documented *American Negro Slave Revolts*, p. 50. Aptheker defines a revolt as a minimum of ten slaves plotting for freedom, and counted 250 such conspiracies in the history of American Negro slavery. He points out that flight to the North drained off most potential leaders of insurrection, and that countless single acts of rebellion took place, consisting of stealing, arson, sabotage, neglecting or abusing farm animals, self-mutilation, suicide, and occasional murder. See also Stampp, *The Peculiar Institution*, pp. 91ff.

14. *Life and Times of Frederick Douglass, Written by Himself*, p. 148.

15. *Cong. Globe*, 31 Cong., 1 session, App. I:153. For a detailed and sympathetic examination of the Southern defense of slavery see esp. Avery Craven, *The Growth of Southern Nationalism, 1848–1860*, and Ulrich B. Phillips, *Life and Labor in the Old South*.

16. As Melville J. Herskovits, *The Myth of the Negro Past*, and John Hope

Franklin, *From Slavery to Freedom,* have expertly demonstrated.

17. W. E. B. DuBois has stated in *Black Reconstruction,* p. 638, that there were 3,651 Negro children in schools supported by free Negroes in the slave states.

18. August 1853. See Helen Catterall, ed., *Judicial Cases Concerning American Slavery and the Negro,* III:33. See also Nye, "Abolitionism and Academic Freedom," in *Fettered Freedom,* pp. 70–94.

19. For details of these laws see H. Catterall, *ibid.,* I:73, 276; II:480; III:3, 361–362, 655. See also Wm. S. Jenkins, *Pro-Slavery Thought in the Old South,* pp. 90, 105–106; and Stampp, *The Peculiar Institution,* pp. 233ff.

20. Stampp, *ibid.,* p. 235.

21. For complete text see *Cong. Globe,* 31 Cong., 1 sess., February 20, and June 10, 1850, App. I:141–143, 765–768.

22. *Cong. Globe,* 31 Cong., 1 sess., February 21, April 3, 1850, App. I:186, 407.

23. *Ibid.,* April 10, 1850, App. I:462.

24. *Ibid.,* June 10, 1850, App. I:766–767.

25. Quoted by John L. Rockey, *op. cit.,* 1917, VII:371.

26. *Cong. Globe,* 31 Cong., 1 sess., February 20, 1850, App. I:143. David M. Potter, in *Lincoln and His Party in the Secession Crisis,* p. 15, describes this tactic ironically: "Southerners threatened disunion, while their Northern partisans explained to the onlookers that a victory for their party would prevent any rupture. This little act always ended with Southern disunionists and Northern Union-savers walking off arm in arm, dividing the spoils. It had all the earmarks of a political confidence game."

27. *Cong. Globe,* 31 Cong., 1 session, February 13, 1850, App. I:154.

28. *Ibid.,* June 10, 1850, App. I:768.

29. October 6, 1847. Quoted in George W. Julian, *Life of Joshua R. Giddings,* p. 209. Julian, as Giddings' son-in-law, had access to his correspondence.

30. Basler, ed., *Collected Works,* II:318; letter from Springfield, Ill., to George Robertson of Lexington, Ky., August 15, 1855.

31. Benjamin Perley Poore, *Reminiscences of Sixty Years,* I:365. Claude M. Fuess, *Daniel Webster,* doubts the story's authenticity. George Ticknor Curtis, *Life of Daniel Webster,* II:403, states: "There was but little *written* preparation for it. All that remains of such preparation is on two small scraps of paper." Poore was a Washington journalist who became Clerk of the Senate and later editor of the *Congressional Globe.*

32. Most of this was edited out when the speech was printed in the *Congressional Globe.* One handbill printing some of these extracts was published by Allan Nevins in his *Ordeal of the Union,* I:295. For other extracts, see E. L. Pierce, *Memoir and Letters of Charles Sumner,* III:198.

33. W. U. Hensel, "Thaddeus Stevens as a Country Lawyer," *op. cit.,* X:276. See also Samuel H. Adams, *The Godlike Daniel,* p. 354.

34. *Cong. Globe,* 31 Cong., 1 session, June 10, 1850, App. I:768.

35. See Holman Hamilton, "Democratic Senate Leadership and the Compromise of 1850," *Mississippi Valley Historical Review,* XLI:403–418, December, 1954.

36. Robert E. Russel, "What was the Compromise of 1850?" *Journal of Southern History,* XXII:292–309, August 1956.

37. See Carl Schurz, *Henry Clay,* II:377–378. Webster followed Clay in threatening Whigs who would not support the compromise. See Nevins, *Ordeal of the Union,* I:350–351. For Sumner's statement, see E. L. Pierce, *Memoir and Letters of Charles Sumner,* III:295.

38. *Cong. Globe,* 31 Cong., 1 session, p. 1106.

CHAPTER 10 *Born Out of Violence*

1. Letter to Joshua F. Speed. Basler ed., *Collected Works,* II:321.

2. Nye, *Fettered Freedom,* p. 209. Nye reports that the *Anti-Slavery Bugle*

listed twenty-three kidnappings in 1846, and that after 1850 this number tripled.

3. Parker's account of what happened in the Christiana riot was published in "The Freedman's Story," *Atlantic Monthly,* February–March, 1866.

4. Quoted in Nevins, *Ordeal of the Union,* I:381.

5. Speech at Peoria, October 16, 1854. Basler, ed., *Collected Works,* II:268.

6. See U. S. Reports, Circuit Court, 3rd. Circuit. *Cases . . . reported by John W. Wallace,* United States v. Hanway, II:140–207; W. U. Hensel, "The Christiana Riot and the Treason Trials of 1851," *Lanc. Co. Hist. Soc. Papers,* 1911, XV:1–134.

7. C. F. Adams, *Richard Henry Dana,* I:182, quoted in Nevins, *Ordeal of the Union,* I:388.

8. February 16, 1851. John Weiss, *Life and Correspondence of Theodore Parker,* I:103.

9. *New York Tribune,* May 10, 1851, cited in Nevins, *Ordeal of the Union,* I:388. Nye, in *Fettered Freedom,* pp. 197–216, counted 81 "important cases" out of several hundred between 1850 and 1860. There are no certain statistics on the number of slaves who escaped annually from the South. The 1850 census listed 1,011 for that year; the 1860 census, 803. Allan Nevins, *Emergence of Lincoln,* App. V, p. 489, has estimated the monetary loss in 1860 as possibly $800,000. Stampp, *The Peculiar Institution,* p. 418, believes to be reasonable the estimate of a Southern judge in 1855 that the South had lost upwards of 60,000 slaves to the North.

10. T. Harry Williams, *Lincoln and the Radicals,* p. 66.

11. Letters of February 10, 1852; November 9, 1850; and December 8, 1854; Lieber Papers, Huntington Library. Hillard was bitterly anti-abolitionist.

12. Charles Sumner to George Sumner, November 15, 1848; Speech at Faneuil Hall, November 6, 1850; Theodore Parker to Charles Sumner, April 26, 1851; Charles Sumner to William Jay, February 19, 1850. All quoted or described in Pierce, *Memoir and Letters of Charles Sumner,* III:185, 212, 229, 250. The school fight is described in III:40–41.

13. *Cong. Globe,* 32 Cong., 2 session, March 3, 1853, p. 1164.

14. Speech at Faneuil Hall, November 2, 1855. Pierce, *op. cit.,* III:421.

15. August 24, 1855. Basler, ed., *Collected Works,* II:323.

16. This is attested by several contemporaries. See John W. Forney, *Address on Religious Intolerance and Political Proscription,* p. 47, and *Anecdotes of Public Men,* I:381; *Philadelphia Daily News,* September 30, 1854; *History of the Rise, Progress, and Downfall of Know-Nothingism in Lancaster County,* by Two Expelled Members; Alexander Harris, *op. cit.,* p. 164; and Oscar J. Harvey, *History of Lodge No. 61,* p. 86.

17. McClure, *Old Time Notes of Pennsylvania,* I:198, 209, 215. See also Nevins, *Ordeal of the Union,* II:398.

18. See House Executive Document No. 7, 36 Cong., 2 session, 648 pages dealing with this subject.

19. A. Lincoln, October 1, 1856, *Complete Works,* Nicolay and Hay, eds., 1905, II:304. Thaddeus Stevens, Speech at Cooper Institute, New York, September 27, 1860, Stevens Papers.

20. "Fragment on Formation of the Republican Party," February 28, 1857. Basler, ed., *Collected Works,* II:391. See also Wm. Starr Myers, *The Republican Party;* and Andrew W. Crandall, *Early History of the Republican Party.*

21. Cash, *The Mind of the South,* p. 43.

22. See George W. Julian, *Political Recollections, 1840 to 1872,* p. 173; and John F. Hume, *The Abolitionists . . . 1830–1864,* p. 13.

23. Hints of this feeling even among Northerners may be seen in the Francis Lieber-George Hillard correspondence in the Huntington Library. For the text of Sumner's Speech, see *Cong. Globe,* 34 Cong., 1 sess., App. pp. 530ff.

24. For a detailed description of this episode see 34 Cong., 1 session, House Committee Reports, I: No. 182; also the *New York Herald, New York Tribune,* and

New York Times for May 23, 1856; and Pierce, *op. cit.*, III:471ff.

25. Pierce, *ibid.*, III:487, 496.

26. *New York Tribune*, July 15, 1856.

27. Letter from Columbia, South Carolina. Lieber Papers, Huntington Library. The imputation that Sumner was a coward became a favorite Southern theme. Jefferson Davis reiterated it at a private party June 28, 1861, as reported by Mary Boykin Chesnut in her *Diary from Dixie*, pp. 71–72. It is still echoed by pro-Southern historians. See Avery Craven, *The Coming of the Civil War*, p. 367, and George Fort Milton, *The Eve of Conflict, Stephen A. Douglas and the Needless War*, pp. 231–236.

28. Quoted in Nevins, *Ordeal of the Union*, II:445.

29. Letter to N. W. Senior, June 22, 1858, from Paris, and letter to Samuel G. Howe, November 30, 1858, from Nismes, France. Huntington Library.

30. In a conversation with George William Curtis, reported in Pierce, *op. cit.*, III:524.

CHAPTER 11 *The Road to War*

1. See Chapter XII for further comment.

2. In 1848 Lincoln had written Stevens a deferential letter: "You may possibly remember seeing me at the Philadelphia Convention—introduced to you as the lone whig star of Illinois. Since the adjournment, I have remained here, so long, in the Whig document room. I am now about to start for home; and I desire the undisguised opinion of some experienced and sagacious Pennsylvania politican, as to how the vote of that state, for governor, and president, is likely to go. In casting about for such a man, I have settled upon you; and I shall be much obliged if you will write me at Springfield, Illinois." Basler, ed., *Collected Works*, II:1.

3. Footnote in the Ninian B. Edwards Papers, edited by Washburne, *Chicago Historical Society Collections*, 1884, III:246–247n.

4. Hale, *Horace Greeley, Voice of the People*, p. 193. See also Nevins, *Frémont, Pathmarker of the West*. The *Richmond Enquirer* slogan is quoted in Nye, *Fettered Freedom*, p. 20.

5. August 24, 1856. McPherson Papers.

6. *Cong. Globe*, 37 Cong., 2 sess., January 27, 1862, p. 495.

7. Hood, *op. cit.*, p. 576. This story was denied by Carpenter's daughter. See Claude Bowers, *The Tragic Era*, p. 221.

8. *Dollar Weekly Pennsylvanian*, October 18, 1856, quoted in Current, *op. cit.*, p. 106.

9. See Nevins, *Emergence of Lincoln*, I:176–197, for a discussion of the complicated causes of the Panic, also pp. 133–175, 229ff., for an analysis of the continuing Kansas problem.

10. See Nevins, *Emergence of Lincoln*, I:90ff., and Fred Rodell, *Nine Men, a Political History of the Supreme Court from 1790 to 1955*, p. 133.

11. Speeches of June 26, 1857; August 21, 1858; and September 15, 1858. Basler ed., *Collected Works*, II:403, III:27, III:130.

12. September 27, 1860. A reprint of this speech is in the Stevens Papers.

13. Speech at Springfield, Illinois, June 26, 1857, Basler, ed., *Collected Works*, II:401 and II:404. See also Lorenzo Sears, *Wendell Phillips*, p. 185.

14. October 15, 1858. John Bassett Moore, ed., *James Buchanan*, X:229.

15. Hensel, "Thaddeus Stevens as a Country Lawyer," *op. cit.*, X:275.

16. Address at Cooper Institute, N. Y., February 27, 1860; Basler ed., *Collected Works*, III:538.

17. Oswald Garrison Villard, *John Brown*, pp. 459, 496, 554.

18. Henry Thoreau, "Plea for Captain John Brown," October 30, 1859, in *A Yankee in Canada, with Anti-Slavery and Reform Papers*, pp. 155, 161; Wendell

Phillips, *Speeches, Lectures, and Letters,* speech of November 1, 1859; Thaddeus Stevens, *Cong. Globe,* 38 Cong., 2 sess., January 24, 1865, p. 400.

19. William Salter, *Life of James W. Grimes,* p. 121. There were said to be 300 loaded pistols in the hall and galleries of the House, according to Justin Morrill, "Notable Letters from My Political Friends," *Forum,* October, 1897, XXIV:141.

20. *Cong. Globe,* 36 Cong., 1 session, December 6, 1859, pp. 24–25. Stevens' reported "Saxon taunts" seem to have been edited out of the *Globe.* See also *New York Evening Post,* January 14, 1860, and Alfred R. Conkling, *Life and Letters of Roscoe Conkling,* pp. 96–97.

21. Memoir of Stevens, undated, in the Stevens Papers, Box 65-G. It is unsigned, but internal evidence indicates it was written by Galusha A. Grow. *Cong. Globe,* 36 Cong., 1 session, January 25, 1860, p. 586.

22. The fight took place during a debate on Kansas, February 6, 1860. See J. T. DuBois and G. S. Mathews, *Galusha A. Grow,* pp. 172–181.

23. *New York Tribune,* April 6, 7, and 17, 1860.

24. Julian, *Political Recollections,* p. 92. Congressman Haskell of Tennessee said Joshua Giddings should be "hanged as high as Haman." See also Julian, *Life of Joshua R. Giddings,* pp. 243–244.

25. A. G. Riddle, *The Life of Benjamin F. Wade,* p. 236; James M. Scovel, "Thaddeus Stevens," *Lippincott's Magazine,* April 1898, p. 550.

26. Speech of April 10, 1861, as reported in the *Charleston Mercury.* See Edward McPherson, *Political History of . . . the Great Rebellion,* p. 112; also David M. Potter, *Lincoln and His Party in the Secession Crisis,* p. 213.

27. See Murat Halstead, *Caucuses of 1860,* and Reinhard H. Luthin, *The First Lincoln Campaign,* p. 157.

28. Howard C. Perkins, *Northern Editorials on Secession,* I:9.

29. George T. Curtis, *Life of James Buchanan,* II:355.

30. Wm. Salter, *Life of James W. Grimes,* p. 132. This was a common Republican view. Kenneth Stampp, *And the War Came, the North and the Secession Crisis, 1860–1861,* pp. 48ff., has pointed out, however, that actually Buchanan's Union-saving efforts were not very different from Lincoln's before Sumter. For other detailed accounts of Buchanan in the crisis, see Roy F. Nichols, *The Disruption of American Democracy,* pp. 392ff., and Nevins, *Emergence of Lincoln,* II:360ff.

31. December 19, 1860. Stevens Papers.

32. See the Rodman Price letter in the Newark *Mercury,* April 4, 1861, quoted in Horace Greeley, *The American Conflict,* I:439; also the *New York Times,* January 8, 1861; Philip Foner, *Business and Slavery, the New York Merchants and the Irrepressible Conflict,* pp. 286–288; Howard C. Perkins, *Northern Editorials on Secession,* I:11, II:144–422.

33. George Fort Milton, *The Age of Hate, Andrew Johnson and the Radicals,* pp. 99, 101.

34. Stampp, *And the War Came,* p. 74.

35. Wendell Phillips, *Speeches,* pp. 347, 370; *Liberator,* January 4, 1861; and *New York Tribune,* November 9, 1860.

36. As Kenneth Stampp, in *And the War Came,* says, Sumner's attitude was "a kind of intellectual excursion into political theory." See Thurlow Weed's statement in the *Albany Evening Journal,* cited in the *New York Tribune,* November 27, 1860.

37. Basler, ed., *Collected Works,* IV:151. See also his letter to Lyman Trumbull, December 10, 1860, and to Representative Kellogg, Illinois member of the House Committee of Thirty-Three, December 11, 1860, with similar instructions.

38. *Cong. Globe,* 36 Cong., 2 session, January 29, 1861, p. 621.

39. *Ibid.,* pp. 621–624, and also for March 1, 1861, p. 1332.

40. *Ibid.,* February 20, 1861, II:1068; and Memoir of Galusha Grow, Stevens Papers, Box 65-G.

41. Chandler to Lyman Trumbull, November 17, 1860, Trumbull Papers; Grimes

to Samuel J. Kirkwood, January 28, 1861, quoted in Salter, *Life of James W. Grimes*, p. 136.

42. Pierce, *Memoir and Letters of Charles Sumner*, IV:17.

43. *Cong. Globe*, 36 Cong., 2 session, February 28, 1861, p. 1284. Lincoln had apparently suggested this amendment through Thurlow Weed. See his letter to Lyman Trumbull, December 21, 1860, Basler ed., *Collected Works*, IV:158; see also Stampp, *And the War Came*, p. 138.

44. The New Mexico territorial legislature had passed a slave code in 1859. Stevens deplored this code as "infamous" in the House, January 29, 1861. *Cong. Globe*, 36 Congress, 2 session, p. 515. The bill to admit New Mexico was tabled March 1861. The territory remained neutral through the war and repealed the slave code November 1861. See Loomis M. Ganaway, *New Mexico and the Sectional Controversy, 1846–1861*.

45. Speech to the Illinois Legislature, quoted in James G. Randall; and Richard N. Current, *Lincoln the President*, I:378.

46. *Cong. Globe*, 36 Cong., 2 session, January 29, 1861, p. 621.

47. Quoted in Horace Greeley, *The American Conflict*, I:417–418.

CHAPTER 12   *Stevens and Lincoln—the Secession Crisis*

1. McClure, *Lincoln and Men of War-Times*, p. 260.

2. Forney, *Anecdotes of Public Men*, I:37.

3. Quoted in Emanuel Hertz, *The Hidden Lincoln, from the Letters and Papers of Wm. H. Herndon*, p. 230.

4. *Cong. Globe*, 40 Cong., 3 session, December 17, 1868, p. 149; Carl Schurz, *Reminiscences*, III:215.

5. *Lincoln and Men of War-Times*, p. 262. This is in striking contrast with judgments of some revisionist historians, like Claude Bowers who, in *The Tragic Era, the Revolution after Lincoln*, p. 25, called Stevens Lincoln's "most inveterate foe."

6. See especially T. Harry Williams, *Lincoln and the Radicals*.

7. Quoted in David Donald, *Lincoln Reconsidered*, pp. 121–122.

8. McClure, *Lincoln and Men of War-Times*, pp. 256–258.

9. Stevens Papers. See also Lee F. Crippen, *Simon Cameron, Ante-Bellum Years*, p. 231.

10. January 19, 1861. Robert T. Lincoln Collection, Library of Congress.

11. Chase Papers, Historical Society of Pennsylvania. For Lincoln's letter to Cameron, January 3, 1861, see Basler, ed., *Collected Works*, IV:169, 174.

12. *Cong. Globe*, 37 Cong., 2 session, April 28, 1862, pp. 1852–1853.

13. Samuel W. McCall, *Thaddeus Stevens*, pp. 311–312.

14. *Cong. Globe*, 40 Cong., 3 session, December 18, 1868, p. 145.

15. McClure, *Lincoln and Men of War-Times*, p. 261.

16. *Cong. Globe*, 37 Cong., 2 session, April 28, 1862, pp. 1852–1853.

17. Albert G. Riddle, *Recollections of War Times, 1860–1865*, p. 180.

18. By March 29, however, only Seward and Caleb Smith held out for evacuation. Scott, who had urged the re-enforcement of Sumter on Buchanan, now indicated he would prefer four separate confederacies to the horrors of civil war. See Stampp, *And the War Came*, pp. 51, 274–278; Roy F. Nichols, *The Disruption of American Democracy*, p. 502; Laura A. White, "Charles Sumner and the Crisis of 1860–61," *Essays in Honor of Wm. E. Dodd*, Avery Craven, ed. Even Lincoln seems to have considered evacuating Sumter if it would ensure Virginia's adherence to the Union. See Randall and Current, *Lincoln the President*, I:326.

19. *Cong. Globe*, 36 Cong., 2 session, February 20, 1861, II:1068; Stevens Papers, No. 54913, June 24, 1868. Andrew Johnson, alone among Southern senators, looked upon the secessionists as traitors. "Were I the President of the United States," he said on March 2, 1861, ". . . I would have them arrested, and, if convicted, within the meaning and scope of the Constitution, by the Eternal

God I would execute them." *Cong. Globe,* 36 Cong., 2 session, II:1354. See also Stampp, *And the War Came,* p. 269.

20. Riddle, *Recollections of War Times,* p. 43.

21. *Cong. Globe,* 37 Cong., 1 session, July 4, 1861, p. 415.

22. McClure, *Lincoln and Men of War-Times,* p. 265; the *Nation,* August 20, 1858.

23. *Cong. Globe,* 37 Cong., 3 session, February 28, 1863, p. 1418.

24. *Cong. Globe,* 37 Cong., 1 session, July 10, 1861, p. 54; July 11, 1861, pp. 54, 72; July 25, 1861, p. 267; July 27, 1861, p. 307. The *New York Times* on July 12, 1861, reported Stevens' urging Congress "to give everything the government asks."

25. *Cong. Globe,* 37 Cong., 1 session, July 29, 1861, p. 325.

26. *Cong. Globe,* 38 Cong., 1 session, April 11, 1864, June 2, 1864, March 21, 1864, pp. 1535, 2693, 1223.

27. *New York World,* August 13, 1868.

28. See *Cong. Globe,* 36 Cong., 2 session, January 29, 1861, p. 624.

29. As reported in the *New York Herald,* July 8, 1867. For Lincoln's proclamation of blockade, April 19, 1861. See Basler ed., *Collected Works,* IV:338–339.

30. *Cong. Globe,* 37 Cong., 1 session, July 4, 1861, pp. 414–415.

31. Nicolay and Hay, *Abraham Lincoln, a History,* VIII:34.

CHAPTER 13 *Stevens, Lincoln, and the Negro*

1. Cable, *The Negro Question,* p. 24.

2. Quoted in Hofstadter, *American Political Tradition,* p. 129.

3. *Cong. Globe,* 37 Cong., 1 session, July 4, 1861, p. 415.

4. As reported by Charles Edward Lester, quoted in Carl Sandburg, *Abraham Lincoln, The War Years,* I:356–357.

5. Basler, ed., *Collected Works,* IV:506. In December 1861, when Cameron without consulting Lincoln recommended in his official War Department Report that the slaves of the rebels be freed and armed, Lincoln had the reports returned and reprinted with the offending paragraph modified.

6. The slaves were to be paid for in government bonds. Two-thirds of the border-state members of Congress rejected the scheme. For the whole story of this struggle, see Henry Wilson, *History of the Antislavery Measures of the Thirty-seventh and Thirty-eighth United States Congresses, 1861–64.*

7. *Cong. Globe,* 37 Cong., 2 session, March 11, 1862, p. 1154; March 12, 1862, pp. 1199–1200.

8. *Cong. Globe,* 37 Cong., 2 session, April 11, 1862, p. 1643. Stevens "moved the laying aside successively of each bill preceding it on the calendar, and thus reached this one." Henry Wilson carried it through the Senate. Horace Greeley, *The American Conflict,* II:259; Isaac N. Arnold, *The Life of Abraham Lincoln,* p. 243.

9. *Cong. Globe,* 37 Cong., 2 session, May 9, 1862, p. 2054.

10. Quoted in Major-General Oliver O. Howard, *Autobiography,* II:174.

11. Oliver O Howard, *Autobiography,* II:167. Cornelia Hancock, a nurse in the Army of the Potomac, writing from the "contraband hospital," reported as late as January 20, 1864, that "a sort of second hand slavery has been going on some time." *South After Gettysburg,* p. 40.

12. Don C. Seitz, *Lincoln the Politician,* p. 333.

13. Basler, ed., *Collected Works,* V:388–389.

14. Stevens Papers.

15. To Sergeant J. L. Stradling, in the presence of Ben Wade and others; Sandburg, *Abraham Lincoln, the War Years,* II:84. Thurlow Weed, who was afraid of emancipation, wrote to John Bigelow December 19, 1862: "I labored earnestly with Mr. Lincoln against this Proclamation." Bigelow, *Retrospections of an Active*

Life, I:580.

16. Isaac Arnold, *Life of Lincoln*, p. 251.

17. As recounted in the Chase Diary, September 22, 1862. See David Donald, ed., *Inside Lincoln's Cabinet, the Civil War Diaries of Salmon P. Chase*, p. 150. See also Gideon Welles, *Diary*, I:143.

18. *Lancaster Intelligencer*, September 23, 1862.

19. *Cong. Globe*, 37 Cong., 3 session, January 8, 1863, p. 243.

20. *Cong. Globe*, 37 Cong., 2 session, July 5, 1862, p. 3127. See also Dudley T. Cornish, *The Sable Arm, Negro Troops in the Union Army, 1861–1865*, pp. 98–99.

21. See especially Chase's diary of July 22, 1862, in Donald, ed., *op. cit.*, pp. 96–99, 100. Governor Kirkwood's statement was quoted in Wm. B. Hesseltine, *Lincoln and the War Governors*, p. 203.

22. Speech in Pennsylvania reported in the *New York Tribune*, September 11, 1862. See also Benjamin Quarles, *The Negro in the Civil War*, pp. 183ff.; and Cornish, *The Sable Arm*, pp. 33ff.

23. By the end of the war there were 178,895 colored troops, and perhaps 300,000 other Negroes were utilized as laborers. Lincoln admitted later that "without the military help of black freedmen, the war against the South could not have been won." See Carter G. Woodson, *The Negro in Our History*, p. 373; W. E. B. DuBois, *Black Reconstruction*, p. 716; and Dudley T. Cornish, *The Sable Arm*. More than 38,000 Negro soldiers lost their lives in the Civil War. John Hope Franklin, *From Slavery to Freedom*, p. 290.

24. *Cong. Globe*, 38 Cong., 1 session, April 30, 1864, p. 1995.

25. Welles, *Diary*, I:152.

26. August 25, 1862. Salmon P. Chase Papers, Historical Society of Pennsylvania.

27. According to Sumner's friend, C. Edwards Lester, as quoted in Sandburg, *Abraham Lincoln, the War Years*, I:578.

28. From the *New York Tribune*, August 15, 1862; see also Basler, ed., *Collected Works*, V:371–372.

29. *Life and Times of Frederick Douglass*, p. 422; Douglass, "Lincoln and the Colored Troops," in Allen T. Rice, *Reminiscences of Abraham Lincoln*, p. 322.

30. To James Redpath, who reported it to a journalist on the *Springfield Republican*, quoted in Sandburg, *Abraham Lincoln, the War Years*, I:578.

31. *Cong. Globe*, 38 Cong., 1 session, January 7, 1864, p. 133.

32. As late as 1865 he asked Benjamin F. Butler to study the question of deportation. "If these black soldiers of ours go back to the South," he said, "I am afraid that they will be but little better off with their masters than they were before, and yet they will be free men. I fear a race war, and it will be at least a guerilla war because we have taught these men how to fight." *Autobiography . . . of Benjamin F. Butler*, p. 903.

33. Sandburg, *op. cit.*, I:523; W. L. Fleming, *General W. T. Sherman as a College President*, p. 88.

34. See Kenneth P. Williams, *Lincoln Finds a General*, and T. Harry Williams, *Lincoln and His Generals*. For a pro-Southern discussion of McClellan's political attitudes see Avery Craven, *The Coming of the Civil War;* H. J. Eckenrode, *McClellan, the Man Who Saved the Union;* and Warren W. Hassler, *General George B. McClellan, Shield of the Union.*

35. *War of the Rebellion, Official Records of the Union and Confederate Armies*, series i, II:48–49; Welles, *Diary*, I:107.

36. *Cong. Globe*, 37 Congress, 2 session, July 5, 1862, p. 3125.

37. O. O. Howard, *Autobiography*, II:172; Sandburg, *op. cit.*, I:512, 561.

38. Kenneth P. Williams, *Lincoln Finds a General*, I:250; Horace Greeley, *The American Conflict*, II:248–249.

39. *Cong. Globe*, 37 Cong., 2 session, May 6, 1862, p. 1956.

40. John Hay's Diary for September 25, 1864, in Tyler Dennett, ed., *Lincoln and the Civil War in the Diaries and Letters of John Hay*, pp. 218–219.

41. *The Life of Thurlow Weed*, Vol. II, *Memoir*, p. 401, edited By Thurlow

Weed Barnes. Even the Democratic *New York World* on December 14, 1861, demanded confiscation of at least two-thirds of each rebel estate, one third to be given to Union soldiers, and the other third to the Negroes.

42. *Cong. Globe,* 37 Cong., 2 session, p. 3127.

43. Wendell Philips, speech at Cooper Institute, New York, December 22, 1863, quoted in the *Liberator,* January 1, 1864.

44. Julian, *Political Recollections,* pp. 212–220.

45. *Cong. Globe,* 38 Cong., 1 session, January 22, 1864, and May 2, 1864, pp. 316, 2041.

CHAPTER 14 *Economic Heretic*

1. See especially T. Harry Williams, *Lincoln and the Radicals,* p. 5. Thomas J. Pressly has written a brilliant analysis of the great complex of American attitudes toward the causes of the Civil War. For his discussion of the economic causes, with special emphasis on Beard, Parrington, and the neo-Marxists, and the subsequent reaction against them, see his *Americans Interpret Their Civil War,* pp. 195ff.

2. McClure, *Old Time Notes of Pennsylvania,* I:413; and George Fort Milton, *Eve of Conflict,* pp. 488–490. Philip S. Foner, in *Business and Slavery: the New York Merchants and the Irrepressible Conflict,* amassed facts showing that most merchants in New York, Boston, and Philadelphia were in favor of compromise up to the day Sumter was shelled. As Allan Nevins, in *Ordeal of the Union,* II:244, concluded after examining the accumulated evidence, "Northern and Southern merchants, manufacturers, and railroad men struggled almost to the last against sectional disseverance. . . . The war was caused primarily by social, moral, and political, not economic forces." See also Stampp, *And the War Came,* pp. 7, 9–10.

3. Roger Shugg has pointed out that in Louisiana the plantation system not only survived but actually expanded after the Civil War. "By 1900 the plantations had multiplied to embrace over half the landholdings in the state. . . . This agrarian monopoly was more harmful to the welfare of Louisiana than all the political evils of reconstruction government." *Origins of Class Struggle in Louisiana, a Social History of White Farmers and Laborers during Slavery and after,* pp. 241, 262.

4. A good many Negroes went to Liberia in 1866 and 1867, their passage paid by colonization societies. About 2,500 went from South Carolina alone. But their letters back to America were so discouraging that few followed. See Francis B. Simkins and Robert H. Woody, *South Carolina During Reconstruction,* p. 234, and Robert S. Henry, *The Story of Reconstruction,* p. 176.

5. Edward S. Stanwood, *American Tariff Controversies in the 19th Century,* II:127, 153.

6. In the Robert Todd Lincoln Papers there is a letter from Samuel Reeves of March 8, 1864, reporting a meeting of the ironmasters in Philadelphia protesting the possible appointment of Robert Walker as Secretary of the Treasury on the grounds that he was a free-trader. Stevens forwarded this to Lincoln with the comment, "This is the universal feeling in Pennsylvania."

7. *Cong. Globe,* 37 Cong., 2 session, June 25, 1862, p. 2939.

8. For Spaulding's own account, see his *History of the Legal Tender Paper Money Issued during the Great Rebellion.* See also Don Carlos Barrett, *The Greenbacks and Resumption of Specie Payments, 1862–1879;* Robert T. Patterson, *Federal Debt-Management Policies, 1865–1879;* Davis R. Dewey, *Financial History of the United States,* pp. 272ff.; and especially Wesley Clair Mitchell, *A History of the Greenbacks . . . 1862–65.*

9. *Cong. Globe,* 38 Cong., 2 session, February 28, 1865, p. 1202, a review of past policy.

10. Milton Friedman has pointed out that the full price rise (as measured by the monthly wholesale price indexes) was almost identical in the three wars, prices

at the peak being 2.1 to 2.3 times their level at the war's beginning. Money income in the Civil War rose at approximately the same or a somewhat higher rate than prices. In the Confederacy, on the other hand, the general price index rose 92 times its prewar base. See Milton Friedman, "The Role of War in American Economic Development," *American Economic Review*, XLII, May 1952, p. 613; and Eugene M. Lerner, "Money, Prices, and Wages in the Confederacy," *Journal of Political Economy*, LXIII, February 1955, p. 24. I am greatly indebted to Andrew W. Marshall of the Economics Department of the Rand Corporation for detailed advice on the economic analysis in this chapter.

11. It was not, of course, as impressive as that of World War II, when three-fifths of the federal expenditures came from tax receipts. In World War I the figure was two-fifths. See Friedman, *op. cit.*, p. 615, and D. R. Dewey, *op. cit.*, p. 299.

12. For his speech on this issue see *Cong. Globe,* 37 Cong., 2 session, February 8, 1862, p. 689.

13. *Cong. Globe,* 37 Cong., 2 session, February 20, 1862, p. 900.

14. *Cong. Globe,* 37 Cong., 3 session, February 24, 1863, p. 1261.

15. Frank B. Carpenter, *The Inner Life of Abraham Lincoln; Six Months at the White House,* p. 84. The Confederates also blamed their own inflation on the speculators in the South. See E. M. Lerner, *op. cit.*, p. 37.

16. *Cong. Globe,* 37 Cong., 3 session, December 23, 1862, and January 20, 1863, pp. 145, 411. See also Wesley C. Mitchell, *A History of the Greenbacks,* pp. 183, 193.

17. See Milton Friedman, *op. cit.*, p. 623. The total supply of money increased in the Civil War only about $1.50 for each $1.00 created directly by the government. World War I saw an increase of $8, and World War II of $5.50. This was due to a variety of causes, including the smaller use of credit and checks in Civil War Times, and to the fact that expansion then was considered more dangerous than it was later.

18. *Cong. Globe,* 38 Cong., 1 session, March 16, 1864, pp. 1145, 1147.

19. This letter was published in the *New York Tribune,* January 20, 1895.

20. Chase to Stevens, June 29, 1864. Robert Todd Lincoln Papers. Chase resigned the next day.

21. *Cong. Globe,* 38 Cong., 1 session, June 23, 1864, p. 3213. See also James G. Blaine's analysis, *Cong. Globe,* 38 Cong., 2 session, December 6, 1864, p. 5.

22. *Cong. Globe,* 38 Cong., 1 session, March 16, 1864, p. 1145; and 38 Cong., 2 session, February 7, 1865, p. 652.

23. As reiterated by Stevens, *Cong. Globe,* 38 Cong., 2 session, January 5, 1865, p. 117.

24. Chauncey W. Ford, ed., *A Cycle of Adams Letters, 1861–1865,* II:232.

25. *Cong. Globe,* 38 Cong., 2 session, January 5, 1865, p. 118.

26. "In my judgment this whole national banking system was a mistake," Stevens said in 1866. "I thought so at the time it was adopted, and I think so still. I think every dollar of paper circulation ought to be issued by the Government of the United States." *Cong. Globe,* 39 Cong., 1 session, July 25, 1866, p. 4153. See also Robert T. Patterson, *op. cit.*, p. 28; Don C. Barrett, *op. cit.*, p. 130; and D. R. Dewey, *op. cit.*, pp. 320ff.

27. *Cong. Globe,* 37 Cong., 3 session, December 23, 1862, p. 146.

28. On July 7, 1868, Stevens said in the House that no honest Secretary of the Treasury would ever pay the debts in anything but lawful money rather than coin. *Cong. Globe,* 40 Cong., 2 session, July 7, 1868, p. 3768.

29. *New York Tribune,* July 6, 1868; *Cong. Globe,* 40 Cong., 2 session, July 17, 1868, p. 4178.

30. Thus avoiding the great error of Britain in returning to the gold standard at pre-war values too soon after World War I. For a concise analysis of the arguments for and against contraction of the currency see D. R. Dewey, *Financial*

History of the United States, pp. 338ff.

31. As reported by the *Baltimore American,* quoted in Carl Sandburg, *op. cit.,* III:150. See also Lloyd Stryker, *Andrew Johnson,* p. 245.

32. The two letters, dated July 6 and July 11, 1863, are in the Stevens Papers.

33. Quoted in the *Washington Weekly Chronicle,* August 22, 1868.

34. See the explicit letter of Stevens on this point in the *Lancaster Intelligencer,* June 4, 1867, quoted in Thomas Woodley, *op. cit.,* p. 359. See also Myra Lloyd Dock, "The Caledonia Furnace, relics and recollections of Thaddeus Stevens in the Iron Country," *Philadelphia Times,* July 14, 1895. A copy is in the Stevens Papers. Stevens' difficulties in getting credit to rebuild his furnaces are hinted at in a letter from his contractor, R. A. Ahl, May 5, 1866, now in the Stevens Papers. It is quoted in part in R. N. Current, *op. cit.,* pp. 246–247n.

35. *Cong. Globe,* 39 Cong., 1 session, April 27, 1866, p. 2241.

36. *Cong. Globe,* 37 Cong., 2 session, May 5, 1862, pp. 1949–1950.

37. See Gaillard Hunt, *Israel, Elihu and Cadwallader Washburne;* George Julian, *Political Recollections,* p. 98; and Thomas Weber, *The Northern Railroads in the Civil War, 1861–1865.* The land-grant policy, which gave alternate sections of land along the route, began with a grant to the Illinois Central Railroad in 1850.

38. See his review, *Cong. Globe,* 40 Cong., 2 session, March 20, 1868, pp. 2135–2137, and March 26, 1868, App. pp. 294ff. See also Elihu Washburne's attack, *Cong Globe,* 38 Cong., 1 session, May 16, 1864, p. 3152.

39. *Cong. Globe,* 38 Cong., 1 session, May 16, May 31, 1864, pp. 2296, 2612.

40. Quoted in Edwin L. Sabin, *Building the Pacific Railway,* p. 130.

41. *Cong. Globe,* 40 Cong., 2 session, March 20, March 26, 1868, pp. 2135, 2137, and App. p. 297. See also U. S. Congress, 42 Congress, 3 session, Senate Report No. 519, Credit Mobilier, p. 106.

42. U. S. Congress, 42 Congress, 3 session, House Report No. 77, Credit Mobilier Investigation (the Poland Report), pp. 88, 421.

43. For Oliver Ames' testimony see U. S. Congress, 42 Congress, 3 session, House Report No. 78, Credit Mobilier and the Union Pacific Railroad (Wilson Report), pp. 301–303. For Thomas C. Durant's testimony see *ibid,* p. 522, and U. S. Cong., 42 Cong., 3 session, House Report No. 77 (Poland Report), pp. 385–386. Durant said under oath: "I deny ever having stated to Mr. Alley that I paid Mr. Thaddeus Stevens any money whatever. . . . I never paid or promised to pay Mr. Stevens any sum of money whatever, or any stock, bonds, or other property. I may have stated that a section introduced by Mr. Stevens, and insisted upon by him in his committee, in the amendment of 1864, had cost this company even a larger sum of money than that named." Stevens' primary interest, Durant indicated, had been to protect the United States Government, and Stevens had ordered him to adjust matters so "as to convince him that the Government lien would be what it purported to be," or else he would "insist upon a clause that would protect the Government." Durant then went on to admit that in adjusting local railroad rivalries "a large amount of money was used." He insisted that he had never purchased any property from Stevens nor had he authorized anyone else to. "I said that I was offered by a broker some land property up in Pennsylvania, but that I would not go into the iron trade." When asked if he knew whether or not Stevens was a stockbroker, he replied that he did not know, but could not know for sure, as there were two or three million dollars' worth of stock floating about.

Durant, more than any other one man, had been responsible for the stupendous achievement of the Union Pacific road. Despite lawsuits, charges of embezzlement, and continual legal feuding with his colleagues, the Ames brothers and John Alley, he had built with a furious obsession for speed and little regard to cost, spending his own and the government's money with extravagant abandon.

44. Dickey, who had been Stevens' law partner at one time, stated that Stevens had always asked $160,000 for the Caledonia property. ". . . we are now negotiating its sale for $130,000, and we have not sold it yet." He listed some national bank stock, Cumberland coal stock and Lancaster turnpike stock, as well as $14,600

worth of Kansas Pacific Railroad bonds, which had been received from John F. Cowan for the sale of a $20,000 tract of Stevens' land. Since the land title had proved dubious, this stock had been returned to Cowan at a loss of several thousand dollars to Stevens' estate.

In addition to the real estate Stevens had $48,616.85, Dickey said, against which there were debts amounting to $20,000. He was certain Stevens had no private bank account save the one in Lancaster. This he had checked for the years 1861 to Stevens' death. "I do not find any deposit in that bank account exceeding ten thousand dollars, with a single exception, and that was the proceeds of a mortgage that he put upon his farm in Franklin County." The largest credits in his account came from the sale of coal lands Stevens had purchased before 1842. U. S. Cong., 42 Cong., 3 session, House Report No. 78, pp. 676–677. The official auditor's report of Stevens' estate, made in 1893, listed small holdings in the Northern Central Railroad and Pennsylvania Railroad. See *Estate of Thaddeus Stevens deceased . . . Auditor's Report*, April 29, 1893.

45. He tried to sell them to Simon Cameron. See his letter of May 10, 1864, in the Simon Cameron Papers, Library of Congress, quoted in part in R. N. Current, *op. cit.*, p. 193.

46. McPherson Papers, Box 60-B. Stevens' foreman, John Sweeney, June 18, 1878, wrote a letter to Edward McPherson calling Simon Stevens "a noted scoundrel." McPherson Papers, Box 61-C.

47. This and other letters were published by McComb in the *New York Sun*, Sept. 4, 1872. This started the Congressional investigation.

48. From April 1867 to December 1869 Credit Mobilier declared dividends of 615% in Union Pacific stock, 280% in Union Pacific first-mortgage bonds and 60% in cash. See David S. Muzzey, *James G. Blaine*, p. 68n, and U. S. Congress, 42 Congress, 3 session, House Report No. 77, p. 40. See also House Report No. 78 and Senate Report No. 519 for this session.

49. Scovel, *op. cit.*, LXI, April 1898, p. 547.

50. Henry L. Dawes, G. W. Scofield, John A. Bingham, William D. Kelley, James A. Garfield, and Henry Wilson were all absolved from any corrupt motive or purpose, though it was generally agreed that they had acted with indiscretion. Others, like George Boutwell, had been approached by Ames but had refused the bait. James Brooks, Oakes Ames, and Senator Patterson were deeply committed and were formally censured by the House and Senate. Brooks and Ames both died within six weeks after the censure vote. Schuyler Colfax, the Vice-President, foolishly lied about his stockholdings, and though not censured, lost his reputation permanently. The Wilson and Hoar Committee concluded that the cost of the Union Pacific Railroad had been $50,000,000, of which the builders received in cash as profit at least $23,000,000. See U.S. Congress, 42 Congress, 3 session, House Report No. 77 and No. 78, and Senate Report No. 519.

51. *Cong. Globe*, 39 Congress, 1 session, July 5, 1866, p. 3587.

52. The critical votes came on March 26 and May 12, 1868. See *Cong. Globe*, 40 Cong., 2 session, pp. 2130, 2428.

53. The *Nation*, October 17, 1867, V:315.

CHAPTER 15 *The Jacobins*

1. The *Nation*, July 2, 1868, VII:4.

2. *American Political Tradition*, pp. 133, 137–138. The agitator, Hofstadter says in reappraising the role of Wendell Phillips, is always vulnerable, but is, nevertheless, "necessary to a republican commonwealth; he is the counterweight to sloth and indifference."

3. This was the platform Phillips ran on in September 1870, when campaigning for Governor of Massachusetts. Lorenzo Sears, *Wendell Phillips*, p. 293.

4. Letter of Wm. H. Herndon to Jesse W. Weik, February 5, 1887, quoted in *The Hidden Lincoln*, Emanuel Hertz, ed., p. 165.

5. *New York World,* March 5, 1868.

6. *Cong. Globe,* 38 Cong., 2 session, January 24, 1865, p. 400.

7. *New York World,* August 13, 1868.

8. Poore, *Reminiscences,* II:43–36.

9. Scovel, *op. cit.,* p. 549, and *Georgetown Courier,* August 22, 1868. For a perceptive study of the psychological gratifications of gambling, see Ralph Greenson, "On Gambling," *Yearbook of Psychoanalysis,* 1948, IV:110–123.

10. Speech before the Democratic Union Association, New York, January 13, 1863, quoted in Samuel S. Cox, *Eight Years in Congress, from 1857–1865,* pp. 286–290. For the striking similarity between the attitudes of many War Democrats and Copperheads and modern "revisionist" historians on this point see Thomas J. Pressly, *Americans Interpret Their Civil War.*

11. *Richmond Examiner,* September 17, 1863; July 8, 1861.

12. Quoted in G. C. Gorham, *Life and Public Services of Edwin M. Stanton,* I:430–431.

13. The *Nation,* August 30, 1866, III:131; Ignatius Donnelly, Representative from Minnesota, *Cong. Globe,* 40 Cong., 3 session, December 17, 1868, p. 139.

14. The *Liberator,* May 16, 1864, December 29, 1865.

15. George H. Haynes, *Charles Sumner,* p. 394.

16. Quoted in Sandburg, *op. cit.,* IV:80.

17. Sears, *op. cit.,* pp. 249–250.

18. For extracts from Blair's speech at Rockville, Maryland, see Wm. E. Smith, *The Francis Preston Blair Family in Politics,* II:228, 238, 269. Blair, according to Nicolay and Hay in *Abraham Lincoln, a History,* IX:340, "wearied the President by insisting upon it that all the leading Republicans were Lincoln's enemies." Senator Wilson wrote to Lincoln on September 5, 1863 (*Ibid.,* IX:339), "Blair everyone hates."

19. The letter to Chase, October 8, 1863, is in the Stevens Papers. The letter to Sumner, dated October 9, 1863, is in the Sumner Papers, Harvard Library.

20. The *Liberator,* June 21, 1864.

21. Several unwary Republican Congressmen endorsed a pamphlet, put out as a hoax early in 1864 by two Democratic New York newspapermen, advocating amalgamation. The Democrats made much political capital out of this. See especially the speech of Representative Samuel S. Cox of Ohio, *Cong. Globe,* 38 Cong., 1 session, pp. 709–712.

22. Letters of July 10, 1860, and July 31, 1862, quoted in W. E. Woodward, *Meet General Grant,* p. 181.

23. *Cong. Globe,* 38 Cong., 1 session, p. 709.

24. *Cong. Globe,* 37 Cong., 2 session, February 24, 1862, pp. 917–918.

25. *Cong. Globe,* January 7, 1864, p. 133; January 5, 1865, p. 125.

26. Speech at Charlestown, Illinois, September 18, 1858. Basler, ed., *Collected Works,* III:145–146.

27. Charles Sumner managed to push these bills through the Senate only by fastening them as riders to appropriation bills, and Stevens had real difficulty getting them through the House. See Henry Wilson, *History of the Antislavery Measures of the Thirty-Seventh and Thirty-Eighth Congress, 1861–64,* for complete details.

28. Basler ed., *Collected Works,* VII:243. Letter dated March 13, 1864.

29. See Basler, ed., *Collected Works,* VIII:403, for his last address, April 11, 1865; and *ibid.,* VII:101–102, for letter to General Wadsworth.

30. Shelby M. Cullom, *Fifty Years of Public Service,* p. 152. See also David Donald, *Lincoln Reconsidered,* pp. 115–127.

31. Letter of May 30, 1864, to the Owen Lovejoy Monument Association, quoted in Frank B. Carpenter, *The Inner Life of Abraham Lincoln,* p. 160, and Basler, ed., *Collected Works,* VII:366–367.

32. Nicolay and Hay, *Abraham Lincoln,* IX:113, and Tyler Dennet, ed., *Lincoln and the Civil War in the Diaries and Letters of John Hay,* November 8, 1864, p. 235.

33. According to John Hay. Quoted in Sandburg, *op. cit.*, III:118. No one has documented the difficulties of Lincoln with the Committee on the Conduct of the War better than Harry Williams, *Lincoln and the Radicals*. Unfortunately, Williams gives the erroneous impression that almost all the Radical Republicans were Lincoln's inveterate enemies.

34. Quoted in Frank Flower, *Edwin McMasters Stanton*, pp. 369-370.

35. See Pierce, *op. cit.*, IV:111, and Charles Sumner to W. W. Story, December 16, 1866, Huntington Library.

36. Stevens Papers.

37. Albert G. Riddle, *Life of Benjamin F. Wade*, p. 273n. Payne is also spelled Paine.

38. Quoted in full in Nicolay and Hay, *Abraham Lincoln, a History*, VII:389. Basler, *op. cit.*, VII:23-24, quotes the Chandler letter in part and the Lincoln reply in full.

39. Basler, *ibid.*, VII:514, quotes Lincoln's memorandum concerning his probable failure.

40. According to Chase, who told Frank B. Carpenter. See Carpenter, *Inner Life of Abraham Lincoln*, p. 38.

41. Isaac N. Arnold, *Life of Abraham Lincoln*, p. 385n.

42. The full details of the Pomeroy Circular were not released till J. M. Winchell, who was the actual author of the circular, described them in a letter to the *New York Times*, September 15, 1874.

43. Nicolay and Hay, *Abraham Lincoln, a History*, IX:367; *Lancaster Intelligencer*, August 18, 1864. On January 24, 1865, Stevens said in the House: "Sir, I venture to declare this day, notwithstanding the recent defeat of General Butler, that if the question could be put to the loyal people of these United States whom they would select for their next President, a majority of them would vote for General Butler." *Cong. Globe*, 38 Cong., 2 session, I:400. Two years later Stevens dismissed Butler as "a false alarm, at once superficial, weak and impracticable. Indeed a 'humbug.' " See his frank interview in the *New York Herald*, July 11, 1867. Still, he cooperated freely with Butler in the impeachment trial of Andrew Johnson in 1868.

44. Quoted in Randall and Current, *Lincoln the President*, IV:225.

45. Carl Schurz, *Reminiscences*, III:101; Wilmer C. Harris, *Public Life of Zacahariah Chandler*, p. 80.

46. *Lancaster Intelligencer*, September 15 and October 13, 1864.

47. Shelby M. Cullom, *Fifty Years of Public Service*, pp. 98-99.

48. Hugh McCulloch, *Men and Measures of Half a Century*, p. 162.

49. Dennett, ed., *Lincoln and the Civil War in the Diaries and Letters of John Hay*, September 30 and October 28, 1863, pp. 97, 108.

CHAPTER 16 *The End of Slavery*

1. James Truslow Adams, *The Epic of America*, p. 275; and Claude G. Bowers, *The Tragic Era, the Revolution after Lincoln*, p. 67.

2. James G. Randall, *The Civil War and Reconstruction*, p. 146; George Fort Milton, *The Age of Hate, Andrew Johnson and the Radicals;* T. Harry Williams, *Lincoln and the Radicals*, p. 371.

3. David Donald, *Lincoln Reconsidered*, p. 126, says: "To picture Lincoln at swords' points with the Radical leaders of his own party, then, is an error. It is also a reflection of a naive view of the nature of American politics. American Presidents are always criticized by members of their own parties. . . . There were pro-Lincoln Radicals and anti-Lincoln Radicals, just as there were pro-Lincoln Conservatives and anti-Lincoln Conservatives."

4. Sumner, July 21, 1863. E. L. Pierce, *op. cit.*, IV:143.

5. Chandler to Trumbull, August 6, 1863, Trumbull Papers, Library of Congress.

6. Basler, ed., *Collected Works*, VII:51; Dennett, *Lincoln and the Civil War in*

the Diaries and Letters of John Hay, pp. 131–132.

7. George Boutwell, *Reminiscences,* II:43; *Cong. Globe,* 38 Cong., 1 session, March 26, 1864, p. 1296.

8. Noah Brooks, *Abraham Lincoln,* p. 402.

9. *Cong. Globe,* 38 Cong., 2 session, January 5, 1865, p. 124.

10. Letter to A. G. Hodges, April 4, 1864, Basler, ed., *Collected Works,* VII:281–282; speech of March 4, 1865, *ibid.,* VIII:333.

11. Arnold, *Life of Lincoln,* pp. 363–364.

12. *Cong. Globe,* 38 Cong., 2 session, January 13, 1865, pp. 265–266.

13. Scovel, *op. cit.,* p. 550.

14. February 1, 1865. "George W. Julian's Journal," *Indiana Magazine of History,* December 1915, XI:327.

15. Basler, ed., *Collected Works,* VIII:254; and Frank B. Carpenter, *The Inner Life of Abraham Lincoln,* p. 90.

16. *Cong. Globe,* 38 Cong., 2 session, January 13, 1865, pp. 265–266.

CHAPTER 17   *Blueprints for Utopia*

1. Basler, ed., *Collected Works,* VII:53–56.

2. *Cong. Globe,* 38 Cong., 1 session, January 22, 1864, pp. 317–318.

3. Basler, ed., *Collected Works,* VII:169, February 5, 1864.

4. *Ibid.,* VII:433.

5. July 10, 1864. Stevens Papers.

6. April 11, 1865. Basler, ed., *Collected Works,* VIII:402–403.

7. *Cong. Globe,* 39 Cong., 1 session, December 18, 1865, p. 73.

8. H. K. Beale, ed., "The Diary of Edward Bates, 1859–1866," American Historical Association, Annual Report, 1930, IV:362.

9. *Cong. Globe,* 37 Cong., 3 session, December 9, 1862, p. 50.

10. *Cong. Globe,* 39 Cong., 1 session, December 18, 1865, p. 74. Stevens figured that the slaves had provided nineteen representatives, and free blacks five more.

11. John Sherman to Wm. Sherman; R. S. Thorndike, ed., *Sherman Letters,* p. 251.

12. Tyler Dennett, ed., *John Hay Diary,* p. 113; and Basler, ed., *Collected Works,* VII:51, for Message to Congress.

13. Letter to Major-General Stephen A. Hurlbut, November 14, 1864. Basler, ed., *Collected Works,* VIII:107.

14. Horace, White, *Life of Lyman Trumbull,* p. 243.

15. "I would myself prefer that it were now conferred on the very intelligent, and on those who serve our cause as soldiers." April 11, 1865, Basler, ed., *Collected Works,* VIII:403.

16. W. W. Holden, *Memoirs,* p. 144; and Benjamin B. Kendrick, *Journal of the Joint Committee of Fifteen on Reconstruction,* p. 370. "Forty acres of land and a hut would be of more value to him than the immediate right to vote," he said in Congress May 8, 1866. *Cong. Globe,* 39 Cong., 1 session, p. 2459.

17. Douglass' speech before the American Anti-Slavery Society, reported in the *Liberator,* January 29, 1864.

18. Undated letter just after Lee's surrender, in the Sumner Mss., Huntington Library.

19. April 11, 1865, Basler, ed., *Collected Works,* VIII:404.

20. Robert Todd Lincoln Papers, Library of Congress.

21. Sandburg, *op. cit.,* IV:58.

22. *Cong. Globe,* 38 Cong., 2 session, February 10, 1865, p. 733.

23. Undated letter just after Lee's surrender, Huntington Library.

24. First printed in the *Galaxy,* April 1872, pp. 525–527.

25. Pierce, *op. cit.,* IV:243.

26. John W. Forney, *Anecdotes of Public Men,* I:38.

27. See Stevens' letter to Mrs. C. C. Clay, July 24, 1865, published in *Lancaster Historical Society Papers*, 1913, XVII:162–163; the interview of Frank A. Burr with Jefferson Davis first published in the *Philadelphia Press*, July 10, 1881; and a letter from Wm. D. Reid to Edward McPherson, January 13, 1869, in which Reid said, ". . . Mr. Stevens was willing and anxious to take part in the defence of Mr. Davis the President of the late Confederate States. I was the recipient of a message to that effect." Stevens Papers.

28. Frank A. Burr, "Jefferson Davis, the Ex-Confederate President at Home," *Philadelphia Press*, July 10, 1881, later reprinted in *Tyler's Quarterly Historical and Genealogical Magazine*, January 1951, pp. 170–180.

29. *Cong. Globe*, 40 Cong., 1 session, July 9, 1867, p. 546.

30. William H. Crook, *Through Five Administrations*, p. 28.

31. Welles, *Diary*, II:237; and Nicolay and Hay, *Abraham Lincoln*, X:133.

32. *Cong. Globe*, 40 Cong., 2 session, July 16, 1868, p. 4136.

CHAPTER 18 *The Tailor in the White House*

1. As quoted by the *Nation* in a description of Andrew Johnson, May 1, 1866, p. 554.

2. According to S. F. Barr. See C. E. Hamlin, *Life and Times of Hannibal Hamlin*, p. 472.

3. Carl Schurz, who visited him in Nashville, later wrote: "To hear him expatiate upon this, his favorite theme, one would have thought that if this man ever came into power, the face of the country would soon bristle with gibbets . . ." *Reminiscences*, III:97. See also George Fort Milton, *Age of Hate, Andrew Johnson and the Radicals*, pp. 111ff.

4. George F. Milton, *Age of Hate*, p. 96.

5. Clement Eaton, *Freedom of Thought in the Old South*, p. 75.

6. Quoted in A. Harris, *op. cit.*, p. 430.

7. Quoted by William G. Brownlow, *Americanism Contrasted with Foreignism, Romanism, and Bogus Democracy*, pp. 22–23. Brownlow, who later became a Radical Republican, was at this time an ardent propagandist for slavery.

8. *Cong. Globe*, 36 Cong., 2 session, p. 769. In a speech in the Senate on December 19, 1860, he had said: "I want to maintain and retain my place here and put down Mr. Lincoln and drive back his advances upon the Southern institutions, if he designs to make any." *Cong. Globe*, 36 Cong., 2 session, p. 139.

9. Quoted in Bower, *The Tragic Era*, p. 34.

10. *Cong. Globe*, 32 Cong., 1 session, May 6, 1852, p. 1278.

11. See the letter criticizing Johnson on this issue from Major-General John M. Palmer, Chattanooga, December 18, 1863, quoted in White, *Life of Trumbull*, p. 214.

12. McClure, *Old Time Notes of Pennsylvania*, I:141. For a detailed discussion of Lincoln's ambiguous role in choosing his vice-president, see Randall and Current, *Lincoln the President*, IV:130–136. There is some evidence that he considered also General Benjamin F. Butler. See Butler's *Autobiography*, p. 633.

13. As reported to Henry L. Dawes, who told it to Hamlin's grandson, April 18, 1896. See C. E. Hamlin, *op. cit.*, p. 480.

14. G. F. Milton, *Age of Hate*, p. 58.

15. For a carefully documented study of the inauguration see G. F. Milton, *Age of Hate*, pp. 145ff. Milton did his best to destroy the legend that Johnson was a drunkard. But it should be noted that Johnson's private secretary, Benjamin C. Truman, wrote in his memoirs, "He did take two or three or four glasses of Robertson County whisky some days; some days less, and some days and weeks no liquor at all." "Anecdotes of Andrew Johnson," *Century Magazine*, January 1913, Vol. 85, p. 438.

16. As reported by the correspondent of the *London Times*, March 20, 1865, the

dispatch dated Washington, March 7, 1865. Johnson's own corrected and expurgated version was published in the *Cong. Globe*, 38 Cong., 2 session, II:1393-1395, March 3, 1865.

17. *New York Herald*, March 6, 1865, and Welles, *Diary*, March 4, 1865, II:252.

18. C. E. Hamlin, *op. cit.*, pp. 498, 505; John W. Forney, *Anecdotes of Public Men*, I:177.

19. *Diary from Dixie*, May 16, 1865, p. 390.

20. "George W. Julian Journal," *Indiana Magazine of History*, December 1915, XI:334. These men had received a garbled account of Lincoln's order to General Weitzel to permit the reassembling of the Virginia Legislature, and were fearful lest Lincoln recognize the rebel legislature. Actually Lincoln had never intended such recognition. See his telegram to General Weitzel, April 12, 1865, in Basler, *op. cit.*, VIII:406-407; also Flower, *Edwin M. Stanton*, p. 272, and Donald, ed., *Inside Lincoln's Cabinet, the Civil War Diaries of Salmon P. Chase*, p. 268.

21. *Cong. Globe*, 40 Cong., 1 session, March 19, 1867, pp. 207-208.

22. "George W. Julian Journal," *op. cit.*, XI:335, and Julian, *Political Recollections*, pp. 255, 257; and *New York Tribune*, April 17, 1865. In defiance of all these facts, the MGM moving picture, *Tennessee Johnson*, portrayed Johnson at this period as a man urging forgiveness and conciliation.

23. See Raoul Naroll, "Lincoln and the Sherman Peace Fiasco—another Fable?" *Journal of Southern History*, November 1954, XX:459-483.

24. As described by George Shea in a letter of January 15, 1876, quoted in Varina Davis, *Jefferson Davis . . . a Memoir by His Wife*, II:782. Shea was informed in March 1866 that Stevens had volunteered as a counsel for Clay.

25. As reported in the *New York Times*, May 4, 1865.

26. Johnson Papers, Vol. 63.

27. E. L. Pierce, *op. cit.*, IV:241, 267-268.

28. Benjamin F. Perry, *Reminiscences of Public Men*, p. 235; and W. W. Boyce, "President Johnson's Policy of Reconstruction," *DeBow's Review*, January 1866, I:18, 24.

29. May 10, 1865, Sumner Papers, Harvard Library.

30. James G. Blaine, *Twenty Years of Congress*, II:76. According to Francis B. Simkins and Robert H. Woody, *South Carolina during Reconstruction*, p. 269, the $20,000 clause excepted 4,418 citizens in South Carolina, Virginia, Georgia, and North Carolina.

31. Quoted in G. F. Milton, *Age of Hate*, p. 183.

32. Stanton, who deliberately withheld Booth's diary, though it contained evidence that would have saved Mrs. Surratt, seems to have been equally culpable with Holt. See the evidence George Fort Milton unearthed concerning this episode. *Age of Hate*, pp. 201-212. The Stevens statement was made in an interview with George M. Drake, May 3, 1867, printed in *Union Springs Times* (Alabama), July 24, 1867.

33. Whitelaw Reid, *After the War*, p. 304.

34. Boutwell, *Speeches and Papers*, p. 546.

35. Johnson Papers, Vol. 70. Stevens complained of Johnson's failure to reply in a letter to Sumner, August 26, 1865. Sumner Papers, Harvard Library.

36. Basler, ed., *Collected Works*, VI:440.

37. Letter to General James W. Wadsworth, Basler, ed., *Collected Works*, VII:101-102. Italics added.

38. See the *Charleston Daily Courier*, March 8, 1865; Edward McPherson, *Political History of the United States during Reconstruction*, p. 40; and Boutwell, *Speeches and Papers*, p. 524.

39. Letter to Governor William L. Sharkey, August 15, 1865, published in Edward McPherson, *A Political Manual for 1866*, p. 19.

40. *Life and Times of Frederick Douglass*, p. 370.

41. Sumner Papers, Harvard Library.

42. *Nation*, November 23, 1865, I:646.

43. Benjamin F. Perry, *Reminiscences,* p. 282.

44. *Journal of the Constitutional Convention of 1865,* Georgia, p. 38, quoted in H. J. Pearce, *Benjamin H. Hill,* p. 118.

45. See Milton, *Age of Hate,* pp. 251–256; W. E. B. DuBois, *Black Reconstruction,* pp. 260–261; and James W. Garner, *Reconstruction in Mississippi,* p. 120.

46. Quoted in the *Nation,* August 10, 1865, I:162.

47. Reid's dispatches were collected in *After the War.* See p. 51.

48. Fernand Baldensperger, ed., *American Reconstruction, 1865–1870,* p. 35. This is a reprint of Clemenceau's dispatches to the Paris *Temps.*

49. See especially the minutes of the special meeting of the American Anti-Slavery Society, January 24, 1866, reported in the *National Anti-Slavery Standard,* February 3, 1866.

50. October 7, 1865. Sumner Papers, Harvard Library.

51. "Diary of Edward Bates," *op. cit.,* IV:512.

52. Referring, of course, to James Buchanan. A copy of this eighteen-page speech may be seen in the Stevens Papers.

CHAPTER 19 *Stevens Views the South*

1. *The Portable Faulkner,* p. 145.

2. John Eaton, *Grant, Lincoln and the Freedmen,* p. 2. The mortality rate was appalling; some Union Army officers placed it as high as 25 per cent. See John Hope Franklin, *From Slavery to Freedom,* p. 271.

3. O. O. Howard, speech at Cooper Union Institute, as reported in *DeBow's Review,* March 1866, p. 324; John W. DeForest, *A Union Officer in the Reconstruction,* J. H. Croushore and D. M. Potter, eds., p. 36.

4. U. S. Congress, 39 Congress, 1 session, House Report No. 30, *Report of the Joint Committee on Reconstruction,* Part IV, p. 37, 1866.

5. Cash, *The Mind of the South,* p. 113.

6. General Howard was Lincoln's choice, though he was not officially installed by Stanton till after Lincoln's death. Howard's *Autobiography* gives a superb picture of the immediate postwar freedmen problems. See especially II:194ff. The speech quoted here was reported in *DeBow's Review,* March 1866, p. 324.

7. Milton, *Age of Hate,* p. 287.

8. As reported in *DeBow's Review,* March 1866, p. 324.

9. Letter from Fisk, Assistant Commissioner in Kentucky and Tennessee, to General Howard. U. S. Congress, 39 Congress, 1 session, 1865–1866. Executive Document No. 27, *Reports of Assistant Commissioners of the Freedmen's Bureau,* p. 6.

10. U. S. Congress, 39 Congress, 1 session, Senate Executive Document No. 2, *Condition of the South,* 1866, p. 17. In Mississippi in 1865 a group of planters seriously planned fighting emancipation through the use of the courts. In remote areas slavery persisted months after the war's end. See Vernon L. Wharton, *The Negro in Mississippi, 1865–1890,* p. 48.

11. Whitelaw Reid, who toured the South with Chief Justice Chase in 1865, pointed out in *After the War,* p. 474, that the rice crop, which in 1860 had been a quarter of a million casks, in 1865 was only seven thousand.

12. Mary Ames, *A New England Woman's Diary in Dixie in 1865,* p. 62.

13. Paul S. Peirce, *The Freedmen's Bureau;* F. B. Simkins and R. H. Woody, *South Carolina during Reconstruction,* pp. 227ff.

14. Howard, *Autobiography,* II:188–189.

15. DeForest, *op. cit.,* pp. 80, 99. DeForest, a distinguished novelist, was an unusually acute observer, and a lively, eloquent writer.

16. Testimony of J. W. Shaffer, January 17, 1866, U. S. Congress, 39 Congress, 1 session, House Report No. 30, *Report of the Joint Committee on Reconstruction,* Part IV, p. 52. See also V. L. Wharton, *op. cit.,* pp. 80ff.

17. For a complete printing of the black codes see U. S. Congress, 39 Congress, 2 session, Senate Executive Document No. 6, *Freedmen's Affairs,* pp. 170–230.

18. George W. Cable, *The Negro Question,* p. 34.

19. Carl Schurz, *Reminiscences,* III:215.

20. Welles, *Diary,* December 3, 1865, II:387.

21. *Cong. Globe,* 39 Cong., I session, December 4, 1865, p. 3ff.

22. Howell Cobb to his wife, December 7, 1865. American Historical Association, Annual Report, 1911, II:672; "The Diary of Edward Bates, 1859–1866," *op. cit.,* 1930, IV:523; December 12, 1865. C. R. Williams, ed., *Diary and Letters of Rutherford B. Hayes,* III:9–10, December 7, 1865.

23. Francis Fessenden, *Life and Public Services of Wm. Pitt Fessenden,* II:21.

24. Theodore Tilton in the *Independent,* April 12, 1866.

25. Seymour vs. McCormick, 16 Howard, 480. They obtained for Cyrus McCormick a decision upholding the validity of his reaper patent.

26. *Cong. Globe,* 39 Cong., 1 session, March 1, 1866, II:1123.

27. *Cong. Globe,* 39 Cong., 1 session, January 11, 1866, p. 203.

28. Testimony of Judge John C. Underwood, *Report of the Joint Committee on Reconstruction,* 39 Congress, 1 session, House Report No. 30, II:7; and testimony of Jaquelin M. Wood, *ibid.,* II:86.

29. Letter from Thompson Powell, Halifax County, Virginia, February 22, 1866. Stevens Papers.

30. Testimony of General George A. Custer, *Report of the Joint Committee on Reconstruction,* 39 Congress, 1 session, House Report No. 30, IV:72; James H. Mathews to Major George D. Reynolds, *ibid.,* III:184–185. On the basis of such reports the *New York Tribune* estimated on March 4, 1867, that 5,000 Negroes had been murdered in the South in the twenty months following the end of the war.

31. *Report of the Joint Committee on Reconstruction,* 39 Congress, 1 session, House Report No. 30, III:104–105.

32. DeForest, *A Union Officer in the Reconstruction,* p. 153.

33. J. W. Alvord, in *Report of the Joint Committee on Reconstruction,* 39 Congress, 1 session, House Report No. 30, II:246–256. Carter G. Woodson, in *The Negro in Our History,* p. 386, noted that the Bureau later officially reported the establishment of 4,329 schools with 247,333 students in the first year after the war.

34. *Report of the Joint Committee on Reconstruction,* IV:64, II:183, III:141.

35. *Ibid.,* IV:134.

36. Quoted in Whitelaw Reid, *After the War,* p. 411. It is impossible to get accurate figures on the decline of the black population during 1865. James W. Garner, using the U. S. Census of 1860 and a special state census in Mississippi in 1866, brought out these astonishing figures: whereas in six years the white population had decreased from 353,899 to 343,400, a loss of 10,499, the colored population had dropped from 437,404 to 381,258, a loss of 56,146—about five times as much. See *Reconstruction in Mississippi,* p. 124. The U. S. Census of 1870 revealed that the colored population of the U. S. had increased only 9.21 per cent between 1860 and 1870, whereas between 1850 and 1860 the slave population had increased 23.39 per cent and the free colored 12.33 per cent. White population from 1860 to 1870 had increased 24.39 per cent, but this included immigration. Carl Schurz wrote later that he believed more Negroes were killed in 1865 than in any year thereafter, including the worst years of the Ku Klux Klan.

37. In a widely reported conversation with Judge Wardlaw. See Benjamin F. Perry, provisional governor of South Carolina, *Reminiscences of Public Men,* p. 250. Johnson actually was apprenticed at fourteen, not ten. See Milton, *Age of Hate,* p. 62.

CHAPTER 20   *The Open Rupture*

1. *Cong. Globe,* 39 Cong., 1 session, December 21, 1865, and January 16, 1866, pp. 116, 255.

2. *Cong. Globe,* 39 Cong., 1 session, December 18, 1865, p. 74.

3. General Wager Swayne worked out a satisfactory agreement in Georgia by promising to transfer all causes for court action to state tribunals in return for the admission of the testimony of Negroes. The results of a similar arrangement in Mississippi were not good, however, "owing to the strong indigenous prejudice against negroes as witnesses." Major-General Oliver O. Howard, *Autobiography,* II:253–254.

4. About 4,000 Negro families were eventually settled on public land in Missouri, Mississippi, Arkansas, and Florida. Paul S. Peirce, *The Freedman's Bureau,* p. 131.

5. Mary Ames in her *Diary from Dixie* gives a moving account of the Negro reaction to the return of the planters on the sea islands. See pp. 96–97 of the *Diary.*

6. *Cong. Globe,* 39 Cong., 1 session, February 5, 1866, p. 658. Eighty years later the U. S. Government met with no opposition at home when it ordered the Japanese Government to break up Japan's landed estates. Five million acres were purchased and eighty per cent of the lands under tenant cultivation offered for resale to the tenants. Thus ninety per cent of Japan's former tenant farmers became landowners. *New York Times,* Section E, January 16, 1955, p. 9.

7. Basler, ed., *Collected Works,* VII:145. Italics added.

8. As pointed out by the *Nation,* January 25, 1866, II:98.

9. *Cong. Globe,* 39 Congress, 1 session, December 18, 1865, pp. 72–75; January 31, 1866, p. 537.

10. Quoted in McPherson, *Political History of Reconstruction,* p. 123.

11. *Cong. Globe,* 39 Cong., 1 session, December 18, 1865, pp. 74–75.

12. Clemenceau, *American Reconstruction,* p. 62. In his first Message to Congress, written in collaboration with George Bancroft, Johnson had not directly opposed Negro suffrage, but had indicated that the matter must be left to the individual states. See Milton, *Age of Hate,* p. 272.

13. *Cong. Globe,* 39 Congress, 1 session, January 31, 1866, pp. 536–537; *Harper's Weekly,* February 17, 1866, March 10, 1866, pp. 99, 146.

14. See Benjamin B. Kendrick, *Journal of the Joint Committee of Fifteen,* pp. 20–88. Stevens always favored delay, but nevertheless worked closely with the committee getting the proper wording for the bill to admit Tennessee.

15. Speech in Cleveland, September 3, 1866. McPherson, *Political History of Reconstruction,* p. 136.

16. *New York Tribune,* March 3, 1866.

17. Quoted in Reid, *After the War,* p. 574.

18. It is clear to anyone who reads carefully the *Journal of the Joint Committee of Fifteen* that the Committee was not controlled by the Radical faction until after the veto of the Freedmen's Bureau bill.

19. *Cong. Globe,* 39 Congress, 1 session, February 20, 1866, p. 945.

20. *Cong. Globe,* 38 Congress, 1 session, February 3, 1864, p. 469.

21. *Cong. Globe,* 39 Cong., 1 session, February 15, 1866, pp. 858–859.

22. McPherson, *Political History of Reconstruction,* p. 72.

23. Carl Schurz, *Reminiscences,* III:227; James R. Doolittle to O. H. Browning, October 7, 1866, quoted in J. G. Randall, ed., *Diary of Orville H. Browning,* II:93n.

24. The *Chicago Times* was quoted in *Harper's Weekly,* April 14, 1866; see also the *Lancaster Intelligencer,* February 23, 1866.

25. Quoted by Senator John B. Henderson, *Cong. Globe,* 39 Cong., 1 session, May 1, 1866, III:2309.

26. *Cong. Globe,* 39 Congress, 1 session, March 10, 1866, II:1308. A modern unfriendly critic of Stevens, Lloyd Paul Stryker in *Andrew Johnson, a Study in Courage,* p. 286, oddly described this scene as possessing "the distinction that might have been discovered in a longshoremen's saloon, where some great bully bleary-eyed held the floor evoking the ribald guffaws of his submissive listeners."

27. The *Nation,* March 16, 1866; "The President on the Stump," *North American Review,* April 1866, Vol. 102, p. 533.

CHAPTER 21   *The Rump Parliament*

1. Welles, *Diary*, March 9, 1866, II:447; *Cong. Globe*, 38 Cong., 1 session, April 21, 1864, p. 1795.

2. *Cong. Globe*, 40 Cong., 3 session, December 18, 1868, p. 148.

3. Ellis, *Sights and Secrets of the National Capital*, p. 147.

4. *Galaxy*, July 15, 1866, I:495.

5. McClure, *Abraham Lincoln and Men of War-Times*, pp. 258–259.

6. *Nation*, November 30, 1867, p. 755.

7. Wm. E. Smith, *The Francis P. Blair Family in Politics*, II:216, 375.

8. Lowell, "The Seward-Johnson Reaction, 1866," *Political Essays*, p. 279.

9. Douglass said this in a public reply to Andrew Johnson, following a private interview with the President in Washington, February 7, 1866. See *Life and Times of Frederick Douglass*, p. 392.

10. Welles, *Diary*, March 23, 26, 1866, II:460–461, 463–464.

11. *Cong. Globe*, 39 Cong., 1 session, April 4, 1866, II:1760.

12. July 8, 1866. Thorndike, ed., *Sherman Letters*, p. 276. Wm. M. Stewart, Senator from Nevada, wrote: "He assured me by all that he held sacred that if his veto of the Freedmen's Bureau bill was sustained he would sign the Civil Rights bill." *Reminiscences*, pp. 199–200.

13. For the veto message see McPherson, *Political History of Reconstruction*, pp. 74ff.

14. E. L. Pierce, *op. cit.*, IV:288.

15. John Lothrop Motley, *Complete Works*, XVII:102.

16. Carl Schurz, *Reminiscences*, III:216.

17. *Cong. Globe*, 39 Congress, 1 session, April 5, 1866, II:1786.

18. Letter to the *Nation*, April 12, 1866. The Civil Rights bill frightened South Carolina into modifying her black code. Georgia, urged by Alexander Stephens, passed what was by Southern standards a liberal civil-rights resolution in March, 1866. Tennessee passed an identical one later.

19. *Sherman Letters*, p. 269.

20. Taylor, *Destruction and Reconstruction*, p. 326.

21. Cullom, *Fifty Years of Public Service*, p. 145.

22. This clipping, with a note from William Wilder, is in the Stevens Papers.

23. General Grant had opposed the use of colored troops to police the South, pointing out that they "must be kept in bodies sufficient to defend themselves." 39 Congress, 1 session, Senate Executive Document No. 2, 1866, "Condition of the South," pp. 106–108.

24. See U. S. Congress, 39 Congress, 1 session, House Report No. 101, "Memphis Riots and Massacres." E. B. Washburne, J. M. Broomall, and G. S. Shanklin interviewed 170 witnesses, and took a 2,000-page manuscript record of the hearings.

25. *Cong. Globe*, 39 Cong., 1 session, May 8, 1866, p. 2459. It is generally forgotten that Stevens had the support of the Conservative Republican leaders, Senator Fessenden and James G. Blaine, who were also active in 1866 devising plans to guarantee Negro suffrage. See John M. Mathews, *Legislative and Judicial History of the Fifteenth Amendment*, pp. 2–20.

26. *Cong. Globe*, 39 Cong., 1 session, May 8, 1866, p. 2459. A provocative comparative study could be made of the difference in the severity of the terms imposed upon the ex-Confederates and those imposed by the United States upon enemies defeated in foreign wars. After World War II, for example, America alone held 950,000 denazification trials in Germany. See Wm. Ernest Hocking, *Experiment in Education*.

27. *Cong. Globe*, 39 Congress, 1 session, May 10, 1866, p. 2544.

28. Robert Dale Owen, "Political Results from the Varioloid," *Atlantic Monthly*, XXXV:660–670, June 1875. Owen's paper, with annotations in Stevens' hand-

writing, is in the Columbia University Library with the manuscript of the Journal of the Joint Committee of Fifteen. See B. Kendrick, *op. cit.;* Horace E. Flack, *The Adoption of the Fourteenth Amendment;* and Howard K. Beale, *The Critical Year,* pp. 196–210.

29. *Cong. Globe,* 39 Cong., 1 session, March 7, 1866, II:1225ff.

30. *Cong. Globe,* 39 Congress, 1 session, May 8, 1866, p. 2459. For Fessenden's attack in the Senate, see *ibid.,* p. 1279. Fessenden wrote to a friend March 10, 1866; "I believe everybody was gratified with the whipping I gave Sumner, for his speech was atrocious. . . . I regret exceedingly that the amendment was lost, for we can get nothing so good." Francis Fessenden, *Life of Fessenden,* II:56.

31. *Cong. Globe,* 40 Congress, 3 session, December 18, 1868, pp. 203–204.

32. See Robert K. Carr, *The Supreme Court and Judicial Review,* p. 146; Robert E. Cushman, *Leading Constitutional Decisions,* p. 41; Edwin S. Corwin, *Liberty Against Government,* p. 176; and Wm. W. Crosskey, *Politics and the Constitution in the History of the United States,* especially "The True Meaning of the Fourteenth Amendment," II:1083–1118.

33. *Cong. Globe,* 39 Cong., 1 session, June 13, 1866, p. 3148.

34. *Cong. Globe,* 39 Cong., 1 session, July 28, 1866, p. 4304.

35. Milton, *Age of Hate,* pp. 79–80, 317; E. Merton Coulter, *William G. Brownlow,* p. 315.

36. Issued May 28, 1866 as House Bill No. 623. *House Journal,* p. 657. It was not printed in full, but an abstract appeared in the *Nation,* June 5, 1866.

37. See his proposed amendment to House Bill No. 623. *Cong. Globe,* 39 Cong., 1 session, July 28, 1866, p. 4304.

CHAPTER 22 *New Orleans*

1. Quoted by Henry C. Warmoth, in *War, Politics and Reconstruction, Stormy Days in Louisiana,* p. 272.

2. See Roger W. Shugg, *Origins of Class Struggle in Louisiana,* p. 211.

3. U. S. Congress, 39 Congress, 2 session, 1866–1867, House Report No. 16, "New Orleans Riots," pp. 5, 32. See also Warmoth, *War, Politics, and Reconstruction,* p. 41.

4. This letter was printed in U. S. Congress, 39 Congress, 2 session, House Report No. 16, "New Orleans Riots," p. 520. Less than a year after the New Orleans massacre, General Philip Sheridan dismissed Governor Wells because of his "subterfuge and chicanery" and replaced him with the Radical Republican, B. F. Flanders. See his telegram to General Grant, June 4, 1867, U. S. Congress, 40 Congress, 1 session, Senate Executive Document No. 4, "Correspondence Relative to Reconstruction."

5. House Report No. 16, "New Orleans Riots," p. 52. The Louisiana Legislature Democrats also wanted to call a Convention to unmake the Radical Constitution of 1864, but when word came that Andrew Johnson was opposed as it would embarrass his Reconstruction policy, they abandoned the plan. House Report No. 16, "New Orleans Riots," p. 29.

6. For a copy of Judge Abell's charge, see House Report No. 16, p. 28.

7. According to Howell's sworn testimony, House Report No. 16, "New Orleans Riots," p. 52.

8. *Ibid.,* pp. 57, 489.

9. This dispatch was sent July 24, 1866. House Report No. 16, "New Orleans Riots," p. 40.

10. Eugene Tisdale testified he saw the letter but not the signatures in the middle of July. (House Report No. 16, "New Orleans Riots," pp. 41, 259–260.) Who wrote the letter was never determined, for a motion to summon Flanders to testify in the hearings was overruled by a majority of the committee. (House Report No. 16, "New Orleans Riots," p. 41.) Thaddeus Stevens testified: "I got

one or two letters from him, and I may have answered them. I keep no copy of such letters, and I receive and answer briefly so many that I cannot say whether I did or not. I have no recollection of it." (House Report No. 16, p. 489.) Since Stevens never tried to hide his support of the Louisiana Convention, there would have been no point in his denying knowledge of this specific letter, had he been one of the co-signers. It seems likely that two other members of the Joint Committee of Fifteen, anxious to avoid being implicated in the massacre in any way, saw that it was suppressed. Every other member of the Joint Committee of Fifteen denied having written it. Boutwell, however, went so far as to say: "I occasionally received letters from people in Louisiana, and I may have answered some letters about that time; but I have no recollection of answering any letter that contained any allusion to the subject of the convention." (House Report No. 16, p. 489.)

11. U. S. Congress, 39 Congress, 2 session, 1866–1867, Executive Document No. 68, "New Orleans Riots," p. 39.

12. U. S. Congress, 39 Congress, 2 session, 1866, House Report No. 16, "New Orleans Riots," Question No. 3348, p. 225.

13. Executive Document No. 68, "New Orleans Riots," pp. 6, 7.

14. Testimony of S. S. Fish, House Report No. 16, "New Orleans Riots," p. 22.

15. As quoted in the *New Orleans Times*, August 3, 1866, and *Appleton's Annual Cyclopedia*, 1866, p. 454. For another version, see the testimony of F. W. Tilton, Executive Document No. 68, "New Orleans Riots," p. 195.

16. Executive Document No. 68, "New Orleans Riots," p. 280.

17. For evidence that there was no riot at this time see House Report No. 16, "New Orleans Riots," p. 21. For the telegram from Voorhies and Herron to Andrew Johnson and his reply see Executive Document No. 68, "New Orleans Riots," p. 4.

18. Andrew Johnson later wrote: "I never saw this dispatch from General Baird until some ten days or two weeks after the riot." *Trial of Andrew Johnson*, I:63.

19. Stanton's explanation at the hearings was lame. "Upon consideration," he said, "it appeared to me that his warning to the city authorities was all that the case then required." (House Report No. 16, p. 27.) Later he sent a message to the Senate: "General Baird's telegram intimated no apprehension of violence, he expected none; as he had done and intended to do what was exactly right, there was no occasion to give him any instructions or apply to the President for instructions." (December 12, 1867, quoted in George C. Gorham, *Life of Edwin M. Stanton*, II:424.)

20. July 30, 1866, republished in Executive Document No. 68, p. 8.

21. Executive Document No. 68, pp. 89, 36–39.

22. *Ibid.*, pp. 160, 36, 89.

23. An account signed by W. P. B. and republished in a 23-page compilation of documents by the *New York Tribune*. See "The New Orleans Riots," *Tribune Tracts* No. 1.

24. House Report No. 16, p. 7.

25. The telegram was sent August 13, 1866. *Tribune Tracts*, No. I, 1866.

26. Executive Document No. 68, p. 143.

27. *Ibid.*, pp. 93, 32. Official report of Assistant Surgeon A. Hartsuff, U. S. A. He carefully counted and treated the injured policemen as well as the Convention and parade participants.

28. *Ibid.*, pp. 9–11. Sheridan at first listed forty killed and about 160 wounded among the Convention and parade members.

29. *Ibid.*, p. 15.

30. Welles, *Diary*, II:569.

31. See especially his telegram to General Sheridan, August 4, 1866. Executive Document No. 68, p. 12.

32. E. L. Pierce, *op. cit.*, IV:298.

33. This version was reprinted in McPherson, *Political History . . . Recon-*

struction, p. 137, and House Report No. 16, pp. 511–513. The shorthand reporter who recorded the speech, L. L. Walbridge, testified in the hearings on the New Orleans massacre on January 26, 1867. He had retained his original notes and insisted on their accuracy. In the version printed here, expressions of cheers and hisses from the crowd are omitted.

34. Johnson's private secretary, Benjamin C. Truman, who frankly described Johnson's drinking habits, denied that he was drunk when he made this speech. "Anecdotes of Andrew Johnson," *Century Magazine,* Vol. 85, January 1913, p. 438.

35. *DeBow's Review,* July 1866, p. 91; August 1866, p. 347.

CHAPTER 23   *The Climate of Reconstruction*

1. Lowell, "The Seward-Johnson Reaction," *Political Essays,* p. 255.

2. James G. Blaine, *Twenty Years of Congress,* II:223; *Proceedings of the National Union Convention . . . Philadelphia, August 14, 1866;* Milton, *Age of Hate,* pp. 350ff.; Howard K. Beale, *The Critical Year,* pp. 131–138.

3. August 18, 1866. McPherson, *Political History of Reconstruction,* p. 127.

4. September 3, 1866. See the *New York Herald,* August 20, 1866, for the full text. In a letter to Justin Morrill, dated October 19, 1866, he reported that he was recovering, and said, "We have certainly grave things to consider and stern things to do, if we are brave enough." See Morrill, "Notable Letters from My Political Friends," *Forum,* October 1897, XXIV:142.

5. Letter to Thurlow Weed, January 2, 1862, quoted in *The Life of Thurlow Weed,* Vol. 2, *Memoir,* edited by Thurlow Weed Barnes, p. 408.

6. *Cong. Globe,* 40 Cong., 1 session, March 19, 1867, p. 207.

7. *The Education of Henry Adams,* p. 104.

8. Rollo Ogden, ed., *Life and Letters* of E. L. Godkin; Welles, *Diary,* III:4. Welles reported that Seward had expressed the latter sentiment in a cabinet meeting of January 4, 1867.

9. James H. Wilson, *Life of John A. Rawlins,* p. 330.

10. See George Fort Milton, *Age of Hate,* pp. 358ff.; Howard K. Beale, *The Critical Year,* p. 368; Lloyd Stryker, *Andrew Johnson,* p. 355.

11. McPherson, *Political History of Reconstruction,* p. 135.

12. *Ibid.,* p. 140.

13. Quoted in Edward B. Callender, *Thaddeus Stevens, Commoner,* pp. 158–161.

14. H. Millis to Stevens, Battle Creek, Michigan, October 23, 1866. Stevens Papers.

15. *Harper's Weekly,* September 22, 1866, p. 594; "The New York Press and Andrew Johnson," *South Atlantic Quarterly,* October 1927, XXVI:415. David Donald has written that "Andrew Johnson's greatest weakness was his insensitivity to public opinion." *American Heritage,* December 1956, p. 22.

16. *Nation,* September 6, 1866, III:190.

17. Speech in New York, August 29, 1866. McPherson, *Political History of Reconstruction,* p. 131.

18. Letter from Bedford Springs, where he was convalescing, September 6, 1866. Stevens Papers. See also *Life and Times of Frederick Douglass,* pp. 395ff.

19. This was the first of the two speeches Stevens made in the campaign. He was too ill to make others. A copy of this one, "The Pending Canvass," made at Bedford, Pa., September 4, 1866, is in the Stevens Papers and the McPherson Papers.

20. *Lancaster Intelligencer,* September 12, 1866.

21. Current, *Old Thad Stevens,* p. 257.

22. W. E. Smith, *The Blair Family in Politics,* II:375, and the *Nation,* July 26, 1866, III:62.

23. Reprinted in an 1866 campaign pamphlet, *Is the South Ready for Reconstruction,* p. 14.

24. *New York Tribune,* January 4, 1867.

25. McClure, *Old Time Notes of Pennsylvania,* II:206–208. For an expertly detailed description of the fight for the Senatorial seat, see Current, *Old Thad Stevens,* pp. 263–267.

26. See Beale, *The Critical Year,* p. 402.

27. Quoted in Theodore C. Smith, *Life and Letters of James A. Garfield,* I:397.

28. James Ford Rhodes, *History of the United States,* V:621; McPherson, *Political History of Reconstruction,* p. 140.

29. September 20, 1866. "Diary of Orville Hickman Browning," *Ill. Hist. Coll.,* XXII:94. Browning was then Secretary of the Interior.

30. See Charles Warren, *The Supreme Court in United States History,* III:140–176; also Samuel Klaus, ed., *The Milligan Case.* The decision actually was known as early as April 3, 1866, but the official ruling did not come till December 17, 1866. That Stevens recognized its implications in April is clear, for from this month onward he planned to circumvent the Court by returning the South to military rule.

31. *New York Independent,* quoted in Charles Warren, *The Supreme Court,* III:165. See also U. S. Congress, 39 Congress, 2 session, House Report No. 23, "Murder of Union Soldiers," February 22, 1867, an investigation into the freeing of several South Carolina citizens convicted of murdering three Union soldiers in 1865.

32. Warren, *op. cit.,* III:167; *Nation,* January 3, 1867, IV:3.

33. *Cong. Globe,* 39 Cong., 2 session, January 3, 1867, p. 251.

34. Warren, *op. cit.,* III:167.

35. The Court originally had 6 members; Congress reduced the number to 5 in 1801; increased it to 7 in 1807; to 9 in 1837; and to 10 in 1863. In April 1866, Congress reduced the number to 7 (though actually nine remained on the bench), and finally settled upon 9 in 1869. "In every instance . . . there is at least some evidence that the change was designed to affect the Court's decisions." Robert K. Carr, *The Supreme Court and Judicial Review,* p. 270. See also the *Nation,* September 19, 1867, V:222.

36. *Cong. Globe,* 39 Cong., 2 session, January 3, 1867, p. 252. Something of this was foreshadowed in his speech in Lancaster, published in the *New York Herald,* September 29, 1866, but he had not then wholly abandoned the concept that the President under the Constitution had other rights than merely obeying Congressional orders.

37. Taylor, *Destruction and Reconstruction,* pp. 327–328.

38. As reported in the *Nation,* March 28, 1867, IV:245.

39. E. L. Pierce, *op. cit.,* IV:365–366.

40. Donn Piatt, *Memories of the Men Who Saved the Union,* p. 136.

41. Howard, *Autobiography,* II:370, 388.

42. See U. S. Congress, 39 Congress, 2 session Senate Executive Document No. 6, "Freedmen's Affairs"; U. S. Congress, 39 Congress, 2 session, House Report No. 23, "Murder of Union Soldiers," p. 30; and *Cong. Globe,* 39 Congress, 2 session, February 19, 1867, pp. 1567–1568.

43. *Cong. Globe,* 40 Cong., 2 session, March 28, 1868, p. 2214. See also the *Nation,* March 14, 1867, IV:203, and *Harper's Weekly,* January 12, 1867, quoting reports from Annapolis and Raleigh.

44. Paul S. Peirce, *The Freedmen's Bureau,* p. 147; the *Nation,* October 24, 1867, V:325.

45. *Nashville Daily Press and Times,* April 19, 1867, quoted in James W. Patton, *Unionism and Reconstruction in Tennessee,* pp. 136–137.

46. For the reports of these Union Army officers see U. S. Congress, 39 Congress, 2 session, Senate Executive Document No. 6, "Freedmen's Affairs," pp. 20, 45, 50–56, 119, 129, 158.

47. Francis B. Simkins and Robert H. Woody, *South Carolina during Recon-*

struction, p. 59.

48. Howard, *Autobiography,* II:350; U. S. Congress, 39 Congress, 2 session, Senate Executive Document No. 6, "Freedmen's Affairs"; U. S. Congress, 40 Congress, 1 session, Senate Executive Document No. 14, "Correspondence Relative to Reconstruction," pp. 62–63.

49. *Cong. Globe,* 39 Cong., 1 session, July 27, 1866, p. 4255.

CHAPTER 24 *Puritan Tyrant*

1. Donald, "Why They Impeached Andrew Johnson," *American Heritage,* December 1956, VIII:103.

2. *Cong. Globe,* 39 Cong., 1 session, April 27, 1866, p. 2245; January 5, 1867, p. 292.

3. *Cong. Globe,* 39 Cong., 2 session, December 14, 1866, p. 139. H. K. Beale, in *The Critical Year,* pp. 400–405, has noted that the first draft of Johnson's message was conciliatory, and believes that the reason the final draft was truculent and bitter was that Johnson had become convinced, after learning of Stevens' activities in Washington two weeks before Congress met, that conciliation with Congress was impossible.

4. As shown by Orville H. Browning's Diary for November 30, 1866, and January 4, 1867, *Illinois Historical Collections,* XXII:114, 122.

5. As related by Boutwell in his *Reminiscences,* II:107.

6. *Cong. Globe,* 39 Cong., 2 session, I:252.

7. *Nation,* November 30, 1865, I:682. Davis died in February 1866.

8. W. E. B. DuBois, *Black Reconstruction,* p. 456.

9. As reported in the *Nation,* March 7, 1867, IV:183, and the *New York World,* July 13, 1867.

10. Paul Lewinson, *Race, Class, and Party, a History of Negro Suffrage and White Politics in the South,* p. 38; and Walter L. Fleming, *Civil War and Reconstruction in Alabama,* pp. 387–388.

11. See W. E. B. DuBois, *Black Reconstruction,* p. 466; Alexander H. Stephens, *Recollections,* pp. 269–270; John R. Ficklen, *History of Reconstruction in Louisiana,* p. 185; and Howard K. Beale, "On Rewriting Reconstruction History," *American Historical Review,* 1940, XLV, pp. 821–822.

12. *Cong. Globe,* 39 Cong., 1 session, pp. 2799–2800.

13. Quoted in the *Nation,* January 10, 1867, IV:23.

14. *Cong. Globe,* 39 Cong., 2 session, January 7, 1867, p. 324.

15. *Harper's Weekly,* January 12, 1867, p. 18.

16. *Cong. Globe,* 39 Cong., 1 session, June 18, 1866.

17. Letter to Samuel Shock, August 26, 1867, published in the *New York World,* August 28, 1867, and *Cong. Globe,* 39 Cong., 2 session, January 15, 1867, p. 478.

18. *Cong. Globe,* 39 Cong., 2 session, February 13, 1867, p. 1214.

19. *Cong. Globe,* 39 Cong., 2 session, February 13, 1867, p. 1215.

20. Scovel, *op. cit.,* p. 549.

21. According to Senator Henry Wilson, who introduced the bill into the Senate. See Wilson, *Rise and Fall of the Slave Power,* III:619.

22. Stevens opposed giving the choice of appointment of the generals to the President, but failed to amend the bill to his liking. See McPherson, *Political History of Reconstruction,* pp. 191–192, 335, for texts.

23. Boutwell, *Speeches,* pp. 380–386.

24. Quoted in the *New York World,* March 9, 1867.

25. *Cong. Globe,* 40 Cong., 1 session, March 19, 1867, p. 205.

26. *American Reconstruction,* p. 76. In 1866 three-fourths of nearly twenty million dollars collected in federal taxes in the South came from the cotton tax. James G. Blaine, *Twenty Years of Congress,* II:59.

27. August 10, 1867, *American Reconstruction,* p. 97; the *Nation,* January 31, 1867, IV:81.

28. *Cong. Globe,* 40 Cong., 2 session, December 10, 1867, p. 108.

29. *Nation,* March 21, May 16, 1867, IV:225, 395.

30. Paul S. Peirce, *The Freedmen's Bureau,* pp. 68, 131. Roger Shugg pointed out in *Origins of Class Struggle in Louisiana,* p. 262, that most of the six million acres opened to homesteaders in Louisiana fell into the hands of railway promoters and lumber magnates.

31. F. B. Leigh, *Ten Years on a Georgia Plantation, Since the War,* p. 79.

32. See the memoirs of Elizabeth H. Botume, a schoolteacher on the sea islands, *First Days among the Contrabands.* General O. O. Howard, head of the Freedmen's Bureau, wrote (*Autobiography,* II:243): "After years of thinking and observation I am inclined to believe that the restoration of their lands to the planters proved for all their future better for the negroes."

33. As late as 1900 there were only 190,111 farm-owning Negro families, out of a total Negro population (including Porto Rico) of 9,204,531. *U. S. Census, 12th Census, 1900.* Supplementary Analyses, pp. 520ff.

34. *Congressional Globe,* 40 Cong., 1 session, March 19, 1867, p. 204.

35. McClure, *Lincoln and Men of War-Times,* p. 256. Maximilian was executed June 19, 1867.

36. *Cong. Globe,* 39 Cong., 2 session, February 13, 1867, p. 1213.

37. *Cong. Globe,* 39 Cong., 1 session, March 10, 1866, II:1308–1309.

CHAPTER 25 *Negro Suffrage—the First Fruits*

1. Copied into the Stevens Papers, No. 54471.

2. As described by Wm. D. Reid in a letter of recollections of Stevens written to Edward McPherson, January 13, 1869. Reid was on his way to interview James Buchanan when he had this interview. Stevens Papers.

3. *Cong. Globe,* 39 Cong., 1 session, July 28, 1866, p. 4304.

4. Stevens Papers.

5. "A Conversation with Thaddeus Stevens," November 7, 1867, signed "Clarence," in the *Washington Weekly Chronicle,* August 29, 1868.

6. *Cong. Globe,* 40 Cong., 3 session, December 18, 1868, p. 149; *American Reconstruction,* p. 138.

7. *New York Tribune,* August 13, 1868.

8. *The Lost Cause Regained,* p. 158.

9. Ben Perley Poore, *Reminiscences,* II:199–200, 278; *New York World,* January 28, 1868.

10. E. L. Pierce, *op. cit.,* IV:337.

11. The Weed editorial is quoted in the *Life,* Vol. II, edited by Thurlow Weed Barnes, p. 456. Paul H. Buck, in *Road to Reunion,* points out that the leading business Journal of the country, the *Commercial and Financial Chronicle,* continuously opposed the Radical Republicans. See especially p. 154 of *Road to Reunion.* See also George W. Smith, "Some Northern Wartime Attitudes toward the Post-Civil War South," *Journal of Southern History,* X:269, August 1944.

12. *Nation,* January 23, 1868, January 30, 1868, VI:65, 84–85.

13. *New York World,* January 27, 1868, February 27, 1868.

14. Letter to Samuel Shock, August 26, 1867, published in the *New York World,* August 28, 1867. See also his frank statement in Congress, *Cong. Globe,* 40 Cong., 2 session, March 28, 1868, p. 2214.

15. George M. Drake, in the Alabama *Union Springs Times,* June 12, 1867.

16. Letter from Port Royal, Va., September 17, 1867. *DeBow's Review,* October 1867, p. 291.

17. This activity was deplored by the *Nation,* June 27, 1867. See also O. O. Howard, *Autobiography,* II:374.

18. H. C. Warmoth, *War, Politics, and Reconstruction*, p. 51.

19. February 4, 1868. Quoted in the *Independent Monitor*, Tuscaloosa, Alabama, February 19, 1868, and in James S. Allen, *Reconstruction*, pp. 123–124.

20. Richard L. Morton, *The Negro in Virginia Politics*, 1865–1902, pp. 40, 763. See also H. J. Eckenrode, *Political History of Virginia during Reconstruction*, p. 76.

21. Leigh, *Ten Years on a Georgia Plantation*, pp. 109–110.

22. The *New York Evening Post* stated on October 7, 1867, that in Louisiana most whites simply refused to register. William A. Russ, Jr., has stated: "it is impossible to make even a fair guess as to the number disabled by the radical policy." See his "Registration and Disfranchisement under Radical Reconstruction," *Mississippi Valley Historical Review*, 1934–1935, XXI:176.

23. *DeBow's Review*, 1867, p. 135.

24. *Nation*, July 13, 1865, I:37.

25. Roger W. Shugg, *Origins of Class Struggle in Louisiana*, p. 220.

26. U. S. Cong., 40 Cong., 1 session, Senate Executive Document No. 4, "Correspondence Relative to Reconstruction," p. 38.

27. As reported by George Boutwell in a speech in the House, July 20, 1866, reprinted in Boutwell, *Speeches*, p. 482.

28. Paul Lewinson, *Race, Class, and Party*, p. 41.

29. James S. Allen, *Reconstruction*, pp. 106–107; Richard L. Morton, *The Negro in Virginia Politics*, p. 30.

30. Allen, *op. cit.*, p. 116. Horace Mann Bond has stated that reports of Negro membership in the Alabama convention vary from twelve to twenty-seven. See his "Social and Economic Forces in Alabama Reconstruction," *Journal of Negro History*, 1938, XXIII:308.

31. W. E. B. DuBois, *Black Reconstruction*, p. 350.

32. *American Reconstruction*, p. 131, November 1, 1867; *Cong. Globe*, 40 Cong., 1 session, July 11, 1867, p. 594; and the *New York World*, April 3, 1868.

33. *Cong. Globe*, 40 Cong., 2 session, December 18, 1867, p. 267.

34. "A Conversation with Thaddeus Stevens," Nov. 7, 1867, published in the *Washington Weekly Chronicle*, August 29, 1868.

35. Quoted in the *New York World*, November 9, 1867. In 1868, Minnesota, Iowa, and Wisconsin all accepted Negro suffrage.

36. Coulter, *The Civil War and Readjustment in Kentucky*, p. 439, and Lewinson, *Race, Class, and Party*, p. 24. All the tricks that were to be used later in the deep South—the "job lash," gerrymanders, inadequate voting facilities, and violence at the polls—were thought up and employed first in Kentucky.

37. *New York World*, October 29, 1867.

38. O. O. Howard, *Autobiography*, II:344.

39. Wm. J. Robertson, *The Changing South*, p. 53. See also Stanley F. Horn, *Invisible Empire, the Story of the Ku Klux Klan*.

40. According to James Ford Rhodes, *History of the United States*, VI:188. Each state was made a Realm under a Grand Dragon; several counties made up a Dominion under a Grand Titan; each county had its Grand Giant, and each den its Grand Cyclops. Leaders were Genii, Hydras, Furies, Goblins, Night Hawks, Magi, Monks, and Turks. Individual members were Ghouls. For an excellent monograph describing the workings of the Klan in a single state, see Vernon L. Wharton, *The Negro in Mississippi, 1865–1890*, pp. 261ff.

41. Stevens papers.

42. Republished in the *New York Tribune*, April 6, 1868. The same issue reported many Klan outrages, all from the Southern press.

43. Pollard, *The Lost Cause Regained*, p. 138.

44. Stevens' haste was further stimulated by the failure of the impeachment trial. After the Senators had filed opinions on May 11, 1868, indicating that conviction was doubtful, Stevens did his best to push the omnibus bill through so that the Republican membership of the Senate would be increased, and con-

viction of the President would be certain. In this he failed.

45. Simkins and Woody, *South Carolina during Reconstruction*, p. 91.

46. *Ibid.*, p. 94.

47. W. E. B. DuBois, *Black Reconstruction*, pp. 396, 437, 721. DuBois has pointed out that Alabama tried to obliterate all printed records of the Reconstruction, and that in Florida many documents were deliberately destroyed. Only three or four states preserved the debates of the Constitutional conventions of 1867–1868. Virginia kept her Reconstruction constitution till 1902.

48. James G. Blaine, *Twenty Years of Congress*, II:266. The Florida constitution had one serious defect. It gave the governor power to appoint practically all county officials. After home rule was restored the Democrats kept this provision, and political democracy in Florida was sadly delayed. See C. Vann Woodward, *Origins of the New South*, p. 55.

49. Quoted in Simkins and Woody, *op. cit.*, p. 93.

50. *Cong. Globe*, 40 Cong., 2 session, March 11, 1868, p. 1822.

51. Warmoth, *War, Politics and Reconstruction*, p. 93. Laws were also passed in South Carolina and Arkansas calling for mixed schools; these too were ignored in practice. See Walter L. Fleming, *Documentary History of Reconstruction*, I:189; Roger Shugg, *Origins of Class Struggle in Louisiana*, p. 226; and W. E. B. DuBois, *Black Reconstruction*, p. 437. The only mixed-school experiment of any consequence was at the University of South Carolina, which permitted Negroes from 1873 to 1877. See Simkins and Woody, *op. cit.*, p. 441.

52. Quoted in the *Nashville Daily Press and Times*, November 15, 1867, and in James W. Patton, *Unionism and Reconstruction in Tennessee*, p. 162.

53. Simkins and Woody, *op. cit.*, p. 429. In the District of Columbia only twenty-seven whites were enrolled in the Freedmen's Bureau schools during 1868–1869. See Lillian G. Dabney, *The History of Schools for Negroes in the District of Columbia*, p. 86.

54. O. O. Howard, *Autobiography*, II:376; James W. Garner, *Reconstruction in Mississippi*, pp. 360–361.

55. *Philadelphia Press*, August 13, 1868. A copy of the bill may be seen in the Stevens Papers. The District of Columbia school system provided for separation of the races, but this had its legal foundation in by-laws and rules of the school board, not in Congressional enactment. See Lillian G. Dabney, *op. cit.*, p. 118.

56. *American Historical Association Annual Report*, 1911, II:694; and the *Nation*, April 2, 1868, VI:262.

57. For a detailed discussion, see Charles Warren, *The Supreme Court*, III:187–196, 211–212.

CHAPTER 26 *Impeachment Beginnings*

1. *American Reconstruction*, p. 103.

2. See *Harper's Weekly*, February 9, 1867, for the Republican reaction.

3. U. S. Congress, 40 Cong., 1 session, House Report No. 2, "Impeachment of the President."

4. Letters from Johnson to his son now in the Huntington Library show that trouble between the two had begun years earlier. See also Milton, *Age of Hate*, p. 325; Welles, *Diary*, II:461, 468, 472–473; Beale, *The Critical Year*, p. 17.

5. *Cong. Globe*, 40 Cong., 1 session, March 7, 1867, p. 19.

6. Had Booth's diary, which was suppressed by Stanton, been put in evidence at the trial, it would have saved Mrs. Surratt from death. Stanton knew the pages were missing when it first came to him; Johnson knew nothing of the diary until the impeachment investigations. See Milton, *Age of Hate*, pp. 202, 410–411. Benjamin Butler later admitted that there was no "reliable evidence" for his suspicions against Johnson. *Autobiography*, p. 930.

7. *Cong. Globe*, 40 Cong., 2 session, July 7, 1868, p. 3786. Mrs. Lucy Cobb,

said to be "a lady of easy virtue" and a frequent visitor to the White House, was accused of selling presidential pardons. See Milton, *Age of Hate*, p. 407.

8. As reported by Ben Perley Poore in his *Reminiscences*, II:229.

9. Quoted by James M. Scovel, *op. cit.*, p. 549.

10. *Cong. Globe*, 40 Cong., 1 session, July 10, 1867, p. 566.

11. Edmund G. Ross, *History of the Impeachment of Andrew Johnson*, p. 56.

12. October 18, 1867, *American Reconstruction*, p. 125.

13. He even effectively opposed, through Attorney-General Stanbery, the attemps of two Southern governors to stop by injunction the enforcement of the Reconstruction Acts. See Carl Schurz, *Reminiscences*, III:253.

14. Secretary of the Interior Orville H. Browning noted this in his diary, March 8, 1867. See *Illinois Historical Collections*, XXII:135.

15. Blaine, *Twenty Years of Congress*, II:297.

16. This "Order No. 40" caused an immediate furor in Congress. "They will crucify me," Hancock said to his wife. ". . . I know I shall have Johnson's sympathy, but he is powerless to help me." A. R. Hancock, *Reminiscences of Winfield Scott Hancock by His Wife*, p. 124. See also Francis A. Walker, *General Hancock*, pp. 297, 301, 303.

17. See the hearings of the House Committee on the elections in 1868, U. S. Congress, 40 Congress, 3 session, House Misc. Documents No. 52–53; the *Nation*, July 16, 1868, VII:42; and Blaine, *Twenty Years of Congress*, II:410.

18. Simkins and Woody, *op. cit.*, pp. 65, 70.

19. McCulloch, *Men and Measures of Half a Century*, p. 391.

20. Welles, *Diary*, III:120.

21. November 1, 1867, John Sherman, *Recollections of Forty Years*, I:415.

22. Marguerite H. Albjerg, "The New York Press and Andrew Johnson," *South Atlantic Quarterly*, October 1927, XXVI:414–415. John Hay, who had just returned from Europe, noted in his diary on February 2, 1867, "It is startling to see how utterly without friends the President is." See . . . *Diaries and Letters of John Hay*, p. 261.

23. Woodward, *Origins of the New South*, p. 77.

24. Welles, *Diary*, III:291.

25. Moore diary, Library of Congress, quoted in Milton, *Age of Hate*, p. 501.

26. McClure, *Lincoln and Men of War-Times*, p. 156.

27. A conversation of "some months ago," reported by Senator Wilson in a letter of August 24, 1867, printed in the *Nation*, September 12, 1867, V:215. See also Frank M. Flower, *Edwin McMasters Stanton*, p. 311; Donn Piatt, *Memories of Men Who Saved the Union*, p. 55; and McClure, *Lincoln and Men of War-Times*, p. 156.

28. Quoted in Frank Flower, *op. cit.*, p. 315, and George C. Gorham, *Life and Public Services, of Edwin M. Stanton*, II:421–422.

29. August 27, 1867. Lieber Papers, Huntington Library.

30. Wm. B. Hesseltine, *Ulysses S. Grant, Politician*, p. 81.

31. As reported in the *Philadelphia Ledger*, February 10, 1868.

32. Welles, *Diary*, January 18, 1868, III:263.

33. Frank Flower, *op. cit.*, pp. 336, 338.

34. *American Reconstruction*, p. 148.

35. *New York World*, February 14, 1868.

36. According to Donn Piatt, *op. cit.*, p. 58.

37. Welles, *Diary*, February 22, 1868, III:289.

38. The whole sequence of events is described in the *Trial of Andrew Johnson*, I:211, 224, 428–429, 449.

39. Welles, *Diary*, III:297, and *New York Herald*, February 28, 1868.

40. *Cong. Globe*, 40 Cong., 2 session, February 22, 1868, pp. 1336–1338.

41. *New York Tribune*, February 25, 1868, and *New York World*, May 5, 1868.

42. *Cong. Globe*, 40 Cong., 2 session, February 24, 1868, pp. 1399–1400.

43. February 28, 1868, *American Reconstruction,* p. 151. See also *Harper's Weekly,* March 14, 1868, p. 164.

CHAPTER 27   *The Trial*

1. *Blackwood's Edinburgh Magazine,* June 1868, Vol. 103, p. 727.
2. *New York Tribune,* April 13, 1868, and February 26, 1868.
3. *Trial of Andrew Johnson,* III:328.
4. *Cong. Globe,* 40 Cong., 2 session, March 2, 1868, p. 1612.
5. *New York Herald,* March 9, 1868.
6. *Ibid.,* April 15, 1868.
7. Blaine, *Twenty Years, of Congress,* II:289.
8. Butler, *Autobiography,* p. 929. The *New York Times* on March 31, 1868, said Stevens lacked the "strength and mental cohesion" to make the opening argument.
9. Butler, *Autobiography,* p. 928.
10. *American Reconstruction,* p. 164.
11. February 22, 1868. Francis Fessenden, *Life and Public Services of William Pitt Fessenden,* II:154.
12. Quoted in Charles H. Coleman, *The Election of 1868,* p. 80.
13. Letter to Col. Wm. B. Thomas, March 10, 1868. Oddly enough, this letter found its way into the Benjamin F. Butler Papers, Library of Congress.
14. According to the President's aide, Colonel W. G. Moore, in his Diary, March 14, 1868, as quoted in Milton, *Age of Hate,* p. 576.
15. Letters to Mr. Ticknor, March 26 and April 10, 1868, *Memoir of Benjamin R. Curtis,* I:416–417.
16. Quoted in Morefield Story, *Charles Sumner,* p. 345. See also Brainerd Dyer, *Public Career of Wm. M. Evarts.* Thomas A. R. Nelson of Tennessee and Wm. S. Groesbeck of Ohio also aided in the President's defense.
17. The *Nation* denounced this attitude April 16, 1868, VI:384.
18. J. B. Henderson, "Emancipation and Impeachment," *Century Magazine,* December 1912, pp. 205–207.
19. Letters to his cousin, March 31, 1868 and April 12, 1868. Francis Fessenden, *op. cit.,* II:184–185.
20. May 10, 1868. Quoted in Francis Fessenden, *op. cit.,* II:205–206.
21. Letter to J. H. Rhodes, May 21, 1868. Theodore C. Smith, *Life and Letters of James A. Garfield,* I:246. The *World* letter was republished in the *New York Tribune,* May 5, 1868.
22. May 15, 1868. Quoted in Charles H. Coleman, *The Election of 1868,* p. 79. Sprague did, however, vote for conviction, though he was one of three ready to vote for acquittal if necessary.
23. Letter to J. H. Rhodes, May 21, 1868. Theodore C. Smith, *op. cit.,* I:426.
24. Julian, *Political Recollections,* p. 356.
25. *Cong. Globe,* 40 Cong., 1 session, March 23, 1867, p. 317; and *New York World,* April 3, 1868.
26. Speech in Lawrence, Kansas, June 10, 1867, reported in the *New York World,* June 11, 1867.
27. As reported in the *New York World,* April 20, 1868.
28. *New York World,* April 4, 1868.
29. *New York Tribune,* April 3, 1868.
30. *Trial of Andrew Johnson,* I:115, 119.
31. *Nation,* February 13, 1868, IV:124.
32. Letter to Wm. T. Sherman, March 1, 1868. John Sherman, *Recollections,* I:424.
33. Carl Schurz, *Reminiscences,* III:252, 282.
34. *Trial of Andrew Johnson,* II:333.

35. April 3, 1868. A reference to the tradition that Butler stole the silver spoons from the house in which he lived in New Orleans, and to the fact that on behalf of the U. S. Army he had seized $800,000 in bullion belonging to Southern owners which had been entrusted with the French consul. He had returned the bullion after protests from European nations. See also *New York Times,* March 7, 1868.

36. *Trial of Andrew Johnson,* I:317.

37. *Ibid.,* II:233.

38. April 10, 1868. *American Reconstruction,* pp. 174–175.

39. *Trial of Andrew Johnson,* II:224. During the trial the President's counsel, T. A. R. Nelson, in an effort to discredit the managers, broke open to public gaze the Alta Vela case. Historians have been arguing ever since about whether or not threats of bribery were involved. Lloyd P. Stryker, Claude G. Bowers, and George Fort Milton have suggested that Jeremiah Black and three of the impeachment managers—and possibly Thaddeus Stevens—were guilty of intriguing to bribe the President with the promise of acquittal in order to fatten their pocketbooks out of Alta Vela profits. But Wm. N. Brigance, who made a meticulous examination of the documents, unearthed convincing evidence to the contrary, and agreed with the older judgment of Wm. A. Dunning, that "there was in the episode nothing whatever discreditable morally to any party concerned." *Jeremiah S. Black* (Philadelphia, 1934), pp. 186ff.

Alta Vela was a small guano island claimed by the Dominican Republic. American speculators working the guano in 1861 had been expelled, and the Santo Domingo authorities had contracted for the guano to be mined by another American firm, in which Thurlow Weed had a financial interest. The original firm then hired the distinguished Democratic lawyer, Jeremiah S. Black, a former member of Buchanan's cabinet and a good friend to Andrew Johnson, to press their claims in Washington. He was promised 1½ per cent of the profits. The case dragged on for six years. Black was bitter against Seward, who he felt was befriending Weed and his firm. Seward however had good legal reasons for not sending a warship to the island, as Black wanted. When the President refused to side with Black, and the release of certain documents put him in an ambiguous position, he resigned as counsel in the impeachment trial.

Meanwhile one of Black's aides had persuaded Benjamin Butler, John A. Logan, John A. Bingham and Thaddeus Stevens to sign a paper endorsing the claims of Black's clients. When the President was shown this paper he interpreted it as a strong hint that if he gave in to Black the impeachment would end in acquittal. As Brigance notes wryly: "Now what historian knowing Stevens would contend that he would trade Johnson's acquittal for a guano dump, or for any monetary price whatsoever?" Stevens said later in the House that the paper had been shown to Andrew Johnson without his sanction, but that he had nothing to retract; it was simply a restatement of his well-known opinion on the Falkland Island case, that the United States Government ought to intervene wherever Americans had been forcibly ejected. *Congressional Globe,* 40 Cong., 2 session, May 8, 1868, p. 2366. The *Nation* of May 7, 1868, said that Stevens privately said he had signed the paper because "Seward has acted the scoundrel." See also *Trial of Andrew Johnson,* II:262, 268, 282–283.

40. *Trial of Andrew Johnson,* II:220, 223.

41. *Ibid.,* I:227.

42. As reported by Clemenceau, February 28, 1868. *American Reconstruction,* p. 153.

43. As described by Alexander McClure, who was present. *Lincoln and Men of War-Times,* p. 263.

44. *Blackwood's Edinburgh Magazine,* June 1868, Vol. 103, p. 717.

45. *Cong. Globe,* 40 Cong., 2 session, July 7, 1868, p. 3790.

46. *Cong. Globe,* 40 Cong., 2 session, May 14, 1868, p. 2464.

47. *Cong. Globe,* 40 Cong., 2 session, July 7, 1868, p. 3786.
48. A reference to Aristotle.
49. *Cong. Globe,* 40 Cong., 2 session, July 7, 1868, p. 3786.

CHAPTER 28   *Defeat*

1. P. 288.
2. Many Senators filed these opinions in writing, and they were published after the voting. Fessenden's appeared in the *New York Times,* May 15, 1868. Others printed in the *Times* were those of Sherman, Van Winkle, Fowler, Henderson, Howe, and Grimes. Several years later Charles Sumner said privately to Senator John B. Henderson, "I want to say that in that matter you were right and I was wrong." John B. Henderson, "Emancipation and Impeachment," *Century Magazine,* Vol. 85, p. 209, December 1912.
3. David M. DeWitt, *The Impeachment and Trial of Andrew Johnson,* p. 521.
4. George W. Julian admitted conversing with her on the subject, but denied threatening her. *Cong. Globe,* 40 Cong., 2 session, pp. 2674–2675.
5. April 1868. *American Historical Association Annual Report,* 1911, II:694.
6. Letter from J. D. Hopkins, Newberry, South Carolina, May 28, 1868. Stevens Papers.
7. May 17, 1868. In the MGM motion picture *Tennessee Johnson* the impeachment trial was grotesquely distorted. A wholly fictional episode was created, with Chase expelling Thaddeus from the Senate Chamber. Names of the Senators were changed, and Andrew Johnson was pictured as going to the Senate to give a speech in his own defense.
8. William B. Crook, *Through Five Administrations,* p. 133.
9. Reported in the *New York Herald,* May 20, 1868, reprinting a letter from Washington dated May 17, 1868.
10. Edmund G. Ross, *History of the Impeachment of Andrew Johnson,* p. 142.
11. A picture of this bust, which seems to have disappeared, may be seen in *Vinnie Ream.*
12. July 21, 1868. The Stevens Papers contain the series of brief notes between Stevens and Vinnie Ream. A letter from T. C. Fletcher, Executive Department, State of Missouri, May 23, 1868, in the Stevens Papers, states that the Missouri Senate formally visited the Stevens statue on May 23, 1868.
13. *Cong. Globe,* 40 Cong., 2 session, July 7, 1868, p. 3786.
14. *Ibid.*
15. This letter came to light in January 1913 when Truman published his "Anecdotes of Andrew Johnson" in the Century Magazine, Vol. 85, p. 440.

CHAPTER 29   *The Last Weeks*

1. See Chapter XIV, pp. 179–180.
2. *Cong. Globe,* 40 Cong., 2 session, July 1, 1868, p. 3661.
3. See the unsigned and undated memorandum in Johnson's handwriting in the Johnson papers quoted in Wm. A. Dunning, "Paying for Alaska," *Political Science Quarterly,* September 1912, XXVII:385–399. See also John Bigelow, *Retrospections of an Active Life,* IV:217.
4. U. S. Congress, 40 Congress, 3 session, House Report No. 35. See also F. A. Golder, "The Purchase of Alaska," *American Historical Review,* 1920, XXV:411–425. Stevens' last speech on behalf of the Alaska appropriation was made July 13, 1868. The House shortly thereafter voted money for the purchase. Stevens for a time had supported the Perkins claim, which was delaying the appropriation, but after consulting with Seward, rejected it. Perkins was an arms

dealer, who claimed the Czar owed him money, and hoped to be paid out of the Alaska purchase fund.

5. McClure, *Abraham Lincoln and Men of War-Times,* pp. 263-264.

6. Georgia in September was temporarily barred after her state legislature banished its twenty-five Negro members.

7. *Cong. Globe,* 40 Cong., 2 session, pp. 1966-1967.

8. Stevens Papers, June 24, 1868. The letter to Forney appeared in the *New York Times,* March 14, 1868.

9. Stevens Papers. The Fifteenth Amendment passed the House February 26, 1869. Boutwell was the chief author in the House and John B. Henderson in the Senate.

10. This interview was first published in the *Cincinnati Commercial,* September 3, 1868. See Walter L. Fleming, *Documentary History of Reconstruction,* II:343. Fleming prints the constitutions of the Klan and other similar organizations, II:347ff. He also gives the constitutions and declarations of the Republican Union League, Lincoln Brotherhood, etc., II:7-29.

11. *Nation,* September 10, 1868, VII:201.

12. As quoted in the *Nation,* November 12, 1868, VII:384, the *Cincinnati Commercial,* July 30, 1868, and the *New York Evening Post,* August 10, 1868. See also Charles H. Coleman, *The Election of 1868,* p. 319.

13. McPherson Scrap Book, Library of Congress, quoted in Charles H. Coleman, *op. cit.,* p. 320.

14. Quoted in the *New York Times,* August 10, 1868.

15. O. O. Howard, *op. cit.,* II:386; the *Nation,* November 12, 1868; Coleman, *op. cit.,* p. 322; and Warmoth, *op. cit.,* p. 67.

16. Stewart Mitchell, *Horatio Seymour of New York,* p. xvii, and Wm. B. Hesseltine, *Lincoln and the War Governors,* p. 269.

17. Quoted in Wm. E. Smith, *The Francis P. Blair Family in Politics,* II:405.

18. *Cong. Globe,* 40 Cong., 2 session, July 1, 1868, p. 3661.

19. McClure, *Abraham Lincoln and Men of War-Times,* pp. 263-264; *New York Tribune,* August 14, 1868; *Christian Cynosure,* September 8, 1868, I:6.

20. *Cong. Globe,* 40 Cong., 2 session, July 7, 1868, p. 3790.

21. February 15, 1868. Stevens Papers. See also the letter from Reverend Alfred Cookman, September 4, 1867, Stevens Papers.

22. Burrowes, *Philadelphia Press,* September 2, 1868.

23. As reprinted in "Out of the Past, 75 Years Ago," *Gettysburg Times,* April 13, 1942.

24. Forney, *Anecdotes of Public Men,* I:37.

25. Stevens Papers.

26. *New York Tribune,* August 12, 1868.

27. Letter from Dr. Henry Carpenter, November 17, 1867. Stevens Papers.

28. McPherson Papers, Box 57. Although the will was brief, and its provisions described with seeming clarity, the use of popular rather than technical words resulted in what the *Philadelphia Times* called "one of the most unique, complicated and generally unintelligible wills of record." Litigation between the executors of the estate and Stevens' heirs continued intermittently for twenty-five years, before all the minor claims were finally paid and the final $50,000 used to endow the orphanage. In 1900 this orphanage became the Thaddeus Stevens Trade School, and is now a junior college financed by the State of Pennsylvania. James H. Hartzell, *History of the Thaddeus Stevens Trade School.*

29. Samuel P. Bates, *Martial Deeds of Pennsylvania,* p. 987.

30. George F. Hoar, *Autobiography of Seventy Years,* I:239.

31. September 13, 1868. The *New York Times,* August 18, 1868, published Stevens' funeral services in full. It was estimated that there were 15,000 in the Lancaster funeral procession.

CHAPTER 30 *The Stern Pen of History*

1. Lincoln was an exception to this, Stevens said, predicting that his reputation would shine more brightly with increasing years. *Cong. Globe,* 40 Cong., 1 session, March 19, 1867, p. 207.

2. *Cong. Globe,* 40 Cong., 3 session, December 17, 1868, p. 139.

3. *Memorial Addresses on the Life and Character of Thaddeus Stevens, Delivered in the House of Representatives, Washington, D. C. December 18, 1868.* The copy inscribed thus by Jn. H. McClellan, Gettysburg banker, April 30, 1872, is now in the possession of Mr. Jacob M. Sheads of Gettysburg.

4. *New York Times,* August 13, 1868; *New York Herald,* August 13, 1868; *London Times,* August 13, 1868; *New York Tribune,* August 12, 1868; *New York World,* August 13, 1868.

5. *Planter's Banner,* August 15, 1868; *New Orleans Picayune,* as quoted in the *Georgetown Courier,* August 22, 1868.

6. See W. E. B. DuBois, *Black Reconstruction,* pp. 265, 300; Bowers, *The Tragic Era,* p. 67; Coulter, *The South during Reconstruction,* p. 119; J. G. Randall, "Johnson and the Vindictives," *Civil War and Reconstruction;* Milton, *Age of Hate,* p. 263; Stryker, *Andrew Johnson,* pp. 248, 440, 691; W. E. Woodward, *Meet General Grant,* p. 376; Paul H. Buck, *The Road to Reunion, 1865–1900,* pp. 15, 88; Gunnar Myrdal, *An American Dilemma, the Negro Problem and Modern Democracy,* I:224, 448.

7. Coulter, *The South during Reconstruction,* p. 164.

8. Letter from Lincoln to Lt. Colonel John Glenn, February 7, 1865, after learning that Glenn was "forcing negroes into Military service, and even torturing them —riding them on rails and the like—to extort their consent." Basler ed., *Collected Works,* VIII:266; also VIII:268; VII:390, for similar protests from Lincoln.

9. Buck, *The Road to Reunion,* p. 25.

10. Harvey Wish, *George Fitzhugh, Propagandist of the Old South,* p. 333.

11. Warmoth, *op. cit.,* p. 92.

12. Cable, *The Negro Question,* pp. 37–38.

13. Beale, "On Rewriting Reconstruction History," *American Historical Review,* XLV:808.

14. C. Vann Woodward, *Origins of the New South,* 1877–1913, p. 206; Jesse T. Wallace, *History of the Negroes of Mississippi from 1865 to 1890,* p. 183; and James Allen, *Reconstruction,* p. 142. In 1880 the land in Georgia was valued at $88,000,-000. The Negroes, who numbered almost half the population, owned land valued at only $1,500,000.

15. See W. E. B. DuBois, *Black Reconstruction,* p. 546; Robert E. Martin, *Negro Disfranchisement in Virginia,* p. 50; Hilary A. Herbert, *Why the Solid South?* p. 101; Simkins and Woody, *South Carolina during Reconstruction,* p. 137. T. Harry Williams has pointed out that the postwar budgets seem high only when compared with the niggardly outlay of the planter-controlled pre-war budgets. "An Analysis of Some Reconstruction Attitudes," *Journal of Southern History,* November 1946, XII:469.

16. DuBois, *Black Reconstruction,* p. 617; and Cable, *The Negro Question,* p. 160.

17. C. Vann Woodward, *Origins of the New South,* p. 205.

18. In North Carolina both Houses of the legislature went Democratic in 1870, though the Republicans retained the governorship till 1876. See Woodward, *Origins of the New South,* pp. 66ff.; David Donald, "The Scalawag in Mississippi Reconstruction," *Journal of Southern History,* November 1944, X:447–461; W. E. B. DuBois, *Black Reconstruction,* pp. 692–693; and C. Vann Woodward, *The Strange Career of Jim Crow.* The ironclad oath was repealed in 1871, readmitting many leaders to eligibility for office. National amnesty in 1872 restored political

rights to all but 600 ex-Confederate officials. The federal Marshalls and supervisors of elections were not wholly withdrawn, however, till 1894, and Negro legislators were elected till 1895.

19. In the Slaughter House Cases of 1873. See W. S. Corwin, *Liberty against Government,* pp. 121, 176.

20. Arthur M. Schlesinger, Sr., *The American as Reformer,* p. 67.

Bibliography

I. Speeches of Thaddeus Stevens *

Speech of Thaddeus Stevens on the School Law, Delivered in the Pennsylvania Legislature, April, 1835. Lancaster, Pa., 1865. 11 pp.

Speech of Thaddeus Stevens, Esq., in Favor of the Bill to Establish a School of Arts in the City of Philadelphia, and to Endow the Colleges and Academies of Pennsylvania, Delivered in the House of Representatives at Harrisburg, March 10, 1838. Harrisburg, 1838. 12 pp.

Argument of Thaddeus Stevens, Esq. Before the Supreme Court of Pennsylvania, at Harrisburg, in the Case of Jacob Specht vs. the Commonwealth. Lancaster, 1848. 14 pp.

Speech of the Hon. Thaddeus Stevens of Pa., on the Subject of the Admission of Slavery in the Territories, February 20, 1850. Harrisburg, 1850, 7 pp.

Speech of Thaddeus Stevens on the California Question, June 10, 1850. 8 pp.

Speech of Hon. Thaddeus Stevens of Pa., on the Public Lands—the Tariff, June 11, 1852. 8 pp.

"The Presidential Question," Speech of Hon. Thaddeus Stevens of Pa., at Cooper Institute, New York City, September 27, 1860. 8 pp.

Speech of the Hon. Thaddeus Stevens of Pa., on the State of the Union, January 29, 1861. 8 pp.

Speech of the Hon. Thaddeus Stevens of Pa., on the Best Means of Subduing the Rebellion, January 22, 1862. 6 pp.

Speech of Hon. Thaddeus Stevens, of Pa., on the Treasury Note Bill, February 6, 1862. 7 pp.

Speech of Hon. Thaddeus Stevens of Pa., on the Tax Bill, April 1862. 4 pp.

Speech of Hon. Thaddeus Stevens of Pa., on Government Contracts, April 28, 1862. 14 pp.

Speeches of Messrs. Colfax of Indiana and Thaddeus Stevens of Pennsylvania in Reply to Messrs. Diven and Blair's Attack on General Frémont. Washington, 1862.

Speech of Hon. Thaddeus Stevens of Pennsylvania "in reply to the Attack on Gen. Hunter's Letter." 1862. 8 pp.

"Reconstruction." Speech of the Hon. Thaddeus Stevens Delivered in the City of Lancaster, September 7, 1865. 8 pp.

* Reprints of these may be seen in either the Stevens Papers or the Edward McPherson Papers in the Library of Congress.

Speech of Hon. Thaddeus Stevens, Gettysburg, Pa., October 2, 1865. 4 pp.
Speech of Hon. Thaddeus Stevens of Pa., on Reconstruction, December 18, 1865. 8 pp.
Speech of Hon. Thaddeus Stevens of Pa., "Basis of Representation," January 31, 1866. 7 pp.
Speech of Hon. Thaddeus Stevens of Pa., on Reconstruction, March 10, 1866. 7 pp.
"The Pending Canvass," Speech of Hon. Thaddeus Stevens, delivered at Bedford, Pa., September 4, 1866. Lancaster, 1866. 12 pp.
Speech of Hon. Thaddeus Stevens of Pa., "Government of Insurrectionary States," February 15, 1867. 4 pp.
Speech of Hon. Thaddeus Stevens of Pa., Bill (H. R. No. 20) Relative to Damages to Loyal Men, and for Other Purposes, March 19, 1867. 8 pp.
Speech of Hon. Thaddeus Stevens of Pa., on "State Governments Republican in Form," March 18, 1868. 7 pp.

II. Government and State Documents

Congressional Globe, 1848–1853, 1859–1869.
Pennsylvania Constitutional Convention, *Proceedings and Debates,* 1837.
Pennsylvania House Journal, 1834–1840.
Pennsylvania Senate Journal, 1838–1839.
Pennsylvania Senate, *Report of the Select Committee appointed to inquire into the cause of an Armed Force, being brought to the capitol of Pennsylvania . . . 4th December, 1838, etc.* Harrisburg, 1839.
U. S. Congress, 39th Congress, 1 session, 1865–1866, Executive Document No. 70, "Freedmen's Bureau."
U. S. Congress, 39 Congress, 1 session, 1866, Executive Document No. 2, Carl Schurz: "Condition of the South."
U. S. Congress, 39 Congress, 1 session, 1866, Executive Document No. 27, "Reports of The Assistant Commissioners of the Freedmen's Bureau."
U. S. Congress, 39 Congress, 1 session, 1866, Executive Document No. 70, "Freedmen's Bureau."
U. S. Congress, 39 Congress, 1 session, 1866, House Report No. 30, "Report of the Joint Committee on Reconstruction."
U. S. Congress, 39 Congress, 1 session, 1866, House Report No. 101, "Memphis Riots and Massacres."
U. S. Congress, 39 Congress, 2 session, 1866–1867, Executive Document No. 68, "The New Orleans Riots."
U. S. Congress, 39 Congress, 2 session, 1866–1867, House Report No. 16, "The New Orleans Riots."
U. S. Congress, 39 Congress, 2 session, 1866–1867, House Report No. 23, "Murder of Union Soldiers."
U. S. Congress, 39 Congress, 2 session, 1866–1867, Senate Executive Document No. 6, "Freedmen's Affairs."
U. S. Congress, 40 Congress, 1 session, 1867, House Report No. 2. "Impeachment of the President."
U. S. Congress, 40 Congress, 1 session, 1867, Senate Executive Document No. 14. "Correspondence Relative to Reconstruction."
U. S. Congress, 40 Congress, 2 session, 1868, House Executive Document No. 342. "General Orders—Reconstruction."
U. S. Congress, 40 Congress, 2 session, 1867–1868, House Report No. 30. "Reconstruction."
U. S. Congress, 40 Congress, 3 session, 1868, House Report No. 30. "Bureau of Freedmen and Refugees."
U. S. Congress, 40 Congress, 3 session, 1868, House Miscellaneous Documents 52–53. *Georgia Affairs, Mississippi Affairs.*

U. S. Congress, 42 Congress, 2 session, 1872. "Ku Klux Conspiracy," 13 vols.
U. S. Congress, 42 Congress, 3 session, 1873. House Reports Nos. 77, 78, 81, 82. "Credit Mobilier Investigation."
U. S. Congress, 42 Congress, 3 session, 1873. Senate Report No. 519. "Credit Mobilier."
U. S. Reports. Circuit Court, 3 circuit. *Cases in the Circuit Court of the United States, reported by John W. Wallace,* Vol. II. Philadelphia, 1854.

III. Books and Articles *

Adams, Charles Francis, *Autobiography, 1835–1915.* Boston, 1916.
Adams, Henry, *The Education of Henry Adams.* New York, 1931.
Adams, James Truslow, *The Epic of America.* Boston, 1931.
Adams, John Quincy, *Memoirs of John Quincy Adams,* edited by C. F. Adams, 14 vols. Philadelphia, 1874–1877.
Adams, Samuel Hopkins, *The Godlike Daniel.* New York, 1930.
Albjerg, Marguerite H., "The New York Press and Andrew Johnson." *South Atlantic Quarterly,* XXVI:404–416 (October, 1927).
Allen, James S., *Reconstruction, the Battle for Democracy, 1865–1876.* New York, 1937.
"The American Constitution and Impeachment of the President," *Blackwood's Edinburgh Magazine,* June 1868, 707–727.
Ames, Mary, *A New England Woman's Diary in Dixie in 1865.* Springfield, 1906.
Aptheker, Herbert, *American Negro Slave Revolts.* New York, 1943.
Arnold, Isaac N., *The Life of Abraham Lincoln.* Chicago, 1891.
Atlee, Benjamin C., "Thaddeus Stevens and Slavery," *Lancaster County Historical Society Papers,* XV:167–187, 1911.
Bancroft, Frederic, *The Life of William H. Seward.* 2 vols. New York, 1900.
Barnes, Gilbert H., *The Antislavery Impulse, 1830–1844.* New York, 1933.
Barnes, Thurlow Weed, *Memoir of Thurlow Weed.* 2 vols. Boston, 1884.
Barnes, Wm. Horatio, *The Fortieth Congress of the United States, 1867–69.* 2 vols. New York, 1871.
Barrett, Don Carlos. *The Greenbacks and Resumption of Specie Payments, 1862–1879.* Cambridge, 1931.
Bates, Edward, "The Diary of Edward Bates, 1859–1866," edited by Howard K. Beale, *American Historical Association Annual Report,* Vol. IV, 1930.
Bates, Samuel P., *History of Pennsylvania Volunteers.* Philadelphia, 1870.
—— *Martial Deeds of Pennsylvania.* Philadelphia, 1876.
Beale, Howard K., *The Critical Year, a Study of Andrew Johnson and Reconstruction.* New York, 1930.
—— "On Rewriting Reconstruction History," *American Historical Review,* XLV:807–827, 1940.
Belden, Thomas G. and Marva R. Belden. *So Fell the Angels.* Boston, 1956.
Bemis, Samuel Flagg, *John Quincy Adams and the Foundations of American Foreign Policy.* New York, 1949.
—— *John Quincy Adams and the Union.* New York, 1956.
Bigelow, John, *Retrospections of an Active Life.* 5 vols. New York, 1909–1913.
Binckley, J. W., "The Leader of the House," *Galaxy,* I:493–500, July 15, 1866.
Blaine, James G., *Twenty Years of Congress: From Lincoln to Garfield.* 2 vols. Norwich, Connecticut, 1886.
Blanchard, Jonathan, "Reminiscences of Thaddeus Stevens," *Christian Cynosure,* September 8–December 29, 1868, April 5, 1883.
Blair, Montgomery, "Address of the National Johnson Club to the People of the United States, written by Montgomery Blair, President." 1866.
Bond, Horace Mann, *Negro Education in Alabama.* Washington, 1939.

* Newspaper and magazine articles not listed here are cited in the notes.

———— "Social and Economic Forces in Alabama Reconstruction," *Journal of Negro History*, XXIII:290–348, 1938.

Botume, Elizabeth Hyde, *First Days Among the Contrabands*. Boston, 1893.

Boutwell, George S., *Reminiscences of Sixty Years in Public Affairs*. 2 vols. New York, 1902.

———— *Speeches and Papers Relating to the Rebellion and the Overthrow of Slavery*. Boston, 1867.

Bowers, Claude G., *The Tragic Era, the Revolution after Lincoln*. Cambridge, 1929.

Brigance, William N., *Jeremiah S. Black*. Philadelphia, 1934.

Brinton, Crane, *The Anatomy of Revolution*. New York, 1938.

———— *The Jacobins, an Essay in the New History*. New York, 1930.

Brooks, Noah, *Abraham Lincoln*. New York, 1888.

Brown, W. H., *Education and Economic Development of the Negro in Virginia*. University of Virginia, 1921–1923.

Browning, Orville H., "The Diary of Orville Hickman Browning," edited by James G. Randall, *Illinois Historical Collections*, Vols. 20, 22, 1930, 1933.

Brownlow, William G., *Americanism Contrasted with Foreignism, Romanism, and Bogus Democracy*. Nashville, Tennessee, 1856.

———— *Sketches of the Rise, Progress, and Decline of Secession*. Philadelphia, 1862.

Buchanan, James, *Works of James Buchanan*, edited by John B. Moore, 12 vols., Philadelphia, 1908–1911.

Buck, Paul H., *The Road to Reunion, 1865–1900*. Boston, 1937.

Bunker, C. A., *100th Anniversary of the Caledonia County Grammar School, 1897*. Peacham, Vt., 1900.

Burgess, John W., *Reconstruction and the Constitution, 1866–1876*. New York, 1902.

Burr, Frank A., "Jefferson Davis, the ex-Confederate President at Home," *Tyler's Quarterly Historical and Genealogical Magazine*, 170–188, (January, 1951).

Burrowes, T. H., "Reminiscences of Thaddeus Stevens," *Philadelphia Press*, Sept. 2, 1868.

Butler, Benjamin F., *Autobiography and Personal Reminiscences of Major-General Benjamin F. Butler, Butler's Book*. Boston, 1892.

Cable, George W., *The Negro Question*. New York, 1890.

———— *The Silent South*. New York, 1885.

Callender, Edward B., *Thaddeus Stevens, Commoner*. Boston, 1882.

Carpenter, Frank B., *The Inner Life of Abraham Lincoln; Six Months at the White House*. New York, 1868.

Carr, Robert K., *The Supreme Court and Judicial Review*. New York, 1942.

Carter, Hodding, *The Angry Scar, the Story of Reconstruction*, New York, 1959.

Cash, W. J., *The Mind of the South*, New York, 1941.

Catterall, Helen T., ed., *Judicial Cases Concerning American Slavery and the Negro*. 5 vols. Washington, D. C., 1926–37.

Catterall, Ralph C. H., *The Second Bank of the United States*. Chicago, 1903.

Chambers, William N., *Old Bullion Benton, Senator from the New West*. Boston, 1956.

Chase, Salmon P., *Inside Lincoln's Cabinet, the Civil War Diaries of Salmon P. Chase*, edited by David Donald. New York, 1954.

Chesnut, Mary Boykin, *A Diary from Dixie*, edited by Ben Ames Williams. Boston, 1949.

Chidsey, Donald B., *The Gentleman from New York: a Life of Roscoe Conkling*. Yale University Press, 1935.

Child, L. Maria, *The Freedmen's Book*. Boston, 1865.

Clemenceau, Georges, *American Reconstruction, 1865–1870*, edited by Fernand Baldensperger. New York, 1928.

Cole, Arthur C., *The Irrepressible Conflict, 1850–1865*. New York, 1934.

Coleman, Charles H., *The Election of 1868, the Democratic Effort to Regain Control*. New York, 1933.

Conkling, Alfred R., *Life and Letters of Roscoe Conkling, Orator, Statesman, Advocate.* New York, 1889.

Cornish, Dudley T., *The Sable Arm, Negro Troops in the Union Army, 1861–1865.* New York, 1956.

Corwin, Edward S., *Court Over Constitution, a Study of Judicial Review as an Instrument of Popular Government.* New York, 1950.

――― *Liberty Against Government.* Louisiana State University Press, 1948.

Coulter, E. Merton, *The Civil War and Readjustment in Kentucky.* Chapel Hill, 1926.

――― *The South During Reconstruction, 1865–1877.* Louisiana State University Press, 1947.

――― *William G. Brownlow, Fighting Parson of the Southern Highlands.* Chapel Hill, 1937.

Cox, Samuel S., *Eight Years in Congress, from 1857–1865.* New York, 1865.

――― *Three Decades of Federal Legislation, 1855 to 1885.* Providence, 1888.

Crandall, Andrew W., *Early History of the Republican Party.* Boston, 1930.

Craven, Avery, *The Coming of the Civil War.* New York, 1942.

――― *The Growth of Southern Nationalism, 1848–1860.* Louisiana State University Press, 1953.

Craven, Avery, ed. *Essays in Honor of Wm. E. Dodd, by His Former Students at the University of Chicago.* Chicago, 1935.

Craven, John J., *Prison Life of Jefferson Davis.* New York, 1866.

Crippen, Lee F., *Simon Cameron, Ante-Bellum Years.* Oxford, Ohio, 1942.

Crook, William H., *Through Five Administrations.* New York, 1907.

Crosskey, William W., *Politics and the Constitution in the History of the United States.* 2 vols. Chicago, 1953.

Cullom, Shelby M., *Fifty Years of Public Service.* Chicago, 1911.

Current, Richard N., *Old Thad Stevens, a Story of Ambition.* University of Wisconsin Press, 1942.

Curti, Merle, *The Growth of American Thought.* New York, 1951.

Curtis, Benjamin R., Junior, ed., *A Memoir of Benjamin Robbins Curtis, with some of his Professional and Miscellaneous Writings,* 2 vols. Boston, 1879.

Curtis, Francis, *The Republican Party, a History of its Fifty Years' Existence . . . 1854–1904.* 2 vols. New York, 1904.

Curtis, George Ticknor, *Life of Daniel Webster.* 2 vols. New York, 1870.

――― *Life of James Buchanan.* 2 vols. New York, 1883.

Cushman, Robert E., *Leading Constitutional Decisions.* New York, 1940.

Dabney, Lillian G., *History of Schools for Negroes in the District of Columbia, 1807–1947.* Catholic University of America, 1949.

Dana, Charles A., *Recollections of the Civil War.* New York, 1898.

Daniel, John M., *The Richmond Examiner During the War; or, the Writings of John M. Daniel.* New York, 1868.

Davis, Henry Winter, *Speeches and Addresses.* New York, 1867.

Davis, Jefferson, *The Rise and Fall of the Confederate Government.* 2 vols. New York, 1881.

Davis, Varina, *Jefferson Davis . . . a Memoir by His Wife.* 2 vols., New York, 1890.

DeForest, John W. *A Union Officer in the Reconstruction,* edited by James H. Croushore and David Morris Potter. Yale University Press, 1948.

Dennett, Tyler, ed., *Lincoln and the Civil War in the Diaries and Letters of John Hay.* New York, 1939.

DeVoto, Bernard, *The Year of Decision, 1846.* Boston, 1943.

Dewey, Davis R., *Financial History of the United States.* New York, 1931.

DeWitt, David M., *The Impeachment and Trial of Andrew Johnson.* New York, 1903.

Dixon, Thomas, Jr., *The Clansman, an Historical Romance of the Ku Klux Klan.* New York, 1905.

Dock, Myra L. "The Caledonia Furnace, Relics and Recollections of Thaddeus Stevens in the Iron Country," *Philadelphia Times,* July 14, 1895.

Dodd, Anna Bowman, *Talleyrand: the Training of a Statesman.* New York, 1927.

Donald, David, *Lincoln Reconsidered.* New York, 1956.

—— "The Scalawag in Mississippi Reconstruction," *Journal of Southern History.* X:447–461, November, 1944.

—— "Why They Impeached Andrew Johnson," *American Heritage.* VIII:20–26ff., December, 1956.

Douglass, Frederick, *Life and Times of Frederick Douglass, Written by Himself.* Hartford, 1881.

DuBois, James T., and Gertrude S. Mathews, *Galusha A. Grow, Father of the Homestead Law.* Boston, 1917.

DuBois, W. E. Burghardt, *Black Reconstruction.* New York, 1935.

Dumond, Dwight L., *The Secession Movement, 1860–1861.* New York, 1931.

Dumond, Dwight L., ed., *Southern Editorials on Secession.* New York, 1931.

Dunning, William A., *Essays on the Civil War and Reconstruction.* New York, 1898.

—— "The Impeachment and Trial of Andrew Johnson," *Papers of the American Historical Association,* IV:145–717. 1890.

—— "Paying for Alaska," *Political Science Quarterly,* XXVII:385–399, (September, 1912).

Dyer, Brainerd, *The Public Career of William M. Evarts.* University of California Press, 1933.

—— *Zachary Taylor.* Louisiana State University Press, 1946.

Early, Jubal, *Memoir of the Last Year of the War for Independence in the Confederate States of America.* Lynchburg, 1867.

Eaton, Clement, *Freedom of Thought in the Old South.* Durham, North Carolina, 1940.

—— *A History of the Southern Confederacy.* New York, 1954.

Eaton, John, *Grant, Lincoln, and the Freedmen, Reminiscences of the Civil War.* New York, 1907.

Eckenrode, Hamilton J., *McClellan, the Man Who Saved the Union.* Chapel Hill, 1941.

Eckenrode, Hamilton J., *Political History of Virginia During Reconstruction.* Baltimore, 1904.

Elliott, Charles W., *Winfield Scott, the Soldier and the Man.* New York, 1937.

Ellis, John B., *Sights and Secrets of the National Capital.* New York, 1869.

Erikson, Erik M., "Thaddeus Stevens, 'Arch Priest of Anti-Masonry,'" *Grand Lodge of Iowa Bulletin,* XXVII:no. 2, February, 1926.

Estate of Thaddeus Stevens, Deceased. Audit. Notes of Testimony. Lancaster, Pennsylvania, 1893. Including also, *Appeal from the Orphans' Court of Lancaster County. Estate of Thaddeus Stevens, Deceased, Appeals of Thaddeus, J. B. Stevens, and others, heirs-at-law of Thaddeus Stevens, deceased.* Supreme Court of Pa., Eastern District. January term, 1894.

Faulkner, William, "The Unvanquished," *The Portable Faulkner,* edited by Malcom Cowley. New York, 1946.

Fertig, James W., *Secession and Reconstruction of Tennessee.* Chicago, 1898.

Fessenden, Francis, *Life and Public Services of William Pitt Fessenden.* 2 vols. Boston, 1907.

Ficklen, John R., *History of Reconstruction in Louisiana through 1868.* Baltimore, 1910.

Flack, Horace E., *The Adoption of the Fourteenth Amendment.* Baltimore, 1908.

Fleming, Walter L., *Documentary History of Reconstruction.* 2 vols. Cleveland, 1906.

—— *Civil War and Reconstruction in Alabama.* New York, 1949.

—— *General W. T. Sherman as a College President.* Cleveland, 1912.

Flower, Frank A., *Edwin McMasters Stanton.* New York, 1905.

Foner, Philip S., *Business and Slavery, the New York Merchants and the Irrepressible Conflict.* Chapel Hill, 1941.

Ford, Chauncey W., ed., *A Cycle of Adams Letters, 1861–1865.* 2 vols. Boston, 1920.

Forney, John W., *Anecdotes of Public Men.* 2 vols. New York, 1873, 1881.

—— *Address on Religious Intolerance and Political Proscription,* 1854.

Franklin, John Hope, *From Slavery to Freedom, a History of American Negroes.* New York, 1948.

Frazier, E. Franklin, *The Free Negro Family, a Study of Family Origins Before the Civil War.* Nashville, Tennessee, 1932.

Freeman, Douglas Southall, *Robert E. Lee, a Biography.* 4 vols. New York, 1935.

Free-Masonry Unmasked: or Minutes of the Trial of a Suit in the Court of Common Pleas of Adams County, wherein Thaddeus Stevens, Esq., was Plaintiff, and Jacob Lefever Defendant. Gettysburg, Pennsylvania, 1835.

Friedman, Milton, "The Role of War in American Economic Development," *American Economic Review,* 42:612–638 (May, 1952).

Fuess, Claude M., *Daniel Webster.* 2 vols. Boston, 1930.

Gabriel, Ralph, *The Course of American Democratic Thought.* New York, 1940.

Ganaway, Loomis M., *New Mexico and the Sectional Controversy, 1846–1861.* Albuquerque, New Mexico, 1944.

Garner, James W., *Reconstruction in Mississippi.* New York, 1901.

Garrison, Wendell P. and Francis J., *Wm. Lloyd Garrison, the Story of his Life as Told by his Children.* 4 vols. New York, 1885–1889.

Garrison, William Lloyd, *The Words of Garrison.* Boston, 1905.

Giddings, Joshua, *History of the Rebellion.* New York, 1864.

Glover, Gilbert G., *Immediate Pre-Civil War Compromise Efforts.* Nashville, Tennessee, 1934.

Godkin, Edwin L., *Life and Letters,* edited by Rollo Ogden. 2 vols. New York, 1907.

—— *Reflections and Comments, 1865–1895.* New York, 1895.

Golder, Frank A., "The Purchase of Alaska," *American Historical Review,* 25:411–425, (April, 1920).

Gorham, George C., *Life and Public Services of Edwin M. Stanton.* 2 vols. Boston, 1899.

Grace, Sister M. Grace Madeline. *Monetary and Banking Theories of Jacksonian Democracy.* Philadelphia, 1943.

Grant, Ulysses S., *Personal Memoirs.* 2 vols. New York, 1885.

Greeley, Horace, *The American Conflict: a History of the Great Rebellion in the United States of America, 1860–64.* 2 vols. Hartford, Connecticut, 1864–1866.

—— *Recollections of a Busy Life.* New York, 1868.

Gurowski, Adam, *Diary, 1863–1864–1865.* Washington, 1866.

Haecker, Theodor, *Kierkegaard the Cripple.* New York, 1950.

Hale, William Harlan, *Horace Greeley, Voice of the People.* New York, 1950.

Hall, William M., *Reminiscences and Sketches, Historical and Biographical.* Harrisburg, Pennsylvania, 1890.

Halstead, Murat, *Caucuses of 1860, a History of the National Political Conventions.* Columbus, Ohio, 1860.

Hamilton, Holman, "Democratic Senate Leadership and the Compromise of 1850," *Mississippi Valley Historical Review,* 41:403–418, December, 1954.

Hamlin, Charles E. *Life and Times of Hannibal Hamlin, by his Grandson.* Cambridge, 1899.

Hammond, Bray, *Banks and Politics in America from the Revolution to the Civil War.* Princeton, 1957.

Hancock, A. R., *Reminiscences of Winfield Scott Hancock, by his Wife.* New York, 1887.

Hancock, Cornelia, *South After Gettysburg, Letters of Cornelia Hancock from the Army of the Potomac, 1863–1865.* University of Pennsylvania Press, 1937.

Harper, Robert S., *Lincoln and the Press*. New York, 1951.

Harris, Alexander, *A Review of the Political Conflict in America . . . Comprising also a Résumé of the Career of Thaddeus Stevens*. New York, 1876.

Harris, Wilmer C., *Public Life of Zachariah Chandler, 1851–1875*. Lansing, Michigan, 1917.

Hartzell, James H., *History of the Thaddeus Stevens Trade School*. Lancaster, Pennsylvania, 1955.

Harvey, Oscar J., *History of Lodge No. 61, F. and A. M.* Wilkesbarre, Pennsylvania, 1897.

Hassler, Warren W., *General George B. McClellan, Shield of the Union*. Louisiana State University Press, 1957.

Hayes, Rutherford B., *Diary and Letters*, edited by C. R. Williams, 5 vols. Ohio State Arch. and Historical Society, 1924.

Haynes, George H., *Charles Sumner*. Philadelphia, 1909.

Hefelbower, Samuel G., *The History of Gettysburg College, 1832–1932*. Gettysburg, 1934.

Helper, Hinton Rowan, *The Impending Crisis of the South: How to Meet It*. New York, 1857.

Henderson, John B., "Emancipation and Impeachment," *Century Magazine*, LXXXV:196–209, December, 1912.

Hendrick, Burton J., *Lincoln's War Cabinet*. Boston, 1946.

Henry, Robert S., *The Story of Reconstruction*. New York, 1938.

Hensel, W. U., "The Christiana Riot and the Treason Trials of 1851," *Lancaster County Historical Society Papers*, Vol. 15. Lancaster, 1911.

——— "Jacob Eichholtz, Painter," *Pennsylvania Magazine of History and Biography*, Vol. 37, 1913.

——— "Thaddeus Stevens as a Country Lawyer," *Lancaster County Historical Society Papers*, X:247–290. Lancaster, 1906.

Herbert, Hilary A., and others, *Why the Solid South? or, Reconstruction and its Results*. Baltimore, 1890.

Herskovits, Melville J., *The Myth of the Negro Past*. New York, 1941.

Hertz, Emanuel, *The Hidden Lincoln, from the Letters and Papers of Wm. H. Herndon*. New York, 1938.

Hesseltine, William B., *Lincoln and the War Governors*. New York, 1948.

——— *Ulysses S. Grant, Politician*. New York, 1935.

History of Perseverance Lodge No. 21, F. and A. M. Harrisburg, 1901.

History of the Rise, Progress and Downfall of Know-Nothingism in Lancaster County, by two Expelled Members. Lancaster, Pennsylvania, 1856.

Hoar, George F., *Autobiography of Seventy Years*. 2 vols. New York, 1903.

Hocking, Wm. Ernest, *Experiment in Education*. Chicago, 1954.

Hoffer, Eric, *The True Believer, Thoughts on the Nature of Mass Movements*. New York, 1951.

Hofstadter, Richard, *The American Political Tradition*. New York, 1954.

Holden, W. W., *Memoirs*. Durham, N. C., 1911.

Hood, Alexander H. "Thaddeus Stevens," *A Biographical History of Lancaster County*, edited by Alexander Harris. Lancaster, 1872.

Horn, Stanley F. *Invisible Empire, the Story of the Ku Klux Klan*. Boston, 1939.

Howard, Major-General Oliver Otis, *Autobiography*. 2 vols. New York, 1907.

Hulbert, Archer B., *The Great American Canals*. Cleveland, 1904.

Hume, John F., *The Abolitionists . . . 1830–1864*. New York, 1905.

Hunt, Gaillard, *Israel, Elihu and Cadwallader Washburne*. New York, 1925.

Hyman, Harold M., *Era of the Oath. Northern Loyalty Tests During the Civil War and Reconstruction*. University of Pennsylvania Press, 1955.

Jenkins, William S., *Pro-Slavery Thought in the Old South*. Chapel Hill, 1935.

Johnson, Oliver, *William Lloyd Garrison and His Times*. Boston, 1880.

Julian, George W., *The Life of Joshua R. Giddings*. Chicago, 1892.

———— *Political Recollections, 1840 to 1872.* Chicago, 1884.

"George W. Julian's Journal," *Indiana Magazine of History,* December 1915, XI: 324ff.

Kendrick, Benjamin B., *Journal of the Joint Committee of Fifteen on Reconstruction, 39th Congress, 1865–1867.* New York, 1914.

Klaus, Samuel, ed., *The Milligan Case.* New York, 1929.

Klein, Frederic S., *Lancaster County, 1841–1941.* Lancaster, Pennsylvania, 1941.

Koch, Adrienne, and William Peden, eds., *The Life and Selected Writings of Thomas Jefferson,* New York, 1944.

Korngold, Ralph, *Thaddeus Stevens, a Being Darkly Wise and Rudely Great.* New York, 1955.

Landis, Charles I., "A Refutation of the Slanderous Stories Against the Name of Thaddeus Stevens . . ." *Lancaster County Historical Society Papers,* 28:49–52, March, 1924.

Leigh, Frances B., *Ten Years on a Georgia Plantation, Since the War.* London, 1883.

Lerner, Eugene M., "Money, Prices, and Wages in the Confederacy, 1861–65," *Journal of Political Economy,* 63:20–41, February, 1955.

Lewinson, Paul, *Race, Class, and Party, a History of Negro Suffrage and White Politics in the South.* New York, 1932.

Lincoln, Abraham, *Collected Works,* edited by Roy P. Basler, Marion D. Pratt and Lloyd A. Dunlap, 9 vols. Rutgers University Press, 1953–1955.

Lincoln, Abraham, *Complete Works,* edited by John G. Nicolay and John Hay, 12 vols. New York, 1905.

Logan, John A., *The Great Conspiracy, its Origin and History.* New York, 1886.

Lonn, Ella, *Reconstruction in Louisiana after 1868.* New York, 1918.

Lothrop, Thornton K., *William Henry Seward.* Boston, 1899.

Love, John L., "The Disfranchisement of the Negro," *American Negro Academy, Occasional Papers,* No. 6. Washington, 1899.

Lowell, James Russell, *Political Essays.* Boston, 1888.

Lowrie, Walter, *A Short Life of Kierkegaard.* Princeton University Press, 1942.

Luthin, Reinhard H., *The First Lincoln Campaign.* Harvard University Press, 1944.

Lynch, John Roy, *The Facts of Reconstruction.* New York, 1913.

Martin, Robert E., *Negro Disfranchisement in Virginia.* Washington, 1938.

Mathews, John M., *Legislative and Judicial History of the Fifteenth Amendment.* Baltimore, 1909.

May, Samuel J., *Some Recollections of our Antislavery Conflict.* Boston, 1869.

Mayo, Bernard, *Henry Clay, Spokesman of the New West.* 2 vols. Boston, 1937.

McCall, Samuel W., *Thaddeus Stevens.* Boston, 1899.

McCarthy, Charles H., *The Antimasonic Party: A Study of Political Antimasonry in the United States, 1827–1840.* (American Historical Association Annual Report, 1902) Washington, 1903.

———— *Lincoln's Plan of Reconstruction.* New York, 1901.

McClure, Alexander K., *Abraham Lincoln and Men of War-Times.* Philadelphia, 1892.

———— *Old Time Notes of Pennsylvania.* 2 vols. Philadelphia, 1905.

———— *Recollections of Half a Century.* Salem, Mass., 1902.

McCulloch, Hugh, *Men and Measures of Half a Century.* New York, 1888.

McPherson, Edward, *Political History of the United States during the Great Rebellion.* Washington, 1876.

———— *Political History of the United States during the Period of Reconstruction.* Washington, 1875.

———— *A Political Manual for 1866.* Washington, 1866.

Memorial Addresses on the Life and Character of Thaddeus Stevens, Delivered in the House of Representatives . . . December 17, 1868. Washington, 1869.

Merriam, George S. *Life and Times of Samuel Bowles.* 2 vols. New York, 1885.

Miller, Alphonse B., *Thaddeus Stevens*. New York, 1939.

Milton, George Fort, *The Age of Hate, Andrew Johnson and the Radicals*. New York, 1930.

—— *The Eve of Conflict, Stephen A. Douglas and the Needless War*. Boston, 1934.

Mitchell, Stewart, *Horatio Seymour of New York*. Harvard University Press, 1938.

Mitchell, Wesley Clair, *A History of the Greenbacks . . . 1862–65*, Chicago, 1903.

Morrill, Justin, "Notable Letters from my Political Friends," *Forum*, 24:141–142, October, 1897.

Morton, Richard L., *The Negro in Virginia Politics, 1865–1902*. University of Virginia, 1918.

Motley, John Lothrop, *Complete Works*. 17 vols. New York, 1889.

Mueller, Henry R., *The Whig Party in Pennsylvania*. New York, 1921–1922.

Muzzey, David S., *James G. Blaine, a Political Idol of Other Days*. New York, 1935.

Myers, William Starr, *The Republican Party, a History*. New York, 1928.

Myrdal, Gunnar, *An American Dilemma, The Negro Problem and Modern Democracy*. 2 vols. New York, 1944.

Naroll, Raoul S., "Lincoln and the Sherman Peace Fiasco—Another Fable?" *Journal of Southern History*, 20:459–483, November, 1954.

National Union Convention, Proceedings, Philadelphia, August 14, 1866.

Nevins, Allan, *The Emergence of Lincoln*. 2 vols. New York, 1950.

—— *The Emergence of Modern America, 1865–1878*. New York, 1927.

—— *Frémont, Pathmarker of the West*. New York, 1939.

—— *Ordeal of the Union*. 2 vols. New York, 1947.

—— *The Statesmanship of the Civil War*. New York, 1953.

"The New Orleans Riot," *Tribune Tracts*. No. 1. New York, 1866.

Nichols, Roy F., *The Disruption of American Democracy*. New York, 1948.

Nicolay, John G., and John Hay, *Abraham Lincoln, a History*. 10 vols. New York, 1917.

Nye, Russel B., *Fettered Freedom, Civil Liberties and the Slavery Controversy, 1830–1860*. Michigan State College Press, 1949.

Nye, Russel B., *George Bancroft, Brahmin Rebel*. New York, 1944.

Oberholtzer, Wm. P. *Jay Cooke, Financier of the Civil War*. 2 vols. Philadelphia, 1907.

Ogden, Rollo, ed., *Life and Letters* (of Edwin L. Godkin). 2 vols., New York, 1907.

Olmstead, Frederick Law, *The Cotton Kingdom*, edited and with an introduction by Arthur M. Schlesinger, New York, 1953.

Owen, Robert Dale, "Political Results from the Varioloid," *Atlantic Monthly*, 35:660–670, June, 1875.

—— *Wrong of Slavery and Right of Emancipation*. Philadelphia, 1864.

Patterson, Robert T., *Federal Debt-Management Policies, 1865–1879*. Duke University Press, 1954.

Patton, James W., *Unionism and Reconstruction in Tennessee, 1860–1869*. Chapel Hill, 1934.

Pearce, Haywood J., *Benjamin H. Hill, Secession and Reconstruction*. Chicago, 1928.

Peirce, Paul Skeels, *The Freedmen's Bureau*. State University of Iowa, 1904.

Penrose, Charles B., *Address of, together with speeches of Messrs. Fraley, Williams, Pearson and Penrose, on the Subject of the Insurrection at Harrisburg, in December of 1838*. Harrisburg, 1839.

Perkins, Howard C., ed., *Northern Editorials on Secession*. 2 vols. New York, 1942.

Perry, Benjamin F., *Reminiscences of Public Men*. Greenville, South Carolina, 1889.

Phillips, Ulrich B., *Life and Labor in the Old South*. Boston, 1929.

Phillips, Ulrich B., ed., "Correspondence of Robert Toombs, Alexander H. Stephens, and Howell Cobb," *American Historical Association, Annual Report*, 1911, Vol. 2. Washington, 1913.

Phillips, Wendell, *Speeches, Lectures, and Letters.* Boston, 1863.

Piatt, Donn, *Memories of the Men Who Saved the Union.* New York, 1887.

Pierce, Edward L., "The Freedmen at Port Royal," *Atlantic Monthly,* XII:296–297. September 1863.

Pierce, Edward L., *Memoir and Letters of Charles Sumner.* 4 vols. Boston, 1893.

Pollard, Edward A., *The Lost Cause, a New Southern History of the War of the Confederates.* New York, 1867.

———— *The Lost Cause Regained.* New York, 1868.

Poore, Benjamin Perley, *Perley's Reminiscences of Sixty Years in the National Metropolis.* 2 vols. Philadelphia, 1886.

Popper, Karl R., *The Open Society and its Enemies.* Princeton University Press, 1950.

Potter, David M., *Lincoln and his Party in the Secession Crisis.* Yale University Press, 1942.

Pratt, Fletcher, *Stanton, Lincoln's Secretary of War.* New York, 1953.

"The President on the Stump," *North American Review,* 102:530–544, April, 1866.

Pressly, Thomas J., *Americans Interpret Their Civil War.* Princeton University Press, 1954.

Proceedings of the National Union Convention, held at Philadelphia, August 14, 1866.

Proceedings of the United States Anti-Masonic Convention. Philadelphia, September 11, 1830.

Quarles, Benjamin, *The Negro in the Civil War.* Boston, 1953.

Ramsdell, Charles W., *Reconstruction in Texas.* New York, 1910.

Randall, James G., *The Civil War and Reconstruction.* New York, 1937.

Randall, James G., and Richard N. Current, *Lincoln the President.* 4 vols. New York, 1945–1955.

Reid, Whitelaw. *After the War: a Southern Tour, May 1, 1865 to May 1, 1866.* Cincinnati, 1866.

Rhodes, James Ford, *History of the United States, From the Compromise of 1850, to the Restoration of Home Rule, 1877.* 7 vols. New York, 1893–1906.

Rice, Allen T., *Reminiscences of Abraham Lincoln by Distinguished Men of His Time.* New York, 1888.

Riddle, Albert G., *The Life of Benjamin F. Wade.* Cleveland, 1886.

———— *Recollections of War Times, 1860–1865.* New York, 1895.

Rockey, John J., "Pennsylvania's Free School Laws of 1834 and Their Great Defender, Thaddeus Stevens," *Lebanon County Historical Society Papers,* VII:1917.

Rodell, Fred. *Nine Men, a Political History of the Supreme Court from 1790 to 1955.* New York, 1955.

Ross, Edmund G., *History of the Impeachment of Andrew Johnson.* Santa Fe, New Mexico, 1896.

Russ, William A., "Registration and Disfranchisement under Radical Reconstruction," *Mississippi Valley Historical Review,* 21:163–180, 1934.

Russel, Robert E. "What Was the Compromise of 1850?" *Journal of Southern History,* XXII:292–309. August, 1956.

Russell, Charles Edward, *Blaine of Maine, his Life and Times.* New York, 1931.

Russell, William H., *The Civil War in America.* Boston, 1861.

Sabin, Edwin L., *Building the Pacific Railway.* Philadelphia, 1919.

Salter, William, *The Life of James W. Grimes.* New York, 1876.

Samuelson, Paul A., *Economics.* New York, 1948.

Sandburg, Carl, *Abraham Lincoln, the War Years.* 4 vols. New York, 1939.

Schlesinger, Arthur M., Sr., *The American as Reformer.* Cambridge, Mass., 1950.

Schlesinger, Arthur M., Jr., *The Age of Jackson.* Boston, 1946.

———— "The Causes of the Civil War," *Partisan Review,* 18:969–981, October, 1949.

Schofield, John M., *Forty-Six Years in the Army.* New York, 1897.

Schurz, Carl, *Condition of the South.* 39 Congress, 1 session, Senate Executive

Document No. 2, 1866.

—— *Henry Clay.* 2 vols. Boston, 1887.

—— *Reminiscences of Carl Schurz.* 3 vols. New York, 1908.

—— *Speeches, Correspondence and Political Papers,* edited by Frederick Bancroft, 6 vols. New York, 1913.

Scovel, James M., "Thaddeus Stevens," *Lippincott's Magazine,* 61:545–551. April, 1898.

Sears, Lorenzo, *Wendell Phillips, Orator and Agitator.* New York, 1909.

Seitz, Don C., *Lincoln the Politician.* New York, 1931.

Sellers, Charles G., *James K. Polk, Jacksonian, 1795–1843.* Princeton University Press, 1957.

Sergeant, T., and Wm. Rawle, *Cases Adjudged in the Supreme Court of Pennsylvania, 1814–1828.*

Seward, Frederick W., *Reminiscences, 1830–1915.* New York, 1916.

Seward, Frederick W., ed., *William H. Seward: An Autobiography from 1801 to 1834.* New York, 1891.

Seward, William H., *Works of William H. Seward,* edited by George C. Baker, 5 vols. Boston, 1884.

Sherman, John, *Recollections of Forty Years in the House, Senate and Cabinet, An Autobiography.* 2 vols. New York, 1895.

Sherman, William T., *Personal Memoirs of General W. T. Sherman.* 2 vols. New York, 1891.

Shugg, Roger W., *Origins of Class Struggle in Louisiana, a Social History of White Farmers and Laborers during Slavery and After, 1840–1875.* Louisiana State University Press, 1939.

Simkins, Francis B., "New Viewpoints of Southern Reconstruction," *Journal of Southern History,* V:49–61, 1939.

Simkins, Francis B. and Robert H. Woody, *South Carolina During Reconstruction.* University of North Carolina Press, 1932.

Singletary, Otis A., "The Negro Militia During Radical Reconstruction," *Military Affairs,* 19:177–186, Winter, 1955.

Singmaster, Elsie, *I Speak for Thaddeus Stevens.* Boston, 1947.

Smedes, Susan Dabney, *Memorials of a Southern Planter.* Baltimore, 1888.

Smedley, R. C., *History of the Underground Railroad in Chester and the Neighboring Counties of Pennsylvania.* Lancaster, Pennsylvania, 1883.

Smith, Samuel Denny. *The Negro in Congress, 1870–1901.* University of North Carolina Press, 1940.

Smith, Theodore C., *Life and Letters of James A. Garfield.* 2 vols. New Haven, 1925.

Smith, William E., *The Francis Preston Blair Family in Politics.* 2 vols. New York, 1933.

Spaulding, E. G., *History of the Legal Tender Paper Money Issued During the Great Rebellion,* Buffalo, New York, 1869.

Stampp, Kenneth M., *And the War Came, the North and the Secession Crisis, 1860–1861.* Louisiana State University Press, 1950.

—— "Lincoln and the Strategy of Defense in the Crisis of 1861," *Journal of Southern History,* II:297–323.

—— *The Peculiar Institution, Slavery in the Ante-Bellum South.* New York, 1956.

Stanwood, Edward, *American Tariff Controversies in the Nineteenth Century.* 2 vols. Boston, 1903.

Staples, Thomas S., *Reconstruction in Arkansas, 1862–1874.* New York, 1923.

Stephens, Alexander H., *Recollections of Alexander H. Stephens.* New York, 1910.

Stewart, William M., *Reminiscences of Senator Wm. M. Stewart of Nevada.* New York, 1908.

Stone, William L., *Letters on Masonry and Anti-Masonry.* New York, 1832.

Storey, Moorfield, *Charles Sumner.* Boston, 1900.

Stryker, Lloyd Paul, *Andrew Johnson, a Study in Courage.* New York, 1929.

Sumner, Charles, "Our Domestic Relations; or, How to Treat the Rebel States," *Atlantic Monthly,* 12:507–529 (October, 1863).

Swanberg, W. A., *Sickles the Incredible.* New York, 1956.

Swint, Henry Lee. *The Northern Teacher in the South, 1862–1870.* Vanderbilt University Press, 1941.

Sydnor, Charles S., *The Development of Southern Sectionalism, 1819–1848.* Louisiana State University Press, 1948.

Taylor, A. A., "Historians of the Reconstruction," *Journal of Negro History,* 23:16–34, 1938.

Taylor, Richard, *Destruction and Reconstruction.* London, 1879.

Thompson, C. Mildred, *Reconstruction in Georgia.* New York, 1915.

Thoreau, Henry D., *A Yankee in Canada, with Anti-slavery and Reform Papers.* Boston, 1866.

Thorndike, R. S., ed., *Sherman Letters.* New York, 1894.

Tindall, George B., *South Carolina Negroes, 1877–1900.* University of South Carolina Press, 1952.

Trefousse, Hans, *Ben Butler.* New York, 1957.

Trial of Andrew Johnson, President of the United States, Before the Senate of the United States, on Impeachment by the House of Representatives for High Crimes and Misdemeanors. 3 vols. Washington, 1868.

Truman, Benjamin C., "Anecdotes of Andrew Johnson," *Century Magazine,* 85:435–440, January, 1913.

Turner, Edward R., *The Negro in Pennsylvania, 1639–1861.* Washington, 1911.

Van Deusen, Glyndon G., *The Life of Henry Clay.* Boston, 1937.

Villard, Oswald G., *John Brown, a Biography Fifty Years After.* Boston, 1910.

Vinnie Ream. Washington Press of Gibson Bros., 1908.

Walker, Francis A., *General Hancock.* New York, 1894.

Wallace, Jesse T., *A History of the Negroes of Mississippi from 1865 to 1890.* Clinton, Mississippi, 1927.

Warden, R. B., *An Account of the Private Life and Public Services of Salmon P. Chase.* Cincinnati, 1874.

Wardlaw, Ralph, "Negro Suffrage in Georgia, 1867–1930." *University of Georgia Bulletin,* Vol. 33, September, 1932.

Ware, Edith Ellen, *Political Opinion in Massachusetts During Civil War and Reconstruction.* New York, 1916.

Warmoth, Henry Clay, *War, Politics and Reconstruction, Stormy Days in Louisiana.* New York, 1930.

Warren, Charles, *The Supreme Court in United States History.* 3 vols. Boston, 1923.

Weber, Thomas, *The Northern Railroads in the Civil War, 1861–1865.* New York, 1952.

Webster, Daniel, *Writings and Speeches.* 18 vols. National Edition, Boston, 1903.

Weed, Thurlow, *The Life of Thurlow Weed,* Vol. II, *Memoirs* edited by his grandson, Thurlow Weed Barnes. *Autobiography* is Vol. I, edited by Harriet A. Weed. 2 vols. Boston, 1883.

Weiss, John, *Life and Correspondence of Theodore Parker.* 2 vols. New York, 1864.

Welles, Gideon, *Diary.* 3 vols. New York, 1911. New edition, with introduction, notes, and annotations by Howard K. Beale, New York, in press.

Wharton, Vernon L., *The Negro in Mississippi, 1865–1890.* University of North Carolina Press, 1947.

White, Horace, *The Life of Lyman Trumbull.* Boston, 1913.

White, Laura A., "Charles Sumner and the Crisis of 1860–61," *Essays in Honor of Wm. E. Dodd.* Chicago, 1935.

Williams, Kenneth P., *Lincoln Finds a General, a Military Study of the Civil War.* 2 vols. New York, 1949.

Williams, T. Harry, *Lincoln and His Generals.* New York, 1952.

———— *Lincoln and the Radicals.* University of Wisconsin Press, 1941.

Wilson, Henry, *History of the Antislavery Measures of the Thirty-seventh and Thirty-eighth United States Congresses,* 1861–64. Boston, 1864.

———— *History of the Reconstruction Measures of the Thirty-ninth and Fortieth Congresses.* Boston, 1870.

———— *History of the Rise and Fall of the Slave Power in America.* 3 vols. Boston, 1877.

Wilson, James H., *Life of John A. Rawlins.* New York, 1916.

Wise, Henry A., *Seven Decades of the Union.* Philadelphia, 1872.

Wish, Harvey, *George Fitzhugh, Propagandist of the Old South.* Louisiana State University Press, 1943.

Witmer, T. Richard, "Some Hitherto Unpublished Correspondence of Thaddeus Stevens," *Lancaster County Historical Society Papers.* Vol. 35, 1931.

Woodburn, James A., *The Life of Thaddeus Stevens.* Indianapolis, 1913.

Woodley, Thomas F., *Great Leveler, the Life of Thaddeus Stevens.* New York, 1937.

Woodson, Carter G., *The Negro in Our History.* Washington, D. C., 1947.

Woodward, C. Vann, *Origins of the New South, 1877–1913.* Louisiana State University Press, 1951.

———— *Strange Career of Jim Crow.* New York, 1957.

Woodward, W. E., *Meet General Grant.* New York, 1928.

Woolley, Edwin C., *The Reconstruction of Georgia.* New York, 1901.

Index